Coy Hunt

Coy Hunt

Software
Risk
Management

Software
Risk
Management

Barry W. Boehm

IEEE Computer Society Press
Los Alamitos, California

Washington • Brussels • Tokyo

IEEE COMPUTER SOCIETY PRESS TUTORIAL

Published by the
IEEE Computer Society Press
10662 Los Vaqueros Circle
PO Box 3014
Los Alamitos, CA 90720-1264

IEEE Computer Society Press Order Number 1906
Library of Congress Number 89-80295
ISBN 0-8186-5906-8 (microfiche)
ISBN 0-8186-8906-4 (case)

Second Printing, 1993

Additional copies can be ordered from

IEEE Computer Society Press
Customer Service Center
10662 Los Vaqueros Circle
PO Box 3014
Los Alamitos, CA 90720-1264

IEEE Computer Society
13, avenue de l'Aquilon
B-1200 Brussels
BELGIUM

IEEE Computer Society
Ooshima Building
2-19-1 Minami-Aoyama
Minato-ku, Tokyo 107
JAPAN

Production Editor: Robert Werner
Printed in the United States of America by Braun-Brumfield, Inc.

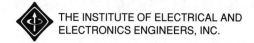

THE INSTITUTE OF ELECTRICAL AND
ELECTRONICS ENGINEERS, INC.

Preface

Like many fields in their early stages, the software field has had its share of project disasters. Most post-mortems of these software disaster projects have indicated that their problems would have been avoided or strongly reduced if there had been an explicit early concern with identifying and resolving their high-risk elements. Frequently, these projects were swept along by a tide of optimistic enthusiasm during their early phases, which caused project managers to miss some clear signals of high-risk issues that proved to be the project's downfall later.

Although enthusiasm for new software capabilities is a good thing, it needs to be tempered with a concern for early identification and with a resolution of a project's high-risk elements. Therefore people can get these high–risk elements resolved early and can continue to focus their enthusiasm and energy on the positive aspects of their software product.

Current approaches to the software process make it too easy for software project managers to make high-risk commitments that they will later regret. The sequential, document-driven "waterfall" process model tempts people to overpromise software capabilities in contractually-binding requirements specifications before they understand the risk implications. The code-driven evolutionary development process model tempts people to say, "Here are some neat ideas I'd like to put into this system. I'll code them up, and if they don't fit other people's ideas, we'll just evolve things until they work." This sort of approach works fine in some well-supported mini-domains such as spreadsheet applications, but in more complex application domains, it often creates or neglects intrinsic high-risk elements and leads the project to disaster.

At TRW and elsewhere, I have had the good fortune to observe first–hand many software project managers at work and to try to understand and to apply the factors that distinguished the more successful project managers from the less successful ones. Some were able to successfully use a waterfall approach, others successfully used an evolutionary development approach, and others successfully orchestrated complex mixtures of these and other approaches involving prototyping, simulation, commercial software, executable specifications, tiger teams, design competitions, subcontracting, and various kinds of cost-benefit analyses.

One pattern that emerged very strongly was that **the successful project managers were good risk managers.** Although they generally didn't use such terms as risk identification, risk assessment, risk management planning, or risk monitoring, that's what they were doing. And their projects tended to avoid pitfalls and to produce good products.

This pattern has led me and others to try to formalize these risk–oriented correlates of software project success into a discipline of software risk management. The structure of this discipline is organized into two main branches:

- *Risk assessment,* which includes risk identification, risk analysis, and risk prioritization
- *Risk control,* which includes risk management planning, risk resolution, and risk monitoring

In the process of researching software risk management as a discipline, I found that it can benefit from a long tradition of studying risk management in other situations. The use of risk analysis has been traced back to the Babylonians in 3200 B.C. Pascal and Bernoulli analyzed many risk situations that occur in games of chance. Bernoulli's classic paper, "Exposition of a New Theory on the Measurement of Risk," was published in 1738.

The insurance business is founded on the ability to assess and deal with risk. Large corporations have risk management departments whose responsibility is to assess corporate risks and to establish appropriate risk management programs that involve various kinds of insurance, contract provisions, preventative measures, policies, and practices to deal cost–effectively with the corporation's risk exposure. The classic book in the field, Allan Willett's *The Economic Theory of Risk and Insurance* [Willett, 1951], was first published in 1901.

Dealing with risk is central to the modern discipline of economics, particularly in such areas as decision theory, utility theory, and game theory. The study of risk-seeking or risk-averse behavior bridges economics and psychology. There is also a quarterly journal called *Risk Analysis,* published by the Society for Risk Analysis.

It turns out that this material provides software risk management with some valuable concepts and principles, but that its particular application to software and project management situations requires a good deal of tailoring. This process is in its early stages. Thus, there is no large body of software risk management literature to date, but there is now enough good material to make a tutorial volume of this nature feasible. And, given the critical leverage risk management can have on a project's success, it seems important to disseminate this information as early and as extensively as possible.

The primary *objectives* of this tutorial volume are therefore to enable readers of the volume and participants in the tutorial to:

- Identify the major sources of risk on a given software project
- Understand the essential concepts and techniques involved in software risk assessment and risk control
- Apply these concepts and techniques to practical day-to-day software project situations.

With regard to *scope,* some approaches to risk management confine themselves to operational risks involving reliability, safety, and/or security. In this tutorial, we use a broad definition of "risk," since it is most effective to address all sources of project risk in a uniform way. Thus, the "risks" one is assessing and controlling in this tutorial involve all potential aspects of a project's "unsatisfactory outcome:" overrunning budget and schedule; causing operational problems because of errors, performance shortfalls, inappropriate functionality, or user interface mismatches; or creating a product that is difficult to maintain or reuse.

The overall risk management *concept of operation* presented in this tutorial is not that of a discipline separately practiced on the side by a few specialists, but that of a discipline integrated into the practice of all of the project participants. These participants include customers, users, and maintainers as well as developers; and software engineers and system analysts as well as managers. Its primary emphasis is in the early phases of a software product's definition (concept definition, requirements analysis, and design), since the major risk reduction leverage is in the early phases. But it can and should continue to be applied throughout the software life cycle.

Each of the four sections in this tutorial consists of a text portion followed by several reprinted articles. The text portion for each section begins with the author's tutorial material, and ends with a short description of each of the reprinted articles.

Section 1, the Introduction and Overview, defines software risk management and its component parts, provides some motivation for why software risk management is important, introduces some of the fundamental concepts, and presents a case study of a poorly risk-managed project which will be used as context in subsequent sections.

Section 2, Risk Management Practices, constitutes the heart of the tutorial. It addresses the six basic risk management steps: the risk assessment steps of risk identification, risk analysis, and risk prioritization; and the risk control steps of risk management planning, risk resolution, and risk monitoring.

Section 3, Risk Resolution Techniques, elaborates on some of the most effective techniques available for risk resolution, particularly in the areas of prototyping, performance engineering, and software reliability, security, and safety assurance.

Section 4, Implementing Risk Management, discusses the application of risk management throughout the software life cycle, and presents some examples of applying risk management techniques to large software-intensive programs.

I would like to acknowledge the help of a good many people who have improved the material in this tutorial by applying or constructively critiquing earlier versions of it. At TRW, these have included Eric Anderson, Frank Belz, Mark Gerhardt, Ed Goldberg, Larry McLaughlin, Isabel Muennichow, Lolo Penedo, Al Peschel, Walker Royce, Richard Sansom, George Spadaro, Don Stuckle, Bob Williams, and Herb Woodward. I have received other valuable insights and feedback from Vic Basili, Tom Bell, Lee Cooper, Tom DeMarco, Tom Gilb, Rony Ross, Win Royce, Art Salwin, Col. Tony Shumskas, and Jerry Smith, along with Ez Nahouraii and the IEEE Computer Society reviewers for this tutorial volume. I would also like to thank Margaret Brown of the IEEE Computer Society and my secretary, Nancy Donato, for their tremendous help in putting the material together.

Table of Contents

Section 1: Introduction and Overview

1.1: Outline

This section of the tutorial establishes the context and foundations for the sections that follow. The next subsection defines software risk management and its components. Subsection 1.3 discusses the primary reasons why software risk management is important. Subsection 1.4 presents the fundamental concepts involved in risk management, particularly the concepts of risk exposure and risk reduction leverage (RRL). Subsection 1.5 presents a case study of the UniWord project, a typical example of a project that did not do much risk management. By reading and analyzing this case study you will receive some very good practice in the identification and assessment of risk items; the experience will be very valuable for the assimilation of the material that follows. Subsection 1.6 provides an overview of the tutorial articles in Section 1, by showing how the articles contribute to the motivation, context, and foundations for the discipline of software risk management.

1.2: What Is Software Risk Management?

Software risk management is an emerging discipline whose objectives are to identify, address, and eliminate software risk items before they become either threats to successful software operation or major sources of software rework.

As may be seen in Figure 1.1, the practice of risk management involves two primary steps, risk assessment and risk control, each with three subsidiary steps. Risk assessment involves risk identification, risk analysis, and risk prioritization. Risk control involves risk management planning, risk resolution, and risk monitoring.

Risk identification produces lists of the project-specific risk items likely to compromise a project's satisfactory outcome. Typical risk identification techniques include checklists, decomposition, comparison with experience, and examination of decision drivers.

Risk analysis produces assessments of the loss-probability and loss-magnitude associated with each of the identified risk items, and assessments of compound risks involved in risk-item interactions. Typical techniques include network analysis, decision trees, cost models, and performance models.

Risk prioritization produces a prioritized ordering of the risk items identified and analyzed. Typical techniques include risk exposure analysis, RRL analysis, and Delphi or group-consensus techniques.

Risk management planning produces plans for addressing each risk item, including the coordination of the individual risk-item plans with each other and with the overall project plan (e.g., to ensure that enough up-front schedule is pro-

vided to properly develop, exercise, and learn from a prototype). Typical techniques include checklists of risk resolution techniques, cost-benefit analysis, and statistical decision analysis of the relative cost and effectiveness of alternative risk-resolution approaches.

Risk resolution produces a situation in which the risk items are eliminated or otherwise resolved (e.g., by relaxing requirements). Typical techniques include prototypes, simulations, benchmarks, mission analyses, key personnel agreements, design-to-cost approaches, and incremental development.

Risk monitoring involves tracking the project's progress toward resolving its risk items and toward taking corrective action when appropriate. Typical techniques include risk management plan milestone tracking and a top–10 risk-item list that is highlighted at each weekly, monthly, or milestone project review.

In addition, risk management provides an improved way of addressing and organizing the software life cycle. Risk-driven approaches such as the spiral model of the software process and its refinements, described in three of the tutorial articles in Section 1 [Boehm, 1988a; Boehm-Belz, 1988; Boehm,1988b], avoid many of the difficulties that can be encountered by using previous process models such as the waterfall model and the evolutionary development model. Such risk-driven approaches also show how and where to incorporate new software technologies such as rapid prototyping, fourth-generation languages, and commercial software products into the software life cycle, and to help managers determine how much of a given software activity (i.e., prototyping, verification and validation, configuration management, and testing) is enough.

1.3: Why Is Software Risk Management Important?

Software risk management is important primarily because it helps people avoid disasters, avoid rework, avoid overkill, and stimulate win-win situations on software projects.

1.3.1: Avoiding Disasters

The [McFarlan, 1981], [Rothfeder, 1988], and [Neumann, 1988] tutorial articles in this section provide several examples of software disaster projects and some sobering statistics on their frequency. The Rothfeder article cites a Peat Marwick Mitchell & Co. survey of 600 client firms, which indicated that 35 percent of them had at least one "runaway" data-processing project at the time. These disaster projects generally trace back to one or more risk items that either were not identified, were improperly assessed, or were improperly dealt with. The risk management techniques in this tutorial can help you properly identify, assess,

1

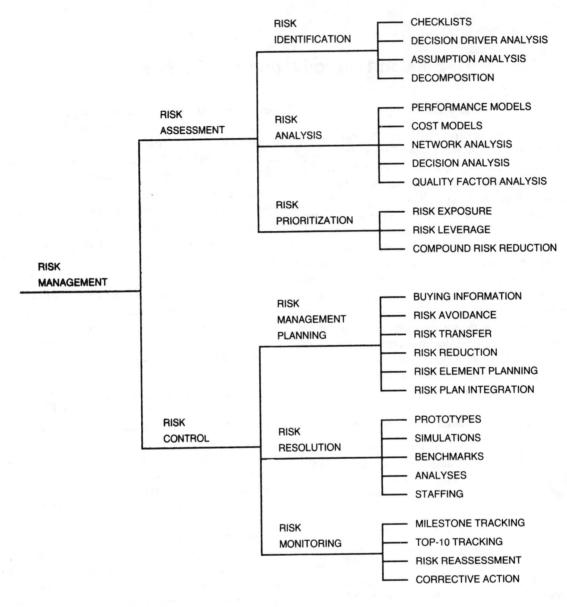

Figure 1.1: Software Risk Management Steps

and deal with such risk items, and thus keep your project from the disaster file.

1.3.2: Avoiding Rework

Several studies of the software process [Jones, 1986; Boehm, 1987] indicate that rework of erroneous requirements, design, and code typically consumes 40-50 percent of the total cost of a software development. Avoiding rework is thus one of the prime opportunities to improve software productivity. Software risk management helps avoid these rework costs by focusing project effort on the early identification and elimination of high-risk software problems. As may be seen in Figure 1.2, reworking a software requirements problem once the software is in operation generally costs about 100 times more than it would take to rework the problem in the requirements phase. Figure 1.3 provides an even stronger rationale for risk

management. It shows that typically 80 percent of the cost to fix software problems is spent on the highest-risk 20 percent of the problems. Thus, a strong emphasis on software risk management will identify and eliminate these top-20 percent problems while their rework costs are relatively low, and thus maximize the rework-reduction and productivity improvement leverage.

1.3.3: Avoiding Overkill

Many software project managers spend much more effort and money than necessary on redundant and demotivating activities in such areas as testing, documentation, configuration management, and quality assurance. These activities are very important, but they frequently spend most of their effort on low-leverage activities. For example, a software test program may plan, prepare, run, analyze, and document hundreds or thousands of tests that redundantly cover nomi-

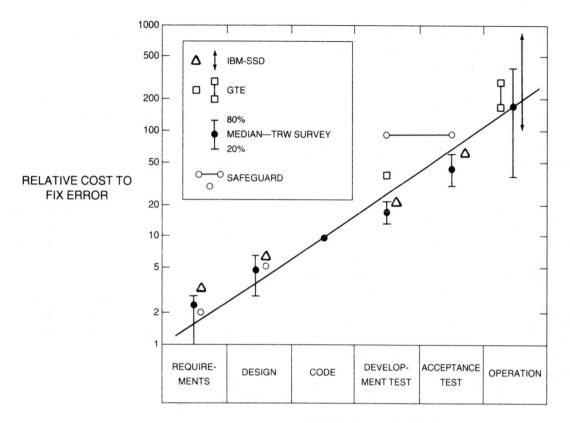

RELATIVE COST TO FIX ERROR

PHASE IN WHICH ERROR DETECTED

Figure 1.2: Escalation of Software Rework Costs with Phase

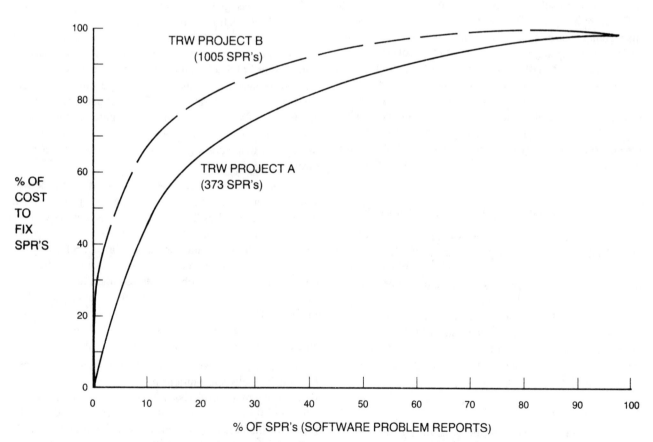

% OF COST TO FIX SPR'S

% OF SPR's (SOFTWARE PROBLEM REPORTS)

Figure 1.3: Rework Costs Concentrated in a Few High-Risk Items

nal or low-risk functions, while neglecting to test high-risk off-nominal cases with critical operational consequences. A risk-management approach to these areas will focus effort on the critical areas that make a difference; that is, saving project resources and establishing more meaningful jobs for project personnel.

Also, risk management will help avoid software requirements overkill or gold-plating by focusing on such questions as, "What is the risk if we don't add this questionable feature to the product?"

1.3.4: Stimulating Win-Win Situations

Many software projects fail because their principals allow themselves to set up win-lose or lose-lose situations by neglecting high-risk items, by sweeping problems under the rug, or by forcing project performers into no-win situations. Common examples are "best and final offer" negotiations on software contracts, "success-oriented" schedules, and unrealistic assumptions about technology or support capabilities. Most win-lose situations on software projects eventually turn into lose-lose situations, because the losing parties can usually find some way of fulfilling the letter of their commitment by compromising the product's quality or utility.

The "Theory W" paper in this part of the tutorial [Boehm-Ross, 1988] indicates that the creation and sustenance of the win-win conditions for all of the major participants in the software process (i.e., make everyone a winner) constitutes a necessary and sufficient set of conditions for a successful software project. The Theory W framework highlights risk management as a key to sustaining win-win conditions. Thus, one of the major sources of risk to be covered by risk management is the risk of turning one of the participants in the software process (developers, customers, users, maintainers, and bosses) from a winner into a loser. Viewed in this way, risk management is not a negative and pessimistic approach to software project management, but is a means for ensuring positive win-win outcomes for all of the software process participants.

1.4: Fundamental Risk Management Concepts

This section provides definitions of the term "risk" and other fundamental risk management concepts. It presents a typical risk management situation, and identifies the primary risk management options available to address this and other situations. It explains the key concepts of risk exposure (RE) and RRL, and shows how they apply in an example involving nuclear powerplant software. Finally, it addresses the question, "Isn't all software management risk management?" by distinguishing between generic software risks and project-specific software risks.

1.4.1: Definitions

Webster defines "risk" as "the possibility of loss or injury." This definition can be translated into the fundamental concept of risk management: the concept of RE, sometimes

also called risk impact. RE is defined by the relationship

$$RE = Prob(UO) * Loss(UO)$$

where Prob(UO) is the probability of an unsatisfactory outcome, and Loss(UO) is the loss to the parties affected if the outcome is unsatisfactory.

To relate this definition to software project situations, we need a definition of "unsatisfactory outcome." Here, the Theory W "Make everyone a winner" principle provides a key: Outcomes are unsatisfactory when they keep a major participant in the software process from becoming a winner. Table 1.1 identifies the major participants in the software process, and the corresponding dimensions of software risk involved in providing a satisfactory outcome to these participants.

These dimensions provide a top-level checklist for the identification and assessment of software project risk items. More detailed checklists will be covered under risk identification in Subsection 2.3 of this tutorial.

1.4.2: A Typical Risk Management Situation

Figure 1.4 shows a typical situation in which risk considerations are important. It shows the net payoff (value of throughput minus cost of development and operation) for a transaction processing system (TPS). The TPS may be delivering message packets, answering credit queries, making travel reservations, dispatching emergency vehicles, or the like. The net payoff is shown as a function of the level of investment in computer cycles necessary to process the transactions. TPS solutions at the left of Figure 1.4, such as point A, represent systems based on single small processors. They provide a moderate level of throughput for a relatively small level of investment. Point B in Figure 1.4 represents a system based on a single large processor. It provides more throughput than solution A, but its higher cost reduces the throughput/$ ratio.

Point C in Figure 1.4 represents a range of multiprocessor solutions with a number of smaller parallel processors. In the best case, if all of the processor cycles were devoted to processing transactions, this would be a very high-payoff solution, since the smaller processors incur a relatively low cost. However, such multiprocessor solutions often encounter performance problems due to distributed operating system overhead, resource contention, or context-switching inefficiencies. Thus, the worst-case outcome for the multiprocessing solution C is less attractive than any of the single–processor solutions to the left in Figure 1.4.

If we consider a manager's decision problem with respect to choosing between solutions of class A, B, or C, it is clear that there are several risk management considerations. Choosing solutions A or B will run the risk of underperformance or inefficient operation. Choosing solution C will be very attractive in the best case, but very risky if the worst case is true.

Table 1.1: Major Software Participants and Risk Dimensions

MAJOR PARTICIPANTS	RISK OF UNSATISFACTORY OUTCOME
CUSTOMER, DEVELOPER	BUDGET OVERRUN
	SCHEDULE SLIP
USER INTERFACE	WRONG FUNCTIONALITY, USER
SHORTFALLS	PERFORMANCE, RELIABILITY
MAINTAINER	POOR-QUALITY SOFTWARE

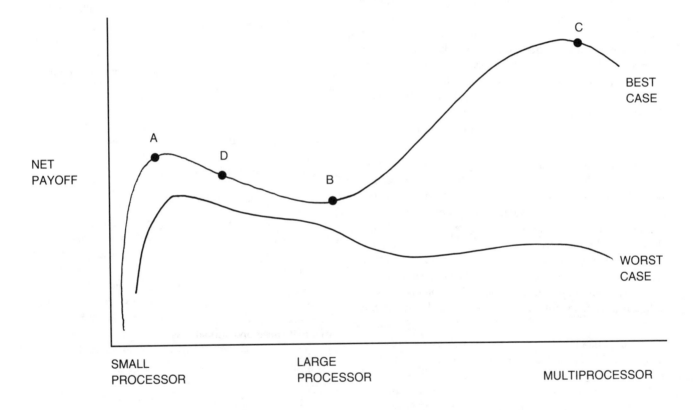

Figure 1.4: Typical Risk Management Situation

How should we choose between these alternatives?

Before reading further, try to work out for yourself what conditions might affect the choice of preferred solution in Figure 1.4, and to identify some risk management options that you could exercise to ensure a solution with acceptable risk.

1.4.3: Primary Risk Reduction Options

To determine our best risk management approach to this situation, it is best to begin by assessing our risks with respect to the unsatisfactory outcome criteria in Table 1.1. To begin, we need to assess the relative performance of the solutions with respect to the system's performance needs. If we do not need the levels of throughput available via the multiprocessor solution, we can choose lower-risk options such as solution A. Or, we might find that the users would be satisfied with a lower level of functionality per transaction, in which case the low-risk solution A would deliver adequate throughput. These are examples of a class of risk management options called *risk avoidance*. They are focused on reducing risk by pursuing less ambitious objectives.

Another example of risk avoidance is illustrated by point D in Figure 1.4. Choosing point A could be very risky if your payoff analysis were based on assumptions about workload, average transaction size, or processor speed which were somewhat inaccurate, so that your actual payoff were somewhere down the steep slope to the left of point A. Choosing point D reduces your calculated payoff a little bit, but it would avoid the risk of a major drop in payoff if your assumptions and calculations were somewhat off.

A related option is *risk transfer*: reallocating sources of risk from one portion of a system to another. For example, the need for additional transaction processing power may have come from an expert-system rule checker for credit references. Transferring the responsibility for credit pattern checking from software to human operators would reduce the software performance risk, but would transfer the risk to the operators. Clearly this would not be a unilateral decision you could make by yourself, but it represents an option for consideration.

Another major option is *risk control*: accepting the existence of the risk, preparing plans to handle it as well as possible, and establishing contingency plans in case the risk items turn out to be unresolvable. A risk control approach to solution C of the TPS problem in Figure 1.4 could involve developing the multiprocessor operating system and applications; doing careful planning, instrumentation, and monitoring to track whether the system is being developed successfully; and preparing a reduced-functionality type-A solution should the multiprocessor option be clearly heading for failure.

The final major option is to reduce risk by *buying information*. This can be done in concert with any of the other options, but it is best done in advance of the other risk reduction options, in order to assess how best to proceed with the other options. Examples of TPS information-buying options for solution C are:

- Developing a prototype of the performance-critical multiprocessor operating system functions

- Performing analytic modeling, simulation, or benchmarking studies to determine performance drivers and solution options

- Performing reference checks or surveys on the performance characteristics of proposed or alternative multiprocessor operating systems or applications

Thus, for example, we might develop a rapid prototype of the performance-critical multiprocessor operating system features in solution C. If the prototype indicated a very low probability of a worst-case outcome, we would go forward with solution C. If the prototype indicated a very high probability of a worst-case outcome, we could choose one of the risk-avoidance or risk-transfer solutions such as A or D. If the prototype indicated that there were still some fundamental uncertainties remaining, we could either try to buy more information, go with a risk-avoidance or risk-transfer option, or use a risk-control option with solution C.

These risk reduction options of risk avoidance, risk transfer, risk control, and buying information are not just specific to this situation. They can be used as the generic elements of risk management strategies applying to any risk management situation. Also, they can be combined. An incremental development approach, starting with a reduced-functionality type-D approach and growing with experience to a type-C approach, would combine risk avoidance, risk control, and buying information.

Some sources, such as the Air Force "Software Risk Abatement" pamphlet [AFSC, 1988], also include another option: software risk assumption, or the acceptance of a risky situation and the possibility of failure. Here, we have included this option under risk control, by using the rationale that one generally should try to anticipate and prepare alternative or fallback options should the risk of failure materialize. However, one could consider high-risk exploratory research projects as examples of risk assumption.

Having examined the basic risk management options, let us now look at the two fundamental concepts available to assess and deal with risk situations: RE and RRL.

1.4.4: Two Fundamental Concepts

There are two fundamental concepts that help us to deal with risk assessment and risk prioritization in a quantitative way: the concepts of RE and RRL. As an example of their definition and use, we will present them in the context of a verification and validation (V&V) program for a nuclear powerplant software project. The unsatisfactory outcomes whose risks are addressed in a V&V program are software errors that cause operational losses. For nuclear powerplant software, the most critical losses are those dealing with powerplant meltdown and shutdown, although other unsatisfactory outcomes such as performance degradation are also important: A powerplant that produces little power is not very useful.

1.4.4.1: Risk Exposure

As mentioned earlier, the quantity RE, sometimes also called risk impact, is defined by the relationship

$$RE = Prob(UO) * Loss(UO)$$

where Prob(UO) is the probability of an unsatisfactory outcome and Loss(UO) is the loss to the parties affected if the outcome is unsatisfactory.

Figure 1.5 shows RE contours as functions of Prob(UO) and Loss(UO), where Loss(UO) is assessed on a scale of 0 (no loss) to 1 (complete loss). The lower left portion of

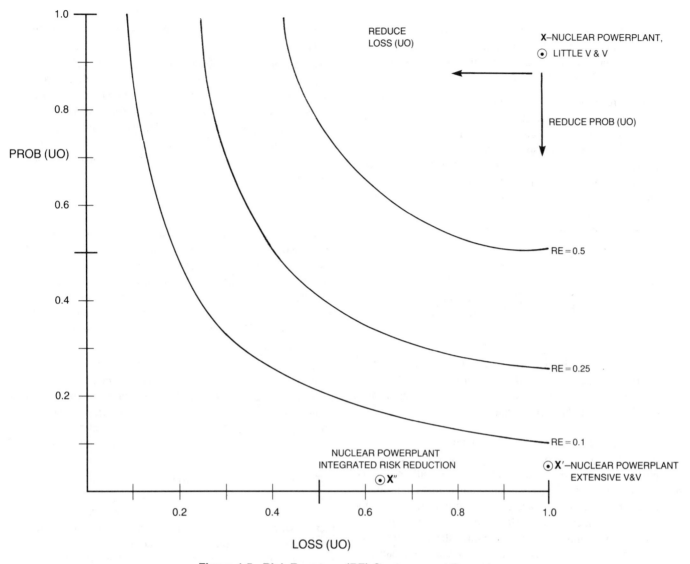

Figure 1.5: Risk Exposure (RE) Contours and Examples

Figure 1.5 is the area of low RE; the upper right portion is the area of critical RE. A project with a risk item in this area, such as point X, should attempt to reduce its RE by reducing the Prob(UO), reducing the Loss(UO), or some combination of both, as indicated by the arrows emanating from point A in Figure 1.5.

Software risk management and V&V: In a typical verification and validation (V&V) situation, the unsatisfactory outcome (UO) is produced by a software error that causes an operational loss. If a software project does relatively little V&V, the probability of an operational error is relatively high. If the software is controlling a nuclear powerplant, the software error could result in a major loss of human life, a situation corresponding to point X in Figure 1.5. Thus, for nuclear powerplant software, a significant investment in V&V is appropriate if it can reduce Prob(UO) far enough to bring the RE down to an acceptable level (point X' in Figure 1.5).

Of course, there may be other methods besides V&V that can help reduce Prob(UO) and RE to an acceptable level as well. For example, an integrated risk reduction strategy

involving additional procedural safety features, fault tolerance, and other software error elimination techniques as well as V&V could reduce the nuclear powerplant's software RE to the level of point X'' in Figure 1.5.

A risk management example with a different V&V conclusion is illustrated by point Y in Figure 1.5, which might reflect a software program involved with astronomical data reduction. Here, the effect of a software error is relatively minor and recoverable, and the resulting RE level is relatively low. In this case, RE may already be at an acceptable level, and relatively little investment in V&V may be necessary.

This RE view of software V&V suggests the following two major points:

- The level of investment in software V&V is a function of the relative loss caused by a software error in a system

- Software V&V should be part of an integrated risk reduction strategy that also includes other error elimination techniques (constructive correctness methods, walkthroughs, cleanroom techniques, redundancy), software fault-tolerance techniques, and operational loss limiting techniques

With respect to the key question, "How much V&V is enough?" the first point shows that the answer is a function of the relative loss caused by a software error. The second point shows that it is also a function of the relative cost-effectiveness of V&V with respect to other techniques that reduce software risk exposure. This consideration is covered by another key risk management (RM) concept: RRL.

1.4.4.2: Risk Reduction Leverage

The RRL quantity is defined as follows:

$$RRL = \frac{RE_{before} - RE_{after}}{Risk\ Reduction\ Cost}$$

where RE_{before} is the RE before initiating the risk reduction effort and RE_{after} is the RE afterwards. Thus, RRL is a measure of the relative cost-benefit of performing various candidate risk reduction activities.

To consider a V&V example, suppose that the loss incurred by having a particular type of interface error in a given software product is estimated at one million dollars, and that from experience we can estimate that the probability of this type of interface error being introduced into the software product is roughly 0.3. (As with the other loss and probability numbers in this example, these numbers are representative but purely notional examples.) We can then compare two approaches for eliminating this type of error: a requirements and design interface checker, whose application will cost $20,000 and will reduce the error probability to 0.1; and an interface testing approach, whose application will cost $150,000 and will reduce the error probability to 0.05. (The relative costs reflect data on the relative costs to find and fix software errors as a function of the software phase.) We can then compare the RRL of the two approaches:

$$RRL(R\text{-}D\ V\&V) = \frac{\$1000K^*(0.3) - \$1000K^*(0.1)}{\$20K} = 10$$

$$RRL(Testing) = \frac{\$1000K^*(0.3) - \$1000K^*(0.05)}{\$150K} = 1.67$$

Thus, the RRL calculation confirms that V&V investments in the early phases of the software life cycle generally have high payoff ratios, and that V&V is a function that needs to begin early to be most cost-effective. Similar calculations can help a software project determine the most cost-effective mix of defect removal techniques to apply across the software life cycle. Example approaches can be found in Chapter 3 of [Jones, 1986] and Chapter 24 of [Boehm, 1981].

This quantitative approach to RE and RRL makes it sound as if risk management is a precise and easily quantifiable discipline, primarily concerned with formulating and evaluating sets of equations. As will be discussed next, however, the estimates of probabilities and losses are usually imprecise, and the resulting approaches are more judgment-oriented strategies than they are fully quantitative optimal policies.

1.4.5: Using Risk Exposure to Prioritize Risk Items

One difficulty with the RE and RRL quantities is the problem of making accurate estimates of the probability and loss associated with an unsatisfactory outcome. In many cases, however, one can use approximate methods that provide sufficient information to support risk management decisions. For example, one useful approach for estimating and prioritizing RE quantities is to assess the risk probabilities and losses on a relative scale of 0 to 10.

Figures 1.6 and 1.7 show an example of this risk prioritization process as it might be applied to a nuclear powerplant software project. Figure 1.6 shows a tabular summary of a number of unsatisfactory outcomes (UOs) with their corresponding ratings for Prob(UO), Loss(UO), and their resulting RE estimates. Figure 1.7 plots each UO with respect to the RE contours defined in Figure 1.5.

Two key points emerge from Figures 1.6 and 1.7. First, projects often focus on factors having either a high Prob(UO) or a high Loss(UO), but these may not be the key factors with a high RE combination. One of the highest Prob(UOs) comes from item G (accounting system errors), but the fact that these errors are recoverable and not safety-critical leads to a low loss factor and a resulting low RE of 8. Similarly, item I (insufficient memory) has a high potential loss, but its low probability leads to a low RE of 7. On the other hand, a relatively low-profile item such as item H (hardware delay) becomes a relatively high-priority risk item because its combination of moderately high probability and loss factors yields a RE of 30.

The second key point emerging from Figures 1.6 and 1.7 deals with the probability rating ranges given for items A, B, and C. It often occurs that there is much uncertainty in estimating the probability or loss associated with an unsatisfactory outcome. This uncertainty is itself a major source of risk, that needs to be reduced as early as possible. The primary example in Figures 1.6 and 1.7 is the uncertainty in item C about whether the operating system safety features are going to cause an unacceptable degradation in performance. If Prob(UO) is rated at 4, this item has only a moderate RE of 28; but if Prob(UO) is 8, the RE has a top-priority rating of 56. Thus, some operating system prototyping or performance analysis would help in buying information to reduce risk.

It should also be mentioned that these relative 0-to-10 scales oversimplify some concerns (e.g., the loss due to a

UNSATISFACTORY OUTCOME (UO)	PROB(UO)	LOSS(UO)	RISK EXPOSURE
A. OS ERROR CAUSES MELTDOWN	3-5	10	30-50
B. OS ERROR CAUSES SHUTDOWN	3-5	8	24-40
C. OS SAFETY FEATURES CAUSE UNACCEPTABLE PERFORMANCE	4-8	7	28-56
D. DISPLAY SOFTWARE REPORTS UNSAFE CONDITION AS SAFE	5	9	45
E. DISPLAY SOFTWARE REPORTS SAFE CONDITION AS UNSAFE	5	3	15
F. APPLICATION ERROR CAUSES INEFFICIENT OPERATION	6	4	24
G. ACCOUNTING SYSTEM ERRORS CAUSE EXTRA WORK	8	1	8
H. HARDWARE DELAY CAUSES SCHEDULE OVERRUN	6	5	30
I. PROCESSOR MEMORY INSUFFICIENT	1	7	7
J. DBMS SOFTWARE LOSES HISTORY DATA	2	2	4

Figure 1.6: Example Risk Exposure Factors—Nuclear Powerplant Software

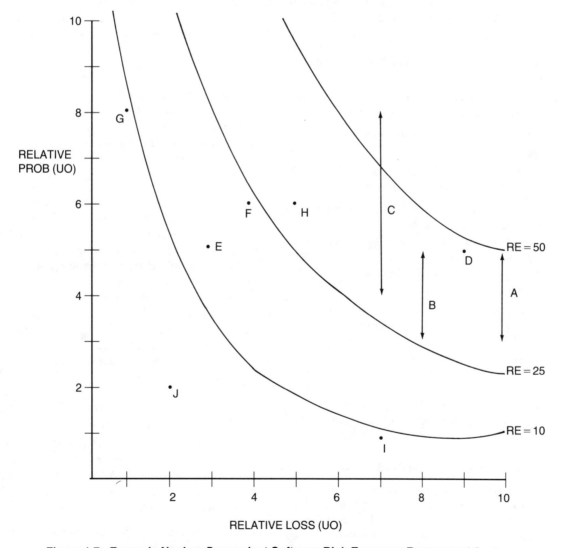

Figure 1.7: Example Nuclear Powerplant Software Risk Exposure Factors and Contours

meltdown is orders of magnitude higher than any losses due to performance and memory constraints). Thus, although they are very useful for early "ballpark" risk prioritization activities, they should not be used in analytical calculations of optimal risk reduction strategies. Even with these qualifications, however, the RE quantity provides a useful conceptual tool for comparing and prioritizing a project's risk items.

1.4.6: Generic and Project-Specific Risks

We can see from the previous examples that risk management concepts such as RE and RRL add value to the software process by focusing projects on the issues with the highest impact on the project's success or failure. However, one question that software project managers often ask is, "It seems like everything I do on a software project is done to avoid some sort of risk. If all management is risk management, how can the risk management concept add any value?"

The important distinction here is the distinction between the project's *generic risks* (items that are common to all projects, and are covered by the project's basic software development plan) and its *project-specific* risks, which are addressed by a project-specific risk management plan.

Examples of a software project's generic risks are:

- Error-prone products, which are addressed by testing and verification

- Costly, late fixes, which are addressed by early requirements and design verification and validation

- Out-of-control projects, which are addressed by project planning and control functions

- Out-of-control products, which are addressed by configuration management and quality assurance functions

Project-specific risks deal with characteristics that are not common to all projects, such as user-interface uncertainties, ambitious performance requirements, tight budget and schedule constraints, or reliance on advances in computer science. These are the items to be addressed by project risk assessment and risk control activities.

Even for the generic portions of the project, though, risk management concepts are useful in tailoring the software development plan, particularly in determining how much of a given activity is enough. As discussed earlier in considering project verification and validation functions, the relative risk exposure associated with a product's software errors determines the extent of nominal-case testing, off-nominal testing, stress testing, formal verification, or independent V&V that should be included in the project's plan.

1.5: Case Study: The UniWord Project

The UniWord case study presented in the next subsection describes a project, which did not perform much risk management, and therefore had poor results. It is described in terms of the assessment portion of an audit report done by a consultant hired to assess the status of the project. The case study is a synthesis of two projects, which between them experienced risk items very similar to the ones described.

The case study is provided as an opportunity for you to practice identifying risk items, and as a context for the risk management material to be covered in Section 2.

Before going on to the rest of the tutorial, read the case study and identify project risk items that could have been better addressed by the UniWord project.

Answers will be discussed within the various parts of Subsection 2.3 on Risk Identification. In addition, UniWord will be used to illustrate the application of many of the risk assessment and risk control techniques presented in Section 2.

1.5.1: Audit Report: UniWord Project

Scope

This report presents the results of a two-week audit of the UniWord project. The project was undertaken by SoftWizards, Inc., under contract to Universal Micros, Inc., to develop a word processing system for Universal Micro's UniWindow workstation. The report will cover the audit's charter, procedures, findings, and recommendations. In this draft of the report, the recommendations are still to be determined.

Charter

The audit's charter was to determine the technical, financial, and management status of the UniWord project, to identify problems needing solution, and to recommend solutions. The audit was to be performed by one person within a two-week period.

Procedures

A kickoff meeting was held with Joan Black, Universal Micro's product line manager for the UniWindow product; George Green, SoftWizards, Inc. president; and Bill Brown, SoftWizards' project manager for UniWord. We agreed on the scope, charter, procedures, and information sources to be used in the audit. Interviews were held with all five remaining SoftWizards project personnel, one previous project member, and three Universal Micros personnel. Documents reviewed included the contract, project plans, and UniWord specifications, plus selected portions of the code listings, user documentation, and accounting records.

Findings

The audit findings are summarized in a project chronology and a project status assessment.

Project chronology: Universal Micros, Inc., has been developing a new product: An advanced personal computer or workstation called the UniWindow. It will be driven by two Universal 3215 32-bit, 15-megahertz microprocessors, and will have the following major features:

- A high-resolution bit-mapped color display device

- 1 megabyte of main memory

- A 20-megabyte Winchester disk drive
- The UniWindow operating system, an extension of Unix (TM Bell Labs) supporting fast, powerful window management.

Universal is contracting with several software houses to produce software packages for the UniWindow. Universal developed a set of high-level functional specifications for a word-processing package called UniWord, and used these specifications as the basis for a request for proposals (RFP) which was sent to a number of software houses on July 15, 1983. Universal's schedule for the procurement was keyed to have a demonstrable set of products to exhibit at the 1984 National Computer Conference in Las Vegas, July 9-12, 1984. Thus, they scheduled one month for proposal response, one month for source selection, and nine months for software development, as follows:

July 15, 1983: RFP

August 15, 1983: Proposals due

September 15, 1983: Project go-ahead

June 15, 1984: Product delivery

The competition (July-September 1983): Five companies responded to the RFP. Three more declined to bid, saying that nine months was insufficient time to develop the amount of software specified. Two of the five bidders were clearly not qualified to do the job, and one company's price was much higher (over $1 million) than the two remaining bidders, SoftWizards and Text Products, Inc., each of which bid around $400K. Universal Micros asked these two companies to submit a Best and Final Offer.

George Green, SoftWizards' president, felt that the Uni-Word job was a key win for his company. SoftWizards had done some text editors, but never a full word-processing package. UniWord would help SoftWizards achieve a leading position in developing software for multi-color, window-oriented personal computers and workstations, clearly the wave of the future for software products. Also, some of his systems programmers needed some contract coverage for their salaries.

As a result, SoftWizards' Best and Final Offer proposed even more functionality than requested by Universal, reduced the price to $300K, and still committed to deliver the product in nine months. There was a $10.00 per workstation license fee for UniWord also in the package, so George Green felt that he could recover his $100K if 10,000 Uni-Windows were sold.

This bid was so much more attractive than Text Products' bid that Universal Micros accepted it at once. Final contract negotiations ($300k, fixed price) went smoothly, and work commenced on September 15, 1983.

Project startup (September-October 1983): Six people were assigned to the UniWord project. The two key people were:

- Bill Brown, the project manager, had experience in developing a CP/M-based editor, but no experience

with Unix or with other components of a word-processing system

- Karen Gray, the deputy project manager, had considerable Unix experience, was an expert user of the Unix text editor "vi," but had no word-processor system development experience

Brown and Gray had significantly different ideas as to how the text editor should operate. Brown preferred to use a few simple commands invoked by function keys and menu choices. Gray preferred to use a powerful, extensive set of one-letter commands and a separate mode for text entry. All six project members gravitated into discussing and researching this issue, with little consideration going into the other components of the product. After about a month, Brown felt he needed to get the other parts of the project moving along, and decided to let Gray proceed to implement her model of a text editor. He then went on to develop the other components by using his approach.

Early problems (October 1983-February 1984): Around January, some pieces of the product had been coded and debugged, and Bill Brown began to put them together to test them. This was initially difficult, because of a lack of test data and test drivers, but by mid-February some initial capabilities were available.

Brown then found that the pieces didn't fit together very well. Karen Gray's file structures, edit buffer conventions, and window controls were incompatible with their counterparts in the format/runoff and file manager components.

Clearly, some compromises were needed to get the components to play together, but after some extended arguments with Brown, Karen Gray left the company rather than compromise on her approach. Fortunately, her programs were extremely well-structured, but they capitalized on so many exotic capabilities of Unix and C that they were still hard to understand and modify.

The file manager was proving too much of a challenge for the two junior personnel developing it. Key features were missing (e.g., list and delete files), and the features present were slow and cumbersome. Sam Silver, SoftWizards' DBMS expert, was brought aboard the project to rescue the file manager.

Problem interactions (February-April 1984): By mid-March, work was proceeding on the various rescue efforts. Although he didn't have a specific schedule of events, Bill Brown was optimistic that the project's problems were solved, so he continued to report that the project was on schedule.

Unfortunately, there were more problems than he realized, and even further problems were developing. Attempts to modify Karen Gray's text editor frequently encountered mysterious side effects, so it was decided to leave the text editor as is, and to build an outer layer around it to communicate with users and with the other UniWord components. This was harder to do, particularly for the user interface, than originally envisioned.

Another difficulty resulted from a conversation between Sam Silver and an enthusiastic Universal Micros marketer, who said that UniWord really needed a relational database management system (DBMS) and a full-capability query language, rather than a simple file system. Although this was not formal customer direction, Sam Silver responded eagerly. He quickly began to develop a good-sized relational DBMS with extensive natural language query capabilities.

The extent of this redirection was not evident to Bill Brown until mid-April. When he found out about it and discussed it with Silver, he was concerned that it was a much bigger job than Silver could carry out in the time available. But Silver assured him that he could do it, and said that he had to proceed this way because that was what the customer wanted. Brown decided not to make an issue of this with the customer, as he was not eager to discuss other issues with the customer as well.

Brown's main difficulty was in integrating the components of UniWord. It was taking virtually all of his time and attention. Each component now existed in several versions, and it was hard to determine which was the right one to use at any given time. Also, there were no interface specifications between the components, so when interface problems occurred, they were hard to diagnose. Worse yet, when an interface problem was identified, there was no foundation for determining who was responsible for fixing it. All of the UniWord developers were already busy trying to catch up on their own components, and nobody wanted to change their programs just to accommodate someone else's. This led to further arguments, delays, and loss of morale.

SoftWizards' rescue attempt (April-May 1984): By this time, it was late April, and Bill Brown knew that there was no way that his current team could solve their problems and deliver UniWord by June 15. So he appealed to George Green, saying that customer wishes had caused SoftWizards to add some new capabilities such as the relational DBMS. These functions would be very valuable to SoftWizards, but they were causing him to have schedule problems with integration. If Green could provide him with four experienced people for six weeks to help with integration, the rest of Brown's team could concentrate on getting their components finished, and he could deliver on schedule.

George Green considered going to Universal Micros to ask for schedule and budget relief to compensate for the added UniWord capabilities. Bill Brown recommended against this, saying that there was no written request from Universal Micros for the added features, and the likely result of the request would be a nonproductive delay. Green therefore decided to pull four people off some other SoftWizards projects for six weeks to work on integrating the UniWord components.

The four rescuers were capable people, but they knew nothing about UniWord. There was very little documentation available, and it was generally out of date. So the new people had to spend a great deal of time asking questions of the component developers, with the result that the developers' progress slowed down even further.

Universal Micros assesses the situation (May-June 1984): By the end of May, it was clear that very little progress had been made, and that a June 15 delivery was impossible. George Green decided to present the strongest situation possible to Universal Micros. He arranged a meeting with Universal Micros at which he:

- Demonstrated the strongest features of Karen Gray's text editor
- Presented a summary of the added UniWord capabilities requested by Universal Micros personnel
- Stated that by June 1, SoftWizards could deliver a package of software that literally satisfied the rather loose terms in the contract, but said that nobody would be happy with that outcome
- Cited SoftWizards' additional $50K investment in getting UniWord to work, and requested another $100K and three months' calendar time from Universal Micros to deliver the full UniWord product

Joan Black and the Universal Micros people were not at all pleased by this proposal. They did not like the Karen Gray text editor. They felt that it did not take advantage of the UniWindow workstation's strengths: its advanced mouse pointing-device and its rapid, flexible window management capabilities. Universal had prepared a great deal of publicity for the National Computer Conference, and the SoftWizards text editor came nowhere near fulfilling Universal's claims for UniWord. Some people at Universal felt that they should take SoftWizards to court, but others felt that Universal's legal case would be weak. In any event, what Universal really needed was a word processor, not a lawsuit.

In a meeting on June 7, Universal's top management decided not to include UniWord in their UniWindow exhibit at the National Computer Conference, and to engage an external consultant to assess the situation and to evaluate Universal's options. George Green agreed to have SoftWizards fully support the consultant's audit. As a result, the author of this report performed a two-week audit of the UniWord project between June 14 and June 29, 1984.

Project Status

The status of the UniWord project is summarized in six categories;

1. Product features: user interface
2. Product features: other
3. Product control
4. Management
5. Personnel
6. Finance

Product features: user interface: The most serious problem with UniWord is that its three main components have three entirely different approaches to the user interface:

- The *format/runoff* component has the best match to the capabilities of the UniWindow workstation: a separate control window for menu options and user feedback, and the use of the mouse for menu selection
- The *text editor* component has two modes: one for commands and one for text entry. An overpowering variety of one-letter commands are available. They combine in powerful but obscure ways. There is relatively little user feedback on results
- The *file manager* has an English-like query language approximating free text. It operates in a separate control window that provides user feedback, but otherwise it does not capitalize on UniWindow capabilities

In addition, the three components vary significantly in their use of color.

An attempt was made to provide a front-end for the text editor to make its user interface comparable to that of the format/runoff component, but it was not very successful. Making the text editor and file manager consistent with the format/runoff user interface would require a major effort (at least four months' full-time effort of two highly experienced persons, one for each component).

Product features—other: Structured code: One strong feature of all the UniWord components is that the code is highly modular and well-structured:

Organization into components: The separation of the text editor and format/runoff components meant that the project missed the opportunity to integrate these functions into a single, "what you see is what you get (WYSIWYG)," text composition capability. This capability is particularly well-suited to the high-resolution, window-oriented UniWindow workstation.

Overlaps and inconsistencies: There are a number of overlaps and inconsistencies among the components. Some examples are:

- The text editor "quit" command has options for saving and naming files that don't match those of the file manager
- Format/runoff has edit features for formatting commands, page headers, etc. that don't match those of the text editor

Inter-component interfaces: There are many interface inconsistencies between components. Some examples are:

- Files with embedded format commands are structured differently than pure text files, complicating interfaces with the file manager
- Format/runoff assumes that an end-of-sentence is any occurrence of a period, question mark, or exclamation point followed by two blanks. The text editor has more complex rules, considering quotation marks, parentheses, brackets, etc.
- There are numerous inconsistencies in parameter passing, edit buffer conventions, and window controls

UniWindow interfaces: Universal Micro made several changes in the UniWindow workstation (window management procedures, mouse button interpretations, escape key conventions) that were only informally communicated to the UniWord project staff. This resulted in irregular and inconsistent accommodation of these changes among the various UniWord components.

Missing capabilities: Several UniWord capabilities specified in the contract have not been implemented. Some examples are table processing and section numbering capabilities.

Unspecified capabilities: Several Uniword capabilities have been implemented that were not specified in the contract. Some examples are: the large number of text editor commands and the relational DBMS capabilities.

Product control: The UniWord project does not have a change control system. There are no baselined master versions of specifications or programs. Many versions of programs and documents are in circulation. There is no central directory of the product's components or deliverables. These factors cause many problems and delays in project activities, particularly in product integration and test.

Product Management

Project plan: Beyond some high-level Gantt charts, there was no evidence of a project plan. As a result, no preparation was made for a number of downstream activities. Some examples are:

- Preparation of test drivers and test data for integration and test activities
- Preparation of library capabilities for programs and documents

Reviews: No project reviews were held to determine customer satisfaction with the user interface or other product features, or to ensure that the project was ready to proceed to the next phase.

Milestones: Other than the high-level Gantt charts, there were no individual milestones established to track progress. Team members' weekly status reports included percent-complete estimates. These would generally reach 90 percent about halfway through the job, and would be useless thereafter.

Scope changes: Changes in the project's scope of work were initiated without consultation with the customer, or consideration of their impact on schedule and budget.

Also, as indicated earlier, there were overlaps and gaps in project responsibilities, and a lack of internal as well as external change control.

Personnel: Morale is very low among the project personnel. There are major doubts that the product can become successful, and a great deal of uncertainty about the project's future.

There are still major unresolved differences among project personnel about technical issues: the user interface style, the use of color, the use of windowing, the type of modularization, and the extension of Unix capabilities.

Some team members are not well qualified for their assignments. Details can be provided separately.

Finance: Universal Micros has paid $300,000 to SoftWizards in three equal installments. SoftWizards' financial reporting and control system is rather loosely structured. Their charges to the UniWord project are:

Expenditures	$298,541
Outstanding Commitments	6,022
Total	$304,563

SoftWizards has agreed to pay the additional $4,563 in outstanding commitments.

Options and Recommendations

To be determined.

This is the end of the case study. Its risk issues will be covered in the various parts of Section 2.

1.6: Overview of Tutorial Articles

The first five articles in Section 1 of this tutorial (McFarlan, three Boehm articles, and Gilb) establish an overall context for addressing risk management issues throughout the data processing and software life cycle. The next three articles (Rothfeder, Neumann, and Tate) present a wide range of examples that provide motivation for the importance of risk management in a software manager's career, and illustrate some specific characteristics of software risk items. The final article on Theory W software management provides a more positive context for risk management: providing assurance that a software project will make winners of all of its major participants (developers, customers, users, maintainers, and bosses).

1.6.1: Software Risk Management Overview and Context Articles

The first article, McFarlan's "Portfolio Approach to Information Systems" [McFarlan, 1981], alerted the mainstream business data processing (DP) community to the importance of risk considerations in determining the ensemble or portfolio of DP applications an organization chooses to implement and operate. Previously, DP portfolio decisions tended to be made by using a nominal-case or expected-value cost-benefit comparison. Relatively little attention was given to high-risk elements that could seriously compromise the organization's bottom line.

McFarlan's article cites examples showing the importance of risk considerations in DP portfolio management. It then identifies three primary risk dimensions—project size, experience with DP technology, and project structure—and provides examples of a questionnaire for determining the relative risk level of a project with the use of the three risk dimensions. It then discusses what types of management tools and approaches are most likely to ensure project success for the various combinations of project size, technology experience, and project structure. The paper's final conclusion is that there is no single monolithic DP project management approach that is optimal for all projects, but that it is preferable to tailor the project management approach to the primary sources of project risk.

The next paper, Boehm's "A Spiral Model of Software Development and Enhancement" [Boehm, 1988a], provides a specific process for tailoring a project's management approach to its sources of risk. The paper begins with descriptions and comparative analyses of current and previous software process models (build and fix, waterfall, evolutionary development, and transform). It then proceeds to describe the spiral model and its use of risk analysis to determine the preferred ordering and emphasis of candidate software-project activities (prototyping, requirements specification, simulation, reuse analysis, etc.).

This paper also provides an extensive example of the spiral model's use on a successful project to develop a large corporate software engineering environment. The example shows how risk management considerations were used to evolve the system's objectives, to evaluate architectural alternatives, to establish increments of system capability, and to employ combinations of prototypes and risk-driven specifications to elaborate the system's definition.

The paper concludes with a discussion of issues needing further refinement to bring the use of the spiral model to the level of maturity of existing process models such as the waterfall model. One of the key conclusions was the need to bring the processes of risk management (risk identification, risk analysis, risk management planning, etc.) to a higher level of definition and maturity. That has been one of the primary motivating factors for developing this tutorial.

Another challenge for the spiral model was to accommodate the increasing use of commercial off-the-shelf (COTS) products within software systems. If one has the opportunity to choose among a group of similar COTS products with somewhat different combinations of capabilities (e.g., electronic publication systems), the use of a complete, frozen requirements specification to determine the choice is both time inefficient and overconstraining. It is much more effective to use an approximate set of system requirements to determine a set of evaluation criteria for choosing the best COTS product. Then, once the best COTS product is selected, its strengths and remaining deficiencies can be used to determine a set of requirements for any remaining custom-developed portions of the system.

The next tutorial paper, "Applying Process Programming to the Spiral Model" [Boehm-Belz, 1988], addresses the COTS challenge by providing an elaboration of the spiral model. This elaboration provides a way to apply risk management and the spiral cycle to the software *process* as well as to the software *product*. The paper also provides an example of how this elaborated spiral model was used to determine an effective process for developing TRW's next-generation software engineering environment, the Quantum Leap system.

A third challenge for risk management and the spiral model has been to determine how they can best be used in tailored versions of more traditional software acquisition methods such as the U.S. Department of Defense's software development standard, DoD-STD-2167. The new 2167A version of this standard is much more flexible than its predecessor, 2167, but it is still too easy to inappropriately go with the waterfall model as the default implementation of 2167A.

The next paper, "Rapid Prototyping, Risk Management, 2167, and the Ada Process Model" [Boehm, 1988b], provides a synthesis of the spiral model, DoD-STD-2167A, and Ada technology. It uses an increasingly detailed sequence of risk management plans to determine the phasing of 2167A's milestones with respect to the use of prototyping, COTS products, and other advanced technologies. The paper also includes a set of process tailoring tables showing which process models work best for various classes of commonly-encountered application domains, and showing the critical software activities that must be performed in the early concept-definition phases to determine the best software-acquisition approach. A further refinement of these tables is presented in Subsection 4.1.

The final paper, which covers the context and principles of software risk management, is the chapter on "Estimating the Risk" from Gilb's book, *Principles of Software Engineering Management* [Gilb, 1988]. Gilb provides a number of succinct and useful risk management principles, such as:

- If you don't actively attack the risks, they will actively attack you

- Never make promises you cannot keep, no matter what the pressure

- When something happens during the project that you did not foresee, which increases deviation from planned risk, immediately raise the issue, in writing, with your constructive suggestion as to how to deal with it

- If you don't ask for risk information, you are asking for trouble

As can be seen from these principles, Gilb's main focus is on the individual software project member or manager, and on personal responsibility for risks and their consequences. Particular risk estimation techniques presented tend to be of the "back of the envelope" variety, but very much to the point for practical project situations. The illustrative real-world examples are also very useful in bridging the gap from the principles to everyday practice.

1.6.2: Software Risk Examples and Motivation

Fairly frequently, you will encounter situations in which you believe that software risk management would be a good approach for your project or organization, but you are faced with primarily complacent or skeptical users, marketers, or managers who feel that software risks are too unlikely to justify spending extra effort in dealing with them.

The next few articles provide some help for such situations. They provide strong evidence of the frequency and criticality of software risk items across all of the major software application domains: business, industry, service, and government systems.

The recent *Business Week* article, "It's Late, Costly, Incompetent—But Try Firing a Computer System" [Rothfeder, 1988], provides some current examples in the business data-processing area. Allstate Insurance's integrated-automation system escalated from an $8 million, five-year project to a currently estimated $100 million, 11-year project. Blue Cross-Blue Shield of Wisconsin commissioned a $200 million computer system whose hardware was delivered on schedule in 18 months, but the software didn't work. The system disbursed $60 million in overpayments or duplicate checks in its first year of operation. The article cites a recent Peat Marwick Mitchell & Co. survey of 600 client firms, indicating that 35 percent of them currently have similar major "runaway" data-processing projects.

The article cites some guidelines for keeping such projects under control. Some of the guidelines are good, such as user involvement, key personnel clauses, and contract performance clauses. Others are highly questionable, though, such as putting nontechnical management in charge and setting up 12-month review milestones, which are much too far apart for good risk control. A much preferable approach is the monthly review of progress on the top-10 project risk items discussed under Risk Monitoring in Section 2 of this tutorial.

Peter Neumann, the editor of ACM *Software Engineering Notes*, has performed a valuable service to the software community by publishing a continuing series of "Risks to the Public in Computers and Related Systems" in each issue of *Software Engineering Notes*. The next article in this section [Neumann, 1988] is a recent example of one of these summaries. It includes budget and schedule risk items such as the major Bank of America trust division software overrun; operational risks affecting human safety and major financial losses, and an increasing number of risk items dealing with software viruses and other computer security problems. The fact that a similarly-sized "Risks to the Public" section appears every quarter in *Software Engineering Notes* gives additional perspectives on the relative frequency of software risk situations.

The next article, Tate's "Risk! The Third Factor" [Tate, 1988], focuses on computer security and corporate vulnerability to software and information systems problems. It highlights the trends toward corporate emphasis on information systems for strategic competitiveness, and toward total corporate reliance on the successful functioning of computers, software, and interdependent networks. It describes the strategies being pioneered by corporations such as Aetna, which has integrated the information system risk management function into its corporate risk management department. A typical major benefit has been the identification and resolution of potential critical single-point failures in Aetna's information processing systems. The article also summarizes an 11-point information system security risk management strategy formulated by Sweden's Vulnerability Board.

1.6.3: Software Risk Management and Theory W

As discussed earlier, risk management can engender a somewhat negative and pessimistic attitude toward software development, unless it is incorporated within a more positive overall software management approach. The Boehm and Ross article, "Theory W Software Project Management: Principles and Examples" [Boehm-Ross, 1989], establishes such a positive approach. According to Theory W, a necessary and sufficient set of conditions for a successful software development is the creation and sustenance of a set of win-win conditions for all of the major participants in the software process. These participants include the software developers, customers, users, maintainers, bosses, or other key parties such as the operators of systems that interact strongly with the system under development. The role of risk management under Theory W is the positive role of watching for the win conditions of each of the various parties, and of applying corrective action whenever it appears as if their win conditions may be compromised by a risk item.

The paper establishes a nine-step process for achieving a win-win software process. These steps include understanding how people want to win, establishing reasonable expectations, and identifying and managing your win-lose and lose-lose risks. The paper then shows how one can derive a set of strategic and tactical guidelines for software project management by applying the nine key steps to each of the participants in the software process. It provides a set of techniques for creating win-win situations, and presents an extensive case study of an unsuccessful software project, with an analysis of how Theory W and risk management could have identified and avoided the problems encountered by the project.

Portfolio approach to information systems

F. Warren McFarlan

Assessing the risk of their projects, separately and in the aggregate, will help managers make more informed decisions and ensure more successful outcomes

Despite business's more than 20 years of experience with information systems (IS), disasters in that area still occur with surprising regularity. According to this author, managers, both general and IS, can avert many of these fiascoes by assessing the risks—singly and as a portfolio—in advance of implementation. Also he notes that difficult projects require different management approaches. The chief determinants of risk are the size and structure of the project and the company's experience with the technology involved. Companies can use a series of questions to assess risk and to build a risk profile that will help them choose the best management tools for projects of differing risk.

Warren McFarlan is professor of business administration at the Harvard Business School, where he has taught extensively in the areas of management information systems and information systems administration. This is his third article for HBR.

☐ A major industrial products company discovers one and a half months before the installation date for a computer system that a $15 million effort to convert from one manufacturer to another is in trouble, and installation must be delayed a year. Eighteen months later, the changeover has still not taken place.

☐ A large consumer products company budgets $250,000 for a new computer-based personnel information system to be ready in nine months. Two years later, $2.5 million has been spent, and an estimated $3.6 million more is needed to complete the job. The company has to stop the project.

☐ A sizable financial institution slips $1.5 million over budget and 12 months behind on the development of programs for a new financial systems package, vital for the day-to-day functioning of one of its major operating groups. Once the system is finally installed, average transaction response times are much longer than expected.

Stories from the Stage 1 and Stage 2 days of the late 1960s and early 1970s?[1] No! All these events took place in 1980 in *Fortune* "500" companies (I could have selected equally dramatic examples from overseas). In a fashion almost embarrassing to relate, the day of the big disaster on a major information systems (IS) project has not passed. Given business's more than 20 years of IS experience, the question is "Why?"

My analysis of these cases and first-hand acquaintance with a number of IS projects in the past ten years suggest three serious deficiencies in practice that involve both general management and IS management. The first two are the failure to assess individual project risk and the failure to consider the aggregate risk of the portfolio of projects. The third is the lack of recognition that different projects require different managerial approaches. This article focuses on these deficiencies and suggests ways of redressing them.

1. Richard L. Nolan and Cyrus F. Gibson, "Managing the Four Stages of EDP Growth," HBR January-February 1974, p. 76.

Elements of project risk

The typical project feasibility study covers exhaustively such topics as financial benefits, qualitative benefits, implementation costs, target milestones and completion dates, and necessary staffing levels. In precise, crisp terms, the developers of these estimates provide voluminous supporting documentation. Only rarely, however, do they deal frankly with the risk of slippage in time, cost overrun, technical shortfall, or outright failure. Rather, they deny the existence of such possibilities by ignoring them. They assume the appropriate human skills, controls, and so on, that will ensure success.

By *risk* I am suggesting exposure to such consequences as:

Failure to obtain all, or even any, of the anticipated benefits.

Costs of implementation that vastly exceed planned levels.

Time for implementation that is much greater than expected.

Technical performance of resulting systems that turns out to be significantly below estimate.

Incompatability of the system with the selected hardware and software.

These kinds of risk in practical situations, of course, are not independent of each other; rather, they are closely related. In discussing risk, I am assuming that the manager has brought appropriate methods and approaches to bear on the project (mismanagement is obviously another element of risk). Risk, in my definition here, is what remains after application of those tools.

In my discussion, I am also not implying a correlation between *risk* and *bad*. These words represent entirely different concepts, and the link between the two normally is that higher-risk projects must yield higher benefits to compensate for the increased downside exposure.

At least three important dimensions influence the risk inherent in a project:

1 *Project size.* The larger it is in dollar expense, staffing levels, elapsed time, and number of departments affected by the project, the greater the risk. Multimillion-dollar projects obviously carry more risk than $50,000 projects and also, in general, affect the company more if the risk is realized. A related concern is the size of the project relative to the normal size of a systems development group's projects. The implicit risk is usually lower on a $1 million project of a department whose average undertaking costs $2–$3 million than on a $250,000 project of a department that has never ventured a project costing more than $50,000.

2 *Experience with the technology.* Because of the greater likelihood of unexpected technical problems, project risk increases as familiarity of the project team and the IS organization decreases with the hardware, operating systems, data base handler, and project application language. A project that has a slight risk for a leading-edge, large systems development group may have a very high risk for a smaller, less technically advanced group. Yet the latter group can reduce risk through purchase of outside skills for an undertaking involving technology that is in general commercial use.

3 *Project structure.* In some projects, the very nature of the task defines completely, from the moment of conceptualization, the outputs. I classify such schemes as highly structured. They carry much less risk than those whose outputs are more subject to the manager's judgment and hence are vulnerable to change. The outputs of these projects are fixed and not subject to change during the life of the project.

An insurance company automating preparation of its agents' rate book is an example of such a highly structured project. At the project's beginning, planners reached total agreement on the product lines to be included, the layout of each page, and the process of generating each number. Throughout the life of the project, there was no need to alter these decisions; consequently, the team organized to reach a stable, fixed output rather than to cope with a potentially mobile target.

Quite the opposite was true in the personnel information project I mentioned at the beginning, which was a low-structure project. In that situation, the users could not reach a consensus on what the outputs should be, and these decisions shifted almost weekly, crippling progress.

Assessing risk

Exhibit I, by combining the various dimensions of risk, identifies eight distinct project categories, each carrying a different degree of risk. Even at this gross intuitive level, such a classifica-

Exhibit I

Effect of degree of structure on project risk

	High	Low
Low company relative technology	Large – low risk	Large – low risk (very susceptible to mismanagement)
	Small – very low risk	Small – very low risk (very susceptible to mismanagement)
High company relative technology	Large – medium risk	Large – very high risk
	Small – medium-low risk	Small – high risk

tion is useful to separate projects for quite different types of management review. IS organizations have used it successfully to distinguish the relative risk for their own understanding and as a basis for communicating these notions of risk to users and senior corporate executives.

A legitimate concern is how to ensure that different people viewing the same project will come to the same rough assessment of its risks. While the best way to assess this is still uncertain, several companies have made significant progress in addressing the problem.

Exhibit II presents, in part, a method one large company developed for measuring risk: a list of 54 questions about a project that the project manager answers both prior to senior management's approval of the proposal and several times during its implementation.

This company developed the questions after carefully analyzing its experience with successful and unsuccessful projects. I include some of them as an example of how to bridge concepts and practice. No analytic framework lies behind these questions, and they may not be appropriate for all companies; however, they represent a good starting point and several other large companies have used them.

Both the project leader and the key user answer these questions. Differences in the answers are then reconciled. (Obviously, the questionnaire provides data that are no better than the quality of thinking that goes into the answers.)

These questions not only highlight the risks but also suggest alternative ways of conceiving of and managing the project. If the initial aggregate risk score seems high, analysis of the answers may suggest ways of lessening the risk through reduced scope, lower-level technology, multiple phases, and so on. Thus managers should not consider risk as a static descriptor; rather, its presence should encourage better approaches to project management. Numbers 5 and 6 under the section on structure are particularly good examples of questions that could trigger changes.

The higher the score, the higher must be the level of approval. Only the executive committee in this company approves very risky projects. Such an approach ensures that top managers are aware of significant hazards and are making appropriate risk strategic-benefit trade-offs. Managers should ask questions such as the following:

Are the benefits great enough to offset the risks?

Can the affected parts of the organization survive if the project fails?

Have the planners considered appropriate alternatives?

On a periodic basis, these questions are answered again during the undertaking to reveal any major changes. If all is going well, the risk continuously declines during implementation as the size of the remaining task dwindles and familiarity with the technology grows.

Answers to the questions provide a common understanding among senior, IS, and user managers as to a project's relative risk. Often the fiascoes occur when senior managers believe a project has low risk and IS managers know it has high risk. In such cases, IS managers may not admit their assessment because they fear that the senior executives will not tolerate this kind of uncertainty in data processing and will cancel a project of potential benefit to the organization.

Portfolio risk profile

In addition to determining relative risk for single projects, a company should develop an aggregate risk profile of the portfolio of systems and programming projects. While there is no such thing as a correct risk profile in the abstract, there are appropriate risk profiles for different types of companies and strategies. For example, in an industry that is data processing intensive, or where computers are an important part of product structure

Exhibit II	**Risk assessment questionnaire**
	sample from a total of 54 questions

Size risk assessment		Weight
1.	**Total development man-hours for system** [*]	5
	100 to 3,000	Low – 1
	3,000 to 15,000	Medium – 2
	15,000 to 30,000	Medium – 3
	More than 30,000	High – 4
2.	**What is estimated project implementation time?**	4
	12 months or less	Low – 1
	13 months to 24 months	Medium – 2
	More than 24 months	High – 3
3.	**Number of departments (other than IS) involved with system**	4
	One	Low – 1
	Two	Medium – 2
	Three or more	High – 3

Structure risk assessment		Weight
1.	**If replacement system is proposed, what percentage of existing functions are replaced on a one-to-one basis?**	5
	0% to 25%	High – 3
	25% to 50%	Medium – 2
	50% to 100%	Low – 1
2.	**What is severity of procedural changes in user department caused by proposed system?**	5
	Low – 1	
	Medium – 2	
	High – 3	
3.	**Does user organization have to change structurally to meet requirements of new system?**	5
	No	– 0
	Minimal	Low – 1
	Somewhat	Medium – 2
	Major	High – 3
4.	**What is general attitude of user?**	5
	Poor – anti data-processing solution	High – 3
	Fair – some reluctance	Medium – 2
	Good – understands value of DP solution	– 0
5.	**How committed is upper-level user management to system?**	5
	Somewhat reluctant or unknown	High – 3
	Adequate	Medium – 2
	Extremely enthusiastic	Low – 1

6.	**Has a joint data processing/user team been established?**	5
	No	High – 3
	Part-time user representative appointed	Low – 1
	Full-time user representative appointed	– 0

Technology risk assessment		Weight
1.	**Which of the hardware is new to the company?**	5
	None	– 0
	CPU	High – 3
	Peripheral and/or additional storage	High – 3
	Terminals	High – 3
	Mini or micro	High – 3
2.	**Is the system software (nonoperating system) new to IS project team?** [†]	5
	No	– 0
	Programming language	High – 3
	Data base	High – 3
	Data communications	High – 3
	Other – specify	High – 3
3.	**How knowledgeable is user in area of IS?**	5
	First exposure	High – 3
	Previous exposure but limited knowledge	Medium – 2
	High degree of capability	Low – 1
4.	**How knowledgeable is user representative in proposed application area?**	5
	Limited	High – 3
	Understands concept but no experience	Medium – 2
	Has been involved in prior implementation efforts	Low – 1
5.	**How knowledgeable is IS team in proposed application area?**	5
	Limited	High – 3
	Understands concept but no experience	Medium – 2
	Has been involved in prior implementation efforts	Low – 1

Note: Since the questions vary in importance, the company assigned weights to them subjectively. The numerical answer to the questions is multiplied by the question weight to calculate the question's contribution to the project's risk. The numbers are then added together to produce a risk score number for the project. Projects with risk scores within 10 points of each other are indistinguishable, but those separated by 100 points or more are very different to even the casual observer.
[*] Time to develop includes systems design, programming, testing, and installation.
[†] This question is scored by multiplying the sum of the numbers attached to the positive responses by the weights.
Source: This questionnaire is adapted from the Dallas Tire case, no. 9-180-006 (Boston, Mass.: HBS Case Services, 1980).

(such as banking and insurance), managers should be concerned when there are no high-risk projects. In such a case, the company may be leaving a product or service gap for competition to step into. On the other hand, a portfolio loaded with high-risk projects suggests that the company may be vulnerable to operational disruptions when projects are not completed as planned.

Conversely, in less computer-dependent companies, IS plays a profitable, useful, but distinctly supporting role, and management often considers this role appropriate. In such cases, heavy investment in high-risk projects appropriately may be smaller than in the first type of company.

Even here, however, a company should have some technologically exciting ventures to ensure familiarity with leading-edge technology and to maintain staff morale and interest. Thus the aggregate risk profiles of the portfolios of two companies could legitimately differ. *Exhibit III* shows in more detail the issues that influence IS toward or away from high-risk efforts (the risk profile should include projects that will come from outside software houses as well as those of the internal systems development group).

In summary, it is both possible and useful to talk about project risk during the feasibility study stage. The discussion of risk can be helpful both for those working on the individual project and for the department as a whole. Not only can this systematic analysis reduce the number of failures, but, equally important, its power as a communication link helps IS managers and senior executives reach agreement on the risks to be taken in line with corporate goals.

Contingency approach

Now the organization faces the difficult problem of project operation. Much of the literature and conventional wisdom about project management suggest that there is a single right way of doing it. A similar theme holds that managers should apply uniformly to all such ventures an appropriate cluster of tools, project management methods, and organizational linkages.

While there may indeed be a general-purpose set of tools, the contribution each device can make to planning and controlling the project varies widely according to the project's characteristics. Further, the means of involving the user—through steering committees, representation on the team, or as leader (not DP or IS professional)—

Exhibit III	Factors that influence risk profile of project portfolio		
		Portfolio low-risk focus	Portfolio high-risk focus
	Stability of IS development group	Low	High
	Perceived quality of IS development group by insiders	Low	High
	IS critical to delivery of current corporate services	No	Yes
	IS important decision-support aid	No	Yes
	Experienced IS systems development group	No	Yes
	Major IS fiascoes in last two years	Yes	No
	New IS management team	Yes	No
	IS perceived critical to delivery of future corporate services	No	Yes
	IS perceived critical to future decision-support aids	No	Yes
	Company perceived as backward in use of IS	No	Yes

should also vary by project type. In short, there is no universally correct way to run all projects. The general methods for managing projects fall into four principal types:

☐ *External integration tools* include organizational and other communication devices that link the project team's work to the users at both the managerial and the lower levels.

☐ *Internal integration* devices ensure that the team operates as an integrated unit.

☐ *Formal planning tools* help to structure the sequence of tasks in advance and estimate the time, money, and technical resources the team will need to execute them.

☐ *Formal control* mechanisms help managers evaluate progress and spot potential discrepancies so that corrective action can be taken.

Exhibit IV gives examples of the tools in each category commonly used by companies. The next paragraphs suggest how the degree of structure and the company-relative technology influence the selection of items from the four categories.

High structure—low technology

Projects that are highly structured and that present familiar technical problems are not only the lowest-risk projects but are also the easiest to manage (see *Exhibit I*). They are also the least common. *High structure* implies that the outputs are very well defined by the nature of the task, and the possibility of the users changing their minds as to what these outputs should be is essentially non-existent. Consequently, the leaders do not have to develop extensive administrative processes in order to get a diverse group of users both to agree to a design structure and to keep to that structure. External integration devices such as inclusion of analysts in user departments, heavy representation of users on the design team, and formal approval by users of design specifications are cumbersome and unnecessary for this type of undertaking. Other integrating devices, such as training users in how to operate the system, remain important.

The system's concept and design, however, are stable. At the same time, since the technology involved is familiar to the company, the project can proceed with a high percentage of persons having only average technical backgrounds and experience. The leader does not need strong IS skills. This type of project readily gives opportunity to the department's junior managers, who can gain experience that may lead to more ambitious tasks in the future.

Project life cycle planning concepts, with their focus on defining tasks and budgeting resources against them, force the team to develop a thorough and detailed plan (exposing areas of soft thinking in the process). Such projects are likely to meet the resulting milestone dates and keep within the target budget. Moreover, the usual control techniques for measuring progress against dates and budgets provide very reliable data for spotting discrepancies and building a desirable tension into the design team to work harder to avoid slippage.

A portfolio comprised of 90% of this type of project will produce little excitement for senior and user managers. It also requires a much more limited set of skills for the IS organization than might be needed for companies whose portfolios have quite a different mixture of projects. An example of this type of project is the agent's rate book project mentioned earlier.

High structure—high technology

These projects, vastly more complex than the first kind, involve some significant modifications from the practice outlined in project management handbooks. A good example of this type is the conversion of systems from one computer manufacturer to another with no enhancements

Exhibit IV	Tools of project management

External integration tools	Internal integration tools
Selection of user as project manager	Selection of experienced DP professional leadership team
Creation of user steering committee	Selection of manager to lead team
Frequency and depth of meetings of this committee	Frequent team meetings
User-managed change control process	Regular preparation and distribution of minutes within team on key design evolution decision
Frequency and detail of distribution of project team minutes to key users	
Selection of users as team members	Regular technical status reviews
Formal user specification approval process	Managed low turnover of team members
Progress reports prepared for corporate steering committee	Selection of high percentage of team members with significant previous work relationships
Users responsible for education and installation of system	Participation of team members in goal setting and deadline establishment
Users manage decision on key action dates	Outside technical assistance

Formal planning tasks	Formal control tasks
PERT, critical path, etc., networking	Periodic formal status reports versus plan
Milestone phases selection	Change control disciplines
Systems specification standards	Regular milestone presentation meetings
Feasibility study specifications	Deviations from plan
Project approval processes	
Project postaudit procedures	

(which is, of course, easier said than done). Another example of this kind of project is the conversion of a set of manual procedures onto a minicomputer with the objective only of doing the same functions more quickly.

The normal mechanisms for liaison with users are not crucial here (though they are in the next type of project), because the outputs are so well defined by the nature of the undertaking that both the development of specifications and the need to deal with systems changes from users are sharply lower. Liaison with users is nevertheless important for two reasons: (1) to ensure coordination on any changes in input-output or other manual procedure changes necessary for project success and (2) to deal with any systems restructuring that must follow from shortcomings in the project's technology.

It is not uncommon in this kind of project to discover during implementation that the technology is inadequate, forcing a long postponement while new technology is chosen or vital features pruned in order to make the task fit the available technology. In one such situation, a major industrial products company had to convert some computerized order-entry procedures to a manual basis so that the rest of an integrated materials management system could be shifted to already-purchased, new hardware.

Such technological shortcomings were also the main difficulty in the financial institution I described at the start of this article. In such a case, where system performance is much poorer than expected, user involvement is important both to prevent demoralization and to help implement either an alternative approach (less ambitious in design) or a mutual agreement to end the project.

The skills that lead to success in this type of project, however, are the same as for effective administration involving any kind of technical complexity. The leader needs this experience (preferably, but not necessarily, in an IS environment) as well as administrative experience, unless the project is not very large. The leader must also be effective in relating to technicians. From talking to the project team at various times, the ideal manager will anticipate difficulties before the technicians understand that they have a problem. In dealing with larger projects in this category, the manager's ability to establish and maintain teamwork through meetings, a record of all key design decisions, and subproject conferences is vital.

Project life cycle planning methods, such as PERT (program evaluation and review technique) and critical path, identify tasks and suitable completion dates. Their predictive value is much more limited here, however, than in the preceding category. The team will not understand key elements of the technology in advance, and seemingly minor bugs in such projects have a curious way of becoming major financial drains.

In one company, roughly once an hour an on-line banking system generated garbage across the CRT screen. While simply hitting a release key erased this screen of zeroes and x's, four months and more than $200,000 went into eliminating the so-called ghost screen. The solution lay in uncovering a complex interaction of hardware features, operating system functions, and application traffic patterns. Correction of the problem ultimately required the vendor to redesign several chips. And formal control mechanisms have limits in monitoring the progress of such projects.

In summary, technical leadership and internal integration are the keys in this type of project, and external integration plays a distinctly secondary role. Formal planning and control tools give more subjective than concrete projections, and the great danger is that neither IS managers nor high-level executives will recognize this. They may believe they have precise planning and close control when, in fact, they have neither.

Low structure—low technology

When these projects are intelligently managed, they have low risk. Over and over, however, such projects fail because of inadequate direction. In this respect they differ from the first type of project, where more ordinary managerial skills could ensure success. The key to operating this kind of project lies in an effective effort to involve the users.

Developing substantial user support for only one of the thousands of design options and keeping the users committed to that design are critical. Essential aspects of this process include the following:

> A user either as project leader or number 2 person on the team.

> A user steering committee to evaluate the design.

> An effort to break the project into a sequence of very small and discrete subprojects.

> Formal user review and approval on all key project specifications.

> Distribution of minutes of all key design meetings to users.

> Strong efforts to keep at least chief subproject time schedules below normal managerial and staff turnover times in the user areas (since a consensus on approach with the predecessor of a user manager is of dubious value).

The personnel information debacle I mentioned at the start of this article is an example of what can happen when this process does not take place. Soon after work started, the director of human resources decided that his senior staff's par-

Exhibit V

Relative contribution of tools to ensuring project success

Project type	Project description	External integration	Internal integration	Formal planning	Formal control
I	High structure, low technology, large	Low	Medium	High	High
II	High structure, low technology, small	Low	Low	Medium	High
III	High structure, high technology, large	Low	High	Medium	Medium
IV	High structure, high technology, small	Low	High	Low	Low
V	Low structure, low technology, large	High	Medium	High	High
VI	Low structure, low technology, small	High	Low	Medium	High
VII	Low structure, high technology, large	High	High	Low+	Low+
VIII	Low structure, high technology, small	High	High	Low	Low

ticipation in the design was a waste of their time, and he made sure none of them was involved.

Instead of immediately killing the undertaking, the IS manager attempted to continue work under the leadership of one of his technically oriented staff who had little experience dealing with the human resources department. Bombarded by pressures from the human resources staff that he did not understand, the project manager allowed the systems design to expand to include more and more detail of doubtful merit until the system collapsed. The changing design made much of the programming obsolete. Tough, pragmatic leadership from users in the design stage would have made all the difference in the outcome.

The importance of user leadership increases once the design is final. Almost inevitably, at that stage users will produce some version of "I have been thinking. . . ." Unless the desired changes are of critical strategic significance to the user (a judgment best made by a responsible user-oriented project manager), the requests must be diverted and postponed until they can be considered in some formal change control process.

Unless the process is rigorously controlled (a problem intensified by the near impossibility of distinguishing between the economies of a proposed alternative and those implicit in the original design), users will make change after change, and the project will evolve rapidly to a state of permanent deferral, with completion always six months in the future.

If the project is well integrated with other departments, the formal planning tools will be very useful in structuring tasks and helping to remove any remaining uncertainty. The target com-pletion dates will be firm as long as the systems target remains fixed. Similarly, the formal control devices afford clear insight into progress to date, flagging both advances and slippages. If integration with outside departments is weak, use of these tools will produce an entirely unwarranted feeling of confidence.

By definition, the problems of technology management are usually less difficult in this type of project than in the high technology ventures, and a staff with a normal mixture of technical backgrounds should be adequate.

In fact, in almost every respect management of this type of project differs from the previous two. The key to success is close, aggressive management of external integration, supplemented by formal planning and control tools. Leadership must flow from the user rather than from the technical side.

Low structure—high technology

Because these projects are complex and carry high risk, their leaders need technical experience and knowledge of, and ability to communicate with, users. The same intensive effort toward external integration described in the previous class of projects is necessary here. Total commitment on the part of users to a particular set of design specifications is critical, and again they must agree to one out of the many thousands of options.

Unfortunately, however, an option desirable from the user's perspective may turn out to be infeasible in the selected hardware-software system. In the last several years, such situations have occurred particularly with stand-alone minicomputer systems designs, and they commonly lead either to significant restructuring of the project or elimination of it altogether. Consequently, users should be well represented at both the policy and the operations levels.

At the same time, technical considerations make strong technical leadership and internal project integration vital. This kind of effort requires the most experienced project leaders, and they will need wholehearted support from the users. In approving such a project, managers must face the question whether it can or should be divided into a series of much smaller problems or use less innovative technology.

While formal planning and control tools can be useful here, at the early stages they contribute little to reducing uncertainty and to highlighting problems. The planning tools do allow the manager to structure the sequence of tasks. Unfortunately, in this type of project new tasks crop up with monotonous regularity, and tasks that appear simple and small suddenly become complex and protracted. Time, cost, and resulting technical performance turn out to be almost impossible to predict simultaneously. In the Apollo moon project, for example, technical performance achievement was key, and cost and time simply fell out. In the private sector, all too often this is an unacceptable outcome.

Contingency approach

Exhibit V shows the relative contribution that each of the four groups of project management tools makes to ensure maximum control, given a project's inherent risk. It reveals that managers need quite different styles and approaches to manage the different types of projects effectively. Although the framework could be made more complex by including more dimensions, that would only confirm this primary conclusion.

The usual corporate handbook on project management, with its unidimensional approach, fails to deal with the realities of the task facing today's managers, particularly those dealing with information services. The right approach flows from the project rather than the other way around.

The need to deal with the corporate culture within which both IS and project management operate further complicates the problems. Use of formal project planning and control tools is much more likely to produce successful results in a highly formal environment than in one where the prevailing culture is more personal and informal. Similarly, the selection and effective use of integrating mechanisms is very much a function of the corporate culture.

Thus the type of company culture further complicates my suggestions as to how different types of projects should be managed. (Too many former IS managers have made the fatal assumption that they were in an ideal position to reform corporate culture from their position!)

The past decade has brought new challenges to IS project management, and experience has indicated better ways to think about the management process. My conclusions, then, are threefold:

1 We will continue to experience major disappointments as we push into new fields. Today, however, the dimensions of risk can be identified in advance and a decision made whether to proceed. If we proceed, we will sometimes fail.

2 The work of the systems development department in aggregate may be thought of as a portfolio. Other authors have discussed what the appropriate components of that portfolio should be at a particular point in time. The aggregate risk profile of that portfolio, however, is a critical (though often overlooked) strategic decision.

3 Project management in the IS field is complex and multidimensional. Different types of projects require different clusters of management tools if they are to succeed. ▽

A Spiral Model of Software Development and Enhancement

Barry W. Boehm, TRW Defense Systems Group

Reprinted from *Computer*, May 1988, pages 61–72. Copyright ©1988 by The Institute of Electrical and Electronics Engineers, Inc. All rights reserved.

"Stop the life cycle—I want to get off!"
"Life-cycle Concept Considered Harmful."
"The waterfall model is dead."
"No, it isn't, but it should be."

These statements exemplify the current debate about software life-cycle process models. The topic has recently received a great deal of attention.

The Defense Science Board Task Force Report on Military Software[1] issued in 1987 highlighted the concern that traditional software process models were discouraging more effective approaches to software development such as prototyping and software reuse. The Computer Society has sponsored tutorials and workshops on software process models that have helped clarify many of the issues and stimulated advances in the field (see "Further reading").

The spiral model presented in this article is one candidate for improving the software process model situation. The major distinguishing feature of the spiral model is that it creates a *risk-driven* approach to the software process rather than a primarily *document-driven* or *code-driven* process. It incorporates many of the strengths of other models and resolves many of their difficulties.

This article opens with a short description of software process models and the issues they address. Subsequent sections outline the process steps involved in the

This evolving risk-driven approach provides a new framework for guiding the software process.

spiral model; illustrate the application of the spiral model to a software project, using the TRW Software Productivity Project as an example; summarize the primary advantages and implications involved in using the spiral model and the primary difficulties in using it at its current incomplete level of elaboration; and present resulting conclusions.

Background on software process models

The primary functions of a software process model are to determine the *order of the stages* involved in software development and evolution and to establish the *transition criteria* for progressing from one stage to the next. These include completion criteria for the current stage plus choice criteria and entrance criteria for the next stage. Thus, a process model addresses the following software project questions:

(1) What shall we do next?
(2) How long shall we continue to do it?

Consequently, a process model differs from a software method (often called a methodology) in that a method's primary focus is on how to navigate through each phase (determining data, control, or "uses" hierarchies; partitioning functions; allocating requirements) and how to represent phase products (structure charts; stimulus-response threads; state transition diagrams).

Why are software process models important? Primarily because they provide guidance on the order (phases, increments, prototypes, validation tasks, etc.) in which a project should carry out its major tasks. Many software projects, as the next section shows, have come to grief because they pursued their various development and evolution phases in the wrong order.

Evolution of process models. Before concentrating in depth on the spiral model, we should take a look at a number of others: the code-and-fix model, the stagewise model and the waterfall model, the evolutionary development model, and the transform model.

The code-and-fix model. The basic model used in the earliest days of software

EH0291-5/89/0000/0026$01.00 ©1988 IEEE

26

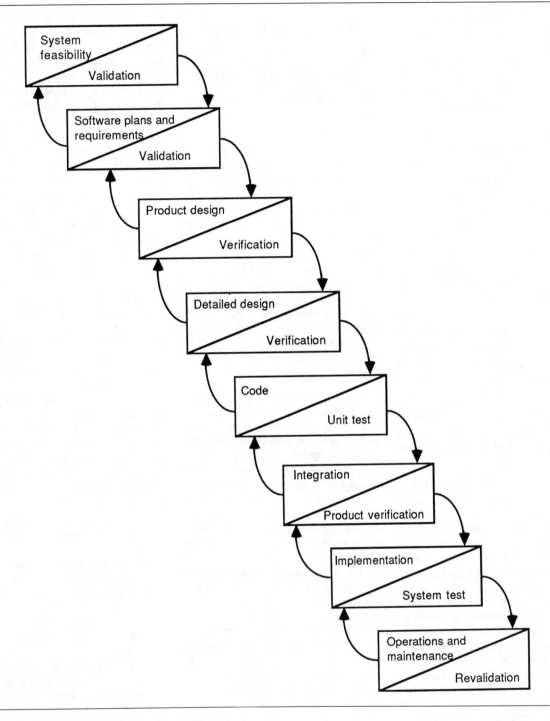

Figure 1. The waterfall model of the software life cycle.

development contained two steps:

(1) Write some code.

(2) Fix the problems in the code.

Thus, the order of the steps was to do some coding first and to think about the requirements, design, test, and maintenance later. This model has three primary difficulties:

(a) After a number of fixes, the code became so poorly structured that subsequent fixes were very expensive. This underscored the need for a design phase prior to coding.

(b) Frequently, even well-designed software was such a poor match to users' needs that it was either rejected outright or expensively redeveloped. This made the need for a requirements phase prior to design evident.

(c) Code was expensive to fix because of poor preparation for testing and modifi-

COMPUTER

cation. This made it clear that explicit recognition of these phases, as well as test-and-evolution planning and preparation tasks in the early phases, were needed.

The stagewise and waterfall models. As early as 1956, experience on large software systems such as the Semi-Automated Ground Environment (SAGE) had led to the recognition of these problems and to the development of a stagewise model[2] to address them. This model stipulated that software be developed in successive stages (operational plan, operational specifications, coding specifications, coding, parameter testing, assembly testing, shakedown, system evaluation).

The waterfall model,[3] illustrated in Figure 1, was a highly influential 1970 refinement of the stagewise model. It provided two primary enhancements to the stagewise model:

(1) Recognition of the feedback loops between stages, and a guideline to confine the feedback loops to successive stages to minimize the expensive rework involved in feedback across many stages.

(2) An initial incorporation of prototyping in the software life cycle, via a "build it twice" step running in parallel with requirements analysis and design.

The waterfall model's approach helped eliminate many difficulties previously encountered on software projects. The waterfall model has become the basis for most software acquisition standards in government and industry. Some of its initial difficulties have been addressed by adding extensions to cover incremental development, parallel developments, program families, accommodation of evolutionary changes, formal software development and verification, and stagewise validation and risk analysis.

However, even with extensive revisions and refinements, the waterfall model's basic scheme has encountered some more fundamental difficulties, and these have led to the formulation of alternative process models.

A primary source of difficulty with the waterfall model has been its emphasis on fully elaborated documents as completion criteria for early requirements and design phases. For some classes of software, such as compilers or secure operating systems, this is the most effective way to proceed. However, it does not work well for many classes of software, particularly interactive

> ## The waterfall model has become the basis for most software acquisition standards.

end-user applications. Document-driven standards have pushed many projects to write elaborate specifications of poorly understood user interfaces and decision-support functions, followed by the design and development of large quantities of unusable code.

These projects are examples of how waterfall-model projects have come to grief by pursuing stages in the wrong order. Furthermore, in areas supported by fourth-generation languages (spreadsheet or small business applications), it is clearly unnecessary to write elaborate specifications for one's application before implementing it.

The evolutionary development model. The above concerns led to the formulation of the *evolutionary development* model,[4] whose stages consist of expanding increments of an operational software product, with the directions of evolution being determined by operational experience.

The evolutionary development model is ideally matched to a fourth-generation language application and well matched to situations in which users say, "I can't tell you what I want, but I'll know it when I see it." It gives users a rapid initial operational capability and provides a realistic operational basis for determining subsequent product improvements.

Nonetheless, evolutionary development also has its difficulties. It is generally difficult to distinguish it from the old code-and-fix model, whose spaghetti code and lack of planning were the initial motivation for the waterfall model. It is also based on the often-unrealistic assumption that the user's operational system will be flexible enough to accommodate unplanned evolution paths. This assumption is unjustified in three primary circumstances:

(1) Circumstances in which several independently evolved applications must subsequently be closely integrated.

(2) "Information-sclerosis" cases, in which temporary work-arounds for software deficiencies increasingly solidify into

unchangeable constraints on evolution. The following comment is a typical example: "It's nice that you could change those equipment codes to make them more intelligible for us, but the Codes Committee just met and established the current codes as company standards."

(3) Bridging situations, in which the new software is incrementally replacing a large existing system. If the existing system is poorly modularized, it is difficult to provide a good sequence of "bridges" between the old software and the expanding increments of new software.

Under such conditions, evolutionary development projects have come to grief by pursuing stages in the wrong order: evolving a lot of hard-to-change code before addressing long-range architectural and usage considerations.

The transform model. The "spaghetti code" difficulties of the evolutionary development and code-and-fix models can also become a difficulty in various classes of waterfall-model applications, in which code is optimized for performance and becomes increasingly hard to modify. The transform model[5] has been proposed as a solution to this dilemma.

The transform model assumes the existence of a capability to automatically convert a formal specification of a software product into a program satisfying the specification. The steps then prescribed by the transform model are

- a formal specification of the best initial understanding of the desired product;
- automatic transformation of the specification into code;
- an iterative loop, if necessary, to improve the performance of the resulting code by giving optimization guidance to the transformation system;
- exercise of the resulting product; and
- an outer iterative loop to adjust the specification based on the resulting operational experience, and to rederive, reoptimize, and exercise the adjusted software product.

The transform model thus bypasses the difficulty of having to modify code that has become poorly structured through repeated reoptimizations, since the modifications are made to the specification. It also avoids the extra time and expense involved in the intermediate design, code, and test activities.

Still, the transform model has various

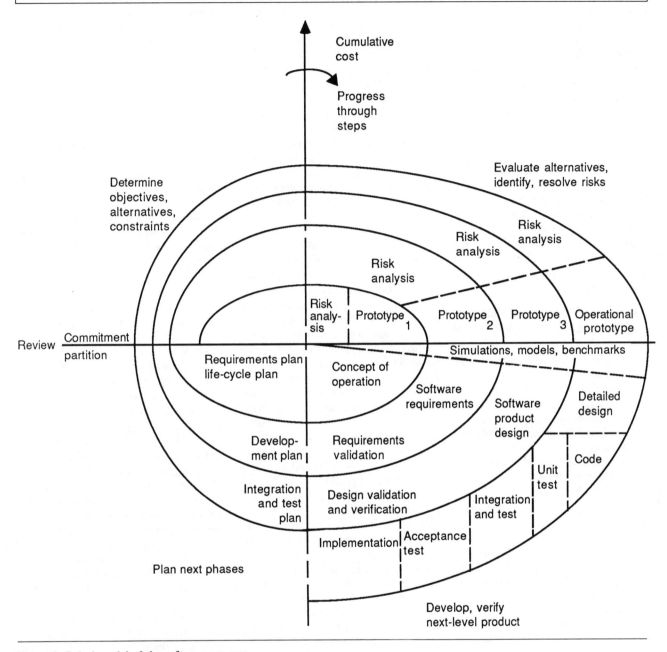

Figure 2. Spiral model of the software process.

difficulties. Automatic transformation capabilities are only available for small products in a few limited areas: spreadsheets, small fourth-generation language applications, and limited computer-science domains. The transform model also shares some of the difficulties of the evolutionary development model, such as the assumption that users' operational systems will always be flexible enough to support unplanned evolution paths.

Additionally, it would face a formidable knowledge-base-maintenance problem in dealing with the rapidly increasing and evolving supply of reusable software components and commercial software products. (Simply consider the problem of tracking the costs, performance, and features of all commercial database management systems, and automatically choosing the best one to implement each new or changed specification.)

The spiral model

The spiral model of the software process (see Figure 2) has been evolving for several years, based on experience with various refinements of the waterfall model as applied to large government software projects. As will be discussed, the spiral model can accommodate most previous models as special cases and further provides guidance as to which combination of previous models best fits a given software situation. Development of the TRW Software Productivity System (TRW-SPS), described in the next section, is its most complete application to date.

The radial dimension in Figure 2 represents the cumulative cost incurred in accomplishing the steps to date; the angular dimension represents the progress made in completing each cycle of the spiral. (The model reflects the underlying concept that each cycle involves a progression that addresses the same sequence of steps, for each portion of the product and for each of its levels of elaboration, from an overall concept of operation document down to the coding of each individual program.) Note that some artistic license has been taken with the increasing cumulative cost dimension to enhance legibility of the steps in Figure 2.

A typical cycle of the spiral. Each cycle of the spiral begins with the identification of

- the objectives of the portion of the product being elaborated (performance, functionality, ability to accommodate change, etc.);
- the alternative means of implementing this portion of the product (design A, design B, reuse, buy, etc.); and
- the constraints imposed on the application of the alternatives (cost, schedule, interface, etc.).

The next step is to evaluate the alternatives relative to the objectives and constraints. Frequently, this process will identify areas of uncertainty that are significant sources of project risk. If so, the next step should involve the formulation of a cost-effective strategy for resolving the sources of risk. This may involve prototyping, simulation, benchmarking, reference checking, administering user questionnaires, analytic modeling, or combinations of these and other risk-resolution techniques.

Once the risks are evaluated, the next step is determined by the relative remaining risks. If performance or user-interface risks strongly dominate program development or internal interface-control risks, the next step may be an evolutionary development one: a minimal effort to specify the overall nature of the product, a plan for the next level of prototyping, and the development of a more detailed prototype to continue to resolve the major risk issues.

If this prototype is operationally useful and robust enough to serve as a low-risk base for future product evolution, the subsequent risk-driven steps would be the evolving series of evolutionary prototypes going toward the right in Figure 2. In this case, the option of writing specifications would be addressed but not exercised. Thus, risk considerations can lead to a project implementing only a subset of all the potential steps in the model.

On the other hand, if previous prototyping efforts have already resolved all of the performance or user-interface risks, and program development or interface-control risks dominate, the next step follows the basic waterfall approach (concept of operation, software requirements, preliminary design, etc. in Figure 2), modified as appropriate to incorporate incremental development. Each level of software specification in the figure is then followed by a validation step and the preparation of plans for the succeeding cycle. In this case, the options to prototype, simulate, model, etc. are addressed but not exercised, leading to the use of a different subset of steps.

This risk-driven subsetting of the spiral model steps allows the model to accommodate any appropriate mixture of a specification-oriented, prototype-oriented, simulation-oriented, automatic transformation-oriented, or other approach to software development. In such cases, the appropriate mixed strategy is chosen by considering the relative magnitude of the program risks and the relative effectiveness of the various techniques in resolving the risks. In a similar way, risk-management considerations can determine the amount of time and effort that should be devoted to such other project activities as planning, configuration management, quality assurance, formal verification, and testing. In particular, risk-driven specifications (as discussed in the next section) can have varying degrees of completeness, formality, and granularity, depending on the relative risks of doing too little or too much specification.

An important feature of the spiral model, as with most other models, is that each cycle is completed by a review involving the primary people or organizations concerned with the product. This review covers all products developed during the previous cycle, including the plans for the next cycle and the resources required to carry them out. The review's major objective is to ensure that all concerned parties are mutually committed to the approach for the next phase.

The plans for succeeding phases may also include a partition of the product into

increments for successive development or components to be developed by individual organizations or persons. For the latter case, visualize a series of parallel spiral cycles, one for each component, adding a third dimension to the concept presented in Figure 2. For example, separate spirals can be evolving for separate software components or increments. Thus, the review-and-commitment step may range from an individual walk-through of the design of a single programmer's component to a major requirements review involving developer, customer, user, and maintenance organizations.

Initiating and terminating the spiral. Four fundamental questions arise in considering this presentation of the spiral model:

(1) How does the spiral ever get started?
(2) How do you get off the spiral when it is appropriate to terminate a project early?
(3) Why does the spiral end so abruptly?
(4) What happens to software enhancement (or maintenance)?

The answer to these questions involves an observation that the spiral model applies equally well to development or enhancement efforts. In either case, the spiral gets started by a hypothesis that a particular operational mission (or set of missions) could be improved by a software effort. The spiral process then involves a test of this hypothesis: at any time, if the hypothesis fails the test (for example, if delays cause a software product to miss its market window, or if a superior commercial product becomes available), the spiral is terminated. Otherwise, it terminates with the installation of new or modified software, and the hypothesis is tested by observing the effect on the operational mission. Usually, experience with the operational mission leads to further hypotheses about software improvements, and a new maintenance spiral is initiated to test the hypothesis. Initiation, termination, and iteration of the tasks and products of previous cycles are thus implicitly defined in the spiral model (although they're not included in Figure 2 to simplify its presentation).

Using the spiral model

The various rounds and activities involved in the spiral model are best understood through use of an example. The spiral model was used in the definition and development of the TRW Software Productivity System (TRW-SPS), an integrated software engineering environment.[6] The initial mission opportunity coincided with a corporate initiative to improve productivity in all appropriate corporate operations and an initial hypothesis that software engineering was an attractive area to investigate. This led to a small, extra "Round 0" circuit of the spiral to determine the feasibility of increasing software productivity at a reasonable corporate cost. (Very large or complex software projects will frequently precede the "concept of operation" round of the spiral with one or more smaller rounds to establish feasibility and to reduce the range of alternative solutions quickly and inexpensively.)

Tables 1, 2, and 3 summarize the application of the spiral model to the first three rounds of defining the SPS. The major features of each round are subsequently discussed and are followed by some examples from later rounds, such as preliminary and detailed design.

Round 0: Feasibility study. This study involved five part-time participants over a two- to three-month period. As indicated in Table 1, the objectives and constraints were expressed at a very high level and in qualitative terms like "significantly increase," "at reasonable cost," etc.

Some of the alternatives considered, primarily those in the "technology" area, could lead to development of a software product, but the possible attractiveness of a number of non-software alternatives in the management, personnel, and facilities areas could have led to a conclusion not to embark on a software development activity.

The primary risk areas involved possible situations in which the company would invest a good deal only to find that

- resulting productivity gains were not significant, or

- potentially high-leverage improvements were not compatible with some aspects of the "TRW culture."

The risk-resolution activities undertaken in Round 0 were primarily surveys and analyses, including structured interviews of software developers and managers, an initial analysis of productivity leverage factors identified by the constructive cost model (Cocomo[7]; and an analysis of previous projects at TRW exhibiting high levels of productivity.

The risk analysis results indicated that significant productivity gains could be achieved at a reasonable cost by pursuing an integrated set of initiatives in the four major areas. However, some candidate solutions, such as a software support environment based on a single, corporate, maxicomputer-based time-sharing system, were found to be in conflict with TRW constraints requiring support of different levels of security-classified projects. Thus, even at a very high level of generality of objectives and constraints, Round 0 was able to answer basic feasibility questions and eliminate significant classes of candidate solutions.

The plan for Round 1 involved commitment of 12 man-months compared to the two man-months invested in Round 0 (during these rounds, all participants were part-time). Round 1 here corresponded fairly well to the initial round of the spiral model shown in Figure 2, in that its intent was to produce a concept of operation and a basic life-cycle plan for implementing whatever preferred alternative emerged.

Round 1: Concept of operations. Table 2 summarizes Round 1 of the spiral along the lines given in Table 1 for Round 0. The features of Round 1 compare to those of Round 0 as follows:

- The level of investment was greater (12 versus 2 man-months).

- The objectives and constraints were more specific ("double software productivity in five years at a cost of $10,000 a person" versus "significantly increase productivity at a reasonable cost").

- Additional constraints surfaced, such as the preference for TRW products (particularly, a TRW-developed local area network (LAN) system).

- The alternatives were more detailed ("SREM, PSL/PSA or SADT, as requirements tools etc." versus "tools"; "private/shared" terminals, "smart/dumb" terminals versus "workstations").

- The risk areas identified were more specific ("TRW LAN price-performance

Table 1. Spiral model usage: TRW Software Productivity System, Round 0.

Objectives	Significantly increase software productivity
Constraints	At reasonable cost Within context of TRW culture • Government contracts, high tech., people oriented, security
Alternatives	Management: Project organization, policies, planning, control Personnel: Staffing, incentives, training Technology: Tools, workstations, methods, reuse Facilities: Offices, communications
Risks	May be no high-leverage improvements Improvements may violate constraints
Risk resolution	Internal surveys Analyze cost model Analyze exceptional projects Literature search
Risk resolution results	Some alternatives infeasible • Single time-sharing system: Security Mix of alternatives can produce significant gains • Factor of two in five years Need further study to determine best mix
Plan for next phase	Six-person task force for six months More extensive surveys and analysis • Internal, external, economic Develop concept of operation, economic rationale
Commitment	Fund next phase

within a "$10,000-per-person investment constraint" versus "improvements may violate reasonable-cost constraint").

• The risk-resolution activities were more extensive (including the benchmarking and analysis of a prototype TRW LAN being developed for another project).

• The result was a fairly specific operational concept document, involving private offices tailored to software work patterns and personal terminals connected to VAX superminis via the TRW LAN. Some choices were specifically deferred to the next round, such as the choice of operating system and specific tools.

• The life-cycle plan and the plan for the next phase involved a partitioning into separate activities to address management improvements, facilities development, and development of the first increment of a software development environment.

• The commitment step involved more than just an agreement with the plan. It committed to apply the environment to an upcoming 100-person testbed software project and to develop an environment focusing on the testbed project's needs. It also specified forming a representative steering group to ensure that the separate activities were well-coordinated and that the environment would not be overly optimized around the testbed project.

Although the plan recommended developing a prototype environment, it also recommended that the project employ requirements specifications and design specifications in a risk-driven way. Thus, the development of the environment followed the succeeding rounds of the spiral model.

Round 2: Top-level requirements specification. Table 3 shows the corresponding steps involved during Round 2 defining the software productivity system. Round 2 decisions and their rationale were covered in earlier work[6]; here, we will summarize the considerations dealing with risk management and the use of the spiral model:

• The initial risk-identification activities during Round 2 showed that several system requirements hinged on the decision between a host-target system or a fully portable tool set and the decision between VMS and Unix as the host operating system. These requirements included the functions needed to provide a user-friendly front-end, the operating system to be used by the workstations, and the functions necessary to support a host-target

operation. To keep these requirements in synchronization with the others, a special minispiral was initiated to address and resolve these issues. The resulting review led to a commitment to a host-target operation using Unix on the host system, at a point early enough to work the OS-dependent requirements in a timely fashion.

• Addressing the risks of mismatches to the user-project's needs and priorities resulted in substantial participation of the user-project personnel in the requirements definition activity. This led to several significant redirections of the requirements, particularly toward supporting the early phases of the software life-cycle into which the user project was embarking, such as an adaptation of the software requirements engineering methodology (SREM) tools

for requirements specification and analysis.

It is also interesting to note that the form of Tables 1, 2, and 3 was originally developed for presentation purposes, but subsequently became a standard "spiral model template" used on later projects. These templates are useful not only for organizing project activities, but also as a residual design-rationale record. Design rationale information is of paramount importance in assessing the potential reusability of software components on future projects. Another important point to note is that the use of the template was indeed uniform across the three cycles, showing that the spiral steps can be and were uniformly followed at successively detailed levels of product definition.

Table 2. Spiral model usage: TRW Software Productivity System, Round 1.

Objectives	Double software productivity in five years
Constraints	$10,000 per person investment Within context of TRW culture • Government contracts, high tech., people oriented, security Preference for TRW products
Alternatives	Office: Private/modular/. . . Communication: LAN/star/concentrators/. . . Terminals: Private/shared; smart/dumb Tools: SREM/PSL-PSA/. . .; PDL/SADT/. . . CPU: IBM/DEC/CDC/. . .
Risks	May miss high-leverage options TRW LAN price/performance Workstation cost
Risk resolution	Extensive external surveys, visits TRW LAN benchmarking Workstation price projections
Risk resolution results	Operations concept: Private offices, TRW LAN, personal terminals, VAX Begin with primarily dumb terminals; experiment with smart workstations Defer operating system, tools selection
Plan for next phase	Partition effort into software development environment (SDE), facilities, management Develop first-cut, prototype SDE • Design-to-cost: 15-person team for one year Plan for external usage
Commitment	Develop prototype SDE Commit an upcoming project to use SDE Commit the SDE to support the project Form representative steering group

Succeeding rounds. It will be useful to illustrate some examples of how the spiral model is used to handle situations arising in the preliminary design and detailed design of components of the SPS: the preliminary design specification for the requirements traceability tool (RTT), and a detailed design rework or go-back on the unit development folder (UDF) tool.

The RTT preliminary design specification. The RTT establishes the traceability between itemized software requirements specifications, design elements, code elements, and test cases. It also supports various associated query, analysis, and report generation capabilities. The preliminary design specification for the RTT (and most of the other SPS tools) looks different from the usual preliminary design specification, which tends to show a uniform level of elaboration of all components of the design. Instead, the level of detail of

the RTT specification is risk-driven.

In areas involving a high risk if the design turned out to be wrong, the design was carried down to the detailed design level, usually with the aid of rapid prototyping. These areas included working out the implications of "undo" options and dealing with the effects of control keys used to escape from various program levels.

In areas involving a moderate risk if the design was wrong, the design was carried down to a preliminary-design level. These areas included the basic command options for the tool and the schemata for the requirements traceability database. Here again, the ease of rapid prototyping with Unix shell scripts supported a good deal of user-interface prototyping.

In areas involving a low risk if the design was wrong, very little design elaboration was done. These areas included details of all the help message options and all the

report-generation options, once the nature of these options was established in some example instances.

A detailed design go-back. The UDF tool collects into an electronic "folder" all artifacts involved in the development of a single-programmer software unit (typically 500 to 1,000 instructions): unit requirements, design, code, test cases, test results, and documentation. It also includes a management template for tracking the programmer's scheduled and actual completion of each artifact.

An alternative considered during detailed design of the UDF tool was reuse of portions of the RTT to provide pointers to the requirements and preliminary design specifications of the unit being developed. This turned out to be an extremely attractive alternative, not only for avoiding duplicate software development but also for bringing to the surface several issues involving many-to-many mappings between requirements, design, and code that had not been considered in designing the UDF tool. These led to a rethinking of the UDF tool requirements and preliminary design, which avoided a great deal of code rework that would have been necessary if the detailed design of the UDF tool had proceeded in a purely deductive, top-down fashion from the original UDF requirements specification. The resulting go-back led to a significantly different, less costly, and more capable UDF tool, incorporating the RTT in its "uses-hierarchy."

Spiral model features. These two examples illustrate several features of the spiral approach.

• It fosters the development of specifications that are not necessarily uniform, exhaustive, or formal, in that they defer detailed elaboration of low-risk software elements and avoid unnecessary breakage in their design until the high-risk elements of the design are stabilized.

• It incorporates prototyping as a risk-reduction option at any stage of development. In fact, prototyping and reuse risk analyses were often used in the process of going from detailed design into code.

• It accommodates reworks or go-backs to earlier stages as more attractive alternatives are identified or as new risk issues need resolution.

Overall, risk-driven documents, particularly specifications and plans, are important features of the spiral model. Great amounts of detail are not necessary unless the absence of such detail jeopardizes the

Table 3. Spiral model usage: TRW Software Productivity System, Round 2.

Objectives	User-friendly system
	Integrated software, office-automation tools
	Support all project personnel
	Support all life-cycle phases
Constraints	Customer-deliverable SDE $\Rightarrow$ Portability
	Stable, reliable service
Alternatives	OS: VMS/AT&T Unix/Berkeley Unix/ISC
	Host-target/fully portable tool set
	Workstations: Zenith/LSI-11/. . .
Risks	Mismatch to user-project needs, priorities
	User-unfriendly system
	• 12-language syndrome; experts-only
	Unix performance, support
	Workstation/mainframe compatibility
Risk resolution	User-project surveys, requirements participation
	Survey of Unix-using organizations
	Workstation study
Risk resolution results	Top-level requirements specification
	Host-target with Unix host
	Unix-based workstations
	Build user-friendly front end for Unix
	Initial focus on tools to support early phases
Plan for next phase	Overall development plan
	• for tools: SREM, RTT, PDL, office automation tools
	• for front end: Support tools
	• for LAN: Equipment, facilities
Commitment	Proceed with plans

project. In some cases, such as with a product whose functionality may be determined by a choice among commercial products, a set of weighted evaluation criteria for the products may be preferable to a detailed pre-statement of functional requirements.

Results. The Software Productivity System developed and supported using the spiral model avoided the identified risks and achieved most of the system's objectives. The SPS has grown to include over 300 tools and over 1,300,000 instructions; 93 percent of the instructions were reused from previous project-developed, TRW-developed, or external-software packages. Over 25 projects have used all or portions of the system. All of the projects fully using the system have increased their productivity at least 50 percent; indeed, most have doubled their productivity (when compared with cost-estimation model predictions of their productivity using traditional methods).

However, one risk area—that projects with non-Unix target systems would not accept a Unix-based host system—was underestimated. Some projects accepted the host-target approach, but for various reasons (such as customer constraints and zero-cost target machines) a good many did not. As a result, the system was less widely used on TRW projects than expected. This and other lessons learned have been incorporated into the spiral model approach to developing TRW's next-generation software development environment.

Evaluation

Advantages. The primary advantage of the spiral model is that its range of options accommodates the good features of existing software process models, while its risk-driven approach avoids many of their difficulties. In appropriate situations, the spiral model becomes equivalent to one of the existing process models. In other situations, it provides guidance on the best mix of existing approaches to a given project; for example, its application to the TRW-SPS provided a risk-driven mix of specifying, prototyping, and evolutionary development.

The primary conditions under which the spiral model becomes equivalent to other main process models are summarized as follows:

• If a project has a low risk in such areas

All of the projects fully using the system have increased their productivity at least 50 percent.

---

as getting the wrong user interface or not meeting stringent performance requirements, and if it has a high risk in budget and schedule predictability and control, then these risk considerations drive the spiral model into an equivalence to the waterfall model.

• If a software product's requirements are very stable (implying a low risk of expensive design and code breakage due to requirements changes during development), and if the presence of errors in the software product constitutes a high risk to the mission it serves, then these risk considerations drive the spiral model to resemble the two-leg model of precise specification and formal deductive program development.

• If a project has a low risk in such areas as losing budget and schedule predictability and control, encountering large-system integration problems, or coping with information sclerosis, and if it has a high risk in such areas as getting the wrong user interface or user decision support requirements, then these risk considerations drive the spiral model into an equivalence to the evolutionary development model.

• If automated software generation capabilities are available, then the spiral model accommodates them either as options for rapid prototyping or for application of the transform model, depending on the risk considerations involved.

• If the high-risk elements of a project involve a mix of the risk items listed above, then the spiral approach will reflect an appropriate mix of the process models above (as exemplified in the TRW-SPS application). In doing so, its risk-avoidance features will generally avoid the difficulties of the other models.

The spiral model has a number of additional advantages, summarized as follows:

It focuses early attention on options involving the reuse of existing software. The steps involving the identification and evaluation of alternatives encourage these options.

It accommodates preparation for life-cycle evolution, growth, and changes of the software product. The major sources of product change are included in the product's objectives, and information-hiding approaches are attractive architectural design alternatives in that they reduce the risk of not being able to accommodate the product-charge objectives.

It provides a mechanism for incorporating software quality objectives into software product development. This mechanism derives from the emphasis on identifying all types of objectives and constraints during each round of the spiral. For example, Table 3 shows user-friendliness, portability, and reliability as specific objectives and constraints to be addressed by the SPS. In Table 1, security constraints were identified as a key risk item for the SPS.

It focuses on eliminating errors and unattractive alternatives early. The risk-analysis, validation, and commitment steps cover these considerations.

For each of the sources of project activity and resource expenditure, it answers the key question, "How much is enough?" Stated another way, "How much of requirements analysis, planning, configuration management, quality assurance, testing, formal verification, etc. should a project do?" Using the risk-driven approach, one can see that the answer is not the same for all projects and that the appropriate level of effort is determined by the level of risk incurred by not doing enough.

It does not involve separate approaches for software development and software enhancement (or maintenance). This aspect helps avoid the "second-class citizen" status frequently associated with software maintenance. It also helps avoid many of the problems that currently ensue when high-risk enhancement efforts are approached in the same way as routine maintenance efforts.

It provides a viable framework for integrated hardware-software system development. The focus on risk-management and on eliminating unattractive alternatives early and inexpensively is equally applicable to hardware and software.

Difficulties. The full spiral model can be successfully applied in many situations, but some difficulties must be addressed before it can be called a mature, universally applicable model. The three primary challenges involve matching to contract software, relying on risk-assessment expertise, and the need for further elaboration of spiral model steps.

Matching to contract software. The spiral model currently works well on internal software developments like the TRW-SPS, but it needs further work to match it to the world of contract software acquisition.

Internal software developments have a great deal of flexibility and freedom to accommodate stage-by-stage commitments, to defer commitments to specific options, to establish minispirals to resolve critical-path items, to adjust levels of effort, or to accommodate such practices as prototyping, evolutionary development, or design-to-cost. The world of contract software acquisition has a harder time achieving these degrees of flexibility and freedom without losing accountability and control, and a harder time defining contracts whose deliverables are not well specified in advance.

Recently, a good deal of progress has been made in establishing more flexible contract mechanisms, such as the use of competitive front-end contracts for concept definition or prototype fly-offs, the use of level-of-effort and award-fee contracts for evolutionary development, and the use of design-to-cost contracts. Although these have been generally successful, the procedures for using them still need to be worked out to the point that acquisition managers feel fully comfortable using them.

Relying on risk-assessment expertise. The spiral model places a great deal of reliance on the ability of software developers to identify and manage sources of project risk.

A good example of this is the spiral model's risk-driven specification, which carries high-risk elements down to a great deal of detail and leaves low-risk elements to be elaborated in later stages; by this time, there is less risk of breakage.

However, a team of inexperienced or low-balling developers may also produce a specification with a different pattern of variation in levels of detail: a great elaboration of detail for the well-understood, low-risk elements, and little elaboration of the poorly understood, high-risk elements. Unless there is an insightful review of such a specification by experienced development or acquisition personnel, this type of project will give an illusion of progress during a period in which it is actually heading for disaster.

Another concern is that a risk-driven specification will also be people-dependent. For example, a design produced by an expert may be implemented by non-experts. In this case, the expert, who does not need a great deal of detailed documentation, must produce enough additional documentation to keep the non-experts from going astray. Reviewers of the specification must also be

Table 4. A prioritized top-ten list of software risk items.

Risk item	Risk management techniques
1. Personnel shortfalls	Staffing with top talent, job matching; teambuilding; morale building; cross-training; pre-scheduling key people
2. Unrealistic schedules and budgets	Detailed, multisource cost and schedule estimation; design to cost; incremental development; software reuse; requirements scrubbing
3. Developing the wrong software functions	Organization analysis; mission analysis; ops-concept formulation; user surveys; prototyping; early users' manuals
4. Developing the wrong user interface	Task analysis; prototyping; scenarios; user characterization (functionality, style, workload)
5. Gold plating	Requirements scrubbing; prototyping; cost-benefit analysis; design to cost
6. Continuing stream of requirement changes	High change threshold; information hiding; incremental development (defer changes to later increments)
7. Shortfalls in externally furnished components	Benchmarking; inspections; reference checking; compatibility analysis
8. Shortfalls in externally performed tasks	Reference checking; pre-award audits; award-fee contracts; competitive design or prototyping; teambuilding
9. Real-time performance shortfalls	Simulation; benchmarking; modeling; prototyping; instrumentation; tuning
10. Straining computer-science capabilities	Technical analysis; cost-benefit analysis; prototyping; reference checking

Table 5. Software Risk Management Plan.

1.	Identify the project's top 10 risk items.
2.	Present a plan for resolving each risk item.
3.	Update list of top risk items, plan, and results monthly.
4.	Highlight risk-item status in monthly project reviews. • Compare with previous month's rankings, status.
5.	Initiate appropriate corrective actions.

sensitive to these concerns.

With a conventional, document-driven approach, the requirement to carry all aspects of the specification to a uniform level of detail eliminates some potential problems and permits adequate review of some aspects by inexperienced reviewers. But it also creates a large drain on the time of the scarce experts, who must dig for the critical issues within a large mass of non-critical detail. Furthermore, if the high-risk elements have been glossed over by impressive-sounding references to poorly understood capabilities (such as a new synchronization concept or a commercial DBMS), there is an even greater risk that the conventional approach will give the illusion of progress in situations that are actually heading for disaster.

Need for further elaboration of spiral model steps. In general, the spiral model process steps need further elaboration to ensure that all software development participants are operating in a consistent context.

Some examples of this are the need for more detailed definitions of the nature of spiral model specifications and milestones, the nature and objectives of spiral model reviews, techniques for estimating and synchronizing schedules, and the nature of spiral model status indicators and cost-versus-progress tracking procedures. Another need is for guidelines and checklists to identify the most likely sources of project risk and the most effective risk-resolution techniques for each source of risk.

Highly experienced people can successfully use the spiral approach without these elaborations. However, for large-scale use in situations where people bring widely differing experience bases to the project, added levels of elaboration—such as have been accumulated over the years for document-driven approaches—are important in ensuring consistent interpretation and use of the spiral approach across the project.

Efforts to apply and refine the spiral model have focused on creating a discipline of software risk management, including techniques for risk identification, risk analysis, risk prioritization, risk-management planning, and risk-element tracking. The prioritized top-ten list of software risk items given in Table 4 is one result of this activity. Another example is the risk management plan discussed in the next section.

Implications: The Risk Management Plan. Even if an organization is not ready to adopt the entire spiral approach, one characteristic technique that can easily be adapted to any life-cycle model provides many of the benefits of the spiral approach. This is the Risk Management Plan summarized in Table 5. This plan basically ensures that each project makes an early identification of its top risk items (the number 10 is not an absolute requirement), develops a strategy for resolving the risk items, identifies and sets down an agenda to resolve new risk items as they surface, and highlights progress versus plans in monthly reviews.

The Risk Management Plan has been used successfully at TRW and other organizations. Its use has ensured appropriate focus on early prototyping, simulation, benchmarking, key-person staffing measures, and other early risk-resolution techniques that have helped avoid many potential project "show-stoppers." The recent US Department of Defense standard on software management, DoD-Std-2167, requires that developers produce and use risk management plans, as does its counterpart US Air Force regulation, AFR 800-14.

Overall, the Risk Management Plan and the maturing set of techniques for software risk management provide a foundation for tailoring spiral model concepts into the more established software acquisition and development procedures.

Wecan draw four conclusions from the data presented:

(1) The risk-driven nature of the spiral model is more adaptable to the full range of software project situations than are the primarily document-driven approaches such as the waterfall model or the primarily code-driven approaches such as evolutionary development. It is particularly applicable to very large, complex, ambitious software systems.

(2) The spiral model has been quite successful in its largest application to date: the development and enhancement of the TRW-SPS. Overall, it achieved a high level of software support environment capability in a very short time and provided the flexibility necessary to accommodate a high dynamic range of technical alternatives and user objectives.

(3) The spiral model is not yet as fully elaborated as the more established models. Therefore, the spiral model can be applied by experienced personnel, but it needs further elaboration in such areas as contract-

ing, specifications, milestones, reviews, scheduling, status monitoring, and risk-area identification to be fully usable in all situations.

(4) Partial implementations of the spiral model, such as the Risk Management Plan, are compatible with most current process models and are very helpful in overcoming major sources of project risk.☐

Acknowledgments

I would like to thank Frank Belz, Lolo Penedo, George Spadaro, Bob Williams, Bob Balzer, Gillian Frewin, Peter Hamer, Manny Lehman, Lee Osterweil, Dave Parnas, Bill Riddle, Steve Squires, and Dick Thayer, along with the *Computer* reviewers of this article, for their stimulating and insightful comments and discussions of earlier versions of the article, and Nancy Donato for producing its several versions.

References

1. F.P. Brooks et al., *Defense Science Board Task Force Report on Military Software*, Office of the Under Secretary of Defense for Acquisition, Washington, DC 20301, Sept. 1987.

2. H.D. Benington, "Production of Large Computer Programs," *Proc. ONR Symp. Advanced Programming Methods for Digital Computers*, June 1956, pp. 15-27. Also available in *Annals of the History of Computing*, Oct. 1983, pp. 350-361, and *Proc. Ninth Int'l Conf. Software Engineering*, Computer Society Press, 1987.

3. W.W. Royce, "Managing the Development of Large Software Systems: Concepts and Techniques," *Proc. Wescon*, Aug. 1970. Also available in *Proc. ICSE 9*, Computer Society Press, 1987.

4. D.D. McCracken and M.A. Jackson, "Life-Cycle Concept Considered Harmful," *ACM Software Engineering Notes*, Apr. 1982, pp. 29-32.

5. R. Balzer, T.E. Cheatham, and C. Green, "Software Technology in the 1990s: Using a New Paradigm," *Computer*, Nov. 1983, pp. 39-45.

6. B.W. Boehm et al., "A Software Development Environment for Improving Productivity," *Computer*, June 1984, pp. 30-44.

7. B.W. Boehm, *Software Engineering Economics*, Prentice-Hall, 1981, Chap. 33.

Further reading

The software process model field has an interesting history, and a great deal of stimulating work has been produced recently in this specialized area. Besides the references that appear at the end of the accompanying article, here are some additional good sources of insight:

Overall process model issues and results

Agresti's tutorial volume provides a good overview and set of key articles. The three recent *Software Process Workshop Proceedings* provide access to much of the recent work in the area.

Agresti, W.W., *New Paradigms for Software Development*, IEEE Catalog No. EH0245-1, 1986.

Dowson, M., ed., *Proc. Third Int'l Software Process Workshop*, IEEE Catalog No. TH0184-2, Nov. 1986.

Potts, C., ed., *Proc. Software Process Workshop*, IEEE Catalog No. 84CH2044-6, Feb. 1984.

Wileden, J.C., and M. Dowson, eds., Proc. Int'l Workshop Software Process and Software Environments, *ACM Software Engineering Notes*, Aug. 1986.

Alternative process models

More detailed information on waterfall-type approaches is given in:

Evans, M.W., P. Piazza, and J.P. Dolkas, *Principles of Productive Software Management*, John Wiley & Sons, 1983.

Hice, G.F., W.J. Turner, and L.F. Cashwell, *System Development Methodology*, North Holland, 1974 (2nd ed., 1981).

More detailed information on evolutionary development is provided in:

Gilb, T., *Principles of Software Engineering Management*, Addison Wesley, 1988 (currently in publication).

Some additional process model approaches with useful features and insights may be found in:

Lehman, M.M., and L.A. Belady, *Program Evolution: Processes of Software Change*, Academic Press, 1985.

Osterweil, L., "Software Processes are Software, Too," *Proc. ICSE 9*, IEEE Catalog No. 87CH2432-3, Mar. 1987, pp. 2-13.

Radice, R.A., et al., "A Programming Process Architecture," *IBM Systems J.*, Vol. 24, No.2, 1985, pp. 79-90.

Spiral and spiral-type models

Some further treatments of spiral model issues and practices are:

Belz, F.C., "Applying the Spiral Model: Observations on Developing System Software in Ada," *Proc. 1986 Annual Conf. on Ada Technology*, Atlanta, 1986, pp. 57-66.

Boehm, B.W., and F.C. Belz, "Applying Process Programming to the Spiral Model," *Proc. Fourth Software Process Workshop*, IEEE, May 1988.

Iivari, J., "A Hierarchical Spiral Model for the Software Process," *ACM Software Engineering Notes*, Jan. 1987, pp. 35-37.

Some similar cyclic spiral-type process models from other fields are described in:

Carlsson, B., P. Keane, and J.B. Martin, "R&D Organizations as Learning Systems," *Sloan Management Review*, Spring 1976, pp. 1-15.

Fisher, R., and W. Ury, *Getting to Yes*, Houghton Mifflin, 1981; Penguin Books, 1983, pp. 68-71.

Kolb, D.A., "On Management and the Learning Process," MIT Sloan School Working Article 652-73, Cambridge, Mass., 1973.

Software risk management

The discipline of software risk management provides a bridge between spiral model concepts and currently established software acquisition and development procedures.

Boehm, B.W., "Software Risk Management Tutorial," Computer Society, Apr. 1988.

Risk Assessment Techniques, Defense Systems Management College, Ft. Belvoir, Va. 22060, July 1983.

Barry W. Boehm is the chief scientist of the TRW Defense Systems Group. Since 1973, he has been responsible for developing TRW's software technology base. His current primary responsibilities are in the areas of software environments, process models, management methods, Ada, and cost estimation. He is also an adjunct professor at UCLA.

Boehm received his BA degree in mathematics from Harvard in 1957 and his MA and PhD from UCLA in 1961 and 1964, respectively.

Readers may write to Boehm at TRW Defense Systems Group, One Space Park, R2/2086, Redondo Beach, CA 90278.

APPLYING PROCESS PROGRAMMING TO THE SPIRAL MODEL

Barry Boehm and Frank Belz
TRW, DSG
Redondo Beach, California

The primary thesis of this position paper is that process programming is analogous to programming in an key respect not previously emphasized: that it will proceed more effectively if preceded by a set of activities to determine the requirements, architecture, and design of the process.

1. The Spiral Model

The Spiral Model [Boehm,1986; Belz,1986] provides a candidate approach to determining the requirements, architecture, and design of a software process. The Spiral Model activity of determining mission objectives and constraints addresses the requirements for the process: the nature of the product required; budget and schedule constraints; organizational and procedural (e.g. contracting) constraints, etc. The Spiral Model "alternatives" activity addresses process architecture and design considerations: the use of prototypes, simulations and competitive concept definition phases; the choice of incremental products, cutover strategies, and integration strategies; the use of design-to-cost, independent V & V contractors, etc. The choice of process architecture is obtained in the Spiral Model by determining which alternative process architecture minimizes the risk of not meeting the system objectives within the system constraints.

2. Applying Process Programming to the Spiral Model

Applying process programming to the Spiral Model appeared to the authors to be a useful exercise in two main respects:

- to see how well process programming approaches addressed process architecture and design issues;
- to better understand the ramifications of the Spiral Model

The authors developed an initial top-level formulation of the Spiral Model, using a rather conventional process programming approach. The language we used was a version of Ada based partly on [Osterweil,1986] and informally (though, we hope, precisely) adapted to our purpose. The resulting process program contained roughly 150 lines. It was expressed as an iterative loop through the four main elements of the Spiral Model (see Figure 1), with succeeding cycles through the spiral represented as a refinement of a project database of product and process objects such as objectives, constraints, alternatives, plans, specifications, designs, and programs. The objects in this database would inherit attributes from the objects defined in earlier cycles of the spiral, and then be refined into more detailed starting points for the next cycle.

3. Lessons Learned The process programming exercise is not yet complete; however, we have already learned some lessons about the Spiral Model itself, and about process programming issues.

3.1. Spiral Model Issues The primary lessons learned about the Spiral Model were:
- Some ambiguities about how to initiate, terminate, and iterate within the spiral were discovered. An approach to some of the iteration concerns was presented at the previous workshop [Boehm-Belz, 1986].

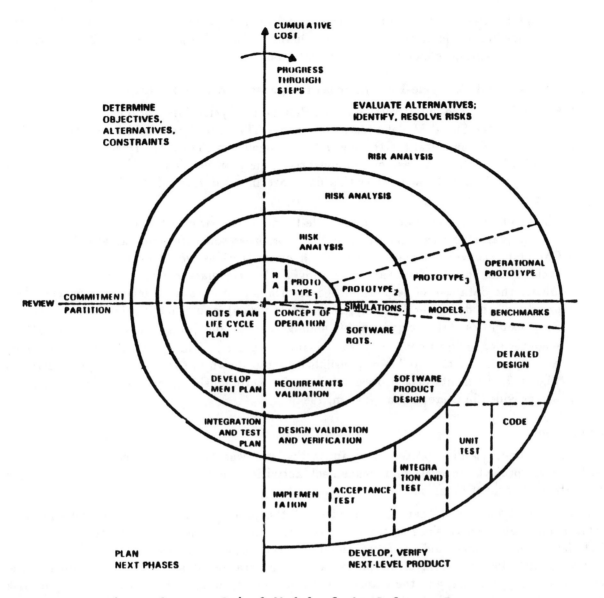

Figure 1   Spiral Model of the Software Process

- Some complexities in handling incremental development were discovered: e.g., what does a new increment inherit from the previous increment in such areas as plans and specifications?

- Some processes appeared to involve too much creativity to be able to formalize well: e.g., identifying and refining alternatives.

- Some key areas needed more formalization in order to address them as process programs, e.g., risk management. This lesson has led to an extensive activity to better elaborate the steps in risk management.

- Some Spiral Model steps were more complex than were previously envisioned. An example is the "Refine life-cycle plan" step. It was initially represented as a sequence of process-PDL steps elaborating each component of the life-cycle plan. When this program was compared with experience on a recent TRW project, a different model emerged. In this revised model, the "Refine life-cycle plan" activity was best represented as a repeat of the Spiral Model steps as applied to the process, yielding an approach to the development and refinement of the software process requirements, architecture, and design for a given project. Section 3.1.1 below elaborates on the original process program and its evaluation. Section 3.1.2 provides an example from the TRW Quantum Leap Project. Section 3.1.3 discusses the resulting refinement of the Spiral Model.

3.1.1. The Refine-Life-Cycle-Plan Process Program and Its Evaluation

Figure 2 shows the initial version of the Refine-Life-Cycle-Plan procedure developed as a portion of the Spiral Model Process program. The procedure would be invoked during each cycle of the spiral (at the lower left as shown in Figure 1). During each cycle, it would inherit the database of components of the plan developed in the previous cycles (Life-Cycle-Plan-DB), and refine this database into the level of detail required for the next cycle.

The top-level structure of the Life-Cycle-Plan-DB is shown in Figure 3. It represents a generic plan structure which can be used for other software plans as well (test plans, CM plans, conversion plans, etc.). Each of its sections would be refined during each cycle of the spiral. For example, during an intermediate cycle, the procedure might inherit the database of responsibilities determined to date (e.g., lead agency, customer project office, developer company, developer division), and refine it into the next level of Responsibilities data (e.g., project manager, assistant project managers for system engineering, programming, integration and test, etc.). This particular step would be accomplished by the "Refine-responsibilities" step shown in the process program given in Figure 2. Elements of a process program for accomplishing this particular refinement are provided in Chapter 7 of [Boehm, 1981].

Evaluation

The Refine-Life-Cycle-Plan process program in Figure 2 was evaluated by comparing its steps with several project life cycle plan refinement activities, particularly TRW's Quantum Leap software environment program.

The evaluation concluded that the net effect of the procedure was about right: to produce refined, more detailed versions of the plan sections inherited from earlier cycles of the spiral. But the sequence of steps did not follow the linear, sequential model shown in the Figure 2 process program. Instead, it involved the parallel consideration of a number of candidate life-cycle process approaches, and the determination of a preferred approach based strongly on risk considerations as applicable to the process objectives, constraints, and alternatives.

The result of the evaluation was to reformulate the "Plan Next Phases" portion of the Spiral Model. Instead of the relatively simple elaboration of previous plans depicted in the lower-left portion of the spiral in Figure 1, this portion was revised into the process shown in Figure 4. It indicates that the objectives/alternatives/ evaluation/risk resolution/elaboration process is applied twice during each cycle of the spiral; initially to refine the *product* requirements, architecture, and implementation in the first three quadrants of Figure 4, and subsequently to refine the *process* requirements, architecture, and implementation in the fourth quadrant. (Actually, these would be considerable process look-ahead during the product refinement, and product feedback during the process refinement.) The next section provides an example from the TRW Quantum Leap project.

3.1.2. Quantum Leap Project Example

The TRW Quantum Leap project is chartered to develop an advanced Ada-oriented Software Engineering Environment (SEE), based on lessons learned during the development and use since 1981 of the previous TRW Software Productivity System SEE. One of these lessons was the necessity of coupling the SEE to an initial host project. For Quantum Leap, a host project was chosen which required an Initial Operational Capability (IOC) SEE by July 1988. Another lesson was the necessity to maximize the use of commercial off-the-shelf (COTS) software in order

```
with
    Life_cycle_plan,
    Risk_management_DB,
    Management_plan,
    Objectives_DB,
    Constraints_DB,
    Alternatives_DB,
    Risk-issues_DB;
procedure Refine_life_cycle_plan
is
    . . .
begin
    Refine_plan_objectives;
    Refine_milestones_and_deliverables;
    Refine_responsibilities;
    Refine_approach;
    Refine_resources;
    Validate_refined_plan;
end Refine_life_cycle_plan;
```

Figure 2   Refine-Life-Cycle-Plan Process Program

to minimize in-house SEE software maintenance costs. In particular, TRW wanted to use a COTS SEE "framework": a complex of software providing virtual operating system, software project object management, user interface, and other utility services.

During the initial rounds of the spiral, the Quantum Leap project developed an Operational Concept Document and a top-level Life Cycle Plan organized in consonance with the outline given in Figure 3. The next round of the spiral produced an initial System Requirements Specification in the first three quadrants, and prepared to produce the next-level refinement of the life cycle plan.

Process Objectives, Constraints, and Alternatives

The actual procedure Quantum Leap used to do this is summarized in Figure 5. The process objectives and constraints are largely those introduced in the paragraphs above. The process alternatives included a pure waterfall model, a pure evolutionary-development model, incremental development, and a COTS-driven model. The COTS-driven model uses the following procedure:

(1) The initial requirements specification is used to determine a weighted set of evolution criteria for COTS candidates.

(2) The COTS candidates are evaluated, and a winning set of candidates chosen (often after considerable negotiation).

(3) Given that the COTS candidates are not identical in functionality or performance, the requirements specification is modified to reflect the winning candidates' capabilities and the need to compensate for any of their deficiencies.

As a parenthetical note, we would like to point out that the COTS-driven model, and its associated reinterpretation of the term "requirements" (the most cost-effective combination of capabilities emerging from a comparison of similar but non-congruent products) is rapidly gaining attractiveness as a candidate approach in an increasingly COTS-oriented software world.

1.   Objectives (the "why")
1.1 Software Product Objectives
1.2 Development Plan Objectives

2.   Milestones and Products (the "what" and "when")
2.1 Overall Development Strategy
2.2 Detailed Schedule of Deliverables
2.3 Detailed Development Milestones and Schedules

3.   Responsibilities (the "who" and "where")
3.1   Organizational Responsibilities
3.1.1 Global Organization Charts
3.1.2 Organizational Commitment Responsibilities
3.2   Development Responsibilities
3.2.1 Development Organization Charts
3.2.2 Staffing
3.2.3 Training

4.0   Approach (the "how")
4.1   Risk Management
4.2   Development Phases
4.2.1 Plans and Requirements Phase
4.2.2 Product Design Phase
4.2.3 Programming Phase
4.2.4 Test Phase
4.2.5 Implementation Phase
4.3   Reviews
4.4   Documentation
4.5   Configuration Management
4.6   Quality Assurance
4.7   Facilities and Related Concerns

5.0   Resources (the "how much")
5.1   Work Breakdown Structure
5.2   Budgets
5.3   Status Monitoring and Control

Figure 3   Software Plan Database Structure: Top Levels

Process Alternative Evaluation and Risk Resolution

The results of the Quantum Leap risk identification and resolution activities shown in Figure 5 show that the pure evolutionary development model was rejected as being unlikely to produce a sufficiently robust large-project SEE in 18 months, and that the pure waterfall model was rejected as being too constraining. Specifically, it was judged that a large number of arbitrary choices would have to be made to arrive at a detailed requirements specification, and that these arbitrary specifications would strongly limit the available degrees of freedom in choosing between COTS candidates. Thus, the COTS-driven model, used in conjunction with incremental development, emerged as the minimal-risk process architecture for Quantum Leap.

The other primary process risk item involved the scope and timely maturity of the available COTS SEE frameworks. In late 1986 and early 1987, these frameworks were judged to be insufficiently robust, mature, and fully defined to commit to a single framework choice and use

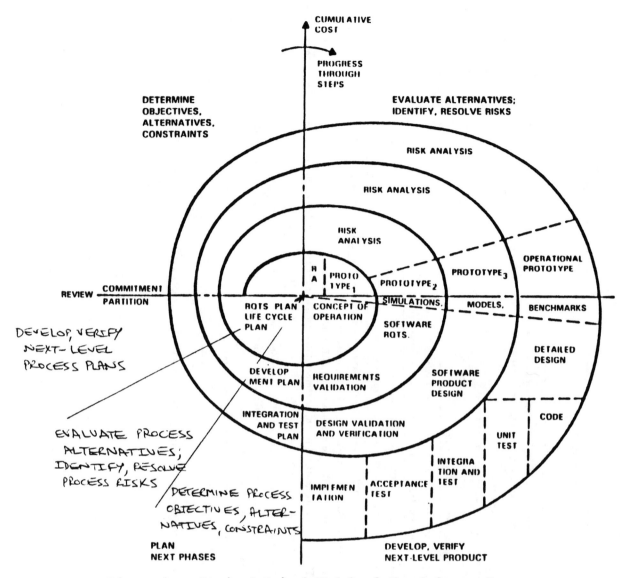

Figure 4   Revised Spiral Model of the Software Process

it as the basis of a large-project support system in 18 months. The risk resolution result in this case was to develop the 18-month IOC SEE without a COTS framework, to continue to evaluate the candidate COTS frameworks, and to plan to upgrade the Quantum Leap SEE to include a COTS framework in the 42-month time frame. (Note also that the revised process approach fed back into a revision of the product definition as well.)

Once these process risk resolution decisions were determined, the Quantum Leap project proceeded to elaborate its earlier life-cycle plan into a more detailed set of schedules, milestones, responsibilities, and budgets, along the lines indicated in Figure 5.

3.1.3. Revised Spiral Process Program

Based on the initial attempt to express the Refine-Life-Cycle-Plan procedure as a process program and its evaluation, we were able to reach a better understanding of the planning segment of the Spiral Model. Rather than a linear sequence of tasks to elaborate each section of the plan as in the original process program, the planning process turned out to be better represented as a repeated application of the earlier Spiral Model objectives-alternatives-evaluation-risk resolution steps, focussed on the requirements and architecture of the development *process* as compared to the focus on the *product* in the earlier steps of the spiral. Thus,

Process Objectives, Constraints	• SEE support of host project in 18 months • SEE budget for 25-person effort • Functionality defined by SEE requirements spec • Maximum use of COTS tools, SEE framework • Robust support of large projects, Ada, DoD-STD-2167
Process Alternatives	• DoD-STD-2167 style waterfall • Pure prototype/evolutionary development • COTS-driven requirements; evaluation; choice; tailoring of requirements and COTS • Incremental development re tools
Process Risks	• Objectives unachievable within budget, schedule • Scope, compatability, maturity of COTS tools, frameworks
Risk Resolution	• Evaluate, benchmark COTS tools, frameworks • Analyze alternative plans, budgets, detailed schedules
Risk Resolution Results	• Scope, maturity of COTS framework insufficient for robust large-scale Ada project support in 18 months. • 2167-style waterfall overconstraining re COTS, schedule • Pure prototype/ED unlikely to produce robust SEE in 18 months • COTS-driven requirements approach, incremental devevelopment re tools viable with design-to-schedule tools choice • Revise increment objectives: 18-month IOC SEE without COTS framework; 42-month full SEE with COTS framework
Next-level Process Plans	• COTS-driven, incremental approach with revised increments • Revised, elaborated, objectives: 18-month toolset with inter-tool moderators in place of framework • Elaborated milestones and deliverables • Revised project responsibilities (e.g., re framework) • Revised, elaborated approach, resource plan

Figure 5. SPIRAL PROCESS ARCHITECTURE STEPS: QUANTUM LEAP EXAMPLE

44

the process programming experiment led to a revised process program better reflecting the realities of Spiral Model application. In particular, it identified the importance of early process requirements, architecture, and design activities, and the appropriateness of the Spiral Model risk-driven approach in guiding these activities.

3.2. Process Programming Issues The primary lessons learned about process programming issues were:

- A model for the meaning of the process program is essential: What role does the process program play in the coordination of human and computer resources? In our experiment, we took a relatively naive view that the process program was to specify the entire process without regard to the fact that some aspects of the process (but not all) were to be "executed" by the human organizational system and some by, for example, an automated project support environment.

- Along the same lines, the limits of process programming must be dealt with explicitly: e.g., when some portions of the process are not to be formalized, how should that fact be represented; to what extent should the results of unformalized process be formalized, and in what fashion?

- Data representation issues are significant: e.g., How are prioritized objectives and constraints determined and represented?

- Data visibility issues are significant: not all aspects of the process need make references to all objects in the project data base, but different process programs appear to require different visibility disciplines. How should the variations be handled?

- Relationships among data objects are a central issue; in our experiment, the relationships were, for the most part, implicit. The opposite approach appears to be called for: the relationships need to be made explicit, and the process programming language and system need to support the management of these explicit relationships as they change over time. Our version of Ada was totally inadequate to deal with this issue.

- Change of the process during its elaboration is critical. In the Spiral Model, the plan can change at regular and identified points in the process, yet the nature of the change cannot be determined a priori. In what manner is this incremental specification of the plan and its realization in a yet-to-be-executed process program to be handled?

- The process program must accurately capture parallelism in the process; parallelism is inherent in the Spiral Model. In our experiment, it was difficult to capture parallelism in a satisfactory way. This was largely due to the fact that our adaptation of Ada did not initially include tasking, and the introduction of Ada tasking did not appear to be sufficient for our needs. (The Ada "compile time" model of binding all named structures did not seem compatible with our need for incrementally defining parallelism in the plan.)

4. Conclusions

Spiral Model Conclusions

We found process programming using our adaptation of Ada to be useful as an initial "PDL" for representing process architectures and designs. The process-PDL activity helped identify a number of incomplete and ambiguous aspects of the Spiral Model. In particular, the process programming approach helped us better understand the nature of the planning activity as a repeat of the Spiral model objectives-alternatives-evaluation-risk resolution-elaboration paradigm, focussed on determining the requirements, architecture, and design of the software process as well as the product.

Another significant process modeling conclusion deals with the need to reflect the increasing importance of commercial off the shelf (COTS) software to the architecture of both software products and software processes. The COTS-driven process model presented here provides an initial candidate process architecture component to cover such situations.

Process Programming Language Conclusions

On the basis of our experimentation, we believe some Process Programming Language (PPL) features to be very important for supporting process design activities:

- Mechanisms supporting the partitioning of the process specification into (sub) process specifications, and similarly to partition the objects into separate classes.

- Mechanisms to characterize the relationships among objects and the changes that occur among them.

- Mechanisms to represent process programs as objects and to control the execution disciplines that govern their activation.

- Mechanisms to specify (to various degrees of precision) the results of specific processes, even if the processes themselves are to be accomplished by non-deterministic (human) processors.

These kinds of features are not rare among existing languages; we suspect that broad spectrum languages with some mixture of conventional and as-yet-untried features will be required to deal effectively with the various aspects of the process design process.

An additional set of software process issues is important and so far largely unaddressed: the most appropriate derivation methods and representation schemes for software process requirements, architectures, and designs. The Spiral Model provides an initial cut at a derivation method for software process architectures and designs, and a PPL provides an initial cut at a representation scheme, but much more needs to be done.

5. References

[Boehm,1986] B. W. Boehm, "A Spiral Model of Software Development and Enhancement", *ACM Software Engineering Notes,* August 1986, pp.14-24.

[Belz,1986] F. C. Belz, "Applying the Spiral Model: Observations on Developing System Software in Ada", *Proceedings, 1986 Annual Conference on Ada Technology,* Atlanta, GA, 1986, pp.57-66.

[Boehm-Belz,1986] B. W. Boehm and F. C. Belz, "Reasoning about Iteration: A Cost-Benefit Approach", *Proceedings, Third International Software Process Workshop,* November 1986, pp. 40-42.

[Osterweil,1986] L. Osterweil, "Software Process Interpretation and Software Environments", University of Colorado Report CU-CS-324-86, April 1986.

[Boehm,1981] B.W. Boehm, *Software Engineering Economics,* Prentice Hall, 1981.

Rapid Prototyping, Risk Management, 2167, and the Ada Process Model

Barry Boehm
TRW

Introduction

DoD-STD-2167A offers sufficient degrees of freedom to appropriately accommodate rapid prototyping into a software development, given that one has an appropriate process model to substitute for the waterfall model, which otherwise tends to be used as the default implementation of 2167A.

TRW has been developing an Ada process model that incorporates the strengths of Ada, rapid prototyping, risk management, and the spiral model into a model that can be expressed as a tailored version of DoD-STD-2167A. We have also been developing an Ada version of the constructive cost model (COCOMO) for software cost estimation, which reflects the added efficiencies of using Ada and the Ada process model.

The Ada Process Model and Its Effects

The Ada process model focuses on the programming-in-the-large features of Ada (primarily, compiler-checkable package specifications) to define a software-development process model that minimizes the primary sources of inefficiency on most previous projects. These are the inefficiencies of process thrashing, turbulence, and interpersonal communication overhead brought on when large numbers of project personnel are working in parallel on tasks that are closely intertwined, incompletely defined, continually changing, and not well prepared for downstream integration. These factors primarily account for the high exponent value of 1.20 used in the standard-COCOMO nominal-effort equation for embedded mode projects (typical of the type of aerospace projects addressed by Ada). The resulting inefficiency can be seen from the fact that doubling a software product's size will increase its nominal effort by a factor of $(2)^{1.20} = 2.30$.

The primary features of the Ada process model that address these inefficiencies are its requirements to:

- Produce compilable, compiler-checked package specifications (and body outlines) for all top-level and critical lower-level Ada packages by the project's preliminary design review or PDR

- Identify and eliminate all major risk items by PDR

- Use a phased incremental development approach, with the requirements for each increment stabilized by the increment's PDR

These conditions ensure that many people can work on a software project in parallel (a necessary feature for achieving timely schedules), without the turbulence and inefficiencies usually experienced.

Additional features of the Ada process model include the use of:

- Small up-front system engineering and design teams

- Intermediate technical walkthroughs in the early requirements and design phases. These focus the pre-walkthrough effort on problem-solving and architecture definition, and post-walkthrough effort on document production

- Individual detailed design walkthroughs instead of a massive Critical Design Review (CDR). Instead, an efficient CDR is held to cover the highlight issues of the walkthroughs

- Continuous integration via compiler checking of Ada package specifications, rather than beginning integration at the end of unit test

- Well-commented Ada code and big-picture design information instead of massive as-built software detailed design documents (SDDDs)

The resulting Ada process model can be and has been used as a tailored version of DoD-STD-2167, initially on a small TRW-internal project, and currently on a large Air Force project: the Command Center Processing and Display System-Replacement (CCPDS-R) project.

Because of the reduction in project communications overhead and diseconomies of scale, the use of the Ada process model leads to an overall reduction in project effort. The overall schedule for a single-shot development is lengthened somewhat, but the use of incremental development means that users receive their initial operating capability earlier. The phase distribution of effort and schedule also changes. Use of the Ada process model involves more effort and schedule for requirements analysis and design, and considerably less for code, integration, and test.

Descriptive Figures

Figure 1 presents a graphic comparison of the Ada process model and what might be called the "all too frequent" process model, which often results from a superficial application of 2167A or the waterfall model, with unrealistically

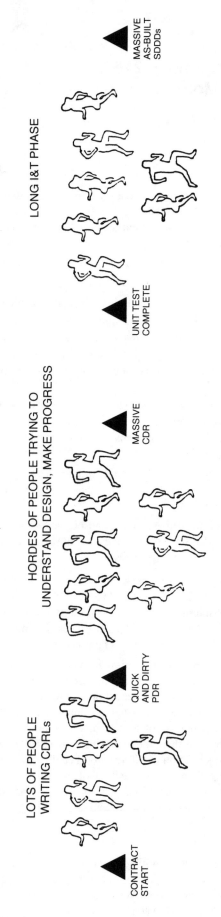

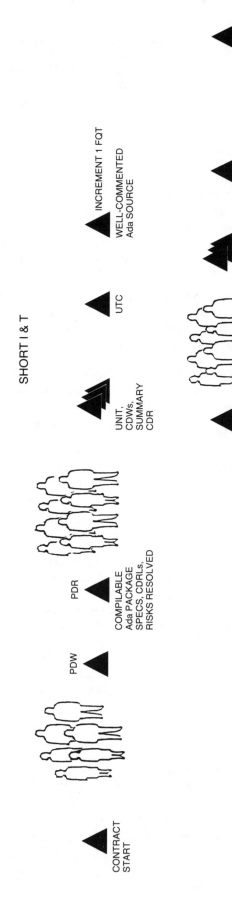

Figure 1: Ada Process Model: Key Distinctions

$$MM_{NOM} = (2.8)(KDSI)^{1.04 + \sum_{i-1}^{4} W_i}$$

WEIGHTS W_i	0.00	0.01	0.02	0.03	0.04	0.05
EXPERIENCE WITH Ada PROCESS MODEL	SUCCESSFUL ON >1 MISSION-CRITICAL PROJECT	SUCCESSFUL ON 1 MISSION-CRITICAL PROJECT	GENERAL FAMILIARITY WITH PRACTICES	SOME FAMILIARITY WITH PRACTICES	LITTLE FAMILIARITY WITH PRACTICES	NO FAMILIARITY WITH PRACTICES
DESIGN THOROUGHNESS AT PDR: UNIT PACKAGE SPECS COMPILED, BODIES OUTLINED	FULLY (100%)	MOSTLY (90%)	GENERALLY (75%)	OFTEN (60%)	SOME (40%)	LITTLE (20%)
RISKS ELIMINATED BY PDR	FULLY (100%)	MOSTLY (90%)	GENERALLY (75%)	OFTEN (60%)	SOME (40%)	LITTLE (20%)
REQUIREMENTS VOLATILITY DURING DEVELOPMENT	NO CHANGES	SMALL NONCRITICAL CHANGES	FREQUENT NONCRITICAL CHANGES	OCCASIONAL MODERATE CHANGES	FREQUENT MODERATE CHANGES	MANY LARGE CHANGES

ALL 0.04'S: COCOMO EMBEDDED MODE

- TYPICAL MM_{NOM}'S

ΣW_i	0.00	0.04	0.08	0.12	0.16	0.20
100 KDSI	336	405	487	585	703	846
500 KDSI	1,795	2,302	2,951	3,784	4,852	6,221

Figure 2: Ada COCOMO Scaling Equation

early schedules for completing the software requirements and design. The chart indicates some of the resulting inefficiencies as compared to the effects of the Ada process model in reducing project communications overhead and rework.

Figure 2 shows the major effects of using elements of the Ada process model on software project costs, as incorporated into Ada COCOMO. A typical 100,000-line (100 KDSI) software project fully experienced and compliant with the Ada process model would choose the 0.00 ratings in the table, and generate an estimated development effort of 336 nominal man-months (MM nom). A typical 100-KDSI "all too frequent" project would choose ratings averaging 0.04 each and generate an MM nom estimate of 703. Ada COCOMO has been calibrated to two contract Ada projects, and subsequently validated on three more completed Ada projects.

Figure 3 shows an elaboration of the progress through each of the early software definition cycles, by using the full synthesis of the Ada process model with risk management and the spiral model. It shows that prototyping is one of the project risk-resolution techniques employed as a result of the project's risk-assessment activities. It is guided by a risk management plan (required by 2167A), which establishes the necessary budgets and schedules for the risk reduction activities, and ensures that they are compatible with those in the project's overall software development plan.

In particular, Figure 3 shows the process of going from the review of one level of definition of a software product (either a specification, an executing portion of the product, or a mix of both) to the review of the next level of definition of the product. The review covers the current definition of the product and the plan for the next phase or cycle, which is strongly driven by the risk management (RM) plan for the phase (to begin the process, an initial version of these is generated). If the successive products are primarily system and software requirements and design specifications, then the reviews will follow the System Requirements Review, System Design Review, Software Specification Review, and Preliminary Design Review sequence of DoD-STD-2167A.

If the review process produces a concurrence on and a commitment to the plan for the next cycle, then the next steps involve an elaboration of the objectives and constraints for the software product and process, an identification of alternative approaches for satisfying the objectives within the constraints, an evaluation of the alternatives, and a risk assessment activity. The following step involves the elaboration and refinement of the RM plan for the current cycle, plus a draft of a RM plan to cover the primary RM functions to be performed during the following cycle (including the necessary budget and schedule for performing them).

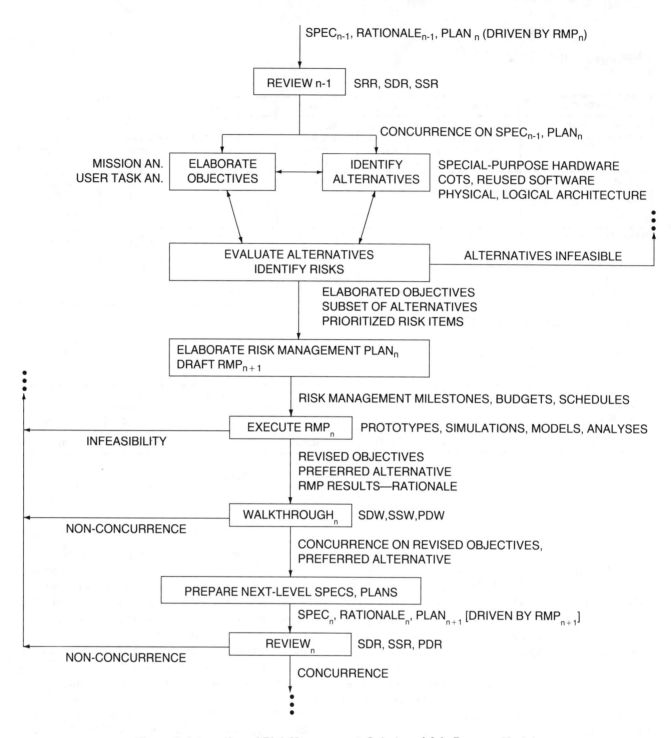

$SPEC_{n-1}$, $RATIONALE_{n-1}$, $PLAN_n$ (DRIVEN BY RMP_n)

REVIEW n-1 | SRR, SDR, SSR

CONCURRENCE ON $SPEC_{n-1}$, $PLAN_n$

MISSION AN.
USER TASK AN.

ELABORATE OBJECTIVES

IDENTIFY ALTERNATIVES

SPECIAL-PURPOSE HARDWARE
COTS, REUSED SOFTWARE
PHYSICAL, LOGICAL ARCHITECTURE

EVALUATE ALTERNATIVES
IDENTIFY RISKS

ALTERNATIVES INFEASIBLE

ELABORATED OBJECTIVES
SUBSET OF ALTERNATIVES
PRIORITIZED RISK ITEMS

ELABORATE RISK MANAGEMENT $PLAN_n$
DRAFT RMP_{n+1}

RISK MANAGEMENT MILESTONES, BUDGETS, SCHEDULES

EXECUTE RMP_n

INFEASIBILITY

PROTOTYPES, SIMULATIONS, MODELS, ANALYSES

REVISED OBJECTIVES
PREFERRED ALTERNATIVE
RMP RESULTS—RATIONALE

$WALKTHROUGH_n$ | SDW,SSW,PDW

NON-CONCURRENCE

CONCURRENCE ON REVISED OBJECTIVES,
PREFERRED ALTERNATIVE

PREPARE NEXT-LEVEL SPECS, PLANS

$SPEC_n$, $RATIONALE_n$, $PLAN_{n+1}$ [DRIVEN BY RMP_{n+1}]

$REVIEW_n$ | SDR, SSR, PDR

NON-CONCURRENCE

CONCURRENCE

Figure 3: Integration of Risk Management, Spiral, and Ada Process Models

Once the RM plan is executed (along with risk monitoring and any necessary corrective actions), the resulting revised objectives, preferred alternatives, and their rationale are covered in a technical walkthrough involving the key developer, customer, user, and maintainer participants. A non-concurrence on the results of the walkthrough will cause an iteration of the appropriate previous steps. Given a concurrence, the project will proceed to develop the next level of definition of the product (specification executing portion, or mix) and the plan for the next cycle, which is driven by the draft RM plan for the next cycle. In this model, therefore,

the early 2167A phases are mapped onto early cycles of a spiral model software development.

Thus, Figure 3 provides a roadmap for using risk management techniques to navigate through the critical and difficult early phases of a software development. The project's relative risk exposure factors provide guidance on when and what to prototype, simulate, benchmark, or V&V; and on how much of these activities will be enough.

Figures 4 and 5 provide additional context on the use of prototyping and alternative software process models. They

DOMAIN CHARACTERISTICS	PROCESS MODEL	EXAMPLES
• WELL-UNDERSTOOD APPLICATION • SEVERAL COMMERCIAL PACKAGES AVAILABLE	ACQUIRE COTS	• ELECTRONIC PUBLISHING • BASIC FINANCIAL FUNCTIONS • BASIC INVENTORY CONTROL
• STRONG EVOLUTION-SUPPORT CAPABILITY AVAILABLE: 4GL, TRANSFORM, FORMS MGMT. • APPLICATION FUNCTIONS POORLY UNDERSTOOD • STANDALONE APPLICATION	EVOLUTIONARY DEVELOPMENT	• SMALL-ORGANIZATION MIS • SPREADSHEET APPLICATION • FORMS-PROCESSING APPLICATION
• APPLICATION FUNCTIONS WELL UNDERSTOOD • SYSTEM ARCHITECTURE WELL UNDERSTOOD • NO MAJOR RISK ITEMS • 4GL-TYPE CAPABILITIES INSUFFICIENT	WATERFALL (Ada-ENHANCED)	• MEDIUM-LARGE INVENTORY CONTROL • OFFLINE DATA REDUCTION • SIMPLE MESSAGE HANDLING
• MAJOR ISSUE POORLY UNDERSTOOD • PARTIAL, FRAGILE CAPABILITIES SATISFACTORY	EXPLORATORY RISK REDUCTION	• EXPERT SYSTEMS • PATTERN RECOGNITION • SITUATION ASSESSMENT
• MAJOR ISSUES POORLY UNDERSTOOD • STABLE CAPABILITIES REQUIRED	EXPLORATORY RISK REDUCTION FOLLOWED BY WATERFALL (Ada-ENHANCED)	• LARGE USER-INTENSIVE SYSTEMS — C&C, INTEL, ADVANCED SDE'S • STRONGLY EMBEDDED SYSTEMS • MAJOR REUSE OPPORTUNITIES, UNCERTAINTIES
• DOWNSTREAM FUNCTIONS POORLY UNDERSTOOD • NEED FOR EARLY SUBSET CAPABILITY • MANPOWER CONSTRAINTS • NEED TO STABILIZE REQUIREMENTS DURING DEVELOPMENT	INCREMENTAL DEVELOPMENT	• LARGE USER-INTENSIVE SYSTEMS • VERY LARGE SYSTEMS — CORPORATE MIS, SDI, CORPORATE LOGS. MGMT. • MANPOWER-CONSTRAINED DEVELOPMENTS

Figure 4: Major Software Process Models and Their Preferred Domains

were prepared for a recent National Research Council/Air Force Studies Board summer study on software technology and acquisition management. Figure 4 summarizes the primary alternative software process models (COTS, evolutionary development, waterfall, explanatory risk reduction, exploratory risk reduction followed by waterfall, and incremental development, which can be combined with the earlier alternatives), in terms of the project domains to which they best apply, with examples provided for each.

Figure 5 provides more context on how software risk management and the alternative process models fit into the overall DoD system acquisition process. It shows the critical software activities which need to be done during the concept definition and demonstration/validation phases, including the determination of which process model will be used during the full-scale development phase. For each of these process models, it also shows the critical software activities to be performed during the full-scale development phase.

References

V.R. Basili et al., "Use of Ada for FAA's Advanced Automation System," *MITRE MTR—87W77,* MITRE Corporation, McLean, Va., April 1987.

PHASE	CRITICAL SOFTWARE ACTIVITIES
CONCEPT DEFINITION	ANALYZE, PROTOTYPE CRITICAL SOFTWARE ISSUES — HARDWARE-SOFTWARE TRADEOFFS, PERFORMANCE, RELIABILITY, MULTILEVEL SECURITY, USER INTERFACE, DISTRIBUTED OS/DBMS, SYSTEM INTERFACES, PORTABILITY LAYERS, GROWTH POTENTIAL. DEVELOP DEM/VAL SOFTWARE RISK MANAGEMENT PLAN.
DEMONSTRATION/ VALIDATION	EXECUTE DEM/VAL SOFTWARE RISK MANAGEMENT PLAN ⎫ SKIP THESE STEPS IF PROTOTYPE CRITICAL SOFTWARE ISSUES IN SYSTEM CONTEXT ⎬ DEM/VAL RISK IS LOW ESTABLISH ACQUISITION PROCESS MODEL AND FSD RISK MANAGEMENT PLAN DEVELOP SYSTEM RQTS, DESIGN, LC PLAN, TAILORED ACQUISITION STANDARDS
FULL-SCALE DEVEL. —COTS	• "REQUIREMENTS" BECOME COTS EVALUATION CRITERIA • SELECTED COTS CAPABILITIES REDEFINE REQUIREMENTS
—EVOLUTIONARY DEVELOPMENT	• TIME & MATERIALS OR TASK-ORDER CONTRACT TO EVOLVE SYSTEM • AWARD FEES BASED ON USER SATISFACTION
—WATERFALL	• Ada PROCESS MODEL ENHANCEMENTS • REQUIREMENTS—BASED ACQUISITION CONTRACT
—EXPLORATORY RISK REDUCTION	• COMPETITIVE BUILD-TO-COST EXPLORATORY DEVELOPMENT CONTRACTS • MINIMIZE CONTRACTING OVERHEAD
—EXPLORATORY RISK REDUCTION & Ada ENHANCED WATERFALL	• DRIVEN BY SDP, PARTICULARLY RISK MANAGEMENT PLAN • COMPETITIVE PRELIMINARY DESIGN WHERE BOUNDARY CONDITIONS ALLOW

Figure 5: Critical Software Activities in System Development

B.W. Boehm and W. Royce, "Ada COCOMO: TRW IOC Version," *Proceedings, Third COCOMO User's Group Meeting, CMU/SEI*, Carnegie Mellon University, Software Engineering Institute, Pittsburgh, Penn., November 1987.

B.W. Boehm, *"Tutorial: Software Risk Management,"* IEEE Computer Society Press, Washington, D.C., 1989.

B.W. Boehm. "A Spiral Model of Software Development and Enhancement," *Computer,* May 1988, pp. 61-72.

B.W. Boehm, and F.C. Belz, "Applying Process Programming to the Spiral Model," *Proceedings, Fourth Software Process Workshop,* Association for Computing Machinery, Inc., New York, 1989.

W. Royce, "TRW's Ada Process Model for Incremental Development of Large Software Systems," *Proceedings, Tri-Ada Conference*, Pittsburgh, Penn., October 1989 (to appear).

Estimating the risk

■ Introduction

Chapter 6 gives an overview of some of the ways in which we can handle uncertainty and risk.

■ 6.1 Risk

We have taken a brief look at some tools which can help us to define and analyze problems, and identify and evaluate possible solutions. However, the implementation of a solution which is based (as we have shown it is bound to be) on plans containing estimates, approximations and uncertainties, involves risk. The idea of risk is a particularly important one, and deserves more extended treatment.

> 'One of the most rigorous theorems of economics (Boehm–Bawerks Law) proves that the existing means of production will yield greater economic performance only through greater uncertainty, that is, through greater risk. While it is futile to try to eliminate risk, and questionable to try to minimize it, it is essential that the risks taken be the right risks. . . .
>
> We must be able to choose rationally among risk-taking courses of action, rather than plunge into uncertainty on the basis of hunch, hearsay, or incomplete experience, no matter how meticulously quantified.'
>
> Peter Drucker (1975), *Management*, Heinemann

6.1.1 A policy statement on risk control

Here is an example of an attempt to control risk for a software development group of 300 persons. This is the first element of the case study material which is used to illustrate Part Two of this book, the International Banking Corporation. Similar policies have been adopted by a computer manufacturer employing thousands of software engineers.

Example: IBC.Policy

1. *Basic goal*
   Our basic goal, and therefore our measure of success, is to develop systems (computerized or not) which have the *user-value-to-cost ratio* within acceptable limits. This implies that *user-value* of systems must be planned and controlled at all times, and project and operation system *cost* must be planned and controlled at all times.

Reprinted with permission from Chapter 6 of *Principles of Software Engineering Management*, by Tom Gilb, Addison-Wesley Publishing Company, 1988.

2. *Future-shock-proof organization*

   The organization shall be able to succeed in spite of *future shock change* (i.e. unexpected high-impact changes) in any part of the environment – e.g. inflation, new business types, people turnover, new organizational forms, organization growth, technological changes, etc.

3. *Goal oriented people*

   Each of our professionals (managers and technicians) shall be selected, managed, and trained to be competent to help us reach planned goals.

   The goal type and planned level shall only be set by group top management, and it is our responsibility to be able to respond to these goals.

4. *Risk identification*

   All *risk elements* shall be explicitly identified and controlled by us at all stages of planning, design and management – i.e., written documentation for risk control must be present in all planning.

5. *Management by objectives*

   All activity (be it managerial, technical or system project) shall be *controlled in all critical attributes*, at all stages of development – that is what we mean by 'management by objectives'.

The risk principle:
If you don't actively attack the risks, they will actively attack you.

■ 6.2 Being responsible for risk

We can draw conclusions for action from what we see, at a fairly early stage, if we are willing to accept a certain risk that such conclusions may be incorrect, partially misleading, or have a calculable degree of error in them.

   If we make the mistake of insisting on 100% safe conclusions, then we may be committed to continuing our investigations forever, and no practical change will be implemented. We should rather concentrate on knowing and controlling the degree of risk involved. We should let other people know that we are intentionally doing so. And we should take it upon ourselves to inform others of the degree of risk they run of being wrong when they accept any of our statements as a basis for action.

   Knowing that there is a risk, and knowing even approximately what the level of that risk is, is a sign of professional competence. There are too many professionals who mistakenly believe that to raise issues of risk is a sign of incompetence – because it shows that they do not have full control. This is wrong. Knowing that we must share this understanding of risk with others on our own initiative is a sign of sound professional ethics.

The risk sharing principle:
The real professional is one who knows the risks, their degree, their causes, and the action necessary to counter them, and shares this knowledge with his colleagues and clients.

■ 6.3 Expecting overruns

If we attempt to carry out large projects with unclear goal statements, inadequate planning, less than wholly competent people, and weak management methods, in areas which are so uncharted as to justify the use of research funds, we should expect overruns of resource expenditure.

We should remember that a professional engineer is expected to make a clear distinction between predictable costs (usually those based on some sort of experience data), and highly unpredictable cost factors (those based on techniques which have an inadequate or incomplete cost history). The question is, how can we, as managers, avoid the worst effects of systems full of unknowns when they 'go wrong on us'?

The risk prevention principle:
Risk prevention is more cost-effective than risk detection.

The promise principle:
Never make promises you cannot keep, no matter what the pressure.

The written promise principle:
If you do make any promises, make them yourself, and make them in writing.

The promise caveat principle:
When you make a promise, include your estimate of how much deviation could occur for reasons outside of your control, for reasons within your control, and for reasons others in the company can control.

The early reaction principle:
When something happens during the project that you did not foresee, which increases deviation from planned risk, immediately raise the issue, in writing, with your constructive suggestion as to how to deal with it.

The implicit promise principle:
If you suspect someone else – your boss or a client – of assuming you have made promises, then take the time to disclaim them, and repeat the promises you *have* made, if any, in writing.

The deviation principle:
When indicating possible deviation, make a list of the possible causes of deviation, as well as a list of the actions you could take to control those risks.

The written proof principle:
Hang the following sign near your desk: If you haven't got it in writing from me, I didn't promise it.

■ 6.4 Specifying the degree of uncertainty

Management involves constantly making judgements, with varied degrees of risk that these judgements lead to incorrect or inadequate decisions. We are referring here to perfectly ordinary deviations for factors such as human resources requirements, costs, implementation time, effective promised results, and capital investment.

It is common to find that when project goals, budgets and plans are drawn up for management approval, not only are the critical goals vaguely stated, as I have already indicated, but their very vagueness is not stated clearly enough!

For example, it is a poor guide for planning when we state our goals in a form such as 'must be completed as soon as possible.' It is an improvement when we say 'must be completed by 24 December at 17.00 hours G.M.T.' But it would be even more useful, if the realities dictate it, to express the goal like this: 'The project has a planned completion date of 24 December, which is also the earliest conceivable date of completion. There is a high probability of up to one week slippage due to staff sickness conditions, and a slight possibility of a delay of up to one month should the hardware supplier fail to deliver as agreed in the contract.'

In short: '24 Dec. (+7, staff sickness) and (+31, sub-contract delivery).'

When the uncertainty of the estimate is not clearly documented, management lacks information which is vital to its own proper performance.

The principle of risk exposure:
The degree of risk, and its causes, must never be hidden from decision-makers.

Present practices in this area reflect badly on the many managers who do not insist explicitly and regularly on getting clearly documented risk estimates for every significant estimate in every budget and plan. The first planning document you look at will give you examples of this failure. But it is an equally poor reflection on responsible planners and problem solvers who do not take it upon their own professional initiative to provide the 'passive' manager with the stimulant of clear written risk estimates. I have on several occasions suggested, and had accepted as planning policy, a version of the following statement:

'All significant, large and critical-to-success estimates are to be accompanied by an explicit written estimate of plus and minus deviations from the planned number, date or amount. This will be done even when no deviation is 'expected' or 'allowed.' Footnotes will explain the probable causes or reasons why such deviations could occur, so that management can evaluate the deviation estimates themselves, take action to limit the causes, and so become responsible for accepting these conditions as known risks.'

This was one of five policy statements in 'IBC. POLICY,' see Section 6.1.

You might like to consider the effect of such a policy in your own working environment. It will probably take no more than a single trial – of insisting on it being done thoroughly on one single project – to convince you that you must continue to do so for your own future protection and peace of mind.

The asking principle:
If you don't ask for risk information, you are asking for trouble.

■ 6.5 The most critical part of an estimate

The most important part of a result, a measure, an estimate, a conclusion, or a prediction is not the quantitative statement itself. It is the confidence we can place in the figures.

The cost of a project is estimated at, say, 500 work-months effort, and this has been accepted. The estimator is the first to be criticized when the actual effort turns out to be 750 work-months. If, on the other hand, the estimate was originally 500 plus or minus 300 work-months ('depending on the quality of the work-force'), then the manager who accepts the estimates is in a very different position. If he does not act to get the necessary quality of people actually working on the project, or even find out what is meant by 'quality' here, he has only himself to blame when the actual figure turns out to be 790 work-months.

I am suggesting that managers be more exposed to criticism on these grounds. But I am also suggesting that they be given more opportunity to get control of such unpleasant realities before they take effect in the real world.

One other simple way of expressing a risk element, and one which we can combine with the 'plus-or-minus deviation' idea, is the use of 'best,' 'worst,' 'planned' and 'now' levels when specifying attribute goals. (See Sections 9.7, 9.8, 9.9, 9.10 for details on these attribute levels.) Each one of these sheds light on the others, and provides a focal point for discussion as to how big the difference really is, why there is a difference, and how reliable each one of those figures actually is.

For example, if the best known performance level for a system is 99.98% availability, and the planned level is set at 99.999%, then these two pieces of information together tell a manager that a state of the art breakthrough is needed to meet the planned level. The risk of failure, or at least higher than expected costs, is very high. If, in addition, the worst acceptable level is set at only 99% while the present level is also 99%, the manager might feel better about the risk involved. After all, the level was achieved in the old system. That does not make it taken-for-granted in a new system, but at least the way to get there has been explored.

■ 6.6 A software maintenance cost example

An example follows showing software maintenance cost per line of code changed:

> *Present cost:* $100 per line of code changed (varies between $55 and $205 depending on volume ordered).
> *Planned cost (by today plus two years):* $45 (+ $20 due to design uncertainty).
> *Worst acceptable case cost:* $90 (management refuse to sponsor a new system which does not result in a net saving).
> *Best observed case:* $30 to $50 ('a corresponding company in town reported reducing their costs to the $30 level last year. Nothing better is recorded or promised.').

We should not be afraid of bringing out the truth here, because even great uncertainty, if made clear and public at an early stage, can lead directly to efforts to avoid the 'worst case' from happening, to make the planned level happen, and even to move in the direction of the best case.

■ 6.7 The 'best case delivery date' example

A project team member in New York, when we asked about the 'best case' delivery date for a software application development project, gave it as 'right now.' His colleagues tried actively to suppress his oral statement and avoid recording it. They were afraid that management would misinterpret it, and expect the entire project, with all whistles and bells, to be available immediately, instead of in the six months time which was planned.

When it was clearly explained that this early delivery date was only a valid estimate for the most critical and basic functions of the new system, things quietened down a bit. It turned out that management were both surprised and pleased by this information, and wanted to exercise the early partial delivery option.

The possibility of early delivery had never been discussed, up to that point, by anyone. Management almost missed an important competitive advantage by not asking for the 'best case.' They had also failed to create a climate where project members were unafraid to discuss such notions of deviation from 'the main plan.'

The 'why not the best?' principle:
The 'best imaginable' can be a reality, if you are willing to risk or sacrifice any other planned attributes.

■ 6.8 Try your own risk estimation

You might like to try out this on a few elements in a project of your own. Here are some simple ways in which we can specify the risk element by:

- determining various levels of an attribute (best, worst, planned, now);

- finding plus and minus deviation estimates for each figure;

- estimating the probability (which is also an uncertainty, but is still a useful way of expressing things) that a certain result will occur;

- listing the factors which can contribute to the stated variations in a particular estimate;

- simply putting a '?' after the estimate (e.g. best = 300 months ? – TG 880731). Include 'who' and 'when' information as well.

■ 6.9 Create the motivation for getting control

Common sense, openness, imagination, simple ways of expressing yourself, and the will to communicate with others effectively will all go a long way towards making predictions realistic. Realistic predictions, and the promises implied by them, are one step towards controlling the ultimate results.

Bear in mind that strong motivation (in managers and planners alike) to get and keep control over results, has an observable and decisive influence on whether or not results tend to be achieved satisfactorily, in spite of the mischievous nature of the world around us.

What have you done to create motivation to achieve results? Does everybody get paid the same no matter how badly the project runs? Do the people who keep promises, if any, get ample rewards and honors? Does your staff have a real slice of the action – like shares in your small software house, or a share of the profits via a bonus scheme? Do people who cannot keep their promises get smoked out early and corrected in their ways? Have you or your company executives created the fear that makes people make silly promises, and then make excuses. Or are people unafraid to be realistic?

6.9.1 A motivational example: Fridays free

In one case, with an application product software subsidary of a computer manufacturer, I got the Director's agreement (much to our surprise) to the following motivation idea. The development teams would plan for weekly incremental delivery of 'something working.' If they succeeded in getting it demonstrable by the end of Thursday, they could use Friday for professional purposes other than their project work. For example: attend lectures, study trips to exhibitions, research projects, write technical papers, read technical literature, or study other parts of the organization.

The group was left free to make its own plan, however small. The important thing was to be oriented towards live software results to be delivered every week, which the Director could see, and show his colleagues, as visible evidence of progress. He had been very disturbed, as was I, by a culture which allowed months to slip by with no visible progress in terms of working usable systems. We both felt that the groups would get more useful work done in those four days, than five days with no focus on results.

I stayed on for the initial planning of projects on the weekly basis. It was surprising to learn how wrong we could be about how much (or how little) we could actually get done in a week. But we kept on iterating the plans until we learned to be more realistic. This process helped us to reduce the danger of being wrong in relation to plans. It was a good thing we were doing this learning on a weekly scale rather than a yearly scale!

The uncertainty motivation principle:
Uncertainty in a technical project is half technical and half motivational, but with good enough motivation, uncertainty will not be allowed to lead to problems.

■ 6.10 Uncertainty and risk specification using impact estimation

Those who wish to get a really detailed evaluation of risk elements should refer to Chapter 11 for the description of impact estimation tables. See particularly Section 11.7 safety factors, Section 11.5 side-effect estimation, Section 11.3 limitations, Section 11.10 justification of an estimate, and other parts of this chapter.

Impact estimation is an application of the concept of 'cost estimation' to all the other attributes of a planned system. Impact estimation is limited to early planning stages. It is a modelling idea, when you need something more precise than the general risk estimation methods discussed earlier in the chapter.

However, there comes a stage when it is necessary to get 'risk feedback' from the project implemented in the real world. At this point we will use a different tool entirely, evolutionary delivery. See Chapter 7 for an initial discussion of evolutionary delivery methods.

Paper models (such as impact estimation) of complex systems can never replace the more certain knowledge of a real system working with a real user. This is where evolutionary delivery is vital, because it gives us that certain knowledge before we have committed too many of our resources to the wrong ideas. Even then there are uncertainties about the future and about scaling up.

Ng's visibility principle:
We don't trust it until we can see it and feel it.

The reality principle:
Theoretical estimation is as accurate as our oversimplified estimation models backed by obsolete historical data. The real thing is a somewhat more reliable indicator.

■ 6.11 The software import risk example

One European client, a computer manufacturer, decided to base the software for a new line of computers on the UNIX operating system and the C programming language. They found they could buy a basic package for this from a software house in California which was supplying many of my client's competitors with the same software. This decision was dictated by top management; the development team was given no say, nor was their advice asked. The marketing decision was that their market wanted (or would want) UNIX and importing the basic software for adaptation was obviously the best way to do it.

At one point I began to explore, with the quality manager, exactly what we knew about the quality requirements for the project, and for the imported component. It was quite clear that the quality requirements for our product were quite high. They included zero defects to customers in our final product, and no more than two minutes downtime per 48-hour period for the entire hardware-software delivery to our customers.

The imported component was a large part of our total delivery, much more than half, and furthermore was central to all other components. If it failed, they failed. I asked what we knew ot error rates, etc. for the imported components. Nothing – what we were going to get was the 'latest,' of which there was, of course, no experience.

I asked if we had contractually committed the supplier to any particular quality levels, and appropriate acceptance tests, which were critical to our product. Apparently this had been considered unnecessary by the managers who had started all this, because, I was told, 'no matter how bad it is, our competitors will have the same bad software.'

All this was a breach of the formal company guidelines designed to improve the quality of all products, as my quality manager colleague and I knew quite well. I helped write them – and he was among the leaders in implementing them. But the decisions were apparently taken so high up (lab director level, I believe, but even this was unclear) that nobody dared challenge them.

What is the risk that the project will fail?

The final chapter of this story is not known as I write this so the reader is left with an exercise to guess what the risks are.

Here is a set of questions you can ask yourself in order to analyze a situation like the example given above.

1. What is the probability that the product will ever meet the quality specifications?
2. What is the probability that the product will be severely delayed while they try to bring it up to some minimally acceptable specifications?
3. What is the probability that at least one competitor will handle this situation in a smarter manner?
4. What is the probability that the lab director will try to lay the blame on the software development team?
5. What should the software development team do to defend themselves, and their company, against this situation?
6. What is the probability that the lab director will lose face and power – if he regularly violates company policy regarding quality, and takes quality out of the hands of the developers?

■ Further reading

Peters, T., and Waterman, R., 1982, *In search of excellence*, Harper and Row/Warner Books, New York. (Ng's Principle source)

IT'S LATE, COSTLY, INCOMPETENT —BUT TRY FIRING A COMPUTER SYSTEM

Companies get stuck with 'runaways' that trample all over their budgets and reputations

It's a project that, for Allstate Insurance Co., has redefined the concept of sparing no expense. The Sears, Roebuck & Co. subsidiary set out in 1982 to build the insurance industry's most sophisticated computer system, one that would make its competitors quake. The system was supposed to automate Allstate's office operations and shorten the normal three-year period needed to introduce new types of policies to one month. Allstate hired Electronic Data Systems Corp., the systems-integration company, to develop the software and help install it on the firm's hardware. The target date for completion was December, 1987; the target cost was $8 million. Some $15 million later, Allstate has a new project consultant, a new deadline, and a new cost estimate: $100 million.

The Allstate case is a classic example of a computer runaway, a system that's millions over budget, years behind schedule, and—if ever completed—less effective than promised. A recent Peat Marwick Mitchell & Co. survey of 600 of the accounting firm's largest clients highlighted the problem: Some 35% currently have major runaways. Indeed, experts say, such diverse systems integrators as the Big Eight accounting firms, computer suppliers, and even in-house data processing staffs are fast building a record of mediocrity. Says James A. Willbern, a management consultant at Peat Marwick: The industry's "ability to install systems is pretty crummy."

The problem is so acute that it has created a lucrative industry of its own. In 1986, Willbern set up a group at Peat Marwick to rein in runaways. Since then, he has had $30 million in revenues from nearly 20 clients, including Allstate.

BLOWN DEADLINES. Allstate's project ran on track for about a year before it went awry. First, deadlines for programming and for testing hardware started slipping by. Then Allstate technical staffers quarreled over the dimensions of the project and each other's roles. By 1987, the huge project had changed from savior to albatross, and Allstate had had enough. It started over with Peat Marwick, which helped revamp and train the in-house staff working on the system, now targeted for completion in 1993.

Although there are many explanations for the epidemic of runaways, there seems to be a common thread: Neither buyers nor builders of computer systems have adjusted their deadlines to reflect the increased complexity of computer projects. A decade ago, a $2 million computer system that took longer than a year to build was a rarity. Such systems were self-contained units with no interweaving of technologies and data bases. Connectivity was a foreign word. Today, although companies are developing systems of such magnitude that entire businesses are sculpted around them, many designers still use the old approach. Far better, consultants say, is to divide major projects into modules that can be finished one at a time.

"It's the difference between counting the number of people in a small room and doing a U. S. census," says Wayne Stevens, a leading systems-design theorist. "It takes two different skills, and when you go from the simpler to the more complex project, you'd better do things differently."

Tom Hefty learned this the hard way when a runaway carried Blue Cross & Blue Shield United of Wisconsin to the brink of disaster. In 1983, three years before Hefty became chief executive of the Milwaukee-based insurer, it hired EDS to build a $200 million system to coordinate all the services then being handled by five computers. The system was completed on time—in just 18 months. But it didn't work. One example: Because of an entry error, the computer sent out hundreds of checks to the fictitious hamlet of None, Wis. A month later the checks arrived back at Blue Cross for readdressing. During its first year, the system disbursed $60 million in overpayments or duplicate checks.

Before the runaway was stopped, Blue Cross lost 35,000 members—a setback it attributes to the computer problems. EDS contends foul-ups were inevitable because of the multitude of data to be converted from the old system to the new. But Blue Cross wants EDS to reimburse it for some of the lost revenues. The dispute is now in arbitration.

Inheriting this mess in 1986, Hefty immediately instituted tough quality-control measures. He found that the system's developers never adequately used checkpoints during the project to evaluate whether the system was on track. Only that, he says, would have ensured a more successful outcome. Others concur. "In larger projects, you should have a detailed review every 12 months," says Jack Epstein, a vice-president at the research firm International Data Corp. "In shorter-term projects, you could meet every six months. These meetings, Hefty adds, should include senior management. Most nontechnical executives are unwilling to take an active role in developing a computer system—until costs spiral out of control. "I let it slip, that's the problem," says the president of a medical diagnostic firm. "I kept hands off, and it hurt me in the end."

'PROMISING EVERYTHING.' This company experienced a nightmare last year when its new computer system, during its first day in operation, lost information pertaining to thousands of crucial medical tests. The software couldn't handle the volumes of data it had to deal with. Luckily, the loss was not permanent—but it took 30 days to reconstruct the records. At that point, the company's president decided to "take a clean look at this thing." He fired the data processing chief, hired a new technical staff, and announced that he would be closely involved with all future systems develop-

A SAMPLING OF 'RUNAWAY' PROJECTS

ALLSTATE INSURANCE In 1982, with software from Electronic Data Systems, the insurer began to build an $8 million computer system that would automate it from top to bottom. Completion date: 1987. An assortment of problems developed, delaying completion until 1993. The new estimated price: $100 million

CITY OF RICHMOND In 1984 it hired Arthur Young to develop a $1.2 million billing and information system for its water and gas utilities. Completion date: March, 1987. After paying out close to $1 million, Richmond recently canceled the contract, saying no system had been delivered. Arthur Young has filed a $2 million breach of contract suit against the city

BUSINESS MEN'S ASSURANCE In 1985 the reinsurer began a one-year project to build a $500,000 system to help minimize the risk of buying insurance policies held by major insurers. The company has spent nearly $2 million to date on the project, which is in disarray. The new completion date is early 1990

STATE OF OKLAHOMA In 1983 it hired a Big Eight accounting firm to design a $500,000 system to handle explosive growth in workers' compensation claims. Two years and more than $2 million later, the system still didn't exist. It finally was finished last year at a price of nearly $4 million

BLUE CROSS & BLUE SHIELD UNITED OF WISCONSIN In late 1983 it hired Electronic Data Systems to build a $200 million computer system. It was ready 18 months later—on time. But it didn't work. The system spewed out some $60 million in overpayments and duplicate checks before it was harnessed last year. By then, Blue Cross says, it had lost 35,000 policyholders

DATA: BW

ment. A new system is expected to be completed by the end of this year.

One problem with giving data processing professionals and outside suppliers free rein over a new computer system is that they tend to be overly optimistic: "They sell expectation, not reality," says Dave Elenburg, who last year led a group that cleaned up a multimillion-dollar runaway in the workers' compensation system in Oklahoma. "DPers feel they have to keep the executives happy by promising even what they can't deliver. And suppliers are out for sales."

One common gripe among customers is that after they hire a supplier to direct the development of a system, the work is frequently assigned to "students straight out of tech school," as Elenburg puts it. The more talented professionals who represented the supplier in the initial meetings are busy trying to bring in new business. Robert C. Bobb, city manager of Richmond, Va., was so incensed two years ago when Arthur Young sent inexperienced technicians to develop the management system for the city's utilities that he now writes into all consult-

ing contracts the names of the people who must work on the project. Arthur Young says that its senior consultants were "heavily involved" in the Richmond project. But Bobb says that's not enough: "The partners have to begin to do the grunt work."

DISMAL PICTURE. So do the people who ultimately will use the system. Too often, a runaway occurs because during the planning stages the staffers who eventually will be operating the computers are not consulted for ideas about how the system should work. "User involvement cannot be casual," says George Hathaway, a runaway-buster at the Index Group, a Cambridge (Mass.) consultancy. "The mind-set has to be emphasized more to users that the computer works for you; you don't work for it."

As dismal as the picture is, there are glimmers of light. Many runaway consultants feel that the recent round of failures has taught buyers caution. "Corporate executives are becoming very wary about dropping millions of dollars into a bottomless bucket," says Phil Dressler, a Dallas-based runaway salvager. Moreover, Dressler adds, as such executives become more computer-literate over the next few years, they will be less afraid to take charge of technical projects. And data processing professionals are becoming better managers, increasingly using the modular approach to building systems. What's more, unyielding competition in the $5 billion-a-year systems-integration field will sooner or later force the companies in it to be more attentive to customers' needs or be losers in a booming market.

These trends are cause for hope. But until they spread, it seems inevitable that millions more will be squandered on computer systems that fail to work or even to see the light of day.

By Jeffrey Rothfeder in New York

HOW TO KEEP A PROJECT UNDER CONTROL

▶ Before designing the system, get suggestions from the people who will use it

▶ Put senior, nontechnical management in charge of the project to help ensure that it is finished on time and within budget

▶ Set up 12-month milestones—interim deadlines for various parts of the project

▶ Insist on performance clauses that hold suppliers legally responsible for meeting deadlines

▶ Don't try to update the system in midstream, before the original plan is finished

DATA: BW

CATY BARTHOLOMEW

Reprinted with permission from *ACM Software Engineering Notes*, April
1988, pages 5–18. Copyright ©1988 by P.G. Neumann.

RISKS TO THE PUBLIC IN COMPUTERS AND RELATED SYSTEMS

Peter G. Neumann [*SEN* Editor and Chairman of the ACM Committee on
Computers and Public Policy], plus contributors as indicated

Multimillion Dollar Fraud Failed Due to Computer Error (From Frans Heeman)

In the Dutch newspaper "De Volkskrant" of 12 January and 13 January 1988, two articles appeared on a computer fraud that was discovered by ... an error of that same computer:

An employee of a bank in Amsterdam (name of the bank not mentioned) transferred $15.1 million to a Swiss account, using the computer. To make an international money transfer, two persons must give permission. Each of them has a secret password. The employee knew the password of one of his collegue's, and had a password himself, and thus could make the money transfer on his own.

On 24 December 1987 the employee tranferred $8.4 million and $6.7 million to a bank in Zurich. Due to a technical malfunctioning, the transfer of $6.7 million failed. After Christmas, other employees saw on their terminal screen that the transfer had failed, got suspicious, and reported to their superiors. [The employee was arrested.]

According to the Volkskrant, many banks use the same system, and this method of fraud "occurs presumably more often, although the banks are very quiet about this".

[This makes me wonder about fail-safe computers: a fail-safe computer would have failed to save the bank from *this* fraud. Frans Heeman]

$9.5 million computer-based check fraud

Four employees of the DCASR (Defense Contract Administration Services Region) office in El Segundo CA are accused of having "prepared some false documents and tricked some coworkers" to rig the DCASR computer to issue a check for $9.5 million to one of them individually as payment for a legitimate invoice from a legitimate contractor. A bank officer apparently became suspicious when the person trying to deposit the check wanted $600,000 in cash on the spot, and called in the law. One of the defense lawyers blamed the events on *other* DCASR employees. "Because of incompetence, lack of control and violation of regulations, it's impossible to know exactly what happened in this case, who did what and when they did it." [Source: Evening Outlook, Santa Monica CA, 4 February 1988, courtesy of Donn B. Parker]

First Boston Losses (From Dave Curry)

First Boston has confirmed that the company faces a substantial loss due to inaccuracies in its system that inventories mortgage-backed securities. The company won't comment on the cause of the inventory error until an internal audit is completed, but it's expected that losses will range between $10 million and $50 million. (Source: Information Week, March 7, 1988, p. 8)

Computer glitch stalls 3 million bank transactions for a day (From Rodney Hoffman)

The 24 Dec 1987 Los Angeles Times reports that "an unexplained computer glitch caused a one-day delay in posting an estimated $2 billion in transactions at First Interstate Bank of California last week." The data processing problem affected all checking account transactions last Thursday -- 3 to 4 million, both deposits and checks, an estimated $2 billion total. For unexplained reasons, the entire record of Thursday's transactions from the bank's branches was rejected by the computer when posting was attempted at 10:30 pm Thursday. DP employees worked on the problem all night and the following day, and the transactions were finally posted late Friday afternoon. The problem was corrected in time to avoid any widespread effect on customer accounts. A bank executive VP said, "We did not have a disaster. We had a systems problem that we are still diagnosing to make sure it doesn't happen again."

Getting a raise out of your computer (From Dave Horsfall)

The Australian Commonwealth Bank's computer gave many of its customers a raise -- in fact, it doubled their pay. To make matters worse, as well as doubling the usual Thursday salary transfer, the computer doubled every other transaction. The bank's computer malfunctioned overnight and had to be controlled manually. It finished up processing transactions twice. Customers all over Australia with Keycard or cheque accounts found they had twice the amount debited or credited in their accounts. "These are the hazards of computing -- they are only limited by your imagination," said the bank's general manager, electronic data processing, Mr Peter Martin. (From the Sydney Morning Herald, Friday 26th February 1988)

Details of BofA's costly computer foul-up (From Rodney Hoffman)

[This is a follow-up to the story "$23-million computer banking snafu" in *SEN* 12 4, which was also contributed by Rodney Hoffman.] ''B of A's Plans for Computer Don't Add Up'', Douglas Frantz, Los Angeles Times, 7 February 1988, p. 1.

Bank of America acknowledged that it was abandoning the $20 million computer system after wasting another $60 million trying to make it work. The bank will no longer handle processing for its trust division, and the biggest accounts were given to a Boston bank. Top executives have lost their jobs already and an undisclosed number of layoffs are in the works. ... The total abandonment of a computer system after five years of development and nearly a year of false starts raises questions about the bank's ability to overcome its technological inadequacy in an era when money is often nothing more than a blip on a computer screen...

In 1981, the bank had fallen far behind in the computer race. Then-new chairman Armacost launched a $4-billion spending program to push B of A back to the technological forefront. The phrase he liked was "leap-frogging into the 1990s," and one area that he chose to emphasize was the trust department... The bank was mired in a 1960s-vintage accounting and reporting system. An effort to update the system ended in a $6-million failure in 1981 after the company's computer engineers worked for more than a year without developing a usable system...

In the fall of 1982, bank officers met Steven M. Katz, a pioneer in creating software for bank trust departments... In 1980, he had left SEI Corp. in a dispute and founded rival Premier Systems. Katz insisted on using Prime instead of B of A's IBM computers. He boasted that he could put together a system by 1983. Within six months, a B of A - led consortium of banks agreed to advance Premier money to develop a new, cutting-edge system for trust reporting and accounting. Nearly a year was spent on additional research... The go-ahead to fund to project came in March, 1984. While it was not a deadline, the goal was to have the new system in operation by Dec. 31, 1984.

What followed was a textbook structure for designing a computer system. A committee was formed of representatives from each B of A department that would use the system and they met monthly to discuss their requirements. DP staff gathered for a week each month to review progress and discuss their needs with the Premier designers. Some of the DP experts found Katz difficult to deal with occasionally, especially when they offered views on technical aspects of the project. "Don't give us the solutions. Just tell us the problems," Katz often said.

When the ambitious Dec. 31, 1984, goal was passed without a system, no one was concerned. There was progress, and those involved were excited about the unfolding system and undaunted by the size of the task. B of A devoted 20 man-years to testing the software system and its 3.5 million lines of code; 13,000 hours of training, including rigorous testing, were provided to the staff that would run the system...

In spring 1986, the system was about ready. Some smaller parts were already working smoothly. Test runs had not been perfect, but the technicians thought most bugs could be worked out soon. A demonstration run had been successful... Many employees were operating both systems, working double shifts and weekends. Late in 1986, an anonymous letter warned against a "rush to convert" to the new system and told the manager, not a computer expert, that people had "pulled the wool" over his eyes. The executive assured the staff that there would be no conversion before it was time. By then, lines of authority had also changed, making cooperation difficult.

By early 1987, tests had been running with only a few bugs. "There were still bugs, but the users felt they could run with it and work out the bugs as we went along," one former executive said. A conversion date was set: March 2, 1987. Just then, half the DP staff was pulled off the assignment. The conversion lasted one week. On March 7, the first of the 24 disk drive units on the Prime computers blew up, causing the loss of a portion of the database. It was past midnight each night before workers retrieving data from a backup unit left the offices. Over the next month, at least 14 more of the disk drives blew up. None had malfunctioned in the previous months of test. It turned out that the units were part of a faulty batch manufactured by Control Data Corp. But by the time the cause was discovered, delays had mounted and other difficulties had arisen. Taken individually, none would have caused the ensuing disaster. Together, they doomed the system. At the same time, the bank decided to move the main staff 30 miles away. Key people quit and morale sank. Another section of staff was told they would be moving from Los Angeles to San Francisco, with many losing their jobs. [Conflicts, turf battles, consulting firms, temporary employees]

The bank's first public acknowledgement of the problems came in July 1987. An in-house investigation was viewed by many staff members as a witch hunt. The bank announced further costs and then the transfer of the accounts in January 1988.

The bank's one-time head of the program, since resigned, says, "A lot of people lay down on the floor and spilled blood over this system, and why they abandoned it now I cannot understand. A guy called me this morning out of the blue and said that 95% of it was working very well."

Computer error blamed for diplomatic fiasco

The French Foreign Ministry's Protocol Office has committed an extraordinary gaffe by mistakenly inviting the Iranian chargé d'affaires to a party for diplomats at the Elysée Palace. [...] [France had of course broken ties with Iran.] Upon later interrogation, the Quai d'Orsay swore the whole mistake was due to a computer error and formally apologised -- although Mr Mitterand confided that he suspected the foreign minister, Mr Jean-Bernard Raimond, had planned the whole thing to try to get back in the good graces of the Iranians. (From an article by Anne-Elisabeth Moutet, datelined Paris, from the Sunday Telegraph, 10 January 1988, contributed by Bernard de Neumann of Marconi Research in Chelmsford, England.)

The Fable of the Computer that Made Something (From Geraint Jones)

"It has happened before, but is worth documenting that almost all the media here reported the last year's erroneous calculations of the Retail Price Index as a computer error. It was the BBC's flagship evening radio news bulletin on Friday that I heard report that "a computer made a mistake". As far as I can see, this time it was not even the case that 'the computer' was incorrectly instructed; rather it was decided to perform an (almost) entirely unrelated calculation, and it just so happened that a computer was used to do the adding up. Using a computer means never having to say sorry."

UK Logic Bomb Case Backfires

In *SEN* 13 1 we noted the case of the Logic Bomb in the UK, planted by James McMahon, the contract systems programmer accused of planting "logic bombs" in the DEC PDP 11 system of his client, air freight forwarder Pandair Freight. The prosection claimed that one such "logic bomb" locked terminals at Pandair's Heston office, near Heathrow, and a second was set to wipe the memory of the company's Birmingham computer. He has been cleared of all charges, on the grounds that the evidence was inconsistent, incomplete and lacking reliability. The first such case in Britain, it establishes some interesting legal precedents.

McMahon claims he was framed, presumably because of a contract dispute. The original disks containing the supposed bomb were not taken into police custody immediately after the suspected sabotage, but left in the Pandair computer room. The Pandair programmer who produced the printout of file directories and source listings from the disks had sufficient skills in Macro Assembler to insert the bombs the judge said. Further the Pandair development disk went missing shortly after the alleged crime. "There is doubt over who produced the printout and which disks it came from," he said. [Source: Datalink, 11 January 1988]

Computer Accomplice in Overcharging Scheme? (From Dave Wortman)

Hertz Corp allegedly fraudulently overcharged customers who damaged rental cars and were liable for repair charges. Hertz apparently bought repair parts and services at discount rates but billed customers and insurance companies at a higher rate. Hertz has already issued refunds of about $3M and it is estimated that they may have collected $13M through these questionable practices. Hertz's computers were in on the fraud. In some parts of the U.S., company computers generated two estimates, one for the actual repairs and one with higher prices which was sent to customers and insurers.

Gambler Who Wired Himself to Computer Faces Trial (From Arthur Axelrod)

Carson City [AP] -- The [Nevada] state Supreme Court upheld a ruling against a man who wired his athletic supporter to a hidden microcomputer to improve his odds of winning at blackjack. The ruling Thursday revived a charge of possessing a cheating device that had been filed against Philip Preston Anderson in Las Vegas. According to the court, Anderson strapped a microcomputer to his calf. Wires ran to switches in his shoes that he could tap with his toes to keep track of the cards that had been played. The computer calculated Anderson's advantage or disadvantage with the house and sent "vibratory signals to a special receiver located inside an athletic supporter," the Supreme Court said. [Source: Rochester (NY) Democrat and Chronicle, Dec. 13, 1987]

Another Case of Incomplete Deletion (From Brian Randell)

PSION'S MEMORY IS MADE OF THIS, by Tony May (The Guardian, 7 March 1988)

As a drug smuggler, Paul Dye knew that a filofax was of no use to him, but since his highly entrepreneurial business demanded a portable diary, contact list, memory prompter, calculator and note-taking device, he opted instead for a Psion Organiser. At around (pounds)100 for the basic machine, he got a hand-held computer whose memory could hold details of his (pounds)200 million drug smuggling ring, and could be wiped clean if the law caught up with him. But since he has been fined (pounds)202,000 and is now doing 28 years in gaol partly on the strength of evidence obtained from the machine's "erased" memory we may conclude that he potentially has a case under the Trades Description Act. Our computer staff tell us that when he came to erase his file the details were no longer available to him but were retained in the EPROM chip-based storage system which does not actually erase. They also tell me that Psion may have had another walk-on part in the case as members of the ring used corsets bought from Marks & Spencers to carry heroin, and the stores use Organisers for till price checking and chargecard validation. Mr Dye may not have been entirely happy with his purchase, but Psion believes that 300,000 of them will have been sold by the end of year ... [Psion-ARA! PGN]

Safer Programming Languages (From Martyn Thomas)

There is a (draft) definition of a language that is designed to make it harder to write incorrect programs.

The language (defined in terms of its abstract syntax tree, to facilitate program transformation in the language), is called NewSpeak, and is the work of Ian Currie, at the Royal Signals and Radar Establishment, MoD, UK. It is an "unexceptional language" - programs cannot loop infinitely, run out of store at runtime, or cause address errors or numeric overflow. Where the compiler cannot deduce the safety of an operation, the programmer is required to supply a checkable assertion.

The language is designed for safety-critical applications, and the ideal hardware target is VIPER (RSRE's formally-proven 32-bit microprocessor). A design rationale is in "Orwellian programming in safety-critical systems", Proc IFIP working conference on System Implementation Languages, experience and assessment. University of Kent at Canterbury, 1984.

Further details may be available from Ian Currie at RSRE, St Andrews Rd, Gt Malvern, Worcs WR14 3PS, UK. [There is also an article in the 14 March 1988 issue of the Electronic Engineering Times, pp. 55, ff., called to my attention by Tom Berson. PGN]

More Clock Problems

The RISKS Forum has been full of problems relating to the switchover from 31 December 1999 and 1 January 2001. John McLeod commented on COBOL programs with a two-character year field, with the suggestion that no one should have money in the bank at that time. Robert I. Eachus noted that the Ada TIME_OF year field will return an error after 2099, and that MS-DOS will go belly-up on 1 January 2048 (a 7-bit field).

There was also a flurry of problems reported after 29 February 1988, resulting from recently written calendar clock programs to accommodate the Leap year. Various system failures and other glitches resulted, including the Xtra supermarket chain being fined $1,000 for having meat around an extra day because their computer did not recognize Leap Day. You would think that reliable calendar programs were easy to find by now!

April Fool's Pranks

Just as this issue went to press, there were some rather nice April Fool's Day netmail messages. The most enjoyable was a forged message, allegedly from Gene Spafford, warning about such pranks and listing various tell-tale indicators. Alert readers noticed that the message itself contained an instance of each indicator.

Trojan horsing around with bank statements?

Your *SEN* Editor and RISKS Moderator personally received his very own Wells Fargo EquityLine statement of 2 Feb 88 with the following message at the bottom:

> YOU OWE YOUR SOUL TO THE COMPANY STORE. WHY NOT OWE YOUR HOME
> TO WELLS FARGO? AN EQUITY ADVANTAGE ACCOUNT CAN HELP YOU SPEND
> WHAT WOULD HAVE BEEN YOUR CHILDREN'S INHERITANCE.

It took until 11 Feb for Wells Fargo to send out the following letter:

> I wish to extend my personal apology for a message printed on your EquityLine statement dated February 2, 1988.

> This message was not a legitimate one. It was developed as part of a test program by a staff member, whose sense of humor was somewhat misplaced, and it was inadvertently inserted in that day's statement mailing. The message in no way conveys the opinion of Wells Fargo Bank or its employees. You may be assured that the financial information on the statement was correct, and the confidentiality of your individual account information has been maintained. [... James G. Jones, Executive Vice President, South Bay Service Center]

According to reports a few weeks later, Wells Fargo had still not identified the responsible party. I have no inside information that would lead me to believe it was an intentional Trojan horse rather than an accidental leakage, but that is certainly a possibility under the circumstances! PGN

Risks of Advertising Messages Appended to Telex Messages (From Bruce N. Baker)

Bruce Baker at SRI recently sent a TELEX message to Copenhagen. The recipient responded by writing on the message he received from me and returning it by normal post. He thus found that the TELEX carrier had appended text to my original message, which struck him as unprofessional and unethical. The appended text reads:

> FOR 1988 HOROSCOPE FORECASTS CALL USA 62200 CODE 9150

Apparently this message is routinely being added to TELEX messages sent from SRI. Bruce requested that this dubious practice be stopped -- at least for *our* messages!

Finagling Prescription Labels (From Robert Kennedy)

Robert Kennedy reported a similar experience with the label on a bottle of prescription medicine. ''The instructions for use, the name, the Doctor's name, and all the important stuff appeared intact, but down at the bottom of the label, in compressed print (the rest of the label had been printed in a "normal" dot-matrix style) was the question "WILL THIS COMPUTER WORK?" At first, I just thought it was funny -- someone having a good time with some spare space on the label. But then I realized that maybe prescription labels aren't the best thing to be monkeying around with...''

Missouri Voting Decision (From Charles Youman)

The 1 January 1988 edition of the St. Louis Post Dispatch contained a follow up article on the Missouri voting decision. The article by Tim Poor is titled "Blunt Says Ruling Could Make Punch-Card Voting 'Unworkable'", appears on page 9A and is quoted without permission:

> "Missouri Secretary of State Roy Blunt said Thursday that a recent federal court decision could 'make punch-

card voting unworkable' and delay the results of statewide elections. Blunt called the ruling by U.S. District Judge William L. Hungate 'unfair' because it requires a manual review of ballots on which some votes have gone uncounted by St. Louis' automatic tabulating equipment. He said as many as 60,000 ballots--half of all cast--might have to be counted by hand because of the ruling...

Hungate said the board's failure to review the ballots violated the Federal Voting Rights Act. In addition to the manual review, he told the board to target for voter education those wards from which more than 5 percent of the ballots were uncounted. . . .

Blunt said he agreed with the board's position that a manual review of ballots on which some votes were uncast would be unworkable. There would be too many ballots to review; on lengthy ballots, many voters skip some issues, he said.

The ruling 'encourages voters to vote on things they're not interested in,' Blunt said. He explained that people might vote on all items on the ballot if they think that their ballot will be manually inspected if they don't. . . . And he questioned the ability of election officials to determine for whom a voter wanted to vote on ballots that are uncounted because they are improperly punched. 'Engaging in speculation by looking at scratch marks, indentions or double punches requires guessing as to what the voter is thinking,' he said. 'No group of election workers is qualified to do that.'"

There appear to be two distinct categories of votes that are not being counted (1) those with the "scratch marks, indentions or double punches" and (2) those that the voter didn't vote on every issue. It's difficult to tell from the article how many fall into category (1) and how many fall into category (2). I would not expect a computer program to be able to make the judgements needed to deal with those in (1). On the other hand, if a substantial number of votes are in category (1) something is seriously wrong with the overall system design that causes voters to make this error. I see no reason why a computer program couldn't accurately count those votes that fall into category (2). In fact, I would go further and say that a program that makes that kind of error should not be allowed to be used. Perhaps legislation to that effect is in order.

It also appears that the judge was willing to accept a 5% rate of uncounted votes. A lot--A LOT!--of elections are decided by less than 5% of the vote.

I'm not sure how votes in category (1) are dealt with in a manual system. Is the entire ballot voided or are only those issues where the voter's intent is not clear?

It also appears that there need to be extensive procedural controls to prevent someone from voiding ballots by making additional punches after the vote is cast. You could void all the votes that didn't go the way you wanted them to. Does this mean that a checksum needs to be computed and punched into the ballot at the time it is cast? [Charles Youman]

Unusual Computer Risk -- Harem Scarem? (From Mike Bell)

Computer Program Drives Arab to Sexual Exhaustion (Computer Talk, 1 February 1988)

A Saudi Arabian millionaire thought he was heading for conjugal bliss when he had the bright idea of organising his harem by computer. Unfortunately his plan misfired. Instead of leaving him with the satisfied smile of a clever Cassanova, Saleh-el-Modiia's rigorous regime left him completely knackered. A fact which one of his four wives tearfully related to a newspaper in the Saudi city of Riyadh. "The computer has gone haywire. It's making Saleh too exhausted... he just falls asleep in my arms", she said. The computer devised a weekly schedule for the 38-year-old failed Lothario after he had keyed in his wives ages, birthdays, clothes sizes and medical details. The schedule told him who to go to see, what to wear, and what he was meant to do. But even though Modiia's wives are complaining, he refuses to ditch the computer. "It's only gone wrong once. That was when I was in hospital and all four wives came to visit me at the same time", he said.

When in doubt, blame the computer. Mistaken-identity nightmare.

Neil Foster from Marlborough and Neil Foster from Somerset are both 38, with brown hair, moustaches, and almost the same height. One was wanted for motor vehicle violations, but the other one got picked up. The other one also lost his job, his savings, and his car in the process. Wiltshire police blamed their computer. But other police admitted that the computer is "only an aid to identification, and information on it should always be cross-checked..."

The real culprit was found after a three-month search by the other Neil Foster, who explained what had been happening and got the guilty one to go to the police.

The national police computer system currently houses records of stolen and suspect vehicles, fingerprints, names of known criminals, wanted and missing persons, and disqualified drivers. Plans are underway to expand it to use by the courts, the crown prosecution service, probation service and prisons. It currently contains 25 million names. An individual may be identified by name, age, sex, height, and vehicle type. "In theory, with a correctly spelt name and date of birth, a case of mistaken identity should be impossible." [Source: An article by Stephen Davis and Nick Rufford in the Sunday Times, London, 10 January 1988, contributed anonymously.]

[Lousy theory. Even adding birthplace and "unique ID" may not be enough -- see the next item. PGN]

More double troubles -- with Social Security Numbers (From Peter Capek)

Ann Marie O'Connor, 21, Queens NY and Anne Marie O'Connor, 22, of Larchmont NY, both with the same SSN. Both are 5' 5", with brown hair and brown eyes, birthdays in September, and a father and a brother named Daniel. It took the government 9 months to straighten out a request for a name change when the first AMO'C got married, during which time she was being dunned for back taxes based on their COMBINED incomes. [From page 12 of an unspecified issue of MONEY] [So that's where running AMO'C came from!]

James Edward Taylor, NY, NY (Manhattan), Health Department inspector, and James Edward Taylor, NY, NY (Brooklyn), Postal Service employee, share names, birthdates (23 July 1919), and birthstate (Virginia). They also shared the same SSN! The error was detected in 1965, but still had not been corrected 8 years later, with all sorts of interference problems meanwhile. [NY Times, 18 March 1973]

[Here we have three cases of accidentally confused identities -- each involving almost identical information. Other such cases have been reported in RISKS in which computer systems were implicated, but in which human laziness may ultimately have been to blame -- such as the Shirley Jackson and Sheila Jackson case in 1983 (*SEN* 10 3, July 1985). These should be contrasted with the case of Terry Dean Rogan, in which someone assumed his identity and caused him great grief (also in *SEN* 10 3) -- see the next item. PGN]

Terry Dean Rogan concluded? (From Hal Perkins)

Wrong Suspect Settles His Case for $55,000 (N.Y. Times, 6 March 1988, section 1, p.30)

Saginaw, Mich., March 5 [1988] (AP) -- Terry Dean Rogan, who [was] arrested five times in Michigan and Texas for crimes he did not commit, has settled a lawsuit against the City of Los Angeles for failing to remove his name from a crime computer's file. Mr. Rogan, who is 30 years old, sued Los Angeles, its Police Department and two detectives, saying his civil rights were violated when the department neglected to remove his name from a nationwide crime computer file. The settlement, approved by the Los Angeles City Council Friday, calls for Mr. Rogan to receive $55,000. Last July, a Federal district judge in Los Angeles ruled that Mr. Rogan should be paid damages. The murders and robberies he was charged with were ultimately traced to an Alabama jail inmate, Bernard McKandes. Mr. McKandes was found to have assumed Mr. Rogan's identity after Mr. Rogan apparently discarded a copy of his birth certificate.

Police computer problem -- lighting up license-plate matches

John Stapelton, 35, a computer consultant from Yonkers NY was stopped while driving in The Bronx and was frisked because a random check of automobile licenses in the police computer system erroneously turned up his car as that of someone who had killed a state trooper. Strangely the database record did not include the make of the car, which might have been a tip-off that the actual license of the killer had been entered inaccurately.

Stapleton said the cops admitted the car computer system has its faults. "They told me it tilts on them all the time." In this case they let him go after deleting the incorrect entry. Officers of the Bronx' 50th Precinct claimed to have no record of the incident, but that is not surprising because no arrest was made. [Source: An article by Joy Cook and Linda Stevens in the New York Daily News, no date available, contributed by Michael J. Wallach, Innovative Computer Solutions, 31 Tulip Circle, Staten Island NY 10312.]

[The subject of accepting partial matches is a very thorny one, especially in the presence of inaccurate data. One approach is that much greater effort is needed in training personnel who interpret partial matches. Another is that systems that try to do partial matching should *reject* unconfirmed input data and should continually warn the users... PGN]

Cleaning PC's can be bad for your health... (From John McMahon)

The following "SAFE-ALERT" form was distributed at Goddard Space Flight Center (NASA - Greenbelt, MD) about cleaning PC's. The date was 29 July 1987, alert number X7-S-87-01.

''Recently an employee of this installation was cleaning his personal computer screen with a glass cleaner when the screen caught on fire. The computer had been in use for some time and had built up a static charge. When the employee went to wipe off the glass cleaner with a tissue, his finger hit the screen. This action discharged the static charge causing a spark which ignited the alcohol in the window cleaner. A total of 8 personal computers were checked, with only 1 other catching on fire.''

The installation mentioned above was the Naval Weapons Center in China Lake, CA. The action taken was to inform the employees about what could happen, and ask them to use a non-flammable cleaner. If there was a need for a flammable cleaner, then employees were advised to discharge the computer before spraying.

Two More Telephone Bill Problems

Rochester Telephone Corporation (New York) erroneously billed 4,800 customers for phone calls to Egypt when the computer system misread the number dialed. (From the February 1988 issue of Online, contributed by Bill McGarry)

A new AT&T computer billing system caused up to 2 million AT&T telephone customers across the country to be billed for payments they already made. Some accounts have mistakenly been referred to collection agencies. (From the Lafayette (Indiana) Journal & Courier, 1-29-88, Contributed by Dave Curry)

Subsection: RISKS of Trojan horses, ''viruses'', and other security violations

In the previous issue (*SEN* 13 1) we noted the Christmas Trojan horse ''virus'', an Amiga virus, and a few other recent attacks. There was also the ''Lehigh virus'', which altered COMAND.COM files, propagating itself four times and then destroying the disk contents. The past quarter saw a continuation of such perpetrations, including an incursion into Aldus' commercial software, CompuServe Macintosh viri, and the Israeli virus. There were long lists of PC software programs that have been contaminated. There was also much discussion in the on-line RISKS Forum as to what can be done to protect against such perpetrations. Most of the defensive measures are incomplete -- and there have been reports that at least one of the defensive programs itself carries a damaging Trojan horse! Some discussion focused on being able to examine source code, but that is clearly not a panacea. All in all the situation is potentially dangerous, even though most of the attacks to date have been relatively more educational than destructive. However, my Letter From the Editor in *SEN* 13 1 on software engineering, disasters, and terrorism seems to have been timely.

Here is a heavily excerpted collection of the highlights from the past quarter. Readers should note that the terminology is becoming infected as well, in that strictly speaking, a virus is self-propagating rather than something that infects an unsuspecting victim upon contact -- as is the case with several of the so-called viruses.

The Israeli virus (From Mike Linnig)

Hebrew University computers sabotaged by electronic 'virus'
(The Fort Worth Star Telegram's Startext Information Service, 7 Jan 88)

JERUSALEM (AP) -- A saboteur infected Hebrew University computers with an electronic "virus" that threatens to destroy thousands of files and wipe out years of research, a university employee said Thursday. "It is the most devastating thing we've ever come across," said Yisrael Radai, a senior programmer at the university's computer center. A "virus" is computer jargon for a self-propagating set of orders devised by a saboteur that spreads from one computer disk to another to cause mischief or harm. Radai said that soon after the virus was discovered last week, university computer experts developed an antidote to diagnose and treat it. But there is still a danger that many users will not learn they have been affected until it is too late. The virus threatened to wipe out research data, financial statements, ledgers, lists of students and other vital information compiled by administrators, teachers, and students. Radai said other institutions and individuals in Israel have been contaminated. In fact, anyone using a contaminated disk in an IBM or IBM-compatible computer was a potential victim, he said.

The virus was devised and introduced several months ago by "an evidently mentally ill person who wanted to wield power over others and didn't care how he did it," Radai said. He said the saboteur "had to be very clever because he knew how to write directly into the disk controller and evade the computer's ordinary safeguards." The saboteur exploited a standard programming technique to insert the virus into the computer's memory, said Radai. The computer infected all disk files exposed to it and they, in turn, contaminated healthy computers and disks. Radai said the saboteur's target date to wipe out the files was Friday, May 13, 1988. Unless computer users apply the antidote developed by the university, they will lose disks afflicted with the virus on that day. Meanwhile, the saboteur decided to wreak some minor havoc. His virus ordered contaminated programs to slow down on Fridays and the 13th day of the month.

But the prank was the first obvious indication something was wrong with apparently healthy computer disks, said Shai Bushinski, a self-employed computer expert knowledgeable about the virus. Another clue was derived from a flaw in the virus itself. Instead of infecting each program or data file once, the malignant orders copied themselves over and over, consuming increasing amounts of memory space. Computer experts noticed that supposedly static programs were inexplicably growing in size and launched a search for the cause. Bushinsky said experts isolated the malignant commands, which appeared in easily decipherable assembly language. Within a few hours three university computer experts devised a two-phased program, called "immune" and "unvirus," which tells users whether their disks have been infected and applies an antidote to those that have. Bushinsky said the computer virus was a new and dangerous development in the computer world that could penetrate military, industrial and commercial data systems. "It might do to computers what AIDS has done to sex," said Bushinsky. "The current free flow of information will stop. Everyone will be very careful who they come into contact with and with whom they share their information."

More on the Israeli Virus (From Y. Radai) (FROM Info-IBMPC Digest, Mon, 8 Feb 88, Volume 7 : Issue 8)

Issue 74 of the Info-IBMPC digest contained a description of a "virus" discovered at Lehigh University which destroys the contents of disks after propagating itself to other disks four times. Some of us here in Israel, never far behind other countries in new achievements (good or bad), are suffering from what appears to be a local strain of the virus. Since it may have spread to other countries (or, for all we know, may have been imported from abroad), I thought it would be a good idea to spread the word around.

Our version, instead of inhabiting only COMMAND.COM, can infect any executable file. It works in two stages: When you execute an infected EXE or COM file the first time after booting, the virus captures interrupt 21h and inserts its own code. After this has been done, whenever any EXE file is executed, the virus code is written to the end of that file, increasing its size by 1808 bytes. COM files are also affected, but the 1808 bytes are written to the beginning of the file, another 5 bytes (the string "MsDos") are written to the end, and this extension occurs only once.

The disease manifests itself in at least three ways: (1) Because of this continual increase in the size of EXE files, such programs eventually become too large to be loaded into memory or there is insufficient room on the disk for further extension. (2) After a certain interval of time (apparently 30 minutes after infection of memory), delays are inserted so that execution of programs slows down considerably. (The speed seems to be reduced by a factor of 5 on ordinary PCs, but by a smaller factor on faster models.) (3) After memory has been infected on a Friday the 13th (the next such date being May 13, 1988), any COM or EXE file which is executed on that date gets deleted. Moreover, it may be that other files are also affected on that date; I'm still checking this out. (If this is correct, then use of Norton's UnErase or some similar utility to restore files which are erased on that date will not be sufficient.)

Note that this virus infects even read-only files, that it does not change the date and time of the files which it infects, and that while the virus cannot infect a write-protected diskette, you get no clue that an attempt has been made by a "Write protect error" message since the possibility of writing is checked before an actual attempt to write is made.

It is possible that the whole thing might not have been discovered in time were it not for the fact that when the virus code is present, an EXE file is increased in size *every* time it is executed. This enlargement of EXE files on each execution is apparently a bug; probably the intention was that it should grow only once, as with COM files, and it is fortunate that the continual growth of the EXE files enabled us to discover the virus much sooner than otherwise.

From the above it follows that you can fairly easily detect whether your files have become infected. Simply choose one of your EXE files (preferably your most frequently executed one), note its length, and execute it twice. If it does not grow, it is not infected by this virus. If it does, the present file is infected, and so, probably, are some of your other files. (Another way of detecting this virus is to look for the string "sUMsDos" in bytes 4-10 of COM files or about 1800 bytes before the end of EXE files; however, this method is less reliable since the string can be altered without attenuating the virus.)

If any of you have heard of this virus in your area, please let me know; perhaps it is an import after all. (Please specify dates; ours was noticed on Dec. 24 but presumably first infected our disks much earlier.)

Fortunately, both an "antidote" and a "vaccine" have been developed for this virus. The first program cures already infected files by removing the virus code, while the second (a RAM-resident program) prevents future infection of memory and displays a message when there is any attempt to infect it. One such pair of programs was written primarily by Yuval Rakavy, a student in our Computer Science Dept.

In their present form these two programs are specific to this particular virus; they will not help with any other, and of course, the author of the present virus may develop a mutant against which these two programs will be ineffective. On the other hand, it is to the credit of our people that they were able to come up with the above two programs within a relatively short time.

My original intention was to put this software on some server so that it could be available to all free of charge. However, the powers that be have decreed that it may not be distributed outside our university except under special circumstances, for example that an epidemic of this virus actually exists at the requesting site and that a formal request is sent to our head of computer security by the management of the institution.

Incidentally, long before the appearance of this virus, I had been using a software equivalent of a write-protect tab, i.e. a program to prevent writing onto a hard disk, especially when testing new software. It is called PROTECT, was written by Tom Kihlken, and appeared in the Jan. 13, 1987 issue of PC Magazine; a slightly amended version was submitted to the Info-IBMPC library. Though I originally had my doubts, it turned out that it is effective against this virus, although it wouldn't be too hard to develop a virus or Trojan horse for which this would not be true. (By the way, I notice in Issue 3 of the digest, which I received only this morning, that the version of PROTECT.ASM in the Info-IBMPC library has been replaced by another version submitted by R. Kleinrensing. However, in one respect the new version seems to be inferior: one should *not* write-protect all drives above C: because that might prevent you from writing to a RAMdisk or an auxiliary diskette drive.)

Of course, this is only the beginning. We can expect to see many new viruses both here and abroad. In fact, two others have already been discovered here. In both cases the target date is April 1. One affects only COM files, while the other affects only EXE files. What they do on that date is to display a "Ha ha" message and lock up, forcing you to cold boot. Moreover (at least in the EXE version), there is also a lockup one hour after infection of memory on any day on which you use the default date of 1-1-80. (These viruses may actually be older than the above-described virus, but simply weren't noticed earlier since they extend files only once.)

The author of the above-mentioned anti-viral software has now extended his programs to combat these two viruses as well. At present, he is concentrating his efforts on developing broad-spectrum programs, i.e. programs capable of detecting a wide variety of viruses. [...]

Macintosh Viruses (From David HM Spector)

A programmer in West Germany has posted to Compu$erve the *source* for a simple virus that will run on a

Macintosh computer. I normally wouldn't even dare to mention that such a thing exists in a "public" forum, but it's on Compuserve, so it might as well be painted on walls coast to coast. The author insists that it's is a very simple virus, easily defeated, (which it is, having looked at and understood the sources), and is posted for educational uses with the intent of making people aware that such things exist and to inspire them to write defenses against them.

In terms of a program, it's very small, a few pages of Pascal, and maybe 50 lines of assembly code. The installation code has a bunch of flags to control whether or not the virus replicates, whether it gets installed into the current running application, or just the system software, etc, etc. The actual virus is a small piece of code disguised as a resource that inserts itself in a system trap handler...it's alarmingly straight forward.

The author goes on to mention, in the documentation, that this virus was inspired by a number of viruses he has encountered that did damage to his systems, so he wrote a virus that won't let "unknown" programs run on any of his company's machines. (i.e., if the program(s) to be run aren't already infected with *his* virus, they won't be allowed to run at all.)

This is the first time I have ever seen sources to something like this, and it scares me a lot. If this code is any indication, viruses in general are a snap to write -- an could be placed _anywhere_; even in innocent looking HyperCard Stacks (Apple's HyperText software...) that thousands of people and User's Groups download and give out all over the place (and most Mac users aren't computer professionals -- they'll never know what hit'em).

Another Mac virus on the loose? (From Chris Borton via Dave Platt)

Symptoms: INIT 32 in System File, nVIR resources in various applications and the System File.

This sucker is tricky -- it is getting itself loaded before any INITs do (we believe the INIT 32 is just a teaser), like PTCHs do, but it isn't in PTCH. Our two best programmers spent today tracing through it and still haven't found a real solution other than offloading and re-initializing. To our knowledge it is non-malicious (yet). The nVIR resources are usually small, sometimes 8 bytes, sometimes ~360. If you remove them from both System and ResEdit, the virus won't let you run ResEdit because it is looking for those resources and can't find them. It occasionally beeps when running a program.

We have no idea what installed this. We are fairly certain it originated from one of the many small programs that come over the net. Many of these would be perfect 'carriers' -- little demo program that's an "aww, that cute, now let's trash it." I'm not putting down these programs, just pointing out what I feel is obvious.

I don't believe this is any cause for panic -- it hasn't done any known harm yet. I would, however, like to get to the bottom of this! If it's a joke, I don't find it very funny. (unless it de-installs itself completely after April Fool's Day :-)). If it is someone's graduate thesis, you get an A-. But enough is enough!

More on Macintosh Viruses (From David HM Spector, in response to Borton)

There seem now to be (at least) 5 Macintosh viruses on the loose, two are of the "Brandow/MacMag" variety [and the rest are based on the sources described by DHMS above].

It seems you have been bitten by a virus whose sources were uploaded to Compuserve several months ago... The author, a fellow in West Germany, thought it would be educational to distribute these example viruses in source form to encourage people to write defenses against them. His stated intent in writing a virus in the first place was to keep people from running possibly virus ridden program on their production Macintoshes which had been previously hit by viruses.... its signature, in the orignal sources, was a resource type of nVir... its a simple yet potent virus and very easily modified to do bad things. ... unfortunately the only way around most of these viruses is to replace your system folder. (Make sure you do this from a WRITE-LOCKED copy of the Apple System installer... or else you'll end up back where you started, with an infected system.... there is another problems, that being that the virus that was on CompuServe knows how to infect APPLICATIONS, as well as the system itself. Pretty depressing....

MacMag virus infects commercial software (From Dave Platt)

According to an article in the 15 Mar 88 San Jose Mercury News, the "DREW" INIT-virus has been found to have infected a commercial software product.

The virus, which was a "benign" time-bomb designed to display a message of world peace on March 2nd, is present on disks containing Aldus Freehand. The virus was inadvertently passed to Aldus by Marc Canter, president of MacroMind Inc., which makes training disks for Aldus. Canter avisited Canada some time ago, and was given a disk containing a program called "Mr. Potato Head", which lets users play with a computerized version of the toy character. Canter ran the program only once, and his machine was apparently infected by the virus at this time. Subsequently, the virus infected a disk of training software that Canter then delivered to Aldus; at Aldus, the virus infected disks that were then sold to customers.

Although this virus was believed to be harmless, Canter reports that it forced his Macintosh II computer to shut down and caused him to lose some computer information. "My system crashed," Canter said, "I was really angry."

((Not all that surprising... quite a few popular but nonstandard programming tricks used on the classic Mac
    don't work on the Mac II due to its different video card/monitor architecture... many games, etc. don't run on
    the II for this reason and can cause some very impressive system crashes... dcp))

Canter fears that more of his customers may have been infected by the virus. MacroMind's clients include Microsoft Corp., Lotus Development Corp., Apple Computer Inc. and Ashton-Tate. Microsoft has determined that none of its software has been infected, a company spokeswoman said. Apple and Lotus could not be reached for comment. Ashton-Tate declined to comment.

Aldus would not comment on how many copies of FreeHand are infected, but admits that a disk-duplicating machine copied the infected disk for three days. Half of the infected disks have been distributed to retail outlets; the other half are in Aldus' warehouse. Aldus will replace the infected disks with new, uninfected copies to any FreeHand buyer who requests it, according to Aldus spokeswoman Laury Bryant. The company will also replace the infected disks in its warehouse.

German 'Computer Chaos Hacker' arrested in Paris (From Klaus Brunnstein)

A leading German hacker, Mr. Steffen Wernery of 'Computer Chaos Club' of Hamburg, has been arrested in Paris, on March 14. He is accused of having participated in the invasion of a Philips France VAX computer (under a 'buggy' VMS) in 1987; while being a speaker at SECURICOM, Philips officials had arranged a meeting, but police awaited him before. French police wanted to arrest Mr.Wernery since some time, but German institutions refused to deport him due to German law. [...]

Another RISK of viruses (From David Purdue)

A club based in Canberra offerred someone $100 to write a program for the Amiga that would do some timetabling for a conference that the club holds annually. When the conference rolled around, the program was not ready and the timetabling was done by hand, and there were many mistakes made.

A meeting was held recently, some three weeks after the conference. At this meeting the programmer pointed out that although he didn't have a working product, he had done a lot of work for the club, and asked for his $100. He was asked why the program wasn't ready in time. He replied, "It's not my fault. The program was hit by a virus which scrubbed my disk, and I didn't have a backup."

The Risk? Well, it may be true that a virus scrubbed his disk; but there was no mention of it until the meeting. With the proliferation of viruses, and the big fuss that the media are making of them (that includes computing industry newspapers, the major press and discussions on the net), it seems to me that programmers now have a real handy excuse for not meeting their commitments.

Hackers to Face Jail or Fines (From Anne Morrison)

Computer Hackers to Face Jail or Fines (From The Age, Melbourne, 14 March 1988)

Convicted computer hackers will face huge fines under new laws being prepared for Victoria. The State Government is planning to create an offence of computer trespass, with a maximum fine of $2500, under a bill soon to be debated in Parliament.

The Attorney-General, Mr McCutcheon, said yesterday that while many computer hackers were no more than technological voyeurs, there was a need for some kind of deterrent. He said the legislation was the first in Australia to deal specifically with technological crime. The Government had previously thought it sufficient to ensure that computer hackers could be prosecuted if they altered or erased data, Mr McCutcheon said. But submissions from police, the computer industry and legal experts had led to the inclusion of penalties for hackers who simply looked at material after breaking into a computer system. People were understandably concerned that hackers could gain access to sensitive data of great commercial value or of a personal and private nature, Mr McCutcheon said.

The new offence of computer trespass was similar to the offence of willful trespass on property or being unlawfully on premises. The bill before Parliament also creates offences of falsifying or altering data held in a computer system, punishable by fines of up to $100,000 or 10 years jail.

Existing laws applying to criminal damage will be applied to technological crime, enabling prosecution of anyone releasing "viruses" or "bugs" into computer systems to cause damage. People spreading these "viruses" or "logic bombs" -- programming instructions timed to destroy data later -- would face up to 10 years jail or a $100,000 fine, or 15 years jail if they acted for gain, Mr McCutcheon said.

[This raises an interesting point - does "accidentally" spreading a virus or logic bomb (i.e. if you don't know it's there) make you liable for prosecution? Can you prove that you passed on sabotaged software in good faith? This legislation may prove to be a major deterrent to software piracy - *if* it is strictly enforced. Anne Morrison]

Yet Another Virus - The "Brain" Virus (From Bruce N. Baker)

George Washington University, the University of Delaware, and the University of Pittsburgh all have taken steps to eradicate a virus - known as the "brain" virus because it can be identified by "(c) BRAIN" on the directory screen. The virus was created by Basit Farooq Alvi, 19, who claims to be a college student in Lahore, Pakistan. In 1986 Mr. Alvi and his brother Amjad, 23, wrote the computer code for the virus and placed it on a disk that they gave to another student. He did it "for fun," he said and has no idea how it might have reached the United States. A message with Mr. Alvi's name, address, and telephone number appears in the computer code that carries the virus. (Source: The Chronicle of Higher Education, 3 February 1988)

Software theft

Ming Jyh Hsieh, 38, a computer product support engineer who had been fired for "nonperformance" by the Wollongong Group in Palo Alto CA in November 1987, was caught in the act while downloading Wollongong-proprietary software to her PC. She used the "secret password" and privileges that were still valid two months later, and spent 18 hours over several nights copying software. Police placed a "trap and trace" device on Wollongong's computer phone lines to identify her phone line. [Source: Palo Alto Times Tribune, 7 February 1988]

A few comments are in order.

(1) A password is not secret when it is known to more than one person; in this case, it was shared among at least 5 people. (Shared passwords are generally a bad idea.)

(2) A password is not necessarily secret even if it is kept private by one person. Exposures (stored unencrypted, transmitted unencrypted, derivable, guessable, etc.) are often very easy to obtain.

(3) It is extraordinarily bad practice to fire someone and then not change all relevant passwords, revoke their privileges, etc.

(4) This kind of problem of nonrevoked privileges seems to happen amazingly often.

NEXT ISSUE. The deadline for the next issue is 21 June 1988. Thanks. Peter G. Neumann

RISK!

THE THIRD FACTOR

The use of information systems and related technology has provided many benefits to corporations over the years, but the increasing dependence on IS has brought an accompanying need to analyze factors that go beyond traditional computer security, such as organizational, management, and market conditions. The emergence of this third factor in justifying the use of IS has yet to ascend to the forefront of thinking in many companies. The need to do so, however, is becoming more important, as illustrated by the recent Wall Street crash, and management must take up the challenge.

BY PAUL TATE

Do you complain of information overload? Have you ever suffered from a network virus? Were either you or your corporation stung by last October's stock market crash?

If you have experienced any of the above symptoms you are among the growing number of corporations and individuals exposed to a new IS phenomenon—information age vulnerability.

The information systems revolution has brought with it innumerable benefits, but it also has created problems and risks that didn't exist before its onset. The increasing dependence of firms in all industry sectors on IS has created areas of vulnerability with potentially serious consequences, from organizational obsolescence to a loss of control of a firm's IS destiny in such brave new worlds as electronic data interchange and enterprise computing.

Costs, Benefits—and Risk

The traditional equation of costs and benefits is no longer enough to justify a corporate IS strategy. In a world of highly distributed pc power, complex networks, and database systems, risk has become the third factor in the IS equation.

In many ways, the rise to prominence of this factor was inevitable. "When you become dependent on any resource you become vulnerable," warns Mike Moore, information security manager for insurance giant Aetna in Hartford, Conn.

The issues that lie behind corporate vulnerability are not limited to the traditional subject of computer security. They go beyond site, data, and network security issues and cover a broad landscape of corporate concerns: the integrity, volume, and flow of information; the resulting organizational weaknesses; deficiencies in management skills; mutually dependent systems; and the pitfalls of changing business markets around the world.

Strategic thinkers in attendance at a workshop on the Vulnerability of Computerized Society sponsored by the Organization for Cooperation and Economic Development (OECD) in Spain in 1981 made the distinction most succinctly: "Whereas computer security implies a number of passive measures—dealing with a theoretically static set of security problems—the vulnerability of systems is often caused by the continuing changes in technology, applications areas, and information systems themselves. The risk management dealing with the vulnerability of automated information systems, therefore, is a management of change."

Vulnerability has become a business issue. "For years we have been saying that there's something in the shadows, but people argued that everything is dangerous so this isn't any special worry," complains Hans P. Gassmann, head of the Information, Computer, and Communications Policy Division at the OECD in Paris. "Now, after the Wall Street crash in October, people are beginning to pay a lot more

Illustrations by Warren Gebert

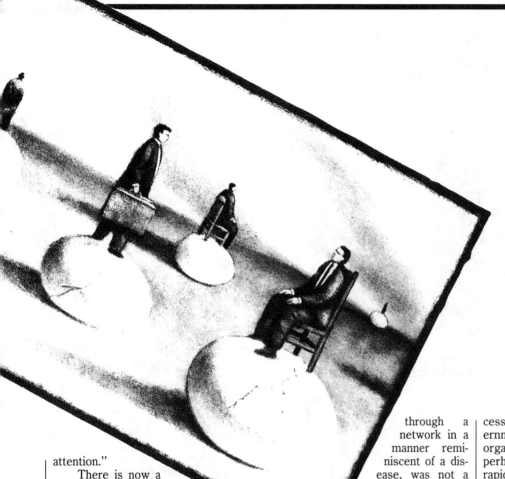

This is the first in a series of articles which will address new management, organizational and systems issues confronting IS.

attention."

There is now a growing consensus among management theorists, social observers, and academicians that the traditional methods and structures of businesses are breaking down. This process is creating new management pressures. Call it what you like, the management of change, of uncertainty, of risk, of crisis, or even of chaos—the bottom line is simply the management of complexity.

Private Message Networks are Targets

Meltdown Monday last Oct. 19th was a prime example of information age vulnerability. It was a global financial and technological event that wiped nearly $1 trillion off the world's balance sheet and shook the world's confidence in the IS revolution. Whatever your own theory about the financial reasons for the crisis, it's impossible to ignore the accelerating effect of private message networks, computer assisted trading systems, and rapid communications links. Like it or not, information systems played a major role in spreading the panic.

It isn't the only recent example. At Christmas, IBM's internal network was brought down by a network virus that drew Christmas trees on the screen before dispatching itself to the next user. It eventually found its way to users on five continents. This program, which is known as a "virus" because it can spread

through a network in a manner reminiscent of a disease, was not a greeting from Big Blue's board in Armonk. Rather, it was a prank perpetrated by a graduate student hacker who accessed the net via a Bitnet node at a university in West Germany.

Only a month later, on Jan. 27, a test message was sent out from the International Atomic Energy Agency in Vienna to weather centers in 25 countries. The message was partially coded and was transmitted on the World Meteorological Association's global telex and communications network. Clearly marked as a test, it referred to a buildup of radiation over the Soviet Bloc. A few days later, the stock markets in Tokyo and Hong Kong shuddered amid sudden rumors of another Chernobyl. In a matter of hours, the fallout spread to markets in the Middle East, Europe, and finally Wall Street. By that time, an early warning monitoring station in Sweden had been put on full alert.

Besides its effect on individuals, industries, and society at large, growing technological dependence creates new risks that affect the resilience and suc-

cess of IS strategies in corporations, government agencies, and international organizations. Some of this risk is the perhaps unavoidable consequence of the rapid information revolution. "Look," says computer crime-fighter Alan E. Brill, director of the information systems and information security bureau of the New York City Department of Investigation, "it's about time people realized that nobody builds perfect software. If you think you have, you simply haven't found all the errors yet."

Those ubiquitous software bugs, along with systems failures, computer crime, and network hacking cost the world's corporations millions of dollars each year. Sometimes, especially in the medical sector, they also can cost lives (see "Software Bugs: A Matter of Life and Liability," May 15, 1987, p. 88). Providing ways for organizations to protect against these sorts of vulnerabilities has become big business for the computer security industry, but events such as the stock market crash suggest that there are much deeper vulnerabilities that the IS community and corporate management must now consider.

A Sense of Responsibility

Information systems suppliers are beginning to realize that there is a problem. "Manufacturers are in danger of

"When you become dependent on any resource you become vulnerable."

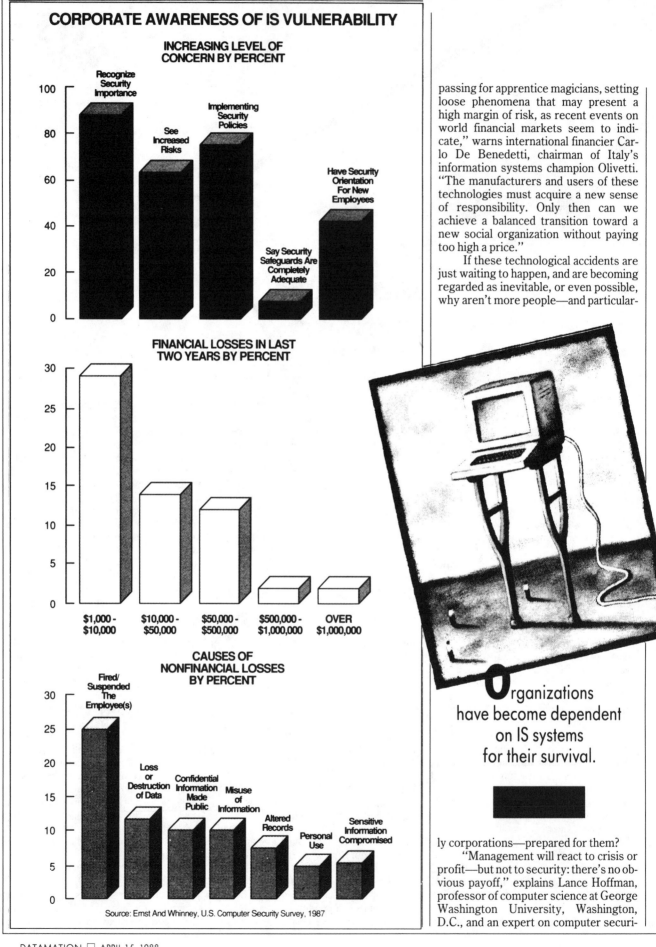

CORPORATE AWARENESS OF IS VULNERABILITY

INCREASING LEVEL OF CONCERN BY PERCENT

- Recognize Security Importance
- See Increased Risks
- Implementing Security Policies
- Say Security Safeguards Are Completely Adequate
- Have Security Orientation For New Employees

FINANCIAL LOSSES IN LAST TWO YEARS BY PERCENT

- $1,000 - $10,000
- $10,000 - $50,000
- $50,000 - $500,000
- $500,000 - $1,000,000
- OVER $1,000,000

CAUSES OF NONFINANCIAL LOSSES BY PERCENT

- Fired/Suspended The Employee(s)
- Loss or Destruction of Data
- Confidential Information Made Public
- Misuse of Information
- Altered Records
- Personal Use
- Sensitive Information Compromised

Source: Ernst And Whinney, U.S. Computer Security Survey, 1987

Chart by Hayes Cohen

passing for apprentice magicians, setting loose phenomena that may present a high margin of risk, as recent events on world financial markets seem to indicate," warns international financier Carlo De Benedetti, chairman of Italy's information systems champion Olivetti. "The manufacturers and users of these technologies must acquire a new sense of responsibility. Only then can we achieve a balanced transition toward a new social organization without paying too high a price."

If these technological accidents are just waiting to happen, and are becoming regarded as inevitable, or even possible, why aren't more people—and particular-

Organizations have become dependent on IS systems for their survival.

ly corporations—prepared for them?

"Management will react to crisis or profit—but not to security: there's no obvious payoff," explains Lance Hoffman, professor of computer science at George Washington University, Washington, D.C., and an expert on computer security. "Awareness varies widely among companies, but, generally, most small- and medium-sized firms, and many large corporations, are not well aware of their vulnerabilities."

Overall vulnerability awareness may be low, but recent reports in the U.S. and Europe indicate that there's growing concern about some basic issues in one specific area of vulnerability: traditional computer security. Nevertheless, awareness in the U.S. and Europe is still limited. In their U.S. survey, consultants Ernst & Whinney, New York, question whether the reported 87% of aware U.S. corporations are really protected or just implementing loose procedures that create a false sense of security.

"In the past," recalls Jon Fitzgerald, managing consultant of the information security group in Ernst & Whinney's U.K. headquarters in London, "it was just the computer that mattered, then networks developed and they were included. Now, we need to look at the whole business. On one side there are people thinking about corporate strategy and normal business risks. On the other side, there are people doing risk analysis for information systems and not thinking in strategic ways. What's missing is a way of bringing the two together."

Security as a Competitive Issue

Some corporations are beginning to respond to this new challenge. "What we have done in Aetna," says Moore, "is to adopt a business risk philosophy, and we have put the information security role into a department covering broad business risk management. I don't know of any other organization that does it this way. So far we're unique."

Aetna has gone further than most of the world's corporations in coordinating the risk management function (see "Aetna Redefines Its Risks"). This approach accepts IS as a strategic factor within the organization, the industry, and the marketplace.

Such an approach is becoming increasingly important. Donn Parker, senior management systems consultant at the Stanford Research Institute (SRI), explains that SRI is now "trying to focus very hard on broad information security. In a shared network, marketplace security becomes a competitive issue. That poses grave new demands on security managers. The companies that provide the greatest integrity, confidentiality, and availability of information will prevail."

At Arthur D. Little in London, con-sultant and security expert Adrian Norman believes that corporations may need to broaden their analyses of vulnerability to include "the effects of systems interdependency, the overload of confusing data for decision makers, and the mismatch of systems design and user needs. There are a thousand other factors."

Two things are driving these new appraisals of technological risk. First, as organizations have become more sophisticated in their use of IS, particularly over the last five years, they've become more dependent on those systems for their survival. Senior managers have begun to get involved in the security process because they feel they should. Systems se-

The sheer supply of information vastly exceeds that which can be individually assessed.

Aetna Redefines Its Risks

Aetna's assistant vice president, Nick Elsberg, is a manager with a broad understanding of risk. At the headquarters of the U.S. insurance giant in Hartford, Conn., Elsberg has created a department that brings corporate-level risk functions together into one group, called Corporate Security/Risk Management (CSRM). Traditional information systems security is a key part of that group.

"We have approached IS security from a business perspective, specifically from a business risk management point of view," he says. "It makes more sense. In the past, we might have talked about backup systems or disaster recovery. Now, we are talking about business continuity, and that involves a wider range of risks and loss control measures."

Elsberg's department of 14 people combines four previously separate functions: IS security, physical site security, loss control, and insurance. Aetna's increasing dependence on its information systems and networks was a key factor in this change of approach.

"IS has become a mainstream part of the business," Elsberg emphasizes. "There was never the feeling before that there would be a complete loss of business if the computers failed, but now we'd be bankrupt if those systems didn't function properly."

By combining IS security together with business risk analysis activities, Aetna has been able to identify areas where its protective controls were weak, particularly in other operational sides of the business. "Those problems have now become more obvious," says Elsberg.

"For example," he continues, "we have a very large computer installation in the commercial insurance division. At the back end of this is a large electronic printing operation with machines built to our own specifications. In the past, the risk of losing that may not have been regarded as all that serious, but we now realize that the commercial insurance business is dependent on the operation, and we must protect against a cascading effect if anything goes wrong. This is just one example. There are many more."

There are other benefits to combining the different corporate risk functions that affect the entire information systems security activity of the company. "Whereas before we may have had difficulty cost-justifying IS security to senior management, it is now much easier because we are talking about corporate risk management; that they understand. I'd recommend it to anyone," he says.

"We now know how dependent we are on technology and can ensure that we protect ourselves properly," adds Elsberg. "After all, if we didn't utilize it, that would be an even greater risk to our business."

curity has become a corporate management issue. That's a step in the right direction, but only a small step. Most managers still delegate the responsibility for coping with vulnerability to people who don't have the corporate perspective needed to appreciate all the consequences.

SRI's Parker adds, "What we have to do is to elevate the security issue within the management structure. Accountability must start to fall on higher-level management where there are people with the appropriate overview."

This is not a marketing ploy on behalf of the security community. It is the inevitable response to the increased involvement of information systems in the development of businesses, markets, and international trade. The situation is going to become more critical in the near future as systems and businesses each become more complex.

Harvard Business School professor of organizational behavior and human resource management, John P. Kotter, notes in his book *The Leadership Factor* (Free Press, 1988) that "the forces of growth, diversification, globalization, and technological development, have been making business more and more complex . . . . Establishing and implementing sensible strategies for businesses is rarely easy. But in many situations today the technological, competitive, market, economic, and political uncertainties make strategic decision-making horrendously difficult."

Unless corporate management understands its strengths—and its vulnerabilities—it will be unable to adapt to this changing business scene (see "The Changing Business Scene"). Since an increasing number of those strengths and vulnerabilities are dependent on the corporate IS strategy, and on corporate links with external technological systems, a broad analysis of its technological risk is becoming critical.

The History of the Debate

The IS community around the world has been trying to assess the broader risks of information technologies for some time. Warnings of unforeseen confusion ahead have surrounded the industry since the pioneering days of Alan Turing and Norbert Weiner, particularly since Weiner's 1947 book, *Cybernetics*.

It was not until the late '70s, however, that the world got its first formal study of the broad effects of technology on society. Concerned about Sweden's security, the Swedish Ministry of Defense set up a committee on the Vulnerability of Computer Systems (SARK) in 1977.

A year later, after much work and numerous interviews with computer users, SARK issued a report, entitled "The Vulnerability of the Computerized Society," which states, "Dp is only one of several causes of the vulnerability of modern society . . . [but] in SARK's opinion the main vulnerability lies in the large central systems and computer installations."

That was in 1978. Since then the debate surrounding information systems' vulnerability has continued on an occasional and erratic basis around the world. In 1981, the Organization for Cooperation and Economic Development (OECD) held a workshop in Sigüenza, Spain, on the Vulnerability of Computerized Society. The workshop was conducted in order to work out ways of minimizing the disadvantages of the widespread use of IS.

By 1984, the American Federation of Information Processing Societies (AFIPS) had completed its own report, which was predominantly concerned with national security, on the vulnerability of U.S. computer installations. Former chairman of the AFIPS Vulnerability Study group Rayne Turn, now working at California State University in Northridge, recalls, "We concluded that we didn't think the country was vulnerable . . . but our general recommendation is that corporations should seriously consider, and make deliberate efforts to develop, a broad contingency plan."

Norway picked up the vulnerability gauntlet in 1986 with its own report called "The Vulnerability of a Computer Dependent Society." Again focused on societal and national security issues, the Norwegian Vulnerability Commission concluded that "the situation is serious. Considerable resources are needed to make data processing vital to society less vulnerable and to reduce the consequences of interference."

That was the most recent full-scale study of network age vulnerability. An international conference on Coping with Computer Age Vulnerability scheduled for last fall by the Netherlands Society for Informatics (NGI) had to be canceled because of poor attendance. While the NGI works out the best time to reschedule the event, it is covering many of the issues in smaller work groups.

Meanwhile, independent organizations around the world are monitoring developments. In the U.S., for example, a Palo Alto group called Computer Professionals for Social Responsibility (CPSR) now has 13 chapters in major U.S. cities and over 2,000 members worldwide. It regularly acts as a consultant to U.S. federal agencies and is affiliated with similar groups in the U.K., West Germany, Canada, Italy, Finland, Australia, and New Zealand. Its goal is to "dispel popular myths about the infallibility of technological systems."

The OECD may soon begin an international study that helps overcome this lack of understanding. Following up on its past work on vulnerability, a proposal was put to the member countries last month to embark on a major international computer audit to investigate the existence and effects of traditional computer security controls, how well systems perform the functions they are designed for, and how effective data privacy and protection laws currently in place around the world are.

The Factor of Network Interdependece

This leads to the second driving factor behind new appraisals of technological risk—the development of industrywide networks and competitive technologies that have created new business environments in which systems have become interdependent. In the finance sector, access to interlinked global information networks is a prerequisite for doing business.

According to a recent survey of financial companies by Coopers & Lybrand, New York, called "Opportunity and Risk in the 24-Hour Global Marketplace," this dependence will increase rapidly and is already a major worry. The report notes that "a majority of the executives are very seriously concerned with issues related to technology, such as transaction settlement, worldwide communication of the trading book, and access to reliable information on prices, quotes, and currency exchange rates."

In the airline sector, operating computerized reservation systems (CRSs) is becoming more lucrative than flying planes. National and global links with other systems are essential; without them, many airlines wouldn't have any passen-

"Most information systems are designed to improve the quantity of the output instead of the quality of the input."

gers. Chris Lyle at the International Civil Aviation Organization in Montreal believes that the rapid development of highly sophisticated CRSs has resulted in "the vulnerability of 'have-not' airlines, travel agents, and passengers."

These brave new business worlds have their own dynamics and can leave many organizations exposed. Even the people now benefiting from the changes don't understand what the eventual consequences will be.

"These are typical examples of the way that systems have become interdependent," says ADL's Norman. "And electronic data interchange networks are supporting the trend. Yet, no analysis has been done of these systems. The main reason is that people have been trained along IBM's lines in hierarchical structures, and this makes it very difficult for them to understand complex networks of shared systems."

EDI Will Force Top-Down Analysis

Norman's point on shared networks is echoed by security consultant Tony Bromfield at Ernst & Whinney. "That kind of top-down analysis isn't being done anything like enough," Bromfield says. "The impending explosion of EDI networks will force the situation to change though. Companies will realize how dependent they are on their networks and how much relationships will change between players in their business. EFTPOS [electronic funds transfer point of sale] networks will have a similar effect."

Systems interdependency is not a new concern for the information systems community. Ten years ago, the world's first study group into computer vulnerability, set up by the Swedish govern-ment, identified such interdependency as one of 15 key vulnerability factors. Vulnerability reports from the U.S., Norway, the OECD, and other groups followed over the next few years (see "The History of the Debate").

The Swedes, however, went further. Though much of their initial study was concerned with societal risks, such as national security and the resilience of community systems to disaster or disruption, a set of guidelines known as "Security by Analysis" was later issued for use by Swedish corporations (see "Sweden's Vulnerability Guide").

"These take a broad approach and are designed to help corporations find

Sweden's Vulnerability Guide

Swedish corporations have been taking a broad view of the risks of IS dependence since the Swedish Vulnerability Board issued a practical guide to vulnerability assessment almost five years ago.

Called "Security by Analysis" (SBA), it is a series of methodologies designed to pinpoint areas of risk, provide an in-depth analysis of each area, identify practical controls, increase corporate awareness of vulnerability, and plan for future security needs.

The SBA guide is divided into the following sections. Some of the sections overlap to provide continuity.

Start: potential corporate risks created by security breaches, unauthorized access, defective data quality, loss of information, etc. are identified and quantified by senior decision-makers.

Dependence: the analysis is conducted on a deeper level, detailing and documenting where each key area of a corporation is dependent on IS, providing an overall picture, and identifying the areas that have the greatest degree of exposure.

Systems: at this point, the analysis is broken down even further to address the problems associated with each individual applications system.

Scenario: current security status is examined, and areas that need further protection are highlighted. Using a series of "What if?" questions, this can also be used as a strategic planning aid.

Action plans: using the results of the previous stages of analysis, this section helps companies put together implementation plans for increasing their IS security. Three alternative methods are suggested, each with a varying degree of support and funding.

Output: procedures for the regular assessment and monitoring of security controls.

Project: using quantitive analysis techniques, the risks to the corporation of problems in a key development project are established. Among other aspects, it includes target dates, budgets, and specifications.

System development: a checklist of security controls that should be built into systems during the development cycle of new systems or the maintenance of old ones.

Key personnel: this is a technique to be used by management to identify those people who are critical to the smooth running of the corporate IS systems and then to assess their degree of importance.

The auditor: this section is a summary of the SBA methodology and a guide for auditors.

Legislation: current and proposed legislation covering data privacy and IS usage is summarized, and techniques for assessing the conformity of corporate systems to the law are discussed.

Source: Swedish Federation of Data Processing Users, Stockholm.

out where they have vulnerabilities and how to introduce controls," explains Ulla-Brit Roslund, a former member of the committee that produced the handbook. Roslund is now with Stockholm-based consultancy Bertil Olssons. "It is still widely applicable and the techniques are regularly used in Swedish corporations," says Roslund. Although these provide a general basis for analysis, they don't cover all the issues. In an international company, for example, there are many areas of vulnerability that are unique. Different and often changing regulations covering telecom links and data privacy in other nations may mean that a firm must adapt its methods to suit the local environment. There also may be problems with the supply and approval of IS products in some countries, so firms must undergo a completely new assessment cycle to find suitable products locally.

The Quality of Data Is Scored

Closer to home, meanwhile, the effects of technological dependency are being felt where it hurts—in the in-box. "A major problem is that most information systems are designed to improve the quantity of the output instead of the quality of the input," argues ADL's Norman. "The result for decision-makers is a data overload and an information underload. They are getting lots of data but not the information they want." That view is supported by an increasing amount of market research. Earlier this year, a U.K. survey from IS supplier Comshare in London revealed that many top executives in Times 1000 companies were being inundated with reports that had to be passed to someone else to refine the data. A large number simply wanted better structured reports and complained of too much data, not too little.

Data overload is also a problem identified by Prof. William Melody, former chief economist at the Federal Communications Commission and currently the director of the U.K.'s Program on Information and Communications Technologies (PICT) sponsored by the Economic and Social Research Council.

Too much information can create confusion and prevent independent thought.

"The sheer supply of information," says Melody, "vastly exceeds that which can be individually assessed. Too much information may be worse than too little because it is more likely to create confusion and suspend independent thought."

He also believes that the problem is compounded by the fact that there is less time for managers to assess this information before decisions must be made.

"Ironically," says Melody, "in an age where information and communication systems are more sophisticated and comprehensive than ever before, the planning horizons for decision-makers of all kinds are continuously being reduced because of a growing inability to forecast even short-term future developments."

So, many of today's managers appear to face a future filled with too much information and too little time to make sense of it. Melody has an answer: the

corporate electronic monks—a 1990s version of the medieval monks who stored and produced information in the past. "It is clear that data and raw information require context and meaning to be understood," he explains. "Once again, society needs a professional class to guide it to the relevant information."

While the creation of such roles in a corporation—now partially filled by secretaries, computer center help desks, and management assistants—may alleviate some of the effects of the information problem, it won't get at the root of the problem. That has to be done in the planning stage.

Raising the profile of computer security and corporate vulnerability issues at a management level will help focus attention on this and other topics during a corporate planning cycle, but observers believe two other major changes are needed—better education for key personnel and a more open attitude to the planning process.

"What is needed is to improve the IS education of generalists and the general education of IS specialists," asserts ADL's Norman.

"We are entering an era of decision-making under ignorance rather than uncertainty," adds Ernst & Whinney's Fitzgerald. "There are going to be unpredictable effects. So all you can do is to build in checks and warnings, and methods for rescuing yourself from oblivion. These are the essential characteristics behind the design principles of highly complex systems today."

Whether the shock of Oct. 19th did enough to open government and corporate minds to the realities of information age vulnerability may not be known. But New York City investigator Brill, for one, is under no illusions about how serious the problem is now, and how different the risks of the near future will be compared with those of the near past.

"We have all been around a while and think we know what's going on," he says. "But we are the last generation that grew up without computers as a normal part of our lives."

If you think today's vulnerabilities are going to be tough to cope with, wait until tomorrow. ∎

THEORY-W SOFTWARE PROJECT MANAGEMENT: PRINCIPLES AND EXAMPLES

Barry Boehm
Rony Ross

UCLA Computer Science Department

ABSTRACT

A good software project management theory should be simultaneously simple, general, and specific. To date, those objectives have been difficult to satisfy. This paper presents a candidate software management theory and shows that it satisfies those objectives reasonably well. Reflecting various alphabetical management theories (X, Y, Z), it is called the Theory W approach to software project management.

Theory W: Make Everyone a Winner

The paper explains the key steps and guidelines underlying the Theory W statement and its two subsidiary principles: *Plan the flight and fly the plan;* and, *Identify and manage your risks*.

Several examples illustrate the application of Theory W, and an extensive case study is presented and analyzed: the attempt to introduce new information systems to a large industrial corporation in an emerging nation. The case may seem unique, yet it is typical. The analysis shows that Theory W and its subsidiary principles do an effective job both in explaining why the project encountered problems, and in prescribing ways in which the problems could have been avoided.

1. INTRODUCTION

Software Project Management today is an art. The skillful integration of software technology, economics and human relations in the specific context of a software project is not an easy task. The software project is a highly people-intensive effort that spans a very lengthy period, with fundamental implications on the work and performance of many different classes of people.

1.1 The Software Project Manager's Problem

The software project manager's primary problem is that a software project needs to simultaneously satisfy a variety of constituencies: the users, the customers, the development team, the maintainance team, the management. As seen in *Figure 1*, each of these constituencies has its own desires with respect to the software project. The *users* -- sometimes too enthusiastic, sometimes too skeptical -- desire a robust, user-friendly system with many functions supporting their mission. The *Customers* desire a product delivered reliably to a short schedule and low budget. The *bosses* of the project manager desire a project with ambitious goals, no overruns, and no surprises. The *maintainers* of the product desire a well-documented, easy-to-modify system with no bugs. The *development team* memebers -- often brilliant, sometimes unmanageable -- desire interesting technical challenges and fast career paths, generally with a preference for design and an inclination to defer documentation.

THE SOFTWARE PROJECT MANAGER'S PROBLEM

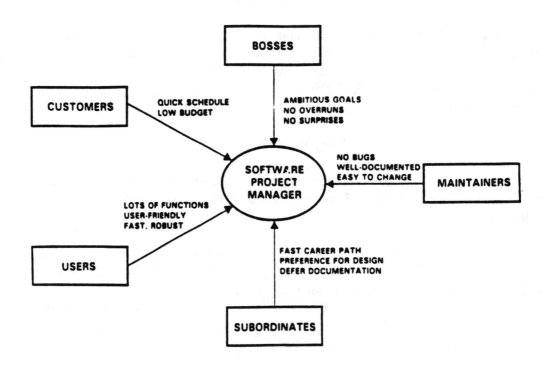

Figure 1

These desires create fundamental conflicts when taken together (e.g., many functions versus a low budget and no overruns). These conflicts are at the root of most software project management difficulties - both at the strategic level (setting goals, establishing major milestones and responsibilities) and at the tactical level (resolving day-to-day conflicts, prioritizing assignments, adapting to changes).

1.2 The Software Management Theory Problem

A good software management theory should help the project manager navigate through these difficulties. As seen in *Figure 2*, a software management theory has a similar challenging set of simultaneous objectives to satisfy. It should be simple to understand and apply; general enough to cover all classes of projects and classes of concerns (procedural, technical, economic, people-oriented); yet specific enough to provide useful, situation-specific advice.

THE SOFTWARE MANAGEMENT THEORY PROBLEM

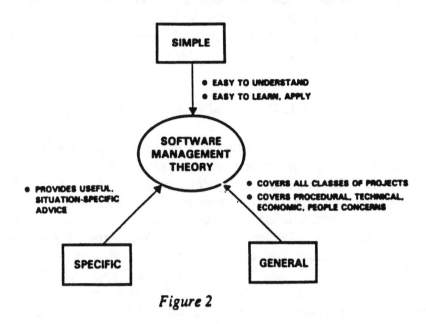

Figure 2

Several attempts have been made to provide a relatively small set of software project management principles which can be easily recalled and applied, and which cover all of the important aspects. Thayer et. al [21] and Reifer [18] provide sets of principles largely organized around the five overall management principles in Koontz-O'Donnell [12] of planning, staffing, organizing, controlling and directing. Boehm [3] provides a set of seven fundamental principles of software development. Although these have been very useful in many situations, none of these to date have produced a sufficient combination of simplicity, generality and specificity to have stimulated widespread use.

This paper presents a candidate fundamental principle for software project management developed by one of the authors (Boehm), and shows how it would apply in avoiding the software project management problems encountered in a case study analyzed by the other author (Ross).

The fundamental principle is called the Theory W approach to software project management.

Theory W: Make Everyone a Winner.

It holds that the primary job of the software project manager is to make winners of each of the parties involved in the software process: the project manager's subordinates and managers; the customers; the users and maintainers of the resulting product; and any other significantly affected people, such as the developers or users of interfacing products.

Making everyone a winner has a number of implications which will be discussed below, including the use of two subsidiary principles:

* Plan the Flight and Fly the Plan.
* Identify and Manage Your Risks.

Section 2 of this paper elaborates on the overall Theory W approach and the software project implications of making everyone a winner. Section 3 elaborates on the two subsidiary principles. Section 4 provides the history of the system involved in the case study. Section 5 analyzes the case study with respect to Theory W and the subsidiary principles, and Section 6 presents the resulting conclusions.

2. THEORY W: MAKE EVERYONE A WINNER

This Section elaborates on Theory W's major principle. We begin in Section 2.1 by placing Theory W in the context of other management theories, particularly Theories X, Y and Z. Section 2.2 presents the key concept involved in Theory W: the distinction between win-win, win-lose, and lose-lose situations. Section 2.3 summarizes the three primary steps suggested to achieve the desired goal of making everyone a winner, and the 9 substeps involved in implementing Theory W. Section 2.3 also elaborates on the first three substeps: those that deal with creating win-win situations, the strongest distinguishing feature of Theory W as a management approach. Section 2.4 elaborates on all of the substeps, and shows how a set of strategic principles for software project management can be generated by applying each of the substeps to each of the project manager's constituencies identified in *Figure 1* above. Section 2.5 shows via an example how the Theory W steps can be used to solve day-to-day tactical project management problems as well as strategic problems.

2.1 Comparison with Theories X, Y and Z

The Theory X approach to management built largely on the "scientific management" ideas of Frederick Taylor [20]. It held that the most efficient way to get a job done was to do more and more precise time and motion studies, and to organize jobs into well-orchestrated sequences of tasks in which people were as efficient and predictable as machines. Management consisted of keeping the system running smoothly, largely through coercion.

Theory Y, introduced in [8], held that Theory X was a poor long-term strategy because it stunted people's creativity , adaptiveness, and self esteem, making the people and their organizations unable to cope with change. Theory Y held that management should stimulate creativity and individual initiative. This led to organizations which were much more adaptive and personally satisfying, but created difficulties in dealing with conflict. This was not a problem in Theory X, but became a major concern in Theory Y organizations, with many individual initiatives competing for resources and creating problems of coordination.

Theory Z, described in [10], holds that much of the conflict resolution problem can be eliminated by up-front investment in developing shared values and arriving at major decisions by consensus. It focuses largely on doing this within an organization, and does not say much about how to deal with other organizations with different objectives and cultures - a particularly common situation with software managers and their diverse constituencies (developers, customers, users etc.). Overall, Theory Z's primary emphasis is at the corporate-culture level rather than at the inter-company level or the individual project level.

Theory W's fundamental principle is well-matched to the problems of software project management. It holds that software project managers will be fully successful if and only if they make winners of all the other participants in the software process: superiors, subordinates, customers, users, maintainers, etc. This principle is particularly relevant in the software field, which is a highly people-intensive area whose products are largely services or decision aids, and whose performers are often unfamiliar with user and management concerns. However, Theory W can be applied to other fields as well.

Rather than characterizing a manager as an autocrat (Theory X), a coach (Theory Y), or a facilitator (Theory Z), Theory W characterizes a manager's primary role as a negotiator between his various constituencies, and a packager of project solutions with win conditions for all parties. Beyond this, the manager is also a goal-setter, a monitor of progress towards goals, and an activist in seeking out day-to-day win-lose or lose-lose project conflicts, confronting them, and changing them into win-win situations.

2.2 Win-Win, Win-Lose, and Lose-Lose Situations

Making everyone a winner may seem like an unachievable objective. Most situations tend to be zero-sum, win-lose situations. Building a quick and sloppy product may be a low-cost, near-term "win" for the software developer and customer, but it will be a "lose" for the user and the maintainer. Adding lots of marginally useful software "bells and whistles" to a product on a cost-plus contract may be a win for the developer and some users, but a lose for the customer.

At worst, software projects can be lose-lose situations. Setting unrealistic schedule expectations; staffing with incompatible people; poor planning; or trying to catch up on a schedule by adding more people will generally make losers of all the participants.

Nonetheless, win-win situations exist, and often they can be created by careful attention to people's interests and expectations. Creating a profit-sharing arrangement for a software subcontractor provides the subcontractor with a motivation to develop a high-quality, widely-sold product, thus increasing the size of the profit pie for both the subcontractor and the top-level product developer. Using better software technology such as structured programming, early error detection techniques, or information hiding will also create wins for all parties.

2.3 Creating Win-Win Situations

The best work on creating win-win situations has been done in the field of negotiation. The book *Getting to Yes* [9] is a classic in the area. Its primary thesis is that successful negotiations are not achieved by haggling from pre-set negotiating positions, but by following a four-step approach whose goal is basically to create a win-win situation for the negotiating parties:

1. Separate the people from the problem
2. Focus on interests, not positions
3. Invent options for mutual gain
4. Insist on using objective criteria

The Theory W approach to software project management expands on these four steps to establish a set of win-win preconditions, and some further conditions for structuring the software process and the resulting software product, as shown in *Table 1*.

1. Establish a set of win-win preconditions
a. Understand how people want to win; b. Establish reasonable expectations; c. Match people's tasks to their win conditions; d. Provide a supportive environment.
2. Structure a win-win software process.
a. Establish a realistic process plan; b. Use the plan to control the project; c. Identify and manage your win-lose or lose-lose risks; d. Keep people involved;
3. Structure a win-win software product.
a. Match product to users', maintainers' win conditions.

Table 1. Theory W Win-Win steps

The remainder of this section elaborates on the first three substeps in *Table 1* which deal primarily with the process of creating win-win situations.

2.3.1 Understand How People Want to Win

One important sub-principle here is to *make sure you identify the key people*. Often, software projects have failed because a key constituency (users' bosses, hardware procurement personnel, subcontractors) has not been included in the win-win scheme.

Another important sub-principle is to *project yourself into others' win situations*. This is often difficult for people to do because it runs counter to strongly-implanted notions of goodness such as the Golden Rule: "Do unto others as you would have others do unto you". But, others may not want what you want as win conditions. Some frequent examples:

*   Managers frequently assume that software professionals win by getting 'promoted' to management. However, the motivating-factors studies done by Couger and Zawacki [6] indicate that the typical data processing professional has a much stronger need for professional growth than for social interaction, while the average manager has the opposite profile. Thus, such promotions can be quite harmful to software people's careers, and dual-track (technical and managerial) career-path ladders can be much more successful in software organizations.

*   Computer-science majors brought up on canonical applications such as compilers and operating systems, where users are programmers, implicitly build up a set of assumptions about software users: that software users like to program, and prefer powerful and terse (but perhaps obscure) command languages and users' manuals. Well-meaning attempts to apply those assumptions to such software users as nurses, doctors, pilots and bank tellers have led to numerous software disasters.

Thus, Theory W suggests a modified form of the Golden Rule: "Do unto others as you would have others do unto you -- if you were like them".

Another key sub-principle is the Peters-Waterman [17] maxim to *get close to the customer*. This involves getting software people to operate more like marketing personnel than like people who wait around to code up whatever specification is provided. It involves much more pro-active use of interviews, surveys, tours of duty, prototypes, scenarios, operations analysis, user-culture analyses, and understanding of users' previous experiences with automation (scars, bruises, traumas, triumphs).

Overall, the field of motivational analysis provides the most comprehensive set of insights on understanding how people want to win. Gellerman [10] provides a good early survey of the field; more recently, Couger and Zawacki [6] have provided a good set of insights related specifically to data processing people.

2.3.2 Establish Reasonable Expectations

Many software problems stem from the fact that software customers and users frequently have little feel for what is easy and what is hard to achieve with computers and software. This leads to a set of unrealistic expectations: either thinking things are too hard to implement (complex scheduling or file management) or too easy (pattern recognition or building 150 man-months worth of software in 6 months). Similarly, software people often have unrealistic expectations of what is easy and what is hard for users to do.

Some important sub-principles here are:

*   Bring your constituencies together to identify and resolve expectation mismatches.

*   Have people look at issues from the other constituent's viewpoints.

*   Have people look for objective, mutually relevant solution criteria.

*   Relate people's expectations to experience: benchmarks, reference checks, expert judgment.

*   Relate people's expectations to well-calibrated models: computer-performance models, software project cost and schedule estimation models.

A related management insight is that "hard-soft works better than soft-hard". A manager who overpromises to his various constituencies and then has to deflate their expectations has an easier time initially, but a much rougher time in the long run, than a manager who deflates initial expectations and provides some management reserve to soften his position later where necessary.

A good recent example of establishing reasonable software project expectations involved the need for improvements in the on-board software of the F-16 aircraft. The aircraft users expected a long list of additional software capabilities to be delivered in 12 months. The developers' expectations were in terms of previous software productivity rates, and indicated a much longer development period. Rather than conduct a positional bargaining exercise resulting in unsatisfied expectations on both sides, the users and developers decided to explore their options using COCOMO, a software cost and schedule estimation model calibrated to experience in similar projects [2].

As a result, both groups developed a much better understanding of the relationships between software functionality, cost, and schedule. The developers found options to increase their software productivity capabilities and expectations. The users were able to establish a series of prioritized annual software increments whose achievability was keyed to their developer-shared productivity expectations. After two years of software deliveries, both groups have experienced satisfactory results relative to their revised expectations.

Overall, the process of reconciling people's expectations is dealt with in the fields of conflict resolution and teambuilding. Walton [22], Kirchof and Adams [11], and Dyer [7] are good sources of additional insight.

2.3.3 Match People's Tasks to Their Win Conditions

The key principles here involve *searching out win-win situations* and *expanding the option space to create win-win situations.*

Some effective techniques available to the software project manager for searching out win-win situations include:

* Breaking options into parts (functions, activities, increments, phases), and configuring combinations of sub-options into win packages for each participant. For example, under some conditions, establishing a separate leader for successive software increments has worked well, particularly if the increments are large, with different technical and/or organizational centers of gravity.

* Realigning options along win-win axes. For example, some projects have successfully shifted the authority and responsibility for software quality assurance from the developer (who may consider it a bore) to the maintainer, who has considered it a major win-leverage opportunity.

Some effective techniques available to the software project manager for expanding the option space to create win-win situations are:

* Linking tasks to future options and career paths ("Quality assurance may be a bore, but it's a ticket to a fast-track career path.")

* Expanding the scope of a task (" Quality Assurance should not be a bore. I think you could lead the way in helping us make quality assurance a more pro-active function in getting us quality products. That would be a real achievement.")

* Linking tasks to extra rewards (" Rescuing this integration and test mess will be a killer, but I'll make sure you get a good bonus and lots of kudos if you succeed.")

* Providing extra support ("This schedule is very ambitious, but I'll provide your team with the first-class workstations and facilities you'll need to meet it.")

* Surfacing new options ("We can't develop all the functions in 12 months, but if we do an incremental development, we can satisfy your top-priority needs in 12 months.")

Overall, the field of negotiation provides the best additional sources of insight in matching tasks to win conditions. Some good books are Fisher and Ury [9] and Nierenberg [15].

2.4   Deriving Strategic Project Guidelines from Theory W Win-Win steps

Most current software management directives, and many of the textbooks, present strategic software management guidelines as a series of relatively unconnected what-to-do lists of activities to perform (e.g., prototype the user interface, configuration-manage the baselined items, set up and follow a set of programming standards).

The power of Theory W becomes evident in *Tables 2 and 3*, which show that one can derive most of the apparently unconnected what-to-do activities by applying the Theory W win-win steps in Table 1 to the various constituencies involved in the software process. Prototyping is a way of understanding the users' win conditions (Table 2). Configuration management is partly establishing a supportive environment for the developers and maintainers, and partly participation in change control by all parties impacted by a proposed change (Table 2). Programming standards contribute to structuring a software product so that its maintainers will be winners (Table 3).

Further, Tables 2 and 3 provide stronger guidance than usual for allocating life-cycle responsibilities to the various software parties. An example is the allocation of the

Win-Win Precondition	Users	Maintainers	Customers	Developer Team
Understand win conditions	Mission anal. Ops. concept Prototyping Rqts. spec Early users' manual	Ops. concept Ops. procedures	Cost-benefit analysis	Career path develop.
Reasonable expectations	*Teambuilding, Negotiating, Conflict resolution* Rqts. scrub		*Resource allocation*	
Match tasks to win conditions	*Change control participation* User-spec reviews Prototype exercise	Quality assurance	Status tracking *Early Error Detection*	Staffing, organizing
Supportive environment preparation	User training Cutover preparation	Maint. training Conversion Deliverable support envir. Config. mgmt.	Customer training	Developer training Support envir. Config. mgmt.
		Modern programming practices		

Table 2 - Strategic Guidelines Derived from Win-Win Preconditions

quality assurance responsibility to the maintainers, as their win conditions are most strongly affected by product quality.

Tables 2 an 3 also show that Theory W provides not just a "what" for the process activities, but also the underlying "why". This is very important in the frequent situations of tailoring the process activities to special circumstances, and determining how much of a given process activity is enough. For example, if the inclusion of machine-generated flowcharts in the maintainance documentation does not help the maintainers, it is not necessary to require their delivery.

Guideline	Users	Maintainers	Customers	Developers
Process planning	Operational plan Installation & training plans	Life-cycle support plan	Development plans	
Process control	*Teambuilding, Negotiating, Communicating*			
	Reviews	Reviews	Status tracking, Controlling Perform. feedback	
Risk management	*Sensitivity analysis* *Risk management plans*			
	User rqts. validation, stability	Quality assurance	Budget, schedule Validation	staffing
Process involvement	Sys. engr, plan participation Review participation Prototype exercise	Sys. engr, plan participation Review participation Quality assurance	Cost-benefit reviews, approvals	Delegation Planning particip.
Product structuring	Service oriented Efficient Easy to learn Easy to use Tailorable	Easy to modify Prog. standards	Efficient Correct Feasible	Easy to Modify Balanced Correct

Table 3 - Strategic Guidelines Derived from Product, Process Guidelines

2.5   Theory W: A Tactical Management Example

Theory W provides specific useful guidance in tactical as well as strategic project management situations. The resulting solutions are often preferable to those derived from previous management theories. Consider the following example:

XYZ Corp. has been developing a large financial system for a Boston bank. A new position on the project is being created to lead a system analysis effort. George and Ann are the two primary candidates for the job. They are equally well qualified: George has somewhat more overall experience, while Ann has more experience specific to this type of application. The project manager must decide whom to choose.

Using Theory X, the manager would make a choice, based on some arbitrary criterion such as seniority. Using Theory Y, the manager would likely ask George and Ann for proposals on how they would do the job, and pick the most ambitious one. Using

Theory Z, the manager would likely concentrate on pre-building a consensus on team objectives, and make a choice based on team priorities.

Theory W would try to avoid the above solutions, each of which creates a win-lose situation between George and Ann. By following the Theory W steps in Table 1, the manager would try to create a win-win situation as follows:

1. *Understand how people want to win.* In talking with George and Ann, the manager finds that George greatly wants the job because of the extensive travel to Boston, where he has a daughter in college. Ann greatly wants the job because it would provide a career path toward marketing.

2. *Match people's tasks to their win conditions.* The manager expands the option space by considering comparable jobs with Boston travel for George and comparable marketing-oriented jobs for Ann.

Frequently, the Theory W approach will help the manager to find and establish such win-win solutions, creating more satisfaction and personal commitment among the participants, fewer disaffected and uncooperative participants, and more satisfactory all-around outcomes.

2.6   Connections between Theory W and Game Theory

Theory W also has fruitful connections to game theory. For example, the case of George and Ann can be formulated as a nonzero-sum game involving three players: George, Ann and the customer. By using the concept of Rational Offer Groups formulated by Rosenschein and Genesereth [19], one can analyze the conditions under which the expansion of George's and Ann's option spaces will produce a win-win-win situation for George, Ann and the customer. An example result is that if the project manager is too successful in finding alternate jobs for George and Ann, neither will take the systems analysis job, and the customer will become a loser.

3. THEORY W SUBSIDIARY PRINCIPLES

Because of their particular importance to the management of the software process, the first three Theory W win-win process substeps in Table 1 are highlighted and combined into two key Theory W subsidiary principles. These are:

> * Plan the flight and fly the plan (steps 2a, 2b);
> * Identify and manage your risks (step 2c).

3.1 Planning the Flight

Establishing a realistic process plan is crucial to the success of the project. As indicated in Table 3, there are several types of plans involved in making everyone a winner : operational plans, installation and training plans, life-cycle support plans, and development plans. Each of these may have a number of subsidiary plans : configuration management plans, quality assurance plans, test plans, conversion plans, etc.

Plans are important in Theory W because:

They record the mutual commitment of the project participants to a set of win-win conditions and their implications.

They provide a framework for detecting deviations from the win-win conditions which require corrective action.

Frequently, each software sub-plan is organized around a totally different outline, making the various plans more difficult to develop, assimilate, and query. Each Theory W plan is organized around a common outline, reflecting a small number of universal interrogatives (why, what, when, who, where, how, and how much):

1. Objectives (*Why* is the activity being pursued?)

2. Products and Milestones (*What* is being produced by when?)

3. Responsibilities (*Who* is responsible for each result? *Where* are they located organizationally?)

4. Approach (*How* is each result being achieved?)

5. Resources (*How much* of each scarce resource is required to achieve the results?).

Figure 3 presents the outline for one of the key software management plans : the Software Development Plan. It shows that the subsections of the plan are particular to software development issues (requirements, product design, programming, configuration management, quality assurance, etc.), but that the major sections of the plan follow the common Theory W outline.

Space limitations preclude further discussion of software project planning here; Some good references are [8] and [14]. Also, some similar concepts are being developed in the draft IEEE standard for Software Project Management Plans.

3.2 *Flying the Plan*

Developing a plan which satisfies everyone's win conditions is not enough to make everyone a winner. You also need to use the plan to manage the project.

This involves making a particular effort to monitor the project's progress with respect to the plan. The nature of this effort should be specified in the plan; see section 5.3 of the plan outline in *Figure 3*. If the project's progress continues to match its plans, the project is in good shape. But usually, there will be some mismatches between the progress and the plans. If so, the manager needs to assess the reasons for the mismatches. It may be that the plans are flawed or out of date, in which case the plans need to be modified. Or the project's progress may be deficient, in which case the project manager needs to apply corrective action.

Applying corrective action is one of the most critical situations for using the "make everyone a winner" principle. It is all too easy to apply snap-judgment corrective actions with win-lose or lose-lose outcomes, or to heap public blame on people so that they feel

1. Objectives (the "why")

   1.1. Software Product Objectives

   1.2. Development Plan Objectives

2. Milestones and Products (the "what" and "when")

   2.1. Overall Development Strategy

   2.2. Detailed Schedule of Deliverables

   2.3. Detailed Development Milestones and Schedules

3. Responsibilities (the "who" and "where")

   3.1. Organizational Responsibilities

      3.1.1. Global Organization Charts

      3.1.2. Organizational Commitment Responsibilities

   3.2. Development Responsibilities

      3.2.1. Development Organization Charts

      3.2.2. Staffing

      3.2.3. Training

4. Approach (the "how")

   4.1. Risk Management

   4.2. Development Phases

      4.2.1. Plans and Requirements Phase

      4.2.2. Product Design Phase

      4.2.3. Programming Phase

      4.2.4. Integration and test Phase

      4.2.5. Implementation Phase

   4.3. Reviews

   4.4. Documentation

   4.5. Configuration Management

   4.6. Quality Assurance

   4.7. Facilities and Related Concerns

5. Resources (the "how much")

   5.1. Work Breakdown Structure

   5.2. Budgets

   5.3. Status Monitoring and Control

Figure 3: Theory W Outline for the Software Development Plan

like losers rather than winners. But it is generally possible to follow the Theory W win-win steps in *Table 1* to find a corrective action strategy which either preserves everyone as winners, or convinces them that their losses are minimal with respect to other strategies. (An example is provided in the case study analysis in Section 5.1.) And it is generally possible to reprimand people's behavior without making them feel like losers. A good example is the "one-minute reprimand" in the book *The One-Minute Manager* [1].

3.3 Risk Management

Planning the flight and flying the plan will make everyone a winner if the plans reflect the participants' win conditions and if the plans are realistic. Ensuring that the plans are realistic is the province of risk management.

Risk management focuses the project manager's attention on those portions of the project most likely to cause trouble and to compromise the participants' win conditions. Risk management considerations can also help the project manager to determine the appropriate sequence of performing project activities. The Spiral Model of software development [4] discusses risk-driven sequencing of project activities in more detail.

Webster defines "risk" as "the possibility of loss or injury". The magnitude of a risk item is generally defined as a quantity called Risk exposure RE:

$$RE = (LP) * (LM).$$

The Loss Probability factor *LP* represents the probability of an unsatisfactory outcome. The Loss Magnitude factor *LM* represents the magnitude of the loss if the outcome is unsatisfactory. The magnitude of the loss is best expressed in terms of the participants' utility functions, which measure the degree to which the participants become losers rather than winners.

There are two primary classes of project risk :

1. *Generic risks* , which are common to all projects, and which are covered by standard development plan techniques.

2. *Project-specific risks* , which reflect a particular aspect of a given project, and which are addressed by project-specific risk management plans. The most common project-specific risks are personnel shortfalls, unrealistic schedules and budgets, inappropriate requirements, shortfalls in external components and tasks, and technology shortfalls or unknowns.

3.4 Risk Management Steps

The practice of risk management involves two primary steps, Risk Assessment and Risk Handling, each with three subsidiary steps. Risk Assessment involves risk identification, risk analysis, and risk prioritization. Risk Handling involves risk management planning, risk management execution, and risk monitoring and control.

Risk Identification produces lists of the project-specific items likely to comprise a project's win-win conditions. Typical risk identification techniques include checklists, decomposition, comparison with experience, and examination of decision drivers.

Risk Analysis produces assessments of the loss-probability and loss-magnitude associated with each of the identified risk items, and assessments of compound risks involved in risk-item interactions. Typical techniques include network analysis, decision trees, cost models, and performance models.

Risk Prioritization produces a prioritized ordering of the risk items identified and analyzed. Typical techniques include risk leverage analysis and Delphi or group-consensus techniques.

Risk Management Planning produces plans for addressing each risk item, including the coordination of the individual risk-item plans with each other and with the overall project plan (e.g. to ensure that enough up-front schedule is provided to properly develop, exercise, and learn from a prototype). Typical techniques include risk-resolution checklists such as the one in *Table 4*, showing the top 10 primary sources of software project risk and the most effective approaches for resolving them. Other techniques include cost-benefit analysis and statistical decision analysis of the relative cost and effectiveness of alternative risk-resolution approaches.

Risk Management Execution produces a resolution of the risk items. Typical techniques are the ones shown in *Table 4*.

A Top Ten List of Software Risk Items	
RISK ITEM	RISK MANAGEMENT TECHNIQUES
1. Personnel shortfalls	-Staffing with top talent; job matching; teambuilding; key-personnel agreements; cross-training; prescheduling key people
2. Unrealistic schedules and budgets	-Detailed multisource cost & schedule estimation; design to cost; incremental development; software reuse; requirements scrubbing
3. Developing the wrong software functions	-Organization analysis; mission analysis; ops-concept formulation; user surveys; prototyping; early users' manuals
4. Developing the wrong user interface	-Prototyping; scenarios; task analysis user characterization (functionality, style, workload)
5. Gold plating	-Requirements scrubbing; prototyping; cost-benefit analysis; design to cost
6. Continuing stream of requirements changes	-High change threshold; information hiding; incremental development (defer changes to later increments)
7. Shortfalls in externally furnished components	-Benchmarking; inspections; reference checking; compatibility analysis
8. Shortfalls in externally performed tasks	-Reference checking; pre-award audits; award-fee contacts; competitive design or prototyping; teambuilding
9. Real-time performance shortfalls	-Simulation; benchmarking; modeling; prototyping; instrumentation; tuning
10. Straining computer science capabilities	-Technical analysis; cost-benefit analysis; prototyping; reference checking

Table 4

Risk Monitoring and Control completes the "flying the plan" counterpart of risk management planning. It involves tracking the progress toward resolving high-risk items and taking corrective action where appropriate. A most effective technique is a Top Ten Risk Item list which is highlighted at each weekly, monthly, or milestone project review.

These steps are supported by a variety of techniques. Space limitations preclude further discussion of the issues here. Further details on each of the software risk management steps are given in [5].

4. THE CASE STUDY

4.1 Corporate Background

BBB Industries is one of the largest manufacturers in the small, yet advanced emerging nation named Optimia. The company started out in the 1950's as a privately owned workshop, and has gone through periods of prosperity and periods of recession. During one of the recession periods in the early seventies, the owners sold their shares to MMM corporation, one of Optimia's largest investment corporations.

In 1983, BBB Industries' sales volume reached $100 million a year, with over 3000 employees. The manufacturing was carried out in several factories while the Marketing, Production Planning, and Financial Services functions were all concentrated at the company's headquarters. BBB Industries manufactured various consumer products that were marketed through diverse distribution channels, including the company's own store. Over half of the sales were directed to export markets in the USA and Europe.

The profitability of the company was very unstable: the world demand for BBB's product line is subject to frequent ups and downs, and BBB Industries was unable to adjust in time to these dynamic changes. This inability was attributed mainly to BBB's old-fashioned production and organizational methods.

BBB's Information Systems in 1983 were of the most archaic type. In the early 1970's a major effort was made to computerize the production and control systems by using a card-operated computer. This effort failed, and a decision was made to transfer the information processing to a service bureau. For technical and political reasons, the various departments adopted different service bureaus, so that in 1983 each of the General-Ledger, Accounts-Receivables, Payroll and Inventory systems used the services of a different service bureau.

4.2 The New Management's Attitude

In 1984, a new General Manager was appointed to BBB Industries. The business results of 1984 were good, and the General Manager decided that the time had come to do something about BBB's Information Systems. To achieve that result, he hired a new manager for the Data Processing department, Mr. Smith.

"It's not going to be an easy job", he told Mr. Smith, "But this is a big challenge. I know this company cannot go on without proper information systems. However, my middle management does not understand information systems concepts. It is up to you to show us the way, and to help me convince the other managers in this company to give a hand to this effort. However - you should not forget that BBB's budget is limited, and that 1985 is not going to be as profitable as 1984. So, we shall have to do our best with a minimal budget. And, of course, since I am trying to cut down on all personnel, you cannot hire any more people to the data processing department right now. First, I want to see some results, and then - the sky is the limit."

4.3 The Initial Survey

The initial survey was done by Mr. Smith himself. The survey consisted of two parts:

    a. A study of BBB's existing systems

    b. An outline of BBB's requirements for new Information Systems

The survey's findings can be summed up as follows:

- Except for the Payroll system, all the existing data-processing systems of BBB did not serve their purposes. These systems were not used in the day-to-day operations, their accuracy was very low, and they therefore required a lot of manual processing.

- The vital Production Design and Control operation could not benefit at all from any of the computer systems, and therefore was slow, inflexible and inefficient.

- There was practically no integration between the different systems, and each served the specific, limited needs of the department that was in charge of it.

- BBB's productivity, manageability and profitability depended on the replacement of these systems by new, better ones.

- The potential users of the systems were quite ignorant of what modern information systems concepts are, and how they could be of use for them in their daily activities. Furthermore, the factory workers had little faith in BBB's ability to adopt new, modern methods.

The survey's recommendations were:

- There is immediate need to replace the existing systems by on-line, interactive systems, based on in-house computers, that will supply the information by both operational and management levels in a timely, accurate and comprehensive fashion. This effort can be done in stages, and the first system to be implemented should be a relatively simple, low-risk system. The success of this implementation will improve the ability to continue with other, more complex systems.

- The development of the first system should be done by an outside contractor, preferably a software house that already has a package for that purpose.

- BBB's middle management personnel should receive special training that will enable them to better understand the potential of on-line computer systems and their applicability to their own problems.

- The problems of the factories are complex, and require more detailed research to analyze and define the information systems requirements of the factories and to evaluate the various modes of operations that are amenable for this problem (Distributed processing vs. centralized processing, interactive vs. autonomous, data collection techniques etc.);

- Even though the task of computerizing BBB is complex, such projects are common nowadays, and the overall timetable should not exceed three years.

The survey was presented to BBB's management, and its conclusions were approved enthusiastically. The Finished-Goods Sales and Marketing system (FGSM) was chosen for first implementation, primarily because it was the easiest to implement, and because the FGSM managers were the strongest in expressing their need for and support of a new system. Mr. Smith was charged with preparing a Request For Proposal that would be presented to potential suppliers of software and hardware. There was no discussion of the required budget, nor additional personnel.

4.4 The Request For Proposal (RFP)

The RFP was based on the initial survey and on the findings of a subsequent two-week survey of the Finished - Goods Sales and Marketing organization. It consisted of the following parts:

a. A general description of BBB, its organization, operations and goals.

b. A thorough, though not detailed, description of the Finished - Goods Marketing and Sales Organization.

c. A list of the requirements for the new system for FGSM:

-   The system should be an on-line, interactive system.

-   The system shall handle all the different types of items and incorporate all the different types of Catalog Codes that are in current use.

-   The system shall handle the Finished Goods inventory in various levels of detail.

-   The system shall handle the various types of clients (Retailers, wholesalers, Department Stores, Company-owned stores).

-   The system shall produce automatic billings to the various clients (Some of the Department Stores required pre-defined forms).

-   The system shall be able to produce different sales and inventory reports.

-   The system shall be able to integrate in the future into the General Ledger and Accounts Receivables Systems

d. A four-page outline of the requirements for the new Financial Systems for BBB.

The RFP was presented to the three leading hardware suppliers in Optimia, and to five software companies that had previous experience in similar systems.

4.5 The Proposals

After the first elimination process, three proposals were left in the game. Since the RFP was rather open-ended, the proposals varied in their scopes and in the extent to which they covered the requirements mentioned. The price quotations ranged from $70,000 to $450,000. The final competitors were:

1. Colossal Computers - The leading hardware distributor in Optimia. Colossal Computers proposed their popular System C computer, and recommended the software packages of SW1 Software as the basis for the implementation. (Colossal refused to take full commitment for both hardware and software)

2. Big Computing Computers - The second largest hardware distributor in Optimia, distributors of Big computers, with their own Financial and Marketing packages.

3. Fast Computing Computers - The distributors of world renowned Fast computers. There were only few installations of Fast computers in Optimia, even though the equipment was excellent. As a result, there were no software packages available on Fast Computers. The owners of Fast Computing Computers was MMM Corp., the owners of BBB Industries. MMM Corp. was deliberating at the time how to increase the sales of Fast Computers.

Table 5 summarizes the results of the evaluation process among the three competitors, as presented to BBB's management.

Mr. Smith's recommendation was to buy Colossal's equipment and to engage SW1 Software as sub-contractor for the Marketing and Financial Systems, relying on SW1's existing Financial package. Mr. Smith had met with two of SW1's executives and was very impressed with their familiarity with Sales and Marketing Systems. It turned out that SW1 had considerable previous experience in developing Marketing systems similar to that required by BBB.

BBB's management informed the three competitors of BBB's choice, and started final negotiations with Colossal Computers.

The next day, BBB's General Manager got a call from Fast Computing Computers' General Manager, and a meeting was set where BBB was asked to clarify why Colossal was chosen. Fast Computing's General Manager explained that the BBB account had a crucial significance to Fast Computing's future. " If In - House companies (that is - MMM owned) won't buy our equipment, who will? Colossal will use this fact as a weapon to beat us even in places where they don't have such an advantage," he said.

"The solution offered by Colossal answers most of our needs", replied BBB's General Manager, " Your equipment may be good, but you simply do not have enough software packages to attract new clients in our line of business".

	Colossal	Big Computing	Fast Computing
HARDWARE EVALUATION			
Speed Factor	Average	Average	V. Good
Memory Factor	Average	Low	V. Good
# of installations (Optimia)	200	50	5
Growth Factor	Average	Low	High
PROPOSED SW SOLUTION			
Financial Package	SW1's package	Own Package	To be developed
Marketing System	SW1	Own devlp.	BBB devlp.
SOFTWARE EVALUATION			
Financial Package	Good	Good	?
Marketing Solution	Good	Average	None
Addt'l Packages	Many	A few	None
GENERAL FACTORS			
Familiarity with Equip.	High	Low	Low
Compatibility with			
BBB's Inventory Sys.	None	None	High
# of SW houses	15	5	2
COMPANY FACTORS			
Company Stability	High	Average	Average
Maintenance Organization	High	Low	Average
Company Commitment	Average	Average	High
ESTIMATED COSTS			
Hardware	$170K	$130K	$140K
Marketing System	$50K	$40K	?
Financial Package	$30K	$30K	$40K
Estimated Modifications to			
Financial Package	$20K-$40K	$30K-$50K	?
TOTAL COSTS	$270K-$290K	$240K-$260K	$180K+?

Table 5

The following day, BBB's General Manager got a call from MMM's Chairman: " I would hate to interfere with BBB's internal management, but will you please give Fast Computers another chance? There must be a way for them to get this account."

BBB's General Manager's reply to that was simple: "Only if we can get the same solution as is available on Colossal equipment, within no more than two months delay, and provided that the software is developed by SW1 and that we get all the required modifications to the Financial Package for free".

When informed by BBB's General Manager of this conversation, Mr. Smith protested: " This is an infeasible solution! It is too expensive for Fast Computing, and I don't believe we will get our systems within this time frame."

"Are you sure it cannot be done?", asked BBB's manager.

"Well - It's not impossible, but it sure requires an extraordinary effort", replied Mr. Smith.

" So, we must make sure that Fast Computing does this extraordinary effort."

"If that's what you want, we can put a clause in the agreement that we will not pay unless we get satisfactory results within a predescribed time-frame. However - I still recommend that we take Colossal's proposal", said Mr. Smith.

A couple of days later BBB signed an agreement with Fast Computing Computers. One of the pre-conditions for payments for both Hardware and Software was that BBB must receive a software solution that satisfied its needs, within the outlined timetable. The total cost of the project to BBB (Hardware, Marketing System, Financial Package and all the required modifications to the Financial Package) was to be 230,000 dollars.

4.6 The Detailed Requirements Specifications for the FGSM System

Fast Computing Computers engaged SW1 Software to develop both the Marketing and the Financial Systems. The Marketing system was to be developed according to BBB's requirements, and the Financial System was to be converted from the Colossal Computer version.

Since the project was to be carried out on Fast computers, SW1 decided not to allocate the same project manager that was proposed to manage the development on Colossal computers (Mr. Brown). A new project manager was recruited to SW1 - Mr. Holmes. Mr. Smith was disappointed, since his decision to choose SW1 as software developer was based partly on Mr. Brown's capabilities and familiarity with marketing systems. But, SW1 insisted (they did not want to waste Mr. Brown's familiarity with Colossal equipment).

A Technical Committee was formed: Mr. Smith, Mr. Holmes and Mr. Watson, the representative of Fast Computing Computers. The Committee agreed upon the time-table outlined in *Table 6* for the development of FGSM system. It was further agreed that, if feasible, the design and development would be divided into modules (increments), thus enabling starting 1986 with the new inventory system for FGSM (the beginning of the 10th month from the start of the project).

Months	Subject
1 - 3	Detailed System Requirements Document for FGSM
4	Requirements Review
5 - 6	Detailed Design of FGSM
7 - 9	Programming
10	Acceptance Tests
11-12	New and Old Systems running concurrently

Table 6

The analysis of FGSM's requirements specifications started off on the right foot. The Specifications Document was ready in time for the Design Review scheduled for month 4. The Design Review lasted two whole days: on top of the technical and supervisory committee members, additional representatives from FGSM's organization participated and contributed their comments and clarifications. However, Mr. Holmes expressed his concern regarding the difficulty in handling the complex form required for the Catalog Number. He complained about the lack of appropriate software tools on Fast Computers: his people were having difficulties in adjusting to the new development environment. They were very hopeful that the new version of operating system, due to be released the next month, would solve these problems. When the discussion narrowed down on the format of the sales reports, it turned out that there was no easy way to develop a report-writer similar to report-writers found in Colossal applications, and SW1 refused to commit to develop a report-writer within the existing budget for the FGSM system. They were willing to commit only to 4 pre-defined sales reports. Mr. Smith would not agree, and the issue remained unsolved. A similar problem arose regarding the development of special reports to Department-Stores, and this issue remained unsolved as well.

The disagreements were outlined in the document that summarized the Design Review.

4.7 The Design and Development of the FGSM System

The real problems started at the detailed design phase. SW1's people discovered that the differences between the Fast computer and other computers were more than they had planned for. SW1 did not have people with previous experience in Fast computers, and so the original estimates, that were prepared for the Colossal computer, were not accurate. So as to enable BBB to start 1986 with a new Inventory system, the development was partitioned into 3 increments: The Inventory Module, the Operations Module, the Sales Reports Module. Mr. Holmes presented to Mr. Smith the updated timetable outlined in *Table 7*.

Mr. Smith pointed out that even though he understood the difficulties SW1 had run into, these problems should be addressed to Fast Computing, and they should be able to help SW1 to keep the original time-tables. BBB was willing to accept only one month of delay in the delivery of the total system, and had agreed to break the system into increments so as to receive the first module sooner, not later, than the original timetable. After a couple of meetings between Mr. Smith, Mr. Holmes and Mr. Watson, the parties agreed that it was possible to improve the timetables by 6 weeks, delivering the first module to BBB before the end of the 8th month.

Months (From beginning of Project)	Subject
5 - 6	Module # 1 - Detailed Design
7 - 9	Module # 1 - Programming and Test
10	Module # 1 - Acceptance Tests
7 - 9	Module # 2 - Detailed Design
10 - 11	Module # 2 - Programming and Test
12	Module # 2 - Acceptance Tests
10	Module # 3 - Detailed Design
11 - 12	Module # 3 - Programming and Test
13	Module # 3 - Acceptance Test

Table 7

Meanwhile, the people of FGSM were full of enthusiasm towards the prospect of the forthcoming installation. Being aware that once the system was installed, it would be hard to request changes and improvements, they began asking for all sorts of small improvements and minor changes. Both Mr. Holmes and Mr. Smith were very satisfied with the users' attitude, and made every possible effort to please the people of FGSM, by incorporating most of these changes into the design.

4.8 The Installation of Module # 1

Module # 1 was installed in the middle of the 9th month - two weeks before the beginning of the New Year. Mr. Holmes, Mr. Smith and the people of FGSM exerted enormous efforts to have the system up and running in time for the New Year. It turned out, however, that the acceptance tests were not comprehensive enough, and after the system was already installed and running, many problems and bugs would still pop up during operations. The many minor design changes that had accumulated in the last 3 months did not help the SW1 programmers to correct these bugs and problems in time, and it was hard to tell which was the latest version of every program. Though the FGSM people were pleased with having an On-Line system, they began to feel pretty un-easy about the system when it went through a whole series of corrections, errors and crashes.

By early 1986, the development of Module # 2 was almost complete, but the amount of man-months invested by SW1 had already exceeded the original estimates that were presented to Fast Computing. When SW1's General Manager discussed this problem with Mr. Watson, Mr. Watson explained that there was not much they could do for the time being: Fast Computing still had not received any money from BBB, and its own investments in support and management attention to this project were very high. Mr. Watson's recommendation was to wait for the successful installation of the 2nd and 3rd module before approaching BBB's higher management.

Mr. Holmes discussed these problems with Mr. Smith. Mr. Smith expressed his opinion, that Fast Computing had misled his management into believing that an impossible effort was possible, and that now Fast Computers were not doing their very best to keep their promise. Mr. Holmes remarked that his company did not like to be in such a situation either: lagging behind timetables and exceeding cost estimates. Both felt pretty bitter about the situation they found themselves in. Mr. Holmes, who was not party to the original cost estimates, began to feel that he was going to be blamed for something that was not of his doing, and secretly began looking for another job. One month later Mr. Holmes announced his decision to resign from SW1. One of SW1's senior Systems Analysts who participated in the project was made Project Manager.

4.9 The Installation of Modules #2 and #3

The installation of Module #2, though two months later than scheduled, was smoother than the installation of Module #1: the acceptance tests were ready, and were carried out properly. However the integration with Module #1 was not an easy task: it was hard to locate the latest versions of the software that were currently in use. Thus, the installation required a lot of time from SW1 programmers. It became evident that Module #3 would not be ready on time; in fact, the delay was estimated at 6 months.

All the partners to the effort were in bad shape. On one hand, the expenses of SW1 and Fast Computing exceeded even the worst projections, and it was obvious that both companies were going to lose money on this project. On the other hand , BBB was not getting the systems according to the promised timetables, and people started to compare the project to former unsuccessful attempts to introduce new systems to BBB.

The disagreements regarding the contents and form of the Sales Reports now surfaced. FGSM was not willing to settle for the 4 reports suggested by SW1. "The system is completely useless unless we get the reports we want", said Mr. Jones. "Not only that, but the Department Stores are threatening to close their account with us unless we automate the special reports they required, like all their other customers".

SW1 claimed that these reports were not part of their original agreement with Fast Computing. In fact, they blamed the Initial Survey for being vague on these points. "Heaven knows how much money we are going to lose in this project", said their General Manager to Mr. Smith. "Either BBB or Fast Computing must make it up to us."

4.10 The Financial Systems Design

The problems of the FGSM system were minor relative to the problems that arose during the analysis of BBB's requirements for the Financial Systems. Fast Computing's commitment was to deliver a complete system, tailored to BBB's requirements, and at the price of an "Off-the-shelf" product. An initial survey of BBB's requirements, carried out by SW1's professionals, estimated the cost of this project at $150K.

The three General Managers of the three companies were summoned by Mr. Watson to a special meeting. BBB was asked to lower its level of requirements from the Financial System, so as to minimize the projected expenses. BBB's General Manager was furious: " We could have had a working system by now, had we purchased Colossal equipment", he exclaimed. "My people want nothing but the best. It took me a great effort to raise their expectations, and I am not going to let them down. Fast Computers knew exactly what they were up against when they signed the agreement with us. They cannot disregard their commitments now!"

"Our original estimates regarding the scope of the project were based upon the prices quoted by SW1 Software ", replied Fast Computing's General Manager "We never intended to make money on this project, but we also never intended to lose that much".

" We based our estimates on BBB's initial survey", retorted SW1's General Manager. "As it turned out, there were too many TBD's, and the problem was that BBB's people wanted the maximum in every case, and would not settle for anything less. They kept coming with more requirements and endless modifications. One of my people has already resigned. We will not take the responsibilities that you two should have taken".

The meeting lasted for four hours, but the parties could not reach an agreement on how to proceed.

5. CASE STUDY ANALYSIS

Clearly, in this case, none of the parties came out a winner. BBB Industries ended up with unsatisfied users, mistrust in information systems, delays, partial systems, low morale, and major unresolved problems. Fast Computing ended up with significant unreimbursed expenditures, a poor reputation in the Sales Information Systems marketplace, and some useless partial products. SW1 also ended up with unreimbursed expenditures, and also a tarnished reputation in Sales Information Systems and poor prospects for future business in the Fast computer user community.

Below is an analysis of how these problems can be traced to lack of responsiveness to the Theory W fundamental principle (Make everyone a winner) and to the two subsidiary principles (*Identify and manage your risks*, and *Plan the flight and fly the plan*). The analysis also indicates ways in which the principles could have been used to avoid the problems and to make the participants winners.

5.1 Make Everyone a Winner

The major source of difficulty was the win-lose contract established between BBB and Fast Computing: no payment unless BBB got everything it asked for, on schedule (Section 4.5). Fast Computing should have made a more thorough analysis of their overrun potential (risk assessment), and a thorough assessment of the benefits of entering the Sales Information System market. If the benefits were high enough, they should have approached MMM's Chairman to authorize their spending additional profit dollars to cover the added costs of software development. Otherwise, they should have dropped out. BBB's General Manager should have heeded Mr. Smith's cautions, and either required a more detailed and realistic plan and cost estimate from Fast Computers, or gone ahead with Colossal. BBB could have made a better win-win situation by not coupling system delivery and cutover to the New Year at a time when the likely development schedules were not well known.

Another major difficulty was SW1's use of Mr. Holmes. If SW1 seriously wanted to penetrate the Fast Computers market, they should have used Mr. Brown (Section 4.6). Holmes should not have accepted responsibility for making people winners until he understood the situation better (section 4.6). SW1 management should have done more to make Holmes a winner: apprised him of the risks, done a better job of recognizing his good work in getting Module 1 running (section 4.8), and of monitoring his frustration level and likelihood of leaving SW1 (section 4.8).

As indicated in Section 2, making people winners involves seeking out day-to-day conflicts and changing them into win-win situations. An excellent opportunity to do this occurred at the Design Review (Section 4.6), when SW1 balked at producing more than four sales reports, and at producing any Department Store reports at all. However, the conflict was not addressed, and the project continued to inflate users' expectations without any attempt to get SW1 to provide the promised capabilities.

A Theory W solution to this problem would consider the conditions necessary to make winners of each of the interested parties:

- BBB and its customers: Furnish the most important reports in the initial delivery, with the other reports as soon as possible thereafter.

- SW1: Provide a realistic schedule and budget for producing the desired reports (and other capabilities).

- Fast Computing: Develop a strong system with further sales potential, within a realistic and affordable budget and schedule.

Subsequently, a much more thorough analysis would be done to determine realistic budget and schedule estimates as functions of the amount of functionality to be delivered at each increment. These levels of functionality, their associated schedules, and Fast Computing's definition of "affordability" provide some degrees of freedom within which may be possible to define a win-win solution. If so, the project can go forward on such a basis. If not, the project should be disbanded: everyone would not be a winner, but they would minimize their losses.

A similar day-to-day problem which was deferred rather than addressed was the Fast Computing payments problem (Section 4.8). A related problem was the addition of changes and improvements to the system without changing the budget or schedule (Section 4.7). This usually leads to a lose-lose situation when the budget and schedule give out and all the original and new capabilities are not completed. A Theory W solution would involve prioritizing the proposed changes with respect to the original desired capabilities, reallocating the top priority capabilities to remain consistent with the three scheduled increments; then defining an Increment 4 and assuring the users that their remaining features would definitely be incorporated in Increment 4 if BBB's management agreed to provide the budget for them.

Some other problems were created by establishing unrealistic expectations. Issuing vague Requests for Proposal (Section 4.4) is a classical example: users tend to interpret the requirements expansively, while developers interpret them austerely, creating an inevitable lose-lose situation. The cost underestimate and specification interpretation for the Financial System is another example (Section 4.10).

On the other hand, some Theory W principles were followed well. The BBB General Manager's initial conversation with Mr. Smith (Section 4.2) established a realistic climate of expectations. The choice of FGSM as the initial system to implement (Section 4.3) was good, given that FGSM's managers were enthusiastic product champions. Had the other situations been handled in similar ways, with the participants trying harder to accommodate the others' interests, the project could have had a good chance of making the participants winners.

5.2 Plan the Flight and Fly the Plan

The project's planning was seriously deficient with respect to the elements of a Software Development Plan shown in Figure 3. Some top-level milestones were established, but no attempt was made to identify dependencies and critical-path items. As discussed in the previous section, the imprecise allocation of responsibilities (e.g. SW1's responsibilities for sales reports) led to serious problems downstream. Several Approach and Resources problems (configuration management, verification and validation planning, reviews, resource control) will be discussed further below.

But the major problem here was in putting the plans on a realistic basis. Budgets and schedules were determined more from optimistic target figures than from any rationale based on cost estimation techniques or task dependency analyses. Thus, although more elaborate approach plans would have avoided some problems, they would not have cured the budget-schedule-functionality mismatch problems.

For example, SW1's projected productivity for the Fast Computer development was considered to be equal to their productivity on Colossal Computer projects. Even a rough analysis using the COCOMO cost model [2] indicated a factor of 3 likely reduction in productivity due to personnel capability and experience, support system volatility, reduced tool support, and schedule compression.

5.2.1 Configuration Management

In this area, we can easily count the following shortcomings from the part of the project management:

* No Change Control System
* No Configuration Management and Control
* No Baselined master version of the specs or programs
* No Quality Assurance (Project standards, technical audits)

All those led to confusion, multiple bugs, problems in integration, installation, unmaintainability of the system, additional costs and errors. There was no controlled mechanism for product changes, no track of product status, no product integrity.

5.2.2 Verification and Validation planning

Most of the basic principles of V&V planning were not implemented in this case:

* No verification of the initial survey or the detailed design
* Insufficient, late test plans (due to untimely, careless preparation)
* No acceptance criteria
* No integration and test plans
* Test phase and System Acceptance combined

As a result, the users got their system before it was completely verified, and were confronted with bugs and problems. The system's reliability was undermined, and the operations forced into a haphazard process.

5.2.3 Review Plans

No Product Design Review was held, only a Requirements Review. However, the problems that arose in the review were not assigned, nor tracked. It is no wonder that most problems were left unattended. The results were that on one hand there were missing capabilities, and on the other that some of the requirements were not really needed. The users were not committed to the final product. Attempts to correct the problems of missing capabilities at later stages were very expensive. A proper treatment of the problem at an earlier stage would have been less costly.

5.2.4 Resources, status monitoring and control

The main problems in this area were:

* Only high-level milestone charts were available.
* No Work Breakdown Structure was prepared.
* No Budget allocations were established.

Therefore, no cost versus progress monitoring and control was possible, and only when the overall budget was exceeded were the problems surfaced. Problems of insufficient personnel and inappropriate budget were discovered only when it was too late. In short, the visibility was poor, both at the overall progress level and the individual trouble-spot level.

5.3 Identify and Manage Your Risks

In some cases, the participants did a good job of identifying and managing risks. In particular, Mr. Smith's recommendation in Section 4.3 to start and pursue an incremental development was very good. But there were many situations in which the lack of risk management caused serious problems.

Allowing two weeks to prepare the RFP (Section 4.4) reflects a serious neglect of risk management. BBB's General Manager should have done a risk analysis on hearing Mr. Smith assess Fast Computing's need for "extraordinary effort" to succeed (Section 4.5); in particular, to carry out an independent estimate of the development cost and schedule.

BBB also did no risk assessment by looking behind the interface between Fast Computing and SW1. They did not investigate whether SW1 would use Mr. Brown on their job, and were taken by surprise when SW1 assigned the unknown Mr. Holmes. Holmes himself did very little analysis of the risks he was getting into.

BBB did not assess the risk of the highly optimistic, highly overlapped incremental development schedule proposed by SW1 (Table 5,Section 4.7). They were too preoccupied with establishing an ambitious schedule for Increment 1 to meet their New Year deadline. Such overlapping increments are major sources of risk, as changes in the earlier increments usually have serious ripple effects on the later increments under development.

In one case, risk avoidance caused an "everyone a winner" problem. Mr. Smith identified several risks due to lack of user management commitment, and addressed these by a strong effort to sell the users on the advantages of information technology. This backfired when the users compared their unrealistic expectations to the project's results. A preferred Theory W solution would be to couch user benefit projections more realistically in terms of expected near-term and long-term benefits, and to involve the users more closely in analyzing and preparing for the benefits.

6. CONCLUSIONS

When applied to a project case study, a good management theory should be able to do two things:

1.   To explain why the project encountered problems;

2.   To prescribe improved approaches which would have avoided the problems.

Analysis of the BBB case study indicates that the Theory W fundamental principle *(Make everyone a winner)* and its two subsidiary principles *(Plan the flight and fly the plan;Identify and manage your risks)* did a good job on both counts. The case study and the other examples provided earlier also indicate that Theory W does a reasonably good job in satisfying the management theory objectives of being simultaneously simple, general, and specific.

REFERENCES

[1]   K. Blanchard and S. Johnson, *The One Minute Manager,* Berkeley Books, 1982.

[2]   B.W. Boehm, *Software Engineering Economics,* Prentice Hall, Englewood Cliffs, N.J., 1981.

[3]   B.W. Boehm, "Seven Basic Principles of Software Engineering", *Journal of Systems and Software* 3 (1983), pp. 3-24.

[4]   B.W. Boehm, *A Spiral Model of Software Development and Enhancement,* ACM Software Engineering Notes, August, 1986.

[5]   B.W. Boehm, "Tutorial Notes: Software Risk Management", *ICSE 10, IEEE,* 1988.

[6]   J.D. Couger and R.A. Zawacki, *Motivating and Managing Computer Personnel,* John Wiley & Sons, 1980.

[7]   W.G. Dyer, *Team Building,* Addison Wesley, 1987.

[8]   M.W. Evans, P. Piazza and B. Dolkas, *Principles of Productive Software Management,* John Wiley & Sons, 1983.

[9]   R. Fisher and W. Ury, *Getting to Yes,* Houghton-Mifflin, 1981. Also Penguin Books, 1983.

[10]   S.W. Gellerman, *Motivation and Productivity,* American Books, New York, 1978.

[11]   N.J. Kirchof and J.R. Adams, *Conflict Management for Project Managers,* Project management Institute, February 1986.

[12]   H. Koontz and C. O'Donnell, *Principles of Management: An Analysis of Managerial Functions* (5th ed), McGraw-Hill,1972

[13]   D. McGregor, *The Human Side of Enterprise,* McGraw-Hill, 1960.

[14]   P.W. Metzger, *Managing a Programming Project,* (2nd ed), Prentice Hall, 1981.

[15]   G.I. Nierenberg, *The Art of Negotiating,* Pocket Books, 1984.

[16]   W.G. Ouchi, *Theory Z,* Addison-Wesley, 1981. Also Avon, 1982.

[17]   T.J. Peters and R.H. Waterman, *In Search of Excellence,* Harper and Row, 1982.

[18]   D.J. Reifer, *Tutorial: Software Management* (third edition) IEEE Catalog No. EHO 189-1, 1986.

[19]   J.S. Rosenschein and M.R. Genesereth, "Deals Among Rational Agents", *Proceedings, IJCAI-85,* pp. 91-99.

[20]   F.W. Taylor, *The Principles of Scientific Management,* Harper and Bros., 1911.

[21]   R.H. Thayer, A. Pyster, and R.C. Wood, "The Challenge of Software Engineering Project Management", *Computer,* August 1980, pp. 51-59.

[22]   R.E. Walton, *Managing Conflict,* Addison Wesley, 1987.

Section 2: Risk Management Practices: The Six Basic Steps

2.1: Outline

In this section, we will address the six basic risk management steps: the risk assessment steps of risk identification, risk analysis, and risk prioritization; and the risk control steps of risk management planning, risk resolution, and risk monitoring.

If you have not read and analyzed the case study in Section 1, you would get a lot more out of this section if you would go back and do it now.

2.2: Risk Assessment

Risk assessment is a process that should be applied during each phase of the project's life cycle, particularly the early phases. Figure 2.1 shows how the risk assessment process (the step called "evaluate alternatives; identify risks" in Figure 2.1) operates in concert with the other phase activities. Preferably, it should start from a baseline risk management plan for the current phase that had been developed during the previous phases. Details of the risk-driven phase approach are provided in the spiral model papers in Section 1; details of the risk management planning process and content are discussed under risk management planning in Subsection 2.7.

Each phase activity begins by elaborating the objectives for the software product and process (essentially the components of "satisfactory outcome" identified in Section 1), and the alternative methods of achieving the objectives (architectural options, reuse, special hardware, or process alternatives such as prototyping and evolutionary development). The risk identification step then involves the application of the risk identification techniques given in Subsection 2.3 to identify potential high risk areas: those in which no alternatives are likely to satisfy the objectives (the "alternatives infeasible" branch in Figure 2.1), or those in which satisfaction of the objectives is highly uncertain. In many cases, these potential high risk areas need further analysis to determine their absolute or relative unsatisfactory outcome probabilities and losses. Based on the results of this risk analysis step, the risk assessment process proceeds to the risk prioritization step, which sorts out the most critical and the less critical risk items to address. The resulting outputs of the risk assessment process are a set of elaborated objectives that are realistic with respect to the risk items, a subset of alternatives to pursue further, and a set of prioritized risk items to deal with in the risk control process.

2.3: Risk Identification

Many projects that have been wiped out by risk items could have avoided them if there had been better means for flagging people's attention that the risk items were potentially present. The UniWord case study is a typical example. Without a set of warning signs, project people frequently get carried away by enthusiasm, optimism, or management pressure caused by unrealistic expectations, and commit themselves to almost certain disaster. This section presents a number of techniques that have served well to identify potential project risks:

- Risk identification checklists
- Decision driver analysis
- Assumption analysis
- Decomposition

As we present these techniques, we will also show how they would have helped in identifying the risk items involved in the UniWord case study.

2.3.1: Risk Identification Checklists

Table 2.1 shows a top-level checklist, based on a survey of experienced project managers, of the top-10 risk items likely to compromise a software project's success. Table 2.1 also presents the managers' identification of the techniques most likely to resolve the risk items.

For some of these risk items, as will be shown next, there can be a considerable gray area blurring the distinction made in Section 1 between generic and project-specific risks.

2.3.1.1: Personnel Shortfalls

The top-ranked risk item, personnel shortfalls, overlaps the generic project concerns of staffing, motivating, team-building, retention, and career development common to all projects. Over and above these generic concerns, however, projects will often have their own unique sources of personnel risk: the need for project-specific critical skills, unrealistic assumptions about the availability of key people, or particular incompatibilities between candidate project personnel.

Table 2.2 provides a next-level checklist for the number 1 risk source of personnel shortfalls. If we apply this checklist to the UniWord case study, we can see that several critical risk items could have been anticipated:

- Critical skills for WYSIWYG-type user interface development and of file management for which nobody was identified
- Pressures to staff with people needing contract coverage for their salaries
- Incompatibilities between key people, particularly Brown and Gray
- Unsatisfied prerequisites of familiarization with the UniWindow technology

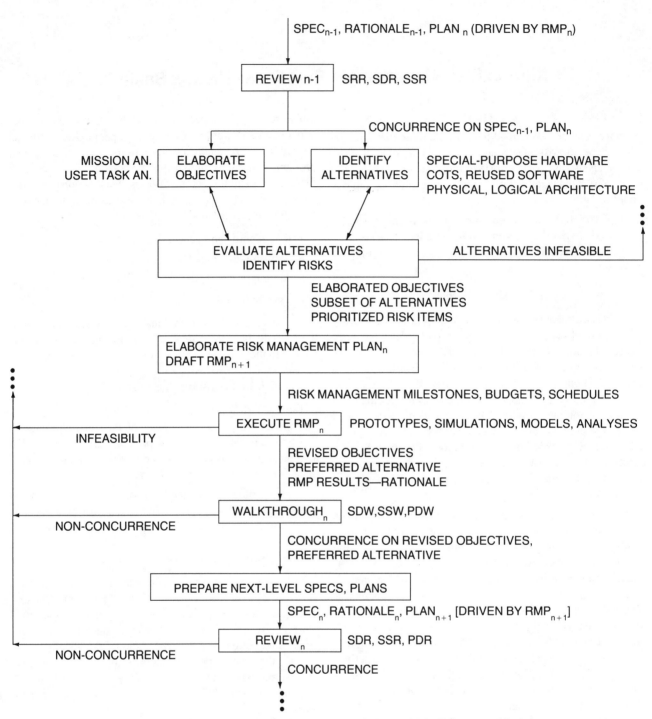

SPEC$_{n-1}$, RATIONALE$_{n-1}$, PLAN$_n$ (DRIVEN BY RMP$_n$)

REVIEW n-1 | SRR, SDR, SSR

CONCURRENCE ON SPEC$_{n-1}$, PLAN$_n$

MISSION AN.
USER TASK AN.

ELABORATE OBJECTIVES

IDENTIFY ALTERNATIVES

SPECIAL-PURPOSE HARDWARE
COTS, REUSED SOFTWARE
PHYSICAL, LOGICAL ARCHITECTURE

EVALUATE ALTERNATIVES
IDENTIFY RISKS

ALTERNATIVES INFEASIBLE

ELABORATED OBJECTIVES
SUBSET OF ALTERNATIVES
PRIORITIZED RISK ITEMS

ELABORATE RISK MANAGEMENT PLAN$_n$
DRAFT RMP$_{n+1}$

RISK MANAGEMENT MILESTONES, BUDGETS, SCHEDULES

EXECUTE RMP$_n$ | PROTOTYPES, SIMULATIONS, MODELS, ANALYSES

INFEASIBILITY

REVISED OBJECTIVES
PREFERRED ALTERNATIVE
RMP RESULTS—RATIONALE

WALKTHROUGH$_n$ | SDW, SSW, PDW

NON-CONCURRENCE

CONCURRENCE ON REVISED OBJECTIVES,
PREFERRED ALTERNATIVE

PREPARE NEXT-LEVEL SPECS, PLANS

SPEC$_n$, RATIONALE$_n$, PLAN$_{n+1}$ [DRIVEN BY RMP$_{n+1}$]

REVIEW$_n$ | SDR, SSR, PDR

NON-CONCURRENCE

CONCURRENCE

Figure 2.1: Integration of Risk Management, Spiral, and DoD Process Models

2.3.1.2: Unrealistic Schedules and Budgets

The number 2 risk item, unrealistic schedules and budgets, happens so often that one might call it a generic software project risk. But most of the particular risk items that cause a project's schedule and budget difficulties are specific to the project and are deserving of special attention in a project's risk assessment and control activities.

Two next-level risk identification checklists for schedule failure and cost failure are shown in Figures 2.2 and 2.3.

These checklists come from an excellent U.S. Air Force guidebook on Software Risk Abatement [AFSC, 1988], which is reproduced in full in this section of the tutorial. If we use these checklists to assess the UniWord project, we note some further risk items that UniWord could have avoided:

1. *Technology experience:* The mouse-and-window WYSIWYG workstation was unfamiliar technology for all of the SoftWizards personnel

116

Table 2.1: A Top Ten Checklist of Software Risk Items

RISK ITEM	RISK MANAGEMENT TECHNIQUES
1. PERSONNEL SHORTFALLS	STAFFING WITH TOP TALENT; JOB MATCHING; TEAMBUILDING; KEY-PERSONNEL AGREEMENTS; TRAINING; PRESCHEDULING KEY PEOPLE
2. UNREALISTIC SCHEDULES AND BUDGETS	DETAILED MULTISOURCE COST AND SCHEDULE ESTIMATION; DESIGN TO COST; INCREMENTAL DEVELOPMENT; SOFTWARE REUSE; REQUIREMENTS SCRUBBING
3. DEVELOPING THE WRONG SOFTWARE FUNCTIONS	ORGANIZATION ANALYSIS; MISSION ANALYSIS; OPS-CONCEPT FORMULATION; USER SURVEYS; PROTOTYPING; EARLY USERS' MANUALS
4. DEVELOPING THE WRONG USER INTERFACE	PROTOTYPING; SCENARIOS; TASK ANALYSIS; USER CHARACTERIZATION (FUNCTIONALITY, STYLE, WORKLOAD)
5. GOLD PLATING	REQUIREMENTS SCRUBBING; PROTOTYPING; COST-BENEFIT ANALYSIS; DESIGN TO COST
6. CONTINUING STREAM OF REQUIREMENTS CHANGES	HIGH CHANGE THRESHOLD; INFORMATION HIDING; INCREMENTAL DEVELOPMENT (DEFER CHANGES TO LATER INCREMENTS)
7. SHORTFALLS IN EXTERNALLY FURNISHED COMPONENTS	BENCHMARKING; INSPECTIONS; REFERENCE CHECKING; COMPATIBILITY ANALYSIS
8. SHORTFALLS IN EXTERNALLY PERFORMED TASKS	REFERENCE CHECKING: PREAWARD AUDITS; AWARD-FEE CONTRACTS; COMPETITIVE DESIGN OR PROTOTYPING; TEAMBUILDING
9. REAL-TIME PERFORMANCE SHORTFALLS	SIMULATION; BENCHMARKING; MODELING; PROTOTYPING; INSTRUMENTATION; TUNING
10. STRAINING COMPUTER SCIENCE CAPABILITIES	TECHNICAL ANALYSIS; COST-BENEFIT ANALYSIS; PROTOTYPING; REFERENCE CHECKING

Table 2.2: Example Risk-Item Checklist: Staffing

- WILL YOUR PROJECT REALLY GET ALL OF THE BEST PEOPLE?
- ARE THERE CRITICAL SKILLS FOR WHICH NOBODY IS IDENTIFIED?
- ARE THERE PRESSURES TO STAFF WITH AVAILABLE WARM BODIES?
- ARE THERE PRESSURES TO OVERSTAFF IN THE EARLY PHASES?
- ARE THE KEY PROJECT PEOPLE COMPATIBLE?
- DO THEY HAVE REALISTIC EXPECTATIONS ABOUT THEIR PROJECT JOB?
- DO THEIR STRENGTHS MATCH THEIR ASSIGNMENT?
- ARE THEY COMMITTED FOR THE DURATION OF THE PROJECT?
- ARE THEY COMMITTED FULL-TIME?
- ARE THEIR TASK PREREQUISITES (TRAINING, CLEARANCES, ETC.) SATISFIED?

SCHEDULE DRIVERS	PROBABILITY		
	IMPROBABLE (0.0 - 0.3)	PROBABLE (0.4 - 0.6)	FREQUENT (0.7 - 1.0)
RESOURCES PERSONNEL	GOOD DISCIPLINE MIX IN PLACE	SOME DISCIPLINES NOT AVAILABLE	QUESTIONABLE MIX AND/OR AVAILABILITY
FACILITIES	EXISTENT, LITTLE OR NO MODIFICATION	EXISTENT, SOME MODIFICATION	NONEXISTENT, EXTENSIVE CHANGES
FINANCIAL	SUFFICIENT BUDGET ALLOCATED	SOME QUESTIONABLE ALLOCATIONS	BUDGET ALLOCATION IN DOUBT

NEED DATES
  THREAT
  ECONOMIC
	VERIFIED PROJECTIONS
	STABLE COMMITMENTS
		SOME UNSTABLE ASPECTS
		SOME UNCERTAIN COMMITMENTS
			RAPIDLY CHANGING
			UNSTABLE, FLUCTUATING COMMITMENTS

POLITICAL GFE/GFP	LITTLE PROJECTED SENSITIVITY AVAILABLE, CERTIFIED	SOME LIMITED SENSITIVITY CERTIFICATION OR DELIVERY QUESTIONS	EXTREME SENSITIVITY UNAVAILABLE AND/OR UNCERTIFIED
TOOLS	IN PLACE, AVAILABLE	SOME DELIVERIES IN QUESTION	UNCERTAIN DELIVERY DATES
TECHNOLOGY AVAILABILITY	IN PLACE	SOME ASPECTS STILL IN DEVELOPMENT	TOTALLY STILL IN DEVELOPMENT
MATURITY EXPERIENCE	APPLICATION VERIFIED EXTENSIVE APPLICATION	SOME APPLICATIONS VERIFIED SOME APPLICATION	NO APPLICATION EVIDENCE LITTLE OR NONE

REQUIREMENTS
  DEFINITION
  STABILITY
	KNOWN, BASELINED
	LITTLE OR NO CHANGE PROJECTED
		BASELINED, SOME UNKNOWNS
		CONTROLLABLE CHANGE PROJECTED
			UNKNOWN, NO BASELINE
			RAPID OR UNCONTROLLED CHANGE

COMPLEXITY	COMPATIBLE WITH EXISTING TECHNOLOGY	SOME DEPENDENCY ON NEW TECHNOLOGY	INCOMPATIBLE WITH EXISTING TECHNOLOGY

REALISTIC, ACHIEVABLE SCHEDULE	POSSIBLE SLIPPAGE IN IOC	UNACHIEVABLE IOC
IMPACT		

Figure 2.2: Quantification of Probability and Impact for Schedule Failure

2. *Requirements definition and stability:* There was no requirements baseline for the UniWord project. The content of components such as the file system changed radically during the project's duration

3. *Personnel:* The UniWord project had weaknesses in all four of the components: availability, mix, experience, and management

4. *Reusable software modifications:* The UniWindow workstation and its system software underwent several considerable changes that impacted the project window management procedures, mouse conventions, etc.

5. *Configuration management:* There were no configuration management controls

Cost models as risk identification checklists: The cost driver factors in software cost-estimation models provide a checklist of risk items that are strongly correlated with cost and schedule increases on past projects. Figure 2.4 summarizes the cost drivers used in each of the major recent software cost-estimation models. This checklist would have picked up some additional UniWord risk items beyond those already identified:

- *Virtual machine experience:* The SoftWizards team's inexperience with the UniWindow type workstation is a source of cost escalation

- *Schedule constraint*: An ambitious delivery schedule such as UniWord's creates additional project costs

COST DRIVERS	PROBABILITY		
	IMPROBABLE (0.0 - 0.3)	PROBABLE (0.4 - 0.6)	FREQUENT (0.7 - 1.0)
REQUIREMENTS SIZE	SMALL, NONCOMPLEX, OR EASILY DECOMPOSED	MEDIUM, MODERATE COMPLEXITY, DECOMPOSABLE	LARGE, HIGHLY COMPLEX, OR NOT DECOMPOSABLE
RESOURCE CONSTRAINTS	LITTLE OR NO HARDWARE-IMPOSED CONSTRAINTS	SOME HARDWARE-IMPOSED CONSTRAINTS	SIGNIFICANT HARDWARE-IMPOSED CONSTRAINTS
APPLICATION	NON-REAL TIME, LITTLE SYSTEM INTERDEPENDENCY	EMBEDDED, SOME SYSTEM INTERDEPENDENCY	REAL-TIME, EMBEDDED, STRONG INTERDEPENDENCY
TECHNOLOGY	MATURE, EXISTENT, IN-HOUSE EXPERIENCE	EXISTENT, SOME IN-HOUSE EXPERIENCE	NEW OR NEW APPLICATION, LITTLE EXPERIENCE
REQUIREMENTS STABILITY	LITTLE OR NO CHANGE TO ESTABLISHED BASELINE	SOME CHANGE IN BASELINE EXPECTED	RAPIDLY CHANGING OR NO BASELINE
PERSONNEL AVAILABILITY	IN PLACE, LITTLE TURNOVER EXPECTED	AVAILABLE, SOME TURNOVER EXPECTED	HIGH TURNOVER, NOT AVAILABLE
MIX	GOOD MIX OF SOFTWARE DISCIPLINES	SOME DISCIPLINES INAPPROPRIATELY REPRESENTED	SOME DISCIPLINES NOT REPRESENTED
EXPERIENCE	HIGH EXPERIENCE RATIO	AVERAGE EXPERIENCE RATIO	LOW EXPERIENCE RATIO
MANAGEMENT	STRONG PERSONNEL	GOOD PERSONNEL	WEAK PERSONNEL
ENVIRONMENT	MANAGEMENT APPROACH	MANAGEMENT APPROACH	MANAGEMENT APPROACH
REUSABLE SOFTWARE AVAILABILITY	COMPATIBLE WITH NEED DATES	DELIVERY DATES IN QUESTION	INCOMPATIBLE WITH NEED DATES
MODIFICATIONS	LITTLE OR NO CHANGE	SOME CHANGE	EXTENSIVE CHANGES
LANGUAGE	COMPATIBLE WITH SYSTEM AND PDSS REQUIREMENTS	PARTIAL COMPATIBILITY WITH PDSS, SOME COMPETITION	INCOMPATIBLE WITH SYSTEM OR PDSS REQUIREMENTS
RIGHTS	COMPATIBLE WITH PDSS AND COMPETITION REQUIREMENTS	PARTIAL COMPATIBILITY WITH PDSS, SOME COMPETITION	INCOMPATIBLE WITH PDSS CONCEPT, NONCOMPETITIVE
CERTIFICATION	VERIFIED PERFORMANCE, APPLICATION COMPATIBLE	SOME APPLICATION-COMPATIBLE TEST DATA AVAILABLE	UNVERIFIED, LITTLE TEST DATA AVAILABLE
TOOLS & ENVIRONMENT FACILITIES	LITTLE OR NO MODIFICATIONS	SOME MODIFICATIONS, EXISTENT	MAJOR MODIFICATIONS, NONEXISTENT
AVAILABILITY	IN PLACE, MEETS NEED DATES	SOME COMPATIBILITY WITH NEED DATES	NONEXISTENT, DOES NOT MEET NEED DATES
RIGHTS	COMPATIBLE WITH PDSS AND DEVELOPMENT PLANS	PARTIAL COMPATIBILITY WITH PDSS AND DEVELOPMENT PLANS	INCOMPATIBLE WITH PDSS AND DEVELOPMENT PLANS
CONFIGURATION MANAGEMENT	FULLY CONTROLLED	SOME CONTROLS	NO CONTROLS

SUFFICIENT FINANCIAL RESOURCES	SOME SHORTAGE OF FINANCIAL RESOURCES, POSSIBLE OVERRUN	SIGNIFICANT FINANCIAL SHORTAGES, BUDGET OVERRUN LIKELY
IMPACT		

Figure 2.3: Quantification of Probability and Impact for Cost Failure

GROUP	FACTOR	SDC, 1965	TRW, 1972	PUTNAM, SLIM	DOTY	RCA, PRICES	IBM	BOEING, 1977	GRC, 1979	COCOMO	SOFCOST	DSN	JENSEN
SIZE ATTRIBUTES	SOURCE INSTRUCTIONS			X	X		X	X		X	X	X	X
	OBJECT INSTRUCTIONS	X	X		X	X							
	NUMBER OF ROUTINES	X				X					X		
	NUMBER OF DATA ITEMS						X			X	X		
	NUMBER OF OUTPUT FORMATS								X			X	
	DOCUMENTATION				X		X				X		X
	NUMBER OF PERSONNEL						X	X			X		X
PROGRAM ATTRIBUTES	TYPE	X	X	X	X	X	X	X			X		
	COMPLEXITY		X	X		X	X			X	X	X	X
	LANGUAGE	X		X				X	X	X	X	X	
	REUSE			X		X		X	X	X	X	X	X
	REQUIRED RELIABILITY					X				X	X		X
	DISPLAY REQUIREMENTS				X						X		X
COMPUTER ATTRIBUTES	TIME CONSTRAINT		X	X	X	X	X	X	X	X	X	X	X
	STORAGE CONSTRAINT		X	X	X	X	X		X	X	X	X	X
	HARDWARE CONFIGURATION	X				X							
	CONCURRENT HARDWARE DEVELOPMENT	X			X	X	X			X	X	X	X
	INTERFACING EQUIPMENT, S/W										X	X	
PERSONNEL ATTRIBUTES	PERSONNEL CAPABILITY					X	X			X	X	X	X
	PERSONNEL CONTINUITY						X					X	
	HARDWARE EXPERIENCE	X		X	X	X	X		X	X	X	X	X
	APPLICATIONS EXPERIENCE		X	X		X	X	X	X	X	X	X	X
	LANGUAGE EXPERIENCE			X		X	X		X	X	X	X	X
PROJECT ATTRIBUTES	TOOLS AND TECHNIQUES			X		X	X	X		X	X	X	X
	CUSTOMER INTERFACE	X					X				X	X	
	REQUIREMENTS DEFINITION	X			X		X				X	X	X
	REQUIREMENTS VOLATILITY	X			X	X	X		X	X	X	X	X
	SCHEDULE			X		X				X	X	X	X
	SECURITY						X				X	X	
	COMPUTER ACCESS			X	X	X	X	X		X	X	X	X
	TRAVEL/REHOSTING/MULTI-SITE	X			X	X					X	X	
	SUPPORT SOFTWARE MATURITY									X		X	
CALIBRATION FACTOR				X		X				X			
EFFORT EQUATION	$MM_{NOM} \cdot C(DSI)^X, X\bullet$		1.0	1.29	1.047		0.91	1.0		1.05-1.2		1.0	1.2
SCHEDULE EQUATION	$t_D \cdot C (MM)^X, X \bullet$			0.333			0.35			0.32-0.38		0.358	0.333

Figure 2.4: Factors Used in Various Cost Models

Besides serving as risk identification checklists, software cost-estimation models provide quantitative estimates of potential overruns, thus making them highly useful as risk analysis tools as well. We will cover this usage in Subsection 2.4.3.2.

2.3.1.3: Requirements Risks

Risk items 3, 4, 5, and 6 in Table 2.1 highlight the importance of software requirements as sources of risk.

1. *Developing the wrong software functions:* Software projects frequently rush into design and development under the assumption that they fully understand the user's requirements. A good many such projects have been completely scrapped because they were built to the wrong requirements, while many others have had to scrap over half of their original code. The risk management tools in the right column in Table 2.1 (e.g., organization analysis, ops-concept formulation, and prototyping) provide a number of valuable capabilities for avoiding or resolving these risks.

2. *Developing the wrong user interface:* A good many other projects did an adequate job on software functionality, but created a very unfriendly user interface. The more fortunate of these projects ended up reworking virtually all of their user interface software; the less fortunate were completely scrapped. This risk item has become increasingly important as more and more software products operate in a user-interactive mode.

3. *Gold-plating:* Many projects assume unnecessary risk by adding complex but marginally useful features to software products. The most frequent causes of gold-plating are marketing speculations, developer ambitions (e.g., the Sam Silver UniWord relational DBMS), and users who say things like, "I'm not sure what features I'm going to need, but if I put everything I can think of into the requirements specification, then what I need will be in there someplace."

4. *Continuing stream of requirements changes:* Some requirements changes are essential, but many are just downstream manifestations of the gold-plating phenomena discussed earlier. Most software projects underestimate the ripple effects that requirements changes have on the project's design, code, testing, documentation, planning and control, configuration management, personnel assignments, management and staff communications, and ultimately on the budget, schedule, and performance. As shown in Table 2.1, key techniques for avoiding these sources of risk are establishing a high threshold for requirements changes; information hiding (anticipating primary sources of change and hiding their effects within individual software modules, thus minimizing the ripple effects of the changes); and use of incremental development (enabling the project to defer many proposed changes to later increments, thus stabilizing the development of the current increment).

Here again, these checklist items identify a number of the UniWord risk items: the assumption that "glass teletype" word processing capabilities would satisfy the users of advanced workstations like the UniWindow; the inadequacy of Universal Micros' high-level functional specifications; the inconsistent user interface across components; and the gold-plating requirements changes involved in the Sam Silver relational DBMS.

2.3.1.4: Shortfalls in External Components and Tasks

External components that can be major sources of risk include:

- Customer-furnished components that may be a poor match to a new application

- Mandated support tools and environments that may be incompatible or poor in performance or functionality

- Commercial components that look great in a vendor brochure and a demo, but turn out to be immature, poorly-supported vaporware.

External tasks that can be major sources of risk include:

- Optimistic statements by customers that they will provide instant turnaround on reviewing and approving the developer's specifications and plans

- Critical-path third-party tasks; legal reviews, procurement approvals, security clearances

- Vendor-product customization and tailoring

- Subcontractor performance versus proposal promises

From the Universal Micros' standpoint, the latter subcontractor issue is the primary risk management area that needed improvement. A pre-award audit based on a questionnaire such as the one in the [Humphrey, 1987] article in this section of the tutorial is one good way to avoid such risks.

2.3.1.5: Performance Shortfalls

Many software projects do not have real-time performance requirements, but many others either neglect the fact that they do have high-performance requirements, or that they unnecessarily create risk items for themselves by skimping on hardware capabilities, by relying on low-performance support software, or by gold-plating the product's performance requirements.

A classic example involved a very large on-line interactive system that supported over 1000 users' access to a huge database. A set of user surveys to determine desired system capabilities led to a response time requirement of 1 second for all queries. This led to a very expensive and risky architecture that involved over 20 intermediate superminis that expedited data around the system. A subsequent prototyping activity determined that virtually all of the users' query needs could be satisfied with a response time of 4 seconds, thus eliminating the need for the expensive, high-risk network architecture. The [Bell, 1987] article in Section 3 provides further performance-risk identification checklists as well as a discussion of performance risk resolution techniques.

2.3.1.6: Straining Computer Science Capabilities

Here again, many projects create high-risk situations for themselves by neglecting to establish whether computer-science technology can meet their stated requirements, or by gold-plating requirements in ways that can turn straightforward software-development projects into high-risk software-research projects. The most common areas of computer-science risk are:

1. *Distributed processing:* Distributed operating systems and data-management systems are still immature, particularly for systems involving heterogeneous processors. Deadlock, race, and synchronization problems do not have efficient and general solutions. Programming language constructs such as CSP and Ada tasking are improvements, but they do not address many distributed-data-processing situations.

2. *Artificial intelligence domains:* Many projects succumb to the temptation to incorporate a pattern-recognition capability, a natural language front end, an expert-system capability, or an AI shell into a system

without any consideration of the relative benefits or risks as compared to a more conventional software approach.

3. *Human-machine performance:* Obtaining well-balanced, synergetic combinations of human and computer performance in such challenging areas as air-traffic control, defense command and control, flight simulators, or other real-time interactive systems involves a high-risk strain on existing knowledge and technology.

4. *Algorithm speed and accuracy:* Complex, high-data rate signal and image processing, computerized tracking and detection systems, complex database-query optimization, and highly parallelized numerical-analysis applications stretch current computer-science capabilities to provide acceptable performance and accuracy.

5. *Information privacy and security protection:* The ability of hackers and penetrators to obtain unauthorized access to information or computer programs creates a high-risk strain on computer-science capabilities to assure selective control of access to sensitive information or systems.

6. *High reliability and fault tolerance:* It is relatively easy to write requirements such as ".999999 reliability" or ".999999 availability" or "graceful degradation" into a software specification, but it is far from easy to achieve (or even define) such requirements with present-day computer science and software fault-tolerance technology.

2.3.2: Decision Driver Analysis

Besides checklists, another good way of identifying potential high-risk software items is to analyze the sources of key decisions on the system. If a decision has been driven by factors other than technical and management achievability, then it will frequently be the source of a critical software-risk item. Some of the most common classes of examples are given in the next few subsections.

2.3.2.1: Politically-Driven Decisions

1. *Choice of equipment:* Has the computer configuration been chosen because it is the best suited for the job, or because of some political connection with the computer vendor? Have the politics of obtaining funding for the project left it with political strings attached to equipment selection that escalate the project's risk?

2. *Choice of subcontractor:* Have subcontractors been chosen based on merit and capability to do the job, or because of some organizational IOU, or political clout in selling the project?

3. *Schedule and budget:* Are these based on a clear assessment of achievability, or on the need to put a system into operation before the next election, board meeting, etc.?

4. *Allocation of responsibilities:* Is the software job divided up (e.g., into configuration items) based on "form follows function" or "encapsulating sources of change" guidelines, or based on organizational (user, customer, or developer) turf considerations?

2.3.2.2: Marketing-Driven Decisions

1. *Gold-plating:* Has the system been encumbered with complex but marginally useful features, based on an unsupported claim that these will increase the software product's sales or customer acceptability?

2. *Choice of equipment:* Has the key equipment been selected based on flashy features (AI, fancy color graphics, raw speed, etc.), or on hardware and software capability to do the job?

3. *Schedule and budget:* Have these been determined by achievability considerations or by marketing considerations (e.g., the UniWord 1984 NCC completion date)?

2.3.2.3: Solution-Driven versus Problem-Driven Decisions

1. *In-house components and tools:* Are these being chosen because they are the best alternatives for the job, or because of Not Invented Here factors, internal marketing pressures, or unawareness of attractive outside alternatives?

2. *Artificial intelligence:* AI can do useful things, but its application has frequently been more solution-driven than problem-driven. A typical example was a logistics productivity improvement effort in which the developers focused on the 2 percent of the system addressable by AI technology, while a high-leverage 80 percent component improvable by conventional database technology was neglected.

3. *Product champions:* Product champions are the key to many positive advances, but also the source of many unnecessary product-risk elements (e.g., the Sam Silver UniWord relational DBMS). A balanced risk-versus-benefit analysis of product-champion solutions is very important.

2.3.2.4: Short-Term versus Long-Term Decisions

1. *Staffing:* In many cases, staffing decisions are made on the basis of which people are available in the short term (usually, the less qualified ones), rather than which people would be best for the project in the long run.

2. *Software reuse:* Often, some available software will be thrown into a software product primarily to show some short-term results. Frequently, this reused software will be flaky and incompatible with the objectives and structure of the rest of the product, creating major life-cycle problems in the long term.

3. *Premature reviews:* Here again, a misguided desire to show some short-term progress will lead a program to establish such early dates for requirements and design reviews that it is impossible to eliminate the major risk items before the requirements and architecture are cast in concrete. Typical examples are 200,000-line software acquisitions by government organizations, with the Software Requirements Review established at 45 days after contract start and Preliminary Design Review established at 90 days.

2.3.3: Assumption Analysis

Many times, major software risk items are hidden behind optimistic assumptions. These arise most frequently from either ignorance about critical issues reflected in non-software people's decisions (accountants, hardware engineers, and user organizations), or from the tendency for software people to avoid conflict. Thus, when pressed to commit to ambitious budgets, schedules, or performance requirements, software people are tempted to say, "Well, we might be able to pull that off if we get all of the best people, if the vendor DBMS is delivered on time with all of the features written up in the brochure, etc." Analyzing these assumptions (or often, just discovering that they were made) is a fruitful source of identifying risks.

2.3.3.1: Comparison with Experience

One effective risk identification technique is to compare software project assumptions with previous experience. For the items mentioned in the earlier example, experience indicates that we generally do not get all of the best people for our project, and that vendor software is often late, full of bugs, and missing advertised features. Other assumptions that bear comparison with experience involve checking the probability that:

1. The reusable software will not require rework.
2. The hardware will be delivered on schedule.
3. The prototype will scale up to large-scale use.
4. The software size is not underestimated.
5. The cost per instruction is consistent with experience for that class of software.

2.3.3.2: Murphy's Law

Murphy's Law states that "If anything can go wrong, it will." As a risk identification device in itself, Murphy's Law is not very effective, since identifying everything on the project as a potential risk item adds no value or information to the situation. However, it can be useful in identifying risks that the software product or project is overoptimized around the nominal or fault-free case. This was one of the top sources of software rework costs in TRW's analysis of high-risk software rework items. Some important product risk items in this regard are shortfalls in backup and recovery capabilities, fault-tolerance features, maintenance and diagnostic software, hardware upgrade capabilities if the workload increases, and performance instrumentation and tuning features.

2.3.4: Decomposition

Another good way to identify risk items is to look within any big, poorly-described blobs to be found within the project's plans and specifications. A frequent phenomenon is for the project personnel to concentrate on the aspects of the system that they best understand or find most technically challenging, and to leave several large, unanalyzed blobs around, with such typical names as "data acquisition," "subcontractor tasks," "DBMS functions," "user interface," or "system integration." These may be simple to develop or perform, but then again they may not. Frequently, they contain serious project risk items: oversimplified problems, complex interactions, major sources of change, or unprepared teams of people. Decomposing these blobs into their constituent elements is a good way to find such risk items.

2.3.4.1: Pareto 80-20 Phenomena

Many software phenomena follow a Pareto distribution: 80 percent of the contribution comes from 20 percent of the contributors. Some frequent examples are:

- 20 percent of the modules contribute 80 percent of the cost
- 20 percent of the modules contribute 80 percent of the errors (not necessarily the same ones)
- 20 percent of the errors cause 80 percent of the down time
- 20 percent of the errors consume 80 percent of the cost to fix
- 20 percent of the modules consume 80 percent of the execution time

It is fairly likely, then, that a large, poorly-described blob will be one of the 20 percent that will cause 80 percent of the project's problems. This has certainly been the case in software cost estimation: one of the best techniques for reducing cost risk is to require the project to perform a further level of breakdown of the 20 percent of the modules contributing 80 percent of the cost.

2.3.4.2: Task Dependencies

A major source of software project schedule risk is the existence of unidentified task dependencies within a poorly-described complex of tasks such as "subcontractor tasks" or "system integration." Decomposing the complex into a PERT chart or task-dependency network will identify many of these schedule risk items. Further detail on this kind of network analysis is provided in Subsection 2.4.2.

One particular source of risk is a task dependency network with high fan-in or high fan-out nodes. Two examples are shown in Figure 2.5. The upper node in Figure 2.5 is an example of a high fan-in node, in which the project has

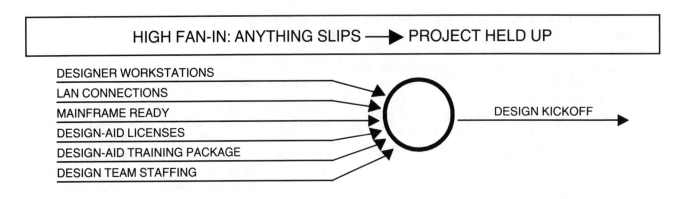

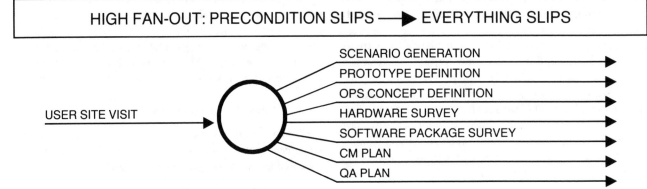

Figure 2.5: High Fan-in or Fan-out Nodes Are a Source of Risk

determined that the design kickoff meeting activity cannot proceed until all of a large number of preceding activities have been completed. Thus, a schedule slip in any of these preceding activities, such as obtaining the licenses and training package for the automated design aid, will slip the schedule of the design kickoff meeting, or throw the project into a high-confusion mode in trying to reorder the activities at the last minute.

It would be preferable to condition the design kickoff meeting start on the completion of its real prerequisites: completion of the contents of the design kickoff briefing, identification of the key issues to be resolved at the meeting, and assembly of the information necessary to resolve the key issues. Use of the design aids should be on a parallel path, with the staffing and training activities preceding the need for all of the hardware and licenses to be in place. If slips in them develop, they should become a key issue in the design kickoff meeting.

The lower node in Figure 2.5 is a similar example of an activity network that has been structured so that many activities cannot start until the completion of a user site visit activity. If the user calls up and says, "We've got a crisis! We can't support your visit for the next six weeks!" then your project will similarly go into high-confusion and schedule-risk mode. We will leave it as a candidate exercise for the reader to restructure this node into a more realistic and lower-risk set of activity dependencies.

2.3.4.3: Uncertainty Areas

One reason that there may be large, poorly-defined blobs in the plans or specifications is that nobody yet understands how to define them. Such situations are certainly strong candidate risk areas to analyze and resolve. Examples of frequent uncertainty areas and unresolved questions are the following:

1. *Mission requirements:* Vague top-level mission statements that the software should support such mission elements as strategic corporate planning, tactical intelligence fusion, optimized personnel planning, or graceful degradation—but with no clear definition of what these are.

2. *Life-cycle concept of operation:* Major unresolved uncertainties such as the lead organization for software maintenance (developer, customer, user, or other); the boundaries between maintenance, incremental development, and preplanned product improvements; system test and evaluation phases and responsibilities; and the degree of software tailoring authorized for user field sites.

3. *System performance drivers:* Uncertainties with respect to which hardware elements will be the primary performance drivers (CPU, main memory, peripherals, communications); software performance-driver

uncertainties (algorithms, data handling, fourth-generation language usage, etc.).

4. *User interface characteristics:* Uncertainties with respect to users' roles within a new mission; potential information overload situations; user differences of opinion on preferred displays or interaction styles; or a number of users saying such things as, "I can't really tell you what I need, but I'll know it when I see it (IKIWISI)."

5. *Interfacing system characteristics:* Uncertainties about whether the interfacing systems are sharing common resources (computers, peripherals, and communications); are sharing common software; are using a common or compatible user-interface approach; or uncertainties about whether the interfacing systems need to mutually resolve application priorities, synchronization, or error handling.

It is easy to let such uncertainty areas persist. However, they frequently become major crises, and, in the meantime, many project commitments are made that will reduce your degrees of freedom in dealing with the crises. Identification of the uncertainty areas as candidate risk items early and their early resolution is a much preferred approach.

2.4: Risk Analysis

Once you have used the risk identification techniques to identify a number of potential risk items, you need to determine how serious they are and what can be done about them. This is the province of risk analysis. In this subsection, we will provide an overview of the most useful risk analysis techniques in the key areas of decision analysis, network analysis, and cost risk analysis. We will also provide some pointers to risk analysis techniques in these and other areas addressed by the tutorial articles included in this volume.

2.4.1: Decision Analysis

One of the fundamental paradigms in risk analysis is the decision tree. The decision tree structures risk situations in terms of the possible decisions one can make, and in terms of the risk exposure factors associated with each decision option. An example is shown in Figure 2.6 in terms of three decision options for creating a geographic database management system (GDBMS): a system supporting not only traditional database transactions but also transactions dealing with spatial information frequently represented on maps. In Figure 2.6, the three decision options are: building a new GDBMS from scratch, reusing some GDBMS modules developed for a similar previous application, and buying a commercial DBMS and modifying it where necessary.

In decision tree analysis, the various options are characterized by their possible outcomes, with their probabilities of occurrence and the resulting cost (or benefit) of each outcome. Thus, for example, the build decision in Figure 2.6 has two possible outcomes. Building the system is estimated to be easy with a probability of 0.4, in which case

the development cost will be $1200K. The probability is estimated to be 0.6 that the job will be hard, in which case the cost will be $1800K.

Given these parameters, we can calculate the total risk exposure (RE) or expected cost of the build option:

$$RE(Build) = 0.4(\$1200K) + 0.6(\$1800K) = \$1560K.$$

We can similarly calculate the total RE for each of the other decision options. As seen in Figure 2.6, the minimum RE of $1400K is achieved by the buy option.

The decision tree paradigm can also be used to analyze the sensitivity of decision options to estimates of the various probabilities or losses. Thus, for example, the probability of the buy option requiring large modifications might have been underestimated. We can calculate that the probability can be as high as 0.450 and still have the buy option be at least as successful as the next-best decision, reuse, which has an RE of $1450K:

$$RE(Buy) = 0.55(\$1000K) + 0.45(\$2000K) = \$1450K.$$

Statistical decision theory: A more generalized decision-oriented risk analysis technique is statistical decision theory, which provides the additional capability to analyze situations that involve the buying of information to reduce risk. It provides a way to characterize the value of information-buying options in terms of the contingent probabilities of the information being correct, given that the system is in a particular state. We can use this information and a powerful equation called Bayes' Formula to calculate the expected values of the possible decisions, and the value of the information acquired to clarify our decision option.

Details of the statistical decision theory paradigm, as it applies to information-buying situations, are provided in the Chapter 20 portion of the tutorial article, "Dealing with Uncertainties, Risk, and the Value of Information" [Boehm, 1981]. This article also includes an example analyzing the relative cost-benefits of different levels of prototyping to buy information about a set of operating system options for a transaction processing system. More details and examples of decision tree analysis are found in the "Risk Assessment Techniques" Handbook [DSMC, 1983] in this tutorial volume, and in such textbooks as Raiffa [Raiffa, 1968] and McCrimmon and Wehrung [McCrimmon-Wehrung, 1986].

2.4.2: Network Analysis

In Subsection 2.3, we identified "unrealistic schedules and budgets" as number 2 in our list of top-10 risk items. We also noted that large, poorly defined blobs in software plans and specifications are likely to contain sources of risk. In the schedule risk area, one of the best techniques for analyzing and reducing this kind of risk is to break down each large schedule blob into an activity network or PERT chart of its constituent tasks.

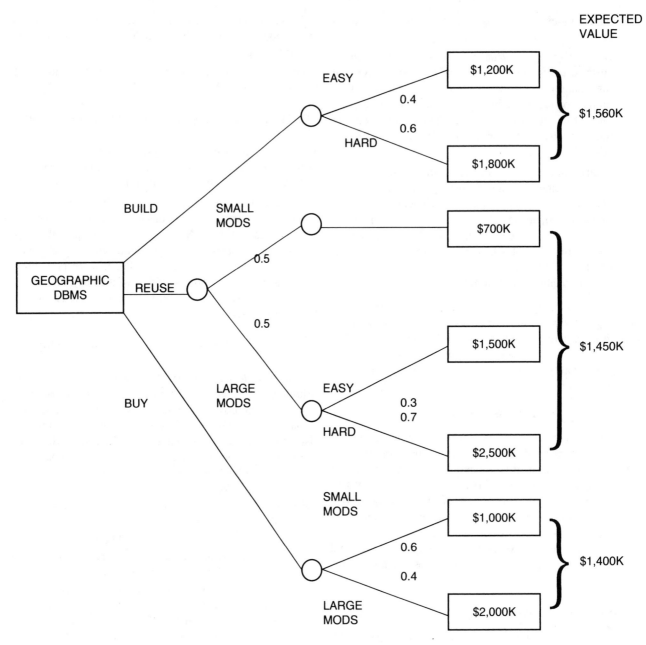

Figure 2.6: Decision Tree Analysis

An example of a PERT chart for a software project is shown in Figure 2.7. The nodes in the network indicate tasks or activities and the number of months each will take. The arrowed lines between the nodes indicate dependency relations; for example, task AP (acceptance plan) cannot start until the tasks upon which it depends—PP (project plan) and RQ (requirements specification)—are complete. The dotted lines in Figure 2.7 indicate the network's critical paths: If tasks on these paths slip their schedule, the overall project will slip its schedule.

Just developing such a PERT chart and understanding task dependencies can create a major risk management benefit in itself. Further, one can analyze various aspects of

the PERT chart for high-risk features. One example, discussed in Subsection 2.3.4.2 was the presence of high fan-in or high fan-out nodes in the network. Another is a multiple critical-path situation, as shown in the incremental development portion of Figure 2.7. Here, slips in any of the multiple critical paths will slip the project's overall schedule.

Another risky item in software PERT charts is the presence of highly overlapped paths. In Figure 2.7, during March-April 1983, the project is simultaneously integrating increment 1, coding increment 2, and designing increment 3. If the integration of increment 1 causes problems that violate the design assumptions of increments 2 and 3, then the project will experience a great deal of design and code

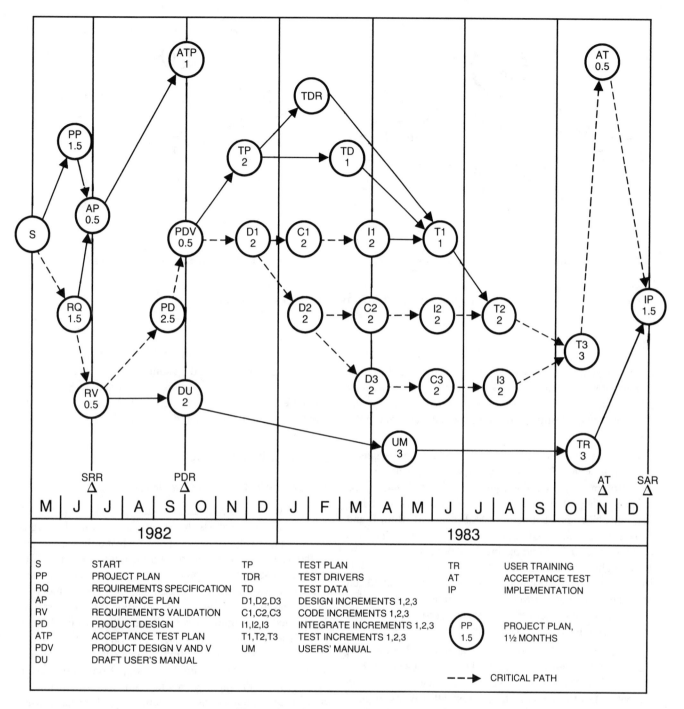

Figure 2.7: Software Project Pert Chart

breakage, confusion, and inefficiency. The effect of the increment 1 problems would be much less serious if the increments were stretched out with less overlap.

Highly overlapped development schedules created to meet unrealistic deadlines are one of the most frequent sources of project schedule risk. One sees them most commonly in project Gantt charts with long, strongly overlapped lines called "design," "code," and "integration and test." (These frequently arise from a project's establishing a fixed deadline, experiencing early slippages, and finding that the

only way to make the project appear to fit its deadline is to put heavy overlaps in the remaining long-duration activities.) Expanding such Gantt charts into PERT charts to analyze the feasibility of such overlaps is often effective in exposing sources of risk and in providing information about how to resolve them.

Probabilistic network analysis: Another quite insidious source of risk in Figure 2.7 is the implicit assumption that the durations of the component tasks are precisely determined. But, as people on software projects have often

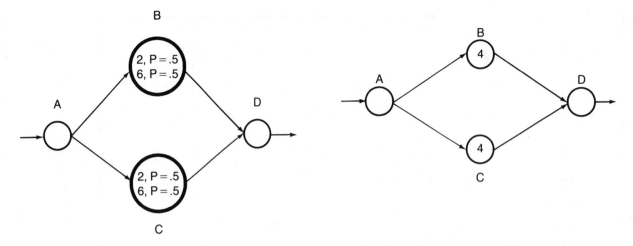

Figure 2.8a: Probabilistic Values   **Figure 2.8b: Expected Values**

Figure 2.8: Are These Two Networks Equivalent?

experienced, these tasks generally go somewhat faster or somewhat slower than predicted. In general, people assume that, if the network analysis uses expected values for the task durations, all of these variations will balance out in the long run.

Alas, desirable as it might be, this assumption is generally untrue. Figure 2.8 shows two network segments that we would often like to treat as equivalent. Figure 2.8a, on the left, shows a portion of a network with two tasks, B and C, that must be completed before task D can start. Both B and C have a probability of 0.5 of completing in 2 months and a probability of 0.5 of completing in 6 months. Figure 2.8b, on the right, shows a simpler network in which the probability distributions of the durations of tasks B and C have been replaced with their expected-value duration of 4 months. This leaves an easy network to analyze; activity D can start 4 months after activity A is complete.

However, if we do a case-by-case analysis of Figure 2.8a, we see that there are four equally likely cases. One-fourth of the time, both B and C will take 2 months, and D can start in 2 months. But for the other three cases, either B or C or both will take 6 months, so D can only start in 6 months. Thus, Ds expected start time is $(0.25)(2) + (0.75)(6) = 5$ months, and we have lost an extra month over the 4-month estimate we made based on expected values of the task durations.

This phenomenon can have even stronger effects on more complex networks. It represents a serious source of schedule risk on software projects, which almost never are aware of its existence. Appendix F of the "Risk Analysis Techniques" article [DSMC, 1983] in this tutorial, discusses more detailed techniques and software packages that deal with probabilistic network analysis. (Subsection 2.4.4.1 also discusses automated risk analysis aids for network and other types of risk analysis.) Even without such sophisticated schedule risk analysis techniques, however, one can guard

against such risks by including some management reserve to compensate for optimistic or highly uncertain task completion times, and by making such tasks high-visibility risk items that can be monitored and highlighted in project reviews.

2.4.3: Cost Risk Analysis

2.4.3.1: Cost Model and Cost Driver Analysis

A software cost-estimation model provides a powerful tool for cost risk analysis. Most software cost models use a series of parameters called cost drivers that describe aspects of the project determined to significantly affect its cost. Example cost drivers are product size, personnel experience and capability, hardware constraints, and use of tools or modern programming practices. Once these parameters are determined for a future software project, the cost model can be used to calculate a reasonably accurate estimate of the project's cost (typically, within 20 percent of the actuals, about 70 percent of the time). Further, if one is uncertain about some of the input parameters, one can use the model to determine the resulting uncertainty or risk in the consequent costs.

An example is provided later in terms of the Intermediate version of the constructive cost model or COCOMO [Boehm, 1981]. Intermediate COCOMO begins by estimating the nominal project effort in man-months as a function of the estimated size of the software product in thousands of delivered source instructions (KDSI). The nominal effort is the amount of effort a project of this size would take if it were perfectly average with respect to the other cost drivers. For the most ambitious type of software project (called an embedded-mode project in COCOMO), the estimating equation for nominal man-months is:

$$MM_{Nom} = 2.8 \, (KDSI)^{1.20}$$

The effects of the project not being perfectly average in all dimensions are then calculated by using Table 2.3. This table shows a set of project effort multipliers as functions of the project's ratings for a set of 15 cost driver variables. For example, a project with high required reliability (e.g., financially-critical software) will require a factor of 1.15 more effort for very thorough testing, analysis, configuration management, and quality assurance. A project with very high required reliability (e.g., life-critical software) will require a factor of 1.40 more effort.

The revised COCOMO man-month estimate is then obtained by multiplying together the individual effort multipliers for each of the cost drivers into an overall effort adjustment factor, and multiplying the nominal man-months by the effort adjustment factor. One can then multiply the estimated project man-months by an average dollar cost per man-month to determine the project's estimated cost.

Example: As an example, suppose we are developing an ambitious microprocessor communications software system. We estimate its size as 50 KDSI, and proceed to rate the project with respect to the other 15 cost drivers in Table 2.3. The results of this rating in terms of effort multipliers and the resulting effort adjustment factor are shown in Table 2.4. This table shows that some of the cost drivers, such as complexity and computer execution time constraint, increase the estimated cost; while others, such as database size and analyst capability, act to reduce the estimated cost. The net result of multiplying all of the effort multipliers together is an effort adjustment factor for the project of 1.17.

We can then compute the nominal man-months and multiply by 1.17 to calculate the estimated effort for the project as:

$$MM = 2.8 (50)^{1.20} (1.17) = 358 \text{ MM}.$$

If our cost per man-month is $10K, the resulting project labor cost is $3,580,000.

At this point, we can do various kinds of risk analysis to determine the effect of uncertainties or sources of risk in the cost drivers on project cost. Suppose, for example, that there was a possibility that the system's size would be more like 60 KDSI than 50 KDSI, and that we would have to staff the project with people whose applications experience and language experience were low instead of nominal (there are objective rating scales for each of these cost driver variables, but they are omitted here for conciseness). The low ratings would change the Figure 1.0 effort multipliers for these cost drivers to 1.13 and Figure 1.07, respectively (see Table 2.3). We could then determine a worst-case man-month estimate to be:

$$MM = 2.8 (60)^{1.20} (1.17) (1.13) (1.07) = 539 \text{ MM},$$

with a resulting dollar cost of $5,390,000, or a 51 percent potential increase in cost or effort.

This is considered to be a worst-case analysis, as it is more likely that only some of the negative possibilities will take place, or that the actual value of the cost driver will be at some intermediate position (e.g., the size might be somewhere between 50 and 60 KDSI). For more sophisticated cost model risk analyses, special tools have been developed for such techniques as Monte Carlo analysis: running the cost model many times, using randomly sampled cost driver rating inputs from user-specified ranges, and compiling the resulting distribution of estimated software costs to determine the probability that the software cost will not exceed a certain value (e.g., the available budget). The RISCOMO tool described in the [Garvey-Powell, 1988] article later in this section of the tutorial operates in this way. The Garvey and Powell article also presents some other cost-risk analysis techniques based on mathematical analysis of the equations used in COCOMO and similar software cost models.

2.4.3.2: Schedule Risk Analysis

Most models such as COCOMO also have a development schedule estimating capability that can be used for risk analysis as well. The COCOMO equation for estimating the project's development time TDEV in months is:

$$TDEV = 2.5 (MM)^{0.32.}$$

If we use the expected and worst-case development man-month estimates given above of 358 and 539 MM in the COCOMO schedule equation, we obtain development schedule estimates of 16.4 and 18.7 months, respectively. We can then compare these with each other and with estimates of the project's schedule from other sources to determine the relative risk of the project's not completing within its available schedule.

The COCOMO schedule estimates previously mentioned are for the project's nominal or unaccelerated schedule. As may be seen on the bottom line of Table 2.3, COCOMO has a cost driver for schedule acceleration. A very low schedule rating involves compressing the schedule to 75 percent of its nominal value, but only at a 23 percent increase in cost. Based on the fact that virtually none of the projects in the COCOMO database were able to reduce their schedule to less than 75 percent of nominal, COCOMO considers such overambitious schedules to be in an unachievable "impossible zone." Thus, reducing the original schedule for the communications processor software project from 16 to 12 months would be a barely feasible high-risk item, while reducing it to 9 months should trigger some type of risk avoidance activity such as reducing functionality or incremental development.

2.4.4: Other Risk Analysis Techniques

A major source of requirements risk involves setting requirements for the software not only to satisfy functional

Table 2.3: Software Development Effort Multipliers

COST DRIVERS	RATINGS					
	VERY LOW	LOW	NOMINAL	HIGH	VERY HIGH	EXTRA HIGH
PRODUCT ATTRIBUTES						
RELY: REQUIRED SOFTWARE RELIABILITY	0.75	0.88	1.00	1.15	1.40	
DATA: DATABASE SIZE		0.94	1.00	1.08	1.16	
CPLX: PRODUCT COMPLEXITY	0.70	0.85	1.00	1.15	1.30	1.65
COMPUTER ATTRIBUTES						
TIME: EXECUTION TIME CONSTRAINT			1.00	1.11	1.30	1.66
STOR: MAIN STORAGE CONSTRAINT			1.00	1.06	1.21	1.56
VIRT: VIRTUAL MACHINE VOLATILITY*		0.87	1.00	1.15	1.30	
TURN: COMPUTER TURNAROUND TIME		0.87	1.00	1.07	1.15	
PERSONNEL ATTRIBUTES						
ACAP: ANALYST CAPABILITY	1.46	1.19	1.00	0.86	0.71	
AEXP: APPLICATIONS EXPERIENCE	1.29	1.13	1.00	0.91	0.82	
PCAP: PROGRAMMER CAPABILITY	1.42	1.17	1.00	0.86	0.70	
VEXP: VIRTUAL MACHINE EXPERIENCE*	1.21	1.10	1.00	0.90		
LEXP: PROGRAMMING LANGUAGE EXPERIENCE	1.14	1.07	1.00	0.95		
PROJECT ATTRIBUTES						
MODP: USE OF MODERN PROGRAMMING PRACTICES	1.24	1.10	1.00	0.91	0.82	
TOOL: USE OF SOFTWARE TOOLS	1.24	1.10	1.00	0.91	0.83	
SCED: REQUIRED DEVELOPMENT SCHEDULE	1.23	1.08	1.00	1.04	1.10	

* FOR A GIVEN SOFTWARE PRODUCT, THE UNDERLYING VIRTUAL MACHINE IS THE COMPLEX OF HARDWARE AND SOFTWARE (OS, DBMS, ETC.) IT CALLS ON TO ACCOMPLISH ITS TASKS.

Table 2.4: Cost Driver Ratings: Microprocessor Communications Software

COST DRIVER	SITUATION	RATING	EFFORT MULTIPLIER
RELY	LOCAL USE OF SYSTEM. NO SERIOUS RECOVERY PROBLEMS	NOMINAL	1.00
DATA	20,000 BYTES	LOW	0.94
CPLX	COMMUNICATIONS PROCESSING	VERY HIGH	1.30
TIME	WILL USE 70% OF AVAILABLE TIME	HIGH	1.11
STOR	45K OF 64K STORE (70%)	HIGH	1.06
VIRT	BASED ON COMMERCIAL MICROPROCESSOR HARDWARE	NOMINAL	1.00
TURN	TWO-HOUR AVERAGE TURNAROUND TIME	NOMINAL	1.00
ACAP	GOOD SENIOR ANALYSTS	HIGH	0.86
AEXP	THREE YEARS	NOMINAL	1.00
PCAP	GOOD SENIOR PROGRAMMERS	HIGH	0.86
VEXP	SIX MONTHS	LOW	1.10
LEXP	TWELVE MONTHS	NOMINAL	1.00
MODP	MOST TECHNIQUES IN USE OVER ONE YEAR	HIGH	0.91
TOOL	AT BASIC MINICOMPUTER TOOL LEVEL	LOW	1.10
SCED	NINE MONTHS	NOMINAL	1.00
EFFORT ADJUSTMENT FACTOR (PRODUCT OF EFFORT MULTIPLIERS)			1.17

requirements but also to satisfy specified *properties:* performance, reliability, availability, maintainability, ease of use, portability, etc. All of these need to be analyzed as potential risk items, as they are easy to overspecify and easy to delay dealing with until it is too late to handle them effectively. Most are difficult to analyze because there is a shortage of quantitative tools and techniques for them (e.g., maintainability and portability). For others, however, there are growing capabilities for analyzing risk items.

For performance risk analysis, such techniques as simulation, benchmarking, modeling, prototyping, instrumentation, and tuning are effective. The [Bell, 1987] and [Swinson, 1985] articles in this tutorial expand on them in more detail. For reliability, availability, and safety analysis, such techniques as checklists, hierarchical design, fault tree analysis, failure mode and effect analysis, and static and dynamic analysis of specifications and programs are effective. The [Cha et al., 1988] and [Neumann, 1986] articles in this tutorial and the [Leveson, 1986] survey article on software safety provide more information on them. For ease of use, prototyping techniques such as those covered in the [Carey-Mason, 1983], [Wasserman et al., 1986], and [Mantei-Teorey, 1988] articles in this tutorial and the more detailed human-computer interface treatments in [Heckel, 1984] and [Smith et al., 1986] provide much valuable information.

For further information on the significant overall problem of specifying, analyzing, and satisfying required software properties, see [Boehm et al., 1978], [Bowen-Wigle-Tsai, 1985], and [Gilb, 1988].

2.4.4.1: Automated Risk Analysis Aids

There are a number of software packages available that calculate schedule, cost, and technical risk quantities based on the user's estimates of the probabilities and criticalities of the project's constituent elements. Schedule risk calculations generally assume a PERT network model, accept probability distributions for the duration of each activity in the network, and use a Monte Carlo approach to run a sequence of possible critical-path schedule outcomes to approximate the probability distribution of the overall project schedule. The cost and technical risk calculations use a similar Monte Carlo approach, but also need the user to define how the component cost and technical risk quantities combine together (additively, multiplicatively, maximum of several candidates, etc.).

Immediately following is a summary, in alphabetical order, of some of the leading candidate risk analysis software packages, based on a 1988 comparative analysis. The usual caveat that software packages evolve rapidly, and that comparative evaluations become progressively less accurate, should be heeded here. Each package below handles schedule, cost, and technical risk estimations, although technical risk analysis is done by the packages in different ways.

- PROMAP V, from LOG/AN, Inc., is a heavyweight program operating on large mainframes. It estimates

technical risk in a somewhat restricted way, as a function of the cost and schedule probability distributions

- PROSIM, from Venture Analytical Associates, is a follow-on to the Army VERT model. It has powerful network modeling capabilities and a flexible approach to modeling cost-schedule-technical relationships

- RISNET, from John M. Cockerham Associates, has strong network logic capabilities. Its approach to technical risk estimation has restrictions similar to those of PROMAP V. RISNET has both a mainframe and a PC capability

- SLAM, from Pritsker and Associates, has powerful network capabilities and flexible cost-schedule-technical risk analysis relationships

In addition, there are several PC-based packages with generally more limited capabilities but lower prices, such as Opera/Open Plan (Welcom Software Technology), PRISM (Tempus Development Corp.), and REP (Decision Sciences, Inc.). Most of the risk analysis packages interoperate with one or more commercial project management support packages.

2.5: Risk Prioritization

The basic concepts of risk prioritization were covered in Subsection 1.4.4.1 on risk exposure (RE), Subsection 1.4.4.2 on risk reduction leverage (RRL), and Subsection 1.4.4.3 on using risk exposure to prioritize risk items. Here, we will cover two complementary topics: assessing risk probabilities and dealing with compound risks.

One of the risks you may encounter after a thorough risk identification activity is that you identify so many potential risk items that you become paranoid and fall into an "analysis paralysis" state, dedicated more to analyzing and worrying about risk items than with getting on with the job. Avoiding this sort of risk is the primary function of risk prioritization. Risk prioritization should actually be going on concurrently with risk identification and risk analysis, so that low-risk areas receive less risk-identification effort and so that low-priority risk items are not overanalyzed.

The overall end result of the risk prioritization activity is to produce a prioritized list of risk items to be addressed by the risk control functions of risk management planning, risk reduction, and risk monitoring.

2.5.1: Assessing Risk Probabilities

Occasionally, you will find situations with enough information that you will be able to calculate risk probabilities directly (e.g., computer availability records, communication line bit-error rates, etc.). In general, however, these probabilities can be only subjectively estimated. One approach to risk probability estimation is the relative scale-of-10 technique discussed in Subsection 1.4.4. Some other approaches are betting analogies, adjective calibration, and Delphi or other group consensus techniques.

The *betting analogy* involves establishing a personally meaningful sum of money (say, $100), establishing a set of betting odds for the occurrence of a satisfactory outcome, and determining whether or not you would be willing to take the bet. For example, suppose that the satisfactory outcome is: "Using Ada will not cause the project to slip its schedule," and the terms of the bet are:

- No schedule slip: you win $100
- Schedule slip: you lose $200

Would you be willing to take this bet?

If you are willing to take the bet, this means that you believe that the Prob(UO) of a schedule slip due to using Ada is less than 0.33. If not, you believe that the probability is higher. By changing the odds on the bet, and seeing which bets you would be willing to take, you can establish a reasonably good range for the probability of the schedule slip. Frequently, also, the immediacy of the betting situation will cause you to identify further risk analysis or risk resolution options such as the need to buy further information on the stability, robustness, vendor support, functionality, and performance of the Ada support environment before making your bet.

Adjective calibration involves using various adjectives connoting levels of probability to obtain judgments on risk item probabilities. For example, you might ask an expert or a group of people whether a risk-significant event is "almost certain," "probable," "likely," "improbable," or "highly unlikely" to happen. Figure 2.9 shows the results of an adjective calibration activity given in [DSMC, 1983] to relate these adjectives to probability estimates. Note that although there is reasonable consensus on the overall location of these adjectives on the probability scale, the location is not precise and is likely to vary significantly from one person to another.

Delphi or group consensus techniques involve getting groups of people to discuss and converge on probability estimates in various more-or-less structured ways. The Delphi approach involves successive rounds of individual estimates, interspersed with feedback on others' estimates and written or verbal discussion of the rationale behind people's estimates, particularly the outlying ones. It frequently results in some convergence of people's estimates. These techniques can be used in conjunction with any of the other probability estimation techniques discussed.

2.5.2: Dealing with Compound Risks

Another risk-assessment risk is that you will treat risk items as independent entities, when actually they are closely coupled in a way that produces a much more serious combined risk exposure than the sum of their individual risk exposures. Some examples are:

- *Pushing technology on more than one front:* An extreme example would be to incorporate an expert-system pilot's associate program into the inner loop of a high-performance, ultra-reliable avionics system with untried, state-of-the-art computer hardware

- *Pushing technology with key staff shortages:* An example from our UniWord case study is SoftWizards' approach to advanced workstation word-processing systems

- *Meeting vague user requirements on an ambitious schedule:* Again, UniWord is a good example: the contract schedule provided little time to prototype or otherwise determine user requirements

- *Untried hardware with an ambitious schedule:* Here, hardware changes and delays are highly likely to compromise the schedule

- *Unstable interfaces with an untried subcontractor:* In the UniWord situation, Universal Micros' hardware and system changes might have worked out all right with a familiar, experienced subcontractor, but not with SoftWizards

The best approach to compound risks is to reduce them to non-compound risks if at all possible. Otherwise, these compound risks should be at the top of your risk prioritization list for extra attention in the risk control phase.

2.6: Risk Control

Risk control follows the classic closed-loop control approach shown in Figure 2.10. Our previous risk assessment steps produce a prioritized list of risk items needing resolution. The risk management planning step produces a coordinated plan for resolving the risk items and integrates the risk management plan with the overall project plan. Next, the risk resolution steps are executed according to the schedules in the risk management plan. They are then monitored with respect to the risk resolution milestones, and also highlighted at the project's periodic upper-management reviews.

The risk monitoring activity can identify four possible situations, as may be seen in Figure 2.10:

1. The risk item is resolved, completing its risk resolution task.

2. The risk resolution activities are tracking the risk management plan, in which case the risk resolution activities continue as planned.

3. Some risk resolution activities are not tracking the risk management plan, in which case corrective action measures are determined and implemented.

4. The situation changes significantly with respect to one or more risk items. This involves a reassessment of the risks and often a replanning activity.

Each situation produces a somewhat different pattern of operation back through the risk management planning and risk resolution steps. Thus, as with the three risk assessment steps, the three risk control steps are generally not performed in a purely sequential order.

STATEMENT

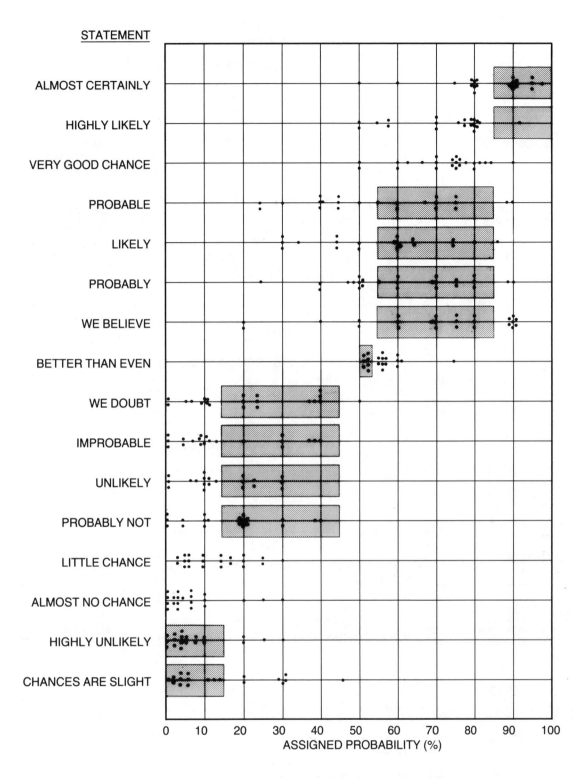

Figure 2.9: What Uncertainty Statements Mean to Different   Readers

133

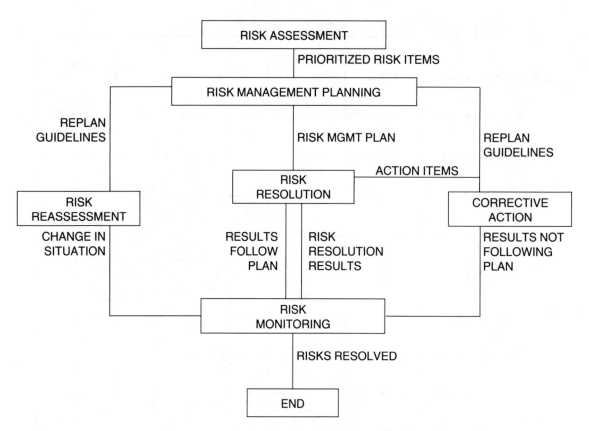

Figure 2.10: Risk Management Control Loop

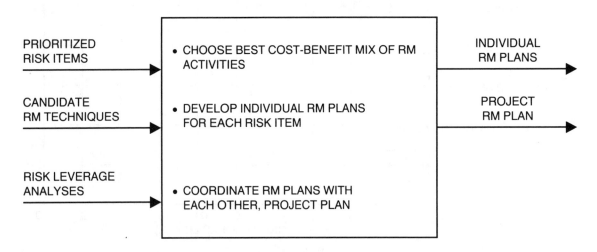

Figure 2.11: Risk Management (RM) Planning Process

The next three subsections expand on the techniques involved in the three risk control elements: risk management planning, risk resolution, and risk monitoring. As the tutorial material on risk resolution techniques is fairly extensive, it is discussed and presented in a separate section of this tutorial (Section 3).

2.7: Risk Management Planning

This subsection begins with a discussion of the overall risk management planning process. It then presents a simple standard form for individual risk management plans, provides an example of the form's use, and discusses the process of coordinating individual risk management plans with each other and with the overall project plan.

2.7.1: Risk Management Planning Process

An overview of the risk management planning process is provided in Figure 2.11. The inputs to the process are:

- The list of prioritized risk items resulting from the risk assessment process

- The candidate risk resolution techniques considered in determining the RRL quantities for each risk item

- The results of the RRL cost-benefit analyses, indicating the levels of budget, schedule, or other scarce resources required to achieve the corresponding reductions in RE

The steps in the risk management planning process are presented sequentially in the box in Figure 2.11, but actually they proceed in a highly concurrent and interactive fashion. The first step, *choosing the best cost-benefit mix of risk resolution activities,* has to some extent already been performed during the risk prioritization process. However, the second step, *developing individual risk management plans for each risk item,* will provide more precise information about the resources necessary to perform each risk resolution activity, and about the value of its results. This information may alter the cost-benefit relations and the resulting risk item priorities. And the third step, *coordinating individual risk management plans with each other and with the project plan,* will often identify cost-effective ways to combine individual risk resolution tasks; sources of conflict for scarce resources (e.g., key people); and needs to rework the risk management plans and the overall project plan when these are in conflict.

An example of the latter would be a situation in which the schedule for developing and exercising a prototype to determine key system requirements will take 4 months, while the schedule in the project plan only allows 2 months for producing the definitive system requirements specification.

Since the risk management planning process is also strongly intertwined with the process of determining the system's requirements and architecture, it is likely that additional system objectives, constraints, and alternatives will surface during the risk management planning process, requiring some further backtracking to the risk assessment

process. It is also valuable to review the risk management plan to ensure that the most effective techniques possible are being used to resolve the risk items. The checklist of top-10 risk items and their corresponding risk resolution techniques (Table 2.1) is a valuable guide for reviewing risk management plans; see Section 3 on risk resolution techniques for a discussion of its key elements.

2.7.2: Risk Management Plan Formulation and Coordination

To many people, the word "plan" conjures up a vision of a thick, ponderous document with a large number of hard-to-remember sections. Plans don't have to be this way; in fact, the best plans emphasize conciseness and decision content rather than generalized "boilerplate."

The outline presented in Table 2.5 for a risk management plan follows this concise, easy-to-remember, decision-oriented philosophy. It organizes the risk management plan (or any other type of plan as well) into five major sections, which serve to answer the familiar common set of interrogatives we all learn in our first few years of school: why, what, when, who, where, how, and how much? Answering these questions provides the essential decision information we need for a plan, allows the length and formality of the answers to be tailored to the situation (risk-driven!), and organizes the information in a way that is easy to find and remember.

Table 2.6 shows an example of an individual risk management plan covering the development, exercise, and iteration of a prototype what-you-see-is-what-you-get (WYSI-WYG) word-processor user interface which could have been used in the UniWord case study to resolve the key word-processor user-interface risk items. The 10-week schedule for the prototyping effort was determined on the basis of engineering judgment to be long enough to create and exercise a representative prototype addressing the major risk issues, but not so long as to compromise the required delivery schedule for (a viable initial increment of) the UniWord product.

Note that although the plan requires only one page, it provides enough information to serve as the basis of monitoring milestone progress (specific milestone events at weeks 3, 7, and 10); identifying responsibility for each of the 10 identified tasks; and establishing what resources are being allocated to implement the various portions of the plan.

The *project risk management plan* consists of each of the individual risk management plans, plus an overview showing how the individual plans fit together with each other and with the overall project plan. Depending on the project's size and criticality, the project risk management plan may consist of a set of briefing charts, a section of the project plan, or a standalone document. Or, it may consist of a series of risk management plans, one for each of the project's major phases. The most important thing is that the risk management plan be used to drive the budget and

Table 2.5: Risk Management Plan Outline

> # FOR EACH RISK ITEM, ANSWER THE FOLLOWING QUESTIONS
>
> 1. WHY?
>   RISK ITEM IMPORTANCE, RELATION TO PROJECT OBJECTIVES
>
> 2. WHAT, WHEN?
>   RISK RESOLUTION DELIVERABLES, MILESTONES, ACTIVITY NETS
>
> 3. WHO, WHERE?
>   RESPONSIBILITIES, ORGANIZATION
>
> 4. HOW?
>   APPROACH (PROTOTYPES, SURVEYS, MODELS, . . .)
>
> 5. HOW MUCH?
>   RESOURCES (BUDGET, SCHEDULE, KEY PERSONNEL)

Table 2.6: Example Risk Management Plan: Uniword WYSIWYG Editor Product Features

> **OBJECTIVES (WHY?)**
> - DETERMINE WYSIWYG EDITOR PRODUCT FEATURES
> - CREATE PROJECT-COMPATIBLE WYSIWYG DEVELOPMENT PLAN
>
> **DELIVERABLES AND MILESTONES (WHAT, WHEN?)**
> - BY WEEK 3:
>   1—TECHNICAL EVALUATION OF EXISTING WYSIWYG PRODUCTS
>   2—USER EVALUATION OF EXISTING WYSIWYG PRODUCTS
>   3—ASSESSMENT OF REUSABLE COMPONENTS
>   4—STRAWMAN PRODUCT FEATURE DESCRIPTION
>
> - BY WEEK 7:
>   5—OPERATING PROTOTYPE WITH KEY USER FEATURES
>   6—STRAWMAN DEVELOPMENT PLAN
>   7—REPRESENTATIVE USERS TO EXERCISE PROTOTYPE
>
> - BY WEEK 10:
>   8—USER EVALUATION; ITERATION OF PROTOTYPE
>   9—REVISED PRODUCT FEATURE DESCRIPTION
>   10—REVISED DEVELOPMENT PLAN
>
> **RESPONSIBILITIES (WHO, WHERE?)**
> - SYSTEM ENGINEER   : TASKS 4, 6, 9, 10
> - MARKETING MANAGER   : TASKS 2, 7, 8a
> - LEAD PROGRAMMER   : TASKS, 1, 5, 8b; SUPPORT TASKS 6, 10
> - PROTOTYPE PROGRAMMER: TASK 3; SUPPORT TASKS 1, 5, 8b
>
> **APPROACH (HOW?)**
>
> - DESIGN-TO-SCHEDULE PROTOTYPING EFFORT
> - EMPHASIZE REUSE, STANDARD INTERFACES
> - USE C LANGUAGE, SHELL SCRIPTS WHERE FEASIBLE
>
> **RESOURCES (HOW MUCH?)**
>
> - DEDICATED S.E., L.P., P.P. (10 WK) (3 FSP) ($2/FSP—WK) $60K
> - M.M. DEDICATED IN WKS 1-3, 8-9; PROVIDED BY SOFTWARE HOUSE   0
> - 4 DEDICATED UNIWINDOW WORKSTATIONS: PROVIDED BY U. MICRO   0
> - 2 DEDICATED, 2 PART-TIME USERS IN WKS 8-9; PROVIDED BY M. MANAGER   0
> - CONTINGENCIES   20K
> $80K

schedule parameters of the overall project plan, particularly in the early phases, so that there is enough time and effort available to resolve risk items early before they become major project crises.

Larger software projects tend to have more formalized risk management plans and approaches. Frequently, they will establish such mechanisms as:

- A project risk management director, typically a senior member of the project's system analysis group, who is responsible for the risk management planning and control process and its integration with the project planning and control process

- A project risk resolution board, typically chaired by the project manager and composed of the project's senior managers, which meets on a regular schedule (typically biweekly or monthly) to monitor risk resolution progress and to prioritize newly-surfaced risk items

- A risk management working group, involving the project and representatives of the customer, user, and other interested parties, which reviews and prioritizes risk items and risk resolution activities as they affect the project's external aspects (completion budgets and schedules, product functionality, performance, or interfaces)

Large projects typically also have risk item-tracking forms and manual or automated systems for keeping forms up to date and for summarizing the project's risk resolution status. Two examples of such forms are provided in Tables 2.7 and 2.8. Table 2.7 is a less formal, single-page form suitable for most projects; Table 2.8 is a much more extensive and structured form suitable for very large or complex projects.

2.8: Risk Resolution

This subsection presents a summary discussion of the risk resolution process. An overview of the key risk resolution techniques and detailed tutorial articles on selected risk resolution techniques are presented in Section 3.

Fundamentally, the risk resolution process involves executing the risk management plan: communicating objectives, establishing responsibilities, and performing to satisfy the milestone criteria in the plan.

Particularly in the risk management area, however, it is important to strike a balance between controlled performance to milestone schedules and not following the risk management plan too slavishly. Risk involves a certain amount of unpredictability, and often you can find unanticipated solutions for risk items:

- A top person may become available who can make a big difference in resolving several critical risk items, if you can redistribute some of the risk resolution tasks

- Performers may discover some reusable or commercial off-the-shelf (COTS) software that can resolve some technical, budget, or schedule risk items

- A faster processor may become available to resolve performance risk items

In striking the balance between plan-compliance and opportunity-exploitation, it is also important not to be hasty in jumping to an attractive-looking new solution. The new processor may be as fast as the wind, but it also may be less stable, weaker with respect to support software, or unfamiliar to your project team.

A further key point in the risk resolution process is to ensure that the planning and control framework is maintained whenever a new risk resolution opportunity is exercised. This is another reason not to overburden your risk management plans with hard-to-modify paperwork and boilerplate.

2.9: Risk Monitoring

The final step in the risk control process involves monitoring progress on resolving risk items and taking the appropriate actions indicated in Figure 2.10 to ensure that risk control is a closed-loop process. This subsection describes the major risk monitoring approaches: risk management plan milestone tracking, project plan milestone tracking, and, most significantly, regular top-10 project risk item tracking. It concludes with a discussion of risk reassessment and its appropriate consequences.

Risk management plan milestone tracking involves the straightforward monitoring of the milestones in each individual risk item's risk management plan, and any aggregate project risk management milestones as well. For example, consider the process of monitoring progress with respect to the UniWord user interface prototype risk management plan in Table 2.6. One would hold a milestone review at the end of week 3 to verify that the week-3 completion items (technical evaluation, user evaluation, reuse assessment, and strawman product feature description) have indeed been successfully completed, and that all of the prerequisites for successfully completing the week-7 completion items are satisfied. If any of these conditions are not satisfied, then an appropriate course of corrective action must be determined and effected.

For example, if the strawman product description is not complete, a short (1-2 day) special effort should be scheduled to provide the prototype developers with all of the product-description information they need to create the prototype. Also, some of the contingency funds should be used to provide the system engineer with some help in completing both the strawman product description and the strawman development plan.

Project plan milestone tracking involves monitoring progress in completing those risk management milestones that coincide with overall project plan milestones. Due to their criticality to project success, these items should be highlighted in the milestone reviews. A particularly important project milestone review is the preliminary design review (PDR), since the resolution of all major risk items by PDR is a strong precondition for efficient product development.

Table 2.7: One-Page Risk Item Tracking Form

RISK IDENTIFIER				STATUS	DATE
SEVERITY	SCHEDULE RISK	TECHNICAL RISK	COST RISK	NUMBER/REVISIONS	

RISK ITEM DESCRIPTION

_____

SUBMITTED BY

MITIGATION PLAN

START DATE _____

COMPLETION DATE _____

ACCEPTANCE

_____

RESPONSIBLE MANAGER

MITIGATION PLAN STATUS

CLOSEOUT APPROVAL _____

RISK REVIEW BOARD CHAIRMAN

Table 2.8: Two-Page Risk Item Tracking Form (Page 1)

RISK IDENTIFICATION	
RISK IDENTIFIER:	DATE OPENED:
STATUS:	LAST UPDATED:
RISK ITEM DESCRIPTION:	
	SUBMITTER:
PRIORITY (TIMING, IMPACT):	

RISK ASSESSMENT	
RISK ASSESSMENT LEADER:	STAFF:
START DATE:	DUE DATE:
MILESTONES:	
INTERIM REPORT:	
	DATE:
IMPACT ASSESSMENT:	
	COMPLETION DATE:

RISK MITIGATION STUDY	
STUDY LEADER:	STAFF:
START DATE:	DUE DATE:
MILESTONES:	
INTERIM REPORT:	
	DATE:
MITIGATION OPTION 1	
MITIGATION OPTION 2	
MITIGATION OPTION N	

Table 2.8: Two-Page Risk Item Tracking Form (Page 2)

RISK REDUCTION PLAN		
RISK REDUCTION LEADER:	STAFF:	
REDUCTION PLAN:		
REDUCTION SCHEDULE:		
REDUCTION BUDGET:		
ABATEMENT STATUS 1:	DATE:	
ABATEMENT STATUS 2:	DATE:	
ABATEMENT STATUS N:	DATE:	
RISK CLOSEOUT APPROVAL DATE:		

2.9.1: Project Top-10 Risk Item Tracking

One of the most significant contributions of risk management to overall project management is the technique of top-10 risk item tracking, which focuses periodic management reviews of the project on the progress in resolving the project's top-10 risk items. (The number could be 7 or 12 without any change in intent or effectiveness.) This technique involves the following steps:

- Ranking the project's most significant risk items.
- Establishing a regular schedule of reviewing the project's progress by higher management. The review should be chaired by the equivalent of the project manager's boss. For large projects (over 20 persons), the reviews should be held monthly. For smaller, fast-track projects such as UniWord, a weekly project review is more appropriate
- Beginning the project review with a summary of progress on the top-10 risk items. The summary should include each risk item's current top-10 ranking, its rank at the previous review, the number of times it has been on the top-10 list, and a summary of progress in resolving the risk item since the previous review
- Focusing the project review on dealing with any problems in resolving the risk items

The use of the project top-10 list is best explained via an example. Figure 2.12 shows how a project top-10 list could have been working for the UniWord project, as of week 3 of the project. The project's top-risk item is the difficulty of prioritizing UniWord capabilities to fit the available development schedule. Even with considerable work, it has remained the project's top risk item, and it continues to require full management attention in coordinating priorities with customer management at Universal Micros.

The number 2 risk item, up from number 4, is another that requires careful coordination with Universal Micros' management: A reversal of previous progress in resolving some critical uncertainties in the interfaces between Universal Micros' software and UniWord software. SoftWizards' management needs to nip this negative trend in the bud, and to sensitize Universal Micros' management about the risks to their success of unstable interface definitions.

As shown in Figure 2.12, some risk items are going down in priority or going off the list, while others are escalating upward or coming onto the list. The ones going down the list, such as the staffing items and the UniWord performance risks, still need to be monitored but frequently do not need further management action. The ones going up or onto the list, such as the delay in Universal Micros' workstation deliveries and the reusable software item, are generally the

THIS WEEK	LAST WEEK	WEEKS ON LIST	RISK ITEM	RISK RESOLUTION PROGRESS
1	1	3	SCOPING PRODUCT TO FIT REQUIRED SCHEDULE	FILE MANAGER PRIORITIES COORDINATED WITH UNIVERSAL MICROS
2	4	3	RESOLVING U-MICROS OS INTERFACE UNCERTAINTIES	NEW CHARGES PROPOSED BY UNIVERSAL MICROS
3	2	3	WYSIWYG WORD PROCESSOR FEATURES	PROTOTYPE ON SCHEDULE
4	6	2	WORKSTATION AVAILABILITY	DELAY IN UMICRO DELIVERIES BEING WORKED
5	5	3	UNI WORD USER INTERFACE DEFINITION	USER STUDY COMPLETE; AWAITING PROTOTYPING RESULTS
6	3	3	STAFFING LEAD DEVELOPER FOR FILE MANAGER	CANDIDATE IDENTIFIED; BEING NEGOTIATED
7	—	1	REUSABLE TEXT-FORMATTING SOFTWARE UNCERTAINTIES	EVALUATION UNDERWAY
8	7	3	UNI WINDOW PERFORMANCE RISKS	BENCHMARK RUNS OK; ALMOST COMPLETE
9	9	2	CONFIG. MGMT. PROCEDURES FOR INCREMENTAL DEVEL.	CM PROCEDURES IDENTIFIED; BEING TAILORED TO UNIWORD
—	8	2	STAFFING PROGRAMMER FOR FILE MANAGER	PROGRAMMER ON-BOARD FULL-TIME

Figure 2.12: Uni Word Project Top-10 Risk Item List

ones needing higher management attention to help in getting them resolved quickly.

As shown in this example, the top-10 risk item list is a very effective way to focus higher management attention onto the project's critical success factors. It is also very efficient with respect to management time; many monthly reviews spend most of their time on things the higher manager can't do anything about. Also, if the higher manager surfaces an additional concern, it is easy to add it to the top-10 risk item list to be highlighted in future reviews.

2.9.2: Risk Item Reassessment

Another valuable function of the monthly top-10 risk item reviews is the redetermination of the risk items' rank order, which ensures a regular risk item reassessment process. Such reassessments frequently determine that a risk item's nature and criticality have changed considerably, which implies a need to change the nature and priority of its risk management plan.

In some cases, the risk level may be reduced: A faster processor may become available for a performance-critical function, or a prototype may determine that a system's requirements may be simplified. In other cases, the risk level may be increased: Some key hardware components may be delayed or changed, or the project's available budget may be reduced. Thus, a periodic reassessment of the risk items and a corresponding revision of their risk management plans is an important management activity.

One frequently asked question relating to risk item reassessment is, "How can I detect the emergence of new risk items?" Several of the most effective techniques are the following:

- *Emerging win-lose or lose-lose conditions:* If one of your constituents starts becoming unhappy with how things are developing, it's important to follow up and identify the source of the concern as a potential new risk item

- *Risk identification checklists:* It is worth revisiting the checklists in Subsection 2.2.3 periodically to identify any conditions that may be developing into serious risk items

- *Control limits:* A good generic risk management technique involves the setting of control limits on key project variables (budget, schedule, earned value, main memory allocations, accuracy allocations, etc.) and establishing an exception reporting mechanism that triggers a risk assessment when a control limit is exceeded (e.g., the number of software units passing their unit test criteria is 10 percent less than the scheduled number)

- *Cost and schedule model monitoring:* A useful policy on larger projects is to have projects re-estimate their cost model inputs at major project milestones, re-run the model, and compare the results with both the previous model estimates and the actual expenditures to date. Any significant discrepancies are good candidate risk items to investigate

- *Behavior monitoring:* For example, if a performer (person or organization) who has been extensively reporting good progress starts submitting short, vague progress reports, or escalates their level of grousing about managers or other participants, it is worth checking their performance for possible sources of risk

- *Teambuilding and incentives:* The best way to surface potential risk items is to have your team members detecting them and reporting them as early as possible. Encouraging this approach (the opposite of "shooting the messenger") will nip most risk items in the bud

2.10: Overview of Tutorial Articles

The first article, the U.S. Air Force pamphlet on Software Risk Abatement, provides an overview of recommended Air Force techniques for software risk management. Compared to this tutorial, the terminology of the Air Force pamphlet is somewhat different, but its overall approach is quite similar, as the material in the pamphlet evolved in parallel with the TRW Software Risk Management course upon which this tutorial is based.

The next four articles cover the overall process of risk assessment. The Ruthberg-Fischer article expands the top-level risk assessment approach developed by McFarlan in the article in Section 1 of this tutorial. The Boehm article deals with software risk assessment as an extension of the verification and validation process to the early phases of software requirements analysis and design. The Humphrey article provides a technique for assessing the risks of contracting for software development with an ill-prepared software house. The U.S. Defense Systems Management College Handbook on Risk Assessment Techniques covers risk assessment techniques in general; the excerpt included here is its summary of primary risk assessment methods such as network analysis, decision analysis, and estimating relationship analysis.

The next two articles focus on techniques for assessing and budgeting for software cost risk. Edgar's article covers cost risk in general and shows how several techniques have been applied to large system developments. Garvey and Powell specifically address software cost risk assessment via the use of software cost estimation models.

The final three articles mainly address the assessment of prototyping as a risk management option. The 1974 Boehm article is an early application of decision theory to the question of when to prototype. The subsequent material from Boehm's *Software Engineering Economics* book provides a more general decision theory treatment of the prototyping question that applies to other risk-management techniques as well. The Mantei and Teorey article provides more detail on assessing the specific costs and benefits involved in performing risk analyses of user-interface prototyping and other human-factors risk-reduction techniques.

2.10.1: Overall Risk Management Approaches

The U.S. Air Force Pamphlet 800-45 on "Software Risk Abatement" [AFSC,1988] is the most comprehensive document on software risk management prepared to date within the software customer community. It was developed largely in response to recommendations in a 1983 Air Force Scientific Advisory Board summer study [AFSAB,1983] on software acquisition management. This study found that software project predictability and control were the prime causes of Air Force software difficulties, and recommended an emphasis on risk management as a method of dealing with the problem. The Air Force has since been a pioneer in the development and application of risk management techniques; this pamphlet summarizes their current recommended approach.

The pamphlet provides an overall set of guidelines for applying risk management during the various phases of software acquisition. The emphasis is on the use of risk management to focus software managers on high-leverage activities rather than on the production of voluminous documentation. It thus provides a way to streamline software acquisition, particularly in government organizations that have been previously locked into inflexible document-driven approaches.

The primary risk areas covered by the pamphlet are performance, cost, schedule, and support risks. (These are similar to the "unsatisfactory outcome" categories of risk in this tutorial, which expands the performance category into four components: functionality, user interface, performance (run-time efficiency), and reliability.) The pamphlet provides a set of tables for top-level identification and assessment of risk items in each of its four risk areas. It uses a three-level breakdown of risk probabilities (frequent, probable, improbable) for the assessment. This probability assessment can then be combined with the results of another table for the assessment of the relative criticality of a risk item (with the use of a four-level breakdown for criticality: catastrophic, critical, marginal, and negligible), to produce a top-level estimate of relative risk exposure for the risk item.

The pamphlet's approach to risk handling or risk control is similar to the approach in this tutorial. An overall risk control flowchart is provided on pages 6 and 7 of the pamphlet. The risk handling options identified in the pamphlet (risk avoidance, control, assumption, and transfer) are slightly different than the ones used in this tutorial. Here, risk assumption is considered as a part of risk control, in order to emphasize the importance of contingency planning, and the additional option of buying information is included.

The overall life-cycle approach chart on page 26 of the pamphlet, which shows the phased risk management responsibilities of the customer and the developer, is again very similar to the one included in Section 4 of this tutorial.

The pamphlet also has some good phase-specific guidelines on the use of risk management techniques during the various phases of Air Force system acquisition (mission analysis, concept exploration and definition, demonstration and validation, full-scale development, production, deployment, and operational support), and a good set of guidelines for the use of a software risk abatement team.

2.10.2: Risk Assessment Techniques: General

The first of this group of articles, "Work Priority Scheme for EDP Audit and Computer Security Review," [Ruthberg-Fischer, 1986], provides an elaboration of the [McFarlan, 1981] portfolio approach to risk management. It provides a set of risk identification criteria that elaborates the McFarlan triad of project size, experience with technology, and project structure. It uses a four-step risk prioritization scheme: identification of risk dimensions; identification of risk characteristics; analysis of risk characteristics; and use of risk assessment to prioritize risk items. This scheme is quite similar to the three-step scheme used in this tutorial: identify risk items, analyze risk items, and prioritize risk items.

The article also provides a good summary of the various overall risk analysis and prioritization approaches that can be used: auditor judgment, dollar risk analysis, risk attribute weighting, and risk assessment software packages, including Monte Carlo extensions of software cost estimation models. It establishes a good overall system risk priority hierarchy, with mission criticality at level 1 and other lower risk factors—complexity, stability, reliability, and technology—established at level 2. Level 1 criteria are always used to assess system risk, with level 2 criteria used only if there are high-risk level 1 items. Each of the level 1 and level 2 risk factors is elaborated into a more detailed risk identification checklist as well.

Compared to the top-10 risk item list in this tutorial, the article's checklists underemphasize several critical risk areas such as key personnel experience and capability, user interface characteristics, reliance on external products and services, and software and network security and vulnerability other than physical access control. It also does not go very far in addressing risk reduction and risk control considerations. Overall, however, the article provides a very good set of checklist items and guidance for both risk item identification and risk assessment. It further provides a useful identification of frequent risk assessment difficulties and recommended methods for overcoming them.

The next article, "Verifying and Validating Software Requirements and Design Specifications" [Boehm, 1984], provides an example of initial attempts to embed risk management into the software life cycle via early verification and validation (V&V). The article's context is shown in Figure 2.13 [Boehm, 1976], which added V&V activities to each of the phases of the waterfall model. Verification and validation were interpreted in the following ways:

- Verification: "Am I building the product right?"
- Validation: "Am I building the right product?"

Thus, requirements and design validation are focused on eliminating all of the risks of building the wrong product—overambitious performance requirements, inappropriate user interfaces, and straining computer science capabilities—before finalizing the requirements and design specifications. The article summarizes the criteria for V&V requirements specifications (including completeness, consistency, testability, and various attributes of feasibility, including technical, cost-schedule, and environment risk). It discusses the primary V&V or risk resolution techniques available (prototypes, scenarios, automated models, automated completeness and consistency checkers, etc.). The article then provides a matrix (Table 2.1) that evaluates the relative efficacy of each V&V or risk resolution technique to eliminate each of the sources of risk. Thus, from Table 2.1 we can see that prototypes are very strong for resolving user interface, performance, or accuracy risk items, but less strong in addressing maintenance or reliability risks.

This requirements and design V&V approach to risk management worked well in many situations, but the overall document-driven nature of the waterfall model focused too many projects on the early production of rapid (or hasty) specifications rather than on early risk identification and resolution. Given that these hasty specifications generally locked developers, customers, and users into high-risk, contractually binding software commitments, it was clear that a stronger break from the waterfall model was needed. The risk-driven spiral model and its variations presented in Section 1 of this tutorial are examples of candidate solutions to the need for better software process models.

Another aspect of risk assessment is provided in the next article, "A Method of Assessing the Software Engineering Capability of Contractors" [Humphrey et al., 1987]. This article presents a set of 101 graded questions for determining the relative maturity level of a software organization. There are five maturity levels associated with the organization's process of developing software:

1. *Initial:* ill-defined procedures and controls

2. *Repeatable:* uses basic standards and methods

3. *Defined:* uses thorough, consistent standards and methods

4. *Managed:* uses quantitative, closed-loop management methods

5. *Optimized:* methods optimized with respect to quantitative experience base

These maturity levels correlate strongly with the level of risk that the software organization will run out of control, particularly when developing an unfamiliar product within a tight budget and schedule. Thus, although it is possible that a software contract with a group of inspired, free-spirited level 1 superhackers will get you an excellent product, it is

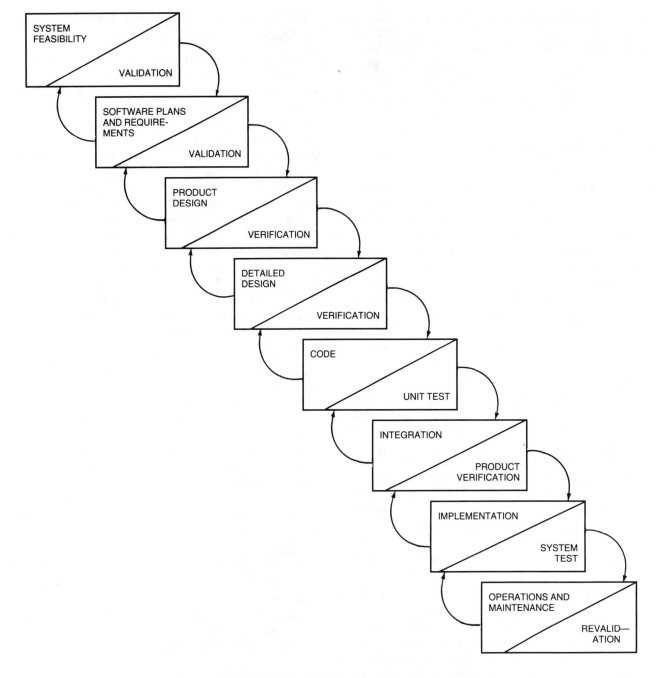

Figure 2.13: The "Waterfall" Model with Stagewise V&V

much more probable that you will get the sort of unsalvageable pile of junk that resulted from the UniWord case study. If Universal Micros had used the process maturity questionnaire given in this article, and had been able to verify the existence of a qualified level 3 bidder, they would have been much better off choosing the level 3 bidder even if the contract price had been considerably higher.

This assessment instrument is undergoing a further refinement, particularly at the higher levels (4 and 5) of process maturity. It has also been incorporated into a draft U.S. Air

Force regulation for possible general use on Air Force software procurements.

Another U.S. Department of Defense aid to software risk management is the Defense Systems Management College Handbook on "Risk Assessment Techniques" [DSMC, 1983]. It deals with general methods of risk assessment, but the techniques generally apply well to software-specific risk issues. The article's definition of "risk assessment" corresponds with the term "risk analysis" used in this tutorial, in that the article does not deal explicitly with risk identification and risk prioritization.

The Handbook as a whole is a 200-page document that also covers such topics as technique selection, implementation, presentation of results, and related policy directives. The material considered most useful is included here: a basic summary of the primary quantitative methods of risk analysis, plus a more detailed summary of network risk analysis techniques.

Each of the method descriptions includes an overall summary of the method; its inputs and outputs; its resource requirements; and its applications to real projects. The methods presented are:

- *Network methods:* These represent the project task dependencies as a network, and support the analysis of schedule and budget risks as functions of the probabilities of overruns in each individual task. Besides the initial summary, more details on network methods are provided in the Appendix F material included at the end of the methods section, and in the earlier discussion of risk analysis in Subsection 2.4.2

- *Decision analysis methods:* These represent the outcomes of major program decisions in terms of decision trees, using estimates of the probabilities and costs associated with the possible decision outcomes. These can be used to calculate expected values of decision outcomes or related decision risk quantities. These are also discussed earlier in Subsection 2.4.1

- *Method of moments:* This is a generalized case of the PERT sizing risk analysis method frequently used in software cost estimation [Putnam-Fitzsimmons, 1979]. The PERT sizing technique covers the first two moments of the Beta probability distribution: the mean and the standard deviation. The method of moments generalizes this to higher order moments and arbitrary probability distributions, although practical use of this generality is infrequent

- *Work breakdown structure simulation methods:* This class of methods consists of breaking down a large project into a hierarchy of work breakdown structure (WBS) elements. Each of the bottom-level WBS elements can then be described in terms of a range or probability distribution of costs or other additive resource requirements. These can then be combined statistically to produce overall system risk ranges

- *Graphic method:* This method involves graphing and combining risk probabilities on "normal probability paper:" a special type of graph paper whose vertical lines follow a normal probability distribution. It does not appear to have been used very much

- *Estimating relationship methods:* This class of methods uses probability distributions of individual project cost drivers or cost estimating relationships (CERs) to derive the cumulative effects over several CERs. The

[Garvey-Powell, 1988] article later in Section 2 uses this technique in concert with the COCOMO software cost model to compute such cost risk probability distributions

- *Risk factor:* This is a simple example of a WBS-oriented method, in which the various WBS components of the system are compared with respect to their levels of risk (by using expert judgment, group consensus, or other methods of choice), to determine a set of risk factors for the components. These are multiplicative factors that provide a suitable increment of budget or schedule to serve as a management reserve to cover risk items

The portion of the Handbook included here includes three acronyms that need further explanation:

- *PDF:* Probability Distribution Function, exemplified on pp. F-7 and F-8 of the article

- *CDF:* Cumulative Distribution Function, also exemplified on those pages

- *GS-12 through GS-15 analysts:* Analysts with the equivalent of a BA degree plus roughly 5 through 15 years' experience

2.10.3: Cost Risk Analysis Techniques

The next two articles elaborate on the cost risk analysis techniques summarized in the DSMC Handbook. The first article, "Controlling Murphy: How to Budget for Program Risk," [Edgar, 1982], describes how some of the techniques have been used on U.S. Department of Defense (DoD) programs. Three of these techniques have been bundled into a package called TRACE (total risk assessing cost estimate), which includes the risk factor method discussed previously, the probabilistic event analysis, an extension of the decision tree method, and a set of network risk-analysis methods.

The article describes the practical use of these and other related methods on DoD programs, and concludes that the explicit treatment of risk was very healthy because it encouraged up-front identification of risk items and placed an emphasis on the development and application of risk management plans. As Edgar says, "The real benefit comes from having thought about and planned for unpredictable events." The applications cited in the article were not software-exclusive, although some included software components.

The next article, "Three Methods for Quantifying Software Development Effort Uncertainty" [Garvey-Powell, 1988], provides some software-oriented variants and extensions of the cost risk analysis methods in the previous two articles. The three methods are based on the typical form used in software cost-estimation models. These models estimate software development effort as a function of the size of the software product and a number of other cost drivers such as product complexity, personnel experience and capability, support system capability and maturity, and hardware constraints.

The first two methods in the article, an analytic probability model and a Taylor series model, are somewhat advanced and are not yet frequently used. The most frequent use of software cost estimation models for risk analysis is exemplified by the third method, the RISCOMO tool. This is an extension of the Constructive Cost Model or COCOMO [Boehm, 1981]. It uses probability distributions of the estimated software product size and the COCOMO cost drivers for each WBS element or software component, to perform a Monte Carlo approximation of the resulting combined probability distribution of the estimated effort. This involves running the COCOMO model a large number of times and using cost driver inputs randomly selected from each cost driver's probability distribution (similar to multiple spins of a Monte Carlo roulette wheel).

The resulting distribution of effort estimates obtained from larger and larger sets of model runs is an increasingly good approximation of the probability distribution of estimated development effort. Thus, RISCOMO can provide an estimate of the probability that the software effort will be within the budgeted effort for a project. Several other software cost estimation models have Monte Carlo risk analysis extensions.

2.10.4: Use of Prototyping

The author's first experiences in attempting to apply risk management to the software process involved prototyping and its role in the software life cycle. When I joined TRW in 1973, I got involved in a long series of software process discussions with Winston Royce, the originator of the waterfall model of the software process [Royce, 1970]. The Royce version of the waterfall model had a "build it twice" step (see Figure 2.14), which was a good early approximation to today's prototyping approach. This "build it twice" approach seemed much better in general than the pure phase-by-phase approach built into government software procurement methods at the time, but it didn't seem to apply to all situations. It didn't seem, for example, that you would need to build a payroll system twice if you already knew pretty much what you wanted the payroll system to do and how to build it.

In trying to determine what distinguished "build it twice" software situations from "build it once" situations, the best I was able to do was to formulate the decision theory approach shown in the next tutorial article, "Software System Design and Development: Top-Down, Bottom-Up, or Prototype" [Boehm, 1974]. This approach basically says that you want to prototype in situations in which you aren't sure how to build the right product, and in which the prototype can significantly help you reduce the probability or risk of producing the wrong product. If you already know how to build the right product, as with a payroll system, then there is no risk and no need to prototype.

This decision theory approach to prototyping and risk reduction was elaborated considerably in the next tutorial items: Chapters 19 and 20, "Dealing with Uncertainties, Risk, and the Value of Information," of *Software Engineering Economics* [Boehm, 1981]. Chapter 20 shows how decision theory can be applied to determine an optimal level of investment in a prototype, given that one can determine the prototype's ability to reduce risk probabilities as a function of the level of investment in the prototype (see Figure 20-1). Chapter 20 also shows that this decision theory approach can be applied to other software project situations, such as in determining optimal levels of testing, simulation, formal verification, reference checking, or other forms of buying information about one's software product.

Of course, this approach will work in practice only where one can estimate the risk probabilities well, which rarely happens. But the approach provides an excellent paradigm for dealing with practical situations in which one wishes to buy information to reduce risk. The value-of-information guidelines in Chapter 20 provide a translation of the decision theory approach into English, showing the five key conditions under which it makes good sense to decide on investing in more information before committing to a particular alternative (see Section 20.11). The chapter also identifies situations in which the value of information guidelines help avoid common software pitfalls.

The TPS referred to at the beginning of Chapter 19 is a transaction processing system, such as an airline reservation system or a bank teller support system. Option B in developing the TPS refers to an option of custom-building a multiprocessor operating system to run the TPS.

The use of prototyping to resolve software risks is of particular importance in the human factors area. The most serious difficulties with the document-driven waterfall model have been in the area of specifying user interfaces. Giving a user (travel agent, doctor, pilot, etc.) a software requirements specification to review has been a particularly unsuccessful way to ensure getting the user interface right, while prototypes have had a good deal more success in eliminating the risks of developing software with the wrong user interface.

The next article, "Cost/Benefit Analysis for Incorporating Human Factors in the Lifecycle" [Mantei-Teorey, 1988], provides a good example analysis of a particular set of human factors risk reduction activities. These include performing user surveys and product mockups, constructing laboratory facilities and prototypes, and performing mockup or prototype evaluation and iteration. The overall cost of this set of activities is then compared with the estimated cost of developing various sizes of software products, to determine the size of the product for which this set of risk reduction activities would be cost-effective.

The article needs to be read and applied carefully, as there are a number of simplifying assumptions that may not hold across all user-intensive systems. For example:

- The particular sequence of activities shown may not be optimal for all products (small products, safety-critical products, and multi-version products)

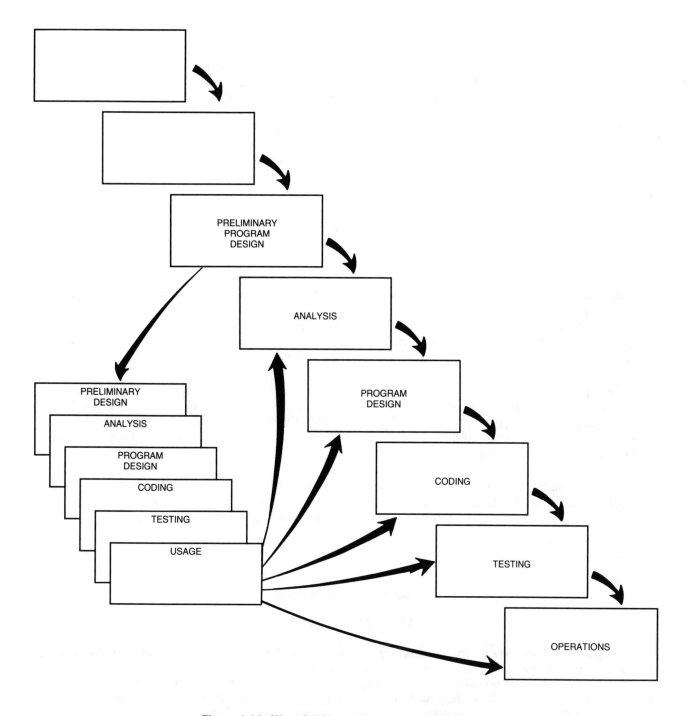

Figure 2.14: Waterfall Model with "Do It Twice" Step

- The items prototyped may vary (DBMS features, group effects, I/O media, and commercial software products)
- Additional benefits may be quantifiable (operational efficiencies, inventory reductions, and liability reductions)

Thus, it would be valuable for the elements of the cost-benefit model to be further parameterized, given that most of the generalizations would be reasonably straightforward.

Also, the particular sequence of activities shown in Figure 2 of the article will not be optimal for all classes of user-intensive systems. Many developments will involve decision trees with downstream options based on such decisions as the choice of workstation or a commercial software package. A more flexible risk-driven model such as the spiral model will support such options, with cost-benefit analyses and decisions made stage-by-stage rather than all at the project's beginning.

Nevertheless, the paper provides a very good example of the type of cost-benefit risk analysis that generally needs to be performed for user-intensive systems. Some of the risk drivers discussed—prototyping of noncritical user-interface issues, unreasonable user interface expectations, and over-design or gold-plating—are of paramount importance in the risk management of user-intensive systems.

DEPARTMENT OF THE AIR FORCE
HEADQUARTERS AIR FORCE SYSTEMS COMMAND
ANDREWS AIR FORCE BASE DC 20334-5000

FOREWORD

Risk abatement is a vital part of system development and acquisition. Software plays a major role in weapon systems. Therefore, the software components of system risk must be more rigorously addressed. Managing the software component of risk can be enhanced by using generic risk abatement tools to examine software data already being collected.

This pamphlet provides a set of tools and techniques to assess risk and to enhance software risk abatement. It should be used in conjunction with the software data by-products of DOD-STD-2167, DOD-STD-2168, AFSC/AFLCP 800-5, AFSCP 800-14, and AFSCP 800-43 to reduce software risk and improve system performance and support.

This pamphlet should be tailored to the specific needs of a program. The widespread use of this pamphlet will reduce software risk as well as improve the software that makes weapon systems versatile and combat capable.

Acquisition Management

SOFTWARE RISK ABATEMENT

This pamphlet describes software risk abatement processes, composed of risk identification, analysis, and handling techniques, that can significantly contribute to improving the acquisition of mission-critical computer resources. This pamphlet is intended to help program directors by integrating software risk abatement with system-level risk-handling techniques. Risk abatement techniques can help the contractor and program office improve the performance and support of the software in weapon systems. This pamphlet applies to all AFSC and AFLC activities involved with software acquisition management. It does not apply to the Air National Guard or to US Air Force Reserve units and members.

DEPARTMENT OF THE AIR FORCE
Headquarters Air Force Systems Command
Andrews Air Force Base DC 20334-5000

Headquarters Air Force Logistics Command
Wright-Patterson Air Force Base OH 45433-5001

AFSC/AFLC PAMPHLET 800-45

30 September 1988

Chapter 1

INTRODUCTION TO SOFTWARE RISK ABATEMENT

1-1. Risk is the traditional manner of expressing uncertainty in the systems life cycle. In a quantitative sense, risk is the probability at a given point in a system's life cycle that predicted goals cannot be achieved with the available resources. Due to the complexity of risk components and the compounding uncertainty associated with future sources of risk, risk is normally not treated with mathematical rigor during the early life cycle phases. As the system progresses through the life cycle and uncertainty diminishes, the degree of mathematical precision increases.

1-2. Successful acquisition management and fielding of systems depends on the effective use of risk identification, analysis, and handling techniques. MIL-STD-499 provides a mechanism to address system risks in terms of identification, quantification, control, priority, and abatement. Traditionally, there are four kinds of risk associated with system acquisition: performance, support, cost, and schedule. Software often presents a significant source of risk in all these areas. Identifying, analyzing, and handling software risk are the key factors in the reduction of system risk. Both AFR 800-14 and DOD-STD-2167A require the program office and the contractor to address software risk components. The purpose of this pamphlet is to allow program offices and contractors to identify software risk components easily.

1-3. This pamphlet is intended to be a practical guide and reference for program office personnel and not a textbook dealing with the theories of risk abatement. It defines a framework for software risk assessment and abatement that is compatible with risk handling techniques applicable to hardware. This pamphlet should be used in coordination with specialists in program control, engineering, and support to ensure a viable risk abatement process. Attachment 1 discusses the collection and uses of software risk analysis data.

1-4. Within AFLC, this pamphlet is intended to show system program managers, item managers, and software engineering personnel how AFSC intends to address software support requirements from a risk abatement point of view during acquisition of systems. AFLC personnel participate in defining support concepts, requirements, and action items through the computer resources working groups (CRWG) and the contract data requirements lists. Support requirements must be provided to AFSC system program offices (SPO) early in the acquisition cycle through CRWG channels to ensure inclusion of those requirements in budgets, contracts, and statements of work (SOW). AFLC participation on the software risk abatement team, discussed in para-

graph 7-4b, is a means to verify those support requirements. This pamphlet may also be used for determining risk abatement for major AFLC support contracts as indicated in paragraph 7-2e.

1-5. Risk abatement is an iterative process requiring program directors to establish objectives and regularly assess their program for impediments to achieving these objectives. Risk abatement should be used to place in perspective the magnitude of the cause and effects of changes, to develop options, and to make decisions to control the outcome.

1-6. The risk abatement framework described in this pamphlet accommodates both qualitative and quantitative risk assessment. For each software risk area, a brief synopsis of the types of information needed, the analysis required, and the risk reduction behavior expected is provided. Rules of thumb useful for identifying, analyzing, and handling risk are also identified.

1-7. Rules of thumb are intended to be broadly applicable to the weapon systems that are acquired by each product division. This broad nature means that the rules of thumb are inherently not absolute. Special cases may exist that legitimately violate the rules provided. Product divisions are encouraged to develop their unique rules of thumb for the software risk elements. Copies of product division rules of thumb should be sent to HQ AFSC/PLR.

1-8. Each software risk component area (performance, support, cost, and schedule) is discussed in a separate chapter. Each chapter contains the inputs required, associated software indicators and/or metrics that support the estimates and evaluations, recommended risk control frequency, data analysis guidelines, and rules of thumb. Risk-handling techniques for each area follow the software risk abatement process described in chapter 2.

1-9. **Terms Explained:**
   a. **Cost Risk.** The degree of uncertainty associated with system acquisition life cycle budgets and outlays that may negatively impact the program.
   b. **Performance Risk.** The degree of uncertainty in the development and deployment process that may keep the system from meeting its technical specifications or that may result in the system being unsuitable for its intended use.
   c. **Risk.** The condition of having outcomes with known probabilities of occurrence, not certainty of occurrence.
   d. **Risk Abatement.** The process of reducing the amount of risk to a system.
   e. **Risk Analysis.** Examining the change of out-

comes with the modification of the risk drivers. This examination is more involved than risk assessment and should result in the identification of the most critical variables, with insights into desired options for risk handling.

f. Risk Assessment. The process of examining a program and identifying areas of potential risk.

g. Risk Control. The process of achieving the desired outcomes by continual application of management techniques to the risk drivers.

h. Risk Drivers. Those variables that cause probabilities of cost, schedule, performance, or support risk to fluctuate significantly.

i. Risk Handling. The identification of options available to reduce or control selected risk drivers.

j. Schedule Risk. The degree of uncertainty associated with the ability of the program to achieve desired milestones (outcomes) on time.

k. Support Risk. The degree of uncertainty associated with the ability of the support organization to maintain, change, or enhance software of the fielded system within the planned support concepts and resources.

Chapter 2

THE SOFTWARE RISK ABATEMENT PROCESS

2-1. General Introduction. The software risk abatement process involves determining the need for abatement procedures, identifying software risk components, analyzing risk component drivers, developing risk-handling options, and controlling risk drivers. The process is iterative and is shown in figure 2-1. This process flowchart shows the general pattern for establishing risk control and initiating risk abatement in building-block fashion. It is strongly emphasized that this pamphlet, to be effective, be used with the publications listed below. Also, this pamphlet uses existing data to the maximum extent possible.

a. AFSCP/AFLCP 800-5, Software Independent Verification and Validation (IV&V). OPR: HQ AFSC/PLR, Andrews AFB DC.

b. AFSCP 800-14, Software Quality Indicators. OPR: HQ AFSC/PLR, Andrews AFB DC.

c. AFSCP 800-43, Software Management Indicators. OPR: HQ AFSC/PLR, Andrews AFB DC.

d. DOD-STD-2167A, Defense Systems Software Development. OPR: SPAWAR-3212, Wash DC.

e. DOD-STD-2168, Defense Systems Software Quality Program. OPR: HQ ARDEC/SMCA-R-FSC, Picatinny Arsenal NJ.

2-2. Determining Need. Before applying software risk abatement techniques, it is necessary to determine whether software significantly contributes to system risk. Use the following checklist:

a. Could software faults cause loss of life, personnel injury, mission failure, or equipment damage?

b. Are software costs more than 15 percent of system life cycle costs?

c. Are computer software configuration items more than 15 percent of the system configuration items?

d. Will software significantly contribute to the operational or support costs of the system?

e. Is software essential to the successful performance of primary mission objectives? If the answer is "yes" to any of the preceding questions, then software risk will most likely be a significant contributor to system risk. In these cases, program offices are expected to initiate software risk abatement techniques by identifying software risk components.

2-3. Identifying Risk Components. Software risk may be divided into performance, support, cost, and schedule components. Program office personnel from multiple disciplines must examine their program data to identify and assess software risk components. Data sources include analogous program histories, lessons learned, preaward surveys, past performance, and previous studies on similar pro-

grams. The expected outputs of this task are the identification of software risk components and associated impacts on the system. The risk components must then be analyzed to determine risk drivers.

2-4. Analyzing Risk Components. Analysis of each risk component can and should be performed by various technical disciplines, including software experts assigned or matrixed to the program office. Baseline estimates, assumptions, requirements documents, and software indicator data are used to determine where and when the consequence of risk is likely to occur, magnitude of exposure, risk impact, drivers, and areas of greatest concern. Particular emphasis should be placed on determining the drivers that significantly influence multiple components of risk. For example, the use of immature software tools or providing government-furnished software can adversely affect software performance, cost, and schedule.

a. Before risk can be assessed for each of the four components (performance, support, cost, and schedule), the impact of each must be determined. Figure 2-2 identifies the four categories that the components can fall into: catastrophic, critical, marginal, and negligible. The categories are determined by the potential consequences if the desired outcome is not achieved or by the potential consequences of undetected software errors or faults. For example, the performance component would have a catastrophic impact if the mission fails due to a performance requirement not being met.

b. Once the impact has been assessed for each component, the probability of occurrence must be determined. The probability for each risk component is determined in figures 3-2, 4-2, 5-2, and 6-2.

c. After the impact and the probability of occurrence has been assessed, the degree of risk can be determined. The degree of risk is broken into four areas: high, moderate, low, and none. Figure 2-3 determines the level of risk for the four components. For example, if performance has a catastrophic impact and has a probability of improbable, then the performance risk assessment is moderate.

2-5. Handling and Controlling Risk Drivers. Once software risk components have been identified and analyzed, risk-handling can be undertaken. This task manipulates the risk drivers to reduce risk exposure. Risk-handling alternatives divide into four categories: avoidance, control (prevention), assumption, and transfer. The technique selected will depend on where the program is in the acquisition process and the options available. Once a risk-handling technique is selected, the outputs of the technique must be compared to expectations to determine the need for continued or further action.

2-6. General Summary. This pamphlet merely formalizes for software management the simple risk abatement process of identifying a project's top software risk items, generating a plan of action to resolve each risk item, updating the plans of action regularly, highlighting the status of risk items at project reviews, and initiating appropriate corrective actions. Software risk abatement is a continuous, iterative task throughout program management. It is a means by which the program office identifies and handles areas of vulnerability and concern. The frequency of risk area evaluations should normally be complimentary to other management control tools. For example, if program cost, schedule, and control criteria are reported on a monthly basis, then software risk abatement information should also be reported on a monthly basis to allow synergetic assessment and intervention. Continuous use of risk abatement techniques provides the information needed for timely and effective decisions by program office and contractor personnel.

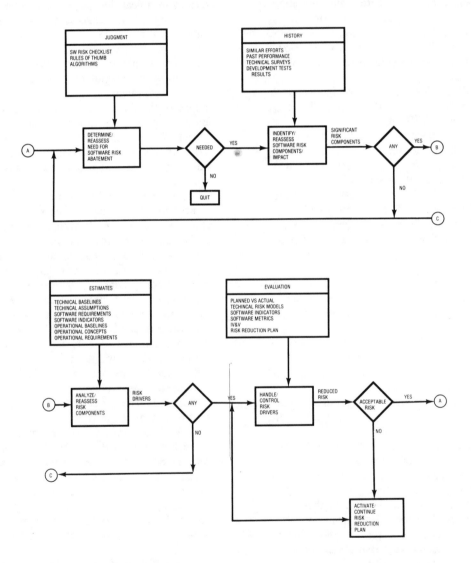

Figure 2-1. Software Risk Abatement Process.

CATEGORY / COMPONENTS		PERFORMANCE	SUPPORT	COST	SCHEDULE
CATASTROPHIC	1	Failure to meet the requirement would result in mission failure		Failure results in increased costs and schedule delays with expected values in excess of $500k	
	2	Significant degradation to nonachievement of technical performance	Nonresponsive or unsupportable software	Significant financial shortages, budget overrun likely	Unachievable IOC
CRITICAL	1	Failure to meet the requirement would degrade system performance to a point where mission success is questionable		Failure results in operational delays and/or increased costs with expected value of $100K to $500K	
	2	Some reduction in technical performance	Minor delays in software modifications	Some shortage of financial resources, possible overrun	Possible slippage in IOC
MARGINAL	1	Failure to meet the requirement would result in degradation of secondary mission		Costs, impacts, and/or recoverable schedule slips with expected value of $1K to $100K	
	2	Minimal to small reduction in technical performance	Reponsive software support	Sufficient financial resources	Realistic, achievable schedule
NEGLIGIBLE	1	Failure to meet the requirement would create inconvenience or non-operational impact		Error results in minor cost and/or schedule impact with expected value of less than $1K	
	2	No reduction in technical performance	Easily supportable software	Possible budget underrun	Early achievable IOC

Note: (1) The potential consequence of undetected software errors of faults.
(2) The potential consequence if the desired outcome is not achieved.

Figure 2-2. Impact Assessment.

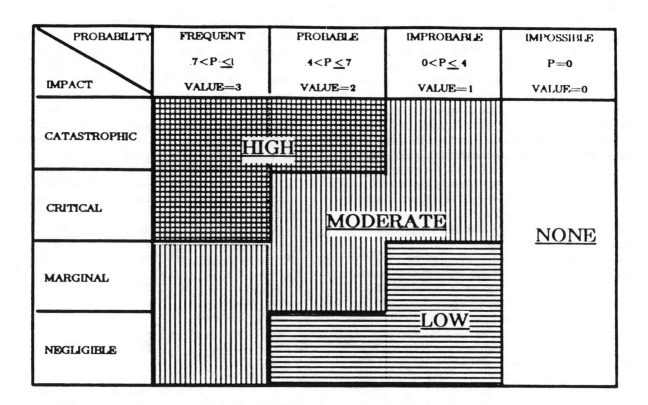

Figure 2-3. Risk Assessment.

Chapter 3

PERFORMANCE RISK

3-1. When performance risk is identified as a significant risk component, it must be assessed as the cornerstone element of risk abatement. Uncertainties and risks inherent in the performance aspects of software development can have major impact on the likelihood of attaining system objectives. Software performance risk can significantly impact the likelihood (probability) of cost and schedule overruns, achievement of required operational capabilities, and the ability to correct errors and implement enhancements in the post-deployment software support (PDSS) environment.

3-2. One way to analyze software performance risk is to assess performance risk inputs that allow risk drivers to be identified. By identifying the drivers, program office personnel can seek the appropriate tools to handle software performance risk effectively. The primary variables affecting software performance risk drivers are: requirements, constraints, available technologies, and development approaches.

a. Requirements can be broken into a series of key elements that provide the greatest amount of uncertainty in achieving technical and performance objectives. Typically these elements are: complexity of the system requirements implemented by software, magnitude of the software to be developed, requirements stability, impact of PDSS requirements on software design, and ability to decompose and allocate system-level requirements to the various software components.

b. Constraints can take the form of resource limitations such as the physical characteristics of the computer resource hardware, availability of technically experienced personnel, and secondary limitations due to cost and schedule. Other constraints that can contribute to uncertainty include the boundaries of the performance envelope, the application of standards, and mandatory use of unsuitable government-furnished equipment (GFE) and government-furnished products (GFP).

c. Available technologies may drive the choice of languages used to implement the software design; the choice of the software tools necessary to develop, test, and accept operational software; the selection of data rights; and identification of the level of experience required for software personnel.

d. Development approaches can impact software performance risk through the use or nonuse of prototypes and reusable software; availability of adequate documentation to support prototype transition and reuse of existing software; availability of tools and resources (facilities, terminals, access time, etc.) for the development environment; application of sufficient management controls to provide discipline, structure, and visibility to the software development process; complexity of interfaces with other systems, those internal to the prime contractor and external to any subcontractors; and uncertainty due to software integration at system, computer software configuration item (CSCI), computer software component, and computer software unit levels.

3-3. The program office can identify the inputs necessary for an effective risk control program from the following sources (fig 3-1):

a. History. Review of similar development effort and contractor's past performance for this type of software development can aid in identifying performance uncertainty. Assessing and reassessing the contractor's capability and capacity to develop the required software can be useful in identifying the contractor's workplace changes that could reduce technical risk. Surveys of technical literature and related laboratory efforts can contribute to assessing technical risk, especially in the areas of prototyping, software reuse, language utilization, and technology insertion.

b. Estimates. Comparing the proposed performance baselines with performance baselines from similar development efforts can provide insight into the variables that can drive and control risk. Insight gained by comparing predevelopment and postdevelopment baselines can aid in assessing validity of the proposed performance baseline for the new development. Critical analysis of technical assumptions, especially allocation of functions between hardware and software, should be accomplished as early as possible but, to determine performance drivers, no later than system and software requirements analysis. During requirements analysis, the scope and nature of software risk components should be clarified, with further refinement as the development effort matures. Performance baselines can be analyzed to determine which management indicators will be useful during development (such as computer resource utilization, software requirements definition and stability, and software development tools indicators (discussed in AFSCP 800-43, Software Management Indicators)).

c. Evaluations. For risk control, periodic evaluations should be performed to ensure that performance risk has not increased to unacceptable levels. Evaluation frequency should be based on degree of risk exposure the program office is willing to accept. During development, primarily during full-scale development (FSD) and earlier if software prototypes may transition into final software products, comparison of actual and planned performance baselines should be initiated. Deviations from planned baselines should be considered as sources of change in performance risk. AFSCP 800-43 indicators provide a useful tool for visual representation of these deviations. AFSCP 800-14, Software Quality Indicators, can be used to gain insight into the quality and maturity of software products being developed. Appropriate choice and use of software quality factors can contribute to the evaluation process. Evaluation results can be tailored for use in existing risk models, such as described in the Defense Systems Management College Risk Assessment Techniques Handbook. AFSCP/AFLCP 800-5, Software Independent Verification and Validation (IV&V), can also be an effective risk abatement tool.

3-4. Potential performance risks should then be assigned according to two categories: (1) the probability that the desired outcome will not occur and (2) impact assessment of the potential consequences if the desired outcome is not achieved and the potential consequences of undetected software errors or faults (fig 2-2). Total performance risk can then be assessed by evaluating the combined results of these two categories (fig 2-3). Figure 3-2 presents a sample set of rules of thumb that can help determine the probability that the desired outcome will not occur. After each driver has been assigned a probability of occurrence value, compute the performance overall probability value. There are several ways to do this. The performance overall probability value can be determined by (1) taking the average value (2) incorporating weighting factors to each driver and then taking the weighted average or (3) taking the driver with the highest probability of occurrence value and using it as the overall value. Once the probability of occurrence and the impact assessment has been de-

termined from figures 3-2 and 2-2, respectively, the overall performance risk can be assessed by using figure 2-3. Analysis should be performed to ensure that the correct performance risk drivers for a particular application have been identified. For risk control, possible courses of action are:

a. Avoidance. Performance risk is best avoided by securing complete system requirements definition before preliminary design and preventing requirements creep during FSD. Risk avoidance may also involve descoping performance objectives to a more achievable level, changing developmental approach, or using a preplanned product improvement (P3I) approach to achieving desired performance objectives. These approaches should be accomplished through successive enhancements to a more technically achievable baseline. Avoidance techniques are viable primarily during the early stages of development. Late application often takes the form of risk transfer.

b. Control. The program office could apply parallel development efforts, intense management reviews, or rapid prototyping or conduct additional tradeoff studies.

c. Assumption. The program office can accept the performance risk, manage the software development effort appropriately, and remain aware of decreased probability of success.

d. Transfer. Software requirements could be realigned through the requirements analysis process and, in some cases, be implemented by hardware instead of software. Another possibility, in some integrated systems, is to reassign the requirement to other elements of the system. Under no circumstance should software performance risk be transferred to the PDSS phase of the system life cycle.

HISTORY	ESTIMATES	EVALUATION
Similar Efforts	Technical Baseline	Planned vs Actual
Past Performance	Technical Assumptions	Technical Risk Models
Technical Surveys	Software Requirements	Software Indicators
Development Test Results	Operational Baselines	Software Metrics
Software Preaward Survey	Operational Concepts	IV&V
	Operational Requirements	
	Software Indicators	

Figure 3-1. Software Performance Risk Abatement Inputs.

PROBABILITY OF DRIVERS ADVERSELY AFFECTING IMPACT

PERFORMANCE DRIVERS	IMPOSSIBLE to IMPROBABLE (0.0<P< 0.4) Value = 0 or 1	PROBABLE (0.4<P<0.7) Value = 2	FREQUENT (0.7<P<1.0) Value = 3	Value
REQUIREMENTS				
COMPLEXITY	Simple or easily allocatable	Moderate, can be allocated	Significant or difficult to allocate	
SIZE	Small or easily broken down into work units	Medium, or can be broken down into work units	Large, cannot be broken down into work units	
STABILITY	Little or no change to established baseline	Some change in baseline expected	Rapidly changing or no baseline	
PDSS	Agreed to support concept	Roles and missions issues unresolved	No support concept or major unresolved issues	
R&M	Allocatable to hardware and software components	Requirements can be defined	Can only be addressed at the total system level	
CONSTRAINTS				
COMPUTER RESOURCES	Mature, growth capacity within design, flexible	Available, some growth capacity	New development, no growth capacity, inflexible	
PERSONNEL	Available, in place, experienced, stable	Available, but not in place, some experience	High turnover, little or no experience, not available	
STANDARDS	Appropriately tailored for application	Some tailoring, all not reviewed for applicability	No tailoring, none applied to the contract	
GFE/GFP	Meets requirements, available	May meet requirements, uncertain availability	Incompatible with system requirements, unavailable	
ENVIRONMENT	Little or no impact on design	Some impact on design	Major impact on design	
PERFORMANCE ENVELOPES	Operation well within boundaries	Occasional operation at boundaries	Continuous operation at boundaries	
TECHNOLOGY				
LANGUAGE	Mature, approved HOL used	Approved or non-approved HOL	Significant use of assembly language	
HARDWARE	Mature, available	Some development or available	Totally new development	
TOOLS	Documented, validated, in place	Available, validated, some development	Unvalidated, proprietary, major development	
DATA RIGHTS	Fully compatible with support and follow-on	Minor incompatibilities with support and follow-on	Incompatible with support and follow-on	
EXPERIENCE	Greater than 4 years	Less than 4 years	Little or none	
DEVELOPMENT APPROACH				
PROTOTYPES and REUSE	Used, documented sufficiently for use	Some use and documentation	No use or no documentation	
DOCUMENTATION	Correct and available	Some deficiencies, available	Nonexistent	
ENVIRONMENT	In place, validated, experience with use	Minor modifications, tools available	Major development effort	
MANAGEMENT APPROACH	Existing product and process controls	Product & process controls need enhancement	Weak or nonexistent	
INTEGRATION	Internal and external controls in place	Internal or external controls not in place	Weak or nonexistent	

Figure 3-2. Quantification of Performance Probability.

Chapter 4

SUPPORT RISK

4-1. As systems become increasingly sophisticated, with more emphasis on the need for computers and software to implement critical functions, software is rapidly becoming the key element in overall mission effectiveness. PDSS costs and associated concerns play a major role in the overall supportability of major systems. There are several issues that complicate the control of risk in the PDSS environment. Among these issues are: determination of what facilities, personnel, and procedures are necessary for PDSS; PDSS requirements; and available resources for PDSS. Perhaps the most important issue to address when attempting to reduce support risk is the early identification of a responsive system-level support concept. The people who will support the software and where the software will be supported during the demonstration validation phase are two of the greater support risk reduction tools. Software support risk control must address several important issues. First, it must be applied throughout the system life cycle. Second, in order to control risk, an estimate of the PDSS activities (personnel, procedures, number of change requests, facility availability, etc.) should be obtained. Third, the computed risk must measure the inability and unavailability of PDSS resources to meet predicted software support requirements.

4-2. PDSS estimates are often impacted by several competing support drivers and the approaches used to manage and control all of the software risk areas. Typically, software support risk drivers divide into four categories: design, responsibilities, tools and environments, and supportability.

a. Software design characteristics are probably the most controllable support risk drivers. The characteristics affecting software supportability include such elements as complexity of software design, including related attributes of software size, structure, and interrelationship; adequacy of deliverable documentation to support PDSS; completeness of software development effort; extent and implementation of configuration management practices for operational and support software; and stability of the design itself.

b. AFR 800-14 contains some guidance on how software support responsibilities can be allocated for PDSS. Allocation should address: who is responsible for PDSS management and at what levels of the software products; who is responsible and at what level for configuration management of both system and software products; who is responsible for technical management of the software; and who is responsible for software modifications.

c. Availability of software tools, engineering data, documentation, and facilities necessary for PDSS is another significant driver. How many PDSS facilities exist or must be built and at how many locations and how much compatibility there is with the "expected" support workload have major impact on support risk. Adequacy of the existing software support tools and those tools that are to be delivered as part of the development effort also contribute to support risk. Compatibility of support computer hardware (of both host and target computers) with the facilities and software support tools can have major impact on the ability to support PDSS requirements. Another element that can affect both support risk and performance risk is the distribution system that will be used physically to implement software changes in the system.

d. Software supportability can be driven by the magnitude, type, complexity, and priority of the anticipated changes. The degree to which software modifications affect operational interfaces, both internal to a given system and external to other systems, can greatly impact the timeliness of change implementation and amount of testing required before incorporating the modification into the operational configuration. Supportability can also be affected by the experience, discipline mix, and availability of personnel to fulfill the PDSS mission. Compatibility of the planned release cycle for software updates with operational needs and changes in threat could significantly impact support risk. Procedures used by the various PDSS activities can have major impact if they are incompatible with each other and do not contribute to the net quality improvement of operational software.

4-3. The program office can identify the inputs necessary for an effective software support risk control program from the following sources (fig 4-1).

a. **History.** Historical PDSS profiles and the quality of delivered software products for similar systems can aid in estimating the amount of PDSS change activity. Information gathered on development processes, schedules, and initial quality of delivered software products for similar systems can be useful in determining the amount of software development that must be completed during PDSS. Responsiveness of the corrective action system during development, especially during development, test, and evaluation (DT&E) and operational test and evaluation (OT&E), can be an indicator of the responsiveness of software design to change and the adequacy of available documentation and support tools. Requirements stability during FSD can also be an indicator of how performance and support expectations have changed since FSD began. During operations and support phases and latter stages of FSD, the software progress indicators (see AFSCP 800-43) and fault density, test coverage, test sufficiency, and documentation indicators (see AFSCP 800-14) can contribute to the historical data base for a specific program.

b. Estimates. A key element of support risk is recognition that supportability is important to both the user and supporter of software. Any risk assessment methodology that ignores the interests of one of these parties may escalate a risk that is unacceptable to the other. One way to avoid this is through use of a user/supporter software support baseline that, according to AFR 800-14, is documented in a computer resources life cycle management plan (CRLCMP). This baseline should include an agreed-upon understanding of the PDSS software release cycle; the projected level of change activity; and projected personnel, facility, tools, and resources needed for PDSS. A combination of the PDSS baseline, support concept, and requirements can be used to refine and influence software development requirements and to produce software with increased supportability at a lower total life cycle cost. The software development tools indicator (AFSCP 800-43) can be helpful in identifying support tools necessary during PDSS. Continued use of the indicators mentioned can contribute to refining PDSS estimates.

c. Evaluations. Tracking PDSS baseline changes (timeliness, completeness, product adequacy, etc.) can play a major role in evaluating software support risk. Comparing test results and responsiveness of the corrective action system can provide valuable insight into the relative ease of modifying and supporting software. All of the software management and quality indicators can contribute to the evaluation of support risk. Using selected software quality factors can assist in the evaluation process. NOTE: While software indicators and quality factors are targeted for software development phases, they can be applied with equal effectiveness during PDSS.

4-4. A sample set of rules of thumb that can assist in the evaluation of probability are in figure 4-2. The overall support risk can be determined in the same manner as performance risk in paragraph 3-4. Following in-depth assessments of the types of inputs described above, potential support risks should be handled. Possible courses of action include:

a. Avoidance. Support risk avoidance should be accomplished before transition of software to the operational and PDSS environments. To avoid unnecessary support risk, plan support requirements early and avoid overly ambitious FSD schedules; control extensive and frequent changes in functional requirements; do not delay planning for PDSS requirements; develop adequate configuration management plans, procedures, and practices; and avoid low priority for automated tool support.

b. Control. According to AFR 800-14, the program office should actively solicit user and supporter involvement in ensuring that contractors understand the nature of support and operational environments and that support requirements are adequately balanced with other system requirements. Additionally, the program office should attempt to balance developmental risks with total life cycle risk and, in particular, support risk. The CRWG and CRLCMP should be integral components of support risk control.

c. Assumption. Support risk assumption is not solely within the purview of the program office; it will require coordination with the support command. The user and supporter are the ultimate agencies responsible for assumption of support risk. Political sensitivities can also be a major contributor in "forcing" support risk onto the using and supporting activities. One risk reduction technique is to have all or a portion of IV&V performed by the software support organizations (AFSCP/AFLCP 800-5 and AFR 800-14/AFSC/AFLC Sup 1).

d. Transfer. Transfer of software support risk should be avoided. Identification of support requirements during the concept exploration and demonstration validation phase is the key to reducing support risk. However, it may be possible to implement some software support requirements later in the development cycle. When a system has been placed in the operational and PDSS environment, there is very limited opportunity for support risk transfer.

HISTORY	**ESTIMATES**	**EVALUATIONS**
Similar Efforts Past Performance Requirements Stability	Support Baseline Support Concepts Support Requirements Software Indicators	IV&V Reports Planned vs Actual Operational Test Results Software Indicators Software Metrics

Figure 4-1. Software Support Risk Abatement Inputs.

PROBABILITY OF DRIVERS ADVERSELY AFFECTING IMPACT

SUPPORT DRIVERS	IMPOSSIBLE to IMPROBABLE (0.0<P<0.4) Value = 0 or 1	PROBABLE (0.4<P<0.7) Value = 2	FREQUENT (0.7<P<1.0) Value = 3	Value
DESIGN				
COMPLEXITY	Structurally maintainable	Certain aspects difficult	Extremely difficult to maintain	
DOCUMENTATION	Adequate	Some deficiencies	Inadequate	
COMPLETENESS	Extensive PDSS incorporation	Some PDSS incorporation	Little PDSS incorporation	
DATA RIGHTS (Including COTS)	Unlimited	Limited	Restricted	
CONFIGURATION MANAGEMENT	Sufficient, in place	Some shortfalls	Insufficient	
STABILITY	Little or no change	Moderate, controlled, change	Rapid or uncontrolled change	
RESPONSIBILITIES				
MANAGEMENT: Hardware Software	Defined, assigned responsibilities	Some roles and missions issues	Undefined or unassigned	
CONFIGURATION MANAGEMENT	Single point control	Defined control points	Multiple control points	
SOFTWARE IDENTIFICATION	Consistent w/support agency control system	Some inconsistencies	Inconsistent	
TECHNICAL MANAGEMENT	Consistent with operational needs	Some inconsistencies	Major inconsistencies	
CHANGE IMPLEMENTATION	Responsive to user needs	Acceptable delays	Nonresponsive to user needs	
TOOLS & ENVIRONMENT				
FACILITIES	In place, little change	In place, some modification	Nonexistent or extensive change	
SOFTWARE TOOLS	Delivered, certified, sufficient	Some resolvable concerns	Not delivered, certified, or sufficient	
COMPUTER HARDWARE	Compatible with "ops" system	Minor incompatibilities	Major incompatibilities	
PRODUCTION	Sufficient for fielded units	Some capacity questions	Insufficient	
DISTRIBUTION	Controlled, responsive	Minor response concerns	Uncontrolled or nonresponsive	
SUPPORTABILITY				
CHANGES	Within projections	Slight deviations	Major deviations	
OPERATIONAL INTERFACES	Defined, controlled	Some "hidden" linkages	Extensive linkages	
PERSONNEL	In place, sufficient, experienced	Minor discipline mix concerns	Significant discipline mix concerns	
RELEASE CYCLE	Responsive to user requirements	Minor incompatibilities	Nonresponsive to user needs	
PROCEDURES	In place, adequate	Some concerns	Nonexistent or inadequate	

Figure 4-2. Quantification of Support Probability.

Chapter 5

COST RISK

5-1. Cost estimating is fundamental to program management. Normally, cost estimates are deterministic. Costs for individual program line items are expressed as a single value representing the "best" available estimate. Software cost estimates are usually determined by using one or more cost estimating technique, such as analogies, bottom-up, and available cost estimating models (for example, SOFTWARE RESOURCES, COCOMO, SLIM, and PRICE-S). Use of a range of estimates allows for software cost risk analysis. Analysis should combine uncertainties for the various cost elements, determine software cost range (minimum and maximum costs), identify the "most likely" or "best" estimate, and assess the risk of overrunning budget.

5-2. Software cost estimates are affected by competing drivers and the approaches used to manage and control technical and schedule risks. It should be noted that system integration can have an enormous effect on cost if an error is found during this time. Statistically, an error found during system integration costs at least 10 times more to correct than the same error found during preliminary software design. The escalating cost of correcting latent software errors is the primary reason that software maintenance accounts for as much as 70 percent of systems life cycle cost. Cost drivers come in four categories: requirements complexity, personnel, reusable software, and tools and environment.

a. Requirements complexity directly affects cost estimation. Critical cost model complexity inputs include software size (magnitude of development effort), identification of computer resource constraints that can affect design approach and may limit implementation of required functions, type of application (real-time, embedded, criticality to system function, etc.), security requirements, and technology availability. These inputs can directly impact costs associated with design and implementation. Requirements stability provides a link that enhances certainty of all other requirements-related inputs.

b. Software development is labor-intensive. Personnel factors can contribute significantly to controlling software cost risk. Factors such as availability of personnel to meet proposed staffing profiles, proper mix of disciplines (systems and software engineering, configuration and documentation management, quality, etc.), use of automation to increase productivity, and use of environment to manage and resolve personnel issues should be included in the program office's cost risk management approach.

c. Reusable software is often presented as a means of reducing cost risk. There are several areas associated with reuse that should be investigated to verify the claim, including availability of software for reuse, extent of modification to meet the "new" application, evaluation of specific software language requirements before reuse, and access to sufficient software data rights and documentation.

d. Software development facilities and tools (host computer hardware, terminals, access time, software development and test tools, simulators, etc.) should be evaluated to assess their availability and applicability to the development effort and availability of data rights.

5-3. The program office can identify the inputs necessary for an effective cost risk control approach from the following sources (fig 5-1).

a. **History.** Reviewing similar development efforts and contractors' past cost performance for this type of software development can contribute to the identification of budgetary uncertainty. This review can also help determine the types of software cost estimation models that are best fitted for a specific software development effort. Comparing the historical projections with the actuals for previous efforts can be beneficial in calibrating cost estimates provided by the contractor as part of the request for proposal (RFP) response and during the development effort. Caution: History from prior development efforts also forms the foundation for most software cost estimation models. Most of these models do not have sufficient empirical data from software efforts accomplished under a structured approach, such as that specified in DOD-STD-2167A. Consequently, several cost models have been modified to present a "best" guess at the cost of software developed in a DOD-STD-2167A-type environment.

b. **Estimates.** Proper selection of software cost estimation models is crucial in controlling cost risk. Selection of the wrong model could cause the development to be underfunded. Input assumption validation for the selected models should be accomplished by management, technical, and program control personnel. Once this is finished, the cost estimate should be baselined. The staffing profile associated with development should be baselined, as staffing is one of the primary cost drivers. These baselines can then be used to form the planned portion of software development manpower and cost/schedule deviations management indicators (AFSCP 800-43).

c. **Evaluations.** Programs can suffer from scarcity of financial resources and misapplication of those resources. The net effect, in either case, can significantly delay program completion and add to the total cost of the development effort. An effective software cost risk control function can aid considerably in ensuring that costs do not increase to unacceptable levels. Monitoring planned versus actual expenditure rates, through the use of cost/schedule control system criteria techniques, can be applied to software developments just as they are to hardware developments. As cost model input assumptions are refined, cost models can be rerun to obtain better cost estimates at completion. The AFSCP 800-43 indicators can be used as a tool for visual representation of deviations from cost and staffing baselines. Completeness, defect density, fault density, test coverage, and documentation indicators (AFSCP 800-14) can also be used to identify the potential for cost overruns due to poor quality of software.

5-4. Following a detailed assessment of the types of inputs described above, potential cost risks can be handled. Figure 5-2 contains a sample set of rules of thumb that can aid in the evaluation of probability. The overall cost risk can be determined in the same manner as performance risk (para 3-4).

5-5. Cost risk control should always be accomplished on a total system life cycle cost analysis basis. Possible courses of action for cost risk control include:

a. Avoidance. Software cost avoidance is normally achieved by reducing the scope of the software development effort, obtaining additional resources, "streamlining" acquisition practices, and using preplanned product improvement (P3I) software development. Because these avoidances severely impact the ability of the support agency to perform its function, extreme caution should be exercised if cost avoidance techniques, such as reducing the amount of formal documentation, reducing the nature and scope of test, and reducing the software quality requirements, are used.

b. Control. Cost control can be achieved through stringent management reviews, continuous updating of cost estimates based on real-time inputs of technical and schedule accomplishments, and additional cost trade-off studies. Appropriate tailoring and application of standards and early user involvement in performance requirements analysis can also contribute to controlling cost risk.

c. Assumption. The program office can accept the cost risk, manage the software development accordingly, and remain cognizant of probability of successful program accomplishment within available financial resources. IV&V can also help lower a system's life cycle cost by revealing and fixing software errors when it is least expensive to do so.

d. Transfer. Software functions that have a high cost risk could be transferred to related programs that have resources to implement these functions successfully. Under no circumstances should cost risk be transferred to operational and PDSS phases of the system life cycle. Cost risk transferred to these phases is counterproductive to reducing life cycle costs.

HISTORY	ESTIMATES	EVALUATIONS
Similar Efforts Past Performance Cost Surveys	Cost Baseline Cost Model Input Assumptions Software Indicators	Planned vs Actual Cost Estimation Models Software Indicators Software Metrics

Figure 5-1. Software Cost Risk Abatement Inputs.

PROBABILITY OF DRIVERS ADVERSELY AFFECTING IMPACT

COST DRIVERS	IMPOSSIBLE to IMPROBABLE (0.0<P<0.4) Value = 0 or 1	PROBABLE (0.4<P<0.7) Value = 2	FREQUENT (0.7<P<1.0) Value = 3	Value
REQUIREMENTS				
SIZE	Small, noncomplex, or easily decomposed	Medium, moderate, complexity, decomposable	Large, highly complex, or not decomposable	
RESOURCE CONSTRAINTS	Little or no hardware-imposed constraints	Some hardware-imposed constraints	Significant hardware-imposed constraints	
APPLICATION	Non real-time, little system interdependency	Embedded, some system interdependency	Real-time embedded, strong interdependency	
TECHNOLOGY	Mature, existent, in-house experience	Existent, some in-house experience	New or new application, little experience	
REQUIREMENTS STABILITY	Little or no change to established baseline	Some change in baseline expected	Rapidly changing or no baseline	
PERSONNEL				
AVAILABILITY	In place, little turnover expected	Available, some turnover expected	High turnover, not available	
MIX	Good mix of software disciplines	Some disciplines inappropriately represented	Some disciplines not represented	
EXPERIENCE	High experience ratio	Average experience ratio	Low experience ratio	
MANAGEMENT ENVIRONMENT	Strong personnel management approach	Good personnel management approach	Weak personnel management approach	
REUSABLE SOFTWARE				
AVAILABILITY	Compatible with need dates	Delivery dates in question	Incompatible with need dates	
MODIFICATIONS	Little or no change	Some change	Extensive changes	
LANGUAGE	Compatible with system & PDSS requirements	Partial compatibility with requirements	Incompatible with system or PDSS requirements	
RIGHTS	Compatible with PDSS & competition requirements	Partial compatibility with PDSS, some competition	Incompatible with PDSS concept, noncompetitive	
CERTIFICATION	Verified performance, application compatible	Some application compatible test data available	Unverified, little test data available	
TOOLS AND ENVIRONMENT				
FACILITIES	Little or no modifications	Some modifications, existent	Major modifications, nonexistent	
AVAILABILITY	In place, meets need dates	Some compatibility with need dates	Nonexistent, does not meet need dates	
RIGHTS	Compatible with PDSS & development plans	Partial compatibility with PDSS & development plans	Incompatible with PDSS & development plans	
CONFIGURATION MANAGEMENT	Fully controlled	Some controls	No controls	

Figure 5-2. Quantification of Cost Probability.

Chapter 6

SCHEDULE RISK

6-1. Schedule estimation has a direct link with cost estimation. Like cost estimates, schedule estimates are usually deterministic. Both can normally be broken down into components that make up the system's overall cost or schedule. In schedules, this breakdown includes critical paths, networks, interim milestones, review points, etc. Schedule risk control includes determining range of times covering the span between earliest and latest dates for program completion, with accompanying detailed activity schedules and risks. Schedules are not realistic unless resources to complete individual activities are available when needed. Schedule risk control should combine uncertainties of the various activities, the range between shortest and longest time-frames, "most likely" or "best" schedule, and the risk of not meeting desired initial operating capability (IOC).

6-2. Schedule estimates are impacted by several competing drivers, some of which are not controllable by the program director. Approaches used to manage and control cost and performance risks can also impact software schedule risk. Typical software schedule drivers include resources, need dates, dependencies, and requirements.

a. The primary resources that can affect schedule include personnel, facilities, and money. Personnel resources impact software development in a slightly different manner than the way they impact hardware development. Too many personnel can negatively impact schedule in the same way that too few can. Facilities and financial resources impact software schedules in the same way they impact hardware schedules.

b. Need dates are usually composed of aspects program directors can and cannot control. Among the aspects outside program directors' control are threat changes; economic factors such as changes in budgetary constraints or in actual inflation rates; and political changes that influence IOC and financial commitments. Need dates that program directors can control to some extent include delivery dates of GFP and GFE, acquisition dates of software development and test tools, and internal interim milestone dates.

c. Technology can also directly influence schedule. New technology insertion may not be compatible with an externally imposed IOC due to immaturity of the technology, availability of the technology (for example, need dates that are incompatible when the technology can transition out of the laboratory environment into the applications environment), and the degree of experience the developer has using the technology.

d. Another driver that can have a direct bearing on schedule is requirements. If requirements are not known, defined, and consistent with given desired outcomes, schedule risk can be adversely affected. Just as in the technical and cost risk areas, the complexity and stability of the requirements can also influence schedule risk.

6-3. When appropriate software schedule risk drivers have been determined, it is then necessary to identify the necessary inputs for schedule risk control (fig 6-1).

a. **History.** A review of similar development efforts and contractors' past performance for this type of software development and application can significantly help identify areas of schedule uncertainty. Particular attention should be payed to the impact that requirements instability has had on schedules for these other programs. Comparison of planned and actual schedules for historical developments, along with determining the reasons for differences, can also aid in defining ways to control risk.

b. **Estimates.** By comparing pre- and post-schedule baselines for related historical development efforts, the validity of the proposed software development schedule can be assessed. Critical analysis of the assumptions used in the development of the schedule baseline should also be accomplished. Schedule baselines can then be used to form the planned portion of the software progress (development and test) indicator (AFSCP 800-43).

c. **Evaluations.** In performing risk control, periodic evaluation should be performed to ensure that the degree of schedule risk has not significantly increased. This evaluation should balance the realities of the development effort with any artificial or political constraints that may be imposed. Evaluation frequency should be based on degree of risk exposure the program office is willing to accept. In comparing schedule baselines with the actuals, deviations should be considered as sources of change in the risk assessment. The software progress indicator can be a useful tool in visually portraying these deviations throughout the software development effort. The correctness, fault density, test coverage, and documentation indicators (AFSCP 800-14) can help determine if product quality could have an impact on schedule.

6-4. Schedule risk control begins with an in-depth assessment of inputs. This is followed by determining the probability that the desired schedule will not be achieved and the assessment of the impact. By evaluating the combination of these two categories (probability and impact) (figs 6-2 and 2-2), total schedule risk can then be assessed as described in paragraph 3-4. When schedule risk has been evaluated, composite risk factors could be ranked to identify those needing most attention and those with high potential for risk reduction. Analysis should be conducted to ensure that correct risk drivers have been identified. Following completion of the evaluations and assessments, the program office's course of action for risk control should be established. Possible courses of action are:

a. Avoidance. This might include descoping the program's technical objectives to a more achievable level within available schedule and IOC needs. Other approaches may be to combine descoping with a P3I effort or to provide an initial capability and grow to the desired IOC through successive enhancement programs. Obtaining additional resources may also contribute to avoiding schedule risk. NOTE: Caution should be used if the last approach is used. Too many people can have a negative impact on schedule achievement.

b. Control. The program office could implement frequent informal or contractor internal management reviews to attempt to control schedule. Other possibilities include continuous updating of the schedule based on real-time inputs of interim milestone completions, but not a "floating" schedule baseline; conducting additional system trade-off studies; and streamlining the acquisition process.

c. Assumption. While remaining aware of the probability of schedule accomplishment, the program office could accept the inherent schedule risk and manage the development effort appropriately.

d. Transfer. The realignment of some software requirements to hardware or other system elements may be possible courses of action. Caution: Schedule risk should not be transferred to either the operational or PDSS phases of the program. This can often cause severe political and public criticism that could cause program cancellation and degrade military preparedness.

HISTORY	ESTIMATES	EVALUATIONS
Similar Efforts Past Performance Requirements Stability	Schedule Baseline Schedule Assumptions Software Indicators	Planned vs Actual Schedule Models Software Indicators Software Metrics

Figure 6-1. Software Schedule Risk Abatement Inputs.

PROBABILITY OF DRIVERS ADVERSELY AFFECTING IMPACT

SCHEDULE DRIVERS	IMPOSSIBLE to IMPROBABLE (0.0<P< 0.4) Value = 0 or 1	PROBABLE (0.4<P<0.7) Value = 2	FREQUENT (0.7<P<1.0) Value = 3	Value
RESOURCES				
PERSONNEL	Good discipline mix in place	Some disciplines not available	Questionable mix and/or availability	
FACILITIES	Existent, little or no modification	Existent, some modification	Nonexistent, extensive changes	
FINANCIAL	Sufficient budget allocated	Some questionable allocations	Budget allocation in doubt	
NEED DATES				
THREAT	Verified projections	Some unstable aspects	Rapidly changing	
ECONOMIC	Stable commitments	Some uncertain commitments	Unstable, fluctuating commitments	
POLITICAL	Little projected sensitivity	Some limited sensitivity	Extreme sensitivity	
GFE/GFP	Available, certified	Certification or delivery questions	Unavailable and/or uncertified	
TOOLS	In place, available	Some deliveries in question	Uncertain delivery dates	
TECHNOLOGY				
AVAILABILITY	In place	Some aspects still in development	Totally still in development	
MATURITY	Application verified	Some applications verified	No application evidence	
EXPERIENCE	Extensive application	Some application	Little or none	
REQUIREMENTS				
DEFINITION	Known, baselined	Baselined, some unknowns	Unknown, no baseline	
STABILITY	Little or no change projected	Controllable change projected	Rapid or uncontrolled change	
COMPLEXITY	Compatible with existing technology	Some dependency on new technology	Incompatible with existing technology	

Figure 6-2. Quantification of Schedule Probability.

Chapter 7

USE AND INTEGRATION OF RISK ABATEMENT

7-1. Application and interpretation of software risk abatement is not a "rote" process. Software risk assessments are not to be used for comparing the software development efforts of program A with program B, except in the global sense that one program may have different top-level risks in one or more risk area. The primary purpose of applying software risk abatement techniques is to be able to determine degree of risk in each area, evaluate and select different risk control approaches, and proactively manage software development. Guidelines presented in chapter 2 for each risk area are generic and need to be tailored to each program's requirements and critical aspects of software development. This chapter provides some acquisition phase-specific guidelines for software risk abatement as well as a sample use in each risk area.

Section A—Phase-Specific Guidelines

7-2. Figure A1-1 identifies the time-phased availability of software risk abatement data. This section presents some generic guidelines on how and when to apply risk abatement techniques throughout the system life cycle (fig 7-1). For brevity, only phases associated with AFR 800-series regulations will be used.

   a. **Mission Analysis.** During mission analysis, performance and support risk assessments from existing systems can significantly contribute to defining the approaches necessary to meet new or changed threats. These assessments can help determine whether existing systems can or should be modified or enhanced to meet the threat or new systems need to be developed. Planning and initial assessments of performance, cost, and schedule risks associated with new system and existing system modification should also be initiated.

   b. **Concept Exploration and Definition.** As various types of system approaches are considered in concept exploration, initial developmental risks associated with performance, cost, and schedule of the competing system should be updated and risk drivers defined. In conjunction with development risk update, feasibility assessments of various risk control alternatives for high-risk areas should be initiated. Revised development risks and control alternatives can be used to identify initial performance and support risks. Initial risk assessments should be used to assist in selecting system approaches that should be considered during demonstration and validation.

   c. **Demonstration and Validation.** In demonstration and validation, development risk abatement should be formally initiated, with contractual mechanisms in place to obtain and use available risk input

data. Data and associated assessments can be used to further monitor risk drivers and to update performance and support risk planning. The risk abatement results can be used in deciding which system approaches should transition to FSD.

   d. **Full-Scale Development.** During FSD, the program office's total risk management program should be in place. The program should include appropriate involvement of using and supporting agencies and contractors. Contractual vehicles for software risk abatement and mechanisms for input data collection for each risk area should have been implemented.

   e. **Full-Rate Production and Deployment and Operational Support.** In production and deployment, responsibility for the risk management program may often transfer from the program office to another agency that assumes responsibility for systems management. Transfer is normally documented in a program management responsibility transfer plan. Software risk abatement continues to be a viable management tool during operational support, especially in control and implementation of software changes that correct deficiencies and implement additional capabilities.

7-3. Overlapping the systems acquisition phases are the contractual "phases" of preaward, source selection, and contract execution.

   a. **Preaward.** The program office should consider software risk abatement activities and input data requirements in the preparation of the RFP. Prospective bidders to the RFP can provide initial industry perspectives of proposed software risk abatement contractual requirements and promote understanding between the program office and industry on the need for risk control. Such dialog should occur in a presolicitation conference before RFP release. Have industry consider and comment on software risk abatement requirements when reviewing the draft RFP.

   b. **Source Selection.** Software risk abatement techniques can be used as part of the selection process to identify "success-oriented" RFP responses. These techniques can also identify specific areas in which responses may be weak, increase risk, or be a possible discriminator in source selection.

   c. **Contract Execution.** Risk abatement can be used to identify software areas in which development is proceeding faster than the supporting structure, both engineering and quality, allows. Risk assessment and control can aid in determining the impact of program changes, where such changes are best implemented, and how to best respond to externally driven changes. How the software risk abatement data is used by the contractors and program office can also provide insight into the level of management involvement and visibility into the software aspect of systems.

Section B—Sample Use of Risk Abatement

7-4. Two samples are included in this section: one, during source selection for entry into FSD and, two, for 3 years into FSD. A retrospective assessment of both risk interpretations is provided. Since risk abatement interpretations are program-unique, the following assumptions concerning the program and program office apply to the samples.

a. Program Requirements. The sample program is to develop a new command, control, communications, intelligence system. The system is to be developed using the new EXTRA programming language for implementation. EXTRA, for example purposes only, is a DOD-approved higher-order language (HOL). Size of the software development effort is estimated in excess of 2 million lines of code, with some software components to be procured as unmodified commercial off-the-shelf (COTS) software. Some prototyping was accomplished during demonstration and validation (DEM/VAL) as proof of concept. System is planned for worldwide installation, used by one command and supported by another command. Due to the great success of the DEM/VAL prototyped software, FSD is planned to take 4 years.

b. Program Office. A new program director (PD) was assigned before source selection and is to remain for 3 years. The PD has had extensive experience with related software-intensive systems and strongly believes in system risk management. To incorporate a strong software risk abatement influence into the system's risk management program, the PD has established a software risk abatement team (fig 7-2) and charged it with the tasks in figure 7-3. In response, the team developed and implemented its approach to managing software risk throughout the life cycle (fig 7-4). After 2 years, the PD was reassigned and replaced by an individual without as strong a software development background. The sample interpretations in paragraphs 7-5 and 7-6 are based on a worst-case scenario; that is, where things can go wrong, they will, and not always in the areas expected.

7-5. During source selection, as the first sample, the risk management team made the following determinations and software risk assessments that were common to all the submitted proposals and were based on the DEM/VAL development strategies and results.

a. Team Determinations:

(1) All the prototyping was accomplished in a rather loosely controlled environment, with insufficient documentation to support direct reuse during FSD. None of the prototyping was done using EX-

TRA. In fact, a large amount of the prototyping was done using non-HOL languages in order to get them to work.

(2) While EXTRA was an approved HOL, the associated software environment (development, implementation, and test tools) was still maturing. EXTRA, though, did have a design structure that could be effectively used independent of implementing HOL. With this in mind, the team recommended EXTRA's use in FSD and made allowances for proposals that contained an implementation option using a more mature HOL.

(3) An agreed-to and signed CRLCMP was not available. The primary reason for its unavailability was the different PDSS concepts of the using and supporting commands. Recognizing the differences, each command felt that PDSS requirements were adequately defined to influence software design and that PDSS concept agreement could be reached before preliminary design review (PDR).

(4) Although the COTS software were proven independent entities, much of the COTS software had not been integrated into a system similar to the one under development. The team recommended that "extra credit" be given to those proposals that addressed the possibility and impact of COTS integration problems.

(5) All of the responding contractors had some limited experience with EXTRA. Most, but not all, had effective methods for gaining visibility into the quality of software products and the software development process and for controlling the development process. All the contractors had experience with similar-type systems and were planning to use DOD-STD-2167A and DOD-STD-2168, as tailored by the program office.

(6) All the proposals were within the program office's planned funding profile. The team still had concerns whether sufficient funds were being allocated to software development.

(7) Based on proposal review and preaward survey results, the team estimated that software development would take a minimum of 6 years, 2 years more than planned. IOC was a directed date and, if COTS software integration went as planned, there was a possibility of success.

b. Software Risk Assessment:

(1) Performance Risk: High. The probability was assessed as frequent and the impact assessment was considered catastrophic due to the size of the software effort, immaturity of the EXTRA development environment, and history associated with the development based on unique, undocumented prototypes.

(2) Support Risk: Moderate to High. The probability was assessed between frequent and probable while the impact was assessed as critical primarily because of the concerns over the lack of COTS software data rights for the concept and the open issues between the using and supporting commands.

800 SERIES REGULATIONS	Mission Analysis	Concept Exploration	Demonstration and Validation	Full Scale Development	Production and Deployment
700 SERIES REGULATIONS	Planning	Concept	Definition	Development and Test	Operation and Maintenance
PERFORMANCE RISK	Plan/Use	Refine	Implement	- - - - - - - - →	
SCHEDULE RISK	Plan	Refine	Implement	- - - - - - - - →	
COST RISK	Plan	Refine	Implement	- - - - - - - - →	
SUPPORT RISK	Use	Plan	Refine	Implement	- - - - - →

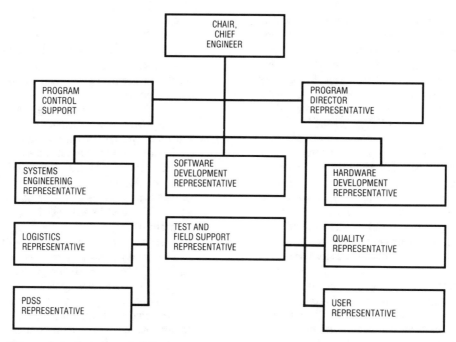

Figure 7-2. Software Risk Abatement Team.

(3) Cost Risk: Moderate to High. The probability was between frequent and probable. Impact was critical. These assessments were driven by the use of COTS software and lack of software engineering discipline while prototyping. Risk was presented as a range to account for schedule concerns.

(4) Schedule Risk: High. The probability was frequent. Impact was critical. Primary causes were a fixed IOC date and the EXTRA development environment.

c. PD Assessment. The PD agreed with the team's risk assessments. Based on previous experience, the PD decided that all the risk areas were controllable within the established risk management framework.

7-6. As the second sample, 3 years later and with a PD change, management involvement in the software development effort has significantly decreased. The software risk management team remains, although with diminished influence. Due to the fixed IOC, the PD has agreed with a contractor proposal to incorporate "unmodified" prototype software in order to maintain schedule. COTS software integration has not proceeded well. Integration has caused some extensive modification to COTS software; the modification has been hampered by the lack of necessary support documentation. Program funding has remained constant. The number of PDSS issues has increased between using and supporting commands. At the PD's request, the team has been tasked to

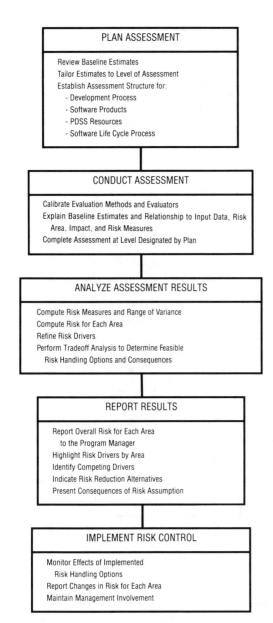

PLAN ASSESSMENT

Review Baseline Estimates
Tailor Estimates to Level of Assessment
Establish Assessment Structure for:
 - Development Process
 - Software Products
 - PDSS Resources
 - Software Life Cycle Process

CONDUCT ASSESSMENT

Calibrate Evaluation Methods and Evaluators
Explain Baseline Estimates and Relationship to Input Data, Risk
 Area, Impact, and Risk Measures
Complete Assessment at Level Designated by Plan

ANALYZE ASSESSMENT RESULTS

Compute Risk Measures and Range of Variance
Compute Risk for Each Area
Refine Risk Drivers
Perform Tradeoff Analysis to Determine Feasible
 Risk Handling Options and Consequences

REPORT RESULTS

Report Overall Risk for Each Area
 to the Program Manager
Highlight Risk Drivers by Area
Identify Competing Drivers
Indicate Risk Reduction Alternatives
Present Consequences of Risk Assumption

IMPLEMENT RISK CONTROL

Monitor Effects of Implemented
 Risk Handling Options
Report Changes in Risk for Each Area
Maintain Management Involvement

Figure 7-3. Team Functions.

update its software risk assessments.

a. Team Determinations:

(1) Use of the software prototypes would most likely not help the contractor maintain schedule due to their non-HOL nature and lack of previous documentation. There was also increased probability that the software would not meet performance requirements and that support costs would increase.

(2) In conjunction with prototype reuse, the contractor was also allowed to postpone software documentation efforts and reduce testing. This action raised significant concerns about software reliability and supportability.

(3) With diminished PD software development involvement, the contractor has correspondingly loosened software development controls in hopes of maintaining cost and schedule.

(4) Development gains expected from the use of EXTRA had been realized. Life-cycle gains were

being diminished by "unmodified" prototype reuse. Problems were also being experienced in the test and integration of the EXTRA code that were primarily attributed to the immaturity of the tool environment.

(5) PDSS requirements were in a state of flux due to lack of agreement between the using and supporting commands on support issues and software partitioning. Previously expected early resolution of these issues has not been reached. The program office defined what it thought would be the best software support concept and incorporated this approach in contract requirements to influence software design for supportability. Software design is now inconsistent with the user's perceived support needs.

(6) Although PDR was conducted on schedule, additional PDRs were required to address design deficiencies at both the software and system levels. A hardware CDR was conducted and the hardware design baselined. The software CDR followed 1 year later and raised several concerns over the compatibility of the baselined hardware with the software requirements and design.

b. Revised Risk Assessments:

(1) Performance Risk: High. Use of the "unmodified" prototypes and the integration problems associated with the COTS software were the key drivers. Additionally, key software design engineers were leaving the program to begin work on a new company. In spite of unusual stability in user operational requirements, the technical performance characteristics were suffering from a lack of reliability, flexibility, and supportability. System responsiveness was also in question due to the new mix of EXTRA code, modified COTS code, prototype incorporation, and reduced testing.

(2) Cost Risk: High. While management actions were controlling development cost, software life cycle costs appeared to be increasing exponentially with each reduction of software requirements implemented to control cost.

(3) Schedule Risk: High. Trying to implement undocumented prototypes into a revised software design combined with a rigid IOC date were the key elements. The loss of experienced software personnel also had a perceived negative impact on schedule.

(4) Support Risk: High. Needed documentation would most likely not be available to support PDSS. Configuration management was suffering from the new software mix and lack of visibility into the modified COTS software. PDSS responsibility issues had not been resolved and were growing. There was also increased likelihood that extensive PDSS modifications would be necessary to bring the IOC-delivered software to full operational capability.

c. PD Assessment. The PD disagreed with the team's risk assessments and evaluations. While the development effort had some difficulties, the contractor appeared to have things under control. The team was tasked with revising its assessments to bring them more in line with political realities.

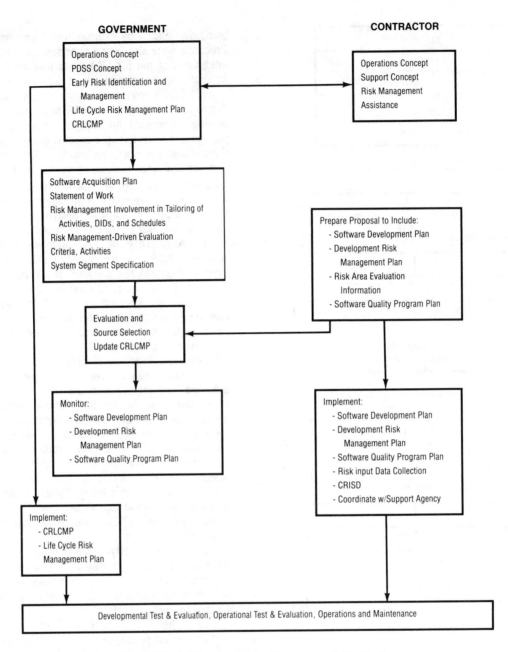

GOVERNMENT

CONTRACTOR

Operations Concept
PDSS Concept
Early Risk Identification and
    Management
Life Cycle Risk Management Plan
CRLCMP

Operations Concept
Support Concept
Risk Management
Assistance

Software Acquisition Plan
Statement of Work
Risk Management Involvement in Tailoring of
    Activities, DIDs, and Schedules
Risk Management-Driven Evaluation
Criteria, Activities
System Segment Specification

Prepare Proposal to Include:
    - Software Development Plan
    - Development Risk
        Management Plan
    - Risk Area Evaluation
        Information
    - Software Quality Program Plan

Evaluation and
Source Selection
Update CRLCMP

Monitor:
    - Software Development Plan
    - Development Risk
        Management Plan
    - Software Quality Program Plan

Implement:
    - Software Development Plan
    - Development Risk
        Management Plan
    - Software Quality Program Plan
    - Risk input Data Collection
    - CRISD
    - Coordinate w/Support Agency

Implement:
    - CRLCMP
    - Life Cycle Risk
        Management Plan

Developmental Test & Evaluation, Operational Test & Evaluation, Operations and Maintenance

Figure 7-4. Software Risk Abatement Life Cycle.

7-7. Possible retrospective assessments of the program office's software risk evaluations are:

a. Source Selection. Risk estimates appeared to be accurate. Concerns about the EXTRA HOL did

not form during FSD, possibly due to increased management interest in promoting and intelligently controlling EXTRA's use. Original optimism about resolving roles and mission issues between the using and supporting commands was not justified, possibly related to changes in personnel representing both commands. Fears associated with reuse of the DEM/VAL prototypes were justified. The team's recommendation for extra credit for those proposals that addressed COTS software integration problems was also valid.

b. Full-Scale Development. The change in PD appears to have had a negative impact on use of risk management techniques to influence program decisions. Decisions to reduce documentation, testing, and quality requirements and to use DEM/VAL prototype software should have included risk impact assessments before implementing the decisions. Management actions to control new risks should be investigated and implemented as soon as possible. The present course presents even more difficulties in achieving IOC.

Section C—Other Analysis Tool Considerations

7-8. The SPO must perform an analysis to determine the need for software IV&V before release of the FSD RFP. The use of an experienced IV&V contractor to review appropriate software configuration items can also help control risk. Many IV&V agents have a considerable repository of software tools to assist in this task (see AFSCP/AFLCP 800-5). Although there are no widespread automated tools available to support the application of software risk abatement techniques, the program office should consider using the same tools it currently uses for technical and schedule risk assessment of hardware. Tools that incorporate methods such as networks, decision analysis, methods of moments, work breakdown structure simulation, graphics, estimating relationships, and risk factors can be adopted for use in addressing software risk.

7-9. Cost risk can be successfully addressed by using one or more of the available software cost estimating models to bound and refine software cost estimations. COCOMO is probably the most widespread model and does have features in many of its newer versions that can be useful in refining estimates for modern software development.

7-10. Software support risk models are in their infancy. The Air Force Operational Test and Evaluation Center (AFOTEC) is doing some pioneering work in this area. Contact AFOTEC/LG5 at Kirtland AFB NM for additional information on its approach to software support risk.

7-11. The Defense Systems Management College has available at no cost (other than supplying them with blank floppy disks) a Program Director's Support System, which is an application of decision support systems technology to the defense acquisition program management environment. Some functional models address cost analysis, software cost estimating, and schedule risk assessment.

OFFICIAL

BERNARD P. RANDOLPH, General, USAF
AFSC Commander

DENIS R. NIBBELIN, Colonel, USAF
AFSC Director of Information Management

ALFRED G. HANSEN, General, USAF
AFLC Commander

JAMES E. GIBBONS, Major, USAF
AFLC Director of Administration

AFSC—Andrews AFB DC 1988

NBSIR 86-3386

WORK PRIORITY SCHEME FOR EDP AUDIT AND

COMPUTER SECURITY REVIEW

Editors:

Zella G. Ruthberg
Institute for Computer Sciences and Technology
National Bureau of Standards

and

Bonnie T. Fisher
Department of Health & Human Services
Office of Inspector General

March 1986

Issued August 1986

U.S. DEPARTMENT OF COMMERCE, Malcolm Baldrige, *Secretary*

NATIONAL BUREAU OF STANDARDS, Ernest Ambler, *Director*

Reprinted from *National Bureau of Standards Technical Report NBSIR 86-3386*, March 1986, pages iii–B-14. U.S. Government work not protected by U.S. copyright.

ABSTRACT

This report describes a high level risk analysis for Automated Information Systems (AISs) that can be used by computer security reviewers and EDP auditors to prioritize their non-discretionary and discretionary review activities for these AISs. It divides the risk analysis problem into five areas of risk concern (called dimensions) with each area defined by a set of characteristics. The five dimensions are: Criticality/Mission Impact, Size/Scale/Complexity, Environment/Stability, Reliability/Integrity, and Technology Integration. The report presents two possible two-level risk scoring schemes, each of which calculates the level of risk for each dimension, uses the Criticality score as a first order system risk score, and then combines all five dimension risk scores for a second order system risk score. One scoring method is simple and intuitive; the other scoring method is more detailed. An approach for deriving an EDP audit or computer security review plan using these scores is outlined.

KEYWORDS

audit/review plan
automated information system risk analysis
computer security review
Criticality/Mission Impact
discretionary audit/review
EDP audit
Environment/Stability
non-discretionary audit/review
Reliability/Integrity
risk score
Size/Scale/Complexity
Technology Integration

1. INTRODUCTION

1.1 The Work Priority Scheme in Perspective

This report describes a methodology for prioritizing the work to be performed by EDP Auditors and Computer Security Reviewers. It is based largely on the results of a Spring 1985 public/private sector workshop of EDP auditors and systems developers who explored the criteria for assessing risk in computer systems. The workshop was co-sponsored by NBS and the EDP Systems Review and Security Work Group of the President's Council on Integrity and Efficiency (PCIE). The Work Group was established in October of 1983 under the auspices of the PCIE Computer Security Project, chaired by Richard P. Kusserow, Inspector General (IG) of the Department of Health and Human

Services (HHS). (See Appendix A for membership in and further description of the Work Group.) The methodology described in this report is to be included in the EDP system development audit guide currently being developed by this Work Group for joint publication by the PCIE and the National Bureau of Standards (NBS).

1.2   Internal Controls and Security Safeguards

Although it may at first appear strange to have the same methodology applicable to both EDP audit and computer security review, further analysis of these two activities reveals the similarity of their focus. EDP audit is concerned with the review of internal controls in an Automated Information System (AIS), while Computer Security review examines the security safeguards in an AIS. Security must be recognized as only one, albeit a major category of internal controls. A study performed by Arthur Young for the Department of Energy [1], recognized that computer security controls are a _subset_ of the internal controls to be found in an AIS. The major difference between these two sets of controls is that internal controls address efficiency and effectiveness _in addition to_ security issues. The Office of Management and Budget, in their OMB Circular A-130 (a re-write of OMB Circular A-71 TM1 (Computer Security)), acknowledges the interrelationship between internal control and security concerns in both their definition of key terms and their acceptance of internal control reviews and documentation in lieu of security reviews. OMB Circular A-123 also reflects this correlation.

1.3   Brief Overview of the Scheme

The Scheme described in this report enables its user to systematically perform a risk-based evaluation of the subjects for EDP audit/security review within an organization (i.e., the universe of its AISs), and to arrive at a risk measurement for each AIS. This final risk measure (or score) is based on an analysis of risk in key areas of concern (dimensions for describing risk) in that system. These scores enable the user to rank the systems by determining which AISs offer the highest levels of risk to the organization and which dimensions within each AIS contribute most to this high level of risk. Based on this analysis, the user can then draw up an EDP audit or security review work plan for the organization in question. The work plan would include annual coverage along with a basis for formulating the scope of specific AIS reviews. Considering the generality of the dimensions and their associated characteristics, the scheme is equally appropriate for public and private sector review subjects.

The scheme employs a two-level review and the characteristics associated with the five dimensions. The levels for the dimensions are:

Level I
      Criticality/Mission Impact

Level II
      Size/Scale/Complexity
      Environment/Stability
      Reliability/Integrity
      Technology Integration

Each dimension is defined by a related set of characteristics
which are used to estimate or calculate the amount of risk posed
by that dimension to the failure of the system. A Level I review
looks at Criticality/Mission Impact of the system to the organization and develops a risk score for each AIS with respect to
this dimension. Since this dimension is the most important of
the five risk areas, it can be used as a first approximation to a
system risk score. The AISs can then be placed in sequence from
high to low risk and the low risk systems eliminated from further
review consideration. Organizations with very limited resources
could stop at a Level I review and plan their work based on these
results.

     To refine the risk scores further, the high criticality risk
AISs are reviewed at Level II. Risk scores are obtained for the
four remaining dimensions for each high criticality risk AIS.
These four dimension risk scores are summed and added to the
Level I risk score to yield the system risk score for that AIS.
The AISs reviewed at Level II can then again be placed in
sequence from high to low risk and thus enable the reviewer to
prioritize his work.

     Two possible risk scoring methods are suggested and describ-
ed briefly in Section 4 and in detail in Appendix D. The first
is a simple intuitive approach based on a minimal collection of
information on the AIS; the second is more elaborate and is based
on more detailed information on the AIS. Organizations with
limited resources could use the simple scoring method to obtain
system risk scores while those with more resources could use the
more elaborate approach.

2. THE NEED FOR THE SCHEME

2.1 Dependence on Computers

     As part of the Fiscal Year 1986 budget, the President
highlighted systems management as one of the Federal Government's
major initiatives for FY 1986 and beyond [2]. The Federal
Government continues to develop 90 percent of its software, which
constitutes the controlling mechanism for the approximately $14
billion spent annually on information technology. More than
120,000 federal employees are involved in programming and
managing the resultant systems which will ultimately control and
distribute the almost $1 trillion dollars in outlays projected
for 1986. Obviously, the Federal commitment to the computer
hardware, software, and management arenas has reached gigantic
proportions with no tapering off in sight of either the size or
the growth rate.

2.2 EDP Audits/Security Reviews - A Form of Control

In the past ten years there has been a slowly growing recognition of the need for controls in the Federal Government's automated systems. Although there often is resistance among program sponsors or user management to employing internal controls within AISs because of the cost, time, and overhead that such controls can introduce, the interest in and use of controls in AISs is continuing to grow. This growth is augmented by the increasing emphasis OMB has placed on internal controls since the passage of PL97-255, the Federal Managers' Financial Integrity Act of 1982 [3], and the completion and revision of their own Circular A-123. (See Section 2.3 for descriptions of these control requirements.) The General Accounting Office (GAO), at Congressional request, has closely followed the Federal agencies' implementation of A-123, and, thus far, has been dissatisfied with agencies' compliance--especially in the area of internal controls in AISs.

Internal audit organizations, whose activities existed long before the computer age, have long recognized and stressed the need for internal controls in manual (primarily financial) systems and the need for independent audits as a critical component of the oversight of an organization's systems. With the advent of computerized AISs in organizations, career fields specializing in EDP audit (generally found in audit organizations) and security review (often found in audit or management) have developed. Recognition and revision of their role in the review of automated systems is continuing, and increasing rapidly.

2.3 Formal Requirements for Audits and Reviews

The major legal requirements for EDP audits and security reviews within Federal agencies are found in three OMB circulars: A-130, A-123, and A-127. Circular A-130 (the follow-on to A-71 TM1) outlines specific requirements for establishing agency security programs, and specifies the use of (1) design reviews and system tests for security during development of applications (to be used for certification of application) (2) periodic security audits or reviews of applications for recertification, and (3) periodic risk analyses of installations. OMB Circular A-123, issued in 1981 and revised in 1983, outlines for Federal agencies specific policies and standards for establishing and maintaining internal controls in their programs and administrative activities. This includes requirements for vulnerability assessments and internal control reviews. The main provisions of A-123 were made into law through the enactment of the Federal Managers' Financial Integrity Act of 1982. OMB Circular A-127, issued in 1984, outlines for Federal agencies specific policies and standards for establishing and maintaining internal controls in financial management systems. This includes requirements for annual reviews of agency financial systems which build on reviews required by OMB Circular A-123. In addition to these three key legal directives, internal audit and security are subject to departmental requirements, audit organization recommendations, and GAO audit standards for computer based systems [4].

2.4 Size of Review Task

A major implication of the enormous numbers of computers and our dependence on them, found today in government (see section 2.1) as well as the private sector, is that the universe of AISs that need reviewing is also enormous. However, the number of trained EDP auditors and security reviewers to do this job has not kept pace with the size of this problem. A consistent methodology for obtaining a risk score for an AIS is seen as a major tool for culling through the review work that needs to be done and assigning relevant as well as realistic workloads to the review staff available within an organization.

3. BACKGROUND ON THE METHODOLOGY

3.1 The Invitational Workshop

The PCIE Work Group, in the course of its activities, decided that an essential component of their final product, Guide to Auditing for Controls and Security Throughout the Systems Development Life Cycle, was a methodology for prioritizing the EDP auditor's work. Rather than rely exclusively on the experience and background of the Work Group members, it was decided to hold an invitational workshop on the subject and use the ideas generated during the course of the workshop to develop a work priority scheme.

The 2 1/2 day workshop was held in March of 1985. A "strawman" scheme (see Appendix B), used as a starting point for discussions, was provided by William Perry, based on a Harvard Business Review article [5] by F. Warren McFarlan on predicting the failure of systems under development. The 62 attendees included EDP auditors, senior ADP managers, and computer security specialists from both the Federal Government and the private sector. (See Appendix C for list of attendees.) Presentations, to set the stage, were given on the first morning by attendees from Coopers & Lybrand, Touche Ross & Co., General Motors, International Security Technology Inc., and Management & Computer Services, Inc. The attendees were then divided into five discussion groups, each of which had 1 1/2 days to analyze the "strawman" and come up with their own version of a work priority scheme, based on the "strawman" framework of providing critical risk dimensions with associated characteristics. Each group presented its scheme at the closing session of the workshop.

3.2 Workshop Points of Agreement

Although each group came up with a somewhat different set of major audit/security concerns (dimensions) for the scheme, there was universal agreement on four underlying premises:

1. The entire EDP audit plan[1] must first give consideration to non-discretionary audits (mandated by law, regulation, and/or the agency/organization management). These are reflected in the front end qualifiers. Only if there are remaining resources for EDP audit would the scheme be used as originally intended.

2. The risk based prioritizing evaluation needs to be performed at two levels, Level I and Level II.

3. The first level of inquiry (for its Level I dimension) should concern itself with the criticality of the AIS to the agency/organization mission. Only critical systems should be reviewed further (for its Level II dimensions[2]) and given a more detailed risk score.

4. The ranking and rating of the risk characteristics of each dimension is program and agency/organization specific. Only the risk scoring method is applicable across the board.

4.   A WORK PRIORITY SCHEME FOR THE EDP AUDITOR

4.1 Assumptions and Caveats

The use of the proposed work prioritizing scheme is based on certain ideal assumptions and caveats. These include:

o An inventory of all computer systems (AISs)--operational, under development, or undergoing major change--is maintained, to establish the audit universe.

o The above inventory may not be complete due to user development or system changes made outside the system development process.

o To use the priority scheme, certain minimal information is required or the assessment of the system may not be valid.

o The full priority scheme would most easily be performed by EDP audit groups in order to enlist multiple perspectives, especially where resources are known to be a concern.

---

[1]) It should be understood that the terms EDP audit and security review may be used interchangeably throughout the scheme and the surrounding discussion.

[2]) The four major concerns or dimensions to be addressed in a Level II review (presented in section 4.4) are a synthesis of the conclusions drawn by the five workshop discussion groups. Two analysis approaches for risk measurement (or scoring) are discussed briefly in Section 4.6 and in detail in Appendix D.

o   Auditors in the organization must agree that risk can be
    evaluated by a standardized scheme.

o   Users should always be consulted in the risk evaluation
    conducted by the auditor to ensure appropriate assump-
    tions, and to assure maximum effectiveness.

o   Auditor judgement is still needed!

Within this framework of assumptions and caveats the entire EDP
audit work plan can then be developed. To the degree these
assumptions differ from the reality of the organization's SDLC
environment, the work planning methodology should be adjusted.

4.2 Audit Planning/Prioritization Process

The risk evaluation performed as part of the work priority
scheme must be done within the context of the entire audit
planning process. There are elements of the process that need to
be considered prior to the risk evaluation (such as non-discretionary audit requirements) and other elements that require
consideration afterwards (such as resource constraints). The
following sections contain a suggested model for the entire
prioritization process.

4.3 Non-Discretionary Audits

As can be seen from the model in Figure 1, the audit
planning and prioritization process starts with front end
qualifiers that must be considered by the auditor prior to making
decisions with respect to which system(s) should be audited.
These front end qualifiers consist of nondiscretionary factors
which are beyond the auditor's control. These nondiscretionary
factors include, but are not limited to the following:

o   External directives (e.g., laws, regulations, OMB
    circulars, and audit standards);

o   Internal directives and priorities (e.g., contractual
    requirements; requirements, standards, and policies of
    audit and data processing organizations; upper management
    directives);

o   Business/organizational environment unique to the
    organization (e.g., effect of economy on organization,
    budget of organization, and technology available to or
    used by organization);

o   Organizational unique factors (e.g., presence and
    strength of quality assurance and security functions,
    management and control philosophy, structure, and
    policies);

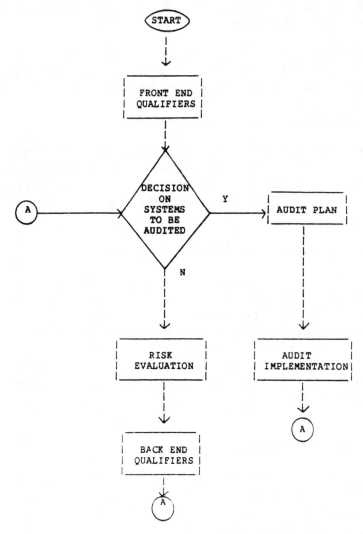

Figure 1   AUDIT PLANNING/PRIORITIZATION PROCESS

o Geo-political environment (e.g., public concern and
   politics);

o Resource constraints/economic health (e.g., dollars,
   time, expertise, training, tools, and techniques);

o Known problems with the system, from current logs or
   previous evaluations and audits (e.g., nature and
   magnitude of problems);

o Evaluations and audits planned by management;

o Auditor's institutional knowledge of organization's
   universe of systems.

     After all of the front end qualifiers have been considered,
it may be that the entire audit plan is dictated by the nondiscretionary work. That is, external directives, internal directives, business environment, unique organization/responsibili-
ties, and/or resource constraints may require that certain audits

be performed and these required audits may use up the limited audit resources available. In this case, the priority scheme may still be useful for determining audit approaches and where to focus efforts.

If, on the other hand, additional audit resources are available for discretionary audits, the risk evaluation of the work priority scheme can be used to identify and rank the systems in greatest need of audit coverage. Ultimately, back end qualifiers may need to be considered for the discretionary audits, as described in Section 5.

4.4 Risk Evaluation Levels and Dimensions

The work priority scheme expresses the risk concerns in terms of two levels and five dimensions. The risk concerns in Level I are reviewed first and those in Level II are reviewed second. Level I has one dimension and Level II has four dimensions. Each dimension is defined as a related set of characteristics which can estimate or measure the amount of risk posed by that dimension to a failure of the system. The chief concern of each dimension can be stated in the form of a question as follows:

1. What is the impact/criticality of the system to the organization?

A poorly developed or controlled system that is mission critical could jeopardize an organization's basic operational or programmatic effectiveness; therefore, an impact/critical system commands audit attention. The larger the impact, the more important it is to audit.

2. How complex is the system? (This includes size considerations.)

The more complex the system, the more difficult is communication and control, and consequently, the higher the risk of failure. The greater the chance for failure, the more important it is to audit the system.

3. How stable is the system internally (structure) and externally (environment)?

The less stable the system, the more difficult it is to develop procedures for communication and control, the greater the chance for failure, and the greater the need to audit.

4. How reliable is the system and the information it processes and generates (i.e., what is the chance of the system failing or the data being wrong)?

The answer to this question is obtained by looking at the controls in the system (integrity controls) and prior audit experience. The less reliable, the more chance for failure and the need to audit.

5. How well is the technology integrated into the organization?

The poorer the system technology is integrated with the skills of the staff and the standards and procedures of the organization, the more chance for failure and the greater the need to audit.

These questions serve as the basis for the five dimensions and their associated characteristics developed for the work prioritization scheme. Identified simply the two levels and five dimensions are:

Level I
   1. Criticality/Mission Impact

Level II
   2. Size/Scale/Complexity
   3. Environment/Stability
   4. Reliability/Integrity
   5. Technology Integration

The five workshop discussion groups believed strongly that the overriding dimension of the five should be Criticality/Mission Impact. Systems that significantly impact the mission of an organization, or key organizational components, would easily take precedence over all other dimensions in allocating EDP audit resources. Because Criticality/Mission Impact was such an overriding dimension, the work priority scheme was developed as a two level scheme. Level I is composed of the dimension Criticality/Mission Impact while Level II is composed of the remaining four dimensions: Size/Scale/Complexity, Environment/Stability, Reliability/Integrity, and Technology Integration.

The two level work priority scheme permits a high amount of flexibility depending on organizational need since it can be applied in any degree of detail required. For example, the results of Level I ranking may be adequate to prioritize all audit work, based on available time and resources. If additional ranking characteristics are necessary, the more detailed Level II can be used to further prioritize audit work. A two level review, additionally, enables the auditor to purge from consideration those systems which will definitely not be reviewed, for any number of reasons. Environment and resource issues enter in here.

The two level work priority scheme follows in outline form, identifying the five dimensions and their related characteristics. [Note that the same characteristic may be used in more than one dimension because the question asked will be different.]

4.5 Two Level Work Priority Dimensions/Characteristics

4.5.1 Level I:

A. <u>Mission Impact/Strategic Value/Organization (Business)
    Criticality and Sensitivity Factors</u>

  o criticality of system to organization mission

  o criticality/sensitivity of system to well being,
     safety or interest of general public/clients/con-
     sumers

  o criticality/sensitivity of data and information
     - competitive advantage
     - confidence of public in program/department
     - privacy/confidentiality/security issues

  o materiality of resources controlled by system

  o fraud potential

  o life cycle costs of system (people and dollars)
     - development cost budget
       . people
       . dollars
           hardware
           software
           facilities
     - operating cost budget
       . people
           data processing/systems (including training)
           users (including training)
       . dollars
           hardware (CPU, peripherals, terminals,
                   telecommunications, etc.)
             - acquisition
             - operation
           software
             - acquisition
             - maintenance
           supplies
           facilities
           configuration change control

  o degree of dependence on AIS

  o criticality of interfaces with other systems and
     external organizations

A Level I review, outlined above, provides a "first cut" at
the total audit universe. This initial review will identify
critical systems that require audit coverage. The additional
dimensions to be reviewed in Level II should be used to

rank these critical systems to find those most deserving of
discretionary audit coverage.

4.5.2 Level II:

B. System[3] Size/Scale/Complexity
_____

[3]The term "system" is used in place of "project" to signify
the entire AIS life cycle and the possibility of auditing at any
point in the development process or operations.

o **size of user area impacted**

o **number/complexity of interfaces/relationships with
 other projects or systems**

o **complexity of AIS technology (e.g., network size,
 communication needs, system configuration, degree of
 centralization, nature of transaction coupling
 mechanisms, nature of security)**

o **size/complexity of system**
 - **size of system budget**
  . **development costs**
  . **maintenance/operation costs**
 - **number/complexity of different inputs**
 - **number/complexity of unique files**
 - **number/complexity of unique outputs**
 - **number/complexity of logical files (views) system
   will access**
 - **number/complexity of major types of on-line
   inquiry**
 - **number of source documents maintained/retained**
 - **number/complexity of computer programs**
 - **complexity of programming language**
 - **complexity of system configuration**
 - **number of human elements interfacing**
 - **number of decision levels**
 - **number of functions by devices**
 - **number, types and complexity of transactions**
 - **number of external organizations impacted**

o **nature of interactions with external organizations**

C. System Environment/Stability

o **organizational breadth (interfaces, dependencies,
 system configuration)**

o **management involvement/commitment**

o **project management approach and structure**
 - **configuration management program**

- management efficiency and effectiveness

o specificity of, agreement on, and support for user requirements

o confidence in estimates -- both cost and time -- premising make-or-buy decisions, vendor selection, system testing/validation, etc.

o number of vendors/contractors involved

o **newness of function/process to user**

o problems associated with current system performance and/or system development effort

o existence/scope of data processing standards, policies and procedures, especially systems development life cycle methodology and documentation requirements

o availability of evidence - document and report preparation and maintenance for entire systems life cycle (e.g., test/validation/certification results, operations manual, system specifications, audit trails, exception reporting)

o quality and completeness of documentation

o general controls
   - physical access controls
   - environmental controls
   - communication controls
   - management controls environment
   - document controls
   - system change and test/validation/certification controls

o on-going concern issues/organization effect (will mission objectives be met in a timely manner?)
   - interruption tolerance
   - ability to maintain performance
   - unsatisfactory system performance (adverse consequences from degradation or failure)
   - unsatisfactory system development completion
   - unsatisfactory conversion

o labor relations (e.g., salary parity, hours, fringe benefits, etc.)

o project team (management and staff effectiveness and training)

o organizational and personnel changes (frequency, magnitude and number)

185

o functional requirements changes (frequency, number, and magnitude)

o technical changes (e.g., frequency, magnitude and number)

o factors affecting cost/economic/budget climate

o availability and adequacy of back-up and recovery procedures

D. Reliability/Integrity

o hazards/risks to information system (data, hardware, communications, facilities)

o general controls
  - environmental (e.g., physical access controls, natural hazards controls)
  - management

o applications controls

o availability and adequacy of audit trails

o quality and quantity of automated error detection/correction procedures

o availability and adequacy of back-up and recovery procedures

o completeness, currency and accuracy of documentation for audit

o prior reviews (e.g., A-123, A-127, A-130, audits--internal, CPA, QA--IRM triennial reviews)

o auditor judgement (intuitively obvious)

E. Technology Integration

o make-up of project team in relation to technology used (number, training, and experience)

o applicability of the data processing design methodologies and standards to the technology in use

o pioneering aspects (newness of technology and/or technological approaches used in this information system for application and organization)

o technical complexity of information system (interrelationships of tasks)

o user knowledge of DP technology

o   margin for error (i.e., is there reasonable time to
    make adjustments, corrections or perform analyses
    before the transaction is completed?)

o   utilization of equipment (tolerance for expansion)

o   availability of automated error detection/correction
    procedures

o   **completeness, currency and accuracy of documentation
    for implementation/maintenance/operation (e.g.,
    operations/maintenance manuals).**

o   amount of hardcopy evidence

4.6 Risk Scoring -- Application of the Work Priority Scheme

4.6.1 Implementation of the Scheme

For the scheme to be of use to the EDP auditor, an analysis
approach for risk scoring must be employed using the dimensions
and characteristics.   Two possible approaches for arriving at a
system risk score are suggested here and described in Appendix D.
The first scoring method is a simple intuitive approach based on
a minimal collection of information on the AIS while the second
one is more elaborate and based on more detailed information on
the AIS.   User experience will undoubtedly lead to modifications
and improvements in the application of the scheme and the risk
scoring methods.   If the EDP reviewer for some reason does not
wish to use a scoring methodology, he/she could still keep the
dimensions and their characteristics in mind when performing a
less formal review.

4.6.2 A Simple Scoring Approach

The simple approach assigns a weight and a risk level to
each dimension, based on a qualitative judgement with respect to
the characteristics associated with each dimension. Criticality/
Mission Impact is always assigned the highest weight. The
product of the weight and risk level of a dimension is the risk
score for that dimension.   The Criticality/Mission Impact risk
score is then the Level I system risk score.   To obtain the Level
II system risk score, the sum of the dimension risk scores over
the four Level II dimensions is added to the Level I system risk
score.   (See Appendix D for details.)

4.6.3 A Detailed Scoring Approach

The more detailed approach looks in depth at the characteristics associated with each dimension.   Each dimension is defined
by a set of characteristics which are used to calculate the
amount of risk posed by that dimension to the failure of the
system.   Each characteristic is given a weight and a risk level.
The product of these two numbers is the risk score of the
characteristic and the sum over the risk scores of the character-

istics of a dimension yields the dimension risk score. Again, the Criticality/Mission Impact risk score is the Level I system risk score. And again, to obtain the Level II system risk score, the sum of the dimension risk scores over the four Level II dimensions is added to the Level I system risk score. (See Appendix D for details.)

5. Discretionary Audits

After the systems have been identified and ranked, using the risk based evaluation, several back end qualifiers must be considered by the auditor in determining how many discretionary audits can be added to the audit plan (See Figure 1). These back end qualifiers can be categorized in two areas:

- Audit Types and Objectives, and

- Audit Resource Constraints

Figure 2 identifies the different audit methodologies that can be used and the different audit objectives that can be accomplished in performing ADP audits. The auditor must consider the audit methodology to be performed and the audit objective to be accomplished in deciding on the number of additional (discretionary) audits that can be performed. Furthermore, these issues must be considered in light of the audit resource constraints (e.g., people, time, dollars, expertise) that exist. For example, to perform a system under development audit which looks at security, confidentiality, and privacy issues requires substantially more resources than an operational system audit which looks at only data reliability issues. Thus, the mix of audit methodologies to be performed, and the existing audit resource constraints must be considered when deciding on the number of discretionary audits that can be added to the audit plan. After these back end qualifiers have been considered, the audit plan can then be finalized, and audits implemented.

6. USES OF THE WORK PRIORITY SCHEME

The risk scores developed during the risk based evaluation can be used for both developmental and operational systems. The major difference between risk based evaluations of these two classes of systems is that (1) the ranking of characteristics may change, and (2) some characteristics may not even be applicable to both. The following is a brief enumeration of some possible uses of the Work Priority Scheme (from "strawman" scheme in Appendix B).

1) To determine relative risk between applications - A risk score of one application is compared to scores developed for other applications in the same department. Thus, risk scoring is used to determine relative risk among applications. The score is not used to determine an absolute measure of risk.

2) To create an audit risk profile - An audit risk profile
is a pictorial representation of the various risk characteristics
measured. While the audit risk score shows audit risk for the
entire automated information system, the risk profile shows the
relational risk among the various risk characteristics. The
objective of the risk profile is to graphically illustrate what
characteristics contribute to the total risk, and in what
proportion.

METHODOLOGY	OBJECTIVES				
	Data Reliability	Security Confidentiality Privacy	Availability of Information Resources	Efficiency Economy Effectiveness	Compliance
(A) System Development Life Cycle Process					
(B) System Under Development					
(C) Operational Systems (Post Implementation)					
(D) Function, e.g., Management, Teleprocessing, Data Processing					

* Decisions on audit methodology and objectives desired will influence:
  - Weights given when ranking risk factors
  - Audit scope, i.e., level of involvement (e.g., tasks, dollars, hours)

Figure 2   AUDIT AREAS OF CONCERN*

3) To modify the characteristics contributing to audit risk
- Both the auditor and data processing management can use the
audit risk scheme to identify those characteristics which may
cause the information system to be less successful than proposed. For example, if the application project personnel do not
understand the computer technology being used, the probability of
success of the information system being developed diminishes.
Once the characteristics that may cause the system to be less
successful than desired are known, those characteristics can be
altered such that the probability of the system being successful
increases.

4) To help allocate audit resources - The information
gathered during the audit risk analysis can be used as a basis
for allocating audit resources to review application systems
and/or review specific aspects of those systems. For example,
high-risk information systems may receive extensive reviews,
medium risk cursory reviews, and low risk no reviews. For those

systems reviewed, the area of review can be selected based on the high-risk characteristics. For example, if computer technology is a high-risk characteristic, the auditors may want to expend time reviewing how effectively the project team is using that technology.

5) To develop a data base of risk characteristics - The information gathered during this process should be saved and used for two purposes. The first use is to improve the audit risk prioritization scheme to make it more predictive of audit risk; and the second use is to assist data processing management in structuring and planning projects such that those projects will have the highest probability of success.

7. PROBLEMS WITH AND SOLUTIONS TO USE OF SCHEME

Potential difficulties in using the work priority scheme and methods for overcoming these difficulties were discussed by the PCIE Work Group participants in order to facilitate the use of the scheme. These follow in outline form.

7.1 Potential Difficulties in Utilization

o Time and resources needed for sufficient data collection

o Inadequate organization data processing planning

o Need to establish an understanding of and agreement on related issues on a consistent basis by all affected parties (auditors/systems developers/users/etc.)

o Need to convince affected management (audit and operations) as to the credibility of scheme and its impact on audit coverage, given a finite level of audit resources

o Initial time and resources needed to adapt the work priority scheme to the organization

o Represents a snapshot at a given point in time which requires maintenance and updating to ensure its continued validity

o Need for audit planning to be separate from and sensitive to data processing and business cycle planning processes

o Requires integrated skill knowledge that includes relevant expertise in pertinent specialty areas

o Work priority scheme just another tool for audit management to consider in its decision-making process

o EDP audit resources still likely to be insufficient to provide coverage suggested by scheme

o   Requires up-to-date and complete inventory of AISs--all
    those which are operational, developmental, and undergo
    ing change

7.2   Methods for Overcoming Difficulties

o   Make underlying questionnaire and data gathering methods
    as simple as possible for administering it.

o   Refine data collection methods through experience and
    learning curve.

o   Educate users (including DP community) regarding needs
    for standards, planning, etc..

o   Audit recommendations should emphasize necessary
    improvements to DP and business executives.

o   Encourage early participation and collective editing to
    reach consensus on data collection instrument.

o   Apply retroactively to existent systems to demonstrate
    the risks that audit coverage would have addressed.

o   Emphasize that initial commitment would have long-term
    benefits; and that once established, maintenance would be
    considerably less costly.

o   Analyze dynamics of the organization and the audit
    component within it to determine the frequency of
    "snapshot". Workload mix and control attributes may be
    affected accordingly.

o   Use means for staying attuned to planning cycles.

o   Consider supplementing EDP audit resources with financial
    and generalist auditors for areas not requiring specific
    technical expertise. They may even be more relevant for
    business and institutional knowledge.

o   EDP audit resources may be supplemented with consultants
    for areas requiring highly skilled data processing
    specialists.

8.   Recommendations

     The workshop attendees came up with a number of recommenda-
tions for further activity in this crucial EDP audit area. A
brief enumeration of these follows.

1) The work priority scheme described here should be tested
within organizations by applying it to the EDP planning considerations of a prior year's workload universe. This might help

ascertain how EDP audit resources may have been allocated differently and whether that allocation may have better assisted management in identifying and overcoming resultant control deficiencies in the systems.

2) Feedback should be captured on institutional knowledge of why and how systems have failed so that one could determine whether the draft scheme would have targeted EDP audit resources on the most vulnerable systems.

3) A prototype needs to be developed which would include a survey questionnaire, a weighting and scoring system, a testing process, a methodology for evaluating results and modifying the prototype, a method for the selection of testing sites, and a method of quantifying qualitative issues that would facilitate a comprehensive cost-benefit evaluation of the work priority scheme.

References

[1.] "ADP Internal Control Guide," U.S. Department of Energy, DoE/MA-0165, August 1984.

[2.] Executive Office of the President, Office of Management and Budget, Management of the United States Government, Fiscal Year 1986. Washington, D.C.: U.S. Government Printing Office, 1985.

[3.] Federal Managers' Financial Integrity Act of 1982, Public Law 97-255, September 8, 1982.

[4.] "Standards for Audit of Governmental Organizations, Programs, Activities, and Functions," U.S. General Accounting Office, 1981 Revision.

[5.] "Portfolio Approach to Information Systems," F. Warren McFarlan, Harvard Business Review, September - October 1981.

APPENDIX B

STRAW MAN PRIORITIZING SCHEME

FOR USE BY AUDITORS IN EVALUATING

AUDIT RISK IN AUTOMATED INFORMATION SYSTEMS

OBJECTIVE OF "STRAW MAN" PRIORITIZING SCHEME

The prioritizing scheme outlined in this paper is proposed as a "straw man" for use by auditors in evaluating the audit risk in automated information systems. An audit risk (sometimes referred to as an exposure) is the probable unfavorable effect associated with the occurrence(s) of an undesirable event. Audit risk needs to be evaluated for two purposes. The first is to determine the need for, and amount of, audit resources that should be assigned to an automated information system; and the second is to point the auditor toward those system characteristics most susceptible to vulnerabilities. The following straw man has been developed primarily for use as a starting point for discussion by the attendees to the NBS/PCIE Work Group Invitational Workshop on "Work Priority Scheme for the EDP Auditor."

BACKGROUND INFORMATION AND ANALYSIS OF EXISTING RISK/PRIORITIZING METHODOLOGIES

Auditors traditionally use audit risk assessment methodologies to allocate audit resources and identify areas for investigation. While various organizations approach audit risk assessment from different perspectives, their chronological approach to audit risk assessment has usually gone through the following four phases or approaches (note that audit groups currently perform risk/exposure assessment using all four approaches):

o   Approach 1 - Audit judgment and instinct

This has been, and is still, the most prominently used method of audit risk assessment. Using this approach, the auditor calls upon his/her personal experiences, coupled with other learning experiences and knowledge of organization mission and external mandates, in order to project those experiences, learning and knowledge to the automated information system (AIS) under review. The auditor intellectually tries to associate the AIS under review with past experience and knowledge to determine comparable characteristics in order to estimate the magnitude of the audit risk/exposure and to select specific system characteristics for investigation. While this method can be effective,it is not a transferable skill, but, rather, one which must be learned over time and is unique to each practitioner.

o   Approach 2 - Dollar risk estimation using the risk formula

Risk is defined as the probability for loss. That probability is expressed through the formula "frequency of occurrence times loss per occurrence equals annual loss expectancy." The "frequency of occurrence" refers to the frequency with which a particular vulnerability (flaw in the system) may combine with a possible threat (a man-made or natural exploitation of the vulnerability). The "loss per occurrence" is then the negative impact of a threat/vulnerability pair. Audit risk based on this formula can be quantified in dollars. This can, under certain circumstances, provide the advantage of projecting, with high precision, risk exposure in terms readily understandable by non-technicians. FIPS PUB 65 is based on this risk assessment method. The disadvantages of projecting risks in dollars are that the base numbers are difficult to get (i.e., frequency of occurrence and loss per occurrence) and it may therefore imply a higher degree of precision than is realistic.

o   Approach 3 - Identifying and weighting risk attributes

The attributes that cause risk/exposure to be realized have been at least partially identified. The relationship among these attributes can be specified through weighting. Using these attributes, an auditor can determine whether or not they are present in the automated information system under review, and through the accumulation of weighted scores rank automated application systems according to their relative audit risks. For example, this method can show that application A is of higher risk than application B. This method is most effective when the attributes are determined through statistical regression analysis.

o   Approach 4 - Use of risk assessment software packages

Vendors have automated approaches two and three and made them commercially available. The first software package on determining dollar risk was marketed by Pansophic as PANRISK, and the first commercially available software package which used the attributes method to project risk was offered by Management and Computer Services as a package called ESTIMACS. The major advantages to the automated version are the ease of use and the opportunity with minimal effort to play "what if" strategies through varying one or more of the risk characteristics.

The ideal audit risk/exposure assessment method has not yet been developed. No current approach can guarantee the completely correct prediction of audit risk. However, approaches 2, 3, and 4 represent transferable skills, and because they have been formalized can be evaluated and proved. One characteristic of a

risk assessment method that appears to be extremely important is
its ease of use. The more difficult the method is to use, the
less likely that an auditor will use it. Lacking a convenient
structured method, the auditor will revert to approach 1 and rely
on instinct and judgment to make audit decisions.

Many internal audit and data processing functions have
developed a prioritizing scheme to evaluate the audit risk of
automated information systems within their own organization.
There appears to be much similarity among the various approaches.
F. Warren McFarlan has attempted to categorize the dimensions of
risk that are common to many of these in-house developed prioritizing schemes.

The Three Dimensions of Risk

F. Warren McFarlan, in a September-October 1981 <u>Harvard
Business Review</u> article entitled "Portfolio Approach to Information Systems," identified three important dimensions which
contribute to the risk exposure inherent in a project:

1) Project size - The larger it is in dollar expense,
    staffing levels, elapsed time, and number of depart-
    ments affected by the project, the greater the risk/ex-
    posure. Multimillion-dollar projects obviously carry
    more risk than $50,000 projects and also, in general,
    affect the company more if the risk is realized. A
    related concern is the size of the project relative to
    the normal size of a systems development Group's
    projects. The implicit risk is usually lower on a $1
    million project of a department whose average
    undertaking costs $2-$3 million than on a $250,000
    project of a department that has never ventured a
    project costing more than $50,000.

2) Experience with technology - Because of the greater
    likelihood of unexpected technical problems, project
    risk increases as familiarity of the project team and
    the IS organization decreases with the hardware,
    operating systems, data base handler, and project
    application language. A project that has a slight risk
    for a leading-edge, large systems development group may
    have a very high risk for a smaller less technically
    advanced group. Yet the latter groups can reduce risk
    through purchase of outside skills for an undertaking
    involving technology that is in general commercial use.

3) Project structure - In some projects, the very nature
    of the task defines completely, from the moment of
    conceptualization, the outputs. The outputs of these
    projects are fixed and not subject to change during the
    life of the project. Such schemes are classified as
    highly structured. They carry much less risk than
    those whose outputs are more subject to the manager's
    judgment and hence are vulnerable to change.

An analysis of the attributes method of risk assessment appears to emphasize these three dimensions. Thus, while it is possible to divide audit risk/exposure into different dimensions, practice appears to support that there is consensus among those working with audit risk/exposure that these are important dimensions. Therefore, the straw man audit prioritizing scheme proposed for this invitational workshop will be constructed around these three dimensions.

NEED FOR AND USE OF AUDIT RISK PRIORITIZING SCHEME

Warren McFarlan, in his "Portfolio Approach to Information Systems" article, states that:

"The typical project feasibility study covers exhaustively such topics as financial benefits, qualitative benefits, implementation costs, target milestones and completion dates, and necessary staffing levels. In precise, crisp terms, the developers of these estimates provide voluminous supporting documentation. Only rarely, however, do they deal frankly with the risk of slippage in time, cost overrun, technical shortfall, or outright failure. Rather, they deny the existence of such possibilities by ignoring them. They assume the appropriate human skills, controls, and so on, that will ensure success."

McFarlan and others have proposed that through proper analysis the auditor should be able to predict the probability of unfavorable consequences such as:

o   Failure to obtain all, or even any, of the anticipated benefits

o   Cost and/or schedule overruns

o   Inadequate system of internal control

o   Technical performance of resulting system that turns out to be significantly below estimate

o   Incompatibility of the system with the selected hardware and software

The internal auditor has only limited resources to perform his mission. Good audit practices dictate that those resources be assigned to activities that offer the greatest payback to the organization. In 1977, The Institute of Internal Auditors issued the report from the research project entitled Systems Auditability and Control. A major conclusion from this project was that the most fruitful use of internal audit time would be participating in the automated information system development process. In addition, the U.S.General Accounting Office issued a standard, which in the 1981 revision was changed to a guideline, regarding auditor participation in system development. The general feeling of the PCIE Work Group, however, is that auditor participation during the System Development Life Cycle (SDLC) is vital to assuring the development of secure and auditable systems. The challenge has been first, what systems should the auditor participate in, and second, if they participate, where should **they spend their review time?**

The audit-risk-based prioritization scheme is developed to answer these challenges. It provides a basis for determining what systems should be reviewed, and for those systems reviewed indicates the characteristics on which audit effort should be expended.

AUDIT RISK PRIORITIZATION SCHEME

An effective audit risk prioritizing scheme has the following four parts:

1) Identification of risk dimensions - Previously defined as project size, experience with technology, and project structure.

2) Identification of risk characteristics - The attributes of an automated information system which permit the auditor to project the performance of an operational information system.

3) Analysis of the audit risk characteristics - Determines the applicability and importance of the characteristic in predicting the operational performance of the automated information system.

4) Use of the audit risk assessment - The objective of the risk prioritization scheme is to assist the internal auditor in using limited resources more effectively. Usage involves the interpretation and application of the risk assessment resulting from the utilization of the first three parts of the audit risk prioritizing scheme.

Part 1 - Identification of the Risk Dimensions

The importance of having risk dimensions is to categorize audit risk by the determinant for that risk. This is important because the audit risk characteristics within a dimension or determinant are more closely related than the characteristics between dimensions. This concept can be helpful in both managing audit risk from the data processing perspective, and selecting specific characteristics to investigate from an audit perspective.

Part 2 - Identification of Audit Risk Characteristics

Risk characteristics are attributes of automated information systems which correlate to operational behavior of the automated information system. The presence or absence of these system attributes can be used to predict behavior. An analogy would be predicting the probability of a heart attack by using an individual's heart attack risk characteristics such as blood pressure, weight, family health history, and amount of cigarettes smoked. The presence or absence of these characteristics can be used to predict whether a specific person might have a heart attack (i.e., a specific human behavior). While the word risk is used, it is not meant to imply that the undesirable event will occur but, rather, that the probability of some type of behavior (e.g., a heart attack) can be predicted. A prioritizing scheme will tell how probable the heart attack is.

The proposed "straw man" characteristics recommended for evaluating each of the three audit risk dimensions are presented in Figure B.1. This straw man risk model is designed to identify and explain the characteristics associated with the three audit risk dimensions. These are the characteristics that most commonly appear in audit risk models currently used by auditors, and are believed to be those which can help auditors predict the operational performance of information systems for audit purposes. Figure B.1 has been placed at the end of this paper so that the attendees may detach it for use in their discussions.

Part 3 - Analysis of the Audit Risk Characteristics

This part of the audit risk prioritizing scheme is designed to measure the degree of audit risk associated with each individual characteristic. The objective of this measurement is twofold. First is to determine the degree of importance of each characteristic in representing the magnitude of audit risk/exposure (i.e., weighting of characteristics among the population of characteristics) and second, to determine the applicability of that characteristic to the specific automated information system being assessed (to determine whether the characteristic is present or absent in a manner that could cause an unfavorable event to occur; for example, if an individual was overweight it would be indicative of a possible undesirable event such as a heart attack).

There are five approaches used to measure the applicability of a characteristic to predict a favorable or unfavorable result. These are:

1) Relational considerations - This asks the auditor to divide the application systems into three risk categories, e.g., high, medium, and low, and then determine into which category the system being assessed falls. For example, an NBS study[1] has shown that the larger the size of a computer program, the more difficult it is to implement. From a relational perspective, the

_____

[1] NBS Special Publication 500-99 entitled "Structured Testing: A Software Testing Methodology Using the Cyclomatic Complexity Metric," issued December 1982.

auditor decides whether the size of the program for the system being assessed will fall within the largest third sizewise for the department, the middle third sizewise, or the lowest third sizewise. The largest third would be considered to have the highest risk.

2) **Factors relating to risk** - This approach attempts to relate specific factors to the expected outcome. The auditor need only determine which factors are applicable to the system under assessment to determine the degree of audit risk. For example, in assessing a data validation characteristic, a factor relating to low risk would be extensive data validation including range, alphabetic, check digit, and relationship tests; while high-risk systems might be those that only use alphanumeric tests.

3) **Dollar risk** - Using the annual loss expectancy formula (i.e., frequency of occurrence times loss per occurrence) the dollar value associated with each characteristic can be used to determine the magnitude of risk for that characteristic.

4) **Audit analysis** - This method requires the auditor to conduct sufficient study to determine the potential vulnerability. The most common approach to doing this is an assessment of the system of internal controls in order to identify vulnerabilities associated with the characteristic in question. Again, if the characteristic was data validation, the audit review could determine the effectiveness of the data validation controls to reduce the specific audit risks reducible by data validation controls.

5) **Statistical regression analysis**- Over a period of time the audit group can record system characteristics and actual operational behavior. Feeding that information into statistical regression analysis, the auditor can determine specific correlation between the various attributes of the characteristics compared to the actual operational behavior of the information system. While this is the statistically proper approach, it can also be very time-consuming and costly to obtain.

Experiences of audit risk model users indicate that the two most popular approaches are relational risk (i.e., high, medium, and low) and risk factors to determine the applicability of the characteristics to the system under review.

Part 4 - <u>Use of the Audit Risk Assessment</u>

The audit risk prioritizing scheme can be used by both data processing and audit personnel. Data processing personnel can use the risk scheme to identify the attributes that may cause the system to be unsuccessful and manage those risks by changing developmental approaches.

The performance of the first three parts of the audit risk scheme will result in the identification of the audit risk characteristics applicable to the automated information system under review, and some indication of the magnitude or degree of applicability. This audit risk information can then be used by internal auditors in any or all of the following manners:

1) Audit risk score - This usage allocates points in accordance with the magnitude of risk associated with each characteristic. The most common scoring method is to divide the risk characteristic into specific subcategories as was illustrated earlier in the data validation example. If the application being assessed falls into the high-risk category, it would be assigned three points, medium risk, two points, and low risk, one point. If a more sophisticated scoring method is wanted, the individual characteristics can be weighted. For example, one characteristic can be considered to be twice as important as another, and thus is multiplied by the weight 2 to give an individual characteristic risk score. The resulting risk score is normally compared to other scores developed for the same department. Thus, risk scoring is normally used to determine relative risk between applications, and the score is not used to determine an absolute measure of risk, such as temperature of the human body, which has an absolute meaning.

2) Create an audit risk profile - An audit risk profile is a pictorial representation of the various risk characteristics measured. While the audit risk score shows audit risk for the entire automated information system, the risk profile shows the relational risk among the various risk characteristics. The objective of the risk profile is to graphically illustrate what characteristics contribute to the total audit risk, and in what proportion.

3) Modification of the characteristics contributing to audit risk - Both the auditor and systems analyst can use the audit risk scheme to identify those characteristics which may cause the information system to be less successful than proposed. For example, if the application project personnel do not understand the computer technology being used, the probability of success of the information system being developed diminishes. Once the characteristics that may cause the system to be less successful than desired are known, those characteristics can be altered such that the probability of the system being successful increases. In our example where the project personnel do not understand the proposed technology, a technology which the project group does know can be substituted and the probability of success will increase.

4)   Allocation of audit resources - The information
     gathered during the audit risk analysis can be used as
     a basis for allocating audit resources to review
     application systems and/or review specific aspects of
     those systems. For example, high-risk information
     systems may receive extensive reviews, medium risk,
     cursory reviews, and low risk, no reviews. For those
     systems reviewed, the area of review can be selected
     based on the high-risk characteristics. For example,
     if computer technology is a high-risk characteristic,
     the auditors may want to expend time reviewing how
     effectively the project team is using that technology.

5)   Data base of risk characteristics - The information
     gathered during this process should be saved and used
     for two purposes. The first use is to improve the
     audit risk prioritization scheme to make it more
     predictive of audit risk; and the second use is to
     assist data processing management in structuring and
     planning projects such that those projects will have
     the highest probability of success.

REFERENCES USED TO BUILD THE "STRAW MAN" AUDIT RISK PRIORITIZING SCHEME

The major references used in creating this "straw man"
prioritizing scheme were:

1)   OMB Circular A-123, "Internal Control Systems," August
     16, 1983.

2)   U.S. General Accounting Office document on internal
     control-- "Evaluating Internal Controls in Computer-
     Based Systems - Audit Guide" June 1981

3)   Computer Control and Audit by William Mair, Keagle
     Davis, and Donald Wood, published by The Institute of
     Internal Auditors (1977)

4)   ESTIMACS software package marketed by Management and
     Computer Services, Valley Forge, PA

5)   PANRISK audit software package and manual, originally
     marketed by Pansophic Systems, Oak Brook, IL and now
     called IST/RAMP and marketed by International Security
     Technology, Inc. of New York City, its originator.

6)   "Portfolio Approach to Information Systems" by F.
     Warren McFarlan, Harvard Business Review, September-Oc-
     tober 1981

7)   FIPS PUB 65, "Guideline for Automatic Data Processing
     Risk Analysis" August 1, 1979

8)   U.S. General Accounting Office "Standards for Internal
     Controls in the Federal Government", 1983

CHARACTERISTICS FOR THE RISK DIMENSION -- PROJECT SIZE

1. Size of user area - Number of employees, size of user budget, number of user functions.

2. Data processing breadth - Size of project as expressed in number of project staff, size of project budget, or number of man-months to produce.

3. Size of information system - Expressed in number of programs, size of programs, number of transactions.

4. Expected frequency of change - The number and/or size of changes that will be made to the initial needs statement.

5. Number of unique logical business inputs that the system will process - Expressed in number of business transactions processed in the course of a day.

6. Number of unique logical business outputs generated by the system - Number of business transactions or reports or messages produced per day by the system.

7. Number of logical files (views) that the system will access - The number of individual files or data base subschemas that will be accessed by the system during the totality of system processing.

8. Number of major types of on-line inquiry expected - The number of requests that will be made by users other than the normal business outputs generated by the information system.

9. Telecommunications - The use of communication facilities in conjunction with automated information systems. Risk associated with the number of terminals, amount of hard-copy documents produced, and the sophistication of processing.

CHARACTERISTICS FOR THE RISK DIMENSION -- EXPERIENCE WITH TECHNOLOGY

1. Makeup of project team in relationship to technology used - The inclusion on the project team of the necessary skills to effectively utilize the information system technology, e.g., the inclusion of data base personnel for data base-related projects.

2. Applicability of the data processing design methodologies and standards to the technology in use - The adaptability of the existing data processing methodologies and standards to the technology being used. For example, if the information system is being developed under prototyping, are the design methodologies and standards applicable to prototyping?

3. Margin of error - The amount of time between the entry of a business transaction and the response to that transaction. For example, is there reasonable time to make adjustments, corrections, or perform analyses before the transaction is completed?

4. Technical complexity of the information system - The number of tasks and interrelationship between those tasks that must be accomplished to satisfy the user needs.

5. Adaptability to change - The ease with which it is expected that changes to the information system requirements can be incorporated into the information system. This will be dependent upon the architecture of the system and its adaptability to the user information needs.

6. Utilization of equipment - How much the information system will push the equipment to its capacity to meet user needs. For example, if a two-second response is needed and given the complexity of the tasks and the volume of work, what is the amount of tolerance within the system capacity to meet those processing needs?

FIGURE B.1 RISK DIMENSION CHARACTERISTICS

7.   Personnel - Skill level, number, and knowledge of user processing of the project team members including any supporting technical staff(s).

8.   Documentation - Amount, currentness, type, and usability of the documents supporting the automatic information system.

9.   Pioneering aspects - The newness of the technology and/or technological approaches used in this application system. The newness can be either within the organization (i.e., the first time any project has used this technology, such as data base technology) or the newness of the technology as offered by the vendors.

1Ø.   How knowledgeable is the user in data processing technology - Determines whether the user personnel can understand the implications of use of data processing technology, and their ability to define requirements and discuss requirements in relationship to its impact on technology.

11.   Data processing knowledge of user tasks - The ability of data processing personnel to challenge the accuracy and need of user requirements in relationship to the mission and tasks performed by the user.

12.   Degree of complexity of processing logic - Measures whether the logic needed to perform the user requirements will be simple, average, or complex.

13.   Need for automated error detection and correction procedures - Measures the complexity of the procedures that need to be incorporated into the information system to detect inaccurate or incomplete input transactions and make automatic correction to those errors.

CHARACTERISTICS FOR THE RISK DIMENSION -- PROJECT STRUCTURE

1.   Organizational breadth - The number of diverse organizational units involved in the application system and/or the number of user organizations that must sign off on the requirements definition.

2.   Political implications of implementing the information system - The level of agreement among all units in the organization as to the need for the system and the approach being used to accomplish the system objectives.

3.   Specificity of user requirements - The level of detail in which the requirements are specified. Measures the amount of additional detail and/or decisions that need to be made before programs can be coded.

4.   Problems associated with current system performance - Measures the amount of problems that are occurring in the current system as implemented. The thesis is that performance problems in current systems may not be correctable by a new system.

5.   Availability of backup hard-copy documents - The number of original source documents and hard-copy format that will be produced and retained during system processing.

6.   Level of user management agreement on system objectives - The agreement within the user(s) department on the stated objectives for the system.

7.   Percentage of the proposed information system that is already performed by the user - Measures the newness of the information system tasks to the user area. Differentiates between existing tasks being automated, and new tasks (new meaning a new method for processing).

FIGURE B.1 (continued)

8.   Importance/criticality of the business system to the user -
Measures the importance of this specific information system to
the user as it relates to the user completing the mission of the
user function.

9.   Project management approach and structure - The organization
of the project in relationship to the size of the project and the
technology being utilized. Includes such consideration as
division of duties within the project, relationship between the
user and data processing personnel, as well as the management and
status reporting structures.

FIGURE B.1 - (continued)

Verifying and Validating Software Requirements and Design Specifications

Barry W. Boehm, TRW

Reprinted from *IEEE Software*, January 1984, pages 75-88. Copyright ©1984 by The Institute of Electrical and Electronics Engineers, Inc. All rights reserved.

> These recommendations provide a good starting point for identifying and resolving software problems early in the life cycle—when they're still relatively easy to handle.

"**D**on't worry about that specification paperwork. We'd better hurry up and start coding, because we're going to have a whole lot of debugging to do."

How many projects start out this way and end up with either a total failure or a tremendously expensive self-fulfilling prophecy? There are still far too many, but more and more projects are turning the self-fulfilling prophecy around. By investing more up-front effort in verifying and validating their software requirements and design specifications, these projects are reaping the benefits of reduced integration and test costs, higher software reliability and maintainability, and more user-responsive software. To help increase their number, this article presents the following guideline information on verification and validation, or V&V, of software requirements and design specifications:

- definitions of the terms "verification" and "validation," an explanation of their context in the software life cycle, and a description of the basic sequence of V&V functions;
- an explanation, with examples, of the major software requirements and design V&V criteria: completeness, consistency, feasibility, and testability;
- an evaluation of the relative cost and effectiveness of the major software requirements and design V&V techniques with respect to the major criteria; and
- an example V&V checklist for software system reliability and availability.

Based on the above, we recommend combinations of software requirements and design V&V techniques that are most suitable for small, medium, and large software specifications.

Verification and validation in the software life cycle

Definitions. The recent *IEEE Standard Glossary of Software Engineering Terminology*[1] defines "verification" and "validation" as follows:

- *Verification.* The process of determining whether or not the products of a given phase of the software development cycle fulfill the requirements established during the previous phase.
- *Validation.* The process of evaluating software at the end of the software development process to ensure compliance with software requirements.

In this article we extend the definition of "validation" to include a missing activity at the beginning of the software definition process: determining the fitness or worth of a software product for its operational mission.

Informally, we might define these terms via the following questions:

- *Verification.* "Am I building the product right?"
- *Validation.* "Am I building the right product?"

Objectives. The basic objectives in verification and validation of software requirements and design specifications are to identify and resolve software problems and high-risk issues early in the software life cycle. The main reason for doing this is indicated in Figure 1.[2] It shows that, for large projects, savings of up to 100:1 are possible by finding and fixing problems early in the life cycle. For smaller projects, the savings are more on the order of 4-6:1, but this still provides a great deal of leverage for early investment in V&V activities. Besides the major cost savings, there are also significant payoffs in improved reliability, maintainability, and human engineering of the resulting software product.

Early life-cycle specifications and phases. In general, experience has shown that the software development process proceeds most cost-effectively if software specifications are produced in the following order:

(1) a requirements specification, which states the functions the software must perform, the required level of performance (speed, accuracy, etc.), and the nature of the required interfaces between the software product and its environment;

(2) a product design specification, which describes the overall architecture of the software product and its components; and

(3) a detailed design specification, which identifies the inputs, outputs, control logic, algorithms, and data structures of each individual low-level component of the software product.

The typical software life cycle includes requirements, product design, and detailed design phases that involve the development, verification and validation, approval or disapproval, and baselining of each of these specifications (see Figure 2). However, the nature of the V&V process causes intermingling of the activities associated with each phase. For example, one cannot validate the feasibility of a performance-critical requirement without doing some design and analysis of ways to implement the requirement. Similarly, some design and development of code in a working prototype may be necessary to validate the user-interface requirements.

V&V functions in the early phases. Verification and validation activities produce their best results when performed by a V&V agent who operates independently of the developer or specification agent. The basic sequence of functions performed by the V&V agent, the specification agent (the analyst or software system engineer), the project manager, and the customer are shown in Figure 2.

The key portions of Figure 2 are the iterative loops in which

- the V&V agent analyzes the specifications and issues problem reports to the specification agent;
- The specification agent isolates the source of the problem and develops a solution resulting in an iteration of the specification;
- the project manager and customer approve any proposed iterations that would perceptibly change the requirements baseline; and
- the V&V agent analyzes the iterated specification and issues further problem reports if necessary.

The process continues until the V&V agent completes his planned activities and all problem reports have been either fixed or assigned to a specific agent for resolution within a given time.

Verification and validation criteria

The four basic V&V criteria for requirements and design specifications are completeness, consistency, feasibility, and testability. An overall taxonomy of their components is given in Figure 3, and each is discussed in turn below.

Completeness. A specification is *complete* to the extent that all of its parts are present and each part is fully developed. A software specification must exhibit several properties to assure its completeness.

No TBDs. TBDs are places in the specification where decisions have been postponed by writing "To be Determined" or "TBD." For example:

- "The system shall handle a peak load of (TBD) transactions per second."
- "Update records coming from

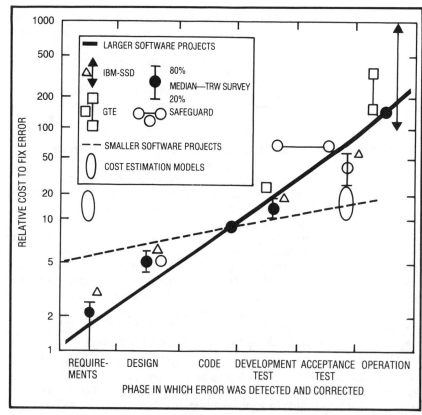

Figure 1. Increase in cost to fix or change software throughout the life cycle.[2]

the personnel information system shall be in the following format: (TBD)."

No nonexistent references. These are references in the specification to functions, inputs, or outputs (including databases) not defined in the specification. For example:

- "Function 3.1.2.3 Output 3.1.2.3.a Inputs
  1. Output option flags obtained from the User Output Options functions...," which is undefined in the specification.
- "A record of all transactions is retained in the Transaction File," which is undefined.

No missing specification items. These are items that should be pres-

ent as part of the standard format of the specification, but are not present. For example:

- No verification provisions
- No interface specifications

Note that verification of this property often involves a human judgment call: a small, stand-alone system may have no interfaces to specify.

No missing functions. These are functions that should be part of the software product but are not called for in the specification. For example:

- No backup functions
- No recovery functions

No missing products. These are products that should be part of the delivered software but are not called for in the specification. For example:

- Test tools
- Output postprocessors

The first two properties—"no TBDs" and "no nonexistent references"—form a subset of the completeness properties called closure properties. Closure is distinguished by the fact that it can be verified by mechanical means; the last three properties generally require some human intuition to verify or validate.

Consistency. A specification is *consistent* to the extent that its provisions do not conflict with each other or with governing specifications and objectives. Specifications require consistency in several ways.

Internal consistency. Items within the specification do not conflict with

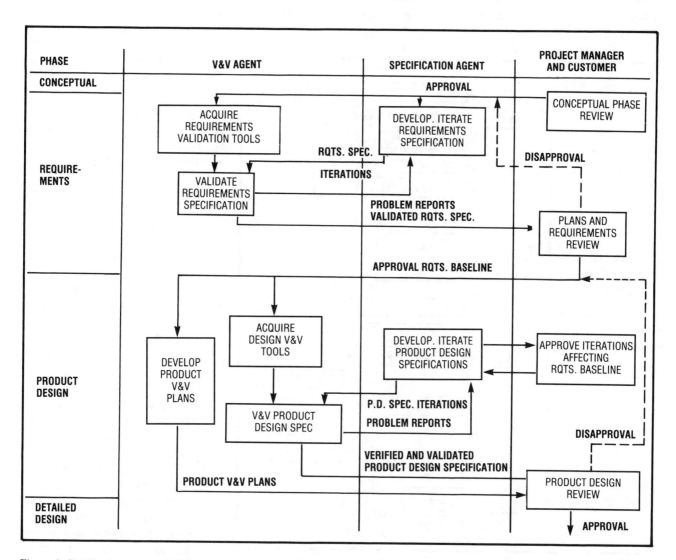

Figure 2. Verification and validation sequences for the requirements and product design phases.

each other, unlike the following counter-examples:

- "Function x
  (1) Inputs: A 4×4 matrix z of reals.
  ⋮
  Function y
  ⋮
  (3) Outputs: A 3×3 matrix z of integers."
- Page 14: "Master real-time control interrupts shall have top priority at all times."
  Page 37: "A critical-level interrupt from the security subsystem shall take precedence over all other processes and interrupts."

External consistency. Items in the specification do not conflict with external specifications or entities,

unlike the following counter-example:

- "Spec: All safety parameters are provided by the preprocessor system, as follows: ..."
  "Preprocessor system spec: The preprocessor initializes all safety parameters except for real-time control safety parameters, which are self-initialized..."

Traceability. Items in the specification have clear antecedents in earlier specifications or statements of system objectives. Particularly on large specifications, each item should indicate the item or items in earlier specifications from which it is derived to prevent

- misinterpretations, such as assuming that "on-line" storage implies a requirement for

random access storage (a dedicated on-line tape unit might be preferable); and

- embellishments, such as adding exotic displays, natural language processing, or adaptive control features that are not needed for the job to be done (and may not work as reliably as simpler approaches).

Feasibility. A specification is *feasible* to the extent that the life-cycle benefits of the system specified exceed its life-cycle costs. Thus, feasibility involves more than verifying that a system satisfies functional and performance requirements. It also implies validating that the specified system will be sufficiently maintainable, reliable, and human-engineered to keep a positive life-cycle balance sheet.

Further, and most importantly, feasibility implies identifying and resolving any high-risk issues before committing a large group of people to detailed development.

Human engineering. Verifying and validation feasibility from a human engineering standpoint involves answering the following questions:

- Will the specified system provide a satisfactory way for users to perform their operational functions?
- Will the system satisfy human needs at various levels?
- Will the system help people fulfill their human potential?

Examples of human engineering considerations are given in Shneiderman[3] and in Smith and Aucella.[4]

Resource engineering. This involves the following verification and validation questions:

- Can a system be developed that satisfies the specified requirements (at an acceptable cost in resources)?
- Will the specified system cost-effectively accommodate expected growth in operational requirements over its life-cycle?

Examples of resource engineering considerations are given in Boehm[1] and Ferrari.[5]

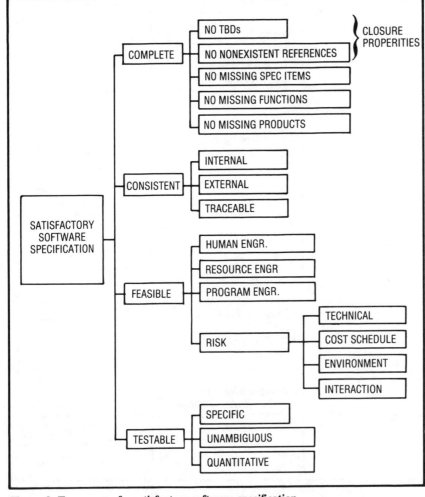

Figure 3. Taxonomy of a satisfactory software specification.

Program engineering. This addresses the following questions regarding a specified system:

- Will it be cost-effective to maintain?
- Will it be cost-effective from a portability standpoint?
- Will it have sufficient accuracy, reliability, and availability to cost-effectively satisfy operational needs over its life cycle?

Examples of these program engineering considerations are given in Lipow, White, and Boehm's[6] checklists on maintainability and portability and in the checklist on reliability and availability on p. 87.

Risk. If the life-cycle cost-effectiveness of a specified system is extremely sensitive to some system aspect that is not well-known or understood, there is a high risk involved in the system. If such high-risk issues are not identified and resolved in advance, there is a strong likelihood of disaster if or when this aspect of the system is not realized as expected.

Four major sources of risk in software requirements and design specifications are technical, cost-schedule, environmental, and interaction effects.

Technical risk, for example, can involve

- achievable levels of overhead in a multiprocessor operating system;
- achievable levels of computer security protection;
- achievable speed and accuracy of new algorithms;
- achievable performance in "artifical intelligence" domains (e.g., pattern recognition, natural language processing); and
- achievable levels of man-machine performance (e.g., air traffic control).

Cost-schedule risks include the sensitivity to cost and schedule constraints of such items as

- availability and reliability of the underlying virtual machine (hardware, operating system,

database management system, compiler) upon which the specified software will be built;
- stability of the underlying virtual machine;
- availability of key personnel; and
- strain on available main memory and execution time.

Some environmental risk issues are

- expected volume and quality of input data;
- availability and performance of interfacing systems; and
- expected sophistication, flexibility, and degree of cooperation of system users.

A particular concern here is the assessment of second-order effects caused by introduction of the new system. For example, several airline reservation systems experienced overloads because new capabilities stimulated additional customer requests and transactions. Of course, this sort of reaction can't be predicted precisely. The important thing is to determine where system performance is highly sensitive and to concentrate risk-avoidance efforts in those areas.

If the development is high-risk in several areas, the risks tend to interact exponentially. Unless you resolve the high-risk issues in advance, you may find yourself in the company of some of the supreme disasters in the software business.

For example, one large government agency attempted to build a huge real-time inventory control system involving a nationwide network of supercomputers with

- extremely ambitious real-time performance requirements;
- a lack of qualified techniques for the operating system and networking aspects;
- integration of huge, incompatible databases;
- continually changing external interfaces; and
- a lack of qualified development personnel.

Although some of these were pointed out as high-risk items early, they were not resolved in advance.

After spending roughly seven years and $250 million, the project failed to provide any significant operational capability and was cut off by Congress.

Testability. A specification is *testable* to the extent that one can identify an economically feasible technique for determining whether or not the developed software will satisfy the specification. To be testable, specifications must be specific, unambiguous, and quantitative wherever possible. Below are some examples of specifications which are *not* testable:

- The software shall provide interfaces with the appropriate subsystems.
- The software shall degrade gracefully under stress.
- The software shall be developed in accordance with good development standards.
- The software shall provide the necessary processing under all modes of operation.
- Computer memory utilization shall be optimized to accommodate future growth.
- The software shall provide a 99.9999 percent assurance of information privacy (or "reliability," "availability," or "human safety," when these terms are undefined).
- The software shall provide accuracy sufficient to support effective flight control.
- The software shall provide real-time response to sales activity queries.

These statements are good as goals and objectives, but they are not precise enough to serve as the basis of a pass-fail acceptance test.

Below are some more testable versions of the last two requirements:

- The software shall compute aircraft position within the following accuracies:
  $\pm$ 50 feet in the horizontal;
  $\pm$ 20 feet in the vertical.
- The system shall respond to
  Type A queries in $\leqslant$2 seconds;
  Type B queries in $\leqslant$10 seconds;

Type C queries in ≤2 minutes; where Type A, B, and C queries are defined in detail in the specification.

In many cases, even these versions will not be sufficiently testable without further definition. For example:

- Do the terms "±50 feet" or "≤2 seconds" refer to root-mean-square performance, 90-percent confidence limits, or never-to-exceed constraints?
- Does "response" time include terminal delays, communications delays, or just the time involved in computer processing?

Thus, it often requires a good deal of added effort to eliminate a specification's vagueness and ambiguity and make it testable. But such effort is generally well worthwhile: It would have to be done eventually for the test phase anyway, and doing it early eliminates a great deal of expense, controversy, and possible bitterness in later stages.

Verification and validation techniques

A number of techniques, outlined in Figure 4 and evaluated below, are effective in performing software requirements and design verification and validation.

Simple manual techniques. Five relatively simple and easily implemented manual techniques—

Simple manual techniques:
  Reading
  Manual cross-referencing
  Interviews
  Checklists
  Manual models
  Simple scenarios

Simple automated techniques:
  Automated cross-referencing
  Simple automated models

Detailed manual techniques:
  Detailed scenarios
  Mathematical proofs

Detailed automated techniques:
  Detailed automated models
  Prototypes

Figure 4. Verification and validation techniques.

reading, cross-referencing, interviews, checklists, and models—can provide much valuable information for meeting verification and validation criteria.

Reading. Having someone other than the originator read the specification to identify potential problems is often referred to as "reviewing." Here, however, we call it "reading" and reserve the term "reviewing" for a more formal activity.

Since reading subjects the specification to another point of view, it is very good for picking up any blind spots or misconceptions that the specification developer might have. This is particularly true if the reader is going to be one of the product's testers, users, maintainers, interfacers, or program developers; a tester can, for example, verify that the specification is testable and unambiguous. Another strength of reading is that it requires little preparation. It is also extremely flexible with respect to when, to where, and to what level of detail it is done.

Reading's strong points can turn into weak points if the "little preparation" it does require is not carried out. Readers can waste a lot of time—looking for the wrong things or looking for nothing in paticular—that could have been spent bringing a valuable perspective to focus on a set of significant issues. This is a particular danger on large projects. For detailed designs, the design inspection or walkthrough described by Fagan[7] can be particularly effective. Still, reading is fundamentally limited in the extent to which it can be used to verify a detailed specification's completeness and consistency, or the feasibility of a complex system's performance requirements.

Manual cross-referencing. Cross-referencing goes beyond reading; it involves constructing cross-reference tables and various diagrams—for example, state transition, data flow, control flow, and data structure diagrams—to clarify interactions among

specified entities. These entities include functions, databases, and interfacing hardware, software, or personnel.

Manual cross-referencing is effective for the consistency (internal, external, and traceability) and closure properties of a specification, particularly for small to medium specifications. For large specifications, it can be quite cumbersome, leading to the suggested use of automated aids. If these are not available, manual methods are still recommended; the payoff will outweigh the cost and time expended.

Manual cross-referencing will not do much to verify the feasibility of performance requirements or to validate the subjective aspects of human engineering or maintainability provisions.

Interviews. Discussing a specification with its originator will identify potential problems. With minimum effort, you can find out a great deal about its strengths and weaknesses; this will allow you to deploy your V&V resources most effectively by concentrating on the weak points. Interviews are particularly good for identifying potential blind spots, misunderstandings, and high-risk issues. But, like spot-checking, they only identify and scope the specification's major problem areas; the detailed V&V work remains to be done.

Checklists. Specialized lists, based on experience, of significant issues for assuring successful software development can be used effectively with any of the manual methods described above.

Checklists are excellent for catching omissions, such as the missing items, functions, and products discussed under "Completeness." They are also valuable aids in addressing some of the life-cycle feasibility considerations: human engineering, maintainability, reliability and availability, portability, security and privacy, and life-cycle efficiency. But they are not much help in verifying the feasibility of performance requirements or in dealing with detailed consistency and closure questions.

One danger with checklists is that items might be considered absolute requirements rather than suggestions. For example, several features in a portability checklist will not be necessary if the software will never be used on another machine; adding them blindly will just incur unnecessary expense.

Manual models. Mathematical formulas can be used to represent and analyze certain aspects of the system being specified. These manual models are very good for analyzing some life-cycle feasibility issues, particularly accuracy, real-time performance, and life-cycle cost. They are also useful for risk analysis. They are not, however, much help in verifying the details of a specification's consistency and completeness or in assessing subjective factors. Their manual nature makes them inefficient for detailed feasibility analysis of large, complex systems, but they are good for top-level analysis of large systems.

Simple scenarios. Scenarios describe how the system will work once it is in operation. Man-computer dialogues are the most common form of simple scenarios, which are very good for clarifying misunderstandings or mismatches in the specification's human engineering aspects but not for checking completeness and consistency details or for validating performance speed and accuracy.

Simple automated techniques. Automation extends the power of two manual techniques—cross-referencing and simple modeling.

Automated cross-referencing. Automated cross-referencing involves the use of a machine-analyzable specification language—for example, SREM-RSL, Software Requirements Engineering Methodology-Requirements Statement Language;[8,9] PSL/PSA, Problem Statement Language/Problem Statement Analyzer;[10] or PDL, Program Design

Language.[11] Once a specification is expressed in such a language, it can be automatically analyzed for consistency, closure properties, or presentation of cross-reference information for manual analysis. Some further automated aids in this category are discussed in the DoD "Methodman" document[12] and its references.

Current automated specification aids have only limited capabilities in addressing accuracy and dynamic performance issues.

Automated cross-referencing is excellent for verifying the detailed consistency and closure properties of both small and large specifications. Using a formatted specification language also eliminates many testability and ambiguity problems because the language forms help prevent ambiguous terms and vague generalities. The automated systems also have less of a problem in checking for additional clerical errors introduced in iterating and retyping a specification.

Current automated specification aids have only limited capabilities in addressing accuracy and dynamic performance issues, and some, particularly SREM-RSL, are not available on many computers. Although their performance on small and medium specifications has improved considerably, they are still somewhat inefficient in performing consistency and completeness checks on very large specifications. Even so, the costs of using them on large specifications are more than repaid by the savings involved in early error detection.

Simple automated models. Mathematical formulas implemented in a small computer program provide more powerful representations than manual models for analyzing such life-cycle feasibility issues as accuracy, real-time performance, and life-cycle costs. Simple automated

models are especially good for risk and sensitivity analysis, but, like manual models, are not much help in verifying detailed consistency and completeness, in assessing subjective factors, or in performing detailed feasibility analysis of large, complex systems.

Detailed manual techniques. Detailed scenarios and mathematical proofs are especially effective for clarifying human engineering needs and for verifying finite-mathematics programs, respectively.

Detailed scenarios. Detailed scenarios, which provide more elaborate—and thus more expensive—operational descriptions, are even more effective than simple scenarios in clarifying a system's human engineering aspects.

Mathematical proofs. Mathematical transformation rules can be applied to a set of statements, expressed in a precise mathematical specification language, to prove desired properties of the set of statements. These properties include internal consistency, preservation of "invariant" relations, and equivalence of two alternate sets of statements (e.g., requirements and design specifications). Automated aids to formal specification and verification such as Special/HDM, Gypsy, Affirm, and Ina Jo, are now available and have been compared by Cheheyl et al.[13]

For certain classes of problems—small problems involving the use of finite mathematics—mathematical proofs offer a near-certain guarantee of the properties proved. But mathematical proofs cannot deal with non-formalized inputs (e.g., noisy sensor data, natural language); cannot deal conveniently with "real-variable" calculations or with many issues in synchronizing concurrent processes; and cannot deal efficiently with large specifications.

Detailed automated techniques. Two final techniques—detailed automated models and prototypes—provide the most complete information.

Detailed automated models. Detailed automated models typically involve large event simulations of the system. While more expensive than simple automated models, they are much more effective in analyzing such issues as accuracy, dynamic consistency, real-time performance, and life-cycle cost. The process of generating such models also serves as a good way to catch specification inconsistencies and ambiguities.

Prototypes. In many situations, the feasibility of a specification cannot be conclusively demonstrated without developing some working software. Examples include some ac-curacy and real-time performance issues, as well as user interface suitability. In such cases, it is often valuable to build a throwaway prototype of key portions of the software: a program that works well enough to resolve the feasibility issues, but lacks the extensive features, error-proofing, and documentation of the final product. The process of building the prototype will also expose and eliminate a number of ambiguities, inconsistencies, blind spots, and misunderstandings incorporated in the specification.

Prototypes can be expensive and do not shed much light on maintainability, but they are often the only way to resolve the critical feasibility issues. (See References 14 and 15 for experiences in prototyping and Chapter 20 of Reference 1 for guidelines on when to prototype.)

An automated aid for requirements V&V

Several available systems—PSL/PSA, SREM, PDL, Special/HDM—provide automated aids to requirements and design verification and validation. To get a feel for what these systems do, let us look at how one of them—the Software Requirements Engineering Methodology, or SREM—handles a simple example, an aircraft engine monitoring system.[16]

Requirements networks. The SREM Requirements Statement Language expresses software requirements in terms of processing paths—that is, the sequences of data processing required to operate on an input stimulus to the software and produce an output response.

The first step in developing an SREM specification is to write it as a description of the processing paths. Thus, if some data is input to a processing path, and a response is required at some other point, we write this in the specification as a fundamental component. To produce several thousand paths for a complex system, a method was developed to integrate simple paths into requirements networks called R_NETS. Thus, all paths initiated by the same input interface are integrated into a common network.

Figure 5 illustrates a network with data coming across an interface (represented by a hexagon). All data coming across the interface have common processing, as indicated by the first two boxes. The AND node is next encountered to indicate a "don't care" parallelism. That is, either branch may be processed first after the AND node. That decision is left as an option for the designer. Validation points (the dark circles) are used to specify performance re-

Figure 5. An example of a path analysis structure. Validation points (dark circles) are added to the paths close to the interfaces (hexagons).

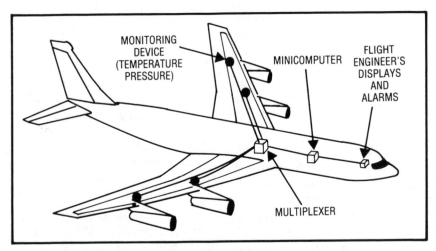

Figure 6. An aircraft engine monitoring system.

quirements in an explicitly testable fashion and are added to the paths close to the interfaces. Data is specified that must be available for testing purposes at those points, and an explicit procedure is described for analyzing those data to give a pass/fail relationship.

One advantage of this type of network is that it is integrated from the collection of paths. Therefore, it can be automatically analyzed, using the rules established for R_NETs. Another advantage is that it is similar to classic logic diagrams and flowcharts used by engineers, making it a natural form of communication between engineers. Finally, it possesses natural test points for assuring that the requirement expressed on a path

is expressly addressed for testing.

R_NETs, then, are the basic tool used by SREM to define functional requirements unambiguously by showing each path of processing required by the input stimuli to the system.

Engine monitoring system. This simple example for an engine monitoring system, or EMS, will show how the R_NET concept is used in describing requirements.

An airplane with multiple engines has a device that is connected to each engine (see Figure 6). This device measures temperatures, pressure, and the state of two switches. All of the devices are connected to the multiplexer, which is interrogated by an on-board computer. The com-

puter senses when a temperature or pressure goes out of an allowed range and gives an alarm in the cockpit.

A partial system specification for the EMS capabilities might look like this:

(1) Monitor 1 to 10 engines.

(2) Monitor (a) 3 temperatures (0 to 1000°C) (b) 3 pressures (0 to 4000 PSIA), and (c) 2 switches (off, on).

(3) Monitor each engine at a specified rate (1 to 10 times per second).

(4) Output a warning message if any parameter falls outside prescribed limits, and an alarm if outside danger limits.

(5) Record history of each engine.

The R_NET approach (see Figure 7) for defining the EMS functional

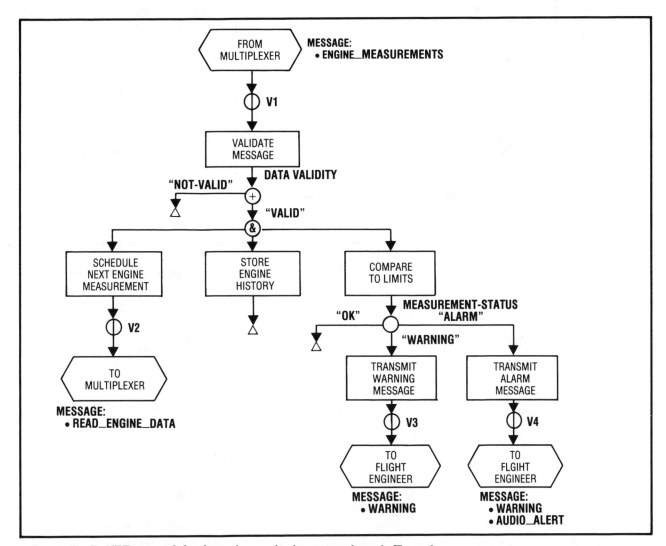

Figure 7. The R_NET approach for the engine monitoring system shown in Figure 6.

requirement presents a clear, unambiguous definition of how each stimulus (called a MESSAGE in SREM terminology) is processed, and where the VALIDATION_POINTs (V1, V2, V3, V4) reside that allow testing of the PERFORMANCE_REQUIREMENTs specified for selected functional processes (paths).

As a result of preparing the R_NET and accomplishing automated error checks, many questions arise. These are typical types of ambiguities resident in system specifications, and

the SREM methodology brings them out early and quite clearly. Answers must be attained before completion of the software specification. Examples for the EMS are

(1) Does "output warning" mean each time or just the first time?

(2) How are "prescribed limits" defined?

(3) How quickly must the system output a "warning" or "alarm?"

(4) What does a "warning message" contain?

(5) What is to be done with the history data for each engine?

Later, we will see how some of these questions were identified by SREM procedures.

Requirements statement language. The SREM approach to attaining explicitness throughout a requirement specification is grounded in the use of the Requirements Statement Language. RSL is a machine-processible, artificial language which overcomes the shortcomings of English in stating requirements. RSL is based on the entity-attribute-relationship model of representing information. Figure 8 illustrates RSL statements related to the R_NET and its data from Figure 7. This figure illustrates the English-like nature of RSL.

Requirements tools and database. The Requirements Engineering and Validation System is an integrated set of tools to support development of the RSL requirements. REVS consists of three segments: a centralized database called ASSM for Abstract System Semantic Model, a translator for the RSL, and a set of automated tools for processing the information in the ASSM. A diagram of the system is shown in Figure 9.

The purpose of the RSL translator is to analyze the RSL statements that are input to it and to make entries in the ASSM corresponding to the

```
INPUT_INTERFACE: MULTI.
    DESCRIPTION: 3 TEMPERATURES 3 PRESSURES 2 SWITCHES.
    ENABLES: R_NET MONITOR_ENGINES.
    PASSES: MESSAGE ENGINE_DATA.
    DOCUMENTED BY
        SOURCE: TRW_CLASS_NOTES.
    COMPLETENESS: CHANGEABLE.

MESSAGE: ENGINE_DATA.
    MADE BY
        DATA: TEMPERATURE
        DATA: PRESSURES
        DATA: SWITCHES.

DATA: TEMPERATURE
    INCLUDES
        DATA: INTAKE_TEMP
        DATA: COMPRESSION_TEMP
        DATA: EXHAUST_TEMP.
```

Figure 8. Sample RSL statements to the R_NET and its data from Figure 7.

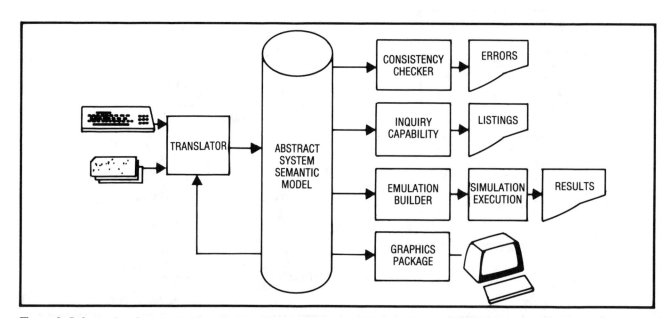

Figure 9. Information flow in the Requirements Engineering and Validation System. REVS is an integrated set of tools that supports the Requirements Statement Language.

meaning of the statements. The translator references the ASSM to do simple consistency checks on the input. This prevents the occurrence of disastrous errors such as the introduction of an element with the same name as a previously existing element or an instance of a relationship that is tied to an illegal type of element. This type of checking catches, at an early stage, some of the simple types of inconsistencies that are often found in requirements specifications.

The information available in the ASSM will support a wide variety of requirements analysis tools. Among these are an interactive graphics package to aid in the specification of the flow paths; static consistency checkers, which check for consistency of information throughout the system; and an automated simulation generator and execution package, which aids in the study of dynamic interactions of the various requirements. Situation-specific reports and analyses, which a particular user or manager may need, are generated through the use of the Requirements Analysis and Data Extraction system. The RADX system is independent of the extensions to RSL so that new concepts added to the language may be included in queries to the database.

A key consideration is that all steps in the SREM approach, including simulations, utilize a common requirements database, which is necessary since many individuals are continually adding, deleting, and changing information about requirements for the data processing system. Centralizaton allows both the requirements engineers and the analysis tools to work from a common baseline and enables implementation of management controls on changes to this baseline.

Automated consistency and completeness checking. Figure 10, a RADX printout for the engine monitoring system, illustrates the RADX query-response capability to test adequacy of engineer inputs to the database.

First, RADX identified that accuracy and response-time limits have not yet been specified. This feature is designed to assure that all appropriate paths are eventually covered by performance requirements.

Next, RADX identified data with no sink—that is, data produced but

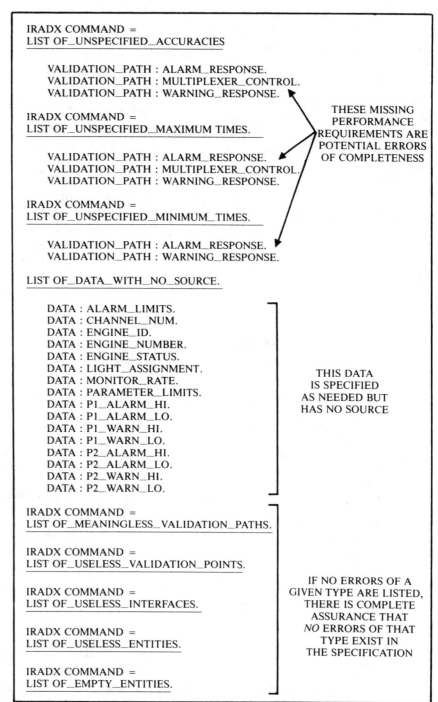

Figure 10. Error checks in the Requirements Analysis and Data Extraction system provide immediate, automatic analysis of requirements completeness and consistency.

never used, since it is not input to a processing step and is not contained in an output message. Thus, the engine history that was required to be maintained is never accessed. This probably represents an incompleteness—that is, an overload set of processing requirements.

Finally, there is a set of error categories with no indicated errors of these types in the specifications. When there are no errors of any type remaining, the database will support a good specification for detailed software design and coding.

In sum, this example shows how an automated verification and validation aid can help us avoid and eliminate problems in our requirements and design specifications. This type of aid is particularly good in resolving completeness and consistency problems, but it does not provide much help in resolving user-interface or maintainability issues. This means that we need to employ a mix of techniques to cover our full range of criteria.

Evaluation and recommendations

Evaluation of V&V techniques. Table 1 provides a way to determine the best mix of V&V techniques for a particular project. It evaluates the techniques discussed above with respect to their ability to help verify and validate specifications. The evaluation is done in terms of the basic V&V criteria discussed earlier.

A retrospective analysis indicated that SREM could have caught 63 percent of the requirements problems on one project.

Some quantitative information is also becoming available on the relative effectiveness of those techniques. For example, one retrospective analysis indicated that SREM could have caught 63 percent of the requirements problems on one proj-

ect. Several studies of design inspections have indicated that they can catch 60 percent of the errors present. Further quantitative information can be found in Chapter 24 of Reference 1.

Small-system V&V. To verify and validate a small specification, the customer and/or project manager should

- outline the specification before opening,
- read the specification for critical issues,
- interview the specification developer(s),
- determine the best allocation of V&V resources, and
- coordinate efforts and resolve conflicts.

The V&V agent should

- read the specification,
- use checklists and manual cross-referencing,
- use simple models if accuracy or real-time performance are critical,

Table 1.
Verification and validation techniques rated according to eight criteria.

	Completeness Small	Large	Consistency Small	Large	Traceability Small	Large	Human Engr.	Re-source Engr.	Maint., Relia.	Accuracy	Relative Economics Small	Large
Simple Manual Techniques												
Reading	**	—	**	—	**	—	**	—	**	—	***	*
Manual Cross-Referencing	***	*	***	*	***	*	*	—	*	—	**	*
Interviews	*	*a	*	*a	**	**a	**a	—	**a	—	***	***
Checklists	*	*	—	—	—	—	***	*	***	*	**	*
Manual Models	—	—	—	—	—	—	—	*b	—	*b	**	**
Simple Scenarios	*	—	*	—	**	*	***c	—	—	—	**	**
Simple Automated Techniques												
Automated Cross-Referencing	***	***	***	***	***	***	—	—	—	—	*d	*d
Simple Automated Models	—	—	—	—	—	—	—	**b	—	**b	*	**
Detailed Manual Techniques												
Detailed Scenarios	*	*	*	*	**	**	***	—	—	—	—	*
Mathematical Proofs	***e	—	***e	—	***e	—	—	—	—	—	—	—
Detailed Automated Techniques												
Detailed Automated Models	**	**	**	**	**	**	—	***	—	**	—	*
Prototypes	**	**	**	**	**	**	***	***	*	***	—	*

Ratings:
*** Very strong
** Strong
* Moderate
— Weak

Notes:
a. Interviews are good for identifying potential large-scale problems but not so good for detail.
b. Simple models are good for full analysis of small systems and for top-level analysis of large systems.
c. Simple scenarios are very strong for small-system and strong for large-system user aspects.
d. Economy rating for automated cross-referencing is strong for medium systems. If the cross-reference tool needs to be developed, reduce the rating to weak.
e. Proofs provide near-certain correctness for the finite-mathematics aspects of software.

- use simple scenarios if the user interface is critical, and
- use mathematical proofs on portions where reliability is extremely critical.

Users should
- read the specification from the user's point of view and
- use a human-engineering checklist.

Maintainers should
- read the specification from the maintainer's point of view,
- use maintainability and relia-

bility/availability checklists, and
- use a portability checklist if portability is a consideration.

Interfacers should
- read the specification, and
- perform manual cross-referencing with respect to the interfaces.

Medium-system V&V. To verify and validate a medium specification, use the same general approach as

Reliability and availability checklist

Rather than being long and exhaustive, this checklist concentrates on high-leverage issues in obtaining a highly reliable and available system.

Reliable input handling

(a) Are input codes engineered for reliable data entry?

Comment: Examples are use of meaningful codes, increasing the "distance" between codes (NMEX, NYRK vs. NEWM, NEWY), and frequency-optimized codes (reducing the number of keystrokes as error sources).

(b) Do inputs include some appropriate redundancy as a basis for error checking?

Comment: Examples are checksums, error-correcting codes, input boundary identifiers (e.g., for synchronization), and check words (e.g., name and employee number).

(c) Will the software properly handle unspecified inputs?

Comment: Options include the use of default values, error responses, and fallback processing options.

(d) Are all off-normal input values properly handled?

Comment: Options are similar to those in (c). "Off-normal" checking may refer not just to the range of values but also to the mode, form, volume, order, or timing of the input.

(e) Are man-machine dialogues easy to understand and use for the expected class of users? Are they hard to misunderstand and misuse?

(f) Are records kept of the inputs for later failure analysis or recovery needs?

Reliable execution

(g) Are there provisions for proper initialization of control options, data values, and peripheral devices?

(h) Are there provisions for protection against singularities?

Comment: Examples are division by zero, singular matrix operations, and proper handling of empty sets.

(i) Are there design standards for internal error checking? Are they being followed?

Comment: These should tell under what conditions the responsibility for checking lies with the producer of outputs, the consumer of inputs, or a separate checking routine.

(j) Are there design standards for synchronization of concurrent processes? Are they being followed?

(k) Are the numerical methods—algorithms, tolerances, tables, constants—sufficiently accurate for operational needs?

(l) Is the data structured to avoid harmful side effects?

Comment: Techniques include "information hiding," minimum essential use of global variables, and use of data cluster (data-procedure-binding) concepts.

(m) Do the programming standards support reliable execution?

Error messages and diagnostics

(n) Are there requirements for clear, helpful error messages?

Comments: These should be correct, understandable by maintenance personnel, expressed in user language, and accompanied by useful information for error isolation.

(o) Are there requirements for diagnostic and debugging aids?

Comment: Examples are labeled, selective traces and dumps, labeled displays for program inputs, special hardware and software diagnostic routines, timers, self-checks, post-processors, and control parameters for easily specifying diagnostic and debugging options.

(p) Are measurement and validation points explicitly identified in the software specifications?

(q) Are database diagnostics specified for checking the consistency, reasonableness, standards compliance, completeness, and access control of the database?

Backup and recovery

(r) Are there adequate provisions for backup and recovery capabilities?

Comment: These include capabilities for archiving programs and data, diagnosing failure conditions, interim fallback operation in degraded mode, timely reconstitution of programs, data, and/or hardware, and operational cutover to the reconstituted system.

(s) Have these provisions been validated by means of a failure modes and effects analysis?

Comment: Potential failure modes include hardware outages and failure conditions (CPUs, memory, peripherals, communications), loss of data (database, pointers, catalogs, input data), and failure of programs (deadlocks, unending loops, nonconvergence of algorithms).

with small systems, with the following differences:

- use automated cross-referencing if a suitable aid is available,
- use simple-to-medium manual and automated models for critical performance analyses,
- use simple-to-medium scenarios for critical user interfaces, and
- prototype high-risk items that cannot be adequately verified and validated by other techniques.

Large-system V&V. Use the same general approach for large specifications as for medium systems, except use simple-to-detailed instead of simple-to-medium models and scenarios.

For special situations, of course, you will have to tailor your own best mix of verification and validation techniques. But in general, these recommendations will provide you with a good starting point for identifying and resolving your software problems while they're still relatively easy to handle. ∎

References

1. *IEEE Standard Glossary of Software Engineering Terminology,* IEEE Std. 729-1983, IEEE-CS order no. 729, Los Alamitos, Calif., 1983.

2. B. W. Boehm, *Software Engineering Economics,* Prentice-Hall, Englewood Cliffs, N.J., 1981.

3. B. Shneiderman, *Software Psychology: Human Factors in Computer and Information Systems,* Winthrop Press, Cambridge, Mass., 1980.

4. S. L. Smith and A. F. Aucella, "Design Guidelines for the User Interface to Computer-Based Information Systems," ESD-TR-83-122, USAF Electronic Systems Division, Bedford, Mass., Mar. 1983.

5. D. Ferrari, *Computer Systems Performance Evaluation,* Prentice-Hall, Englewood Cliffs, N.J., 2nd ed., 1983.

6. M. Lipow, B. B. White, and B. W. Boehm, "Software Quality Assurance: An Acquisition Guidebook," TRW-SS-77-07, Nov. 1977.

7. M. E. Fagan, "Design and Code Inspections to Reduce Errors in Program Development," *IBM Systems Journal,* Vol. 15, No. 3, 1976, pp. 182-211.

8. M. W. Alford, "A Requirements Engineering Methodology for Real-Time Processing Requirements," *IEEE Trans. Software Engr.,* Vol. SE-3, No. 1, Jan. 1977, pp. 60-68.

9. T. E. Bell, D. C. Bixler, and M. E. Dyer, "An Extendable Approach to Computer-Aided Software Requirements Engineering," *IEEE Trans. Software Engr.,* Vol. SE-3, No. 1, Jan. 1977, pp. 49-59.

10. D. Teichroew and E. A Hershey III, "PSL/PSA: A Computer-Aided Technique for Structured Documentation and Analysis of Information Processing Systems," *IEEE Trans. Software Engr.,* Vol. SE-3, No. 1, Jan. 1977, pp. 41-48.

11. S. H. Caine and E. K. Gordon, "PDL: A Tool for Software Design," *AFIPS Conf. Proc.,* Vol. 44, 1975 NCC, pp. 272-276.

12. P. Freeman and A. I. Wassermann, "Ada Methodologies: Concepts and Requirements," DoD Ada Joint Program Office, Nov. 1982.

13. M. H. Cheheyl et al., "Verifying Security," *ACM Computing Surveys,* Sept. 1981, pp. 279-340.

14. S. L. Squires, B. Branstad, and M. Zelkowitz, eds., "Special Issue on Rapid Prototyping," *ACM Software Engr. Notes,* Dec. 1982.

15. B. W. Boehm, T. E. Gray, and T. Seewaldt, "Prototyping vs. Specifying: A Multi-Project Experiment," *IEEE Trans. Software Engr.,* 1984 (in publication).

16. M. W. Alford, R. P. Loshbough, and L. R. Marker, "The Software Requirements Engineering Methodology: An Overview," TRW Software Series, TRW-SS-80-03, May 1980.

Barry W. Boehm is a member of the *IEEE Software* Editorial Board. His photo and biography appear on p. 6.

Technical Report
CMU/SEI-87-TR-23
ESD/TR-87-186
Preliminary Version
September 1987

A Method for Assessing the Software Engineering Capability of Contractors

W.S. Humphrey
W.L. Sweet

Software Engineering Institute

With contributions from

R.K. Edwards
G.R. LaCroix
M.F. Owens
H.P. Schultz

The Mitre Corporation
Burlington Road
Bedford, Massachusetts

Software Engineering Institute
Carnegie Mellon University
Pittsburgh, Pennsylvania 15213

Abstract: This document provides guidelines and procedures for assessing the ability of potential DoD contractors to develop software in accordance with modern software engineering methods. It includes specific questions and a method for evaluating the results.

General Introduction

The purpose of this document is to facilitate objective and consistent assessments of the ability of potential DoD contractors to develop software in accordance with modern software engineering methods. Such assessments would be conducted either in the pre-solicitation qualification process, in the formal source selection process, or both. While this document is intended to guide the assessment of a contractor's overall software engineering capability, it can also be valuable in the assessment of a specific project team's software engineering capability.

Alternatively, this document can be used as an aid to software development organizations in conducting an internal assessment of their own software engineering capability. The document is designed to help an assessment team define the highest priority steps for the improvement of an organization's capability.

Because an understanding of proper software engineering practice is only now developing, standard, well-accepted measures do not yet exist. The assessment questions listed in the body of this document are phrased so that an affirmative answer indicates that an organization has a desirable characteristic. Some of the questions pertain to advanced concepts of software engineering that may not yet be sufficiently refined or disseminated to be incorporated in a contractor's standard practice; therefore, not all assessment questions need be answered affirmatively for an organization to be considered to have a modern software engineering capability.

The capability of a contractor to perform software engineering has been divided into three areas:

1. organization and resource management
2. software engineering process and its management
3. tools and technology.

The qualities that the questions assess are different for each of these areas and are described in the introductions to the questions for each area.

A full assessment of software engineering capability includes some evaluation of the experience level of the software development personnel. Addendum A contains suggested questions for use in this evaluation.

General Approach

This guideline was developed, at the request of the United States Air Force, by the Software Engineering Institute of Carnegie Mellon University with assistance from The MITRE Corporation. The motivation for this work was the increasing importance of software in DoD procurements and the need of all the services to more effectively evaluate the ability of their software contractors to competently perform on software engineering contracts.

A structured assessment approach has been developed to augment the current contractor evaluation methods. The primary objective has been to provide a standardized method that is documented, publicly available for review and comment, and periodically modified as experience is gained with its use.

A further objective is to provide a public process which is defined in advance and for which the contractors can prepare. This assessment guide has therefore been designed to assist software organizations in identifying areas where they should make improvements in their own capabilities. As contractors improve their ability to meet the needs of the services for quality software, the services will improve their ability to serve the national interest by awarding contracts to those with the best capability.

Assessment methodology is based on the principal that prior experience is a good predictor of future performance. Since there are exceptions to this principle, the guidelines suggest that procurement evaluations using this method consider both current capability and future plans for software process improvement.

This method should be used to augment the many steps currently involved in source selection. While the questionnaire structure provides a relatively simplistic numerical evaluation, it also indicates the strong and weak areas of a contractor's software process. This will provide the services with more information on which to base their procurement decisions.

Technical Approach

The assessment process is focused on defining and clarifying the positive attributes of good software engineering practices. It is further recognized that the state-of-the-practice of software engineering is steadily advancing and that additional criteria and a higher level of expectation will be appropriate for judging software engineering capability in the future.

Assessment questions are based on the following premises:

- The quality of a software product stems, in large part, from the quality of the process used to create it.
- Software engineering is a process that can be managed, measured, and progressively improved.
- The quality of a software process is affected by the technology used to support it.
- The level of technology used in software engineering should be appropriate to the maturity of the process.
- Software products developed by contractors for DoD use are acquired under contracts invoking DoD-STD-2167/A, Defense System Software Development, as tailored for each contract.

To provide a structure for assessment, five levels of process maturity and two stages of technology advancement have been postulated. (See Addenda B and C.)

Process Maturity Levels

1. Initial: The initial environment has ill-defined procedures and controls. The organization does not consistently apply software engineering management to

the process, nor does it use modern tools and technology. Level 1 organizations may have serious cost and schedule problems.

2. Repeatable: At Level 2, the organization has generally learned to manage costs and schedules, and the process is now repeatable. The organization uses standard methods and practices for managing software development activities such as cost estimating, scheduling, requirements changes, code changes, and status reviews.

3. Defined: In Level 3, the process is well characterized and reasonably well understood. The organization defines its process in terms of software engineering standards and methods, and it has made a series of organizational and methodological improvements. These specifically include design and code reviews, training programs for programmers and review leaders, and increased organizational focus on software engineering. A major improvement in this phase is the establishment and staffing of a software engineering process group that focuses on the software engineering process and the adequacy with which it is implemented.

4. Managed: In Level 4, the process is not only understood but it is quantified, measured, and reasonably well controlled. The organization typically bases its operating decisions on quantitative process data, and conducts extensive analyses of the data gathered during software engineering reviews and tests. Tools are used increasingly to control and manage the design process as well as to support data gathering and analysis. The organization is learning to project expected errors with reasonable accuracy.

5. Optimized: At Level 5, organizations have not only achieved a high degree of control over their process, they have a major focus on improving and optimizing its operation. This includes more sophisticated analyses of the error and cost data gathered during the process as well as the introduction of comprehensive error cause analysis and prevention studies. The data on the process are used iteratively to improve the process and achieve optimum performance.

Software Technology Stages

- A. Inefficient: Multiple implementations may be available and the practice may be in widespread use, but the technology is no longer effective. An organization that primarily employs inefficient software development technology is likely to be ineffective in developing software. Moreover, at this technology stage some important software engineering practices are not practical in large, complex developments.

- B. Basic: Multiple implementations are available, and they have been demonstrated to be effective. An organization that primarily employs basic software development technologies is likely to be moderately effective and, depending upon the maturity of its process, reasonably consistent in its performance.

Usage Guide

This document is intended for use by DoD development and procurement organizations to assess contractors' software engineering capabilities. When used as part of the formal DoD systems acquisition process, the questions are furnished, for information purposes, to potential contractors with the Request for Proposal (RFP). A qualified assessment team then visits each contractor to obtain responses to the assessment questions and assure accuracy and consistency of interpretation. The assessment results are included in the source selection process as information for the Source Selection Advisory Council.

The effectiveness of an assessment is critically dependent on the process used in the assessment and on the background and training of the personnel conducting it. The following guidelines are recommended for use by procurement agencies for incorporating software capability assessments into the source selection process.

1. Materials
The following basic documents are to be used:

- "A Method for Assessing the Software Engineering Capability of Contractors"

- the Assessment Recording Form (Addendum D)

- the guideline for further questions (Addendum E)

- available training guides and materials.

2. RFP Content
When assessment results will be considered in source selection, a statement of this fact and the above materials must be included with the Request for Proposal.

3. General Assessment Procedure
The answers to the assessment questions are not submitted with the proposal but are provided to an assessment team that visits each contending contractor during the proposal evaluation period. Using the follow-up questions in Addendum E as a guide, the assessment team clarifies what is meant by the responses to the questionnaire. Normally, at least three working days should be scheduled for an assessment to allow for reviewing the questions, obtaining and discussing back-up material, demonstrating support tools, and presenting conclusions. A single assessment team should visit all of the contending contractors to assure consistent interpretation of both the questions and the results.

4. Selection of Assessment Team Members
The assessment team must have a mix of talents. Experienced professionals are required, including professionals knowledgeable in the software development process, the technology, the application area, and the specific procurement. All team members must have been trained in the assessment process.

5. Assessment Training
The training program involves several days of classroom instruction to review the assessment questionnaire in detail and discuss the materials and support tools that should be available to demonstrate performance for each question.

6. Contractor Preparation for Assessment
While making advance arrangements, the assessment team should ask each contractor to provide a listing of the major software development projects at the location, together with a brief indication of their status (e.g., design, implementation, development test, acceptance test). Projects recommended for assessment should also be noted. The assessment team and the contractor should agree in advance on several projects, in different stages of development and indicative of the standard practice in the organization, so that representatives of these projects can be available for participation in the assessment.

7. Conduct of the Assessment
An on-site assessment begins with a briefing explaining the assessment process to the local management and the assessment participants and confirming the planned support for the assessment. The assessment team then goes through the questionnaire with the project representatives as a group, ensuring consistent interpretation of the questions and obtaining an initial set of an-

swers for each project. Based on these initial results, the team makes a preliminary assessment of the organization's process maturity level and technology stage and then requests back-up materials and tool demonstrations to support the affirmative answers that determine the highest likely level and stage. For example, if the preliminary evaluation results (see the following section) indicate that an organization is at maturity level 3, the major focus should be directed to probing the affirmative responses to the maturity level 2 and 3 questions. In each case, the team should request evidence for a specific project at an appropriate phase of development.

8. **Assessment Conclusion**
At the end of the assessment, the local management should be informed of the findings and given an opportunity to offer evidence to refute any disputed findings and to explain their plans for process improvement. Where such plans are material to the procurement, they should be documented and made part of the contract. It is important that the process be completely open because the complexity of the subject matter and the lack of common terms for many of the process elements could lead to confusion and misunderstanding.

9. **Utilization of Results**
The results of the assessments will be made available to the Source Selection Advisory Council for consideration prior to final source selection.

Guidelines for Evaluation of Results

The questions in the body of this document have been designed to require only a "yes" or "no" answer. The method of evaluation presented here incorporates all the questions in this document except those in Addendum A. The questions in Addendum A are provided to assist in the assessment of a contractor's experience relevant to a particular procurement.

Level of Process Maturity
To determine a contractor's level of process maturity, the following procedure is used. **This procedure requires successive qualifications at each level.**

1. Determine the percentage of affirmative answers to all Level 2 questions and to the asterisked questions for Level 2. If the percentage* of affirmative answers to all questions is at least 80% and the percentage of affirmative answers to asterisked questions is at least 90%, the organization has qualified at Level 2; otherwise, it is at Level 1. If Level 2 is achieved, go on to the next step.

2. Determine the percentage of affirmative answers to all Level 2 and 3 questions combined and to the asterisked questions for Levels 2 and 3 combined. Again, if the percentage of affirmative answers to all questions is at least 80% and the percentage of affirmative answers to asterisked questions is at least 90%, the organization qualifies at Level 3, otherwise, it is at Level 2. If it qualifies at Level 3, this procedure is repeated combining Level 2, 3, and 4 answers, again requiring 80% for all questions and 90% for asterisked questions. If the organization qualifies at Level 4, the assessment for Level 5 combines Level 2, 3, 4, and 5 answers, again using 80% and 90% as the criteria.

3. Determine the level for the organization as a whole by averaging the levels of the projects assessed.

---

*Threshold percentages have been arbitrarily established to promote consistency and objectivity.

Software Technology Stages

To determine the technology stage of an organization, a similar procedure is used.

1. Determine the percentage of affirmative answers to all Stage B questions and to the asterisked questions for Stage B. If the percentage of affirmative answers to all questions is at least 80% and the percentage of affirmative answers to asterisked questions is at least 90%, the organization has qualified at Stage B; otherwise, it is at Stage A.

2. Determine the level for the organization as a whole by averaging the levels of the projects assessed.

Combined Process and Technology Evaluation

By placing the levels of process maturity and the stages of technology in a two dimensional matrix, an evaluation can now be made that combines both of these measures. Figure 1 presents process levels on the x-axis and technology stages on the y-axis, and indicates the target region toward which an organization should progress.

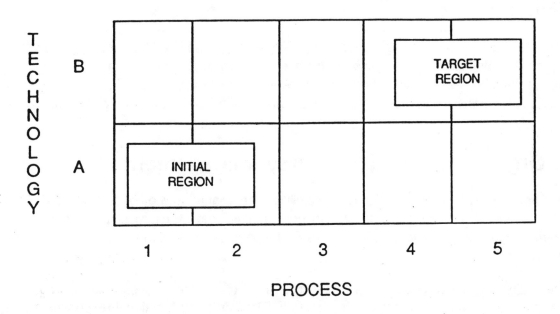

Figure 1: Process/Technology Matrix

Qualifying Considerations

As previously noted, the practice of software engineering is not only complex but is still evolving and is not yet fully defined. In using a specific procedure to assess software engineering capability, some qualifying factors should be considered.

It is recognized that there may be alternative methods to address a given problem, and it is possible that there may be acceptable alternatives to some of the positions taken in this document. Therefore, it is essential that this instrument be used by a competent and adequately trained assessment team if meaningful results are to be obtained. The SEI intends to provide, on a continuing basis, training and/or training materials to facilitate the training of assessment teams.

The process activities and data referred to in the questions are used as indicators of software engineering capability and are assumed to be of value to the internal operations of an organization that develops/maintains significant amounts of DoD software. It is not intended that either the process activities or data be identified as deliverable items in a procurement contract solely because they are referenced in this document. The cost-effectiveness of these activities may vary with different organizations; but available evidence clearly indicates that in the context of total life-cycle cost and performance, investment in these activities is well justified. In this document, software engineering capability is assumed to include the ability to perform large and complex software developments; therefore, the assessment process may not be fully applicable to small projects.

The authors of this document have established, on the basis of extensive experience in software development and acquisition, that the state-of-practice is measurable and that this state can be compared to a norm. This instrument will be used initially to establish the norm. The SEI intends to continue monitoring the use and evolution of this methodology to insure that it is consistent with best current software engineering practice and technology and to correct, whenever possible, those areas where its misuse may be causing problems.

Questions

In order to achieve clarity in the questions, many of the terms used have been given specific explanatory definitions in the glossary at the end of this document. Each use of a glossary term in the Questions section is italicized. Adherence to these definitions is essential for proper and consistent assessments. There is no significance to the order of the questions.

1. Organization and Resource Management

This section deals with functional responsibilities, personnel, and other resources and facilities. Its purpose is to define the magnitude, quality, and structure of the software engineering organization. The questions focus on responsibilities and the quality and quantity of resources.

The major responsibility concerns relate to quality assurance, process management, and configuration control. The intent is to ascertain whether these functional responsibilities are clearly delineated and assigned, not necessarily that an individual is assigned full time to each.

1.1. Organizational Structure

1.1.1. For each project involving software development, is there a designated software manager?

1.1.2. Does the project software manager report directly to the project (or project development) manager?

1.1.3. Does the Software Quality Assurance (SQA) function have a management reporting channel separate from the software development project management?

The answers to the questions should reflect standard organizational practice.

1.1.4.   Is there a designated individual or team responsible for the control of software interfaces?

1.1.5.   Is software system engineering represented on the system design team?

1.1.6.   Is there a software configuration control function for each project that involves software development?

1.1.7.   Is there a software engineering *process group* function?

1.2. Resources, Personnel, and Training

The questions on resources concern software engineering training, process training, and adequacy of the support facilities.

1.2.1.   Does each software developer have a private computer-supported workstation/terminal?

1.2.2.   Is there a required training program for all newly appointed development managers designed to familiarize them with software project management?

1.2.3.   Is there a required software engineering training program for software developers?

1.2.4.   Is there a required software engineering training program for first-line supervisors of software development?

1.2.5.   Is a formal training program required for design and code *review leaders*?

1.3. Technology Management

The questions on technology management relate to the mechanisms used to introduce and control new technologies.

1.3.1.   Is a *mechanism* used for maintaining awareness of the state-of-the-art in software engineering technology?

1.3.2.   Is a *mechanism* used for evaluating technologies used by the organization versus those externally available?

1.3.3.   Is a *mechanism* used for deciding when to insert new technology into the development *process*?

1.3.4.   Is a *mechanism* used for managing and supporting the introduction of new technologies?

1.3.5.   Is a *mechanism* used for identifying and replacing obsolete technologies?

2. Software Engineering Process and its Management

This section concerns the scope, depth, and completeness of the software engineering process and how the process is measured, managed, and improved. The major topics are standards and procedures, metrics, data management and analysis, and process control.

The answers to the questions should reflect standard organizational practice.

2.1. Documented Standards and Procedures

The standards and procedures questions address the scope and usage of conventions, formats, procedures, and documentation during the various software development phases, i.e., requirements, design, code, and test.

2.1.1.   Does the software organization use a standardized and documented software development *process* on each project?

2.1.2.   Does the standard software development *process* documentation describe the use of tools and techniques?

2.1.3.   Is a *formal procedure* used in the management review of each software development prior to making contractual commitments?

2.1.4.   Is a *formal procedure* used to assure periodic management review of the status of each software development project?

2.1.5.   Is there a *mechanism* for assuring that software subcontractors, if any, follow a disciplined software development *process*?

2.1.6.   Are *standards* used for the content of software development files/folders?

2.1.7.   For each project, are independent audits conducted for each step of the software development *process*?

2.1.8.   Is a *mechanism* used for assessing existing designs and code for reuse in new applications?

2.1.9.   Are coding *standards* applied to each software development project?

2.1.10.   Are *standards* applied to the preparation of unit test cases?

2.1.11.   Are code maintainability *standards* applied?

2.1.12.   Are internal design review *standards* applied?

2.1.13.   Are code review *standards* applied?

2.1.14.   Is a *formal procedure* used to make estimates of software size?

2.1.15.   Is a *formal procedure* used to produce software development schedules?

2.1.16.   Are *formal procedures* applied to estimating software development cost?

2.1.17.   Is a *mechanism* used for ensuring that the software design teams understand each software requirement?

2.1.18.   Are man-machine interface *standards* applied to each appropriate software development project?

2.2. Process Metrics

The process metrics questions focus on the degree to which the software engineering process is quantified and measured. Typical metrics concern software quality, the amount of code developed, resources used, and such progress indicators as review coverage, test coverage, and test completion.

2.2.1.   Are software staffing profiles maintained of actual staffing versus planned staffing?

The answers to the questions should reflect standard organizational practice.

2.2.2.   Are profiles of software size maintained for each software configuration item, over time?

2.2.3.   Are statistics on software design errors gathered?

2.2.4.   Are statistics on software code and test errors gathered?

2.2.5.   Are design errors projected and compared to actuals?

2.2.6.   Are code and test errors projected and compared to actuals?

2.2.7.   Are profiles maintained of actual versus planned software units designed, over time?

2.2.8.   Are profiles maintained of actual versus planned software units completing unit testing, over time?

2.2.9.   Are profiles maintained of actual versus planned software units integrated, over time?

2.2.10.   Are target computer memory utilization estimates and actuals tracked?

2.2.11.   Are target computer throughput utilization estimates and actuals tracked?

2.2.12.   Is target computer I/O channel utilization tracked?

2.2.13.   Are design and code *review coverages* measured and recorded?

2.2.14.   Is *test coverage* measured and recorded for each phase of functional testing?

2.2.15.   Are the action items resulting from design reviews tracked to closure?

2.2.16.   Are software trouble reports resulting from testing tracked to closure?

2.2.17.   Are the action items resulting from code reviews tracked to closure?

2.2.18.   Is test progress tracked by deliverable software component and compared to the plan?

2.2.19.   Are profiles maintained of software build/release content versus time?

2.3. Data Management and Analysis

Data management deals with the gathering and retention of process metrics. Data management requires standardized data definitions, data management facilities, and a staff to ensure that data is promptly obtained, properly checked, accurately entered into the database, and effectively managed.

Analysis deals with the subsequent manipulation of the process data to answer questions such as, "Is there is a relatively high correlation between error densities found in test and those found in use?" Other types of analyses can assist in determining the optimum use of reviews and resources, the tools most needed, testing priorities, and needed education.

2.3.1.   Has a managed and controlled *process database* been established for *process metrics* data across all projects?

2.3.2.   Are the *review data* gathered during design reviews analyzed?

2.3.3.   Is the error data from code reviews and tests analyzed to determine the likely distribution and characteristics of the errors remaining in the product?

The answers to the questions should reflect standard organizational practice.

229

2.3.4. Are analyses of errors conducted to determine their *process* related causes?

2.3.5. Is a *mechanism* used for error cause analysis?

2.3.6. Are the error causes reviewed to determine the *process* changes required to prevent them?

2.3.7. Is a *mechanism* used for initiating error prevention actions?

2.3.8. Is *review efficiency* analyzed for each project?

2.3.9. Is software productivity analyzed for major *process* steps?

2.4. Process Control

The process control questions concern the definition of the development process and the mechanisms for identifying process problems, correcting process deficiencies, and preventing their recurrence.

2.4.1. Does senior management have a *mechanism* for the regular review of the status of software development projects?

2.4.2. Is a *mechanism* used for periodically assessing the software engineering *process* and implementing indicated improvements?

2.4.3. Is a *mechanism* used for identifying and resolving system engineering issues that affect software?

2.4.4. Is a *mechanism* used for independently calling integration and test issues to the attention of the project manager?

2.4.5. Is a *mechanism* used for regular technical interchanges with the customer?

2.4.6. Is a *mechanism* used for ensuring compliance with the software engineering *standards*?

2.4.7. Do software development first-line managers sign off on their schedules and cost estimates?

2.4.8. Is a *mechanism* used for ensuring traceability between the software requirements and top-level design?

2.4.9. Is a *mechanism* used for controlling changes to the software requirements?

2.4.10. Is there a formal management *process* for determining if the prototyping of software functions is an appropriate part of the design *process*?

2.4.11. Is a *mechanism* used for ensuring traceability between the software top-level and detailed designs?

2.4.12. Are internal software design reviews conducted?

2.4.13. Is a *mechanism* used for controlling changes to the software design?

2.4.14. Is a *mechanism* used for ensuring traceability between the software detailed design and the code?

2.4.15. Are formal records maintained of unit (module) development progress?

2.4.16. Are software code reviews conducted?

2.4.17. Is a *mechanism* used for controlling changes to the code? (Who can make changes and under which circumstances?)

The answers to the questions should reflect standard organizational practice.

2.4.18.   Is a *mechanism* used for configuration management of the software tools used in the development *process*?

2.4.19.   Is a *mechanism* used for verifying that the samples examined by Software Quality Assurance are truly representative of the work performed?

2.4.20.   Is there a *mechanism* for assuring that regression testing is routinely performed?

2.4.21.   Is there a *mechanism* for assuring the adequacy of regression testing?

2.4.22.   Are formal test case reviews conducted?

3. Tools and Technology

This section deals with the tools and technologies used in the software engineering process. It aims at ascertaining the degree to which the contractor's process employs basic tools and methodologies. (In subsequent revisions of this document, this section will be expanded as the applicability and effectiveness of advanced tools and methodologies become more fully established.)

3.1.   Is automated configuration control used to control and track change activity throughout the software development *process*?

3.2.   Are computer tools used to assist in tracing software requirements to software design?

3.3.   Are formal design notations such as PDL used in program design?

3.4.   Are computer tools used to assist in tracing the software design to the code?

3.5.   Is the majority of product development implemented in a high-order language?

3.6.   Are automated test input data generators used for testing?

3.7.   Are computer tools used to measure *test coverage*?

3.8.   Are computer tools used to track every required function and assure that it is tested/verified?

3.9.   Are automated tools used to analyze the size and change activity in software components?

3.10.   Are automated tools used to analyze software complexity?

3.11.   Are automated tools used to analyze cross references between modules?

3.12.   Are interactive source-level debuggers used?

3.13.   Are the software development and maintenance personnel provided with interactive documentation facilities?

3.14.   Are computer tools used for tracking and reporting the status of the software in the software development library?

3.15.   Are prototyping methods used in designing the critical performance elements of the software?

3.16.   Are prototyping methods used in designing the critical elements of the man-machine interface?

The answers to the questions should reflect standard organizational practice.

231

Addenda

Addendum A: Software Engineering Experience

A complete assessment of a contractor's capability to produce quality software at a particular facility should include an evaluation of the experience level of the software development personnel at that location. The experience level of the development staff significantly and directly influences the cost of software development projects. Information about experience level is normally obtained during source selection from proposals or from review team interviews. However, for the purpose of this evaluation, suggested questions are listed below.

A.1   What is the median number of years of applicable experience of software development managers?

A.2   What is the median number of years of applicable experience of software integration and test managers?

A.3   What percentage of the software development staff has a bachelor degree or higher in computer science or software engineering?

A.4   What is the median number of years of software development experience of the software staff?

A.5   What percentage of the software staff has at least one year of development experience with the design and implementation languages to be used?

A.6   Of those with such experience, what is the median number of years of experience with those languages?

A.7   What is the median size, in source lines of code, of software development projects completed in the last five years? The size of the smallest project? The largest?

A.8   What is the total size of the software development organization, including direct professionals, management, and support personnel?

A.9   What is the total number of software engineers in the organization?

Addendum B: Software Engineering Process Maturity Levels

Five levels of process maturity have been defined for the assessment of software engineering organizations.

- Level 1 Initial
- Level 2 Repeatable
- Level 3 Defined
- Level 4 Managed
- Level 5 Optimized

Level 1 - Initial Process

The initial environment has ill-defined procedures and controls. While positive responses to some of the organizational questions are likely, the organization does not consistently apply software engineering management to the process, nor does it use modern tools and technology.

Level 2 - Repeatable Process

At Maturity Level 2, the organization uses standard methods and practices for managing software development activities such as cost estimating, scheduling, requirements changes, code changes, and status reviews. The organization will provide positive responses to most of the following questions.

1.1.1   For each project involving software development, is there a designated software manager?

1.1.2   Does the project software manager report directly to the project (or project development) manager?

*1.1.3   Does the Software Quality Assurance (SQA) function have a management reporting channel separate from the software development project management?

*1.1.6   Is there a software configuration control function for each project that involves software development?

1.2.2   Is there a required training program for all newly appointed development managers designed to familiarize them with software project management?

1.3.1   Is a *mechanism* used for maintaining awareness of the state-of-the-art in software engineering technology?

*2.1.3   Is a *formal procedure* used in the management review of each software development prior to making contractual commitments?

2.1.4   Is a *formal procedure* used to assure periodic management review of the status of each software development project?

2.1.5   Is there a *mechanism* for assuring that software subcontractors, if any, follow a disciplined software development *process*?

2.1.7   For each project, are independent audits conducted for each step of the software development *process*?

2.1.9   Are coding *standards* applied to each software development project?

*2.1.14   Is a *formal procedure* used to make estimates of software size?

*2.1.15   Is a *formal procedure* used to produce software development schedules?

*2.1.16   Are *formal procedures* applied to estimating software development cost?

2.1.17   Is a *mechanism* used for ensuring that the software design teams understand each software requirement?

2.2.1   Are software staffing profiles maintained of actual staffing versus planned staffing?

*2.2.2   Are profiles of software size maintained for each software configuration item, over time?

*2.2.4   Are statistics on software code and test errors gathered?

The answers to the questions should reflect standard organizational practice.

2.2.7	Are profiles maintained of actual versus planned software units designed, over time?
2.2.8	Are profiles maintained of actual versus planned software units completing unit testing, over time?
2.2.9	Are profiles maintained of actual versus planned software units integrated, over time?
2.2.10	Are target computer memory utilization estimates and actuals tracked?
2.2.11	Are target computer throughput utilization estimates and actuals tracked?
2.2.12	Is target computer I/O channel utilization tracked?
2.2.16	Are software trouble reports resulting from testing tracked to closure?
2.2.18	Is test progress tracked by deliverable software component and compared to the plan?
2.2.19	Are profiles maintained of software build/release content versus time?
*2.4.1	Does senior management have a *mechanism* for the regular review of the status of software development projects?
2.4.5	Is a *mechanism* used for regular technical interchanges with the customer?
*2.4.7	Do software development first-line managers sign off on their schedules and cost estimates?
*2.4.9	Is a *mechanism* used for controlling changes to the software requirements?
*2.4.17	Is a *mechanism* used for controlling changes to the code? (Who can make changes and under which circumstances?)
2.4.20	Is there a *mechanism* for assuring that regression testing is routinely performed?

Level 3 - Defined Process

At Maturity Level 3, the organization not only defines its process in terms of software engineering standards and methods, it also has made a series of organizational and methodological improvements. These specifically include design and code reviews, training programs for programmers and review leaders, and increased organizational focus on software engineering. A major improvement in this phase is the establishment and staffing of a software engineering process group that focuses on the software engineering process and the adequacy with which it is implemented. In addition to the questions for Level 2, organizations at Level 3 will respond "yes" to most of the following questions.

1.1.4	Is there a designated individual or team responsible for the control of software interfaces?
1.1.5	Is software system engineering represented on the system design team?
*1.1.7	Is there a software engineering *process group* function?
1.2.1	Does each software developer have a private computer-supported workstation/terminal?
*1.2.3	Is there a required software engineering training program for software developers?
1.2.4	Is there a required software engineering training program for first-line supervisors of software development?

The answers to the questions should reflect standard organizational practice.

*1.2.5   Is a formal training program required for design and code *review leaders*?

1.3.2   Is a *mechanism* used for evaluating technologies used by the organization versus those externally available?

*2.1.1   Does the software organization use a standardized and documented software development *process* on each project?

2.1.2   Does the standard software development *process* documentation describe the use of tools and techniques?

2.1.6   Are *standards* used for the content of software development files/folders?

2.1.8   Is a *mechanism* used for assessing existing designs and code for reuse in new applications?

2.1.10   Are *standards* applied to the preparation of unit test cases?

2.1.11   Are code maintainability *standards* applied?

2.1.18   Are man-machine interface *standards* applied to each appropriate software development project?

*2.2.3   Are statistics on software design errors gathered?

*2.2.15   Are the action items resulting from design reviews tracked to closure?

*2.2.17   Are the action items resulting from code reviews tracked to closure?

2.4.3   Is a *mechanism* used for identifying and resolving system engineering issues that affect software?

2.4.4   Is a *mechanism* used for independently calling integration and test issues to the attention of the project manager?

*2.4.6   Is a *mechanism* used for ensuring compliance with the software engineering *standards*?

2.4.8   Is a *mechanism* used for ensuring traceability between the software requirements and top-level design?

2.4.11   Is a *mechanism* used for ensuring traceability between the software top-level and detailed designs?

*2.4.12   Are internal software design reviews conducted?

*2.4.13   Is a *mechanism* used for controlling changes to the software design?

2.4.14   Is a *mechanism* used for ensuring traceability between the software detailed design and the code?

2.4.15   Are formal records maintained of unit (module) development progress?

*2.4.16   Are software code reviews conducted?

2.4.18   Is a *mechanism* used for configuration management of the software tools used in the development *process*?

*2.4.19   Is a *mechanism* used for verifying that the samples examined by Software Quality Assurance are truly representative of the work performed?

*2.4.21   Is there a *mechanism* for assuring the adequacy of regression testing?

2.4.22   Are formal test case reviews conducted?

The answers to the questions should reflect standard organizational practice.

Level 4 - Managed Process

At Maturity Level 4, the organization typically bases its operating decisions on quantitative process data, and conducts extensive analyses of the data gathered during software engineering reviews and tests. Tools are used increasingly to control and manage the design process as well as to support data gathering and analysis. The organization is learning to project expected errors with reasonable accuracy. In addition to questions for Levels 2 and 3, organizations at Level 4 will respond "yes" to most of the following questions.

1.3.3   Is a *mechanism* used for deciding when to insert new technology into the development *process*?

*1.3.4   Is a *mechanism* used for managing and supporting the introduction of new technologies?

2.1.12   Are internal design review *standards* applied?

*2.1.13   Are code review *standards* applied?

*2.2.5   Are design errors projected and compared to actuals?

*2.2.6   Are code and test errors projected and compared to actuals?

*2.2.13   Are design and code *review coverages* measured and recorded?

*2.2.14   Is *test coverage* measured and recorded for each phase of functional testing?

*2.3.1   Has a managed and controlled *process database* been established for *process metrics* data across all projects?

*2.3.2   Are the *review data* gathered during design reviews analyzed?

*2.3.3   Is the error data from code reviews and tests analyzed to determine the likely distribution and characteristics of the errors remaining in the product?

*2.3.4   Are analyses of errors conducted to determine their *process* related causes?

*2.3.8   Is *review efficiency* analyzed for each project?

2.3.9   Is software productivity analyzed for major *process* steps?

*2.4.2   Is a *mechanism* used for periodically assessing the software engineering *process* and implementing indicated improvements?

2.4.10   Is there a formal management *process* for determining if the prototyping of software functions is an appropriate part of the design *process*?

Level 5 - Optimized Process

At Maturity Level 5, organizations have not only achieved a high degree of control over their process, they have a major focus on improving and optimizing its operation. This includes more sophisticated analyses of the error and cost data gathered during the process as well as the introduction of comprehensive error cause analysis and prevention studies.

*1.3.5   Is a *mechanism* used for identifying and replacing obsolete technologies?

The answers to the questions should reflect standard organizational practice.

*2.3.5   Is a *mechanism* used for error cause analysis?

*2.3.6   Are the error causes reviewed to determine the *process* changes required to prevent them?

*2.3.7   Is a *mechanism* used for initiating error prevention actions?

Addendum C: Technology

This section defines a method for evaluating the software engineering technology of a contractor. The quality of a software process is affected by the stage of software technology employed. Two stages for describing the level of software technology have been defined.

Stage A - Inefficient Technology
An organization that primarily employs inefficient software development technology is likely to be ineffective in developing software. Many different implementations may be available and the practice may be in widespread use, but the technology is no longer effective. Moreover, at this technology stage some important software engineering practices are not practical in large, complex developments.

Stage B - Basic Technology
An organization that primarily employs basic software development technologies is likely to be moderately effective and, depending upon the maturity of its process, reasonably consistent in its performance. Multiple implementations are available, and they have been demonstrated to be effective. Organizations at Stage B will respond "yes" to most of the following questions.

*3.1   Is automated configuration control used to control and track change activity throughout the software development *process*?

3.2   Are computer tools used to assist in tracing software requirements to software design?

3.3   Are formal design notations such as PDL used in program design?

3.4   Are computer tools used to assist in tracing the software design to the code?

*3.5   Is the majority of product development implemented in a high-order language?

3.6   Are automated test input data generators used for testing?

3.7   Are computer tools used to measure *test coverage*?

3.8   Are computer tools used to track every required function and assure that it is tested/verified?

3.9   Are automated tools used to analyze the size and change activity in software components?

3.10   Are automated tools used to analyze software complexity?

3.11   Are automated tools used to analyze cross references between modules?

*3.12   Are interactive source-level debuggers used?

*3.13   Are the software development and maintenance personnel provided with interactive documentation facilities?

The answers to the questions should reflect standard organizational practice.

*3.14   Are computer tools used for tracking and reporting the status of the software in the software development library?

3.15   Are prototyping methods used in designing the critical performance elements of the software?

3.16   Are prototyping methods used in designing the critical elements of the man-machine interface?

Addendum D: Assessment Recording Form
Contractor Software Engineering Capability

Contractor Code [　　　　]　　　　　　　　Guide Version [093087]

The answers to these questions should reflect standard organizational practice as implemented by a single project.

| Question Number | Additional Information | | | Comments | Shade in Answer |
	Control Number	Level	Follow-up Question		
1.1.1	2	2	1		Y N
1.1.2	3	2	1		Y N
1.1.3	6	2	1		Y N
1.1.4	8	3	1		Y N
1.1.5	11	3	1		Y N
1.1.6	14	2	2		Y N
1.1.7	15	3	2		Y N
1.2.1	16	3	9		Y N
1.2.2	18	2	3		Y N
1.2.3	19	3	3		Y N
1.2.4	152	3	3		Y N
1.2.5	20	3	3		Y N
1.3.1	126	2	4		Y N
1.3.2	127	3	4		Y N
1.3.3	172	4	4		Y N
1.3.4	128	4	4		Y N
1.3.5	129	5	4		Y N
2.1.1	23	3	4		Y N
2.1.2	163	3	4		Y N
2.1.3	24	2	4		Y N
2.1.4	164	2	4		Y N
2.1.5	25	2	4		Y N
2.1.6	28	3	4		Y N
2.1.7	30	2	8		Y N
2.1.8	159	3	4		Y N
2.1.9	31	2	4		Y N
2.1.10	32	3	4		Y N
2.1.11	33	3	4		Y N
2.1.12	37	4	4		Y N
2.1.13	38	4	4		Y N

[　　　　] Of greater importance for indicated maturity level

The answers to the questions should reflect standard organizational practice.

Contractor Software Engineering Capability

Contractor Code [   ]   Guide Version [093087]

The answers to these questions should reflect standard organizational practice as implemented by a single project.

Question Number	Additional Information			Comments	Shade in Answer
	Control Number	Level	Follow-up Question		
2.1.14	42	2	4		Y N
2.1.15	43	2	4		Y N
2.1.16	44	2	4		Y N
2.1.17	124	2	4		Y N
2.1.18	130	3	4		Y N
2.2.1	45	2	5		Y N
2.2.2	46	2	5		Y N
2.2.3	47	3	5		Y N
2.2.4	48	2	5		Y N
2.2.5	49	4	5		Y N
2.2.6	50	4	5		Y N
2.2.7	51	2	5		Y N
2.2.8	52	2	5		Y N
2.2.9	53	2	5		Y N
2.2.10	54	2	5		Y N
2.2.11	55	2	5		Y N
2.2.12	56	2	5		Y N
2.2.13	57	4	5		Y N
2.2.14	58	4	5		Y N
2.2.15	59	3	5		Y N
2.2.16	60	2	5		Y N
2.2.17	61	3	5		Y N
2.2.18	62	2	5		Y N
2.2.19	63	2	5		Y N
2.3.1	64	4	9		Y N
2.3.2	67	4	6		Y N
2.3.3	68	4	6		Y N
2.3.4	70	4	6		Y N
2.3.5	69	5	4		Y N
2.3.6	71	5	7		Y N

[   ] Of greater importance for indicated maturity level

Contractor Software Engineering Capability

Contractor Code [   ]　　　　　　　Guide Version [093087]

The answers to these questions should reflect standard organizational practice as implemented by a single project.

Question Number	Additional Information			Comments	Shade in Answer
	Control Number	Level	Follow-up Question		
2.3.7	72	5	4		Ⓨ Ⓝ
2.3.8	75	4	6		Ⓨ Ⓝ
2.3.9	76	4	6		Ⓨ Ⓝ
2.4.1	77	2	4		Ⓨ Ⓝ
2.4.2	78	4	4		Ⓨ Ⓝ
2.4.3	79	3	4		Ⓨ Ⓝ
2.4.4	81	3	4		Ⓨ Ⓝ
2.4.5	82	2	4		Ⓨ Ⓝ
2.4.6	83	3	4		Ⓨ Ⓝ
2.4.7	84	2	8		Ⓨ Ⓝ
2.4.8	86	3	4		Ⓨ Ⓝ
2.4.9	87	2	4		Ⓨ Ⓝ
2.4.10	88	4	4		Ⓨ Ⓝ
2.4.11	90	3	4		Ⓨ Ⓝ
2.4.12	91	3	8		Ⓨ Ⓝ
2.4.13	92	3	4		Ⓨ Ⓝ
2.4.14	93	3	4		Ⓨ Ⓝ
2.4.15	94	3	5		Ⓨ Ⓝ
2.4.16	95	3	8		Ⓨ Ⓝ
2.4.17	96	2	4		Ⓨ Ⓝ
2.4.18	165	3	4		Ⓨ Ⓝ
2.4.19	98	3	4		Ⓨ Ⓝ
2.4.20	171	2	4		Ⓨ Ⓝ
2.4.21	99	3	8		Ⓨ Ⓝ
2.4.22	162	3	8		Ⓨ Ⓝ

[   ] Of greater importance for indicated maturity level

Contractor Software Engineering Capability

Contractor Code [   ]   Guide Version [093087]

The answers to these questions should reflect standard organizational practice as implemented by a single project.

| Question Number | Additional Information | | | Comments | Shade in Answer |
	Control Number	Stage	Follow-up Question		
3.1	150	B	10		Ⓨ Ⓝ
3.2	103	B	10		Ⓨ Ⓝ
3.3	142	B	9		Ⓨ Ⓝ
3.4	111	B	10		Ⓨ Ⓝ
3.5	151	B	9		Ⓨ Ⓝ
3.6	167	B	10		Ⓨ Ⓝ
3.7	113	B	10		Ⓨ Ⓝ
3.8	112	B	10		Ⓨ Ⓝ
3.9	140	B	10		Ⓨ Ⓝ
3.10	137	B	10		Ⓨ Ⓝ
3.11	143	B	10		Ⓨ Ⓝ
3.12	169	B	10		Ⓨ Ⓝ
3.13	146	B	9		Ⓨ Ⓝ
3.14	114	B	10		Ⓨ Ⓝ
3.15	131	B	9		Ⓨ Ⓝ
3.16	132	B	9		Ⓨ Ⓝ

[▨] Of greater importance for indicated maturity level

Addendum E: Follow-up Questions

It is recommended that, when appropriate, the assessment team ask for amplification of responses to the assessment questions. The team should request actual data supporting the responses. Listed below are ten follow-up questions for amplifying data. The Assessment Recording Form indicates the number of the appropriate follow-up questions for each assessment question.

1. Where responsibility assignments are questioned, request the name of a specific individual, tenure in job, job description, and evidence of activity, such as monthly reports, meeting reports, control logs.

2. Where the existence of a group is questioned, request names of members, the organization represented, and recent meeting agendas and minutes.

3. Where the existence of education or training programs is questioned, request the schedule of recent courses offered, course outlines, names of attendees, and qualifications of instructors and students.

4. Where the existence of a mechanism, procedure, standard, criteria, or guideline is questioned, request a copy of the controlling document, its revision history, the name of individual(s) responsible for tracking, job description(s), and recent issue/activity reports.

5. Where the use of profiles, tracking reports, planned vs. actual comparisons, and measurements are questioned, request the three most recent reports, measurement summaries, or comparisons.

6. Where computations or analysis of data is questioned, request copies of the most recent computations, analysis reports, or summaries showing results or conclusions reached.

7. Where the initiation of actions are questioned, request copies of recent action tracking and/or summary reports.

8. Where the conduct of certain actions or use of facilities is questioned, request evidence in the form of procedures, responsibilities, or tracking systems to demonstrate performance.

9. Where the existence of a facility, capability, practice, or method is questioned, request supporting evidence in the form of inventory lists, tracking and usage reports, instruction manuals, education programs, etc.

10. Where the use of an automated tool or facility is questioned, request a demonstration of that tool or facility.

Glossary

This glossary should be used in conjunction with the *IEEE Standard Glossary of Software Engineering Terminology* (ANSI/IEEE STD729-1983) published by the Institute of Electrical and Electronic Engineers, February 18, 1983. Wherever possible, common software engineering terminology has been used. Where terms in this document are not included in the *IEEE Standard Glossary* or have special meaning in the context used here, they are described in this glossary.

contractor evaluation – A process by which a contracting organization uses the results of contractor assessments and other information to determine the relative capability of contractors.

error prevention analysis – A process that is typically conducted by a working group of software engineering professionals who developed the code in question. It is an objective assessment of each error, its potential cause, and the steps to be taken to prevent it. While placing blame is to be avoided, such questions as mistakes, adequacy of education and training, proper tools capability, and support effectiveness are appropriate areas for analysis.

formal procedure – A documented series of steps with guidelines for use.

mechanism – A means or technique whereby the performance of a task, procedure, or process is assured. The mechanism may involve several organizational elements, and its documentation may include some combination of function statements, operating plans, position descriptions, and/or formal procedures. The documentation defines what should be performed, how it should be performed, and who is accountable for the results.

process – A systematic series of mechanisms, tasks, and/or procedures directed towards an end. The software engineering process documentation defines the sequence of steps used to produce a finished product. Each step is described as a task that is performed by using a software engineering methodology or an administrative procedure, and it prescribes the automated tools and techniques to be used.

process data – The data that is gathered about the software engineering process. It typically includes review, test, and resource data by process phase and change activity. To be most meaningful, this data should be associated with the process documentation, the tools and methods used, and the characteristics of the product being produced.

process database – A repository into which all process data is entered. It is a centralized resource managed by the process group. Centralized control of this database ensures that the process data from all projects are permanently retained and protected.

process group – The software engineering process group is composed of specialists concerned with the process used by the development organization for software development. Its typical functions include defining and documenting the process, establishing and defining

Glossary

This glossary should be used in conjunction with the *IEEE Standard Glossary of Software Engineering Terminology* (ANSI/IEEE STD729-1983) published by the Institute of Electrical and Electronic Engineers, February 18, 1983. Wherever possible, common software engineering terminology has been used. Where terms in this document are not included in the *IEEE Standard Glossary* or have special meaning in the context used here, they are described in this glossary.

contractor evaluation – A process by which a contracting organization uses the results of contractor assessments and other information to determine the relative capability of contractors.

review data – The data that is gathered from design or code reviews. This data is of two types. The first, concerning the review process, typically includes preparation time, lines of code per hour of preparation time, errors identified during preparation (by category), hours per error found in preparation, review time, lines of code (or design statements) reviewed, code (or design statements) reviewed per hour, and errors found per review man-hour (by category). The second type, product data from the review, typically includes errors found per line of code (or design statement), action items identified from each review, action items closed for each review, items needing re-review, re-reviews conducted.

review efficiency – The percentage of errors found through the review process. It is typically stated as a percentage and is calculated by dividing the total errors found during review by the total errors found by both review and test through the completion of product and system integration test. It does not include those errors found during acceptance test or field usage.

review leader – Typically a member of the process or assurance group who is thoroughly trained in the review process. The review leader's role is to ensure that the participants are properly prepared and that the review is efficiently and thoroughly conducted. The review leader is responsible for recording review data, making sure that the actions resulting from the review are completed, and for conducting re-reviews where appropriate.

standard – An approved, documented, and available set of criteria used to determine the adequacy of an action or object.

test coverage – The amount of code actually executed during the test process. It is stated as a percentage of the total instructions executed or paths traversed.

REPORT DOCUMENTATION PAGE

1a. REPORT SECURITY CLASSIFICATION UNCLASSIFIED		1b. RESTRICTIVE MARKINGS NONE			
2a. SECURITY CLASSIFICATION AUTHORITY N/A		3. DISTRIBUTION/AVAILABILITY OF REPORT APPROVED FOR PUBLIC RELEASE DISTRIBUTION UNLIMITED			
2b. DECLASSIFICATION/DOWNGRADING SCHEDULE N/A					
4. PERFORMING ORGANIZATION REPORT NUMBER(S) CMU/SEI-87-TR-23		5. MONITORING ORGANIZATION REPORT NUMBER(S) ESD-TR-87-186			
6a. NAME OF PERFORMING ORGANIZATION SOFTWARE ENGINEERING INSTITUTE	6b. OFFICE SYMBOL (If applicable) SEI	7a. NAME OF MONITORING ORGANIZATION SEI JOINT PROGRAM OFFICE			
6c. ADDRESS (City, State and ZIP Code) CARNEGIE MELLON UNIVERSITY PITTSBURGH, PA 15213		7b. ADDRESS (City, State and ZIP Code) ESD/XRS1 HANSCOM AIR FORCE BASE, MA 01731			
8a. NAME OF FUNDING/SPONSORING ORGANIZATION SEI JOINT PROGRAM OFFICE	8b. OFFICE SYMBOL (If applicable) SEI JPO	9. PROCUREMENT INSTRUMENT IDENTIFICATION NUMBER F1962885C0003			
8c. ADDRESS (City, State and ZIP Code) CARNEGIE MELLON UNIVERSITY SOFTWARE ENGINEERING INSTITUTE JPO PITTSBURGH, PA 15213		10. SOURCE OF FUNDING NOS.			
		PROGRAM ELEMENT NO.	PROJECT NO. N/A	TASK NO. N/A	WORK UNIT NO. N/A

11. TITLE (Include Security Classification)
A METHOD FOR ASSESSING THE SOFTWARE ENGINEERING CAPABILITY OF CONTRACTORS   Preliminary Version

12. PERSONAL AUTHOR(S)
W.S. Humphrey   W. L. Sweet

13a. TYPE OF REPORT FINAL	13b. TIME COVERED FROM _____ TO _____	14. DATE OF REPORT (Yr., Mo., Day) Sept. 1987	15. PAGE COUNT 42

16. SUPPLEMENTARY NOTATION

17.	COSATI CODES		18. SUBJECT TERMS (Continue on reverse if necessary and identify by block number)
FIELD	GROUP	SUB. GR.	contractor assessment software engineering maturity

19. ABSTRACT (Continue on reverse if necessary and identify by block number)

This document provides guidelines and procedures for assessing the ability of potential DoD contractors to develop software in accordance with modern software engineering methods. It includes specific questions and a method for evaluating the results.

20. DISTRIBUTION/AVAILABILITY OF ABSTRACT UNCLASSIFIED/UNLIMITED ☒ SAME AS RPT. ☐ DTIC USERS ☒	21. ABSTRACT SECURITY CLASSIFICATION UNCLASSIFIED, UNLIMITED	
22a. NAME OF RESPONSIBLE INDIVIDUAL KARL SHINGLER	22b. TELEPHONE NUMBER (Include Area Code) (412) 268-7630	22c. OFFICE SYMBOL SEI JPO

RISK ASSESSMENT TECHNIQUES

CHAPTER IV: METHODS OVERVIEW

A. GENERAL.

Reprinted from *Defense Systems Management College (DSMC) Handbook*, Chapter 4 and Appendix F, July 1983, pages iv-1–iv-25 and F-1–F-13. U.S. Government work not protected by U.S. copyright.

Although researchers continue to develop new risk assessment techniques and applications, this chapter will summarily describe only the seven quantitative techniques in predominant current use. The quantitative techniques to be described are:

o   Network analysis

o   The method of moments

o   Decision analysis

o   WBS simulation

o   Graphics

o   Estimating relationships

o   Risk factors

Although there are applications mixing the techniques, these seven constitute the majority of those potentially applicable to ongoing (rather than conceptual) programs.

In addition to the quantitative techniques, there are two non-quantitative methods which in this handbook will be called "structured qualitative" and "engineering analysis". The latter is this handbook's term for the unstructured "problem-immersion" approach discussed in Chapter III; the former is a more structured derivative. These two are mentioned because "engineering analysis" is the approach in predominant military acquisition program use and the "structured qualitative" method (exemplified by [5]) represents an upgrade of the "engineering analysis" method. The "structured qualitative" approach improves on "engineering analysis" by providing explicit criteria for judgment of risk, by adopting a logical structure, and by documenting its rationale.

The seven quantitative risk assessment methods which follow are described briefly in the following sections, and discussed in greater detail in Appendix F.

B. NETWORK METHODS

1. General

Most managers today are familiar with the concept of modeling an acquisition program as a network, such as that in Figure 7, made popular by the Polaris submarine project and termed the Program Evaluation and Review Technique (PERT).

In such a network, each circle represents a decision point or milestone, and each line represents an activity that must be finished to advance the program, that consumes resources, or that takes time. In the PERT approach the objectives were to manage schedule risk by establishing the shortest development schedules, to monitor and project progress, and to fund or apply necessary resources for maintaining the schedule. Successors to PERT included PERT/COST in which the minimum cost path through the network was estimated, and the project was managed to minimum cost. PERT models lacked the capability to include probability information on the cost and/or schedule, however current network models can use computers to arrive at probability statements incorporating evaluations of cost, time, or performance level values by means of a technique called simulation.

Typically, the analysis in PERT models was based on average, and sometimes extreme, values of activity duration. In current techniques, the network is defined, and the activity probabilities of cost or schedule are described. Then, by using computers to simulate a large number of program completions in which events occur according to their probabilities, the probabilities are evaluated for the network as a whole. Subsequently, probability expressions such as confidence levels, etc. (as described in

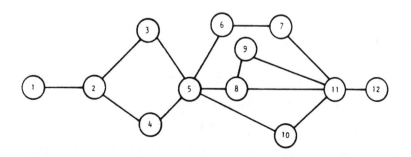

Figure 7 PROGRAM REPRESENTED AS A NETWORK

Chapter II) can be made. Thus the subtle and complex interrelationships of the hundreds of activities required to complete a program can contribute to the same degree they would in the actual program, assuming all activities truly behave as expected. The fact that the activities may not behave exactly as expected, that is, that no model is perfect, is irrelevant. The decisions must be made and must be based on the best information available at the current time. The model represents that best available information, or the analyst must change the model.

2. Inputs/Outputs

a. Inputs

Establishment of a network model requires definition of each program activity, its beginning, its end, its possible predecessors, and its possible successors, at some specified level of detail. The last phrase signifies that activities themselves can almost always be restructured into more detailed activity networks. Part of the art of network modeling, a matter the program manager may wish to review, is the level of detail to use, since increased detail increases complexity, cost, time, and manpower requirements. The inputs described so far say nothing about probability. Each activity must also be described in terms of probability, with the probabilities relating to cost, schedule, manpower, technical level of achievement, or some combination. Also, when it is not certain which activities can occur at a decision point, it is necessary to input probabilities of those activities. Some computer programs limit the characteristics that can be described by probabilities, while some are virtually unlimited but require more computer resources (see Chapter V).

b. Outputs

Network model outputs typically include PDF's, CDF's, and the statistical measures described in Chapter II for the cost or schedule of the entire program or specified parts of it. Other outputs include lists of the activities or groups of activities that have caused program difficulty, in order of their frequency of causing it. This is called "criticality," a term derived from the PERT term "critical path". A PERT critical path is the sequence of activities in a network having the longest duration or highest cost.

3. Resource Requirements

Since most network risk assessments accomplished in the DOD are carried out by functional support offices, risk assessment dollar costs should be estimated from manpower requirements. A comprehensive network analysis for a major program may require definition of between 200 and 1000 activities and require 2 to 6 man-months of GS-12 to GS-14 analyst effort for gathering experts' PDF's and for building the network. The analysts must obtain lists of program activities and information on the sequence of activities from Program Management Office (PMO) personnel and from the members of the organizations supporting the PMO. Obtaining this information consumes more time and requires more re-checking than might seem necessary. This is because the program plan is usually under continual revision and definition, and the support personnel themselves do not fully understand the program activity interdependencies.

Although the difficulty and time required for network definition is a problem, the effort of constructing a consistent and acceptable network model forces the responsible participants to plan more effectively and to understand how their own segments of the program fit into the whole. Program managers have indicated that this benefit can justify all the effort for accomplishment of a formal network risk assessment.

Having recognized the difficulties associated with developing networks for particular acquisition programs, some Army commands (at least MERADCOM and CECOM) have generated "dictionaries" of the activities typically required during the life cycle of a program. These "dictionaries" provide descriptions of the activities, typical durations, and interrelationships with other activities. The activity descriptions, along with a sample network, provide an excellent starting point for PMO personnel and analysts attempting to develop a program network. The existing "dictionaries" are somewhat tailored as they, of course, reflect service and command-peculiar requirements and apply to the types of systems procured by the author commands. They are mentioned here as suggestions of what would be possible in other commands.

4. Applications

Network risk assessment models have been used throughout the Army in support of In Process Review (IPR), Army Systems Acquisition Review Council (ASARC), and Defense Systems Acquisition Review Council (DSARC) program reviews. Navy program offices of NAVSEA have obtained contractor support for network based risk assessments for appraisal and control of both major acquisition programs and overhaul programs. No examples of USAF use of network risk assessment techniques were found during preparation of this handbook.

C. Decision Analysis Methods

1. General

Decision analysis is the examination of decisions by breaking them into the sequences of supporting decisions and the resulting uncertain occurrences. Usually, these sequences are represented as decision "trees" such as that in Figure 8. Interesting and extensive treatment of the subject may be found in [16].

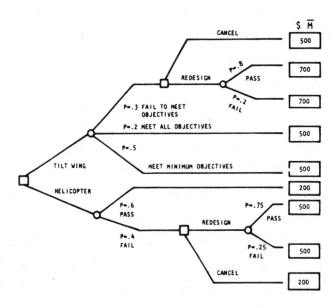

FIGURE 8 DECISION TREE

The first, left-hand square in Figure 8 represents an aircraft conceptual decision that can be made in either of two ways; i.e., select a tilt-wing design or a helicopter. The circles that follow represent test programs that have, on the top branch, three possible outcomes or, on the bottom branch, two possible outcomes. The likelihood of each of these outcomes is shown on the appropriate branch (e.g., P=.3 indicates a probability of 3 in 10 that the tilt wing design will fail to meet test objectives). The next set of squares represent decisions that might have to be made after each outcome. Some of these decisions are followed by new tests. In the boxes on the right-hand side of the tree, the funding consequences of each of the branches are shown.

The complication of managing a large and unwieldly decision tree can be avoided by using a simplified approach, called Probabilistic Event Analysis (PEA) and described in [20]. While the simplified method provides for determining which activities and milestones for major WBS elements contribute to cost, as though milestones were decisions on a decision tree, the tree does not have to be drawn, but the logic is the same. The analyst defines the problems which he feels may effect the program cost or schedule and assesses the likelihoods of their occurrence. The analyst continues by obtaining assessments of the effect of each type of problem on the cost or schedule of the relevant function or milestone. From the probabilities and the magnitude of effects, an "expected value" of cost increment for each effort can be calculated.

A more elaborate method is described in [8], which first orients the assessment around a specific program sequence that allows the analyst to define the program as in a decision flow diagram (decision tree). In this method, time and cost effects of identified problems are estimated as in the former method. A series of simple, but tedious and voluminous, probability calculations allow the analyst to establish cost and schedule probability distributions for each phase. These distributions are then combined by using them as inputs, not to a pencil and paper calculation, but to a simulation on a computer.

Although the mathematics underlying these decision tree approaches are undemanding and the network simulation can be much simpler than those discussed under network methods, analyzing the relationships is not simple, and any computer use requires a degree of sophistication to carry out the programming. It is particularly difficult to ensure comprehensive identification of problems and time/cost effects.

2. Input/Output

a. Inputs

Decision analysis methods require definition of the program decisions to be made, again, as in any model, at some convenient level of detail. These may include many of the milestones that are inputs to a network analysis, but in the decision analysis model, the emphasis is on the points where decisions are made, not on the sequencing of activities. Rather than defining PDF's for activities, usually a specific small number of problem occurrences is defined for any point in the decision logic where chance enters in, and the subject matter experts are polled to obtain probability estimates for all possible occurrences, the problems that could ensue, their cost impacts, and their probabilities. Thus, the inputs for this method are:

DECISIONS

| Potential Problems | Probability of Occurrence | Possible Resolutions | Probability of Success | Cost Impact |

In the method of [8], not only are the problems, their probabilities and their cost (or schedule) impacts obtained, but each problem's resolutions, resolution(s) probabilities of success, and resolution cost (or schedule) impacts are also used.

b. Outputs

The cost oriented Probabilistic Event Analysis output is a reserve to be added to the baseline budget established without consideration of the problems subsequently addressed in the PEA. Nothing similar to a PDF is generated and no statement can be made relative to the probability of exceeding the new budget.

The method described in [8] provides "joint" probability graphs showing program probability of success at given probabilities of needing stated levels of funding (or time).

3. Resource Requirements

Probabilistic Event Analysis was developed to demand less time and analytical skill than network methods. As with other methods, the most time-consuming part of a PEA is probably obtaining comprehensive determination of critical occurrences, their probabilities and their impacts, in other words, data collection. For a program for which the plans have been stabilized, a GS-12 or -13 might require no more than a few days to complete a PEA.

The type of decision analysis described in [8] will probably require an analyst of greater knowledge and skill than a PEA and perhaps than even a network assessment. Some computer programming will be required, data collection is likely to be more comprehensive and demanding, and interpretation of results may require more sophistication. A typical team (that for [15]) consisted of a GS-15 analyst with two lower grade (GS-13/14) team members, and the assessment consumed about 4 months.

4. Applications

No examples of application of the PEA method were found in preparation of this handbook. The method described in [8] has been used at the U.S. Army Air Mobility R&D Laboratory, Ames Research Center, Moffet Field, CA., for a Cobra Armament Program, and for the XV-15 program. No USN or USAF applications of decision analysis applications to risk assessment were found during handbook preparation.

D. THE METHOD OF MOMENTS

1. General

In network risk assessment methods, the program activities are related according to their sequencing, and the combined effects of their probabilities are determined by simulation. In the method-of-moments (developed in [13]) no network sequence relations are defined, and the combined effects of program element probabilities are determined by mathematics instead of simulation. Method-of-moments assessments concern themselves with cost risk and proceed from a framework of costs like a Work Breakdown Structure [14], sometimes called a cost breakdown. Each of the cost elements (not activities, as was the network case) has some probability "statement" (PDF) associated with it. PDF's may be humped and symmetric, indicating that cost is equally as likely to be above as below the most likely; or humped but skewed, indicating a greater likelihood that cost will be on one side of the most likely value than the other. However they are shaped, they combine to produce some total program cost PDF.

As was stated in paragraph D of Chapter II, simplifying assumptions are required in formulation of any mathematical description (model). For example, one of the simplifications used in network models is selecting the level of detail. In the method-of-moments, a major simplification used is that of selecting a total combined PDF, which is assumed to be a type possible to calculate by this technique. While this is a major assumption, it does not render the technique worthless. Typically the assumed PDF exhibits right-hand (positive) skewness, is assumed to have some unspecified lowest possible value (hit the axis on the left), and may or may not have a highest possible unspecified value (hit the axis on the right). Typically, a network simulation cost risk analysis does not produce one of these "well-behaved" PDF's, and some analysts would say that shows that assuming a well-behaved PDF type makes the method-of-moments valueless. It must be remembered, however, that many less-than-major programs are unable to command the resources for a network risk assessment, so a method-of-moments assessment, while less than perfect, can provide otherwise un-available insights.

The method's name comes from the fact that the "moments" of the cost element PDF's are used to form the "moments" of the combined PDF of total cost. Some of the better known moments are the mean and the variance (the standard deviation squared), which describe respectively the "center of gravity" of the distribution and the spread of costs around the mean. There are other moments, such as "skewness", which describes the distribution's assymetry, and others more difficult to visualize. For more on moments themselves, reference should be made to a probability theory or statistical theory textbook.

A PDF is mathematically described by a formula having certain constants (parameters), the values of which establish the PDF's shape. The method-of-moments correctly gives the parameters that determine where the PDF starts, where it peaks, how much it spreads, how quickly it comes down off the peak, and where it ends. The procedures are discussed in more detail in Chapter V.

In theory, even without the method-of-moments, one could compute a resultant PDF describing the multiplication and addition of a number of uncertain element costs. As a practical matter, though, it has been considered heretofore impossible, even when using large computers, which is why analysts have usually had to resort to simulation. Given the method-of-moments, analysts and managers can now make inferences about program cost probabilities with substantially less effort than a network analysis might require. For example, it is possible to carry out the method-of-moments calculations on a hand calculator, although appropriate programs would have to be written to make it convenient.

2. Input/Output

a. Input

As stated above, the framework for a method-of-moments analysis is the program cost breakdown rather than a description of program activities. The cost element probabilities are described using PDF's just as the activities in the network

255

method are. Because some of the cost elements may be costs for exactly the same activities as are described in network assessments, some of the same PDF's may appear, but the overall set of inputs will probably be quite different since in the method-of-moments the effect of schedule cannot be treated independently.

The analyst will perform calculations using information taken from the input PDF's supplied by subject matter experts. This allows him to calculate the specific shape of the assumed PDF type representing the combination of cost elements into a total cost.

b. Outputs

Method-of-moments assessments directly produce the numerical measures associated with PDF's that were described in Chapter II; i.e., mean, standard deviation, and skewness. From these, and using the analyst-assumed PDF type, the specific PDF and its CDF can be drawn. This permits the making of all the same kinds of statements (except those concerning criticality) as can be made following a network risk assessment that addresses cost only.

3. Resource Requirements

The avoidance of the need for computers means that the method-of-moments could be carried out by a single person (a GS-13 analyst, with some reading and study). As with the network method, a large part of his time would be consumed with obtaining experts' PDF's, but definition of a cost breakdown may take much less time than definition of a detailed program network. For the program of less-than-major size, for which this method seems best suited, assuming a cost breakdown has already been constructed, the computations might require less than a week of effort. If pre-written programmable hand calculator programs can be obtained, only a few hours will be needed to organize data, perform calculations and document numerical output. The reader should note that obtaining experts' PDF's can require an hour or more per expert, thus, the total time saved is not in the same proportion as that saved in computation. In other words, cutting

computation time in half does not cut assessment time in half if
data collection time is the same.

4. Applications

No examples of DOD method-of-moments application were found
during preparation of this handbook.

E. WBS Simulation Methods

1. General

WBS (or cost breakdown) simulation methods perform the same
function and use the same concepts as the method-of-moments. As
with the method-of-moments, more than one variant exists and
three are described in [1], [9] amd [17]. The difference between
the method-of-moments and WBS simulation lies in the fact that
the WBS simulation requires a computer and the method-of-moments
does not. The computer is used to generate the PDF for system
total cost by performing large number of simulation runs. These
runs provide sums of elements costs that are generated from the
input cost element PDF's. Specific computer programs that have
been used with this method are described in [1], [9] and [16].

2. Input/Output

a. Input

Inputs are the same as for the method-of-moments, i.e.,
PDFs are obtained for each cost element by consulting experts in
those element categories.

b. Output

Outputs are the same as for the method-of-moments.

3. Resource/Requirements

Skill requirements and costs for this method may be slightly
greater than for method-of-moments assessments since use of a
computer is required. Otherwise, resource requirements should be
nearly equal.

4. Application

The WBS simulation method is used in the Office of the Chief of Naval Operations. A variant of the method is used in the Directorate of Cost Analysis, Deputy for Comptroller, Armament Division, Eglin AFB, FL. A straightforward application is used in the Directorate of Cost and Management Analysis, Comptroller, Headquarters Air Force Systems Command, Andrews AFB, D.C.

F. THE GRAPHIC METHOD

1. General

The graphic method uses graphs of program cost element CDF's and some simple algebra to express program cost uncertainties and to combine the element CDF's to obtain the resultant overall cost CDF. That graph allows the same statements to be made about probabilities of cost as does any CDF.[1]

This method, which is described in [10] and is discussed in more detail in Appendix F, describes the uncertainty of Work Breakdown Structure element costs in terms of normal (bell-shaped) CDF segments and from them finds the CDF of total cost using normal curves. In other words, it performs the same function as the method-of-moments and WBS simulation but makes use of different simplifying assumptions. It also has a more restricted result. The simplifying assumption is that CDF's can be approximated by joining parts of normal CDF's. The assumption greatly weakens the validity of the method but may be acceptable for a speedy approximate solution.

A special tool needed for this method is "normal probability paper"--a special graph paper whose vertical lines are spaced in accordance with the slope of a CDF for a normal (bell-shaped) PDF. Straight lines on this paper have the values that a normal CDF curve has on standard graph paper. A good office supply source should have normal probability paper.

---

[1]Another graphic method uses graphs to determine the moments to be used in a method-of-moments approach. It is discussed in [19], but will not be covered further here.

In this method the analyst determines from experts the cost estimates for WBS elements at 10 percent, 50 percent, and 90 percent confidence levels. These estimates are the expert's beliefs that there are 10 percent, 50 percent, and 90 percent chances that each WBS element will end up costing less than or the same as the corresponding cost.

Having determined the three values for each cost element, the analyst next plots the values as points on a separate piece of the normal probability paper for each cost element as in Figure 9.

For example, if costs are in millions on Figure 9, the plot shows an experts' opinion that there is a 10 percent chance of costs less than about 2 million (V_{10}), a 50 percent chance of costs less than 4 million (V_{50}) and a 90 percent chance of costs less than 9 million (V_{90}) for a given cost element.

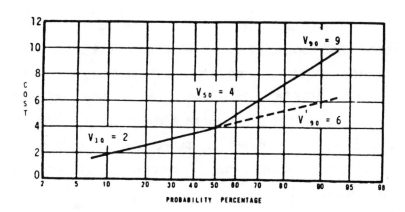

Figure 9   COST ELEMENT UNCERTAINTY

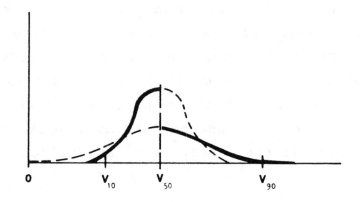

Figure 10 EQUIVALENT PDF FOR GRAPHIC METHOD

259

If V_{90} had been at the point labeled $\overline{V_{90}}$ a straight line would have resulted, and the CDF described would have been that of a normal (bell-shaped) probability. Instead, a CDF is produced that represents a PDF like the darkened lines in Figure 10.

Even though that PDF seems not to fit most people's concepts of how probability should behave, it has two advantages. The first is ease of manipulation. The second is that it exhibits skewness, implying costs are more likely to overrun than underrun which seems generally more realistic.

With V_{10}, V_{50}, and V_{90} from each cost element graph, and with some factors determined from graph values and a table given in Appendix F, the element cost CDF's can be combined and the CDF graph of the overall system cost can be drawn.

2. Input/Output

   a. Input

   Input to this method is of the same type as that required for method-of-moments and WBS simulation, namely PDF's representing subject matter experts estimates of cost element probability. These PDF's, however, are approximations constructed from the experts' statements regarding costs at three levels of probability, one of which must be 50 percent, one less than 50 percent, and one more than 50 percent. Of course, a cost breakdown is also required.

   b. Output

   The output for this method is restricted in the same way that decision analysis methods are limited; the output is solely a CDF. No numerical and not much intuitive information is supplied about uncertainty (since there is no standard deviation information) and skewness. What is provided is an estimate of the most likely cost (that at the 50 percent level), and the probability of underrunning (or overrunning) any selected cost.

3. Resource Requirements

Resource requirements for this method, including skill requirements, should be on the same order as those for an equivalent method-of-moments assessment. (It is worth repeating that the more arguable assumptions in this method suggest that it provides lower quality results).

4. Applications

No examples of DOD uses of this method were found during preparation of this handbook.

G. THE ESTIMATING RELATIONSHIP METHOD

1. General

The estimating relationship, described in [3] and Appendix F, allows a program manager to evaluate his program and enter a curve like that in Figure 11 with a contract rating, explained below, in order to determine a percentage management reserve.

In this method, management reserve represents the amount of funding, above that determined by cost analysis alone, that it is desirable to allocate to a contract to provide for technical

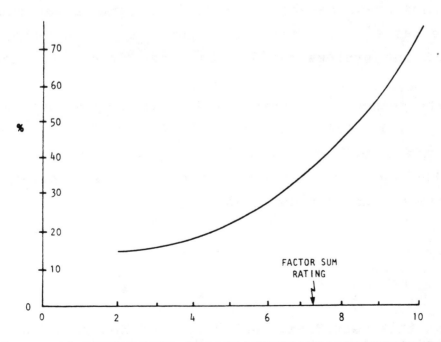

Figure 11 ESTIMATING RELATIONSHIP FOR MANAGEMENT RESERVE

risk.[2] The management reserve is expressed as a percentage of the baseline estimate. The method is called an estimating relationship method because it uses some of the same techniques as the Cost Estimating Relationships (CER's) used in parametric cost estimating.

Cost Estimating Relationships are the result of mathematical methods that determine a relationship between cost and one or more measurable system characteristic such as weight, speed, or volume. The method makes use of a statistical technique called regression analysis to develop an equation to fit a body of data. The data consist of known costs of similar systems, along with their associated sets of data for system characteristics.

The successful use of regression analysis for CER's has led to an attempt to use the same approach for estimating budget requirements to account for technical risk. The application of this approach makes use of categorical definitions for four "factors" derived from an examination of a number of contracts. The "factors", engineering complexity, degree of system definitization, contractor proficiency/experience, and multiple users, are qualities having different levels by which they can be described.

By using descriptions of historical contracts and the amounts of management reserve they used, a formula was contrived which is the basis of the curve in Figure 11. This curve should only be used for systems similar to those from which the data resulted.

To use the method, a contract is described by program management personnel and rated relative to the factor levels. The factor ratings are summed and the result is entered into the Figure 11 curve on the horizontal axis to determine an appropriate management reserve on the vertical axis.

---

[2]Note that this method has been developed and used for contracts, not programs.

2. Input/Output

a. Input

The inputs to the model, the equation of the curve for Figure 11, are the judgemental numbers characterizing the possible contract factor levels.

b. Output

The estimating relationship method provides a percentage figure to be applied to estimated baseline contract cost in determining the amount to supplement the contract for Management Reserve and Engineering Change Order Allowance.

3. Resource Requirements

Resource requirements for this method match those for formulating the baseline contract cost estimate plus a few hours for interviews of PMO personnel.

4. Application

This method is used in the USAF Electronics Systems Division. No other DOD users of this type method were found during preparation of this handbook.

H. THE RISK FACTOR METHOD

1. General

The risk factor method is a determination of factors, or multipliers, by which to increase individual program element costs. The purpose of this risk factor method is to determine a reasonable budget, above that resulting from a baseline cost estimate, to provide for cost growth anticipated as possible by the program manager. The method uses a WBS (or cost breakdown) based on a technical breakdown like Figure 12 (which is taken from [1] but does not necessarily conform to [14]).

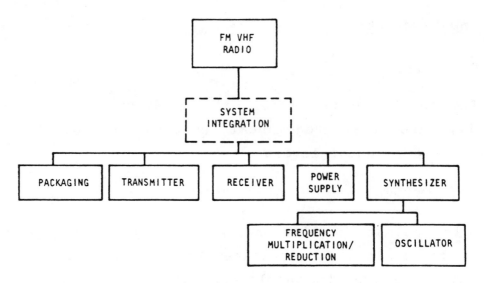

Figure 12 EXAMPLE WBS

The baseline cost estimate is developed for each cost element. Applying whatever considerations are useful, such as those discussed in [11], a risk factor is established, greater than 1, for each cost element. The estimate element costs are then multiplied by these risk factors to obtain the estimates used in the budget for providing a level of funding which will account for technical or other risk.

The assignment of risk factors is the key feature of this method and is the point at which it is both most demanding and has the least objective basis. There is little documented experience upon which the analyst can draw in order to substantiate his factor assignment. Since the application is multiplicative and since such factors cannot reasonably be stated to a greater accuracy than about $\pm$ 0.05, it is just as important as with other methods that the inputs result from a searching probe of highly experienced technical experts. In other words, the apparent simplicity of the method has not relaxed the demand that high quality personnel take key roles in the analysis. On the other hand, once a baseline cost estimate has been formulated by engineering cost estimating methods, the analysts should be able to prepare a cost estimate using risk factors in a relatively short time. The length of time will depend on the difficulty an analyst has in consulting his technical experts and on the level of breakdown of his WBS.

2. Input/Output

a. Input

The primary, and generally pre-existing, "input" of a risk factor assessment is the WBS or cost breakdown of a baseline cost estimate. The risk factors are formulated intuitively based upon analyst or subject matter expert experience and knowledge of program hazards. More detailed discussion of the thinking that might underlie risk factor determination can be found in [11].

b. Output

The "output" of a risk factor application is a budget or cost estimate increased over the baseline budget (or estimate) by an amount anticipated to be sufficient to accommodate otherwise indeterminate, but probable, program costs.

3. Resource Requirements

Resource requirements for this method can be quite flexible. Frequently the same cost estimator responsible for the baseline estimate provides the risk factor result in a few hours. It is assumed that his experience, coupled with his questioning of subject matter experts during formulation of the baseline estimate, is satisfactory.

4. Application

Risk factor methods are the most widely used of those supporting U.S. Army TRACE procedures (see Appendix I), and analysts practiced in carrying them out can be found in the cost analysis offices of any major Army development command.

LIST OF REFERENCES

1. Cost Uncertainty/Management Reserve Analysis, Cost Management and Technology Division, Directorate of Cost Analysis, Deputy for Comptroller, Armament Division, Eglin AFB, FL, January 1982, (#).

2. Crawford, L.P., LCDR USN, A Case Study in Risk/Decision Analysis, Defense Systems Management College, Fort Belvoir, VA, 1973, (AD A046651), (LD32644A).

3. Evriviades, M. <u>Management Reserve Cost Estimating Relation-ship</u>, Cost and Analysis Division, Directorate of Cost Analysis, Comptroller, Hanscom AFB, MA, March 1980 (#).

4. Grover, P.E., and Schneickert, G.D., MAJ USA, <u>Total Risk Assessing Cost Estimate (TRACE): A Field Survey</u>, Systems and Cost Analysis Department, School of Logistics Science, U.S. Army Logistics Management Center, Fort Lee, VA, (#).

5. Hackenbruch, D.J., <u>Risk Assessment of Candidate Mobile Pro-tected Gun Systems</u>, Systems and Cost Analysis Directorate, U.S. Army Tank Automotive Command, May 1981. (#).

6. Hwang, J.D., <u>Analysis of Risk for the Material Acquisition Process, Part I - Fundamentals</u>, U.S. Army Armament Command, Rock Island Arsenal, Rock Island, IL, 1970, (AD 715 394), (LD 25933).

7. Hwang, J.D., <u>Analysis of Risk for the Materiel Acquisition Process, Part II - Utility Theory</u>, U.S. Army Armament Command, Rock Island Arsenal, Rock Island, IL, 1971, (AD 747 365), (LD 25933A).

8. Hwang, J.D., and Kodani, H.M., <u>An Impact Assessment Algorithm for R&D Project Risk Analysis</u>, U.S. Army Air Mobility R&D Laboratory, Ames Research Center, Moffet Field, CA, October 1973 (#).

9. Jordan, H.R., and Klein, M.R., <u>An Application of Subjective Probabilities to the Problem of Uncertainty in Cost Analysis</u>, Office of the Chief of Naval Operations, Resource Analysis Group, Systems Analysis Division, (OP-96D), Pentagon, Washington, D.C., November 1975, (ADA 105 780).

10. Kraemer, G.T., "Quick and Effective Risk Analysis," <u>Trans-action of the AACE Annual Meeting</u>, 21st, Morgantown, WV, 1977, (#).

11. "Letter of Instruction (LOI) for Implementation of RDTE Cost Realism for Current and Future Development Programs," Office of the Deputy Chief of Staff for Research, Development and Acquisi-tion, Department of the Army, Washington, D.C., 6 March 1975 (#).

12. "Letter of Instruction (LOI) for Implementation of the Total Risk Assessing Cost Estimate for Production (TRACE-P)", Head-quarters, U.S. Army Material Development and Readiness Command, Alexandria, VA, 6 October 1982. (#).

13. McNichols, G.R., <u>On the Treatment of Uncertainty in Para-metric Costing</u>, The School of Engineering and Applied Science, The George Washington University, Washington, D.C., February 1976, (#).

14. <u>Military Standard, Work Breakdown Structure for Defense Material Items</u>, 25 April, 1975, (MIL-STD 881A), (#).

15. <u>NASA/Army XV-15 Tilt Rotor Research Aircraft Risk Analysis</u>, XV-15 Tilt Rotor Research Aircraft Project Office, NASA--Ames Research Center, Moffet Field, CA, May 1974, (#).

16. Raiffa, H., <u>Decision Analysis: Introductory Lectures on Choices Under Uncertainty</u>, Addison - Wesley, 1968, (#).

17. "Risk Model Documentation," Letter from Directorate of Cost and Management Analysis, Comptroller, Headquarters Air Force Systems Command, Andrews AFB, MD, 1 June 1981 (#).

18. Sutherland, W., <u>Fundamentals of Cost Uncertainty Analysis</u>; Research Analysis Corporation, McLean, VA, 1971, (AD 881 975).

19. Sutherland, W., <u>A Method of Combining Asymmetric Three-Valued Predictions of Time or Cost</u>; Research Analysis Corporation, McLean, VA, July 1972, (AD 745 404).

20. <u>Total Risk Assessing Cost Estimate (TRACE) Guide</u>; John M. Cockerhand & Associates, Inc., Huntsville, AL, September 1979, (#).

APPENDIX F

TECHNIQUE DESCRIPTIONS

1. <u>GENERAL</u>

This Appendix examines each of the techniques introduced in Chapter IV in greater detail. The goal is for the reader to acquire an appreciation of the most important considerations in accomplishing assessments by use of each individual technique, however the reader wishing to embark on an assessment will need to pursue the subject in the references for the specific techniques.

2. <u>NETWORK METHODS</u>

a. <u>Introduction</u>

The reader who is not familiar with networks and the terms PERT, critical path, arc, and node should refer to any of the excellent introductory works on operations research such as [11] and to the <u>List of Terms</u>, Appendix B.

(#) No AD/LD number for this document

b. The Model

In general, networks like Figure F-1 consist of arcs (lines)
and nodes (end points), the arcs being symbols for program activities and the nodes being symbols for decision points at the
initiation or completion of the activities. Nodes are of three
types: source (or originating) nodes, indicating the initiation
of the program; intermediate nodes, indicating milestones or the
initiation and termination of activities; and terminal nodes,
representing the completion of the program or the failure to
complete some segment of the program. Other means of organizing
networks exist but will not be discussed here.

An awkwardly large comprehensive network can be partitioned
into "sub-networks" when computer space or presentation purposes
dictate.   Figure F-1 shows such a partition and the resulting
simplified network. For example, when a comprehensive network is
too large, it is sometimes possible to run sub-networks independently and to use the derived data as descriptors of arcs in a
simplified network that substitutes for the original sub-network.

While these characteristics are common to most network project models, the techniques with which we are particularly concerned must use "stochastic" (probabilistic) network techniques.
All of the network modeling computer programs cited in this handbook are designed to model probabilistic networks. In a probabilistic network there are two ways in which uncertainty manifests

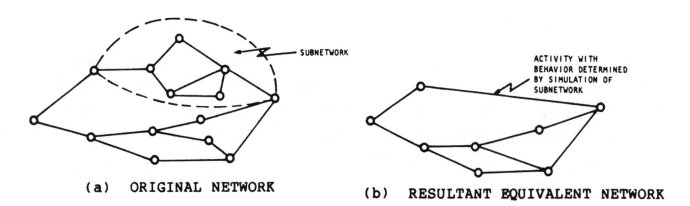

(a) ORIGINAL NETWORK   (b) RESULTANT EQUIVALENT NETWORK

Figure F-1 USE OF SUBNETWORKS

itself. First, activities may have uncertain outcomes in terms of time to complete, cost to complete, or achievement of one or more technical performance levels. Second, the initiation of activities emanating from a node may be predictable only in a probabilistic way. For example, a test outcome (pass/fail) may determine whether the next activity is a progressive continuation of the plan or a corrective action. Since the test outcome cannot be predicted with certainty, it assumes a probabilistic nature. The network model represents this by showing at least two arcs emanating from the node representing test activity completion. The analyst assigns each arc some probability of being selected, depending on the information he has collected from experts. Likewise, he assigns probabilities to the appropriate arcs to represent the relevant probabilities of completing within time or cost constraints or of meeting performance levels.

An important aspect of network models that is needed to permit realistic simulation of programs is varied "node logic". "Node logic" refers to the rules which determine when, for example, a decision point is passed and when it initiates the subsequent activity.

The more advanced computer programs will allow use of both "AND" and "OR" input node logic and "DETERMINISTIC" and "PROBABILISTIC" output node logic. The two types of input logic determine whether all (in "AND" logic) or only one (in exclusive "OR" logic) or some (in "OR" logic) of the possible arcs entering a node must be completed for the node to be actuated. The two output logics determine whether all (in "DETERMINISTIC" logic) or only one (in "PROBABILISTIC" logic) arc (selected at random according to the input probabilities) is initiated upon completion of node actuation. Although later versions of network analyzers elaborate on these rules by allowing use of priorities and other elements, these are the basic node logic concepts.

A principal feature of the stochastic model's handling of both nodes and arcs is its capability to accept a variety of PDF's. One program (VERT) [22] can accept 14 PDF's, ranging from the well-known uniform, triangular, and normal, through the more exotic, such as log-normal, Weibull, and Erlang. If none of these is appropriate, the distribution can be entered as a histogram defined by the analyst. Any or all can be used in a single model. Later network programs also accept large numbers of PDF's.

A significant decision to be made when formulating a network model is the determination of level of detail. Most analysts advise the completion of a "rough-cut" at a fairly aggregated level of detail before attempting to model the fine grained programmatic structure. This allows a more realistic determination of needed level of detail to be made before full commitment, and it also identifies areas which will need to be emphasized in the future. In the earliest stages of program definition (e.g., concept definition), far less than 100 activities can be included. Of course, the inputs are estimates of more highly aggregated sets of activity behaviors, and therefore, they will contain more inherent uncertainty than will be the case as program definition progresses. As plans are defined in more detail, there will be a need to define and include more activities; however, 200-500 have been found adequate by most analysts. Their consensus for analytical (not management control) purposes is that greater detail can tend to obscure major relationships and slow the modeling process unnecessarily.

In the process of structuring the model, analysts do not go directly from activity description sheets to computer terminals. Instead, the actual networks are drawn. Each network computer program users' manual recommends use of a particular set of symbols that define the logic and assist the analyst in ensuring inclusion of necessary inputs. Figure F-2 illustrates some of these symbols.

The work of formulating a network model should not be expected to proceed without some difficulties. Procedure relationships may have to be defined many times as inconsistencies are discovered, weaknesses corrected, and budgets or schedules changed.

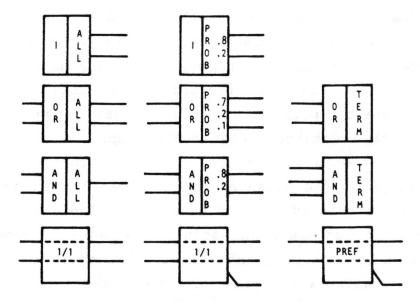

Figure F-2 NODE REPRESENTATION

c. Implementation

When the network is finally judged to be "good enough,"[1] the analysts enter its description into the computer. Specially prepared data formats peculiar to the particular network analysis computer program are used. As can be imagined, the data set may be massive since, for example, in some network models a single activity can require as many as 9 descriptive inputs, and a node as many as 31.

The network analyzers cited herein provide varying amounts of flexibility and realism in their treatment of the variables of time, a statistically independent quantity, or a probabilistic function of time. They may or may not consider technical performance as an uncertain quantity. Another difference is in the treatment of other resources. While VERT, for example, treats only a single resource--cost--others consider a user-defined number (e.g., TRANSIM V)[9], [10].

When the analyst is ready to run his program and has entered his data into the computer, the machine performs a large number

---

[1] A model is an abstraction whose realism is adequate to its purpose.

of simulations of the execution of the acquisition program. This is assisted by use of a computer subprogram known as a "random number generator", which, in concept, produces a number that lies anywhere between zero and one with uniform probability. Whenever an uncertain event is to occur, the computer program compares that number with a data-generated number representing the probability of the event's occurrence. If the "random number" is within the range of the data-generated probability, the computer program initiates that event. Of course, no single simulation of program execution conveys much useful information; however, when that simulation is complete, the computer has collected data from wherever in the network the analysts programmed for it to do so. It then repeats the process, typically 1,000 to 6,000 or more times. Obviously, one simulation tells very little, and 100 may still not give "typical" statistics. How many repetitions are enough? There is no practical way to be sure, but statistical methods can give indications of what is reasonable. Computer time is now cheap enough so that analysts can increase the number of repetitions until percentages of kinds of data being collected appear to have stabilized. The 1,000 to 6,000 replications will consume not much more than five minutes of computer time, and statistical tests can then be performed to see if the results are reasonably stabilized.

d. Outputs

Even the most rudimentary set of outputs obtainable from network analyzers will contain terminal node information like PDF's, CDF's, etc. In fact, VERT outputs include frequency distribution (PDF), Cumulative Frequency Distribution (CDF), mean, standard deviation of the sample, coefficient of variation, mode (most likely), and a measure of skewness, plus other statistical measures for all modeled project completions and specified decision points and activities. This output is in a form similar to the output shown in Figure F-3.

There are many software packages available. Their description here is not intended to be an endorsement. Their indivi-

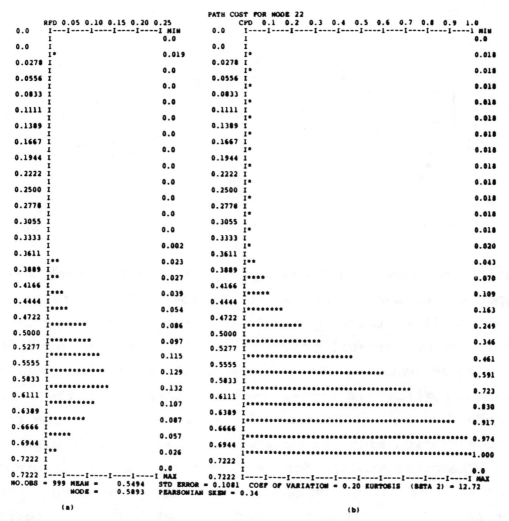

Figure F-3 TYPICAL VERT OUTPUT

dual capabilities must be closely examined for any specific application. Examples described here are only to indicate uses discovered during the survey.

Probability function graphics produced include types such as Figures F-4(a) and F-4(b) below for selected internal nodes (that is, decision points in the program) or terminal nodes (ways in which the program can end).

Figure F-3(a) represents an approximate PDF (in the VERT manual called a Relative Frequency Distribution) and Figure F-3(b), a CDF. The former's shape gives intuitive understanding of probabilities and of uncertainty, whereas the latter's allows the making of probability statements such as, "There is a 72 percent probability of costs being at or under $583,300". The statistical information at the bottom tells the number of times the

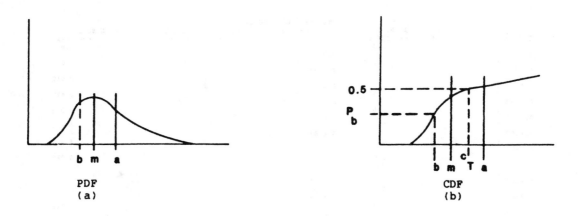

Figure F-4 DISTRIBUTIONS OF COST AT A TERMINAL NODE

simulation was run to get the curves (NO. OBS), which was 999, the expected, or mean, cost, which was $549,400, and certain statistics describing the curves. The Standard Error gives an absolute measure of variability or uncertainty in the units of the variable being assessed (here it is cost), while the Coefficient of Variation gives a relative measure since it is the ratio of the standard error to the mean. A value near 1 for the coefficient of variation might be considered to show fairly high uncertainty. The other two statistics give more abstract information. "Pearsonian skew" (i.e., skewness) indicates the amount the PDF maximum shifted away from the average, and "kurtosis" tells how sharply it is peaked. Skewness tells a manager in a qualitative way the strength of belief that the variable will be different from the average. He will obtain meaningful information, also, by looking at the PDF to see what the most likely value is, and then by looking at the CDF to compare the probability of the value being below or equal to the most likely and below or equal to the average.

By looking for the 50 percent point (median) on the CDF (shown only approximately in Figure F-4(b)) he can, for example, see the point which Army TRACE policy says should be used for a budget and compare that with his baseline estimate's probability.

Other outputs of VERT consist of a bar graph of terminal node probabilities. Since a project may succeed or fail in a number of ways, each may be represented by a terminal node. The bar graph gives the outcome probabilities and allows comparisons to be made. The program can even select an optimum terminal node (that which has least cost and completion time and highest performance), or worst terminal node (that in which highest cost and completion time and worst performance results.)

In many analyzers, this information is supplemented by indices of criticality for specified arcs and nodes. ("Index of criticality" means the probability of an arc or a node being on the critical path.)[2] Other statistics available with various analyzers (e.g., RISNET [23]) include probability of reaching specific terminal nodes (i.e., of a program's ending in a specific way) and joint time and cost distribution (i.e., the probability that final specified limits on both time and cost will be exceeded).

Managers can use these outputs for decision making in the following ways. Suppose Figures F-4(a) and F-4(b) represent the probability density function and cumulative distribution function of cost at a terminal node, which itself represents completion of an important milestone.

Typically, a value such as $\underline{b}$ in the two figures represents the Baseline Cost Estimate submitted by the PMO; but Figure F-4(a) clearly shows that the most likely cost is somewhat higher, at $\underline{m}$, and that the expected value is even greater, at $\underline{a}$.[3] Figure F-4(b) shows even more clearly what the situation is. The probability of not exceeding $\underline{b}$ is only p_b, while the cost level that has an even chance of being exceeded or not is c_T (statistically, the median—also the level of the TRACE). Figure F-4(b) can also be used to set a cost level consistent with the manager's assessment of a reasonable level of risk. For example, if he considers that a risk of failure to cover costs should not be greater than

---

[2]It should be remembered that in probabilistic networks, different variables and paths chosen by the uncertain nature of the program will cause simulations to have critical paths which are not necessarily the same each time. See Appendix B, Definition of Terms for the definition of "Critical Path".

[3]"Expected value" is defined in probability as the average for many runs, not what can be expected to occur. The latter would be a prediction, not a probability statement.

one in five (the 20 percent level), he can set his budget requirement at the 80th percentile cost.

A flexible computer program supporting probabilistic network assessment is TRANSIM V [9] and [10]. This computer model lends itself to use in detailed budgeting and day-to-day project control. The utility of this model is not obtained without effort but is valuable for the insight a manager can have into program status and direction. The data input requirements, however, expand in proportion to the level of detail in the output. For example, for each activity explicitly described in the network a responsibility is named. This allows summaries by name to be included in the output but obviously requires more data preparation.

TRANSIM V provides the following 20 reports: (Note - TRANSIM is but one example of the many programs available that analyze networks).

o List of Names Used in the Model

o Summary of Number of Words of Data Storage Used

o Schedule Risk Report

o Time Summary Graph

o Criticality Analysis Report

o Activity Criticality Report

  - With Predecessors, sorted by Activity/Milestone Code
     and/or Decreasing Criticality

  - With Successors, sorted by Activity/Milestone Code
     and/or Decreasing Criticality

o Activities Delayed Awaiting Resources

o Activity/Milestone Probability of Occurrence Report

o Activity/Milestone Schedule, sorted by

  - Activity/Milestone Code
         and/or
  - Earliest Start Times
         and/or
  - Expected Start Times
         and/or

- Latest Start Times
        and/or
- Earliest Finish Times
        and/or
- Expected Finish Times
        and/or
- Latest Finish Times

o Activity Schedule Graph

o Activity Code and Description for Schedule Graph

o Resource Utilization History

o Resource Requirements Graph

   - Schedule
   - Summary

o Activity Code and Description for Resource Requirements
   Graph

o Aggregate Resource History

o Aggregate Resource History Graph

   - Schedule
   - Summary

o Activity Code and Description for Aggregate Resource
   History Graph

o Cumulative Aggregate Resource History Graph

o Aggregate Resources Summary Graph

o Activity Status Reports

   - Activities Underway for Responsibility
   - Activities Due to Start
   - Activities Due to Complete

These reports can be printed out selectively. To describe each
report in detail would add unnecessary bulk to this handbook. It
is sufficient to summarize as follows:

The reports provide probability of completion by scheduled
date and combine the information with actual calendar dates when
desired. PDF's and CDF's can be obtained for any activity or decision point. Designated risk levels can be used to determine when
each activity is expected to reach that level, and this information can be supplemented by a reading of the number of days
between reaching that level and the date of scheduled completion.

As in other network models, criticalities (probabilities of being on the critical path) are given, but TRANSIM V reports also provide summaries by responsibility. An evaluation is also given of program-wide criticality, which the program manager can use as a general status evaluation. Since each inputs resource is limited (there is a fixed resource pool size) during any activity, and since the resource cost per unit for each activity can also be defined, the manager can obtain detailed and aggregated resource and cost history information plus probability evaluation of future resource and funding requirements. The reports needed to update the model inputs are made periodically, as decided by the program manager, by whatever level of management he decides provides him with necessary detail; therefore, he can establish a system of information and projection which allows him to carry out control functions.

Other variations of outputs concern budget information provided by various network analyzer computer programs. For example, VERT produces two types of cost data for each selected decision point and for each terminal point. The first type, called "path cost", provides the cost distribution of all activities on the path (sequence of activities) which led to that node (during each run). The second type, called "overall cost", provides not only the path cost but adds to it the cost of all activities processed prior to the completion of the decision point and provides the distribution of this value. Such information can be collected to provide overall budget estimates [22]. These costs are illustrated in Figure F-5 by the darkened lines.

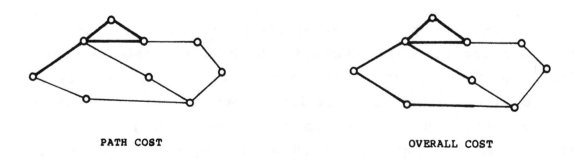

PATH COST   OVERALL COST

Figure F-5 ACCUMULATION OF COST DATA

LIST OF REFERENCES

1. Antunes, Moore, Ed., <u>Army Programs Decision Risk Analysis</u> <u>(DRA) Handbook</u>, U.S. Army Logistics Management Center, Fort Lee, VA, (DARCOM Handbook 11-1.1-79), 1979, (#).

2. Atzinger, E. et al, <u>Compendium on Risk Analysis Techniques</u>, DARCOM Materiel Systems Analysis Activity, Aberdeen Proving Ground, MD, 1972, (AD 746245), (LD 28463).

3. Barclay, Brown, Kelly, Peterson, Phillips, and Selvidge, <u>Handbook for Decision Analysis</u>, Decisions and Designs Inc., McLean, VA, 1977, (#).

4. Brown, R.V., Kahr, A.S., and Peterson, C., <u>Decision Analysis</u> <u>for the Manager</u>, Halt, Rinehart & Winston, New York, NY, 1974, (#).

5. <u>Cost Uncertainty/Management Reserve Analysis</u>, Cost Management and Technology Division, Directorate of Cost Analysis, Deputy for Comptroller, Armament Division, Eglin AFB, FL, January 1982, (#).

6. <u>Cost Uncertainty/Risk Analysis</u>, Headquarters Air Force Systems Command, Andrews AFB, MD, June 1981, (#).

7. Crawford, L.P., LCDR USN, <u>A Case Study in Risk Decision</u> <u>Analysis</u>, Defense Systems Management College, Fort Belvoir, VA 1973, (AD A046651), (LD 32644A).

8. Evriviades, M., <u>Management Reserve Cost Estimating Relation-</u> <u>ship</u>, Cost Estimating and Analysis Division, Directorate of Cost Analysis, Comptroller, Hanscom AFB, MA, March 1980, (#).

9. Feiler, A.M., <u>The TRANSIM V Manual, Volume I, Introduction to</u> <u>TRANSIM V</u>, UCLA-ENG-7848, UCLA School of Engineering and Applied Science, Pasadena, CA., September 1978, (ADA059925)

10. Feiler, A.M., <u>The TRANSIM V Manual, Volume II, TRANSIM</u> <u>User's Manual</u>, UCLA-ENG-7855, UCLA School of Engineering and Applied Science, Pasadena, CA., September 1978 (ADA 060397)

11. Hillier, F.S., and Lieberman, G.J., <u>Operations Research</u>, Second Edition, Holden-Day, Inc., San Francisco, CA, 1974, (#).

12. Hwang, J.D., <u>Analysis of Risk for the Material Acquisition</u> <u>Process, Part I - Fundamentals</u>, U.S. Army Armament Command, Rock Island Arsenal, Rock Island, IL, 1970, (AD 715 394), (LD 25933).

13. Hwang, J.D., <u>Analysis of Risk for the Material Acquisition</u> <u>Process, Part II - Utility Theory</u>, U.S. Army Armament Command, Rock Island Arsenal, Rock Island, IL, 1971, (AD 747365), (LD25933).

\# No AD/LD Number for this Document.

14. Hwang, J.D., and Kodani, H.M., *An Impact Assessment Algorith for R&D Project Risk Analysis*, U.S. Army Air Mobility R&D Laboratory, Ames Research Center, Moffett Field, CA, October 1973, (#).

15. Jordan, H.R., and Klein, M.R., *An Application of Subjective Probabilities to the Problem of Uncertainty in Cost Analysis*, Office of the Chief of Naval Operations, Resource Analysis Group, Systems Analysis Division (OP-96D), Washington, D.C., November 1975, (ADA 105780)

16. Keeney, R.L., and Raiffa, H., *Decisions with Multiple Objectives: Preferences and Value Tradeoffs*, John Wiley & Sons, New York, NY, 1976, (#).

17. Kraemer, G.T., "Quick and Effective Risk Analysis", *Transaction of the AACE Annual Meeting*, 21st, pg. 177; Morgantown, WV, 1977, (#).

18. "Letter of Instruction (LOI) for Implementation of RDT&E Cost Realism for Current and Future Development Programs", Office of the Deputy Chief of Staff for Research, Development and Acquisition, Department of the Army, Washington, D.C., 6 March 1975, (#).

19. Martin, M.D., *A Conceptual Cost Model for Uncertainty Parameters Affecting Negotiated, Sole-Source, Development Contracts*, University of Oklahoma, Norman, OK, 1971, (AD A035482), (LD 37971A).

20. McNichols, G.R., *On the Treatment of Uncertainty in Parametric Costing*, The School of Engineering and Applied Science, The George Washington University, Washington, D.C., February 1976, (#).

21. Military Standard, *Work Breakdown Structures for Defense Material Items*, 25 April 1975, (MIL-STD-881A), (#).

22. Moeller, G.L., *Venture Evaluation and Review Technique*, Decision Models Directorate, U.S. Army Armament Material Readiness Command, Rock Island, IL, November 1979, (AD A076 600).

23. *RISNET Analyst's Guide*, John M. Cockerham & Associates, Inc., Huntsville, AL., (#)

24. *Total Risk Assessing Cost Estimate (TRACE) Guide*, John M. Cockerham & Associates, Huntsville, AL., September 1979, (#)

25. Wheeler, C.F., *Contract Pricing Techniques to Pass Government Cost Credibility Tests - Contractor Viewpoint*, Martin-Marietta Aerospace, (#).

26. Wilder, J.J., and Black, R., "Using Moments in Cost Risk Analysis," in Martin, Rowe, Sherman, Ed., *Proceedings: Management of Risk and Uncertainty in the Acquisition of Major Programs*, University of Southern California, Colorado Springs, CO, 1981, (#).

27. Wilder, J.J., and Black, R., "Determining Cost Uncertainty in Bottoms-Up Estimating", Paper presented at the 1982 Federal Acquisition Research Symposium, The George Washington University, Washington, D.C., May 1982 (#).

28. Williams, J.B., CAPT USAF, An Analysis of Risk Assessment Within Aeronautical Systems Division, The School of Systems and Logistics, Air Force Institute of Technology, Wright-Patterson AFB, OH, 1971, (LD 27458).

29. Williams, C. and Crawford, G., Analysis of Subjective Judgment Matrices, The RAND Corporation, Santa Monica, CA, 1980 (#).

30. Worm, G.H., Application of Risk Analysis in the Acquisition of Major Weapon Systems, Clemson University, Department of Mathematical Sciences, Clemson, SC, 1980, (LD 49124A).

31. Worm, G.H., Applied Risk Analysis with Dependence Among Cost Components, Clemson University, Clemson, S.C., November 1981 (#)

Controlling Murphy: How to Budget for Program Risk

Lieutenant Colonel John D. Edgar, USAF

General George S. Patton once said: "Take calculated risks. That is quite different from being brash." As the quote suggests, taking a risk is not necessarily bad. In fact, in both combat and weapon systems acquisition, taking risks is good, provided the risk-taker recognizes what he or she is doing and plans in advance to cope with potential adverse outcomes. The secret lies in keeping Mr. Murphy and his gremlins under control.

The only reason risk is even an issue is that people set challenging goals. In defense acquisition, there is really no alternative. The only way to remove all risk from an acquisition program is to overfund it, make the schedule too long, or set performance targets too low. It is doubtful that American taxpayers would accept that kind of planning for defense systems. Therefore, what program managers must do, as will be discussed in this article, is select program parameters that provide a reasonable level of risk, and then establish a strategy that allows them to cope with the adverse consequences they might encounter.

Background

Before proceeding, we need to define the term "risk." A typical dictionary defines risk as the possibility of loss or injury. This definition implies that risk has two components—the probability of some event occurring and the adverse consequences of that event, should it occur. Thus, to analyze risk we must be able to estimate both these factors. The first factor may be estimated in terms of some probability distribution, whereas the second factor may be stated in terms of additional dollars and time required to recover.

Risk analysis, as discussed in this article, can be divided into three parts. First, each component of the program must be analyzed to determine what uncertain events could occur, with what probability, and with what impact. Second, the component risks must be combined to arrive at the risk for the total program. Third, the result must be presented in a way that promotes understanding of the risks involved and aids in planning to cope with those risks.

Existing Department of Defense (DOD) and service policy directives clearly state that program managers should indicate bands of uncertainty in cost estimates and "include risk costs and costs of likely contingencies. . . ."[1] In the past, however, program managers who explicitly requested funds to cover program uncertainties have usually found those funds deleted by the services or DOD in the planning, programming, and budgeting system (PPBS), by the Office of Management and Budget (OMB), or by the Congress. Thus, when such adverse events actually occurred, the program manager was faced with some hard decisions. He could delay his program while trying to obtain additional funds through the PPBS or by reprogramming; or he could adjust funds internally by

---

1. U.S. Department of Defense Instruction 5000.2, "Major Systems Acquisition Procedures," 19 March 1980, paragraph E.5.c.; Air Force Systems Command Manual 173-1, *Cost Analysis: Cost Estimating Procedures*, 17 April 1972, paragraph 5-3.i(4); Department of the Army Pamphlet 11-2, *Research and Development Cost Guide for Army Materiel Systems*, 3-5.a.

Lieutenant Colonel John D. Edgar, USAF, is Director of the Research Directorate in DSMC's Department of Research and Information. From 1976 to 1980 he was assigned to Headquarters Air Force, Deputy Chief of Staff/Research, Development, and Acquisition, where he was responsible for congressional liaison activities in support of the Air Force R&D and procurement budgets. Lieutenant Colonel Edgar holds B.S. and M.S. degrees in aeronautics and astronautics and an E.A.A. degree from M.I.T., and an M.B.A. degree from Auburn University. He is also a graduate of DSMC's Program Management course.

Reprinted from *Concepts*, Summer 1982, pages 60–73. U.S. Government work not protected by U.S. copyright.

reducing the program scope, stretching schedules, deleting redundancy in tasks and hardware, and borrowing against the future by deleting test hardware, and reliability and maintainability tasks. Most program managers, whether they would publicly admit it or not, have responded to this problem by budgeting an undisclosed, internal management reserve. This reserve might be spread in small amounts across all the program tasks, or concentrated in the form of a single, "soft" work element that could be deleted without affecting the program.

The Acquisition Improvement Program

This failure of DOD funding policy to allow for evaluation, quantification, and open planning for risk was recognized by the working groups chartered by Deputy Secretary of Defense Frank C. Carlucci to review the acquisition process. As a result, the memorandum on "Improving the Acquisition Process," signed by Deputy Secretary Carlucci on April 30, 1981, included as Action 11, "Incorporate the use of budgeted funds for technological risk."[2] Action 11 recommended that DOD increase its "efforts to quantify risk and expand the use of budgeted funds to deal with uncertainty." The action directed all services to budget funds for risk. In addition, it tasked them to review the Army's total risk assessment cost estimate (TRACE) concept and either adopt it or propose an alternative method.

Total Risk Assessing Cost Estimate (TRACE)

The TRACE concept was initiated by the Army in 1974 under the guidance of Norman R. Augustine, then Assistant Secretary of the Army for Research and Development. The TRACE was designed to provide program managers with a disciplined method of costing for risk, while providing higher authorities with a scientific money management system. An implementing letter of instruction was published in March 1975.[3] The TRACE concept has been accepted by Congress for use in developing the Army's RDT&E budget estimates.

Before discussing the actual techniques used in quantifying the program risks, some terminology and the general management concept require explanation.[4] Figure 1 displays the basic terms used in TRACE. The baseline cost estimate (BCE) budgets the funds required for all planned activities based on the fixed program schedule. The TRACE deferral covers a reasonable percentage of the costs that would be required to deal with forseeable project uncertainties—the "known unknowns"—that can be handled statistically.[5] The TRACE estimate is the total program cost comprising the BCE and the TRACE deferral.

Figure 2 displays the management concept under which TRACE operates. Three important points should be noted. First, the concept is only used in budgeting RDT&E funds. Second, the Army provides only one value, the TRACE estimate, in the budget documentation submitted to Congress. Third, when Congress authorizes and appropriates the program funds, the program manager receives only the BCE amount. The remainder, the TRACE deferral, is held at Department of the Army (DA) headquarters level. The TRACE deferral funds are only released to the program manager after he has submitted proper justification through the Department of the Army's Materiel Development and Readiness Command (DARCOM) headquarters. The funds release must be approved by both the Deputy Chief of Staff for Research, Development and Acquisition (DCSRDA) at DA headquarters and the Assistant Secretary of the Army for Research, Development and Acquisition (ASA(RDA)). Requests for release of TRACE deferral funds are normally approved in one month or less.

2. Frank C. Carlucci, memorandum for the Secretaries of the military departments, and others, subject: "Improving the Acquisition Process," 30 April 1981.

3. "LOI for Implementation of TRACE," U.S. Army Logistics Management Center, Fort Lee, Va., 6 March 1975, ALM-63-4476-H.

4. Department of the Army briefing brochure, "The TRACE Concept," undated.

5. A reasonable percentage is normally taken as the amount which would provide an even chance (50/50 probability) of accomplishing the program within the TRACE estimate.

FIGURE 1
TRACE Terminology

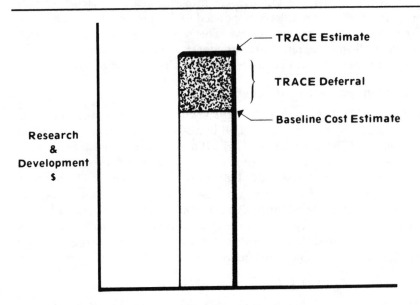

Research
&
Development
$

TRACE Estimate

TRACE Deferral

Baseline Cost Estimate

Baseline Cost Estimate - Funds required for planned activities
TRACE Estimate - Total cost included in budget request
TRACE Deferral - Money withheld by DA Headquarters to cover a percentage
of the cost for program uncertainties

FIGURE 2
TRACE Management Concept

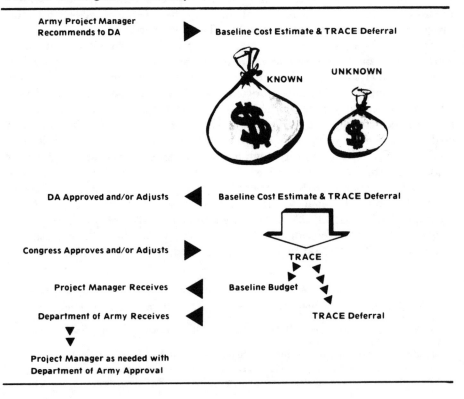

Army Project Manager
Recommends to DA ▶ Baseline Cost Estimate & TRACE Deferral

KNOWN   UNKNOWN

DA Approved and/or Adjusts ◀ Baseline Cost Estimate & TRACE Deferral

Congress Approves and/or Adjusts ▶ TRACE

Project Manager Receives ◀ Baseline Budget

Department of Army Receives ◀ TRACE Deferral

Project Manager as needed with
Department of Army Approval

Normal reprogramming procedures must be used if the deferral funds are transferred outside the program that originally justified them.

Methods for Computing the TRACE

There are several methods program managers may use in computing a TRACE estimate. In all of the methods, the BCE must first be computed using standard estimating procedures. Such procedures include parametric estimating based on cost-estimating relationships (CERs), or "bottoms-up," detailed engineering cost estimating, to name just two.

RISK PERCENTAGE APPROACH

The simplest method for computing the TRACE estimate requires minimum time and resources to apply and has been called the "risk percentage approach."[6] Under this approach the program manager applies a "rule of thumb" and merely increases the BCE by some subjectively derived percentage representing the total program risk. The program manager is not required to consider subelements of his program individually, nor to take account of possible interactions between them. This approach was used by one-fourth (5 out of 20) of the Army program management offices surveyed by the U.S. Army Logistics Management Center in 1980.

RISK-FACTOR METHOD

Moving slightly up the scale of complexity, there is the risk-factor method used by roughly one-half of those surveyed in 1980. This method can be done by hand on any program which has a work breakdown structure (WBS). Figure 3 depicts how this method operates.[7] Basically, a subjectively derived risk factor is assigned to each WBS subelement. Then the BCE for each WBS subelement is multiplied by the appropriate risk factor and the results summed up for all the subelements. In effect, this method computes a weighted average risk factor, which represents the contribution of each subelement risk factor weighted by the dollar value of the subelement.

FIGURE 3
TRACE Risk Factor Method

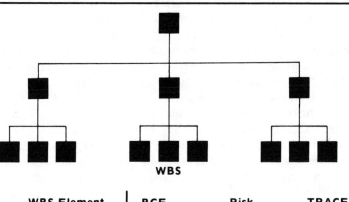

WBS Element	BCE	Risk Factor	TRACE	TRACE Deferral
	a	b	a × b = c	c − a
1	$100M	1.10	$110M	$10M
2	$200M	1.25	$250M	$50M
:	:	:	:	:
Total	$300M	N/A	$360M	$60M

---

6. Major George Schneickert, USA, and Paul Grover, "Don't Be Lost Without a TRACE—Total Risk Assessing Cost Estimate Methodologies," *Program Manager*, November-December 1981, p. 19.
7. "Methodology for Developing Total Risk Assessing Cost Estimate (TRACE)," U.S. Army Logistics Management Center, Fort Lee, Va., ALM-63-4476-H3.

FIGURE 4
TRACE Probabilistic Event Analysis

①	②	③	④	⑤	⑥	⑦	⑧	⑨	⑩	⑪	⑫
		Primary Event A				Secondary Event B				Total Expected Value	FY of Impact
Program Element	Uncertain Event A	Prob. of occurrence	Cost Impact	Expected Value	Secondary Event B	P(B/A)	P(B)	Cost Impact	Expected Value		
Armor	Penetration test failure	.40	$3.0M	$1.2M	Suspension redesign req'd	.75	.30	$2.0M	$0.6M	$ 1.8M	82
Suspension	Additional weight growth	.60	1.0	0.6	—	—	—	—	—	0.6	82
Tracks	Failure to achieve MTBF	.75	2.0	1.5	Add'l delay in integration	1.0	.75	4.0	3.0	4.5	82
Power Train	Extension of testing	.40	1.0	0.4	—	—	—	—	—	0.4	82
Engine	Excessive fuel consumption	.60	3.0	1.8	—	—	—	—	—	1.8	82
Integration	Delay in start of testing	.90	5.0	4.5	Field testing delayed	1.0	.90	6.0	5.4	9.9	83

TRACE Deferrals

$ 9.1M	FY82
$ 9.9M	FY83
$19.0M	Total

PROBABILISTIC EVENT ANALYSIS

The third methodology, called probabilistic event analysis, also begins with the WBS elements, but carries the analysis one step further to consider the interactive effects of one WBS element on the other elements.[8] The end result is a calculation of the "expected value" of uncertain events, including their secondary effects.

A hypothetical probabilistic event analysis is illustrated in Figure 4. In this technique, the first step is to review all the program elements (column 1) and list all the uncertain events that could occur and have an impact on program cost or schedule (column 2). People familiar with the work then estimate the probability of occurrence of each event (column 3) and its impact on the cost of the work element (column 4). The "expected value" of each event (column 5) can then be calculated by multiplying the estimated cost impact by the event probability.

The next step is to identify the secondary effects of the uncertain events (column 6). This step includes assigning a conditional probability of secondary event B occurring given that primary event A has already occurred, $P(B/A)$ (column 7); calculating the probability of event B occurring, i.e. $P(B) = P(B/A) \times P(A)$[9] (column 8); and estimating the cost and schedule impact of the secondary event (column 9). The "expected value" of secondary event B can then be calculated (column 10). The "expected values" of both the primary event and the secondary events it could trigger are summed (column 11) and identified with the fiscal year (FY) in which they could occur (column 12). Thus, the final result is the total "expected value" of uncertain events by fiscal year, which can be used as the TRACE deferral amount.

No programs surveyed in 1980 used this technique, principally because of "difficulty in conceptualizing the interaction effects and lack of trained analysts. . . ."[10] However, subsequent to that survey, the TRITAC AN/TTC-39 family of switches has used the probabilistic event analysis.

---

8. Department of the Army, "Total Risk Assessing Cost Estimate (TRACE) Guide," Contract DAAK40-79-C-0034, 1 September 1979.

9. In this case the equation $P(B) = P(B/A)P(A) + P(B/\bar{A})P(\bar{A})$ is simplified since by definition event B cannot occur without event A causing it, i.e., $P(B/\bar{A}) = 0$.

10. Schneickert and Grover.

The fourth and most demanding methodology is the probabilistic network modeling approach. This approach, shown in Figure 5, uses network models in conjunction with the Monte Carlo simulation technique. The networks are schedule-oriented and can either include only planned, deterministic activities (Type I networks) or both planned and conditional decision activities (Type II networks).[11] Schedule and cost uncertainties, in the form of probability distributions, are estimated for each activity in the network computer model. The model is then run a sufficient number of times, in a Monte Carlo computer simulation, to generate probability distributions of estimated schedule and cost for the total program.

Although this method provides a highly flexible and responsive management tool once it is in place, it initially requires more time and highly skilled analysts to develop the program network model. It also requires access to a computer with a suitable network-evaluation software. At least one type of evaluation software, the risk information system and network evaluation technique (RISNET), is available in-house at the major subordinate commands within DARCOM.[12] Only one-fifth of those surveyed used this method, and half of those who did had the work done under contract by private consultants.

Use of TRACE on Army Programs[13]

Army Regulation (AR) 1000-1, "Basic Policies for Systems Acquisition," states that major programs will use the TRACE concept in developing cost estimates.[14] Over the past 5 years (FY 78–82) roughly 20 programs have designated about $240 million in TRACE deferral funds. Through FY 1981, 99 percent of the deferral funds have been released to the program offices.[15] For example, in FY

FIGURE 5
TRACE Probabilistic Network Modeling Technique

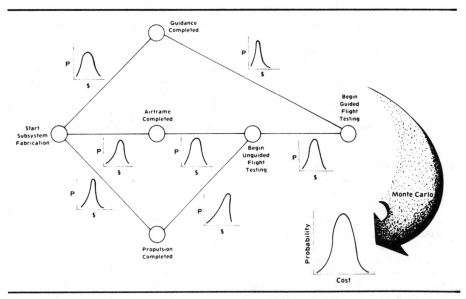

---

11. Type I and II networks are described in the Army briefing brochure on "The Trace Concept," reference (4) above. The Program Evaluation and Review Technique (PERT) uses Type I networks, whereas RISNET uses Type II networks.

12. "Total Risk Assessing Cost Estimate (TRACE)," p. 31.

13. For further information of the Army's use of TRACE contact Patricia Stone, DSCRDA/DAMA-PPR, (202) 697-4988 or Autovon 227-4988.

14. U.S. Army Regulation, "Basic Policies for Systems Acquisition," AR 1000-1, 1 May 1981, paragraphs 2-15.e, and 2-16.d.

15. Lieutenant Colonel James P. McGinnis, USA, and Captain Alan I. Kirschbaum, USAF, "TRACE Risk Assessment and Program Execution," unpublished student research paper, Defense Systems Management College, 7 December 1981.

1981 the advanced attack helicopter (AAH) program used TRACE deferral funds to fabricate equipment and instrumentation for another helicopter following an accident in the test program.

Very few, if any, of the programs underran their TRACE estimates. Less than 1 percent of the total deferral funds have been reprogrammed to other programs. The reason for this is that the TRACE statistical techniques only account for the "known unknowns"; they cannot anticipate the "unknown unknowns" that inevitably occur.

The FY 1983 budget request contains $87.1 million in TRACE deferral funds for 12 programs within the Army's RDT&E budget. As shown in Figure 6, the TRACE deferral amounts range from over 60 percent (HELLFIRE) to under 6 percent (position location reporting system) of the total program cost.

Budgeting for Risk on Navy Programs[16]

Having looked at how the Army is using the TRACE concept, let us now turn our attention to the Navy. The stated policies of the Naval Material Command (NAVMAT) direct program managers to include risk assessment and the means for dealing with that risk as part of their acquisition strategies. This includes "a financial strategy which describes realistic funding necessary to achieve the acquisition objective."[17]

To comply with the direction included in Action 11 of the DOD acquisition improvement program, an *ad hoc* NAVMAT group met to consider the Army's TRACE concept. The result was that the Navy decided to test the TRACE concept on a selected group of Acquisition Category (ACAT) I and II programs in the Naval Air Systems Command (NAVAIR).[18]

The program managers on seven candidate programs were asked to develop TRACE estimates for their programs. The estimates were incorporated into the FY 1984 program objective memorandum (POM) submitted to the Office of the Chief of Naval Operations (OPNAV) by NAVAIR. The seven candidates in-

---

FIGURE 6
FY 1983 TRACE Programs

Program	Total FY 1983 RDT&E Amount	TRACE Deferral
COBRA TOW Missile	12.2	1.0
Army Helicopter Improvement Program	75.8	11.1
PATRIOT Missile	27.5	5.8
HELLFIRE Missile	19.3	12.0
PERSHING II Missile	111.3	29.3
M-1 Tank Gun	31.6	5.6
Tactical Communications	7.9	1.8
Modular Integrated Communication and Navigation System (MICNS) Data Link	14.8	3.5
Position Location Reporting System	9.4	.5
Remotely Piloted Vehicles	73.2	14.4
NAVSTAR Satellite Ground Equipment	11.9	1.0
Tactical Satellite Communications System	17.5	1.1
Total	**$412.4M**	**$87.1M**

---

16. For further information on the Navy's use of TRACE contact Robert Johnson, NAVAIRSYSCOM/AIR-12, (202) 692-7988 or Autovon 222-7988.

17. Naval Material Command Instruction 5000.29, "Acquisition Strategy," October 1981.

18. ACAT I programs are those for which the Secretary of Defense is the decision authority. ACAT II programs have either the Secretary of the Navy or the Chief of Naval Operations as the decision authority.

cluded programs from three general categories: recently initiated programs (pre-Milestone II), programs just entering full-scale development (Milestone II), and ongoing major programs (post-Milestone II). Each program manager was free to select the risk quantification method most appropriate to his program. The methods chosen covered the spectrum of techniques previously described.

The Navy TRACE management concept differs from that used by the Army. The Navy plans to withhold the TRACE deferral funds at the system command level—NAVAIR headquarters. Release of deferral funds will require approval of the commander of NAVAIR. Thus, management of the Navy TRACE funds will occur two levels lower in the Navy management hierarchy than in the Army.

Based on the outcome of the NAVAIR test of the TRACE concept, NAVMAT will decide if the management concept and budgeting methods can be applied to the other system commands.

Budgeting for Risk on Air Force Programs

Like the Navy, the Air Force also evaluated the Army's TRACE concept. In its reply to the Office of the Secretary of Defense (OSD), the Air Force stated that it was using and would continue to use risk assessment techniques that are essentially equivalent to TRACE.[19] One of these techniques, the Air Force Systems Command (AFSC) RISK Model, will be discussed below.

The Air Force has a different philosophy than the Army and Navy on how the funds budgeted for risk should be administered. Whereas in the Army and Navy the TRACE deferral funds are withheld at higher headquarters levels and the program manager must justify their release, the Air Force normally distributes all funds to the program manager. The Air Force does not plan to adopt the deferral concept, because it believes it diminishes the management authority of the program manager, encourages him to budget additional undisclosed reserves, and does not provide higher headquarters with more funding flexibility than it already has. The Air Force believes its approach is in keeping with the management principle of controlled decentralization espoused in the DOD acquisition improvement program.

The AFSC RISK Model

One of the techniques used by the Air Force to evaluate and quantify risk, for

FIGURE 7
AFSC RISK Model

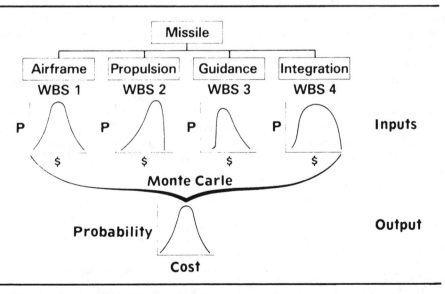

19. James E. Williams, Jr., memorandum for the Under Secretary of Defense for Research and Engineering, subject: "Improving the Acquisition Process," 24 September 1981.

both RDT&E and early production programs, is the RISK Model developed by AFSC's Armament Division at Eglin AFB, Fla.[20] The model is available on the COPPER IMPACT computer time-sharing network. The RISK model is like the Army's risk-factor method in that it is based on the program WBS. However, as shown in Figure 7, the RISK model requires that a cost distribution, rather than a single risk factor, be defined for each WBS element. The inputs that must be made to the model to define the cost distribution include: the point estimate of the cost (equivalent to the TRACE BCE); the highest and lowest costs possible, and the variation of possible costs around the point estimate within this high-low range. In the model, only four discrete variance approximations, which represent the shape of the distribution, are used—"low," "medium low," "medium high," and "high." A lower variance implies a more peaked distribution. The cost range and variance inputs should be based on the estimator's confidence in: the cost-estimating techniques used and their applicability to the program; the firmness of the program schedule; the degree of technology advance required; and the stability of the system configuration. Once these inputs have been made, the model uses a Monte Carlo simulation technique to sum sample cost observations from each WBS element cost distribution into a total program cost distribution.[21]

The computer prints out the total program cost distribution in both tabular and graphic forms. The median value of the cost distribution is considered to be the "best estimate of total program cost," since there is a 50 percent chance that the program can be accomplished within that amount. The difference between the amount the program manager decides to request and the median value represents his management reserve for risk. Unlike the old rule of thumb of adding "X" percent, the RISK model shows the program manager what each dollar increment adds to his program in terms of additional probability of success.

Extension of the TRACE Concept to Early Production

As mentioned earlier, the Army currently uses the TRACE only on RDT&E programs. However, there is a great deal of risk involved in making the transition from development to early production.[22] Because the nature of the risks involved is different, it was not clear if existing TRACE methods could be directly applied to the early production phase.

For this reason, in June 1981, as part of the acquisition improvement program, the Army directed the Army Procurement Research Office (APRO) at Fort Lee, Va., to study the use of a TRACE-like concept for programs entering production. The APRO report submitted to DARCOM headquarters identified the problems encountered in transitioning into production and grouped them into generalized risk categories. These categories are designed to provide a framework for applying conventional cost-estimating techniques to the problem of budgeting for risk

Based on the APRO report, DARCOM refined the risk categories and developed a budgeting methodology and management concept that is now being staffed through DCSRDA. As it now stands, the concept will be applied on a limited basis to selected programs in the Army's FY 1984 POM submission. The management concept used will be similar to that used with RDT&E TRACE—the risk dollars will be identified within the program line and withheld at Army headquarters level until justified and approved for release to the program office.

---

20. Headquarters Air Force Systems Command/ACC letter, subject: "Risk Model Documentation," 1 June 1981. For further information on this model contact A. Fatkin, AFSC/ACCE, (301) 981-4306 or Autovon 858-4306.

21. The RISK model assumes that the cost changes in each WBS element are interdependent as opposed to independent. Thus, a single random number is used to generate observations from all of the WBS element cost distributions as opposed to using a different random number for each WBS element.

22. John D. Nichols, Chairman, *Report of the U.S. Army Ad Hoc Cost Discipline Advisory Committee*, 16 December 1981.

This completes the discussion of where the DOD and the services are in terms of their responses to Action 11. With that background, the next section outlines the advantages and disadvantages of budgeting for risk.

Advantage and Disadvantages of Budgeting for Risk

There are many advantages that can accrue from budgeting for risk. First, and most important, it ensures an open discussion and recognition of the risks involved in the program. That discussion, in turn, facilitates adequate planning to deal with the risks identified. Second, if program funding is based on more realistic cost estimates that account for risk, those programs will be more stable in the long run. Funds will be available quickly to resolve problems as they arise without the need to stretch schedules, reduce program scope, or request reprogramming.

On the other hand, there are both real and perceived disadvantages. Like many of the other actions within the Acquisition Improvement Program, Action 11 required "up-front" funds. That means that fewer programs can be fitted within the total obligation authority (TOA) available. This is probably acceptable if those fewer programs are also more stable programs less subject to stretch-outs. Furthermore, if the risk management reserve funds are openly identified they may prove to be a self-fulfulling prophecy. The funds deferral and release justification procedures, if properly applied, can prevent this from occurring. Finally, unless system discipline is enforced, the risk funds may become an attractive target in budget cutting and redistribution exercises.

Summary

This article has described management concepts used by each of the services in budgeting for risk, as well as several techniques for quantifying risk in dollars terms. The point is that there is no single right way of doing it. What is important for program managers and their staffs, is that they have an approach that forces systematic thinking about program uncertainty and risk before it occurs. The intuitive "X" percent rule-of-thumb approach to budgeting for risk reveals nothing that could improve program management. It would be much more profitable to use one of the more rigorous methods to estimate the level of program risk and the funds needed to cope with that risk. Whether the risk funds are obtained through conventional or "creative" budgeting is immaterial. The real benefit comes from having thought about and planned for unpredictable events. The end result is that you will have Mr. Murphy and his bag of unpleasant surprises firmly under control. ‖

THREE METHODS FOR QUANTIFYING SOFTWARE DEVELOPMENT EFFORT UNCERTAINTY

Paul R. Garvey and Frederic D. Powell
The MITRE Corporation
Bedford, Massachusetts 01730

Reprinted with permission from *Journal of Parametrics*, March 1988, pages 76–92. Copyright ©1988 by The International Society of Parametric Analysts. All rights reserved.

ABSTRACT

Software development effort estimates have several major sources of uncertainty. Among these uncertainties are the size of the project, the development attribute ratings, and the error of the estimation model.

This paper presents three methods which quantify the effects of these uncertainties on development effort estimates. One method takes advantage of the invertibility of the nonlinear effort models to approximate the effort probability distribution. In the case of a single software configuration item, this method yields the exact probability distribution. A second method uses Taylor series to estimate mean and variance of effort, and then specifies its probability distribution by invoking the Central Limit Theorem. The third method, specific to the Constructive Cost Model (COCOMO), invokes a Monte Carlo simulation technique to approximate the effort probability distribution.

The results of case studies based on the COCOMO model are presented and compared. The mathematical details are provided so that analysts may easily review and implement these methods within their organizations.

1.0 Introduction

Large scale software systems being acquired by the Department of Defense face numerous technical and program management uncertainties which challenge the economic integrity and successful delivery of the software system being developed. Among these uncertainties are: technical feasibility, the size of the software system, concurrent hardware development, multisite developments, extensive subcontracting, the availability of a mature programming support environment, the experience of the personnel developing the system, and time and budget constraints. This set of uncertainties is by no means exhaustive, for each software system is unique in character and purpose. Cost studies must identify and assess the economic impact that these and other uncertainties have on software systems being acquired by the Department of Defense.

Uncertainty analyses are needed to support program office budgetary submissions throughout the development life of a system, but never more so than in the concept definition or feasibility planning phases. At this phase, the size of the software system is typically the critical source of uncertainty, and has historically been the most significant driver of cost. Most software resource models exhibit a simple nonlinear relationship between the size of the software

The views and conclusions contained in this document are those of the authors and should not be interpreted as necessarily representing the official policy, either expressed or implied, of the United States government. This work was sponsored by the Electronic Systems Division, Air Force Systems Command, Hanscom AFB, Bedford, Massachusetts under Contract No. F19628-86-C-0001.

system, and the effort required for its development. Analysts using software resource models to generate estimates of effort and duration face additional uncertainties in selecting the appropriate rating levels for development effort multipliers (DEMs) which characterize the technical nature of a Computer Software Configuration Item (CSCI), or a group of CSCIs comprising the system. For instance, the Constructive Cost Model (COCOMO) [1] has fifteen development effort multipliers which modify nominal estimates of effort and duration according to a set of attribute ratings which characterize the software system by product complexity, hardware constraints, personnel skill, and development practices.

In this paper, we look at systems comprised of many CSCIs, and present three approaches which quantify the effects of uncertainty in the size of the software system, and the selection of the rating levels for the development effort multipliers. One approach, the Analytic Software Effort Probability (ASEP) model, evaluates the exact effort mean, variance, and probability distribution for a system consisting of a single CSCI and, in combination with the Central Limit Theorem, provides approximations to these measures for a system comprised of many (two or more) interrelated CSCIs. A second approach uses a Taylor series to approximate the total system effort mean and variance, and then applies the Central Limit Theorem to specify the probability distribution. The third approach, called RISCOMO, is specific to the Constructive Cost Model, and employs a Monte Carlo simulation technique to approximate the effort mean, variance, and probability distribution.

It is assumed in this paper that the uncertainty associated with the size of a CSCI and its development effort multipliers can be adequately bounded by uniform or triangular probability density functions. One approach to bounding this uncertainty is to have the size estimator determine, not an absolute size range, but an 80th or 90th percentile confidence interval from which the analyst may then compute the absolute extremes of the size interval. Within their permissable intervals of definition, the uniform and triangular density functions are characterized by the common feature of unimodality and finite range. Other probability density functions, such as the beta distribution, may be used. However, given the degree of subjectivity typical to: estimates of CSCI size, the rating levels chosen for the development effort multipliers, and the error margins inherent to software resource models; fine-tuning a density function to fit a more elegant mathematical form not only makes the analysis presented in this paper far more complex, but it is not likely to yield meaningful gains in the accuracy of development effort estimates.

1.1 Problem Statement

The general mathematical form of many software resource models is reducible to the expression

$$DE = aI^{\beta}\pi M_j, \quad (j = 1, ..., n) \text{ and } a, \beta > 0$$

where DE is the development effort measured in staff months, a and β are constants specific to be the model type, I denotes the size of the CSCI measured in thousands of delivered source instructions (KDSI), and πM_j is the product of n development effort multipliers which depict unique attributes of the software product, host computer hardware, programmer and analyst experience, and product schedule.

There are a number of software resource models which are reducible to the form shown in the above equation. Examples of such models are the Constructive Cost Model (COCOMO) [1], the Jensen Model [2], the Doty Model [3], and the Walston-Felix Model [3]. It is not within the scope of this paper to discuss the details of these software resource models. The reader is directed to the references if such information is desired.

This paper provides three approaches to solving the following problem. Given a system of multiple CSCIs where their sizes and development effort multipliers are assumed to be random variables, provide expressions for determining the mean, variance, and cumulative probability distribution of the system's development effort.

2.0 The Analytic Software Effort Probability (ASEP) Model

The Analytic Software Effort Probability (ASEP) model, developed by P. R. Garvey, provides analytical expressions which yield exact values for the effort probability distribution, and the effort mean and variance given that the size I of a single CSCI is a random variable. These expressions are first developed for the case of a single CSCI system, and are later modified to the more general problem of determining the approximate effort probability distribution, and the approximate effort mean and variance for a system comprised of many interrelated CSCIs.

The analysis methodology is general to any software resource model of the form

$$DE = \alpha I^\beta, \quad \alpha, \beta > 0 \tag{1}$$

$$\alpha = a \cdot \pi M_j, \quad (j = 1, ..., n)$$

where DE is the development effort measured in staff months, I is a random variable and denotes the size of the CSCI measured in thousands of delivered source instructions (KDSI), a and β are constants specific to the model type, and πM_j is the product of n development effort multipliers (DEMs) which describe unique characteristics of the software product, host computer hardware, programmer and analyst experience, and product schedule.

Assuming that the software development effort DE of a single CSCI system is given by

$$DE = \alpha I^\beta = g(I) \tag{2}$$

where $I \geq 0$ and $\alpha, \beta > 0$, then g(I) is a strictly monotonic function, and $g^{-1}(I)$ exists uniquely. Therefore, the exact probability distribution function of DE, denoted by F_{DE}, is given in equation 3

$$F_{DE}(x) = F_I(g^{-1}(x)) \tag{3}$$

where F_I is the probability distribution function of size. Equation 3 is true since g is a strictly monotonic increasing function, thus

$$F_{DE}(x) = Prob(DE \leq x) \text{ by definition}$$

$$= Prob(g(I) \leq x)$$

$$= Prob(I \leq g^{-1}(x))$$

$$= F_I(g^{-1}(x))$$

where $g(I) \leq x$ if and only if $I \leq g^{-1}(x)$. Since g is a strictly monotonic differentiable function, then the exact density of DE, denoted by f_{DE}, is given below in equation 4.

$$f_{DE}(x) = f_I(g^{-1}(x)) \, d(g^{-1}(x))/dx \tag{4}$$

Equation 5 defines the exact expression for the expected value of the development effort, and is denoted by E(DE).

$$E(DE) = E(aI^\beta \pi M_j) = E(g(I)) = \int_{-\infty}^{\infty} g(u)f_I(u)du \tag{5}$$

The effort variance σ^2_{DE} is

$$\sigma^2_{DE} = E(DE-E(DE))^2 = \alpha^2(E(I^{2\beta}) - (E(DE))^2) \tag{6}$$

where

$$E(I^{2\beta}) = \int_{-\infty}^{\infty} u^{2\beta} \cdot f_I(u)du \tag{7}$$

Table 1 provides a general summary of the equations for f_{DE}, F_{DE}, E(DE), and σ^2_{DE} for the cases where I is uniformly, triangularly, or right triangularly distributed.

Example

Consider a single hypothetical CSCI with the parameters given in Table 2.

Table 3 provides the development effort distribution, mean, and standard deviation which resulted from implementing the ASEP model approach on the technical parameters of the CSCI given in Table 2. Since this case involved a single CSCI, the ASEP model provided the exact development effort distribution, mean, and standard deviation. The ASEP model results were obtained from the equations, given in Table 1, for size being triangularly (Trng) distributed (with $t_a = 30$, $t_m = 50$, $t_b = 80$, and $\alpha = 2.8$, $\beta = 1.2$ — the COCOMO embedded mode parameters).

Table 1
General Summary Equations For
f_{DE}, F_{DE}, $E(DE)$, σ^2_{DE}

Distribution of I	Development Effort Density $f_{DE}(x)$	Development Effort Distribution $F_{DE}(x)$
Unif (t_a, t_b)	$\alpha^{-1}\beta^{-1}(x/\alpha)^{(1/\beta)-1}(t_b-t_a)^{-1}$ if $t_a \leq (x/\alpha)^{1/\beta} \leq t_b$	$\begin{cases} 0 & \text{if } (x/\alpha)^{1/\beta} < t_a \\ (t_b-t_a)^{-1}((x/\alpha)^{1/\beta}-t_a) & \text{if } t_a \leq (x/\alpha)^{1/\beta} < t_b \\ 1 & \text{if } (x/\alpha)^{1/\beta} \geq t_b \end{cases}$
Trng (t_a, t_m, t_b)	$\begin{cases} c(t_m-t_a)^{-1}\beta^{-1}x^{-1}(x/\alpha)^{1/\beta}((x/\alpha)^{1/\beta}-t_a) & \text{if } t_a \leq (x/\alpha)^{1/\beta} < t_m \\ c(t_m-t_b)^{-1}\beta^{-1}x^{-1}(x/\alpha)^{1/\beta}((x/\alpha)^{1/\beta}-t_b) & \text{if } t_m \leq (x/\alpha)^{1/\beta} < t_b \end{cases}$	$\begin{cases} 0 & \text{if } (x/\alpha)^{1/\beta} < t_a \\ (t_b-t_a)^{-1}(t_m-t_a)^{-1}((x/\alpha)^{1/\beta}-t_a)^2 & \text{if } t_a \leq (x/\alpha)^{1/\beta} < t_m \\ 1+(t_b-t_a)^{-1}(t_m-t_b)^{-1}((x/\alpha)^{1/\beta}-t_b)^2 & \text{if } t_m \leq (x/\alpha)^{1/\beta} < t_b \\ 1 & \text{if } (x/\alpha)^{1/\beta} \geq t_b \end{cases}$
RtTrng $(t_a = t_m, t_b)$	$\beta^{-1}x^{-1}(x/\alpha)^{1/\beta}c(t_b-t_a)^{-1}(t_b-(x/\alpha)^{1/\beta})$ if $t_a \leq (x/\alpha)^{1/\beta} \leq t_b$	$\begin{cases} 0 & \text{if } (x/\alpha)^{1/\beta} < t_a \\ 1-(t_b-t_a)^{-1}(t_b-(x/\alpha)^{1/\beta}) & \text{if } t_a \leq (x/\alpha)^{1/\beta} < t_b \\ 1 & \text{if } (x/\alpha)^{1/\beta} \geq t_b \end{cases}$

Note: x is development effort measured in staff-months.
$c = 2/(t_b - t_a)$

Distribution of I	Development Effort Mean $E(DE)$	Development Effort Variance σ^2_{DE}
Unif (t_a, t_b)	$E(DE)_{Unif} = \alpha(\beta+1)^{-1}(t_b-t_a)^{-1}(t_b^{\beta+1}-t_a^{\beta+1})$	$\alpha^2(2\beta+1)^{-1}(t_b-t_a)^{-1}(t_b^{2\beta+1}-t_a^{2\beta+1})-(E(DE)_{Unif})^2$
Trng (t_a, t_m, t_b)	$E(DE)_{Trng} = \alpha c(t_m-t_a)^{-1}\left[(t_m^{\beta+2}-t_a^{\beta+2})/(\beta+2)+(t_a^{\beta+2}-t_a t_m^{\beta+1})/(\beta+1)\right]$ $+\alpha c(t_m-t_b)^{-1}\left[(t_b^{\beta+2}-t_m^{\beta+2})/(\beta+2)+(t_b t_m^{\beta+1}-t_b^{\beta+2})/(\beta+1)\right]$	$\alpha^2 c(t_m-t_a)^{-1}\left[(t_m^{2\beta+1}-t_a^{2\beta+1})/(2\beta+2)+(t_a^{2\beta+2}-t_a t_m^{2\beta+1})/(2\beta+1)\right]$ $+\alpha^2 c(t_m-t_b)^{-1}\left[(t_b^{2\beta+2}-t_m^{2\beta+2})/(2\beta+2)+(t_b t_m^{2\beta+1}-t_b^{2\beta+2})/(2\beta+1)\right]$ $-(E(DE)_{Trng})^2$
RtTrng $(t_a = t_m, t_b)$	$E(DE)_{RtTrng} = \alpha c(t_b-t_a)^{-1}\left[(t_a^{\beta+2}-t_b^{\beta+2})/(\beta+2)+(t_b^{\beta+2}-t_b t_a^{\beta+1})/(\beta+1)\right]$	$\alpha^2 c(t_b-t_a)^{-1}\left[(t_b^{2\beta+2}-t_b t_a^{2\beta+1})/(2\beta+1)+(t_a^{2\beta+2}-t_b^{2\beta+2})/(2\beta+2)\right]$ $-(E(DE)_{RtTrng})^2$

Table 2
Software Cost Model Parameters
For a Single CSCI System

CSCI	Size Distribution KDSI	Mean Size KDSI	πM_j	α
1	Trng (30,50,80)	53.33	1	2.8

Table 3
Development Effort Cumulative Distribution
Generated by the ASEP Model

Development Effort Distribution (F_{DE}) (Percentile)	Development Effort (DE) ASEP Model (Staff Months)
10	234.2
20	263.6
30	286.5
40	306.1
50	325.4
60	347.0
70	371.7
80	401.5
90	440.8
95	468.9
99	506.9
Mean E(DE)	332.3
Standard Deviation σ_{DE}	76.6

2.1 Systems of Multiple CSCIs

In the preceding case (where the system was comprised of a single CSCI), equations which yielded exact values for the effort probability distribution, and the effort mean and variance were derived. The following discussion extends the ASEP model equations for the purpose of approximating the effort mean, variance, and probability distribution for a system comprised of two or more interrelated CSCIs. The Constructive Cost Model (COCOMO) [1] provides the framework around which the extensions to the ASEP model equations are developed. Consider the hypothetical n-CSCI system shown in Figure 1.

The Central Limit Theorem will be used to contend that the development effort distribution is approximately Gaussian. The Central Limit Theorem states that if X_1, X_2, ..., X_n are independent random variables each with finite mean μ_i and variance σ^2_i, then the distribution of their sum is asymptotically normal, with a mean equal to $\Sigma\mu_i$ and variance equal to $\Sigma\sigma^2_i$ for $i = 1$, ..., n. It would be convenient to assert that the total system development effort DE is approximately normal, with mean equal to the sum of the mean efforts for each CSCI, and variance equal to the sum of their variances. However, the Constructive Cost Model applied to a system of interrelated CSCIs exhibits the property that the development efforts DE_1, DE_2, ..., DE_n are not independent random variables. Proposed below is a method of approximating the development effort DE such that DE is expressed as a sum of independent random variables, for which the Central Limit Theorem is then valid.

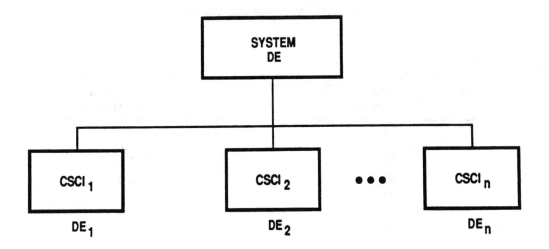

Figure 1. AN n-CSCI SYSTEM

Suppose that the size uncertainty of each CSCI in the n-CSCI system shown in Figure 1 can be characterized as being uniformly or triangularly distributed. The COCOMO nominal development effort relationship is

$$DE = a(\textstyle\sum I_i)^\beta \quad (i = 1, ..., n) \tag{8}$$

The nominal development effort for each CSCI is given by

$$DE_i = (I_i)(\textstyle\sum I_i)^{-1}DE$$

$$= (I_i)(\textstyle\sum I_i)^{-1}a(\textstyle\sum I_i)^\beta$$

$$= aI_i(\textstyle\sum I_i)^{\beta-1} \quad (i = 1, ..., n) \tag{9}$$

Clearly, the development efforts DE_i are not independent since a change in the size of one CSCI affects the estimated development efforts of all the other CSCIs in the system. It is possible to find a constant φ which provides a way to express DE as a sum of independent random variables by solving the expression

$$a(\textstyle\sum \bar{I}_i)^\beta = \varphi a\textstyle\sum \bar{I}_i^\beta, \quad (i = 1, ..., n) \tag{10}$$

for φ, where $\bar{I}_i$ is the mean size of $CSCI_i$.

Let DE, given in equation 8, be approximated by DÊ, where DÊ is defined by equation 11. Thus

$$DE \simeq D\hat{E} = \varphi \sum D\hat{E}_i = \varphi \sum aI^{\beta}_i, \quad (i = 1, ..., n) \tag{11}$$

and DE is now approximated by the sum of independent random variables. Therefore, the mean of DE is approximated by

$$E(DE) \cong \varphi \sum E(D\hat{E}_i), \quad (i = 1, ..., n) \tag{12}$$

and the variance of DE is approximated by

$$\sigma^2_{DE} \cong \varphi^2 \sum \sigma^2_{D\hat{E}_i}, \quad (i = 1, ..., n) \tag{13}$$

where $E(D\hat{E}_i)$ and $\sigma^2_{D\hat{E}_i}$ are computed for each CSCI from the equations provided in Table 1. The Central Limit Theorem implies that for a sufficient number of CSCIs the probability distribution of DE is approximately Gaussian. Therefore, the cumulative probability distribution of DE may be determined from the statistical tables for the normal distribution through the classical transformation

$$z = (DE-E(DE))/\sigma_{DE}$$

where z has a standard normal distribution. The following discussion provides an example which illustrates how the ASEP model is applied to a system of multiple interrelated CSCIs.

Example

Consider a 2-CSCI interrelated system with the parameters given in Table 4.

Table 4
Software Cost Model Parameters
for a 2-CSCI System

CSCI	Size Distribution KDSI	Mean Size KDSI	Development Effort Multipliers			
			RELY	CPLX	DATA	TIME
1	Trng (2,5,10)	5.666	VH	H	*	*
2	Trng (7,9,20)	12.0	VH	*	H	H

Note: These are COCOMO parameter ratings — VH refers to Very High, H refers to High, and * refers to a Nominal rating. It is assumed that the other COCOMO parameters are Nominal.

To use the ASEP model, it was necessary to compute $D\hat{E}_1$ and $D\hat{E}_2$ based on the mean size of each CSCI given in Table 4. Applying COCOMO (embedded mode) to the technical parameters of CSCI 1 using the mean size of 5.666 KDSI yielded a development effort $D\hat{E}_1$ of 36.0 staff months.

From equation 1 (with a = 2.8, β = 1.2, and $\bar{I}_1$ = 5.666)

$$\pi M_{j1} = 1.604$$

$$\alpha_1 = 2.8 \, (\pi M_{j1}) = 4.491$$

where πM_{j1} is the product of the development effort multipliers for CSCI 1.

Similarly, applying the COCOMO model to the technical parameters of CSCI 2 using the mean size of 12 KDSI yielded a development effort $D\hat{E}_2$ of 94.2 staff months. From equation 1 (with a = 2.8, β = 1.2, and $\bar{I}_2$ = 12.0), it may be determined that

$$\pi M_{j2} = 1.705$$

$$\alpha_2 = 2.8 \, (\pi M_{j2}) = 4.775$$

Let DE be the COCOMO-generated total development effort of the system based on the mean size of each CSCI, and modeled as an interrelated hierarchy. From equation 9, the resultant DE was 147.6 staff months. From equation 10

$$147.6 = \varphi \, [36.0 + 94.2]$$

thus φ = 1.133. Using equations 12 and 13, respectively,

$$E(DE) = 1.133[E(D\hat{E}_1) + E(D\hat{E}_2)] = 1.133 \, [36.373 + 94.829] = 148.7$$

$$\sigma^2_{DE} = (1.133)^2[\sigma^2_{D\hat{E}_1} + \sigma^2_{D\hat{E}_2}] = (1.133)^2[158.9 + 738.124] = 1152.8$$

where $E(D\hat{E}_1)$, $E(D\hat{E}_2)$, $\sigma^2_{D\hat{E}_1}$, $\sigma^2_{D\hat{E}_2}$ were computed from the equations provided in Table 1. Therefore, given the technical baseline provided in Table 4, the ASEP model approximation of the development effort mean and standard deviation is

$$E(DE) \cong 148.7 \text{ staff months}$$

$$\sigma_{DE} \cong (1152.8)^{1/2} = 33.9 \text{ staff months}$$

3.0 The Taylor Series Method

In this approach, developed by F. D. Powell, a Taylor series is formed to approximate the development effort mean and variance for a system comprised of many interrelated CSCIs. This series is derived in terms of the size I and the development effort multiplier (DEM) distributions relative to their mean values for each CSCI in the system. These distributions are assumed to be statistically independent. The development effort mean and variance are computed from equations 18 and 19 given below. The Central Limit Theorem is used to determine the overall effort probability distribution of the system.

Although this approach may be generalized for any software resource model of the form shown in equation 1, the hierarchical estimating structure of COCOMO was selected as the basis in which this method is presented. Following the COCOMO methodology, the development effort DE for a system is estimated as a nonlinear function of size I, and a linear function of the DEMs according to

$$DE = \sum_i DE_i = \sum_i (aI_i \, (I)^\beta \, \pi_j M_{ij}) / I \tag{14}$$

where

DE$_i$ is the development effort for CSCI$_i$ (i = 1, ..., n)
a, β are constants specific to the COCOMO model type [1]
I$_i$ is the size of CSCI$_i$
I is the total size of system, I = $\sum I_i$ (15)

and

M$_{ij}$ represents DEM$_j$ in CSCI$_i$.

The variables I$_i$ and M$_{ij}$ for each CSCI in the system are considered to be independent random variables with assumed distributions. The Taylor series expansion of the development effort given by equation 14 about the mean values ~f these random variables is

$$DE = D_0 + \sum_i \frac{\partial(DE)}{\partial I_i} (I_i - \bar{I}_i) + \sum_i \sum_j \frac{\partial(DE)}{\partial M_{ij}} (M_{ij} - \bar{M}_{ij})$$

(16)

$$+ (1/2!) \sum_i \sum_j \frac{\partial^2(DE)}{\partial I_i \, \partial I_j} (I_i - \bar{I}_i)(I_j - \bar{I}_j) + \ldots$$

where the overbars imply means, and the term D$_0$ is

$$D_0 = \sum_i \overline{DE}_i = \left(\sum_i a\bar{I}_i \, (\bar{I})^\beta \, \pi \, \bar{M}_{ij} \right) / \bar{I}$$

(17)

Consistent with the principles of Taylor series, the terms on the right of equations 16 and 17, including the partial derivatives, are evaluated at the mean values of I$_i$ and M$_{ij}$ for each CSCI in the system.

The mean effort for the entire system, computed by taking the expected value of equation 16, is given by

$$E(DE) = D_0 + (1/2!) \sum_i \frac{\partial^2(DE)}{\partial I_i^2} \sigma^2_{I_i}$$

(18)

where $\sigma^2_{I_i}$ is the variance of size of CSCI$_i$. The first partial derivatives vanished due to the use of the mean values for the size, and the development effort multipliers, as the point about which the Taylor series has been expanded. Third and higher derivatives with respect to size have been neglected since they contribute negligible numerical improvement to the estimated mean development effort. The second and higher derivatives with respect to M$_{ij}$ vanish due to the assumption of statistical independence. The rules that the mean of a sum of random variables equals the sum of the means, and that the variance of a sum of independent random variables equals the sum of their variances have been used in equations 18 and 19.

The variance of the development effort is given by

$$\sigma^2_{DE} = \sum_i \left(\frac{\partial(DE)}{\partial I_i} \right)^2 \sigma^2_{I_i} + \sum_i \sum_j \left(\frac{\partial(DE)}{\partial M_{ij}} \right)^2 \sigma^2_{M_{ij}}$$

(19)

---

1. COCOMO embedded mode is given by a = 2.8, β = 1.2.

where $\sigma^2_{M_{ij}}$ is the variance of DEM_i in $CSCI_i$. The error of the COCOMO model is typically zero-mean and approximately normal. Its variance may be added to equation 19 to determine the overall variance of the estimate when calculating the development effort probability distribution. The partial derivatives in equations 18 and 19 are

$$\frac{\partial^2 (DE)}{\partial I_i^2} = (\beta - 1)\left[(\beta - 2)D_0 + 2N\pi \overline{M}_{ij}\right] / \overline{I}^2 \tag{20}$$

$$\frac{\partial (DE)}{\partial I_i} = \left[(\beta - 1)D_0 + N\pi \overline{M}_{ij}\right] / \overline{I} \tag{21}$$

and
$$\frac{\partial (DE)}{\partial M_{ij}} = \overline{DE}_i \cdot \pi \overline{M}_{ik} = \overline{DE}_i / \overline{M}_{ij}, \quad k \neq j \tag{22}$$

where $N = a\overline{I}^\beta$ (23)

Notice that the mean size $\overline{I}$ of the entire system appears in the denominators of equations 20 and 21 to the same power as the standard deviation given in equations 18 and 19. To some extent, this justifies neglecting the higher order terms which involve size in the Taylor series. The second derivative terms with respect to size are so small that neglecting higher order terms appears to be empirically valid. This method is exact for the development effort multipliers since the series terminates for higher powers of these multipliers due to the assumption of statistical independence. The development effort probability distribution is then determined by using the Central Limit Theorem.

Table 5 shows the formulae for the mean and variance of size for uniform and triangular probability functions.

Table 5
Mean and Variance of Size (KDSI) for Uniform and
Triangular Probability Density Functions

Size Distribution	Mean Size	Variance of Size
$Unif(t_a, t_b)$	$(t_a + t_b)/2$	$(t_b - t_a)^2/12$
$Trng(t_a, t_m, t_b)$	$(t_a + t_m + t_b)/3$	$[(t_a^2 + t_m^2 + t_b^2) - (t_a t_m + t_a t_b + t_m t_b)]/18$

Example

Using the technical parameters for the single CSCI system shown in Table 2, the computation procedure for the Taylor series method is shown below. Using Table 5, the mean and standard deviation of size (assumed to be triangularly distributed) are

Mean Size $= (30 + 50 + 80)/3 = 160/3 = 53.33$

Standard Deviation $= \{ [30^2 + 50^2 + 80^2 - (30*50 + 30*80 + 50*80)]/18 \}^{1/2} = 10.27$

Using equations 17 and 18, and the relationship that when $\pi M_{ij} = 1$ then $N = D_0$, yields the mean effort (staff months)

$E(DE) = D_0 + \Delta D = [2.8(53.33)^{1.2}] +$

$2.8(53.33)^{1.2}(1.2)(1.2-1)(10.27/53.33)^2 /2 = 330.8 + 1.5 = 332.3$

Equation 19 yields the standard deviation of effort (staff months)

$\sigma_{DE} = (1.2)D_0(10.27/53.33) = 76.4$

The Taylor series approximations to $E(DE)$, and σ_{DE} compare very favorably (approximately 0.3 percent) with the exact values generated by the ASEP model as shown in Table 3.

4.0 The RISCOMO Tool

Within the family of parametric software resource models described by equation 1, the major source of uncertainty which drives estimates of development effort is the size of the system to be delivered. RISCOMO, developed at MITRE by K.W. Pullen, is a tool which implements a Monte Carlo simulation technique on the COCOMO methodology, by randomly choosing size values for each CSCI according to the distribution defined by the analyst. RISCOMO was developed as a front-end to the WICOMO tool, a commercially available automated implementation of Detailed COCOMO. A project effort estimate is generated for each of the one thousand sets of randomly chosen size values. These one thousand individual estimates for cost, effort, and schedule are then aggregated into frequency distributions.

RISCOMO requires the user to estimate either a single size, or the range of likely size values for each CSCI in a project. For each size estimate, a choice is made between a uniform distribution and a triangular distribution. A uniform distribution is defined by a low and high estimate, and a triangular distribution is specified by a low, high, and most likely estimate. The specific mathematical technique employed to generate the random size variates is the inverse transform method [5]. This method considers size I to be a random variable with cumulative probability distribution $F_I(t)$, that is:

$$\text{Prob}(I \leq t) = F_I(t) = \int_{-\infty}^{t} f_I(z) \, dz$$

This method is illustrated in Figure 2.

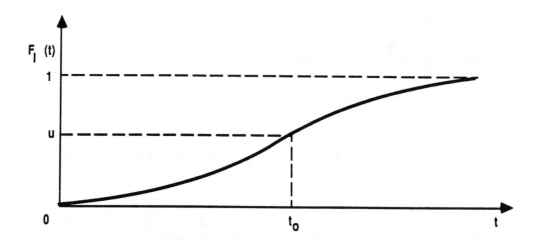

Figure 2. THE INVERSE TRANSFORM METHOD

As shown in the above figure, a random decimal between zero and one is generated using a pseudo-random number generator algorithm. By projecting horizontally from the point on the $F_I(t)$ axis corresponding to the random decimal, to the cumulative curve $F_I(t)$, we find the value of t corresponding to the point of intersection. This value is taken as a sample value for size. This process is repeated for one thousand sets of samples.

Since RISCOMO employs a Monte Carlo simulation approach, it can become expensive in computer usage for systems comprised of a large number of CSCIs. RISCOMO can be applied to a broad set of scenarios. It is particularly useful for approximating the development effort probability distribution for a small number of CSCIs with severely skewed size distributions and widely differing standard deviations. RISCOMO was applied to the software cost model parameters for the single CSCI system shown in Table 2. The results of the RISCOMO simulation, shown in Table 6, compare very favorably (approximately 0.2 percent) with the exact values generated by the ASEP model as shown in Table 3.

5.0 Conclusions

To summarize, the ASEP model has the feature of producing exact values of $E(DE)$, σ^2_{DE}, and the development effort distribution, given the case of a single CSCI, and approximations to these measures in circumstances involving many interrelated CSCIs. It has been enhanced to consider the impact of uncertainty in the selection of rating levels for the development effort multipliers. Its analytic nature makes the ASEP model computationally easy, and inexpensive to execute on a computer.

The Taylor series approach is similar to the ASEP model in the sense that it is an analytic model. A distinguishing feature is that it includes the impact of uncertainty in the selection of rating levels for the development effort multipliers. However, unlike the ASEP model, the Taylor series approach cannot be used to formulate the development effort distribution of a single CSCI due to its reliance on the Central Limit Theorem. By reason of its analytic nature, the Taylor series approach also has the feature of being computationally inexpensive in computer usage.

The assumption of an effort probability distribution being normally distributed is stronger as the number of CSCIs in the system increases, therefore the

Table 6
Development Effort Cumulative Distribution
Generated by RISCOMO

Development Effort Distribution (Percentile)	Development Effort (Staff Months)
10	231.9
20	268.5
30	288.8
40	309.2
50	325.5
60	349.9
70	370.2
80	402.8
90	439.4
95	459.7
99	504.5
Mean E (DE)	334.9
Standard Deviation σ_{DE}	76.5

two analytic methods become more accurate in their formulation of the development effort probability distribution as the number of interrelated CSCIs in the system increases beyond two.

The RISCOMO tool can be applied to a broad set of scenarios, however, it is not computationally straightforward, and can become expensive in computer usage due to its Monte Carlo simulation nature. RISCOMO is especially useful in formulating empirically the development effort mean, variance, and distribution in cases involving a few CSCIs, and in circumstances where the size distributions of a system of CSCIs are *severely* skewed.

1. Boehm, B. W., *Software Engineering Economics*, Englewood Cliffs, NJ, Prentice-Hall, 1981.

2. Jensen, R. W., "Comparison of the Jensen and COCOMO Schedule and Cost Estimation Models," ISPA Conference Proceedings Vol. III, No. 1, San Francisco, CA, 1984.

3. Thibodeau, R., "An Evaluation of Software Cost Estimation Models," General Research Corporation, RADC-TR-81-144, June 1981.

4. Larson, H. J., *Introduction to Probability Theory and Statistical Inference*, John Wiley & Sons, Inc., New York, 1969.

5. Rubinstein, R. Y., *Simulation and the Monte Carlo Method*, John Wiley & Sons, Inc., New York, 1981.

Biography:

Paul R. Garvey is a staff member in the Management Sciences Group at The MITRE Corporation, and is a faculty member in the Department of Mathematics — Northeastern University. His areas of interest include: defense software acquisition practices, software systems cost analysis, and the development of uncertainty analysis methods — an area in which he has published several articles. In July 1986, he served on the OSD/IDA Joint Advisory Council on the use of software resource models in the DOD.

Frederic D. Powell is a staff member in the Management Sciences Group at The MITRE Corporation where his present area of interest is software cost analysis. Prior to joining MITRE in 1986, he was active in several areas of aerospace, and has published a number of articles on automatic control, adaptive systems, digital sampling, and optical fabrication.

SOFTWARE SYSTEM DESIGN AND DEVELOPMENT: TOP-DOWN, BOTTOM-UP, OR PROTOTYPE?

One difficulty which may occur in using the top-down structured programming approach to software development is that of high-risk modules. If one proceeds too routinely through a top-down structuring of a program, he may at times find himself with a fifth-level module which is supposed to "understand natural-language queries," "process a megabit of sensor information in two milliseconds," or something equally impossible. And, in coming up with an acceptable compromise solution for handling this module's task, he may have to rework all of the structure that was painstakingly worked out at levels 1, 2, 3, and 4. It is such practical difficulties that have led some people to consciously reject the top-down approach in favor of the bottom-up approach, and led others to advocate building a throw-away prototype before proceeding to develop the production-engineered software system. However, in straightforward programming projects with no high-risk elements, the prototype approach would generally result in duplicated effort.

There is a formalism which can help determine how much bottom-up prototyping should precede the top-down specification of the overall program structure. This is the statistical decision theory approach, which takes explicit account of risk aspects. It is illustrated below by an example.

The Statistical Decision Theory Approach: An Example

Suppose you are organizing a software project which has within it a requirement to process 30,000 bits of sensor data within 5 milliseconds. You have an algorithm which you are pretty sure will work, and if you proceed top-down to develop the program and it works, you will make an estimated profit of $30,000 on the job. If it does not work, you will have to spend an estimated $40,000 in reprogramming to a less efficient algorithm, and will lose another $40,000 in performance penalties, ending up with a loss of $50,000 on the job. The other alternatives are to develop the program initially with the less efficient algorithm, accepting a loss of $10,000 on the project, or to send $10,000 to quickly develop a bottom-level prototype and test it in a way which gives a much stronger, though still not absolute guarantee that it will work in practice if it passes the tests. How do you decide what to do?

Using statistical decision theory, you would begin by quantifying such words as "pretty sure" and "stronger" into probabilistic terms. This is a very subjective step, but there are various techniques involving expert polling which can help. To begin with, let us suppose that you established a probability of 0.65 that the efficient algorithm would work.

From this, we can see that the expected value of proceeding top-down with the efficient algorithm (Approach A) is:

$$0.65(\$30,000) + 0.35(-\$50,000) = \$2,000$$

clearly better than the $10,000 loss associated with proceeding top-down with the less efficient algorithm (Approach B). However, the positive expected value using Approach A is not completely reassuring, as most software performer organizations have a highly asymmetric utility function such as that shown in Figure 1. It is generally fairly linear on the profit side, but drops off steeply if the project begins to encounter losses. Thus, the expected utility of Approach A is more like:

$$0.65(.4) + 0.35(-.9) = -.055$$

again clearly better than the -.4 utility resulting from Approach B, but still not very satisfactory.

In order to evaluate the expected value and utility of the bottom-level prototype approach (Approach C), we first need to estimate the effectiveness of the prototype as a predictor of the outcome of the success of the project. We do this by estimating two probabilities:

1. The probability that the prototype is successful, given that the project is tractable. Suppose we estimate this as 0.95 (e.g., 5 percent of the time, the prototype would be badly done and fail, but the project would succeed if attempted).

2. The probability that the prototype is successful, but that the project would fail (due perhaps to problems of scale, or unrepresentativeness of the prototype). Suppose we estimate this as 0.15.

Then, we can use Bayes' formula to calculate the probability that the project will succeed, given that the prototype succeeds:

$$P = \frac{(.95)(.65)}{(.95)(.65) + (.15)(.35)} \doteq \frac{.617}{.670} \doteq 0.92$$

Thus, the expected value associated with Approach C is:

$$.670[.92(\$30K + .08(-\$50K)]$$

$$+ .330(-\$10K) - \$10K = \$2.5K ,$$

where .670 is the probability of the prototype being successful and the decision being made to use the efficient algorithm. The expected utility is:

$$.670[.92U(\$20K + .08U(-\$60K)] + .330U(-\$20K) = +.009$$

Thus, in this situation, an expenditure of $10K on a prototype can change the expected utility of the outcome from -.055 to +.009.

If we can estimate costs and probabilities with reasonable accuracy, then, the statistical decision theory approach can help us steer a proper course between top-down, bottom-up, and prototype activities. Currently, given the scanty firm knowledge we have on software cost estimation, and our lack of experience in expressing possible software outcomes in probabilistic terms, the accuracy of the estimates will not support cookbook applications of the method. However, it still has considerable value as a conceptual framework for software development decision making, and provides another reason to press for more collection and analysis of quantitative software data to support cost estimation.

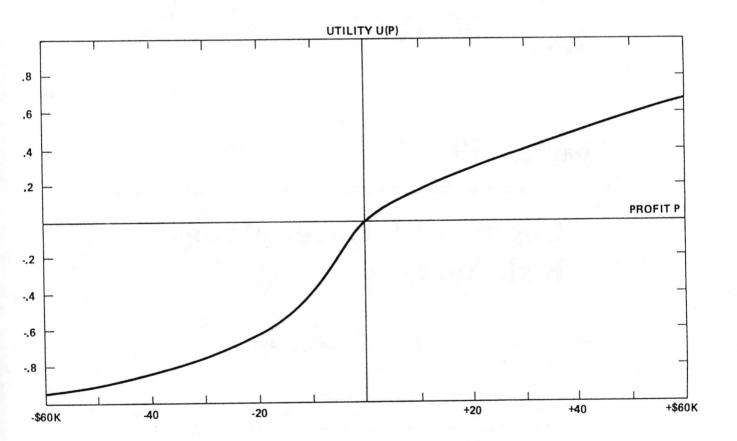

Figure 1. Utility Function for Software Project Outcome

Barry Boehm, *Software Engineering Economics*, ©1981, pages 278–288.
Reprinted by permission of Prentice-Hall, Inc., Englewood Cliffs, N.J.

Part IIIC

DEALING WITH UNCERTAINTIES, RISK, AND THE VALUE OF INFORMATION

The decision techniques we discussed in Part IIIB all assume that we have perfect information about the costs and benefits of alternative systems. Unfortunately, we rarely have perfect information in software engineering decision situations. Part IIIC discusses techniques of *risk analysis* (Chapter 19) and *statistical decision theory* (Chapter 20) that can help in situations of *decisionmaking under uncertainty*. In the process, we will also develop a further appreciation of the *value of information:* that basic phenomenon underlying the demand for software and information processing products in general.

Chapter 19

Coping with Uncertainties: Risk Analysis

19.1   EXAMPLE: OPERATING SYSTEM DEVELOPMENT OPTIONS

Suppose that we have decided to implement TPS Option B in-house, and we now find ourselves confronted with an additional decision problem. After analyzing the various technical approaches to developing the operating system, we find that there are two primary candidates

1. The Option B-Conservative (BC) approach, involving the use of standard operating system techniques. Option BC is sure to work, but will only achieve a peak performance of 160 tr/sec with the eight-processor configuration.
2. The Option B-Bold (BB) approach, involving the use of the recently developed *hypermonitor* concept. If Option BB works, it will achieve a peak performance of 190 tr/sec with the eight-processor configuration. If Option BB doesn't work, though, the team will have to reprogram the system using the conserva-

tive techniques, achieving a performance of 160 tr/sec and an added software cost of $60K.

The potential outcomes of these two approaches (and Option A) are summarized in Table 19–1 below, under the assumption that each tr/sec has a value of $4K.

TABLE 19–1 Operating System Development Options

	Option BB (Bold)		Option BC (Conservative)	Option A
	Successful	Not Successful		
Performance (tr/sec)	190	160	160	120
Value ($4K per tr/sec)	760	640	640	480
Basic cost	260	260	260	130
Total cost	260	320	260	130
Net value NV	500	320	380	350
NV relative to Option A	150	−30	30	0

Which option should we choose, based on net value? One thing is clear: the conservative Option BC is better than Option A. But what are we to do about Option BB? If Nature is favorable, and the bold approach succeeds, we will be rewarded handsomely. But if Nature is unfavorable, we will end up worse off by $30K than if we had stayed with Option A.

19.2 DECISION RULES FOR COMPLETE UNCERTAINTY

The problem of choosing between Options BB and BC, when we have no knowledge of the chance of success of Option BB, is called a problem of *decisionmaking under complete uncertainty.*

There are a number of decision rules for this situation, or any other involving a choice among several alternatives, where

- The outcome or payoff depends on which of several *states of nature* may hold.
- Given any state of nature, the payoff for each alternative is known.
- The probability that any given state of nature holds is unknown.

Table 19–2 is a *payoff table* which summarizes the decision problem. For each alternative and state of nature, it indicates our payoff (here, in terms of net value relative to Option A) if we use the alternative when that state of nature is the case.

The decision rules vary according to their optimism or pessimism about the states of nature. The most pessimistic is the

- *Maximin Rule:* Determine the minimum payoff for each alternative. Choose the alternative which maximizes the minimum payoff.

TABLE 19–2 Payoff Matrix for Operating System Decision Problem

Alternative	State of Nature	
	Favorable	Unfavorable
BB (Bold)	150	−30
BC (Conservative)	30	30

In Table 19–2, this means that we determine the minimum payoff of −30 from Option BB and the minimum payoff of 30 from alternative BC, and choose Option BC.

The maximin rule plays it safe. No matter what nature brings, we are guaranteed a net value of $30K greater than Option A. However, the maximin rule is completely blind to the high potential payoff of Option BB if the state of nature is favorable. Even if the payoff matrix looked like this

	Favorable	Unfavorable
BB	1,000,000	29
BC	30	30

the maximin rule would still choose Option BC.

The most optimistic decision rule is the

- *Maximax Rule:* Determine the maximum payoff for each alternative. Choose the alternative which maximizes the maximum payoff.

The maximax rule would choose Option BB in Table 19–2, because its maximum payoff is the highest. Here again, though, the rule does not have much perspective. Even if the payoff matrix looked like this

	Favorable	Unfavorable
BB	31	−1,000,000
BC	30	30

the maximax rule would still choose Option BB.

One rule that does recognize the relative magnitudes of the payoff values is the

- *Laplace or Equal-Probability Rule:* Assume all of the states of nature are equally likely. Determine the expected value for each alternative, and choose the alternative with the maximum expected value.

Under the equal-likelihood assumption, the expected value* for Option BB in Table 19–2 is $(0.5)(150) + (0.5)(-30) = 60$, and the expected value of Option BC is 30. Thus, we would choose Option BB.

This rule is only as good as the assumption of equal probability, which is often not very good. It is also subject to pitfalls, such as duplication of the states of nature. Suppose, for example, that we split the unfavorable state into two states, U_1 and U_2 (say U_1 = performance failure of hypermonitor and U_2 = reliability failure). Then our payoff matrix, and the expected value, would look like this:

	Favorable	U_1	U_2	Expected Value
BB	150	−30	−30	30
BC	30	30	30	30

Although nothing has changed in the real world situation, our relabeling of the states of nature causes a significant change in the expected value and the recommended decision, because of the equal-probability assumption.

---

* If we have an activity with n possible outcomes whose values are $v_1, v_2, \cdots, v_n$, and whose probabilities of occurrence are $p_1, p_2, \cdots, p_n$, the *expected value* EV of the activity is $EV = p_1 v_1 + p_2 v_2 + \cdots + p_n v_n$.

There are some other decision rules for the total uncertainty situation, but all of them have pitfalls of one sort or another which make them less than totally satisfactory. The best that can be said for these rules is that they provide a well-defined, consistent framework for decisionmaking under complete uncertainty, whose drawbacks are at least well-understood. The main conclusion we can draw is that complete uncertainty about the states of nature is a very difficult position for good decisionmaking.

19.3 SUBJECTIVE PROBABILITIES

One way to improve on our total ignorance of the states of nature is to have some experts give us their subjective estimates of the probabilities of each state. We can refine these into a group estimate, either by some form of averaging or by using a group consensus technique such as the Delphi method [Helmer, 1966], to be discussed in Chapter 22.

Suppose that, after doing so, we have an estimate of 0.4 as the probability that the state of nature is favorable and that Option BB would succeed. We can then compare the expected values

$$BB: 0.4(150) + 0.6(-30) = 42$$
$$BC: 0.4(30) + 0.6(30) = 30$$

and decide that Option BB is preferred.

A related technique is *breakeven analysis.* This involves treating the uncertainties as parameters, and calculating the expected value in terms of the parameters, as shown in Fig. 19–1. Here, the breakeven point is at Prob(favorable) = 0.333. If we feel that the probability of successfully implementing the hypermonitor concept is greater than 0.333, we should choose Option BB; if less, we should choose Option BC.

Note that the previous decision rules are special cases in Fig. 19–1. The pessimistic maximin rule corresponds to the leftmost point, Prob(favorable) = 0. The optimistic maximax rule corresponds to the rightmost point, Prob(favorable) = 1. The Laplace or equal-probability rule corresponds to the midpoint, Prob(favorable) = 0.5.

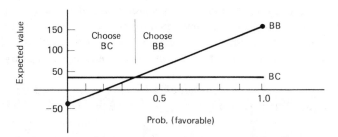

FIGURE 19–1 Breakeven analysis

19.4 GENERAL DISCUSSION: DECISION RULES UNDER COMPLETE UNCERTAINTY

The problem of *decisionmaking under complete uncertainty* involves choosing among a number of *alternatives* (courses of action) under the following conditions:

- The outcome or *payoff* depends on which of several *states of nature* may hold
- Given any state of nature, the payoff for each alternative is known
- The probability that any given state of nature holds is unknown

We have defined and discussed in the previous section the leading decision rules for this situation—the *maximin rule,* the *maximax rule,* and the *Laplace or equal-probability rule*—and illustrated their relative optimism or pessimism, and their strong and weak points.

All of them have serious weak spots. For each rule, there are classes of situations in which the rule counsels a counterintuitive or insensitive decision.*

19.5 THE VALUE OF INFORMATION

It would not be surprising if you finished reading the discussion of these rules with a general feeling of frustration, and thoughts like

> *I can't see myself using a rule like that in a practical software engineering situation. There's got to be a better way*
>
> or
>
> *I don't feel comfortable in this situation at all. If I'm supposed to make a management decision here, I need to know more about those possible states of nature than I'm given here.*

If you felt this way, you were expressing a fundamental human need which provides the main reason for the existence of the software profession: *the need for information which helps people make better decisions.* Virtually all of the models, management information systems, query systems, computer-aided design systems, and automatic test equipment systems developed by the software profession are built because people are willing to pay good money for processed information which will help them make better decisions. In the next chapter, we will focus more on the economic value of information, particularly for making software engineering decisions.

19.6 USE OF SUBJECTIVE PROBABILITIES

One way to buy information to help make software engineering decisions is to acquire information on subjective probabilities, as discussed in Section 19.1. In general, subjective probability information is very useful, and is not very expensive to obtain. It has some practical problems, in that the people most qualified to judge the success probability of an approach on technical grounds are the people closest to the situation, technically or operationally. This closeness often tends to heighten any natural tendencies toward optimism or pessimism they may have, with a resulting bias in their subjective probability estimates. For this reason, the use of group consensus techniques is often valuable.

There are also a number of team-building benefits to be gained by such group-consensus techniques. Further, having the people on the project participate in estimating subjective probabilities gives them a better understanding and feeling of control over their destiny on the project. See Section 22.2 for a discussion of group consensus techniques.

19.7 UTILITY FUNCTIONS

The concept of a *utility function* is often introduced in discussing the use of expected value techniques for decisionmaking. To illustrate the problem they address, suppose you are a manager presented with the following two choices:

- An option which has a guaranteed payoff of $60K
- An option which has a 50% chance of a payoff of $150K, and a 50% chance of a loss of $30K

---

* The same is true of the other rules formulated for decisionmaking under complete uncertainty, such as the Hurwicz rule or the Savage minimax regret rule [Luce–Raiffa, 1957].

Which would you prefer?

Although both options have exactly the same expected value, managers will virtually always prefer Option 1. This is largely because the difference in perception

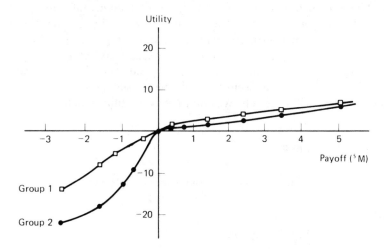

FIGURE 19-2 Utility functions of two groups of managers

between a $60,000 success and a $30,000 failure is much larger than the differences in perception between a $60,000 success and a $150,000 success—and such differences in perception are extremely important to a manager's future career.

Figure 19-2 shows some examples of utility functions which were obtained by asking two groups of managers to express their preferences in various risk situations [Canada, 1971]. A manager in Group 1, for example, has an expected utility of +2 units for the prospect of a $1 million ($1M) gain, and an expected utility of −5 units for the prospect of a $1M loss. Thus, if we presented this manager with a business opportunity which had a 60% chance of earning $1M and a 40% chance of losing $1M, he would refuse it because his expected utility

$$(0.60)(2) + (0.40)(-5) = 1.2 - 2.0 = -0.8$$

is less than zero. His aversion to losses tells him to decline the opportunity even though its expected value is positive

$$(0.60)(\$1M) + (0.40)(-\$1M) = \$0.4M.$$

In order for the manager to accept this business opportunity, he would have to be assured of a positive expected utility, which in this case means a probability of success of at least 5/7 or 71.4%.

19.8 SOFTWARE ENGINEERING IMPLICATIONS

The primary implications of Fig. 19-2 to you as a software engineer are the following:

- You will be dealing largely with managers whose aversion toward losses is much stronger than their desire for gains. Don't expect them to act on an expected value basis in balancing gains and losses.

- On the other hand, managers' utility functions in comparing alternative *positive* payoffs are often reasonably linear, as seen in Fig. 19-2. For such cases, expected value calculations (which are linear) are a reasonable approximation to use in dealing with decisions involving risk.
- Don't assume that everyone has the same or similar utility functions. In Fig. 19-2, the managers in Group 2 have a much stronger aversion toward losses than do the managers in Group 1.

- Don't assume that you can always predict people's utility functions from the type of job they have, although this is often the case. The utility functions in Fig. 19–2 are the results of an experiment to test the hypothesis that research managers (Group 2) have a much smaller aversion to losses than do manufacturing managers (Group 1). To everyone's surprise, the results in Fig. 19–2 show that the opposite was true for the eight managers in this particular study [Canada, 1971].
- Don't assume that people's utility functions are constant. In fact, the utility function is a form of figure of merit which balances a large number of personal variables—needs for money, recognition, security, excitement, belonging, and so on—whose variation with time will cause changes in a person's utility function.

19.9 QUESTIONS

19.1. State the following rules for decisionmaking under complete uncertainty:

- Maximin rule
- Maximax rule
- Laplace or equal-probability rule

19.2. For the following payoff matrix, which alternatives would be chosen by the three decision rules above.

Alternative	State of Nature	
	C	D
A	7	9
B	5	13

19.3. Suppose we are developing software for a spacecraft microprocessor at Precision Products, Inc. (PPI). We wish to decide whether or not to build an emulator of the microprocessor to test the software before the processor is delivered. If we don't develop an emulator, and the processor is delivered on time for testing, PPI will make a profit of $100K. Building the emulator will cost $60K, and will reduce our test costs by $20K if the processor is delivered on time. If the processor is not delivered on time, testing will cost us an additional $20K if the emulator is available, and an added $150K if the emulator is not available.

Set up the payoff matrix for this situation. Determine the best alternative under the maximin rule, the maximax rule, the Laplace rule, and the expected value rule if the probability of on-time processor delivery P(on-time) = 0.8. Compute the breakeven point for P(on-time).

19.4. Consider the utility function shown in Fig. 19–3 for a decisionmaker.
   (a) Based on the payoff matrix of Table 19–2, compute the expected utility of each alternative if the probability of a favorable state of nature is 0.75. Which decision would you make in Table 19–2 if Prob(favorable) >.75? Which if Prob(favorable) <.75?
   (b) Based on the payoff matrix you developed in Question 19.3, compute the expected utility of each alternative if the probability of on-time delivery is 0.8. Which alternative would you choose in this situation?

19.5. Suppose you have a choice of two software programs to develop for a term project in a class: a relatively hard one and a relatively easy one. The payoff matrix below indicates your course grade as a function of the alternative you pick and the state of nature (unfavorable means that the hard project was too hard to do well).

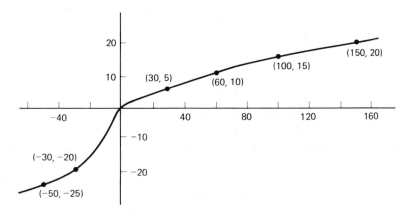

FIGURE 19-3 Possible TPS utility function

Alternative	State of Nature	
	Favorable	Unfavorable
Hard	A	C+
Easy	B	B

Determine your best alternative under the maximin rule, the maximax rule, and the Laplace rule, using the following scale to compute expected values:

A	A−	B+	B	B−	C+	C
10	9	8	7	6	5	4

Does this scale adequately reflect your utility function in this situation? If not, what would be a better one?

19.6. Montana Mining and Manufacturing, Inc. has three times at which it can take delivery of some process control equipment and put its process control system into operation: in 2, 4, or 6 months. Suppose also that there are three possible states of nature: that Montana's process control software will be fully checked out and ready to go in 2, 4, or 6 months. The payoff matrix for this situation is as follows (in $K):

State of Nature / Alternative	Software ready in (months)		
	2	4	6
Deliver equipment in (months) 2	100	60	20
4	70	90	50
6	40	60	80

Determine the best alternative under the maximin rule, the maximax rule, and the Laplace rule. Determine the best alternatives under the following probability distributions of the states of nature.

	Software Ready in (months)		
	2	4	6
Distribution 1	0.2	0.6	0.2
Distribution 2	0.2	0.2	0.6

19.7. Many people are willing to pay hundreds of dollars to go to Las Vegas or Atlantic City in order to play games which, for each dollar they bet, they have roughly a 53% chance of losing the dollar and a 47% chance of winning a dollar. Can you construct a utility function which explains this behavior?

Chapter 20

Statistical Decision Theory: The Value of Information

20.1 EXAMPLE: THE PROTOTYPE APPROACH

In the previous chapter, we analyzed a problem in choosing between a bold and a conservative approach in developing the special-purpose operating system for our TPS. We found that it took the form of a decision problem under uncertainty:

Alternative	State of Nature	
	Favorable	Unfavorable
BB (Bold)	150	−30
BC (Conservative)	30	30

We also found that it was difficult to make a good decision in the absence of any information about the probable occurrence of the states of nature. We thus concluded that such information can be of considerable economic value in decision problems under uncertainty.

In this context, let us look at the idea of building a rough prototype of the key portions of the hypermonitor, which is the high-risk element involved in the Bold approach. Suppose that for $10K we can conduct an investigation to build, exercise, and evaluate a prototype which will tell us whether or not the hypermonitor concept will work for our application, and that the prototype can be developed without any compromise in our schedule.

Then, if the state of nature is favorable, our prototype will work, and we can proceed to develop the production version of the operating system using the hypermonitor concept. Our payoff in this case will be $150K minus $10K for the prototype, or $140K. If the state of nature is unfavorable, our prototype will not work, and we will build the operating system using standard techniques. Our payoff in this case will be $30K minus $10K, or $20K. If these two states of nature are equally likely, our expected payoff would be (0.5) ($140K) + (0.5) ($20K) = $80K.

20.2 EXPECTED VALUE OF PERFECT INFORMATION

Let us compare the expected value and expected utility of the prototype approach with those of Options BB and BC, using the utility function in Fig. 19–3, and assuming that the states of nature are equally likely. We get the following results:

Approach	Expected Value	Expected Utility
Option BB	$60K	0
Option BC	30K	5
Prototype	80K	11.5

Barry Boehm, *Software Engineering Economics*, ©1981, pages 289–303.
Reprinted by permission of Prentice-Hall, Inc., Englewood Cliffs, N.J.

By investing $10K in obtaining information on the actual state of nature, we achieved an expected value which was $20K better than either of the original alternatives. Thus, we could invest up to $30K in obtaining such information and still come out ahead. We can therefore say that the *expected value of having perfect information* on the state of nature is $30K.

20.3 WORKING WITH IMPERFECT INFORMATION

In general, we will not obtain perfect information on the state of nature by developing a prototype, or by other investigations for information to improve our knowledge of the state of nature. There will be two sources of imperfection, which we can express as probabilities

$P(IB|SF)$ Read "the probability of IB given SF"; the probability that the investigation (that is, prototype) would lead us to choose the Bold alternative, in a state of nature in which the Bold option will fail

$P(IB|SS)$ The probability that the investigation would lead us to choose the Bold alternative, in a state of nature in which the Bold option will succeed

The probability $P(IB|SF)$ will generally not be 0.0 because the prototype may not have adequately covered some key technical issue, or because of problems of scaling up from the rough prototype to the production system. Thus the prototype would succeed, and lead us to choose the Bold alternative, but the Bold option would fail. The probability $P(IB|SS)$ will generally not be 1.0 because the prototype may have been developed with implementation errors which would not be repeated in a full production system. This means that there is some probability that the prototype would fail, causing us to choose the Conservative alternative, in a situation where the Bold option would succeed.

20.4 EXAMPLE

Suppose that the best investigation we can perform involving the development of a $10K prototype has the following sources of imperfection, as defined above

$$P(IB|SF) = 0.20, \qquad P(IB|SS) = 0.90$$

Let us now try to calculate the expected value $EV(IB,IC)$ of using this prototype-based investigation to determine whether to use the Bold or the Conservative alternative. In calculating the expected value, we shall assume as before that the states of nature for success and failure of the Bold alternative are equally likely, that is

$$P(SS) = P(SF) = 0.50$$

The expected value is obtained by multiplying each potential payoff by the probability of its occurrence

$$
\begin{aligned}
EV(IB,IC) &= P(IB)(\text{Payoff if use Bold alternative}) \\
&\quad + P(IC)(\text{Payoff if use Conservative alternative}) \qquad (20\text{--}1) \\
&= P(IB)[P(SS|IB)(\$150K) + P(SF|IB)(-\$30K)] + P(IC)(\$30K)
\end{aligned}
$$

This formula calls for a number of probabilities that we do not know directly: $P(IB)$, $P(IC)$, $P(SS|IB)$, and $P(SF|IB)$. The ones that we know from the problem statement are:

$$P(SS) = P(SF) = 0.50, \qquad P(IB|SF) = 0.20, \qquad P(IB|SS) = 0.90$$

20.5 BAYES' FORMULA

Fortunately, given these quantities and their definitions, there is a series of formulas that will give us the values we need to use Eq. (20–1). They are

$$P(IB) = P(IB \mid SS)\,P(SS) + P(IB \mid SF)\,P(SF) \qquad (20\text{–}2)$$

$$P(IC) = 1 - P(IB) \qquad (20\text{–}3)$$

$$P(SS \mid IB) = \frac{P(IB \mid SS)\,P(SS)}{P(IB)} \qquad (20\text{–}4)$$

$$P(SF \mid IB) = 1 - P(SS \mid IB) \qquad (20\text{–}5)$$

Equation (20–2) reflects the fact that there are two different situations in which our prototype investigation will lead us to choose the Bold alternative.

1. Situations in which we choose the Bold approach in a state of nature where the Bold approach will succeed. The probability of doing this is $P(IB \mid SS)\,P(SS)$.
2. Situations in which we choose the Bold alternative in a state of nature where the Bold approach will fail. The probability of doing this is $P(IB \mid SF)\,P(SF)$.

Equation (20–2) thus states that the probability of choosing the Bold approach is the sum of the probabilities of these two mutually exclusive situations.

Equation (20–3) complements Eq. (20–2). It covers the two situations in which the prototype investigation will lead us to the Conservative alternative. It is simply one minus the probability of the Bold alternative.

Equation (20–4) indicates that the probability that the Bold option will succeed, given that our prototype investigation led us to choose the Bold option. It is expressed by the ratio

$$P(SS \mid IB) = \frac{\text{Prob (we will choose Bold in a state of nature where it will succeed)}}{\text{Prob (we will choose Bold)}}$$

Equation (20–4), a form of *Bayes' formula,* is the key to our ability to determine the expected value of using the imperfect prototype, which we can then use as a guide to choosing either the Bold or Conservative approach for system development.

We may now substitute our known probabilities into Eqs. (20–2) through (20–5) to determine the probabilities we need in order to use the expected value formula, Eq. (20–1)

$$P(IB) = (0.50)(0.90) + (0.50)(0.20) = 0.55$$

$$P(IC) = 1 - 0.55 = 0.45$$

$$P(SS \mid IB) = \frac{(0.50)(0.90)}{0.55} = 0.82$$

$$P(SF \mid IB) = 1 - 0.82 = 0.18$$

$$EV(IB,IC) = (0.55)[(0.82)(\$150K) + (0.18)(\$-30K)] + (0.45)(\$30K)$$

$$= (0.55)(\$117.6K) + \$13.5K = \$78.2K$$

Since the largest expected value* we could obtain without developing a prototype was $60K, using the Bold option, the expected value of the imperfect information provided by the prototype investigation is $18.2K. Even though the information is imperfect, it is worth more than the $10K we planned to spend on the prototype.

20.6 MAXIMIZING THE NET EXPECTED VALUE OF THE PROTOTYPE

We can use the Bayes' formula approach above to determine the net values of different levels of investment in prototypes, giving different estimated levels of reliability in their predictions of the states of nature. Such a determination is summarized in Table 20–1 and Fig. 20–1. Thus, for example, an investment in a $20K prototype might eliminate some of the sources of imperfection, decreasing the estimated $P(IB|SF)$ to 0.10 and improving the estimated $P(IB|SS)$ to 0.95. The resulting expected value for the $20K prototype approach would be $86.8K, implying an expected value of the prototype's information of $26.8K and a net expected value of $6.8K, or less than that obtained by the $10K prototype.

TABLE 20–1 Net Expected Value of Prototype versus Cost

Cost of Prototype	Estimated P(IB|SF)	P(IB|SS)	Expected Value	Expected Value of Information	Net Expected Value of Prototype
0			$60 K	0	0
$ 5K	0.30	0.80	69.3K	$ 9.3K	$4.3K
10K	0.20	0.90	78.2K	18.2K	8.2K
20K	0.10	0.95	86.8K	26.8K	6.8K
30K	0.00	1.00	90.0K	30.0K	0

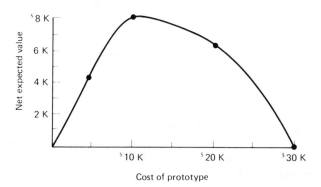

FIGURE 20–1 Net expected value of prototype versus cost

In this situation, the investment of $10K in a prototype is the best decision. Investing less will not produce a sufficient payoff, while investing more will not provide enough of an additional payoff to be worth the additional cost.

20.7 GENERAL DISCUSSION: EXPECTED VALUE OF PERFECT INFORMATION

Definitions. Here is the general form of the problem of *decisionmaking under uncertainty* that we have been discussing

Given a choice between m *alternatives* $A_1, A_2, \ldots, A_m$:

---

* Strictly speaking, we should be calculating expected utilities rather than expected values here. However, since the form of the equations and the resulting conclusion is the same, we have used expected values to simplify the presentation.

- In a situation involving n possible *states of nature* $S_1, S_2, \ldots, S_n$
- Whose probabilities of occurrence are $P(S_1), P(S_2), \ldots, P(S_n)$
- Where the *payoff* value of choosing alternative A_i while in a state of nature S_j is given by the *payoff matrix*

	S_1	S_2	$\cdots$	S_n
A_1	V_{11}	V_{12}	$\cdots$	V_{1n}
A_2	V_{21}	V_{22}	$\cdots$	V_{2n}
$\vdots$	$\vdots$	$\vdots$	$\ddots$	$\vdots$
A_m	V_{m1}	V_{m2}	$\cdots$	V_{mn}

Find the choice of alternative which gives the maximum expected value of the payoff.

In this formulation, the payoff values can be expressed in dollars, figure of merit units, personal utility units, or any other units.

In Chapter 19, we discussed approaches to solving this problem when we had no information about which of the states of nature was actually the case. When we had subjective estimates of the probabilities of the states of nature $P(S_j)$, we used the subjective probability approach: to compute the expected value of choosing each alternative A_i

$$\mathrm{EV}(A_i) = P(S_1)V_{i1} + P(S_2)V_{i2} + \cdots + P(S_n)V_{in}$$

and pick the alternative providing the maximum expected value

$$(\mathrm{EV})_{\text{no info}} = \max_{i=1, \ldots, m} [P(S_1)V_{i1} + \cdots + P(S_n)V_{in}] \qquad (10\text{--}6)$$

If we have perfect information on which state of nature will occur, then for each state of nature we will choose the alternative which provides the maximum payoff for that state of nature. In this situation, the expected value is

$$(\mathrm{EV})_{\text{perfect info}} = P(S_1)\left(\max_{i=1, \ldots, m} V_{i1}\right) + \cdots + P(S_n)\left(\max_{i=1, \ldots, m} V_{in}\right) \qquad (20\text{--}7)$$

Then the *expected value of acquiring the perfect information (EVPI)* is

$$\mathrm{EVPI} = (\mathrm{EV})_{\text{perfect info}} - (\mathrm{EV})_{\text{no info}}$$

$$= \sum_{j=1}^{n} P(S_j)\left(\max_{i=1, \ldots, m} V_{ij}\right) - \max_{i=1, \ldots, m} \sum_{j=1}^{n} P(S_j)V_{ij} \qquad (20\text{--}8)$$

Illustration. Let us refer back to our TPS example with two alternatives (here called A_1 and A_2) and two states of nature SS (Success) and SF (Failure), with equal probabilities of occurrence:

	$S_1 = SS$	$S_2 = SF$
$A_1 = $ Bold	150	-30
$A_2 = $ Conservative	30	30
$P(S_i)$	0.5	0.5

In this case, we have

$$(\mathrm{EV})_{\text{no info}} = \max [(0.5)(150) + (0.5)(-30); (0.5)(30) + (0.5)(30)]$$
$$= \max [60, 30] = 60$$

$$(EV)_{\text{perfect info}} = (0.5) \max (150,30) + (0.5) \max (-30,30)$$
$$= (0.5)(150) + (0.5)(30) = 90$$

$$EVPI = 90 - 60 = 30$$

20.8 EXPECTED VALUE OF IMPERFECT INFORMATION

If our investigations produce perfect information on which state of nature holds, we will always be able to recommend the alternative which maximizes the payoff for that state of nature. In such a case, the alternatives we recommend based on our investigations, IA_i, hold the following relationship with the states of nature, S_j:

$$P\ (IA_i|S_j) = 1.0 \text{ if } A_i \text{ maximizes } V_{ij} \text{ for the state } S_j$$
$$P\ (IA_i|S_j) = 0.0 \text{ otherwise}$$

Usually, the recommended alternatives IA_i will not be based on perfect information on the actual state of nature. Thus, for each alternative A_i and each state of nature S_j, the probability $P\ (IA_i|S_j)$ provides a measure of how often our recommendations are likely to deviate from the ideal (0.0 or 1.0) precision above for that combination of A_i and S_j. For each state of nature S_j, the probabilities $P\ (IA_i|S_j)$ must add up to 1.0, that is

$$\sum_{i=1}^{m} P\ (IA_i|S_j) = 1.0 \qquad \text{for} \qquad j = 1, \ldots , n \qquad (20\text{–}9)$$

The general expression for the expected value of a decision rule based on recommending alternatives $IA_1, \ldots , IA_m$ is

$$EV\ (IA_1, \ldots , IA_m) = \sum_{i=1}^{m} P\ (IA_i)\ EV(\text{payoff using recommendation } IA_i)$$

$$= \sum_{i=1}^{m} P\ (IA_i) \left[\sum_{j=1}^{n} P\ (S_j|IA_i)\ V_{ij} \right] \qquad (20\text{–}10)$$

As in our TPS example (where the IA_i were called IB and IC, and the S_j were called SS and SF), we now need general formulas to calculate $P\ (IA_i)$ and $P(S_j|IA_i)$ from our known values of $P\ (S_j)$ and $P\ (IA_i|S_j)$, in order to calculate $EV(IA_1, \ldots , IA_n)$. These general formulas are the following:

$$P\ (IA_i) = \sum_{j=1}^{n} P\ (IA_i|S_j)\ P\ (S_j) \qquad (20\text{–}11)$$

$$P\ (S_j|IA_i) = \frac{P\ (IA_i|S_j)\ P\ (S_j)}{P\ (IA_i)} \qquad (20\text{–}12)$$

Equation (20–12) is the general form of Bayes' formula.

20.9 THE VALUE-OF-INFORMATION PROCEDURE

Given these formulas, we can describe a *value-of-information procedure* for determining what kind of investigation (simple prototype, detailed prototype, simulation, questionnaire, etc.) will give us the best balance between the cost of performing the investigation and the value we receive from the information produced by the investigation.

1. Formulate a set of alternative information system development approaches $A_1, \ldots , A_m$.

2. Determine the states of nature $S_1, \ldots, S_n$ which influence the outcome of using the alternative approaches.

3. Determine the values V_{ij} of the payoff matrix, where V_{ij} represents the payoff of using alternative A_i if nature is in a state S_j.

4. Determine the probabilities $P(S_j)$ that nature is actually in a state S_j.

5. Compute $(EV)_{no\ info}$, $(EV)_{perfect\ info}$, and EVPI from Eqs (20–6, 7, and 8).

6. If the EVPI is negligible, then it is not worth our time and effort to conduct investigations to determine the actual state of nature. In this case, we would simply choose the development approach which provided the best $(EV)_{no\ info}$, and proceed to implement it. Before doing so, though, we might wish to determine the sensitivity of the EVPI to our assumptions about key payoffs and probabilities, which may cause us to reconsider the prospect of conducting an investigation.

7. If the EVPI is not negligible, it provides a rough* upper bound for the amount of effort we should put into an investigation of the states of nature. Within this limit, determine the most promising type(s) of investigation to perform, and their estimated costs C_k.

8. For each type of investigation, estimate the probability $P(IA_i | S_j)$ that the investigation will recommend alternative A_i when nature is in a state S_j.

9. Compute the expected value of the information provided by investigation k, $EV(I_k)$, using Eqs (20–10, 11, and 12).

10. Compute the net value of each investigation

$$NV(I_k) = EV(I_k) - C_k$$

11. Choose a preferred investigation approach based on the following considerations:
    (a) The relative net values of the investigations
    (b) Whether or not any of the net values are positive
    (c) Whether the results of the investigation will be available in time to aid in choosing which alternative to develop
    (d) The relative magnitude of the side benefits derived from performing the investigations

20.10 USE OF THE VALUE-OF-INFORMATION PROCEDURE IN SOFTWARE ENGINEERING

The value-of-information procedure can help us to resolve a number of key software engineering decisions of the form

How much should we invest in further information gathering and analysis investigations before committing ourselves to a course of action?

The four major issues of this nature in software engineering are

1. How much should we invest in feasibility studies (user questionnaires and interviews, scenarios, concept analyses, models, demand predictions, workload characterizations) before committing ourselves to a particular concept for development?

2. How much should we invest in alternative vendor hardware–software product analysis (workload characterization, benchmarking, reference checking, make-or-buy analysis, rental-versus-purchase analysis) before committing ourselves to a particular product?

3. How much should we invest in risk analysis (simulation, prototyping, user

---

* This is because the investigation may produce *side benefits* of training, concept validation, design sensitivity analysis, user and customer involvement, etc., which are not included in the quantitative calculation of net value.

325

interaction studies, workload characterization, models, sensitivity analyses) before committing ourselves to a baselined requirements specification and a build-to product design specification?

4. How much should we invest in verification and validation (requirements V & V, design V & V, requirements testing, program proving, stress testing, field testing) before committing ourselves to full operational use of the software product?

20.11 VALUE-OF-INFORMATION DECISION GUIDELINES

As the situations above are common in software engineering practice, the value of information procedure is very helpful in providing a stepwise approach for confronting the decision issue, performing the necessary analyses, and communicating our decision rationale to others.

The value-of-information procedure is far from being a cut and dried, cookbook approach. Several steps involve subjective estimates of quantities that are hard to pin down accurately, particularly the payoff values in Step 3, the probabilities of the states of nature in Step 4, and the conditional probabilities $P(IA_i|S_j)$ in Step 8. Thus, we may settle for a more informal version of the procedure in most situations.

Even the informal value-of-information approach will be very useful, because it embodies some basic decision guidelines which will help us avoid some serious common pitfalls, some of which are described in the next section.

Here are the basic decision guidelines embodied in the value-of-information approach, on the *conditions under which it makes good sense to decide on investing in more information* before committing ourselves to a particular alternative.

Condition 1. *There exist attractive alternatives whose payoff varies greatly, depending on some critical states of nature.*

If not, we can commit ourselves to one of the attractive alternatives with no risk of significant loss.

Condition 2. *The critical states of nature have an appreciable probability of occurring.*

If not, we can again commit ourselves without major risk. For situations with extremely high variations in payoff, the appreciable probability level is lower than in situations with smaller variations in payoff.

Condition 3. *The investigations have a high probability of accurately identifying the occurrence of the critical states of nature.*

If not, the investigations will not do much to reduce our risk of loss due to making the wrong decision.

Condition 4. *The required cost and schedule of the investigations do not overly curtail their net value.*

It does us little good to obtain results which cost more than they can save us, or which arrive too late to help us make a decision.

Condition 5. *There exist significant side benefits derived from performing the investigations.*

Again, we may be able to justify an investigation solely on the basis of its value in training, team-building, customer relations, or design validation.

20.12 PITFALLS AVOIDED BY USING THE VALUE-OF-INFORMATION APPROACH

The guideline conditions provided by the value-of-information approach provide us with a perspective which helps us avoid some serious software engineering pitfalls.

The pitfalls below are expressed in terms of some frequently expressed but faulty pieces of software engineering advice.

Pitfall 1. *Always use a simulation to investigate the feasibility of complex real-time software.* Simulations are often extremely valuable in such situations. However, there have been a good many simulations developed which were largely an expensive waste of effort, frequently under conditions that would have been picked up by the guidelines above. Some have been relatively useless because, once they were built, nobody could tell whether a given set of inputs was realistic or not (picked up by Condition 3). Some have taken so long to develop that they produced their first results the week after the proposal was sent out, or after the key design review was completed (picked up by Condition 4).

Pitfall 2. *Always build the software twice.* The guidelines indicate that the prototype (or build-it-twice) approach is often valuable, but not in all situations. Some prototypes have been built of software whose aspects were all straightforward and familiar, in which case nothing much was learned by building them (picked up by Conditions 1 and 2).

Pitfall 3. *Build the software purely top-down.* When interpreted too literally, the top-down approach does not concern itself with the design of low level modules until the higher levels have been fully developed. If an adverse state of nature makes such a low level module (automatically forecast sales volume, automatically discriminate one type of aircraft from another) impossible to develop, the subsequent redesign will generally require the expensive rework of much of the higher level design and code. Conditions 1 and 2 warn us to temper our top-down approach with a thorough top-to-bottom software risk analysis during the requirements and product design phases.

Pitfall 4. *Every piece of code should be proved correct.* Correctness proving is still an expensive way to get information on the fault-freedom of software, although it strongly satisfies Condition 3 by giving a very high assurance of a program's correctness. Conditions 1 and 2 recommend that proof techniques be used in situations where the operational cost of a software fault is very large, that is, loss of life, compromised national security, major financial losses. But if the operational cost of a software fault is small, the added information on fault-freedom provided by the proof will not be worth the investment (Condition 4).

Pitfall 5. *Nominal-case testing is sufficient.* This pitfall is just the opposite of Pitfall 4. If the operational cost of potential software faults is large, it is highly imprudent not to perform off-nominal testing or more rigorous program verification activities.

20.13 VALUE OF INFORMATION: WRAP-UP

Another useful function provided by the value-of-information approach is a means to answer the question posed in Section 15.1: "How do we determine how much cost-effectiveness analysis is enough?" Again, the guideline conditions provide us with a good way to generate a first-cut answer, and the full value-of-information procedure provides a sequence of steps for determining the appropriate size and scope of a large cost-effectiveness analysis in more detail.

Finally, it is worth re-emphasizing that the value of information for improved decisionmaking is the main reason that people build software and information systems. Thus, we will find that the value-of-information guidelines will be very helpful in analyzing the requirements for software and information systems in terms of the types of operational decisions to be supported by the information processing products.

For example, in scoping our airline-reservations TPS, we might receive a suggestion to include information on passenger profiles. The five value-of-information decision guidelines would help us to structure our evaluation of this suggestion. Condition 1, for example, would require us to identify how this information would make a significant difference in our long-range benefits (allowing us to better predict seasonal passenger loads and thus produce better flight schedules; allowing us to give passengers the type of seat and meal they usually request and thus obtain more satisfied customers and repeat business; and so on). The other conditions would help us to evaluate how much expected benefit the passenger-profile information would actually provide in practice.

20.14 QUESTIONS

20.1. State the general problem of decisionmaking under uncertainty. With respect to this statement, give formulas for $(EV)_{\text{no info}}$, $(EV)_{\text{perfect info}}$, and EVPI.

20.2. State the general form of Bayes' formula.

20.3. Consider the TPS example discussed in Section 20.1, with the following changes: P *(SS)* = 0.4, P *(SF)* = 0.6. For this modified problem, compute $(EV)_{\text{no info}}$, $(EV)_{\text{perfect info}}$, EVPI, and the expected value using the $10K prototype investigation.

20.4. Consider the TPS example in Section 20.1, with a different payoff matrix:

Alternative	State of Nature	
	Favorable	Unfavorable
Bold (BB)	150	−100
Conservative (BC)	30	30

Compute the resulting $(EV)_{\text{no info}}$, $(EV)_{\text{perfect info}}$, and EVPI. Develop a counterpart of Table 20–1 for the expected value of various levels of imperfect information.

20.5. Query Systems, Inc. is planning to develop the data base query system for Project Zenith, the community information utility. They have a choice of three data structuring alternatives:
- Alternative A works well if the workload is primarily simple queries
- Alternative B works well if the workload is primarily complex queries
- Alternative C works well if the workload is primarily updates

Below is the payoff matrix in $K for each combination of alternatives and states of nature (actual workload distribution):

Alternative	State of Nature (Primary type of workload)		
	Simple Query	Complex Query	Update
A	1200	600	300
B	800	1000	0
C	400	200	1000
Probability	0.3	0.2	0.5

At this stage, nobody knows which of the states of nature is actually the case.
(a) Compute $(EV)_{\text{no info}}$, $(EV)_{\text{perfect info}}$, and EVPI.
(b) Query Systems wishes to determine whether the following type of user survey would be worthwhile. Its cost would be $200K, and it would have the following accuracy $P(IA_i|S_j)$ in determining the actual states of nature:

	State of Nature		
Alternative	Simple	Complex	Update
A	0.8	0.1	0.1
B	0.1	0.8	0.1
C	0.1	0.1	0.8

Calculate the expected value achieved by using the information from the user survey, and determine whether the survey is worthwhile.

20.6. What are the five value-of-information guideline conditions under which an investment in additional decisionmaking information is worthwhile?

20.7. Elaborate the guideline conditions into a set of guidelines for determining how much one should invest in
(a) Developing a simulation as part of a feasibility study
(b) Developing a prototype or other type of analysis of high risk, low level modules before proceeding into top-down development
(c) Program proving or off-nominal testing before committing a product to full-scale operation.

20.8. The value-of-information approach indicates that the value of information for decision-making is a function of two main factors
(a) The magnitude of the risk involved if the wrong decision is made
(b) The accuracy or reliability of the information
What other factors do you believe influence the value of information for decisionmaking? Are these two the most important factors?

20.9. National Motors, Inc., is developing a microprocessor-based carburetor control system for their next series of automobile models. The software for the system contains 5000 DSI of microprocessor assembly code, packaged in each automobile as a Programmable Read Only Memory (PROM) chip and to be installed in about 5,000,000 automobiles.

Currently, National Motors is investigating the possible use of program proof techniques to reduce the risk of an expensive recall should there be a fault in the software installed in the automobiles. National estimates that conventional test techniques will assure an 0.95 probability that there are no faults in the software. National has two main options for handling a fault, once the 5,000,000 automobiles are in use.

Option A: Take no steps other than to retain the capabilities used in the original software development and chip production. If Nature is favorable and no faults occur, this option incurs no additional cost. If not, and a fault occurs, it will cost National an additional $200 million to service the recall.

Option B: Spend $30 million to develop some additional local service kits to handle the fault correction, should it be needed. This option would cost National an additional $30 million, whether or not a fault occurs.

This situation is summarized in the table below:

	$S_1 = SS$ No Software Fault	$S_2 = SF$ Software Fault
IA_1 = No local service kits	0	200
IA_2 = Local service kits	30	30
$P(S_j)$	.95	.05

The expected cost of Option A_1 is

$$(.05)(200) + (.95)(0) = \$10 \text{ million}$$

The expected cost of Option A_2 is

$$(.05)(30) + .95(30) = \$30 \text{ million}$$

Option A, thus, appears better on an expected cost basis, but National is concerned about its high risk should a fault actually be present in the software. Their investigation of program proof techniques as a way of reducing this risk has produced the following estimates:

$P(IA_1|SF) = 0.01$ (1% of the time, the proof technique will result in the recommendation: "There are no faults; don't produce local service kits," when a fault still exists)

$P(IA_2|SS) = 0.98$ (2% of the time, the proof techniques will result in the recommendation: "This situation is too complex to fully analyze, but the chances of it being in error are high enough that we recommend producing the local service kits," in a situation where no fault exists)

Cost of proof activity = (5000 instr)($200/instr)* = $1,000,000

Calculate the expected cost resulting from the use of the program-proof approach, and determine whether the resulting cost savings are worth the investment in the program-proof activity for National Motors.

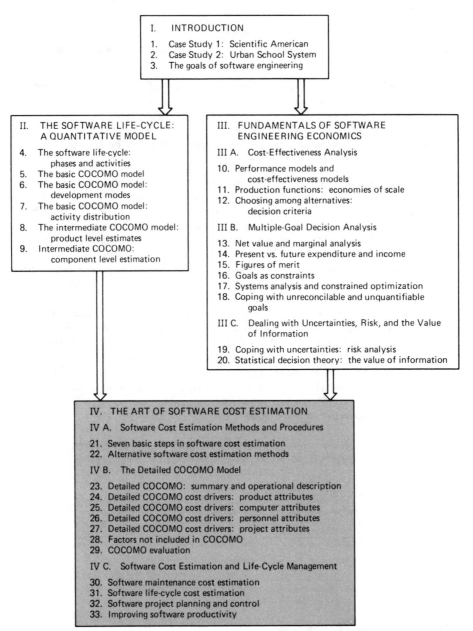

* [Miller, 1980] estimates the cost of a program proof activity in the range $50–500/instruction.

"Cost/Benefit Analysis for Incorporating Human Factors in the Software Lifecycle" by M.M. Mantei and T.J. Teorey from *Communications of the ACM*, Volume 31, Number 4, April 1988, pages 428–439. Copyright ©1988, Association for Computing Machinery, Inc., reprinted by permission.

New software engineering techniques and the necessity to improve the user interface in increasingly interactive software environments have led to a change in traditional software development methods. Methodologies for improvement of the interface design, an overview of the human factors element, and cost/benefit aspects are explored.

COST/BENEFIT ANALYSIS FOR INCORPORATING HUMAN FACTORS IN THE SOFTWARE LIFECYCLE

MARILYN M. MANTEI and TOBY J. TEOREY

Traditional software development breaks the software project into individual components that each perform specific functions in the process of putting together a software product [1, 9, 13, 18, 19, 23, 24, 27, 29, 31, 34, 35]. With the advent of new program development tools and the growing importance of human factors issues in the design and building of software, this accepted way of managing software development has given way to new ways of thinking about the process. In particular, because human factors issues arise at several of the stages and prototypes of the proposed system can be tested long before the final system is in place, many levels of design iteration are now introduced into the development process [7, 8, 17].

These added methods enhance the software product and help ensure its acceptance, in addition to reducing the product's maintenance [26, 30]. Thus, their inclusion is a justified and natural evolution of the software development process. Unfortunately, these methods also add to the dollar cost and the completion time of software projects. We will concentrate on the issue of *when* to include these techniques. An overview of those places within the traditional software development plan where human factors issues are treated, and the type of human factors work that applies will be discussed. Once the techniques are demonstrated, the costs are calculated using models similar to COCOMO

[5], but based on the use of prototyping software. These costs are used to develop cost/benefit analyses for determining when to use and when not to use each of the human factors techniques. These software development techniques were tried in actual development projects; building an integrated software package for a microcomputer and that of building a prototype forms screen interface to a relational DBMS [21].

Many important items related to software development will not be discussed. For example, the problems of staffing the proposed lifecycle, getting the different types of professions working together as a team, or the real issues of product deadlines and organizational structures are not addressed.

A DESCRIPTION OF THE HUMAN FACTORS LIFECYCLE

In order to establish a frame of reference for cost/benefit analysis, we will illustrate the changes to the traditional and prototyping lifecycle brought on by the incorporation of human factors engineering into the final product.

With the advent of prototyping (i.e., the ability to quickly build a preliminary version of the proposed software system), the traditional software lifecycle has undergone major upheaval [4, 6, 32, 33]. In the traditional lifecycle, future users of the software were unable to grasp the functions and support the software would provide until they viewed a finished or nearly finished product. Flowcharts, HIPO Techniques, Dataflow Diagrams, etc. [11, 22] do not adequately convey the actual workings of the system. Therefore, users cannot tell whether the designers have missed their mark and built a functionally useless system until late in the development process. This usually means expensive redesigns.

A prototype replaces the diagram designs of the design stage. With software prototypes, a user can get a *sense* of using the software tool before it has proceeded too far down the implementation trail. Thus, many more iteration and design changes take place early in the lifecycle. These changes to the traditional software lifecycle are shown in bold in Figure 1. The Human Factors Software Lifecycle is illustrated in Figure 2. First, a stage preceding the Feasibility Study called "Market Analysis" has been added. This stage determines the product to be developed, and usually runs focus groups with the intended users. It is different from the traditional Feasibility Study in that it examines people's perceptions and feelings about the information processing tasks that they currently perform. This approach is taken to find out if a software system which aids them in accomplishing these tasks will be adopted.

Following the Requirements Definition, a second human factor's stage has been added called "Product Acceptance Analysis." Now that the particular software product has been proposed, a mockup of what the product does can be presented to a sampling of its intended market. The future users' reactions to the mockup will generate information as to whether the software system, as currently envisioned, will be acceptable. This information is usually acquired via focus group studies and user surveys. Potential users of the system can also recommend changes at this point. This phase is particularly useful for testing whether the appropriate requirements have been specified.

Following the Product Acceptance Analysis, a "Task Analysis" is performed by the human factors specialist on the project. This analysis examines how the user *thinks* about the task and the *mental* data manipulation procedures he or she currently uses. The results of this analysis are applied in the System Design (Global Design and Prototype Construction) stage where the interface is tuned to match the thinking processes of the user. The System Design stage changes dramatically because many of the interface design decisions in the human factors structure are now negotiated with the human factors specialist working on the project.

Once the design of the system is finished, a prototype is built in the Prototype Construction stage. Part of the design stage may incorporate prototype construction, especially if the prototyping software in use separates the interface design from the rest of the software system. The finished prototype is used in the "User Testing and Evaluation" stage. In the testing portion of this stage, projected users perform a cross section of tasks intended for the system [2]. Problems they have with learning the system or with extended use of the system are incorporated into design change recommendations.

These changes are built into new prototypes, and testing continues until the learning and extended use patterns of the system are at acceptable levels of effort and ease-of-use, respectively.

The evaluation stage follows the testing stage. After users have gained some experience with the system, they can assess the system's performance of the desired functions and the adequacy of the provided features for learning the system. If the system does not do what the users require of it, the Requirements Definition stage is reopened and new requirements are drawn up to meet the users' needs.

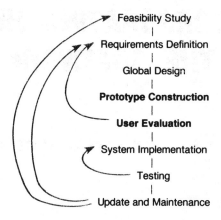

FIGURE 1. Typical Development Stages in a Prototyping Lifecycle

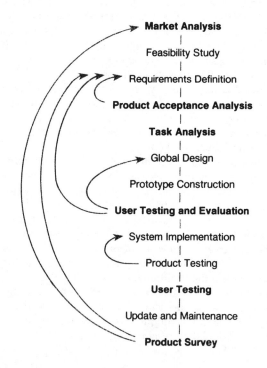

FIGURE 2. Development Stages in a Human Factors Software Lifecycle

Following the "User Testing and Evaluation" stage, the actual system is implemented. Once the system passes the unit and system tests in the "Product Testing" stage (the testing stage in the traditional lifecycle), it is put through a second round of "User Testing." These tests are performed on a working system. The results may differ from the prototype tests because of the differences in response time and complexity in the final system. These test results can also serve as benchmarks for expected human performance levels and learning rates. These values can be used to schedule training, estimate work output and market the software.

When the product is released, user feedback is obtained during the "Product Survey" stage. This is intertwined with Update and Maintenance. The data from this stage is used to drive updates. These updates are put into the system beginning with the Requirements Definition or the Market Analysis. The stage entered depends on the amount of change introduced by the proposed update. If the update dramatically changes the purpose and interface of the software, the entire Software Lifecycle is followed in its re-implementation. If it is a smaller change, the change can be incorporated beginning with a new requirements definition.

The human factors stages can be described within the traditional lifecycle, that is, a feasibility study that consists of a market analysis and cost/benefit studies, a requirements definition that includes the product acceptance analysis and the task analysis, a design stage that includes prototyping and user testing, a test stage that includes the user testing and an update and maintenance stages that includes the product survey. We have separately listed these stages in order to focus on the cost they add to software development and on the situations where they can provide desirable benefits for the project.

COST/BENEFIT ANALYSIS OF THE HUMAN FACTORS ADDITIONS

The projected costs for carrying out the psychological and marketing studies that form the human factors portion of the software lifecycle fall into two categories. Some of these costs and benefits can be quantified but others are ambiguous organizational and sociological gains and losses.

A Breakdown of Tangible Costs

In preparing a cost analysis, we have tried to parallel it with the COCOMO software development model [5] where possible. A $15.00 per hour wage rate is used for hourly employees and a $40.00 per hour wage rate is used for salaried employees. A prototypical software project is used in the calculations. The project is assumed to be built for 250 salaried in-house employees and to fall in the class of medium software projects (i.e., 32,000 lines of delivered source instructions [5]). Using these assumptions, a cost breakdown can be generated for the human factors expenses.

Individual cost components for the analysis can be categorized as either fixed rate or variable rate items, using currently accepted rates in the example:

Salaried employee (SE)	Fixed ($40/hr)
Hourly employee (HE)	Fixed ($15/hr)
External contractor (EC)	Fixed ($60/hr)
Consultant (CN)	Variable
Equipment and supplies (ES)	Variable
Software purchase (SP)	Variable

Only the first two categories (SE, HE) are directly applicable to the COCOMO cost model. Other personnel categories (EC, CN) are assumed in this study to be convertible to worker months (WM) for comparison of lifecycle stages. Furthermore, we do not use the 152 hours/WM recommended in the COCOMO model, that is, 35.3 hours per work week because we are converting the WM to dollars and therefore considering *paid* time as opposed to *worked* time in our model. Based on a 40-hour work week we used 172 hours/WM, applying the figure of 4.3 weeks or 21.5 days/WM. Thus our cost figures are approximately 13 percent higher than COCOMO estimates, or $6,880/WM for a salaried employee at $40/hr.

Eight distinct costs are added to a project by the human factors stages. These are:

(1) the cost of running focus groups;
(2) the cost of building product mockups;
(3) the expense of the initial design of a prototype;
(4) the expense of making a prototyping design change;
(5) the expense of purchasing the prototyping software (UIMS system);
(6) the cost of running the user studies;
(7) the cost of creating a user study environment (laboratory); and
(8) the cost of conducting the user survey.

The prototyping system purchase and the user lab construction are fixed costs with each software project amount reduced in proportion to the volume of software projects that undergo a human factors inclusion in their design. Table I breaks down the various human factors techniques and/or tools used in each of the new stages added to the software lifecycle. Table II breaks down the same human factors stages in terms of worker-months (WM) and total development time (TDEV). The cost of these tools and techniques is discussed further in the paragraphs which follow Table II.

Focus Group Cost Breakdown

The cost of running a focus group is the time cost of the individuals involved in the focus group plus a small equipment cost. This includes the participants, the moderator, the videotaping personnel and any additional staff watching the focus group behind a one-way mirror. Focus groups take approximately three hours to run plus one day to set up and one day to dismantle. A minimum of two days of analysis is needed to assess the results from the focus groups. On the average, ten future users form each focus group population, and a

TABLE I. A breakdown of the costs required to add human factors elements to the development of software

Lifecycle Stage	Cost Item	Total Cost
Market analysis	Focus group (set of 3)	$ 6,285
Product	Focus group (set of 3)	6,285
Acceptance	Product mockup	3,760
Analysis	User survey	7,200
Task analysis	User study	7,320
	Lab construction	17,600
Prototype	Initial design	6,400
construction	Design change (20 @ $320)	6,400
	UIMS system	16,080
User testing and	User study (4 @ $7,320)	29,280
evaluation	User survey	7,200
User testing	User study	7,320
Product survey	User survey	7,200
Total		**$128,330**

support staff of three employees plus the moderator are necessary. The moderator requires time for each focus group plus the two days of analysis. The three support staff are required for the set up, the focus group participation, and the dismantling following the last group. A complete focus group analysis, using three consecutive groups, takes approximately two weeks.

The projected costs for running typical focus groups are shown in Table III. The costs listed for focus group type A are for an in-house focus group using participants and facilities from inside the company. Those costs listed for group type B are for a completely contracted service from a marketing research company. Although the costs are much higher for a type B focus group, the marketing firm provides the appropriate par-

TABLE II. A breakdown of the worker-months (WM) and development time required to add human factors elements to the development of software

Lifecycle Stage	Cost Item	Total WM	TDEV[1]
Market analysis	Focus group (set of 3)	1.11[2]	6 wks
Product	Focus group (set of 3)	1.11	6 wks
Acceptance	Product mockup	.47	2 wks
Analysis	User survey	1.16	4 wks
Task analysis	User study	1.05	4.3 wks[3]
	Lab construction	1.05	5 wks
Prototype	Initial design	.93	4 wks
construction	Design change (20 @ .05 WM)	1.00	4 wks
	UIMS system	1.00	4.3 wks
User testing and evaluation	User study (4 @ 1.05 WM)	4.20	17.2 wks
	User survey	1.16	4 wks
User testing	User study	1.05	4.3 wks
Product survey	User survey	1.16	4 wks
Total		**16.45 WM**	**69.1 wks**

[1] Total development time
[2] E.g., 52 WM(SE) + .44 WM(HE) + .15 WM(CN)
[3] 1 month = 4.3 weeks

ticipants and facilities and carries out a thorough analysis of the participants' reactions.

For each information gathering session, an average of three focus groups are run. This is done because a focus group involves a small segment of the user population and may be a statistical anomaly. Running three groups does not avoid but does reduce the probability of these deviations. An unbiased marketing research firm is essential for running the internal focus groups. It is very unlikely that employees of a company will express their honest opinions unless they are guaranteed complete confidentiality through the external operation. An external research firm is also recommended for a focus group made up of individuals outside of the company. Marketing firms have resources for obtaining participants and expertise in setting up the facilities for a good session that may not be available within the company.

The cost of focus groups are fixed and do not change much with the size of the software project. They are

TABLE III. Estimated costs for conducting focus groups

Type of Expense	Category	Amount
A. Cost of Operating Three Internal Focus Groups		
30 participants, 10 per focus group (3 hrs each)	SE	$3,600
Group moderator (25 hrs)	CN	1,500
Three support staff (25 hrs each)	HE	1,125
Videotape	ES	60
Total		**$6,285**
B. Cost of Contracting Three External Focus Groups		
Fee charged by agency for complete study (3 focus groups and analysis for two weeks)	CN	$10,000

dependent on the variability and size of the expected user group, not on the code under development. More focus groups are necessary to capture data on a large and diverse user population. Table I uses the costs estimated for running an in-house focus group. Both the Market Analysis and Product Acceptance Analysis stages use focus groups.

Estimation of Product Mockup Costs
Building product mockups means constructing a false user interface scenario in software and generating a videotape of the scenario. The script for the voice overlay must be written and someone must be trained to execute the scenario. The videotape should be of sufficient professional quality to avoid negatively influencing future users of the software. Preparation and videotaping (including editing) usually take two weeks. Large companies have an AV department with staff available for preparing such a videotape. Smaller firms can usually rent the appropriate equipment and hire a person to prepare the videotape at minimal cost. Table IV illustrates the basic costs of this task. These are flexible depending on the desired quality of the videotape.

The videotape mockup is used in the Product Acceptance Analysis in two ways. A mockup is shown to focus group participants who are encouraged to vocalize their reactions to the software system. It is also shown to projected users who are asked to fill out a questionnaire designed to assess whether they will learn to use the software being demonstrated. The survey also probes the perceived needs of the user population and asks if the software demonstrated will respond to these needs.

In addition to the human factors uses, the mockup can also be used for marketing. It can be shown to senior managers to demonstrate what the software development group is working on and to potential investors or customers to explain the proposed product.

TABLE IV. Costs incurred in building a product mockup of the proposed software system

Type of Expense	Category	Amount
Preparation of mockup scenario (40 hrs)	SE	$1,600
Videotaping sessions (20 hrs)	SE	800
Splicing/integration of scenarios (20 hrs)	SE	800
Equipment rental for splicing, etc.	ES	500
Videotape	ES	60
Total		**$3,760**

Expense Layout for Conducting the User Survey
A user survey is the distribution of questionnaires to the future or current users. It is designed to collect information from these users on their reactions to the software system. User surveys are employed in the Product Acceptance stage to assess future users' responses to the video showing of the product mockup and to capture their suggestions for changes to the product design. Once the product is released they are used to determine the difficulties users have with the working system, to examine the tasks the system is being used for and to gather suggestions for changes to the existing system.

Survey researchers who are skilled in questionnaire design know where to place particularly difficult questions, when a person will not be able to respond truthfully to a question, how to test for the truthfulness of a response and, in general, how to elicit the maximum amount of information from a respondent with the minimum amount of questions. Without a good design, survey responses are worth little. Thus, a considerable amount of the expense for running a user survey is in the development of the questions. The cost breakdown for conducting a single user survey is listed in Table V.

For the user population of 250 employees in our prototypical example, at least half of the employees would receive a user survey. A typical survey is four pages in length and requires approximately one half hour for an individual to complete. The cost for conducting a user

TABLE V. Cost breakdown for running a user survey for the software product being tested.

Type of Expense	Category	Amount
Development of questionnaire (40 hrs)	SE	$1,600
Pilot testing of questionnaire (40 hrs)	SE	1,600
Distributing and collecting survey (20 hrs)	HE	300
Coding and entering data (20 hrs)	HE	300
Analyzing the results of the survey (40 hrs)	SE	1,600
Cost of time lost in filling out survey (40 hrs)	SE	1,600
Computer time	ES	100
Supplies and duplicating costs	ES	100
Total		**$7,200**

survey is extremely stable. Any increase in cost depends primarily on the number of users who receive the survey. The number of users surveyed need not rise if a good sample is taken. The task of taking an accurate sample, however, increases the overall costs of the user survey by $1,600 or forty additional work-hours. The entire survey requires approximately four weeks to run.

Initial Prototype Building Costs
Although considerable time is spent building a prototype, the cost breakdown for prototype construction excludes much of this time as design time and presents only that time required to build the actual prototype. The estimates shown in Table VI are based on a study that implemented a pre-designed system in three separate prototyping systems [20]. The time required to build the entire prototype is four weeks.

TABLE VI. Costs incurred in the initial design of a prototype of the proposed software system (the prior development of a global design is assumed)

Type of Expense	Category	Amount
Specifications of the screen transitions (80 hrs)	SE	$3,200
Design of the individual screen layouts (80 hrs)	SE	3,200
Total		**$6,400**

Most prototyping systems require a two-stage design specification. In the first stage, the connections between the screen displays must be specified. The second stage then involves the design of each individual screen layout. Advanced prototyping systems do not group design units into screen displays but into states between user interactions. The second stage design process is then the design of the individual states and the alterations that take place because of the user's action. The design work required for each stage is approximately equal.

As the interface grows more complex, the time required to build the prototype increases. If the complexity of the interface is characterized by the number of states required and the average number of new details to be specified in each state, the cost of building a prototype can be written as:

$$C = S(a + bD)$$

where

  C = Cost
  S = Number of states
  D = Average number of new details per state
  a = Constant reflecting the cost of building a single state
  b = Constant reflecting the cost of adding a single detail

The above model assumes little interconnection between states and the ability to copy detailed state descriptions from one state to another. It also ignores the effects of increases in the interconnections and, thus, the complexity of the interface design. These assumptions reflect a large variety of user interfaces and prototyping systems. The time projections for building the prototype also assume a powerful and flexible rapid prototyping package. Limited prototyping packages decrease the prototype building time because they are only able to produce simple interfaces, such as numerical menu selections. Using these systems is a dangerous practice. Their limitations may, in turn, limit the designer's conceptualization of creative interface designs.

Cost Breakdown for Design Changes to the Original Prototype

Once the prototype is built, the user tests will uncover difficulties that the user has in learning and using the system. The causes of these difficulties will be used to suggest design changes. Once the suggested changes are incorporated in the prototype, it will be tested again. The iteration of testing and updating the prototype will occur until the number and type of difficulties a user has with the system reach an acceptable level.

The initial user studies will uncover many problem areas that may lead to redesigns for parts of the system. Later changes are minimal. Since a task analysis and user surveys are used to build the basic design, the prototype is close to the final design. Therefore, any design changes will not constitute a complete redesign of the prototype but only update various parts of the prototype. This time saving allows an average of one day as the time estimated for a design change. The cost of each change is shown in Table VII.

The number of changes expected and the amount of time a change will take is dependent upon the complexity of the interface being constructed. The relationship is the same as the relationship shown for building the prototype.

The Prototyping Software Purchase

Commercially available prototyping systems range in cost from as little as $2,500 to over $15,000. Most systems that are powerful enough to provide graphics capabilities, design tools, and system management tools cost close to $10,000.

The various prototyping systems differ widely in the features and support they provide. The choice of a prototyping system depends on the match of features to the type of interfaces typically constructed by the software staff and the requirements for project management. The review and selection process for a prototyping package is expected to take at least a month. The time spent on making an intelligent purchase and the actual purchase cost constitute the complete price of the package. There is also a learning period in which interface designers acquire the knowledge to use the prototyping system. We do not include this learning in our cost appraisal which we show in Table VIII.

TABLE VII. Costs incurred in incorporating a design change to the original prototype of the proposed software system. These costs assume that the design change does not require a complete revision of the screen transitions

Type of Expense	Category	Amount
Modification of the screen transitions (4 hrs)	SE	$160
Redesign of the individual screen layouts (4 hrs)	SE	160
		——
Total		**$320**

The actual cost of purchasing a software package for a single project is quite low if the cost is distributed over several software projects. This distribution is not assumed in our cost analysis. If it were, the cost of the prototyping software would be negligible.

Cost Breakdown for Running User Studies

A typical user study presents an individual with a set of tasks to perform. As the user performs these tasks, measures are taken on the performance. These user studies are similar to psychological research since they take place in a laboratory and collect data on individuals. They are different from psychological research as they have no hypotheses to prove and no experimental treatments to administer.

TABLE VIII. Costs incurred in examining the market and purchasing a suitable prototyping system (UIMS)

Type of Expense	Category	Amount
Time spent reviewing potential packages (1 month)	SE	$ 6,080
Purchase cost of package	SP	10,000
		————
Total		**$16,080**

The major difficulty in conducting a user study is the preparation of material for the individuals being studied. Since the software system is new, a manual must be written. The manual need not be complete, but it must contain a complete description of those parts of the system which the individual will use in the study. In addition to the manual, a set of directions and a set of tasks are needed for the study.

In the first version of the manual, the directions and tasks will be incomplete, obtuse, and too difficult or easy for the user study. To correct these problems, a pilot of the user study is run on a small number of individuals. The feedback from the pilot is used to rewrite the instructions. Following the testing of the study material, the user study is run and analyzed. The entire process requires a month. Table IX presents a cost breakdown of the worktime used in the process and the videotape required.

TABLE IX. Costs incurred in conducting a single user study on five subjects

Type of Expense	Category	Amount
Development of subject directions (40 hrs)	SE	$1,600
Pilot testing of directions (20 hrs)	SE	800
Redesigning subject directions (20 hrs)	SE	800
Running experiment (40 hrs)	SE	1,600
Analyzing results of lab study (40 hrs)	SE	1,600
Videotape	ES	120
Cost of subjects in experiment (20 hrs)	SE	800
Total		**$7,320**

Three types of user studies are run in the Human Factors Software Lifecycle. The first of these is used in the Task Analysis. Instead of testing a software system on projected users, these users are asked to perform the types of tasks the software system will help them accomplish, but without the software system. Paper and pencil, calculators, file cabinets or an existing computer system may be used to replace the not-yet-built system. The videotapes of these sessions are used to build a model of how the users think about the tasks. This model guides the interface design.

The second and third user studies are more conventional with the second study conducted on prototypes of the system under construction and the final study conducted on the implemented system. A final study is always run because the actual system is different enough from the prototype system, that potentially serious user problems could be embedded in its design.

The cost of a single user study is typically unrelated to the complexity of the user interface being developed. Instead, if a user interface has many complex parts, the number of user studies conducted increases. This occurs naturally by the need to divide the interface into distinct user studies to avoid tiring the participants.

Costing the Construction of a User Laboratory
A laboratory in which to conduct user studies can be a borrowed office or a permanent facility. Permanent space is used when user studies are planned every month for many separate software efforts. A user study laboratory is a mockup of the natural environment where the software system will be used (e.g., an office). The individual being studied works in this environment. Ceiling mounted cameras and a one-way mirror allow human factors staff to record and observe the study session. The observation room is built next to the

TABLE X. Costs of establishing a permanent human factors testing laboratory. These are mid-level costs. Much more sophisticated laboratories can be built

Type of Expense	Category	Amount
Time spent laying out laboratory design and selecting lab equipment (160 hrs)	SE	$ 6,400
Cost of carpenter and electrician (20 hrs)	EC	1,200
Cost of cameras, VCRs, one-way mirror	ES	10,000
Total		**$17,600**

user environment and contains the recording equipment and the monitoring computers. Laboratory design and construction requires approximately five weeks.

Table X presents a cost breakdown for a small permanent facility, one which may be used four months each year for user studies.

The cost of the laboratory is independent of the software system. If it is used to test many software projects, the cost per development effort becomes negligible. The user study area can also be reconfigured for running the focus groups.

The type of laboratory environment generates an image of the software product being tested, so it is important that the furniture and equipment convey the desired image. For example, a machinist trying out numerical control software would not receive the software tests comfortably in a plush office. Nor would a secretary enjoy a user test conducted in a laboratory full of wires and measuring equipment.

Common Tangible Benefits Derived from Human Factors Design.
Although empirically gathered data is not presented here, the direct benefits from adding the human factors aspect to the project can be calculated by making several valid assumptions about the improvements to the interface. These improvements are:

(1) a reduction in user learning times;
(2) a reduction in user errors; and
(3) a reduction in the cost of maintaining the system.

The same size system used in calculating the added costs of human factors stages is used for calculating these estimates, that is, a 32,000 delivered source instructions system to be used interactively by 250 employees. A summary of the first-year savings (for salaried and hourly employees) from the human fac-

TABLE XI. Sample estimates of first year savings incurred through the introduction of human factors elements in the software design process

Type of Savings Incurred	Amount (HE)	Amount (SE)
Training costs (HE or SE)	$15,000	$ 40,000
Error reduction costs (HE or SE)	48,375	129,000
Avoidance of late design changes (SE)	24,000	24,000
Total	**$87,375**	**$193,000**

tors addition to the software development is shown in Table XI.

An Estimate of Potential Training Cost Savings
It is estimated that the learning time for the new system will be cut by one-fourth with the development of a human-factored system. If the turnover rate is fifty (hourly) employees per year and the learning time is typically two weeks of classes, the business has saved $15,000 a year in education costs. The cost savings for salaried employees is $40,000.

(Savings/Year)

= (Turnover) * (Training Time Saved) * (Wage)

= 50 * 20 * $15

= $15,000   for hourly employees

Calculating the Cost of Errors
It is also estimated that at least one *user trap* occurs regularly in each database retrieval scenario. A user trap is defined as a standard sequence of user responses where the user consistently makes an error. The errors are usually negligible and easily corrected, but extremely annoying to the user. These traps are a result of the interface design violating the learned behavior of the user. An analogous example is the experiences a driver has with a car with an automatic shift after driving a standard shift car. The User Testing stage catches these problems.

Suppose a user of the system had ten scenarios which they used regularly and a 0.025 probability of falling into a user trap. For a company with 250 employees using the system at least 3 hours a day and performing approximately 20 scenarios per hour, the company would encounter 375 traps per day. If it took 2 minutes to recover from each trap, a total of 62.5 hours or $937.50 would be lost per week because of these unremoved difficulties. This is a lower bound estimate. The recovery from a number of these traps takes as long as 10 minutes. To estimate the savings per year involved in removing a user trap from the design, the number of worker days per month are taken as 21.5 based on the 172 hrs/WM model. Using the calculations below and assuming the user is an hourly employee, an estimate of $48,375 is saved per year if a user trap with a 2.5 percent chance of happening is caught and removed from the system in the User Testing stages. For a firm with 25 employees, the savings is still considerable, $4,837 per year.

Errors/Year

= (No Emp) * (P[Error]) * (Scenarios/Hr) * (Hrs/Yr)

= 250 * 0.025 * 20 * (21.5 dy/mo) * 3 hr/dy) * (12 mo/yr)

= 96,750

Cost/Year

= (Errors/Yr) * (Hrs/Error Corr) * (Wage/Hr)

= 96,750 * (2 min/err) * (1 hr/60 min) * $15

= $48,375   for hourly employees

If the user is a salaried employee the cost savings per year are $129,000 for 250 employees and $12,900 for 25 employees, respectively.

Potential Savings Achieved by Early Change Detection
Harder to estimate is the amount of system maintenance time that was saved by engineering the system to match the thinking behavior and limitations of the users. The design changes that were incorporated in the prototype and the final system can be estimated to cost one-fourth of what they will cost to make in a released system. Let us assume that twenty-five necessary design changes occurred as a direct result of user tests on the prototypes. If these changes took, on the average, one day to implement in the prototype, then $24,000 was saved through early design changes. It is true that some of these user problems may never have been found and changed, but then, a new cost is incurred via the user's difficulties with the particular system problem.

Early Cost

= (Hr/Change) * (No. Changes) * (Wage/Hr)

= 8 * 25 * $40

= $8,000

Design Change Savings

= (Late Cost) − (Early Cost)

= 4 * (Early Cost) − (Early Cost)

= 4 * $8,000 − $8,000

= $24,000

A final yet very tangible benefit is system adoption. If careful planning is made for the system to meet the psychological and functional needs of the user, the system has a higher probability of acceptance and use. In this case, the benefit is the entire cost of system development which is not lost.

Intangible Costs of Human Factors Software Lifecycles
Intangible costs can occur in a software design project when human factors elements are included in the design process.

The Selection of Non-Critical Design Decisions for User Testing
User interface design can be a nightmare of detailed decisions. Should the selected text have a shadow border when displayed in reverse video or will the existing border be discriminable? If we permit a very large field width on a form, how should the form be displayed when the user types in more information than will fit on the computer screen? These questions cannot always be answered by the direct application of user interface design theory. Therefore, a designer will often opt to build a variety of solutions in a prototype and evaluate these solutions through user studies. Although there are many design decisions made in building an interface, many of them do not affect the quality of the user interface [25].

Human factors researchers often rely on intuition when determining which design issues are important to test, but they can be wrong. For example, the careful selection and testing of icon names to use in the Xerox Star interface did not reveal any differences in performance between the design choices [3]. It is possible to both spend time testing what appear to be crucial design decisions that will not affect the final software and to miss testing design decisions that are essential to the effective operation of the interface. Running the wrong user tests costs time and money. Missing the necessary ones makes their change more expensive when discovered at a later stage of software development.

One approach to this problem is to make the testing process open-ended enough so that information is always acquired from a user test. To uncover missed design problems, follow-up user tests are run on the final product, which do not, unfortunately, prevent the additional expense incurred from the earlier omission.

The Establishment of too High a Level of Usability
The application of human factors elements to software development can incur cost problems when user interface standards are set too stringently for the software system. It is easy to set standards for learnability and usability on paper, but difficult to meet these standards in the design of software. Often, the task of learning a software system is difficult because the task the system is designed for is difficult. Performance requirements for the system to be learned, in one week of training, might be impossible because the actual task cannot be learned in one week.

Few benchmarks exist for describing the level of performance expected of computer users. For example, only two published studies describe benchmarks for text editors. Digital Equipment has collected data on user performance with their "vi" editor [14] and Roberts and Moran [28] have established ballpark performance levels for nine text editors. Since few standard performance levels are available, it is extremely difficult to set performance standards for system use.

Information collected in the Task Analysis stage can be used to set user performance levels for the system tests, but this data is not infallible. It is important to establish incremental levels of improvement from current practices and to recognize that improvements to the user interface are iterative. Increased experience with new designs and new ideas will eliminate user problems in subsequent software systems. If this is not done, considerable time can be spent trying to implement a design to meet unreasonable requirements.

Falling into the Trap of Overdesign
A prototyping system makes it easy to design changes to a user interface, and a designer can fall into the trap of building more and more bells and whistles into the user interface. The additions do not necessarily increase functionality, but add details such as borders that uniquely identify different screen groupings or the installation of a running clock in the corner of the screen. The extra intangible cost is both that of the

designer's time and of the time needed to implement the final design.

The avoidance of overdesign requires strong management control and a regular review of the design process. As with program design, errors can be made both on the side of underdesign and overdesign where necessary features are left out and unnecessary features put in. User tests will not indicate overdesign problems but will pinpoint systems that do not have enough careful user design considerations. Most projects will incur some wasted costs in this area. These amounts will drop as human factors personnel obtain more experience in working with different levels of design complexity.

Communication Problems between Human Factors Specialists and Software Designers
A large problem with current human factors efforts in software development is the knowledge gap between the human factors specialist carrying out the human factors aspects of the user interface design and the computer scientists who are designing and building the system. The human factors specialist has been trained to recognize and interpret a wide variety of human behavior that the computer scientists will miss when observing a computer system user. Although the human factors specialist can recognize problems with system usage, the recognition of these problems has no translation into a software design specification. For example, consider the following user problem that human factors specialists have observed to occur with a pull-down menu. Users find the task of holding the button of the mouse in depressed mode while positioning the mouse to be difficult. Many menu selection mistakes occur with this selection mechanism. The obvious solution is to allow the menu to remain open when selected. Allowing the selected menu to remain open until a selection is made, however, introduces a large number of other design decisions such as whether a *close* selection option needs to be included in each menu and whether the menu should close automatically if the cursor moves away from the menu window. The human factors specialist working with the software team is often not aware of the ramifications a corrected problem has on the rest of the interface.

Individuals with human factor's training do not necessarily understand interface design tricks that software designers have developed through their profession. They cannot easily use a rapid prototyping system to design a user interface on their own. They need to work with individuals who have these design skills. This leads to a large communication cost. The human factors specialist needs to convey the entire nature of the user problem that is being solved and the software scientist needs to convey the possible solutions and their ramifications on other parts of the system. Until more expertise in each area is gained by both types of personnel, a communications overhead will exist on any project that incorporates the human factors methodologies. How much this overhead will cost has never been measured although Gould and Lewis [15] and Grimes, Ehrlich and Vaske [16] have captured a qualitative assessment of the problem.

Intangible Benefits from Human Factors Software Development

A variety of difficulties can occur with software that has not been *tuned* to its user. They cannot readily be measured. Intangible benefits accrue when these difficulties are removed from the software.

Adoption of Features Which Save Time

A reduction in feature adoption occurs when the complexity of the system causes its user to eschew learning advanced features. Davis [10] has shown that users will adopt the less complex software package if they can achieve the same functionality. Thus, if a task can still be carried out, albeit less efficiently, it is unlikely that more powerful features built into the system will be used. The Product Acceptance Analysis and the User Tests avoid the development of the unnecessary features and reduce their complexity, respectively.

Avoiding System Sabotage Problems

Some organizational situations can lead to employee sabotage. Being requested to use a system that is inappropriate, difficult, or inadequate for a task that an employee needs to get done can cause intense frustration. This frustration can be followed by entering inaccurate data or reporting false system failures [12]. The focus groups used in the Market Analysis and Product Acceptance stages are designed to test the receptivity of projected users for the software innovation. The Task Analysis is done to make the final product fit the users' conception of the task as closely as possible.

Enhancing the Ability to Solve Conceptual Problems Using the Software System

If a software system requires an intense amount of concentration on detail in order to carry out a task using the software system, this concentration takes away from an individual's available mental capacity for solving the problem. Although the problem is solved, it may not be solved as creatively. This loss in creativity that occurs with the use of a difficult system is difficult to measure, but the loss may be very large. The User Testing stage is designed to remove system complexities that can hamper creative problem solving.

Although the aforementioned costs and benefits can and do occur, since they are not measurable, they are often discounted in decisions to include or exclude stages in software development. Unfortunately, the dollar figures associated with the intangibles are usually much larger than those associated with the tangibles.

RECOMMENDATIONS FOR HUMAN FACTORS INCLUSION

A large amount of project management data collected over a large variety of projects is necessary to prepare a model for determining when human factors stages are to be included in the software lifecycle. The savings or

the costs of the decision to include human factors in the software are sensitive to a variety of phenomena. These include the type and number of system user, the complexity of the user interface being built and the amount and type of human factors stages that are included in the software development lifecycle. Since a model cannot be built and a tradeoff analysis performed from the small amount of data available, the qualitative aspects of the software project are used to make recommendations about the viability of including various human factors stages in developing the software.

The four factors that make the inclusion of human factors cost effective are listed in Table XII. They are matched with the human factors stages of the software development lifecycle most relevant to reducing the costs associated with these factors.

TABLE XII. The human factors lifecycle stages and the type of software cost reductions they are most likely to affect

Cost Reduction Item	Related Lifecycle Stage
Increased system adoption	Market analysis
	Product acceptance analysis
	User testing and evaluation
Reduced training costs	Task analysis
	User testing
Reduced user errors	Task analysis
	User testing
Transfer of design changes to an earlier stage in the lifecycle	Prototype construction
	User testing (on prototype)
	Product survey (next redesign)

If the use of the software or the software features being developed is discretionary, those stages that measure whether the software meets the needs of the user, both functionally and emotionally are important to add to the lifecycle. Performing a market analysis is a crucial step if the software is being developed for an external market, especially if it is a mass market.

If the software will be used by a large number of employees, the reduction in training costs and the time lost to user errors will make the Task Analysis and the User Testing stages cost effective. The cost of running user studies rises with the complexity of the interface. Since an interface built for many users is somewhat more complex than one built for a few users, the cost of running the user studies increases slightly with the number of users.

The savings incurred from running the user studies rises dramatically as the size of the user population goes up. These two functions intersect, as is shown in Figure 3. For user populations larger than the intersection point, it is appropriate to include the human factors efforts in the software design. The size of the user population is calculated over the life of the software system. If a system has ten users who will use the

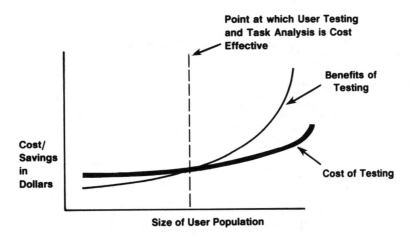

FIGURE 3. Cost of Running User Tests and Benefits Achieved from Running User Tests Graphed Against the Size of the User Population. When the Cost Curve Drops Below the Benefit Curve, these Steps can Achieve a Savings for the Software System

system for the next ten years, the size of the user population is measured as one hundred.

With or without the User Testing, the Prototype Construction stage will cause design changes to occur at an earlier, less expensive stage in the lifecycle. A prototype should always be used on complex projects where a later stage update or design change would be very expensive. A quick rule of thumb is to use a prototype when the cost of the prototype is less than one-fourth of the project cost. This assumes that potential design changes later in the project will cost at least that amount of additional change effort.

TABLE XIII. COCOMO model worker-month (WM) figures for organic mode projects translated to cost, using 172 hrs/WM

Project Size	WM	TDEV (Mo)	Cost @ $6,880/WM
Small (2 KDSI*)	5.0	4.6	$ 34,400
Intermediate (8 KDSI)	21.3	8.0	146,544
Medium (32 KDSI)	91.0	14.0	626,080
Large (128 KDSI)	392.0	24.0	2,696,960

* Thousands of delivered source instructions

In general, the human factors techniques are not recommended for small simple projects but for larger, more complex interfaces, especially those used by a large number of people. Of great interest, however, is the specific point at which human factors could be incorporated into the software lifecycle. To calculate this we must consider the tangible costs as a fraction of total cost of the software lifecycle. For example, if it were

acceptable to allocate a maximum of 25 percent of total project cost to human factors, the minimum project size required that could accommodate human factors would be 75 percent of total cost: 3 × $128,330 or $384,990. According to the COCOMO model, in Table XIII [5], this would require at least a medium-sized project (32,000 lines of delivered source instructions, or 32 KDSI) in any of the three modes of program complexity. A maximum allocation of only 10 percent to human factors would require a large-sized project (128 KDSI) for at least the organic mode of well-defined problems and a medium-sized project for more complex problems.

CONCLUSION

The goal of this article is to give the system analyst and project manager a description of the cost/benefit tradeoffs encountered when human factors methods are applied in software development. These methods are described through their incorporation into the existing management structure of software projects, and an explanation of what they provide to each stage of software development is given. The cost/benefit analysis is presented to provide a quantitative basis for deciding how to budget these methods.

Space is too limited to give a detailed description of the personnel needed to carry out the human factors tasks, to suggest organizational structures or to lay out the variations in the estimates that occur with differing project sizes. In short, this article is intended to fill the current gap that exists between the human-computer interaction research papers and the pragmatic needs of the software developer.

REFERENCES

1. Aron, J.D. *The Program Development Process Part II—The Programming Team.* Addison-Wesley, Reading, Mass., 1984.
2. Bennett, J., Case, D., Sandelin, J., and Smith, M. Eds. *Visual Display Terminals: Usability Issues and Health Concerns.* Prentice-Hall, Inc., Englewood Cliffs, N.J., 1984.
3. Bewley, W.L., Roberts, T.L., Schroit, D., and Verplank, W.L. Human factors testing in the design of Xerox's 8010 'Star' office workstation. In *Proceedings of CHI 83, Human Factors in Computing Systems* (Boston, Mass., Dec. 12–15). ACM, New York, 1983, pp. 72–77.
4. Boar, B.H. *Application Prototyping: A Requirements Definition Strategy for the 80's.* John Wiley & Sons, New York, 1984.
5. Boehm, B.W. *Software Engineering Economics.* Prentice-Hall, Inc., Englewood Cliffs, N.J., 1981.
6. Budde, R., Kuhlenkamp, K., Mathiassen, L., and Zullighoven, H. Eds. *Approaches to Prototyping.* Springer-Verlag, New York, 1984.
7. Buxton, W., and Sniderman, R. Iteration in the design of the human-computer interface. In *Proceedings of the 13th Annual Meeting of the Human Factors Association of Canada* (Point Ideal, Lake of Bays, Ontario, Canada, Sept. 4–6). Human Factors Association of Canada, Mississouga, Canada, 1980, pp. 72–81.
8. Carroll, J.M., and Rosson, M.B. Usability specifications as a tool in iterative development. In *Advances in Human-Computer Interaction,* Vol. 1, H.R. Hartson, Ed. Ablex, Norwood, N.J., 1985, pp. 1–28.
9. Cobb, R.E., Fry, J.P., and Teorey, T.J. The database designer's workbench. *Inform. Sci. 32* (1984), 33–45.
10. Davis, F.D. A technology acceptance model for empirically testing new end-user information systems: Theory and results. Ph.D. dissertation. Sloan School of Management, Massachusetts Institute of Technology, Cambridge, Mass., 1985.
11. De Marco, T. *Structured Analysis and System Specification.* Yourdon Press, New York, 1978.
12. Dowling, A.F., Jr. Hospital staff interference with medical computer systems implementation: An exploratory analysis. Working Paper No. 1073-79. Sloan School of Management, Massachusetts Institute of Technology, Cambridge, Mass., 1979.
13. Gane, C.P., and Sarson, T. *Structured System Analysis: Tools and Techniques.* Prentice-Hall, Englewood Cliffs, N.J., 1979.
14. Good, M., Spine, T.M., Whiteside, J., and George, P. User-derived impact analysis as a tool for usability engineering. In *Proceedings of CHI 86, Human Factors in Computing Systems* (Boston, Mass., Apr. 13–17). ACM, New York, 1986, pp. 241–246.
15. Gould, J.D., and Lewis, C. Designing for usability—Key principles and what designers think. In *Proceedings of CHI 83, Human Factors in Computing Systems* (Boston, Mass., Dec. 12–15). ACM, New York, 1983, pp. 50–53.
16. Grimes, J., Ehrlich, K., and Vaske, J.J. User interface design: Are human factor principles used? *SIGCHI Bulletin 17,* 3 (1986), 22–26.
17. Harrison, T. S. Techniques and issues in rapid prototyping. *J. Sys. Mgmt. 36,* 6 (1985), 8–13.
18. Jackson, M.A. *Principles of Program Design.* Academic Press, New York, 1975.
19. Kolence, K. *An Introduction to Software Physics.* McGraw-Hill, New York, 1985.
20. Mantei, M., and Culver-Lozo, K. A proposed benchmark for testing user interface management systems. Working Paper 479. School of Business Administration, University of Michigan, Ann Arbor, Mich., 1986.
21. Mantei, M.M., and Teorey, T.J. Human factors by example: A case study in applying human factors techniques to the development of a form screen interface to a relational database. Tech. Rep. 100987. Center for Information Technology Integration, University of Michigan, Ann Arbor, Mich., 1987.
22. Martin, J.P., and McClure, C. *Diagramming Techniques for Analysts and Programmers.* Prentice-Hall, Englewood Cliffs, N.J., 1985.
23. Metzger, P.W. *Managing a Programming Project.* Prentice-Hall, Englewood Cliffs, N.J., 1981.
24. Mills, H.D. Software development. *IEEE Trans. Softw. Eng. SE-2,* 4 (1976).
25. Norman, D.A. Design principles for human-computer interfaces. In *Proceedings of CHI 83, Human Factors in Computing Systems* (Boston, Mass., Dec. 12–15). ACM, New York, 1983, pp. 1–10.
26. Norman, D.A., and Draper, S.W. Eds. *User Centered System Design: New Perspectives on Human-Computer Interaction.* Lawrence Erlbaum Associates, Hillsdale, N.J., 1986.
27. Parnas, D.L. On the criteria to be used in decomposing systems into modules. *Commun. ACM 15,* 12 (1972), 1053–1058.
28. Roberts, T., and Moran, T.P. The evaluation of text editors: Methodology and empirical results. *Commun. ACM 26,* 4 (1984), 265–283.
29. Rubin, M.L. Introduction to the System Life Cycle. *Handbook of Data Processing Management, Vol. 1.* Brandon/Systems Press, Princeton, N.J., 1970.
30. Rubinstein, R., and Hersh, H. *The Human Factor: Designing Computer Systems for People.* Digital Press, Bedford, Mass., 1984.
31. Vick, C.R., and Ramamoorthy, C.V. Eds. *Handbook of Software Engineering.* Van Nostrand Reinhold, New York, 1984.
32. Wasserman, A.I. Rapid prototyping of interactive information systems. *Softw. Eng. Notes 7,* 5 (1982), 171–180.
33. Wasserman, A.I. The user software engineering methodology: An overview. In *Information System Design Methodologies.* A.A. Verrijn-Stuart, Ed. North Holland Press, Amsterdam, 1982, pp. 591–628.
34. Wirth, N. Program development by stepwise refinement. *Commun. ACM 14,* 4 (1971), 221–227.
35. Yourdon, E., and Constantine, L.L. *Structured Design.* Prentice-Hall, Englewood Cliffs, N.J., 1979.

CR Categories and Subject Descriptors: D.2.2 **[Software Engineering]:** Tools and Techniques—*user interfaces;* H.1.2 **[Models and Principles]:** User/Machine Systems—*human factors, human information processing;* K.6.1 **[Management of Computing and Information Systems]:** Project and People Management—*life cycle;* K.6.3 **[Management of Computing and Information Systems]:** Software Management

General Terms: Design, Economics, Human Factors, Management

Additional Key Words and Phrases: Human computer interaction, human factors life cycle, productivity, rapid prototyping, software economics, user testing

Received 3/87; revised 11/87; accepted 1/88

Authors' Present Addresses: Marilyn M. Mantei, Center for Machine Intelligence, Electronic Data Systems Corporation, 2001 Commonwealth Boulevard, Ann Arbor, MI 48105-1561 and Toby J. Teorey, Center for Information Technology Integration (CITI) and Electrical Engineering and Computer Science, The University of Michigan, Ann Arbor, MI 48109-2122.

Section 3: Risk Resolution Techniques

Section 2 of this tutorial covered techniques for assessing software risk items, and presented a process for managing their resolution. This section discusses the key techniques available for resolving risk items once they have been identified and assessed to be in need of resolution. Section 3.1 presents an overview of the risk resolution techniques identified as being most effective with respect to the top-10 risk items discussed in Section 2.3. Section 3.2 presents an overview of the tutorial articles in this section, which focus on risk resolution techniques in the key areas of rapid prototyping, performance engineering, and operational reliability and safety assurance.

3.1: Overview of Techniques

This subsection provides capsule descriptions of the key risk-resolution techniques identified in the checklist of top-10 risk items presented in Subsection 2.2.3. The checklist is reproduced here for convenience as Table 3.1. Further details on the most significant risk resolution techniques are provided in the tutorial articles later in this section; these articles are referenced as appropriate in the top-level summaries below.

Staffing and pre-scheduling key people: The biggest risks here are that your project becomes staffed with the most available people rather than with the best qualified people; or that vague promises to provide you with the best people are used as the basis for budgeting and scheduling, but are somehow forgotten once the project is underway. These risks are large: Cost models such as COCOMO indicate that there is a factor of 4 difference in productivity between staffing a project with a very strong team of people versus a team of mediocre people.

The best techniques for resolving such risks involve taking a pro-active approach: lining up the best people for your project, reference checking to ensure that they are a good fit for your project, working out their roles with them personally in advance, getting the appropriate managers to agree to pre-schedule the people for your project, and *documenting* these agreements so that everybody understands the commitments made.

Teambuilding: Teambuilding involves pro-active efforts to ensure that the various participants in a software development activity will be operating as teammates pursuing common, shared objectives rather than as antagonists or totally self-interested parties. The UniWord case study is a good counterexample. As the UniWord project demonstrated, teambuilding is important not only at the development team level, but equally so at the inter-organizational level: Universal Micros and SoftWizards did not make much of an effort to establish a team approach to UniWord. In accordance with the Theory-W principle, teambuilding should involve all of the key participants in the software process, including developers, managers, bosses, customers, users, and maintainers.

Teambuilding objectives involve the development of shared values, appreciation of each party's win conditions, and understanding of how the project approach will realize these win conditions. Teambuilding techniques include participative planning and objective-setting activities, blue-sky sessions, and group-consensus techniques such as the Delphi technique. A particularly effective technique is the "off-site," where participants from each concerned constituency meet in a pleasant, neutral, distraction-free location and focus on understanding individual and common objectives, and ways to achieve them. See [Dyer, 1987] for a more detailed discussion of teambuilding techniques.

Cost and schedule estimation: Techniques for cost and schedule estimation and risk reduction are discussed in Subsection 4.3 and in the [Edgar, 1982] and [Garvey-Powell, 1988] tutorial articles. The TRACE technique discussed in [Edgar, 1982] provides a particularly effective method for cost risk reduction. It involves estimating a cost risk factor—an additional cost increment which may be needed to cover project risk items —and establishes a budget reserve for dealing with such risk items as necessary. As risk items require additional budget to resolve, developers can receive additional funds if they prepare a convincing rationale that the added-funds route is the best way to solve the project's problem. However, developers are incentivized to avoid requesting additional resources: the less they tap into the risk reserve, the greater are their profits. The TRACE approach has been used successfully on several large U.S. Army procurements.

Design to cost: If a project's major risk items involve a fixed budget or schedule (e.g., a timed product announcement or a satellite launch), it makes more sense to make the project's budget and schedule the control variables, and to let the level of delivered functionality of the product be the dependent variable. The design-to-cost or design-to-schedule approach involves an early effort to prioritize software and system requirements into mandatory, desired, and optional capabilities; an architectural approach (e.g., information hiding [Parnas, 1979]) that makes it easy to defer the development of low-priority requirements; and a continuing modulation of the level of delivered functionality to keep it consistent with the available budget or schedule. The [Gilb, 1987] article in this tutorial provides additional guidelines

Table 3.1: A Top Ten Checklist of Software Risk Items

RISK ITEM	RISK MANAGEMENT TECHNIQUES
1. PERSONNEL SHORTFALLS	— STAFFING WITH TOP TALENT; JOB MATCHING; TEAMBUILDING; KEY-PERSONNEL AGREEMENTS; TRAINING; PRESCHEDULING KEY PEOPLE
2. UNREALISTIC SCHEDULES AND BUDGETS	— DETAILED MULTISOURCE COST AND SCHEDULE ESTIMATION; DESIGN TO COST; INCREMENTAL DEVELOPMENT; SOFTWARE REUSE; REQUIREMENTS SCRUBBING
3. DEVELOPING THE WRONG SOFTWARE FUNCTIONS	— ORGANIZATION ANALYSIS; MISSION ANALYSIS; OPS-CONCEPT FORMULATION; USER SURVEYS; PROTOTYPING; EARLY USERS' MANUALS
4. DEVELOPING THE WRONG USER INTERFACE	— PROTOTYPING; SCENARIOS; TASK ANALYSIS; USER CHARACTERIZATION (FUNCTIONALITY, STYLE, WORKLOAD)
5. GOLD PLATING	— REQUIREMENTS SCRUBBING; PROTOTYPING; COST-BENEFIT ANALYSIS; DESIGN TO COST
6. CONTINUING STREAM OF REQUIREMENTS CHANGES	— HIGH CHANGE THRESHOLD; INFORMATION HIDING; INCREMENTAL DEVELOPMENT (DEFER CHANGES TO LATER INCREMENTS)
7. SHORTFALLS IN EXTERNALLY FURNISHED COMPONENTS	— BENCHMARKING; INSPECTIONS; REFERENCE CHECKING; COMPATIBILITY ANALYSIS
8. SHORTFALLS IN EXTERNALLY PERFORMED TASKS	— REFERENCE CHECKING; PRE-AWARD AUDITS; AWARD-FEE CONTRACTS; COMPETITIVE DESIGN OR PROTOTYPING; TEAMBUILDING
9. REAL-TIME PERFORMANCE SHORTFALLS	— SIMULATION; BENCHMARKING; MODELING; PROTOTYPING; INSTRUMENTATION; TUNING
10. STRAINING COMPUTER SCIENCE CAPABILITIES	— TECHNICAL ANALYSIS; COST-BENEFIT ANALYSIS; PROTOTYPING; REFERENCE CHECKING

on design-to-cost and design-to-schedule, and related risk-resolution techniques, including incremental development.

Incremental development: Incremental development involves the organization of the software development into increments of functional capability rather than the more risky one-shot or "all-or-nothing" approach. It is also effective in resolving potential requirements-volatility risk items, as proposed changes in the requirements can often be deferred to later increments. A particularly good set of guidelines for the use of incremental development to reduce and resolve development risks is given in [NSAM, 1987]:

- Early increments should cover high-priority user requirements and high-risk but well-understood requirements
- Late increments should cover poorly-defined or less well-understood requirements
- Device-oriented software increments should be synchronized with device availability

Requirements scrubbing: The requirements prioritization activities discussed under Design to Cost and Incremental

Development are also good for eliminating "requirements" that sound attractive but which are not really necessary to the mission the software is supporting. A cost-benefit analysis is an effective way to scrub unnecessary requirements. Another is an affordability review, specifically organized to identify and eliminate gold-plating and marginally useful capabilities. See [Boehm, 1981, Chapter 11] for a checklist of requirements areas that are frequent sources of gold-plating. Prototypes are also very effective in scrubbing requirements. [Boehm-Gray-Seewaldt, 1983] summarizes the results of a seven-project experiment in which the use of a prototyping approach correlated with resulting software products with roughly equivalent capability but an average of 40 percent less code.

Prototyping: Prototyping involves the development of a representative subset of a software product, primarily for the purpose of buying information to reduce risk. The risks addressed by the prototype generally involve functionality, performance, and user interface issues, but can also involve other risk items (e.g., fault tolerance). Several effective prototyping techniques are available, particularly:

- Spreadsheet and fourth-generation-language capabilities, which support the rapid configuration of small computational and database-oriented software systems

- Object-oriented system development capabilities, which support the rapid configuration of applications organized around hierarchical classes of entities or objects

- Artificial intelligence support systems, which can be quickly configured and interpreted to represent various classes of small applications

- Three-phase conventional language systems, primarily oriented toward rapid prototyping of graphical user interfaces. Phase 1 involves the interactive specification-by-example of a complex of displays and controls. Phase 2 involves compiling the prototype from a set of primitive components. Phase 3 involves executing the resulting prototype and gathering data on its experimental use

Prototypes may be either throwaway or build-upon, depending on the relative risks of using the resulting code operationally. The three-phase and most AI capabilities tend to be fragile and better suited to throwaway prototyping. Spreadsheets, fourth-generation languages, and some object-oriented capabilities are sufficiently robust to support build-upon prototyping of small applications. Further information on prototyping approaches is provided in the [Mantei-Teorey, 1988], [Carey-Mason, 1983], and [Wasserman et al., 1986] papers in this tutorial.

Mission analysis: Several types of mission analysis techniques are available to support risk resolution. The most prominent are:

- *Organizational analysis:* The analysis of a user's mission and its support by constituent organizational elements, including analysis of organizational responsibilities, lines of authority, incentive structures, and information processing support

- *Operational concept formulation:* The characterization of a user's mission in terms of operations, including task sequences, data flows, controls, and operational procedures

- *Cost-benefit analysis:* The analysis of the relative costs and benefits of supporting a user's mission with various combinations of data processing and other capabilities

- *User engineering:* The analysis of data processing system user task support in terms of users' characteristics and workstyles. For example, if a user-workstyle analysis shows that a system's users consistently work better one-task-at-a-time, it will be risky to provide them with a multi-window workstation with several tasks competing for the user's attention

Information hiding: Changes in software requirements are both inevitable and major sources of project risk. A most effective technique for minimizing requirements volatility risk is information hiding. This technique, developed by Parnas and best described in [Parnas, 1979], involves determining the major directions of anticipated changes in software requirements, and hiding these sources of change within individual software modules. Thus, for example, if one anticipates that workstation characteristics will change throughout a software product's life cycle, one can hide these sources of change within a "workstation-handler" module. Then, when the workstation characteristics actually change, the ripple effects of the change are limited to the workstation-handler module.

Reference checking: Many projects have failed because of risks in external components that could have been resolved fairly straightforwardly by reference checking: contacting existing users of the component to verify that it will be satisfactory with respect to ease of use, ease of change, controllability of changes, robustness, scalability, or other critical project risk factors. Frequently, consultants can be very helpful in reference-checking software components as well.

Pre-award audits: A number of checklists and associated techniques are available for performing audits of a software contractor or subcontractor to resolve the risk of their being incapable or unprepared to perform the contracted software tasks. The [Humphrey et al., 1987] assessment technique provided in Section 2 of this tutorial is one good example; another is [Babel, 1985].

Performance engineering: A variety of techniques are available to reduce the risk that a software system's performance will be inadequate. The most effective are:

- *Simulation:* A number of packages are available for simulating the performance of data-processing systems to determine how effectively they will process a given workload. A rapid simulation capability is described in the [Swinson, 1984] article in this tutorial

- *Benchmarking:* Executing the software components under question on a representative workload, and analyzing their resulting behavior

- *Modeling:* Exercising an analytic model of the system's performance (e.g., a queueing theory model) to determine performance capabilities and limitations

- *Prototyping:* Developing and exercising a representative prototype of the performance-critical elements of a software application

- *Instrumentation and tuning:* Measuring a system's performance characteristics and bottlenecks, and tuning the system's parameters (task sequences, task priorities, data distribution, system connectivity, etc.) to eliminate the bottlenecks and improve performance

The [Bell, 1987] article in this tutorial expands on these and related options for performance-engineering risk reduction.

Technical analysis: Analogues to performance analysis are available for other critical success factors that strain computer science capabilities: e.g., AI, distributed processing, fault-tolerance, multilevel security, algorithmic accuracy. For ensuring software trust (reliability, security, fault-tolerance, and graceful degradation), a variety of technical analysis capabilities are available such as fault-tree analysis, failure modes and effects analysis, and static and dynamic analysis of programs and specifications. The [Cha et al., 1988] and [Neumann, 1986] articles in this tutorial provide some particular examples of such analysis capabilities; a more extensive survey of them is provided in [Leveson, 1986]. The [Brown, 1986] and [Hoffman, 1986] articles from the *Proceedings of the Ninth National Computer Security Conference* provide good descriptions of computer security risk analysis and risk resolution techniques.

3.2. Overview of Tutorial Articles

The first two articles address rapid prototyping techniques for risk resolution. The [Carey-Mason, 1983] article addresses rapid prototyping in general; the [Wasserman et al., 1986] article particularly addresses rapid prototyping of interactive information systems, with a strong user-interface component.

The next two articles address techniques for resolution of computer-system-performance risks. The [Bell, 1987], article summarizes overall performance-engineering risk areas and resolution techniques; the [Swinson, 1984] article focuses on rapid simulation as a tool analogous to rapid prototyping for addressing performance risks.

The next three articles address operational reliability and safety risk-resolution techniques. The [Cha et al., 1988] article describes the use of fault-tree analysis tools to resolve software-safety risk items. The [Neumann, 1986] article discusses hierarchical design and development techniques to resolve software security and reliability risk items. The [Kahane, et al., 1988] article addresses backup techniques for resolving data-processing equipment failure risks.

The final article in this section, [Gilb, 1986], presents techniques for resolving risks of meeting (overly) ambitious software development schedules.

3.2.1: Prototyping Techniques

As discussed in Section 2, one of the most attractive ways to reduce software risk is via buying information about the software system by developing, exercising, and iterating prototypes of appropriate high-risk software or system elements. The first paper in Section 3, "Information System Prototyping: Techniques, Tools, and Methodologies" [Carey-Mason, 1983], provides a good summary of the basic concepts of prototyping. It identifies the primary advantage of prototyping as the enhancement of system quality

through better requirements specification. It does not deal explicitly with concepts of risk, but its basic intent of early problem identification and resolution is similar to the risk management approach.

The article considers the three primary benefits of prototyping to be improved functional requirements, improved interaction requirements, and easier evolution of requirements. (Improved performance requirements has also been a major benefit of prototyping.) The article identifies and discusses the pros and cons of three primary prototyping techniques: scenarios, demonstration (throwaway) systems, and version-0 (build-upon) systems. It provides a good survey of the 1976-1981 prototyping literature, and a well-categorized survey of early-1980s prototyping tools (primarily APL, fourth-generation languages, and user-interface tools) in the table constituting the paper's appendix.

The next article, "Developing Interactive Information Systems with the User Software Engineering Methodology" [Wasserman et al., 1986], provides a representative example of a prototyping support system and methodology. These are focused on a class of applications called interactive information systems: systems that provide conversational access to data, typically for persons who are not experts in computing. For such systems, the methodology involves three primary steps: data modeling, characterization of operations on data, and user-interface prototyping.

The support system, RAPID/USE, provides tools that address each of these steps. The user interface prototyping tool is based on a state-transition-diagram representation of the interaction between the user and the information system. It includes a transition-diagram editor for organizing user-interface controls and displays, and a transition-diagram interpreter for interactively exercising them. The system accommodates both throwaway and build-upon prototyping approaches, although it would have some scaling difficulties for very-large interactive-information systems. The system definition aids have evolved into one of the leading commercial software toolsets, Software through Pictures.

The paper provides a good example of the system and methodology's use on an example involving an interactive library information system. It also has a useful summary of the lessons learned in using and evolving the methodology and tools over several years.

3.2.2: Performance Engineering Techniques

Another of the top–10 software risk items discussed in Section 2 was Real-Time Performance Shortfalls. Even with (or especially with) the rapid improvements in computer hardware speed, it is all too easy to develop computer-based systems with insufficient performance. Frequently, this happens because performance risk items are either not identified or are deferred in the hope that they will go away.

The next article, "Performance Engineering: Doing It "Later" on Large Systems" [Bell, 1987], provides a valuable set of checklists of the most frequent performance risk items occurring during each of the system and software development phases. It also provides well-chosen examples of actual systems that failed because of the performance risk items, along with an identification of the performance engineering techniques that would have eliminated the source of risk. The journal containing the article, the *CMG* (Computer Measurement Group) *Transactions,* is a particularly good source of practical guidance and experience on more detailed performance engineering techniques.

Another powerful performance engineering capability is a rapid simulation tool for information systems, particularly distributed-data-processing systems. The next paper, "Workstation-Based Rapid Simulation Aids for Distributed Processing Networks" [Swinson, 1984], describes the architecture, usage, and applications experience with one such tool, called RSA for Rapid Simulation Aids.

RSA enables a systems engineer or performance engineer to operate at a high-performance workstation (here, a Sun) to interactively specify the hardware architecture, software task structure, performance parameters, and workload characteristics of a given distributed-data-processing system. RSA then translates this information into the input parameters of a large VAX-based event simulator for distributed-data-processing systems called ASSIST. Once ASSIST has completed the simulation run, the results are fed back to the Sun workstation, where RSA provides a number of interactive-performance-analysis aids. These include data-view selection, time lines, bar charts, pie charts, probability distributions, report generation, and various hard-copy options. They give the system engineer a way of flexibly navigating through the performance data to investigate problems and critical-performance characteristics such as resource utilization and contention, queue buildups, bottlenecks, and wait times.

An example, which shows the time and effort savings achievable from using RSA for this type of analysis, is given. For a fairly large system (74 processing elements), the RSA-based analysis was completed in 3.5 days; typically, similar analyses had taken 4 to 6 weeks previously. Thus, rapid simulation supports risk management in roughly the same way as rapid prototyping: It provides an efficient way to reduce risk by buying information on the performance characteristics of a complex distributed hardware-software architecture.

3.2.3: Operational Reliability and Safety Risk Resolution

The next three articles present techniques for reducing the risks associated with the operational reliability and safety of complex computer systems. The first article, "Safety Verification in MURPHY Using Fault Tree Analysis" [Cha et al., 1988], describes a methodology and set of tools called MURPHY that identify and analyze the risks of software faults in safety-critical systems.

The methodology involves operational analysis of the system to identify fault conditions and to prioritize them with respect to operational safety risk. Thus, for example, a software fault that loses some scientific data is less critical than one that endangers human life. A top-level checklist is provided of software conditions leading to unsafe behavior: failing to perform a required function, performing a function not required, failing to enforce required sequencing, failing to recognize a hazardous condition requiring corrective action, and producing the wrong response to a hazardous condition.

The next steps in the MURPHY methodology are to perform system-level and code-level fault-tree analyses. Fault-tree analysis involves tracing events backward from undesired fault states to determine their potential causes. If a valid logic path leads from a cause (hardware or software failure) to the undesired state, the failure must either be eliminated or compensated for, to ensure that the undesired fault state is never reached.

The MURPHY toolset includes a fault-tree editor that specifies and modifies fault trees, a fault-tree artist for preparing fault-tree diagram layouts, and the beginnings of a fault-tree generator to analyze Ada code and to produce fault trees. The key to the fault-tree toolset is a set of templates characterizing the fault conditions associated with a type of programming language statement or a logic element. Thus, for Ada, MURPHY provides fault-tree templates for 16 Ada constructs, including assignments, branching, looping, calls, selects, aborts, exceptions, and task rendezvous.

The paper provides an example of the use of MURPHY to perform a fault-tree analysis of an Ada program for controlling traffic lights. The paper also has an extensive list of references to other software-safety-risk management literature, including a very comprehensive *ACM Computing Surveys* article [Leveson, 1986].

To eliminate operational safety and reliability risks, one would like not only techniques for identifying and resolving risk situations, but also system and software design principles for avoiding the occurrence of such risks. The next paper, "On Hierarchical Design of Computer Systems for Critical Applications," [Neumann, 1986], provides a candidate hierarchical design approach for achieving this objective. It involves the structuring of a critical system into design layers such that flaws in, or misuse of, the higher-level layers cannot contaminate the lower layers, and such that faults in the lower-level layers can be contained or recovered from without compromising the operations of the higher layers.

The paper expands on this approach in some detail. It presents principles of hierarchical design, based strongly on Parnas' "uses-hierarchy." It discusses various candidate criticality hierarchies applicable to fault-tolerant operation, networking, hardware-software survivability and vulnerability, and expert-system soundness. It describes hierarchical design approaches that have been used to date, such as multilevel security and integrity kernels, distributed secure-system architectures, capability-based architectures, and network-protocol layers. It also discusses useful design principles such as least privilege, information hiding, and preservation of hierarchical ordering.

Based on these elements, the paper then provides a good candidate five-level design hierarchy for developing critical systems: kernel, generalized trusted computing base, computer-subsystem interface, end-user interface, and user programs. The paper is included in the September 1986 special issue of the *IEEE Transactions on Software Engineering* on *Reliability and Safety in Real-Time Process Control,* which contains several other good articles on the topic as well.

The two previous articles presented techniques for reducing operational risks via analysis of fault cause-effect relationships and via hierarchical design of hardware-software architectures. At an even more aggregated level, many large organizations have to deal with the operational risk of overall computer center failures. Even if the probability of such a failure is low, the potential losses are so high (e.g., corporate bankruptcy) that the combined risk exposure is crucial to address.

There are a number of risk reduction techniques that can be applied in such situations, including the operation of hot backup computer systems, warm backups, split computer sites, cold backups, mutual backup agreements, and backup pools. The next paper, "Computer Backup Pools, Disaster Recovery, and Default Risk" [Kahane et al., 1988], provides an analysis of the last-named backup-pool option. This is an arrangement in which several organizations join a pool to keep a standby backup computer center available for the use of any member suffering a computer center failure.

The paper addresses such issues as the optimal number of members in the pool and the appropriate membership fee to be paid by each member. These are analyzed as functions of the computing capacity available in the pool, each member's required computing capacity, the probabilities of failure of the backup and the members' computing centers, and the members' utility functions for assured computer operation. The analysis provides an interesting bridge between computer and software risk management and classical insurance risk management, in that the membership fees are basically equivalent to insurance premiums.

3.2.4: Schedule Risk Resolution

The risk of a software project exceeding its delivery schedule is simultaneously one of the most serious and one of the most common risk items with which a software project manager must deal. To be commissioned at all, a software product must have some considerable value. Naturally, the beneficiaries of this value would like to have it right away. Thus, there is almost always a strong pressure to accelerate a software project's schedule. All too frequently, the software project manager is insufficiently prepared to cope with such schedule risks, and creates a strong potential win-lose or lose-lose situation by promising a very optimistic software-delivery schedule.

The final paper in this section, "Deadline Pressure: How to Cope with Short Deadlines, Low Budgets, and Insufficient Staffing Levels" [Gilb, 1986], presents ways to resolve project schedule slippage risks (and budget overrun risks also). It defines a number of useful techniques for relieving the schedule pressure, such as:

- Redefining the problem
- Using evolutionary delivery or incremental development
- Refusing to accept the deadline
- Redefining the solution

Of the technical solutions to deadline pressure suggested in Section 3 of the paper, evolutionary delivery is by far the most effective. The other suggestions, Fagan inspections and attribute specifications, are useful techniques, but with considerably less schedule leverage. Techniques with considerably more leverage include most software-cost-estimation models, which add a significant cost penalty for schedule compression, or report that the proposed delivery schedule is infeasible; software reuse; very-high-level languages, or negotiating for more capable and experienced people to staff the project.

INFORMATION SYSTEM PROTOTYPING: TECHNIQUES, TOOLS, AND METHODOLOGIES*

T.T. CAREY AND R.E.A. MASON

University of Guelph

ABSTRACT

"Prototyping" is frequently cited as an effective alternative technique to traditional approaches for the development of systems. This paper reviews recent literature on the subject and categorizes prototyping techniques that appear to be widely used. A large number of tools have been used for prototyping and they are discussed in relation to the technique employed and other factors in the programming environment. Issues of programming methodology raised by prototypes are also discussed.

RÉSUMÉ

Pour la création de systèmes d'information, on choisit souvent, plutôt que les approches traditionnelles, la méthode efficace des prototypes. Dans le présent rapport, nous examinons des documents récents traitant du sujet et rangeons en catégories les différents procédés de mise au point de prototypes les plus souvent utilisés. Un grand nombre d'instruments ont servi à l'élaboration de prototypes; ceux-ci seront étudiés par rapport aux techniques employées et aux autres facteurs relatifs à la programmation. Les points soulevés par les prototypes concernant la méthodologie de la programmation seront aussi analysés.

1. INTRODUCTION

Although the concept of the prototype is widely referenced in the recent computing literature, there appears to be little if any agreement on what a "prototype" is. In broad terms, the prototype attempts to present the user of a system with a relatively realistic view of the system as it will eventually appear. Users are thus able to relate what they see in the form of prototype directly to their requirements.

The use of prototypes appears to have advantages in user communication but raises other issues in system development. Different, non-traditional development tools may be required; the initial cost for the requirements phase of the development cycle may be greater; and there is the possibility of loss of distinction between phases and the development process. Despite such issues, there appears to be a growing consensus that prototypes form an effective component of an application development methodology.

In this paper we present a survey of the literature of application prototyping, and an analysis of the advantages of prototyping. Following distinctions made by Freeman[1], we discuss different categories of prototype techniques, the tools used to support these formal techniques, and some of the management or methodological issues they raise. An appendix summarizes these three parameters in prototype case studies from the literature. We restrict attention throughout to information systems as traditionally understood and as described by Wasserman[2]. Prototyping of systems software[3] is not considered in this paper.

1.1 Prototypes and system requirements

It is well understood that undetected errors that occur in the require-

*Received 9 July 1981; revised 21 December 1982

ments phase of system development are the most costly to repair in later stages. User approval of a requirement specification is mandated by most data processing managements as a means of correcting the requirement specification. Depending upon the application environment and the development methodology, the user may have access to a variety of developer-produced materials before certifying that his requirements have been correctly defined. Software blueprints[5] and SREM[6] are examples of specialized languages as a part of the users/developer interface for real time applications. These requirements languages presuppose sophisticated user representatives operating within the development methodology.

In conventional data processing environments, user participants in the development phase are normally middle managers, and reliance upon such specialized skills is not appropriate. (Zahniser[4] and Mason[7] describe other differences between environments that affect the user / developer interface.) Requirements documentation presented to users can be broadly classified as one of the following three forms:

1. Textual lists of requirements that the proposed system must fulfil. Text description has been the traditional tool. Unfortunately, such descriptions, often lengthy and boring, are psychologically very distant from what the users will eventually receive. Even after significant effort on the part of the user to understand such documents, critical features of the system may not receive appropriate notice. For interactive systems textual description is clearly not an appropriate requirements specification technique.

2. An interpretive model of the proposed system. SADT[8] and USE[9] are examples of interpretive models. These techniques employ top down decomposition to manage relatively complex systems. They maintain distinction between functional specification and design and permit data analysis to be treated separately. Other features of interpretive models are discussed by Scharer[10] and finer classification appears in Peters and Tripp[11]. Again, however, on-line interaction is difficult to communicate with these models.

3. A working model, or prototype, of the proposed system. Prototypes, on the other hand attempt to present the user with a realistic view of the system as it will eventually appear. With prototypes a distinct attempt is made to produce a "specification" which users can directly experience. Communication with users, particularly the non-specialist middle management user, is a major motivator behind the recent interest in prototypes.

1.2 Prototyping as a folk fact: skimming the literature

David Harel's light-hearted article on folk theorems in computing[12] proposes as criteria for a folk theorem that it demonstrate popularity, anonymous authorship, and age. If we examine the assertion "Prototyping reduces specifications error," we can claim that it has the appropriate "folkishness," that is, it has been cited extensively in the literature[13–31]; in each case its origins are attributed either to folklore or the author's discovery,* and DP professionals will frequently state that they were doing it that way in 1401 Autocoder (relatively aged).

Furthermore, the multitude of prototype forms and labels attest to a genuine article of folklore. The assertion never having been proved in a rigorous sense, we are left with a folk fact rather than a folk theorem. Attempts to produce experimental evidence supporting the assertion,

*The lack of any cross-references to other prototype papers may be instructive as to the reading habits of both industry professionals and academics.

rather than simply testimonials, are plagued with the well-known difficulties of creating a long-term and controlled experiment in an industrial management setting of sufficient size to be statistically significant.

The general objectives within which prototypes are referenced in the professional literature are varied. Brittan[13] justifies prototypes in large part by bad example: "look what happens if we don't use them." There is consequently less interest for tools and techniques and more for a change in the attitudes behind the traditional development cycle and its limitations on user participation. Similarly, Berrisford and Wetherbe[14] and McLean[26] are concerned primarily with reducing the "adversarial" nature of a conventional requirements sign-off.

Another direction from which prototypes have been approached involves a specific tool that has made prototypes seem more cost-effective to the developers. Thus Davis and Tweedy[16], Kebel and Marling[20], Bishop and Gore[15], and Goodman[19] all mention prototypes as side effects of program development systems. Each of these systems encompasses a variety of automated techniques, which, as a byproduct, facilitate creation of working views of the system for user comment. Another class of tools frequently referenced is the new set of higher-level languages (sometimes labelled fourth-[29] or even fifth[32]-generation languages). These permit shorter development times for various functional applications. Their promoters have cited quick prototyping as one of the advantages of their use. This is particularly true of APL; see, for example, Jones and Kirk[24], and Martin[27].

Some considerations of prototypes are not directed at the requirements phase of the life cycle. Thus Jones[23] examines prototypes within a careful consideration of techniques for design defect removal. Rosenburger[30] is concerned with an early return on investment, so that a prototype representing 80% of functional capability, but only 20% of the development cost is recommended for its quick payoff to the users. (Some misgivings about this approach from a methodology viewpoint are mentioned in section 5). A measurement of requirements uncertainty is proved by Naumann, Davis, and McKeen[33], suggesting the circumstances under which the cost of a prototype can be most easily justified. The relationships among their situational variables and the point at which a prototype is recommended are recognized as dependent on local management policies and the availability of tools.

Our focus in this paper is on improving the final information system product through use of prototypes to illuminate more clearly the user's real needs. Thus we have not pursued the benefits of improved relationships between developers and users (it can be argued that prototypes merely enforce a communication pattern that should also exist in the traditional development cycle).

In addition, no attempt is made here to detail the relationship between improved product quality and eventual system cost. We are satisfied with the usual consensus that the earlier defects are removed from a product, the lower will be its eventual cost. The somewhat higher costs of development using prototypes are generally agreed by all the literature sources to be more than covered by either lower maintenance costs or better utility for the user.

2. PROTOTYPES AND SYSTEM REQUIREMENTS

From the point of view of enhancing system quality through better requirements specification, the advantages cited for prototypes fall into three categories: improved functional requirements, improved interaction requirements, and easier evolution of requirements. This list is adapted from the thorough description of decision support prototypes by Keen and Gambino[21].

2.1 Improved functional requirements

The prototype system reflects the developer's interpretation of the user's needs, captured previously in either formal or informal communication. When this communication has been distorted by various preconceptions or general unfamiliarity with the environment on either side, the prototype will frequently reveal how the misunderstanding will affect the product. This is particularly necessary for users with limited exposure to information system technology. The degree to which the prototype uncovers errors in functional logic, in addition to the range and type of function to be performed, is dependent on the particular technique employed, as considered in section 4.

2.2 Improved interaction requirements

The interaction requirements for a system are not always directly addressed in requirements specification. This is especially true if the clients are not the (direct) users. While the system may contain the correct functions, the design of the user interface may either discourage its use or introduce errors in usage.

A useful evaluative model for the user interface is Foley's[34] top-down interface design model. This model partitions the interface structure into successively more specific components: conceptual level, semantic level, syntactic level, and lexical level.

On the conceptual level one is concerned with the basic set of concepts underlying the user's view of the application. An example of a flaw in requirements at this level occurred in our development of a small application in which the requirements document specified certain files and certain tables of code interpretation. When the users began to interact with a preliminary version of the system, it became clear that the developer had conceptually separated the files and the tables, but the users did not distinguish them. They were surprised when the tables failed to function as files.

The semantic level deals with the information content that must pass between the user and the (machine) system, without specific regard for its format. When working through a demonstration, the user frequently notes that information is being requested that is not applicable to a given transaction type. Another common flaw at this level is a lack of information from the system for help or error recovery. While a prototype need not be expected to embody all the assistance features of the final program product, the developer can note where more information is likely to be needed.

The syntactic level deals with the structure and format of the interactions, including command syntax and screen layouts. Typical corrections to be incorporated include decreased space for titles, movement of total lines, syntax allowing for multiple report requests, etc.[35] Such alterations may often be made immediately by the analyst and rerun for the user.

At the lexical level one must define the actual command words, menu items, and display symbols. This defining can be related to the incorporation of the user's natural language, for example, renaming a command "insert" from "add," and the removal of the developer's natural language. In a detailed documentation of a prototype case Gomaa and Scott[18] cite examples of the latter problem: removal of expressions like "queue" and

"I6," which were foreign to the users. They give further examples reflecting the other levels.

Foley's model is designed to structure the development of the interface. We have found it a useful framework for the developer to analyse user reactions to a prototype. This is important at the conceptual and semantic levels, where the developer must be willing to interpret user difficulties as requiring re-examination of the application, rather than "educating" the user. (i.e., convert to the developer's conceptual model).

All the changes referenced above from our own studies[35] came after a requirements sign-off, which included printed copies of screen displays. There appears to be no adequate substitute in interactive applications for some kind of prototype to convey the nature of the proposed system. The level of detail in the prototype is partly a function of methodology, discussed in section 6.

2.3 Easier evolution of requirements

The evolution of requirements is of most concern in environments like decision support systems, where the user needs to employ the system in open-ended ways and no pattern of use can be accurately predicted until some experience is available. The case for this development pattern is well documented in standard texts like Keen and Scott Morton[36]. This evolutionary need can be met by successive product releases, but Keen and Gambino[21] note that a prototype methodology implies that the initial version is a program but not a program product in Brook's[37] sense. Accordingly, the initial development time is reduced, and the developer is specifically committed to a large degree of interaction while "version 0" is undergoing test. This testing can be confined to the hardier users. Users known to be reluctant to use the final version need not be exposed to version 0, which would likely confirm some of their fears about the developers not undestanding their application area.

In the summary chart of appendix A we have indicated which of these categories of advantage the authors have explicitly cited. As noted previously, the additional advantage of better relationships between users and developers was also frequently listed. The relationship of these categories to the choice of prototyping technique will be examined in the next section.

3. A CLASSIFICATION OF PROTOTYPING TECHNIQUES

Our literature survey and discussion with system developers* have led us to identify three categories of prototype techniques: scenarios or simulations, demonstration systems, and "version 0"[21] limited working systems.

A *scenario* or simulation presents to the user an example of actual system usage but only simulates the processing of user data or queries. That is, the eventual application logic is not developed, but a script is created that drives the screen for certain fixed entries, as if the system existed. Depending upon the tool used to build the scenario, some of the development work on the scenario may be applied to the production system, as seen in the next section.

A *demonstration* system processes a limited range of user queries or data, using limited files. Frequently, some portion of the system, especially screen displays, is carried over to the production system; these portions are commonly linked by a skeletal processing code, which will be replaced in the final product. Alternatively, the entire demonstration can be coded as a throw-away, as described by Gomaa and Scott[18]. In any case, the user chooses queries and data from a specified type or range.

*In particular, some of our terminology here is due to Art Benjamin of On-Line People.

A *version 0* prototype is a working release of the system intended to receive use under conditions approaching the production environment. While it is specifically designed as a test release, it is usually expected that the final product will build on version 0 by completing the implementation of functions, adding requested alterations, and generating the required documentation, etc. to convert the program into a product.

The three technique categories are clearly points of reference on a spectrum, but the distinction seems to be worth making. It clarifies the intent of a prototype and its expected benefits. A scenario will be expected to address interaction requirements and some functional requirements, although it cannot shed much light on application logic. A demonstration is likely to provide more insight into processing logic but may not be as useful for evolutionary requirements, because the user's exposure is of necessity limited. A related technique, incremental deliveries, has been described by Gilb[43], who distinguishes it from use of demonstrations and version 0.

The differing kinds of return expected from the investment in a prototype also suggest differing tool use. Tools for prototyping are described in the next section.

4. Tools Used for Prototyping

The use of prototypes has been advocated as cost-effective even in the absence of any special tools to support the various techniques[13,22]. But a number of tools do exist to support version 0, demonstrations, and scenario prototypes – some indirectly as by-products of higher-level languages or programming support environments and at least one directly as a requirements tool.

The time and cost of an initial version 0 of an application can be substantially reduced using higher level languages (also known as non-procedural, fourth-generation, even fifth-generation languages). These support applications data aggregates as primitive data types with appropriate built-in operations. When there is a good fit between these predefined structures and the application structure, these tools reduce the amount of programming required to develop an application over a traditional procedural language such as COBOL or PL/1. The most frequently referenced tool in the authors' literature search was APL[21,26,27]. Although this choice may be due more to the nature of the APL community than any other factors, ADF[19] and various other languages[27,29] are also proposed for a first working version.

The distinction between a version 0 prototype and a demonstration is as much the result of the environment in which it receives use as it is the functions provided. Thus, one would expect that demonstration prototypes could be conveniently constructed with tools such as ADF[19] and APL[19]. On the other hand, Berrisford and Wetherbe[14] found it productive to use a relational data base system to implement demonstrations, and several sources construct demonstrations essentially as by-products of programming support environments. This can provide facilities for macro commands (which are replaced once a design is verified) and program stubs to be later enhanced[17] or application generators based on traditional procedural languages[15,20].

The construction of a scenario prototype, since it provides less functionality than a demonstration prototype, must cost less than a demonstration if it is to be worthwhile. Using tools similar to those above, one can implement simple case logic to provide the desired actions when the values in the script are entered (and to ignore or reject all others).

Alternatively, one can use a special-purpose tool, which accepts example actions and automatically constructs the appropriate case logic.

In the chart of appendix A, we have attempted to summarize the literature cited, identifying in each case the prototyping technique employed and the major tool used. Appendix A provides additional comments to amplify the nature of the application development environment or application situation described in the citation.

One is struck in this summary by the wide variety of tools that have been used for prototyping. In their review of prototyping Naumann and Jenkins[44] also note the great variety of definitions of prototyping and the variety of tools employed in different situations. We believe this reflects the use of available tools in the absence of widely available integrated tool sets appropriate to a prototype-oriented development methodology. A tool that would support the evolution of a system prototype from specification through version 0 in an integrated manner is required. The Chevron Program Development System apparently provides such a facility through an "example editor"[16]. ACT/1 (25) allows a developer to script a screen flow by entering examples as a user would and then indicating the next screen to be displayed. In both cases it is envisioned that the screen designs can be transferred into the final product without recoding.

ACT/1 is one of small number of development tools specifically intended to apply an integrated prototype-oriented methodology to the development of information systems. Examples of the use of this and other tools were described in a workshop on rapid prototyping[45]. According to discussion at this workshop, there appears to be a trend towards development of integrated sets of tools which make use of prototypes. Such integrated tools raise many issues in the area of development methodology, some of which are discussed below.

5. METHODOLOGY ISSUES RAISED BY PROTOTYPING

The traditional system life cycle – requirements, design, implementation, test, integration, maintenance – reflects recognition of the need for an organized approach to system development with attendant milestones and approvals. Prototypes can be

1. incorporated into this cycle at the requirements phase (all techniques), or
2. used to bridge or merge the first two or three phases using demonstrations or version 0 in an iterative development, or
3. used to avoid the cycle altogether, when employed by end-users to create their own systems with little or no involvement from professional systems developers (version 0).

The issues raised by these choices are not trivial and include using a prototype as "throwaway" code or building upon it; preserving Brook's distinction between a program and a system product; the use of a prototype in documentation and maintenance; and the roles of development staff and users. In this section we discuss some of these issues.

5.1 Use of prototype materials in the product
Many proposals for prototypes assume that the traditional life cycle will be followed, so that at some point the users will agree to the requirements as specified by the prototype and supporting documentation. A design phase follows, which assumes the design of the prototype to be a black box

that need not be examined. Some tools permit the screen display components to be transferred to later phases without recoding while the remainder of the program is replaced.

It is possible to think of the prototype in this instance as a part of the system documentation rather than an accessory to a specification document. In that case, one must consider maintenance of the system to nclude versions of the prototype, and the tools involved must support explicit version control. The cost involved in a version 0 prototype will sometimes make it unsuitable for this approach.

5.2 Iterative development

Other proposals for prototypes assert that the separation in time of requirements specification, design and implementation is either unnecessary or counter-productive, at least for certain application types. Peters[28,38] would encourage "hybrid" life cycles that merge specification and design. It is unlikely that a scenario prototype would be used alone here, since the extra cost of a demo or version 0 is treated as design expense.

Others feel just as strongly that their application environments require that the prototype be treated as part of the requirements process only (for example Gomaa and Scott[18]). We lack a sufficiently full understanding of those application characteristics that help determine when the phases need to be kept separate.

An important corollary issue is the necessity of allowing life-cycle time for converting a program into a system product. Keen and Gambino[21] suggest that the proportion of time required for these activities may be more or less independent of the implementation tool used. The checklist provided by Waters[39] is helpful in this regard; he distinguishes the specification of an application subsystem from the other subsystems required in a system product (recovery, control, monitor, etc.).

5.3 Prototypes and end users

Some authors suggest that an iterative development cycle as outlined above is well suited to end-users developing their own application systems. The existence of tools of sufficient simplicity and ease of change provides the user the opportunity to implement a version 0 prototype and evolve it to suit the requirements.

Like iterative development, we need a better grasp on the situations in which this is an appropriate choice, as well as a readiness to welcome such user involvement. The issue of fulfilling the requirements for a system product occurs here also. Suitable roles for professional system staff are evolving to address this need, in particular the concept of an Information Centre that helps users choose either a traditional development methodology or one of those outlined above. Martin[40] provides a helpful summary in this area.

It should be noted that the word prototype is also occasionally used for a test version demonstrated to users long after requirements sign-off, as part of system test. This seems to represent either an implicit iterative development cycle or a failure to include interaction requirements in the original specification.

Conclusion

We have examined some of the published accounts of prototypes as employed in information system development, and tried to categorize the techniques, tools and methodologies employed. The particular combination to be used in a given situation is determined by the application structure, the skills of the developers and users, and the tools and management practices available. Any prototype should be developed with a clear idea of the kinds of advantages it is hoped to achieve.

The current emphasis on prototyping represents, we believe, a return to basics in systems development, particularly in the domain of business information systems. Interest in prototyping reflects a recognition that traditional approaches to the management and conduct of systems development are not adequate. Prototyping, however loosely defined, reflects a renewed effort to meet user requirements for ever more complex system function in a more timely and productive manner.

It is our feeling that the prototyping approaches to system development should be expected to differ in different application domains. In the domain of business information systems there is reason to be optimistic that integrated tools that will have this desired effect are available and evolving.

REFERENCES

(1) P. Freeman, "A perspective on requirements analysis and specification," in *Tutorial on Software Design Techniques*, P. Freeman, and A.I. Wasserman, eds. IEEE Press, 1979, 86–96

(2) A.I. Wasserman, Information system design methodology, J. of ASIS 3/(1), 1980

(3) M.V. Zelkowitz, A case study in rapid prototyping," Soft. Pr. and Exp. 10, 1980

(4) R.A. Zahniser, "How to navigate the user fog," Computerworld, March 16, 1981

(5) P.H. Baucom, "Software blueprints," Proc. ACM Conference, 1978, 385–92

(6) M. Alford, "A requirements engineering methodology for real-time processing requirements," IEEE Trans. Software Eng., January 1977

(7) R.E.A. Mason, "A model of programming," Technical Report 80-001, Department of Computing and Information Science, University of Guelph, 1980

(8) M.E. Dickover, L.L. McGowan, and D.T. Ross, "Software design using SADT," Proc. 1977 ACM National Conference

(9) A.I. Wasserman, and S.K. Stinson, "A specification method for interactive information systems," in *Tutorial on Software Design in Techniques*, P. Freeman and A.I. Wasserman, eds. 1980, 187–96

(10) L. Scharer, "Pinpointing requirements," Datamation, April 1981

(11) L.J. Peters and L.L. Tripp, "A model of software engineering," Proc. ICSE 3, 1978

(12) D. Harel, "On folk theorems," CACM 23(7), 1980

(13) L. Bally, J.N.G. Brittan, and K. Wagner, "A prototype approach to information system design and development," Information Management 1, 1977

(14) T. Berrisford and J. Wetherbe, "Heuristic development: a redesign of systems design," MIS, March 1979, 11–19

(15) T.C. Bishop, and E.J. Grace, "CS magic improved program generation with interactive COBOL," Data Base 11(3), 1980, 56–63

(16) D.P. Davis and K.F. Tweedy, Chevron's integrated and automated approach to applications development," Data Base 11(3), 1980, 10–27

(17) Anon., Programming work-stations," EDP Analyzer 17(10), 1979

(18) H. Gomaa and D.B. Scott, "Prototyping as a tool in the specifications of user requirements," ICSE 5, 1981

(19) A.M. Goodman, IMSADF – a tool for programmer productivity," Data Base 11(3), 1980, 106–13

(20) K.N. Kebel and S.C.R. Morling, "Interactive program generator for IMS application," Data Base 11(3), 1980, 35–9

(21) P. Keen and T.J. Gambino, "The mythical man-month revisited," Proc. APL 1980, 630–48

(22) E. Keppel and D. Kropp, "Interactive programming by end-users," Proc. APL 77

(23) T.C. Jones, "A survey of programming design and specification techniques," Proc. of Conf. on Reliable Software, 1979, 91–103

(24) W.T. Jones and S.A. Kirk, "APL as a software design specification language," Computer Journal 23(3), 1980, 230–

(25) R.E.A. Mason and T. Carey, "Productivity experiences with a scenario tool," Proc. Compcon Fall 81, 1981

(26) E.R. McLean, "The use of APL for production applications," Proc. APL 1976, 303–7

(27) B.R. Martin, "Improving productivity with APL," Proc. Share 53, 1979

(28) L. Peters, "Relating software requirements and design," Proc. NCC 1980

(29) N.S. Read and D.L. Harmon, "Assuring MIS success," Datamation 27(2), 1981

(30) R. Rosenberger, "The information center – a productivity tool for end-user support," Proc. Share 53, 1979

(31) A.I. Wasserman, "User software engineering and the design of interactive systems," Proc. ICSE 5, 1981

(32) J.M. Grochoci, "Application generators anticipate requirements," Computerworld 15: SR/30-2, March 30, 1981

(33) J.D. Naumann, C.B. Davis, and J.D. McKeen, "Determining information requirements," J. of Systems and Software 1(4), 1980

(34) W. Myers, "Computer graphics: the human interface," Computer 13(6), 1980

(35) R.E.A. Mason, "Preliminary experiments with a requirements definition aid," Technical Report 80-0002, Department of Computing and Information Science, University of Guelph, 1980

(36) P. Keen and M. Scott Morton, *Decision Support Systems*. Addison-Wesley Publ. Co., 1978

(37) F.P. Brooks, *The Mythical Man Month*. Addison-Wesley Publ. Co., 1975

(38) L.J. Peters, "Relating software requirements and design," Proc. Software Quality and Assurance Workshop, 1978

(39) J. Waters, "Towards comprehensive specifications," Computer Journal 22(3)

(40) J. Martin, "Application development without programmers," Savant Institute, 1981

(41) J.N.G. Brittan, "Design for a changing environment," Computer Journal 23(1), 13–19

(42) E.R. McLean, "End users as application developers," MIS, December 1979, 37–46

(43) T. Gilb, "Evolutionary development," Software Engineering Notes, April 1981

(44) J.D. Naumann and A.A. Jenkins, "Prototyping: the new paradigm for systems development," MIS Quarterly, September 1982, 29

(45) W.V. Zilkowitz, ed., "Workshop notes, ACM SIGSOFT," Workshop on Rapid Prototyping, Columbia, Maryland, 19–21 April 1982

To illustrate the mix of techniques, tools, and methodologies, we summarize in the following table the characteristics of prototype case studies from the professional literature. The comments, especially under environment and advantages cited, represent our interpretations of the original experience.

Technique	Tool	Methodology	Environment	Advantages Cited	Reference
Scenario	Chevron PDS PL/1 base)	Simulation of screen operation post requirements	Information systems	Interaction	(16)
Scenario	ACT/1 Architect tool	Prototype in requirements phase	Information systems	Functional interaction	(25, 35)
Scenario and demonstration	APL	Advocates writing specifications in APL to be interpreted for verification	(Proposal only)	Functional	(24)
Scenario, demonstration, version 0	Dialogue design interpreter linked to DBMS	Prototype in requirements phase	Information systems research	Functional interaction	(31)
Demonstration	Interactive program (PL/1 base)	High level application generator, life cycle stage not stated	Information systems	Interaction functional	(20)
Demonstration ("mockup")	CSMAGIC (Cobol base)	Cobol generator, life-cycle stage not stated	Information systems	Functional interaction	(15)
Demonstration	Various	Iterative development ("hybrid" life-cycles merge specification and design)	Information systems		(28)
Demonstration	ADF	Prototype in requirements phase	Data base transactions	Evolutionary	(19)
Probably demonstration	Command language on programmer's workstation	Iterative development cycle: "throw away code"	Information systems	Functional	(17)
Demonstration	APL	Prototype in requirements phase	Production management	Functional interaction	(18)
Demonstration (occasional inadvertent version 0)	Relational DBMS	Iterative development ("heuristic development")	MIS	Functional	(11)
Version 0	Various	Iterative development (80% version)	Information systems	Early ROI. Use version 0 until version 1 produced	(30)
Version 0	APL	APL in design phase; encourage	Information systems	Functional interaction	(27)
Version 0	Local extension of APL	User programming	Data processing interactive forms	Functional	(22)
Version 0	APL	Iterative development cycle	Decision support	Functional interactive evolutionary	(21)
Version	APL or other high level language	Iterative development ("cooperative development") user programming	Decision support	Evolutionary	(26, 42)
Version 0	FOCUS	Iterative development cycle	MIS	Functional	(29)
Version 0	Various	Iterative development cycle, scaled-down production versions	Data processing (incl. batch)	Functional	(13, 41)
Version 0	Various	Prototypes for design defect removal (after specification)	Various	Functional interaction	(23)

Reprinted from *IEEE Transactions on Software Engineering*, Volume SE-12, Number 2, February 1986, pages 326–345. Copyright ©1986 by The Institute of Electrical and Electronics Engineers, Inc. All rights reserved.

Developing Interactive Information Systems with the User Software Engineering Methodology

ANTHONY I. WASSERMAN, MEMBER, IEEE, PETER A. PIRCHER,
DAVID T. SHEWMAKE, STUDENT MEMBER, IEEE, AND MARTIN L. KERSTEN

Abstract—User Software Engineering is a methodology, supported by automated tools, for the systematic development of interactive information systems. The USE methodology gives particular attention to effective user involvement in the early stages of the software development process, concentrating on external design and the use of rapidly created and modified prototypes of the user interface. The USE methodology is supported by an integrated set of graphically based tools. This paper describes the User Software Engineering methodology and the tools that support the methodology.

Index Terms—Human/computer interaction, interactive information systems, rapid prototyping, RAPID/USE, software development methodology, transition diagrams, User Software Engineering.

I. SOFTWARE DEVELOPMENT METHODOLOGIES

EFFORTS to improve the quality of software systems and the process by which they are produced are at the heart of the field of *software engineering*. The key idea is to use a *software development methodology*, a systematic process for the creation of software. A methodology combines technical methods with management procedures for software development, and includes automated tools in a development support system for additional assistance [1]–[3].

The underlying philosophy is that use of a methodology can improve many aspects of the entire software development process, including a better fit to user requirements, fewer errors in the resulting system, better documentation throughout the entire process, and significantly reduced costs for system evolution.

Most methodologies give primary attention to the functions of the system being developed and the data upon which it operates. They follow a hierarchical decomposition of the problem, working from either a data-oriented or a function-oriented perspective. The user interface to the system is frequently considered only as an afterthought.

For interactive systems, though, these approaches may not work well, since user-oriented considerations must receive attention very early in the development process.

Manuscript received April 30, 1985.

A. I. Wasserman, P. A. Pircher, and D. T. Shewmake are with the Section of Medical Information Science, University of California, San Francisco, CA 94143.

M. L. Kersten is with the Centrum voor Wiskunde en Informatica, Amsterdam, The Netherlands.

IEEE Log Number 8405407.

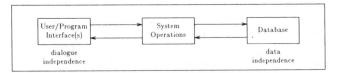

Fig. 1. Logical structure of interactive information systems.

Furthermore, user concerns and user preferences must have priority over some system-oriented considerations.

Accordingly, we created a methodology, named User Software Engineering (USE), that includes many user-oriented considerations in the framework of a software development methodology. User Software Engineering focuses on a particular type of interactive system, termed an interactive information system (IIS). An IIS may be characterized as providing conversational access to data, typically for persons who are not experts in computing.

Interactive information systems are used for applications such as airline reservations, bibliographic searching, medical record management, and banking. From a software perspective, an IIS may be seen as a human/computer dialog, a database, and a set of transactions (operations, functions), where many of the transactions involve access to or modification of a database, as shown in Fig. 1.

From a user standpoint, the interface to the IIS is often most critical and is certainly the first thing that is noticed by the user. There is growing evidence of the relationship between the quality of the user interface and the ease of use of a system [4], [5]. Accordingly, User Software Engineering gives early attention to the design of the user interface, and employs what may be termed an *outside-in* approach to software development and design. The methodology is supported by a collection of tools that support design and testing of the user interface, and the integration of the executable user interface specification with programmed actions written in programming languages and/or the data manipulation language for a relational database management system.

In the remainder of this paper, we outline first the goals of the USE methodology, and then show how systems are designed and built using the methodology and its tools, especially the RAPID/USE application development system. We shall illustrate the use of the USE methodology with the University library database example presented at the 1984 Workshop on Models and Languages for Software Specification and Design. (See *Computer*, vol. 18, no. 3, pp. 103–108.)

II. GOALS OF THE USE METHODOLOGY

The User Software Engineering project was undertaken in 1975 with the intent of creating a methodology that would support the development of interactive information systems. The development of the User Software Engineering methodology has been guided by seven goals:

• *functionality*—The methodology should cover the entire development process, supporting creation of a working system that achieves a predefined set of requirements.

• *reliability*—The methodology should support the creation of reliable systems, so that users are not inconvenienced by system crashes, loss of data, or lack of availability.

• *usability*—The methodology should help the developer to assure, as early as possible, that the resulting system will be easy to learn and easy to use. The methodology should involve users *effectively* in the development process, particularly in its early stages.

• *evolvability*—The methodology should encourage documentation and system structuring so that the resulting system is easily modifiable and able to accommodate changes in hardware operating environments and user needs.

• *automated support*—The methodology should be supported by automated tools that improve the process of software development and the resulting system; this requirement implies the availability of both a general set of automated aids and a methodology-specific set.

• *improved developer productivity*—The methodology, with its supporting tools, should reduce the time required to create a properly functioning system.

• *reusability*—The methodology should be reusable for a large class of projects and the design products from a given application should be reusable on similar future projects.

The USE methodology, as with most other development methodologies [6], [7], follows a well-defined set of phases beginning with analysis and terminating with a validated operational system. We believe, however, that the traditional life cycle approach has several flaws when applied to the creation of interactive systems, and that evolutionary approaches involving the orderly construction of a sequence of prototype systems are frequently more effective.

III. REQUIREMENTS ANALYSIS IN THE USE METHODOLOGY

As with any methodology, the first step in User Software Engineering is to gain an understanding of the problem domain and specific application constraints. This section describes the requirements analysis process of User Software Engineering, showing the information that is obtained for later use. Most of the techniques used in this

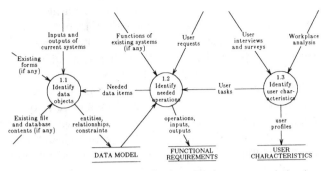

Fig. 2. Dataflow diagram showing requirements analysis in USE methodology.

process are similar to those used with other methods, and are therefore presented very briefly.

A. Aspects of Requirements Analysis

In User Software Engineering, four aspects of analysis are important: data modeling, activity modeling, analysis of user characteristics, and analysis of usage characteristics. It is largely an *informal* process, intended to gain understanding of the problem domain, the context in which a system could be developed, and the nature of the expected usage of such a system. The USE requirements analysis process is summarized in the dataflow diagram shown in Fig. 2.

We begin this phase with an object-oriented approach, identifying, informally, objects and the operations (actions) performed upon them. Conceptual data modeling techniques such as the semantic hierarchy model of Smith and Smith [8] and the entity-relationship model [9] have been used successfully for this step. These techniques are used to identify the primary entities of concern in a system, their attributes, and their relationship to one another. As these entities and relationships are identified, the operations that create and modify these entities are also identified. The USE approach resembles many other approaches in this phase, notably the Entity-Action Step of the Jackson System Development method [10].

Activity modeling is also useful for identifying entities, relationships, and operations. We have successfully used several different techniques for activity modeling, including the A-graphs of ISAC and the dataflow diagrams of Structured Systems Analysis [11], [12].

Regardless of the precise technique used, the names of entities, their attributes, and the operations are collected into a "data dictionary," so that the names may be used consistently throughout the development process. This data dictionary, part of the User Software Engineering project database, eventually obtains information about the user interface, too.

B. Levels of Abstraction in User Software Engineering

The User Software Engineering approach uses these data and activity modeling methods as a means to achieve multiple levels of abstraction based on data independence. The first level is physical data independence. The mere fact of using a database model rather than a file-oriented model provides a level of independence from the physical structure of the data on a secondary storage device; this level of independence is the traditional data independence as the term is used in the database community.

The second level of abstraction is *data-model* independence. The result of the data modeling and activity modeling is the identification of a set of abstract operations (functions, modules, transactions), with well-defined inputs and outputs. These operations, as they are refined through the development process, provide a *complete* set of operations on the database, regardless of the underlying representation or data model.

Of course, not all of the operations in an interactive information system necessarily access or modify a database. However, the same principles of abstraction can be applied, so that the nondatabase operations of the system can also be named.

In summary, all of the programs comprising the interactive information system will use the operations so defined. It should be noted that while the vast majority of these operations can be identified and specified through a typical process of requirements analysis, others will not be identified until a later phase of the software development process. For this reason, User Software Engineering does not proceed with a rigorous formal specification at this stage. The defined operations may later be refined into formal specifications following a state model approach [13]–[15].

The same ideas that provide data model independence also provide *dialog independence*, the separation of the precise syntax of the user interface to the system from the operations of the system [16].

Logical separation of the dialogue from the operations allows several different dialogs to be specified for the same system. This approach facilitates the design of multilingual programs, of different interfaces for novices and experts, for low and high speed terminals, and for different styles of interaction, such as commands versus menu selection.

These operations now provide the first version of the desired abstract operations interface to the library system. To achieve both dialog independence and data model independence, the operations invoked by a user's input to the system must be limited to those in this set.

In practice, this set would be expanded to include certain housekeeping operations, such as opening and closing the database. During the development process, "hidden" operations would also be identified. Such hidden operations are not visible to the end user, but are required by the visible operations to perform their tasks.

Thus, it is necessary to define additional abstract operations to check these values, and such operations are normally defined during the development process. As a general rule, primary attention is given to those operations that *create* or *modify* entities or their attributes in the data model, with less attention given to those operations that simply access these entities and attributes. In Parnas'

terms, and as used by SRI International's Hierarchical Design Methodology, definition of the O-functions and the OV-functions take precedence over the V-functions and the hidden V-functions.

C. User Characteristics

Another important aspect of requirements analysis is understanding of user characteristics, so that the interface to the IIS can be properly designed. It is important to recognize the motivation and intended skill levels for the anticipated user population, to identify the needs for various types of output documents, e.g., hard copy versus "soft" copy, and to see whether the IIS must support casual users as well as regular users. Other issues, such as discretionary use versus mandatory use, and the need for alphanumeric keyboard input, are also taken into account at this stage.

Failure to understand the intended user community may lead to poor decisions concerning the user interface and the selection of information system functions. These errors will almost certainly lead to low user satisfaction and the need to make extensive (and expensive) modifications to the implemented system.

D. The Library Example

The example that will be described throughout the remainder of this paper is that of a simple library system, which supports the following transactions:

1) check out a copy of a book.
2) return a copy of a book.
3) add a copy of a book to the library.
4) remove a copy of a book from the library.
5) remove all copies of a book from the library.
6) get a list of titles of books in the library by a particular author.
7) find out what books are currently checked out by a particular borrower.
8) find out what borrower last checked out a particular copy of a book.

Note that this is an informal description of the problem, and furthermore that it does not completely describe the necessary operations for a library, which would include management of information about cardholders, reservations and requests for books, and numerous additional operations.[1] Nonetheless, this example will serve adequately to explain the concepts and applications of the USE methodology.

We begin by creating a data model for the example, and use the entity-relationship model for this purpose. An abbreviated (for reasons of space) model for the library is shown in Fig. 3.

This modeling activity not only yields information that will eventually go into the database that support the application, but also provides names that may be consistently used throughout the subsequent phases of development.

---

[1]The complete example includes restrictions on the transactions and invariants on the database, which we shall take up in a subsequent section.

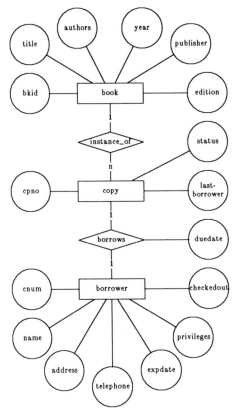

Fig. 3. Entity-relationship model for library database.

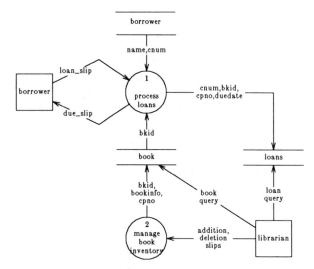

Fig. 4. "Top-level" dataflow diagram for library system.

The next step is to consider the operations that will be needed to create, access, and modify the entities and relationships in the data model. These operations are specified *informally* at this stage. While formal specification of operations is a valuable discipline, formalization can only be done successfully after a substantial amount of information has been obtained. Accordingly, the process is informal at this stage, but follows a pattern and structure that supports formalization at a later stage.

For this example, the major operations are specified by the problem statement, which is rarely the case in a practical system, where a significant amount of problem analysis and modeling is required to detemine the operations that may be supported by a system. User Software Engineering, as noted, typically uses a method such as Structured Systems Analysis, and produces a set of leveled dataflow diagrams that is used to help identify the system operations. A "top-level" dataflow diagram for the library system is shown in Fig. 4.[2]

Fig. 5 shows the operations for the library system, following the problem statement. Note that names for the operations have been chosen, along with names for the inputs and outputs to the operations. The chosen input/output names correspond to the names of entities, relationships, and their attributes in the data model.

Note that operation *checkout* requires several hidden functions to check the validity of the book identification

<hr>

[2]We have taken some liberties with the pure dataflow approach in this example, to provide a better match to the required transactions given in the specifications.

number *bkid*, the copy number *cpno*, and the borrower card number *cnum*. These operations are *checkcard*, *checkbknum*, and *chkbkcopy*.

The problem statement for the library example provides no information about the characteristics of the users or the environment in which the system will be used. Some (not necessarily valid) assumptions may be made, however.

1) Users of the system will be library staff members, who will be regular users of the system. The terminals and printing devices with which they work will have to be located near the users' normal working locations.

2) The nature of the library and the jobs will require certain staff members to become knowledgeable in the use of the system. Some users will become quite adept in use of the system, and will wish to take advantage of any short cuts that may be built into the system. Users must be given the ability to circumvent long or repetitive messages or sequences of steps once they are comfortable with the system operation.

3) These users will not necessarily possess clerical skills, and almost certainly will not be experts in computer science or programming. These requirements imply that an effort should be made to minimize typing by the users, and that the program "lead the user" through each task.

4) There will be several different classes of users, representing several different subsystems of library management. One can easily envisage a subsystem for managing the lending of books to cardholders, and another for acquiring and removing books from the library's collection. The set of operations provided to the different classes of users may be different, but these different classes will share the same database through operations, and should be provided with similar types of user interfaces so that staff members can move from one job function to another without requiring extensive training in the use of the system.

These considerations suggest a menu-oriented interface for initial users of the system, with a command-oriented

```
operation checkout
input bkid,cpno,cnum,duedate,MAX
output status
function
        Processes the checkout of copy cpno of book bkid to cardholder cnum, with a due date of duedate,
        only if cnum has MAX or fewer books already checked out

operation returnbk
input cnum, bkid, cpno
function
        Processes the return of copy cpno of the book with book identification number bkid by cardholder cnum

operation ins_book
input bkid, title, authors, publisher, year
function
        Inserts a new book into the catalog, with information on the book identification
        number bkid, the title, authors, publisher, and year of publication

operation del_book
input bkid, cpno
function
        Removes copy cpno of the book with book identification number bkid
        from the library; no operation performed if (bkid,cpno) pair is invalid

operation removeall
input bkid
function
        Removes all books with a given book identification number bkid from
        the library; no operation performed if the book number is invalid

operation bookbyname
input authorname
output titles
function
        Returns the set of book titles written by authorname

operation borrbooks
input borrower
output titles
function
        Returns the set of book titles presently checked out to borrower

operation lastborr
input bkid, cpno
output cnum
function
        Returns the cardholder cnum of the last person to borrow copy cpno of the book with
        book identification bkid; returns 0 if no such book

operation checkcard
input cnum
output toomany, validcard
function
        Returns true for validcard if cnum is a valid library card number and false
        otherwise; returns true for toomany if too many books are currently checked out to cnum

operation checkbknum
input bkid, cnum
output validbook, loanok
operation
        Returns true for validbook if bkid is a valid book identification and false
        otherwise; returns true for loanok if no copy of book is checked out to cnum

operation chkbkcopy
input bkid, cpno
output validcopy, statloan
operation
        Returns true for validcopy if cpno is a valid copy number for bkid and false
        otherwise; returns true for statloan if that copy is available to be checked out
```

Fig. 5. Informal description of library system operations.

option or a series of "invisible" menu options available for the experienced users.

IV. EXTERNAL DESIGN

To this point, the User Software Engineering methodology resembles many other approaches for information systems development, with its use of data abstraction and data modeling. Here, though, many other methods proceed with formalization of the functional specification, followed by architectural and detailed design, then by implementation, with a parallel activity to assure system quality and reliability.

A. *Top-down Versus Outside-In Design*

From the USE standpoint, this traditional emphasis on functional decomposition and top-down design works poorly in the domain of interactive information systems. In particular, the user community obtains an inappropriate perspective of the system under development, being shown what the system will do without being shown how it will appear to the user. This difference in perspective is important, as can be seen by analogy with obtaining an automobile.

Using a functional orientation, the customer (user) would be told the cost, the dimensions of the vehicle, its horsepower, acceleration, braking, and fuel economy statistics, and would be told when it was scheduled for delivery. But the customer would not have the opportunity to see the vehicle until it was actually delivered, and modifications to the delivered product could only be made with great difficulty and at considerable expense. If the customer had no previous experience with automobiles, coming from a society where bicycles or rickshaws were the common mode of transport, the user probably could not accurately state the desired functions for this new means of transportation. Furthermore, the customer might not understand the technical details about the performance of the automobile and could certainly not understand whether the specific automobile was a good value for the price. As a result, the manufacturer (developer) would make assumptions about the needs and desires of the customer and hope that the customer would be satisfied with the finished product. The customer would be extremely dependent upon the judgment of the manufacturer, who becomes the major determinant of customer satisfaction.

Rather than proceeding with further refinement of the system functions, following a traditional "top-down" approach, the User Software Engineering methodology follows an "outside in" approach, in which the external interface to the system is defined.

There are two major reasons for this choice:

• It is easiest to work with the user community if the system is defined from the user perspective rather than from the system perspective.

• The "outside in" approach also serves the need of functional decomposition, since logical transactions from the user viewpoint often map directly into the previously defined operations.

The subsequent example assumes that the user will work at an alphanumeric terminal with a keyboard (teletypewriter-like or video display, depending on the previous phase).[3] For many common IIS's, the obvious choices for a user interface are then command laguages, multiple choice (menu selection screens), free text, or some combination of these. (Even many forms of nonkeyboard input can be seen as equivalent to one of these.)

We then produce a preliminary design of the user interface. Our method for designing the dialog was initially *ad hoc*, based on our experiences as summarized in a set of guidelines [17]. More recently, though, we have developed and are beginning to use metrics that help evaluate the properties of screen designs [5].

B. Concepts of USE Transition Diagrams

The user program dialog is then specified with a set of USE transition diagrams. We began in 1977 using standard state transition diagrams, following their use in other language processing applications [18]. We associated an

output message with each node (or state), and provided an arc (transition) for each distinguishable class of user input from a given state. An action could be associated with any transition. Others have followed a similar approach [19]–[21]. We found that state transition diagrams were a useful mechanism for modeling interactive systems. However, their basic form was inadequate for the range of user dialogs that one must model. For example, one could not distinguish between buffered and unbuffered input, truncate an input string to fixed length, or terminate user input on some character other than a carriage return. Other situations, such as immediate branching on a specific character, echo versus nonecho of user input, and branching upon expiration of a time limit, simply could not be represented with the basic notations.

Even worse, the complexity of diagrams quickly became unmanageable for all but the smallest dialogs. We therefore introduced "subconversations" in a diagram as a useful structuring technique to manage the complexity of the diagrams. A subconversation is represented by a rectangle, and works in much the same way as a subprogram call in a programming language, suspending transitions in the current diagram and "executing" the called diagram, possibly repeating this process to an arbitrary depth.

In their basic form, transition diagrams are purely syntactic, having no memory and no ability to branch on the results of actions. Both of these restrictions are unrealistic when transition diagrams are used to model interactive information systems.

In an interactive dialog, a user frequently provides input that is subsequently displayed or used as a parameter in some operation. Thus, one must be able to save a user input for additional processing. Variables are the standard means of doing this, so the transition diagrams were extended to allow alphanumeric variables, with optional constraints on string length and values.

Next, the sequence of a dialog is often dependent on the results of actions. For example, if a user types in a name, an action may look up that name in a table. A different path must be followed if the name if found than if it is not found. Therefore, actions must be able to return values *and* it must be possible to branch in the diagram based on those returned values.

Finally, we included cursor and screen management symbols to be able to describe interactive dialog on a full-screen display, not just on a line-oriented basis.

Thus, we have created an extended form of transition diagram notation to support this class of applications [22], and have found them to work well to specify both the user input(s) to the system and the resulting system actions and displays. We found transition diagrams to be preferable to BNF, particularly for users who must comprehend the description. It is important to note that transition diagrams provide an *executable* model of programs, with a highly visible control flow.

As noted in [22], it is important that the descriptive notation cover a broad range of dialog styles and provide the

---

[3]Work is currently underway to extend the user interface specification to handle bit-mapped displays and pointing devices.

Symbol	Meaning
'text'	Branch on receipt of 'text'
name	Assign user input to variable name
!	Unbuffered single key input
+	Transition without user input
@	No echo of user input
"	Time limit in seconds
&x	Transition on receipt of specific character x
list/	Accept input until character in list received
list/m	Truncate input to m characters

Fig. 6. USE transition diagram transition control symbols.

dialog designer with the flexibility to implement dialog design decisions smoothly.

This goal implies the need for a low-level specification capability, in which the dialog designer is given control over the reading and the presentation of every input character typed by the user and every output character displayed by the system. This goal is in contrast to the approach taken in some forms-oriented system, where numerous assumptions are made about the nature of human–computer interaction and about the presentation of information. While the forms-oriented systems are typically simpler to specify, the transition diagram approach envisioned for User Software Engineering is far more general. In other words, it is possible to specify the forms-oriented interfaces using the USE transition diagram approach.

C. Features of USE Transition Diagrams

The USE transition diagrams provide for input specification, output specification, and linkage to system operations.

Input may be obtained on any transition between two nodes, and may optionally be assigned to a declared variable. Input control includes control over the handling of the input, the transition conditions, and the terminator of the user input string. Input control is an important form of transition control, which determines the flow of control through a set of USE transition diagrams. The transition diagram symbols for input transition control are shown in Fig. 6.

Output may be produced at any node, and may consist of literal text, screen control information, and/or display of the contents of variables. Literal text is simply readable text surrounded by quote marks, augmented by control characters and other nonprintable symbols that may be specified as in the C programming language, e.g., "\n" for newline. Screen control information describes the placement of information on the screen, and controls the movement of a cursor representing the current row and column position. The screen control directives are intended to be mnemonic, and are shown in Fig. 7.

Variables are needed since it is frequently necessary to obtain user input, to calculate, and/or to obtain data values prior to using them in system operations or displaying them to users. Since the USE transition diagrams are intended to specify interactive information systems, the variables must support the data types typically needed for such systems, including integer, float, string, date, time, and scalar variables, as in Pascal.

cs	clear screen
rxx	to row xx
cxx	to column xx
r$\pm$n	n rows up or down
c$\pm$n	n columns left or right
hm	row 0, column 0 (home)
rv	reverse video
sv	standard video
il	insert line
cl	clear to end of line
ce	clear to end of screen
c_'text'	center text
i_'text'	insert text at current position
dc	delete character
dl	delete line
mark_a	mark the place a
tomark_a	return to the place a
t_n	move to the column marked by tab n
display (inparam, format)	control the formatting of a given data value

Fig. 7. Screen control directives.

lending

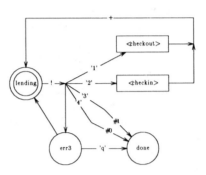

diagram lending entry lending exit done

```
tab t_0 20
tab t_1 25

node lending
        cs,r2,rv,c_'Library System',sv,
        r+2,t_0,'Please choose:',
        r+2,t_1,'1) Check out book',
        r+2,t_1,'2) Check in book',
        r+2,t_1,'3) Exit Book Lending subsystem',
        r+2,t_1,'4) Exit library system',
        r+2,t_0,'Your choice (1-4): '

node done

node err3
        r$-1,rv,bell,'Please type a number from 1 to 4',
        r$,c0,sv,'Press RETURN to continue or "q" to leave this section.'
```

Fig. 8. USE transition diagram for lending subsystem of library system.

D. USE Transition Diagrams for the Library Example

Some of the concepts described in this section can now be illustrated with USE transition diagrams from the library example. We concentrate on the lending subsystem associated with checkin and checkout of books.

The main USE transition diagram for the lending subsystem is shown in Fig. 8. This diagram shows the control flow of the dialog, along with transition control and output display information. The node with two concentric circles is the starting node, named lending. The text associated with node lending below the diagram is screen layout information. In this example, the screen is first cleared. Then the words "Library System" are centered on row 2, followed by six lines that present a "menu selection" on the screen. Note that two tabs are used for alignment of the columns in this menu display. The tabs are set at rows

366

checkout

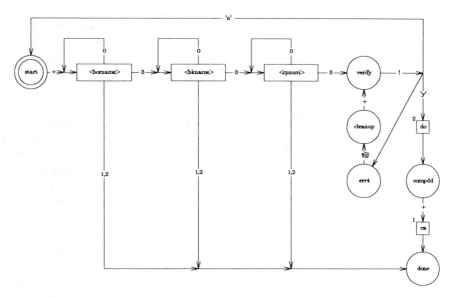

Actions

1   call checkout(cnum,bkid,cpno,duedate,today,MAX ->stat)

2   do newdate(today,loanper ->duedate)

diagram checkout entry start exit done

integer cnum [6:6] range 100000..999999
alpha bkid
integer cpno range 1..1000
integer MAX init 10
date duedate
scalar stat (normal, staff) init normal
integer loanper init 14

node start
        cs,r2,c_'Library System',
        r+2,c0,c_'Checkout Book'

node done

node verify
        r+2,c0,rv,'Is everything OK? (y/n) ',sv,mark_G,cl

node compdd

node err4
        r$-1,c0,rv,'Please type "y" or "n".',sv,
        r$,c0,'Type any character to continue.'

node cleanup
        r$-1,ce,tomark_G

Fig. 9. USE transition diagram for checkout subconversation of lending
subsystem of library system.

20 and 25, and the alignment and/or layout can be changed simply by modifying the tab stops.

The specified system will accept a single character of user input, as shown by the "!" symbol for unbuffered input, and branches accordingly. A response of "1", for example, invokes the ⟨checkout⟩ subconversation, while a response of "4" returns control to the "calling" conversation, returning the value of 0 which is then used to control flow in the calling conversation. Note that any response other than the integers from 1 to 4 causes a transition to node err3, which produces a diagnostic message at the bottom of the screen, using reverse video and an audible bell (control-G on most terminals), giving the user the option to try again or to exit the subsystem. (The help node has intentionally been omitted from this diagram, for reasons of space.)

The checkout diagram (subconversation) is shown in Fig. 9. To check out a book, it is necessary to have a valid

367

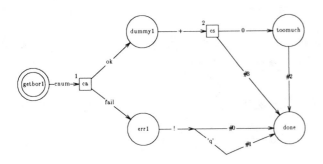

borname

Actions

1   call checkcard (cnum -> toomany)

2   case toomany

diagram borname entry getbor1 exit done

integer cnum [6:6] range 100000..999999
integer toomany init 1

node toomuch
        r$-1,rv,'Cardholder has too many books.',sv

node getbor1
        mark_C,r+2,c0,'Borrower card number: '

node done

node err1
        r$-1,c0,bell,'No such card number.',
        r$,c0,'Press RETURN to try again or "q" to leave this section.',tomark_C,cl

node dummy1

Fig. 10. USE transition diagram for borname subconversation of checkout subconversation of lending system of library system.

borrower, a valid book, and a valid copy number. The checkout diagram calls upon three subconversations, borname, bkname, and cpnum, to perform those checks. In each case, the subconversation returns the value 0 if there was an error and the user wishes to try again, the values 1 or 2 for errors where the checkout operation is to be terminated, and the value 3 for a successful validation. If all three subconversations successively return the value 3, then the user is asked to verify the information, the due date is computed (**do** newdate), and the checkout operation is called.

Each of the three subconversations is similarly structured and we show the first of them, borname, as an example, in Fig. 10. Note that the transition from node getbor1 makes an assignment to variable cnum, representing the card number of the borrower. This value is passed to the checked operation (see Fig. 5), which may succeed of fail. Failure is caused by an invalid card number, and the message at node err1 asks the user to type RETURN to try again or "q" to quit. The former response yields a return value of 0, while the latter returns 1. If the checkcard operation succeeds, the value of its output parameter toomany is checked. If the value is 0, then the borrower has too many books checked out, so that the checkout operation must fail; otherwise, the checkout operation may continue (with the other subconversations). Note the paths in diagram borname that assign the values

2 and 3 as the return value of the diagram. These four values are used as the branching possibilities from the call to the borname subconversation in the checkout diagram.

In earlier versions of the library system, the validation of borrower and book information was implicit in processing the loan of a book to a borrower (the checkout operation). When that operation failed, though, there were numerous possible reasons for the failure, including improper data entry. At that point, the diagram specified that the user would be prompted to type in both the borrower and book identification again, thereby increasing the number of repetitions and the number of user keystrokes, since the user had to provide the information again regardless of the source of the problem.

It was not until the execution of the original diagram was hand simulated that this problem became obvious. In the newer versions of the checkout diagram, as shown here, the checkout operation was changed to do the data entry checking prior to the checkout operation. Once again, it is clear that premature efforts to formalize the operations completely often lead to significant amounts of rework.

This example shows how to combine diagrams for the creation of complex interactive information systems. Values can be communicated between a diagram and its subdiagram through the use of return values. Variables may also be used to store and pass values among diagrams and actions. As will be shown, these variables may be those defined in USE transition diagrams or those defined in the operations that perform the actions required in the interactive information system.

V. Prototype of the Human/Computer Interaction

A. Rationale for Prototypes

Initially (circa 1978), the transition diagrams were used simply as a specification method, since they served both the needs of the developers of the interactive system and the eventual users of the system. When used in combination with hand-drawn "mockups" of the user interface, it was possible to convey some concepts of the intended user interaction with the system.

While this approach worked moderately well, particularly for well-motivated users, it seemed that the users did not really obtain a good sense of the system from the diagrams alone. Furthermore, the developers did not obtain a good indication of the quality of the interface design of the user community's reaction to that design.

To return to the analogy with the automobile, the USE transition diagrams were equivalent to presenting the customer with a brochure describing the features of the automobile. A potential customer with some knowledge of automobiles is able to make some intelligent judgments and rule out certain types of automobiles based on that knowledge; a potential customer who has never before seen an automobile cannot immediately understand the differences (other than price and dimensions) between a Volkswagen and a Rolls-Royce.

What is needed in that case is a test drive, in which the

potential customer has the opportunity to drive the automobile and to see how it performs. The person with knowledge of the automobile will be able to investigate some of the details, while the novice will gain some of the basic concepts and increase his or her understanding of the automobile and what it can do.

The equivalent of the test drive concept in the case of User Software Engineering is an executable version of the user interface to the system—a prototype of the dialog. Without the prototype of the dialog, the user community had only a written description of the system under development. As a result, many changes to the dialog and the functions were made after implementation, with all of the usual problems attendant to evolving systems.

B. The Transition Diagram Interpreter

This observation led to the design and development of the RAPID/USE prototyping system, which contains a Transition Diagram Interpreter (TDI) [23], [24]. This Transition Diagram Interpreter[4] interprets the encoded diagrams, making it possible to allow a user to interact with a "mockup" of the user interface design.

Following the initial design of the user/prototype dialog, the transition diagram(s) are encoded in machine-processable form. This step may either be done automatically with a graphical Transition Diagram Editor (TDE) [25] or manually. We have defined a dialog specification language that supports direct encoding of the USE transition diagrams. Elements of this dialog specification language include diagrams, nodes, arcs, messages, and variables.

The Transition Diagram Editor generates this dialog description language directly, so that it is not necessary for the user to learn the exact syntax of this language (or even to see it!).

This ability to "execute" the dialog, even a portion of it, and even in the absence of operations, is of tremendous value in application of the USE methodology because it gives the user at the terminal a good understanding of the expected behavior of the IIS, and gives the developer a good understanding of the user's problems with the dialog design. It is straightforward to edit the transition diagrams or their textual equivalent as changes are needed. Most cosmetic changes to the dialog can be made in minutes, giving the user a sense of being an active participant in the design process.

For many interactive systems, the optimal design and prototyping approach is to perform the complete dialog design on a major subsystem, and then let the user community work with that interface, making changes dynamically until a workable interface design is achieved. The dialog design for that subsystem then becomes the model for other subsystems to be used by other users having similar skills, to achieve a consistent user interface thoughout the system.

Not only does the executable protype of the interface

give the user a better sense of the planned system, but it also allows objective evaluation of the interface and helps users to think more accurately about the necessary functions for the system.

When the Transition Diagram Interpreter was first developed, the prototype was not built until the complete dialog design was complete or nearly so. Thus, the user community did not see or have the opportunity to work with the user interface until many design decisions had been made. While that process was still an improvement over the traditional means of information systems development, it did not yield as high a degree of user involvement as seemed desirable.

The development of the Transition Diagram Editor has altered the recommended process significantly, since the diagrams are executable without an intermediate encoding step. Users can work with executable versions of the user interface almost immediately, and it is often useful to have "real users" see the emerging system from the outset, occasionally with only a few screens or input opportunities.

This approach has implications for all the initial steps of the USE methodology. Rather than completing the modeling and analysis steps prior to designing the user interface, it is possible to work partly in parallel on these activities and to begin work on the user interface design well before the completion of the data and activity modeling.

In fact, the analysis, dialog design, and dialog prototyping steps can become closely intertwined. Users working with the emerging dialog design obtain a better sense of their own needs, and are therefore better able to aid in the identification of required inputs, outputs, and functions for the system. This information is then "fed back" into the analysis process, possibly causing changes in the data and/or activity models. In this way, the critical User Software Engineering goal of *effective* user involvement in the development process can be achieved.

The dialog prototyping process is iterative and partly experimental. The ability to build and quickly modify interface designs makes it practical to construct alternative interfaces and to give users the opportunity to work with all of them, stating their own likes and dislikes. Because of the dialog independence inherent in the USE approach, it is even possible to customize different interfaces for different individuals, should that be desired.

Empirical observations show that "tuning" of the dialog usually occurs through a sequence of minor changes to node descriptions and control flows. The initial versions of the dialog focus on the major functions and behave properly as long as users provide meaningful inputs. The diagrams are then modified to add nodes for errors and for user assistance (help).

C. Evaluation of the User Interface Design

The objective evaluation of the interface is made possible by the ability to keep session logs of the interaction. Two logs may be maintained: a raw input log and a transition log. The raw input log saves *every keystroke*, so that

---

[4]"Interpreter" is actually a misnomer for the current version of this software, which compiles the dialog description language.

```
diagram lending entry lending exit done

tab t_0 20
tab t_1 25

node lending
        cs,r2,rv,c_'Library System',sv,
        r+5,t_0,'Please choose:',
        r+2,t_1,'1) Check out book',
        r+2,t_1,'2) Check in book',
        r+2,t_1,'3) Exit Book Lending subsystem',
        r+2,t_1,'4) Exit library system',
        r+2,t_0,'Your choice (1-4): '

node done

node err3
        r$-1,rv,bell,'Please type a number from 1 to 4',
        r$,c0,sv,'Press RETURN to continue or "q" to leave this section.'

arc lending single_key
        on '2' to <checkin>
        on '1' to <checkout>
        on '4' to done return 0
        on '3' to done return 1
        else to err3

arc <checkout>
        skip to lending

arc <checkin>
        skip to lending

arc err3 single_key
        on 'q' to done
        else to lending

diagram checkout entry start exit done

integer cnum [6:6] range 100000..999999
alpha bkid
integer cpno range 1..1000
integer MAX init 10
date duedate
scalar stat (normal, staff) init normal
integer loanper init 14

node start
        cs,r2,c_'Library System',
        r+2,c0,c_'Checkout Book'

node done

node verify
        r+2,c0,rv,'Is everything OK? (y/n) ',sv,mark_G,cl

node compdd

node err4
        r$-1,c0,rv,'Please type "y" or "n".',sv,
        r$,c0,'Type any character to continue.'

node cleanup
        r$-1,ce,tomark_G

arc start
        skip to <borname>

arc verify single_key
        on 'n' to start
        on 'y' do newdate(today,loanper -> duedate) to compdd
        else to err4

arc compdd
        skip call checkout(cnum,bkid,cpno,duedate,today,MAX ->stat) to done

arc err4 noecho  single_key
        else to cleanup
```

Fig. 11. Textual representation of USE transition diagrams lending, checkout, and borname.

```
arc cleanup
        skip to verify

arc <borname>
        on 0 to <borname>
        on 1,2 to done
        on 3 to <bkname>

arc <bkname>
        on 0 to <bkname>
        on 1,2 to done
        on 3 to <cpnum>

arc <cpnum>
        on 0 to <cpnum>
        on 1,2 to done
        on 3 to verify

diagram borname entry getbor1 exit done

integer cnum [6:6] range 100000..999999
integer toomany init 1

node toomuch
        r$-1,rv,'Cardholder has too many books.',sv

node getbor1
        mark_C,r+2,c0,'Borrower card number: '

node done

node err1
        r$-1,c0,bell,'No such card number.',
        r$,c0,'Press RETURN to try again or "q" to leave this section.',tomark_C,cl

node dummy1

arc toomuch
        else to done return 2

arc getbor1
        on cnum call checkcard (cnum -> toomany)
                when fail to err1
                when ok to dummy1

arc err1 single_key
        on 'q' to done return 1
        else to done return 0

arc dummy1
        skip case toomany
                default to done return 3
                when 0 to toomuch
```

Fig. 11. (*Continued.*)

it may be serve as a scenario and be replayed later during system testing. Also, keystrokes are easily counted, giving a good measure of usability.

The transition log includes a record for each state transition. Each record includes a time stamp, the diagram name, the node name, any action called, and the user input, and the character that terminated the input. Analysis of this log permits analysis of task completion time, screen viewing times, user error patterns (if all error nodes have recognizable names), and frequency of action calls. A separate tool, rapsum, can do further analysis on the transition log, so that one can, for example, compute the percentage of nodes visited as a measure of test coverage.

RAPID/USE is designed and built specifically as part of the User Software Engineering methodology, and one can see that it supports many of the methodology's goals. It is extremely valuable in verifying and analyzing dialog designs and therefore allows a satisfactory design to be achieved at a very early stage of the IIS development process. In many respects, this use of prototypes and the availability of RAPID/USE are the major contribution of the User Software Engineering methodology.

D. Prototype User Interface for the Library Example

The textual equivalent of the USE transition diagram for the lending, checkout, and borname diagrams is shown in Fig. 11. Careful comparison of this text with the diagrams shown in Figs. 8–10 shows that the encoding of the diagrams is straightforward. The text in Fig. 11 has been generated by the Transition Diagram Editor directly from the diagrams.

The header shows the name of the diagram and the names of the entry and exit nodes. This information is followed by the declaration of the tabs, and then by the nodes and arcs of the diagram, which may be given in any order. Note that the information presented for each node

```
                Library System

        Please choose:

            1) Check out book

            2) Check in book

            3) Exit Book Lending subsystem

            4) Exit library system

        Your choice (1-4):
```

Fig. 12. Screen layout for node lending in diagram lending.

is identicaly to the message associated with a node in the diagram above. For each node, the *arc* statement lists all of the arcs emanating from that node, along with input control and transition conditions. The arc statements provided the structural information about the diagram.

The screen shown upon entry to the borrower subsystem is shown in Fig. 12. The presentation of this screen conveys information that is not apparent from the dialog description language. When this screen design is viewed, one can see that the overall alignment is good, but that the display could be placed closer to the center of the screen by moving the last six lines of text downward by about three lines. Such a change is easily made.

VI. FROM INTERFACE PROTOTYPE TO RUNNING SYSTEM

Following completion of the dialog prototype step, the user interface has been formally specified through the USE transition diagrams, and the system operations have been specified informally. From this point, there are several possible paths that can be followed toward a complete, working system, with three major variants:

1) extend the prototype with programmed actions and database operations;

2) abandon the prototype, and proceed with a system design and implementation using a traditional programming language.

3) abandon the prototype, produce a formal specification of the entire system, and develop a production system using a different set of methods and tools.

The alternative to be taken is highly dependent on local circumstances, including the nature of the application and the structure of the organization(s) involved in the development process. Each of these approaches will be discussed, with emphasis on the first variant, extending the prototype.

A. Relational Database Design

An IIS has been characterized as providing conversational access to data. Thus, an obvious strategy for building such systems is to link a "user interface management system," such as that provided by the Transition Diagram Interpreter, with a database management system (DBMS). In following that approach, the system operations are implemented using the data manipulation language of the DBMS. Many of the commercially available "fourth gen-

eration languages" and "application generators" use this notion.

The semantic data model developed in the analysis phase must be transformed into an executable data model for some DBMS. Since there are few DBMS's that directly support these semantic data models, the most practical transformation is to a normalized relational data model. The transformation from an entity-relationship model or a semantic hierarchy model to relations is straightforward, and simply involves retaining separately the constraints that are lost in making the transformation.

The description of the operations can then be given in terms of definition and manipulation of relations and their attributes, since the database is now defined as a set of relations. All operations that affect the database can be rewritten in a relational data manipulation language, either a nonprocedural, calculus language, such as SQL/DS or QUEL [26]–[28], or a procedural algebraic language, such as that of the Troll/USE relational DBMS [29]. In this manner, the abstract operations are realized as a set of procedures on the relational database and the combination of these procedures with the dialog design provides a substantial part, if not all, of a running system.

The Troll/USE relational DBMS has been designed and developed as a central component in the toolset to support the User Software Engineering methodology. Troll/USE is a compact and efficient system providing a relational algebra-like interface, including operations at the item, tuple, and relation level. Troll/USE supports specification and checking of data types for attributes of relations, including scalar types using enumerated values as in Pascal. An especially valuable aspect of Troll/USE is its support of parameterized scripts, by which named sequences of Troll/USE data manipulation statements may be stored with formal parameters in a "library" of such scripts and may then be invoked by name with actual parameters during a Troll/USE session.

Troll/USE works on a message-passing basis, and has been used as the backend for numerous user interfaces, including the screen-oriented TBE (Troll/USE browser and editor) and the data dictionary subsystem of the Dataflow Diagram Editor developed by Interactive Development Environments, Inc. The message-passing organization makes it suitable for integration with tools in a software development environment. In this way, Troll/ USE may be used both as a DBMS in support of the software development process and as the DBMS for the resulting application systems.

B. Relational Database Design for the Library Example

A relational database definition for the library example is shown in Fig. 13. Note that Troll/USE supports data types of date and variable-length string, as well as providing for user-defined scalar domains and range constraints on domains. These type definitions are enforced by the Troll/USE system to prevent undesirable operations on the database.

```
domain bookstat: scalar (onshelf, checkout);
domain loantype: scalar (regular);
domain cardtype: scalar (normal);
domain cardval: integer (100000..999999);

relation book [key bkid] of
     bkid: string;
     title: string;
     authors: string;
     publisher: string;
     year: date;
end;

relation bookcopy [key bkid,cpno] of
     bkid: string;
     cpno: integer (1..1000);
     ckoutstat: loantype;
     status: bookstat;
     lastborrower: cardval;
end;

relation borrowers [key cnum] of
     cnum: cardval;
     name: string;
     address: string;
     telephone: string;
     expdate: date;
     privileges: cardtype;
     checkedout: integer (0..100);
end;

relation loan [key cnum, bkid, cpno] of
     cnum: cardval;
     bkid: string;
     cpno: integer (1..1000);
     duedate: date;
     checkoutdate: date;
end;
```

Fig. 13. Normalized relations for library example using Troll/USE data manipulation language.

C. Implementing the IIS Operations

While the prototype of the dialog alone is useful, particularly for identifying requirements and for obtaining usable interfaces to an IIS, such a prototype does not *do* anything. Furthermore, the pure dialog prototype makes it difficult to display the dialog alternatives that may sample results, since there is no real database and no actions. The dialog prototype, as implemented with the TDI part of RAPID/USE, provides merely a "façade" for the system.

Thus, it is valuable to be able to implement some (or even all) of the actions specified for the system. The actions performed by an IIS may vary widely, from numerical computation to database management, and from language processing to application generation. Thus, the IIS developer may need access to any of several programming languages and, most importantly, to a database management system.

The logical organization of such an interactive information system is now more accurately represented as shown in Fig. 14, in which the "system operations" of Fig. 1 are partitioned into "database operations" and "computational operations." In the User Software Engineering toolset, the combinations of RAPID/USE with Troll/USE provides the mechanisms required to imple-

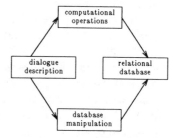

Fig. 14. Logical organization of interactive information systems.

ment both classes of operations. The Action Linker part of RAPID/USE serves this purpose. Routines may be written in C, Fortran 77, or Pascal.[5]

RAPID/USE operates by linking together the TDI with the actions and with libraries that provide terminal and screen handling, access to the Troll/USE DBMS, and the action routines. With that combination, the developer may gradually implement actions, adding operations, error handling, online assistance, and other features as desired.

Because the action mechanism is completely general, one could build the *entire* IIS in this way. Indeed, for systems consisting almost entirely of dialog and database manipulations, such an approach is quite easy. The RAPID/USE approach is also useful for use with programming languages having weak input/output management capabilities, since the dialog specification can be handled with TDI and the actions can be implemented in the desired programming language.

In the User Software Engineering toolset, the combination of RAPID/USE with Troll/USE provides the necessary mechanisms to implement such an IIS quickly and efficiently. Communication between the dialog description and database manipulation is accomplished with the *call* statement in the Transition Diagram Interpreter. The *database* and *library* statements in RAPID/USE dialog description files are passed to Troll/USE at execution time to define the file system location of the database and the location(s) of any libraries that contain Troll/USE scripts needed for program execution. As can be seen in the USE transition diagram for checkout above (and in its textual equivalent), there are calls to operations named check-card, checkbknum, and checkout. Each of these operations is implemented as a parameterized script, written in the Troll/USE data manipulation language. The RAPID/USE-to-Troll/USE linkage passes the parameters from the call statement in RAPID/USE to the Troll/USE script and can similarly return values to RAPID/USE from Troll/USE.

The format of the call statement in RAPID/USE is

call operation (inparamlist → outparamlist)

The parameters are assigned to the Troll/USE global variables $0 through $9 using a positional correspondence and a call-by-reference mechanism. These global variables take

[5]Other languages that share linkage conventions with these languages can be easily added.

the role of formal parameters in the script. Assignments to the global variables within the called Troll/USE script are therefore reflected in changes to the output parameters (RAPID/USE variables).

Of course, not all of the IIS operations involve database manipulation, so it is important to be able to combine the dialog definition part with the computational operations as well. This situation is handled by the Action Linker portion of RAPID/USE and by the *do* statement in the dialog description.

The format of the do statement is identical to that of the call statement except that the word "call" is replaced by "do." While the linkage for the call statement may be accomplished with the Transition Diagram Interpreter, the do statement requires a more general program linkage facility.

The Action Linker accepts programmed routines written in programming languages, either in source or object form, and either as individual files or as archived libraries of routines. Source code is compiled, resulting in a collection of object files and libraries. These objects are linked incrementally, along with the object program that executes the compiled dialog description file. The dialog description file is then compiled and the resulting data structure is linked in to the object program, producing an executable program, which may be invoked in the same way as can any other object program in the environment.

The facilities of RAPID/USE and its Action Linker also support modifications to existing software built without the User Software Engineering methodology and its tools. A useful activity is to take programs that do not support the notion of *dialog independence* and to modify them to do so. That approach is now sketched out.

In many interactive programs, the input/output statements are embedded within the program, rather than separated as is done here. One could begin with existing modules and systems, and find the input and output statements to determine the information that must be communicated between the program and the "outside world." Each of the modules is then treated as an "operation" from the standpoint of User Software Engineering, and the variables that are input and output for that module become parameters passed to it from a *do* statement in the dialog description. These parameters thereby become variables in the USE transition diagrams that describe the dialog and the actions. The input and output statements in the module are then replaced with statements that make assignments to the variables. The existing modules are then combined using the Action Linker of RAPID/USE with the user interface design.

In this way, the tools supporting the User Software Engineering methodology provide direct support not only for the creation of prototypes of user/program interfaces, but also for the extension of those prototypes into running programs and the modification of existing programs.

The benefits of the RAPID/USE-Troll/USE combination are especially evident when the operations for a sys-

```
operation bookbyname (authorname)

    ans1 := book where authors $ authorname;
    {ans1 is the set of books where the set of authors contains a
        string matching the given authorname}


operation checkout (bkid,cpno,cnum,duedate,MAX -> status)

    {everything already checked}
    insert loan [$0,$1,$2,$3,$4];
    bookcopy [$1,$2].lastborrower := $0;
    bookcopy [$1,$2].status := checkout;
    borrowers [$0].checkedout := borrowers[$0].checkedout + 1;
    $5 := normal;

operation ins_book (bkid, title, authors, publisher, year)

    insert book [$0,$1,$2,$3,$4];
    t3 := bookcopy where bkid = $0;
    if count (t3) = 0 then
    begin
         $5 := 1;
    end else
    begin
         $5 := max(t3.cpno)+1;
    end;
    insert bookcopy [$0,$5,normal,onshelf,999999];
    destroy t3;
```

Fig. 15. Troll/USE scripts for library system operations.

tem largely involve database manipulation. In that case, the dialog management is specified in a language well suited to that task, and the database definition and manipulation is similarly specified in a specialized language. The resulting system is built on powerful software development tools without the need for programming in a traditional programming language. Experience has shown that this approach drastically shortens the time needed to produce a running system and the amount of "code" written by the software developer, without giving up anything in performance. Furthermore, the use of the extensively tested application development tools helps to reduce the number of errors in the resulting system.

D. IIS Operations for the Library Example

This combination of tools has been used to implement the operations for the library example. Consider the library operations for displaying all of the books by a given author, for adding a book to the library, and for checking out a book. These operations have been named bookbyname, ins_book, and checkout, respectively. Each of these operations may be described as a Troll/USE procedure, involving a script of database operations that accept parameters. These three operations are shown in Fig. 15. The checkout and ins_book operations are among the most complex operations in the entire library system, yet only involve a small number of lines of code each. All of the operations for the library system, except computation of the due date for a book, are handled by 21 Troll/USE scripts totaling just 96 lines of data manipulation language with comments.

If all of the operations are described in this way, we obtain a precise *executable* specification of the operations. These executable statements, when combined with the dialog description from the USE transition diagrams, yield a running system.

VII. Formal Specification

Whether or not a functional prototype has been created, the previous steps provide sufficient information to produce a formal specification of system behavior, should one wish to do so. The transition diagrams give a formal definition of the input syntax, the output displays, and the possible sequences of state transitions, showing the points at which various operations are invoked. All that remains, then, is to give a formal specification of the behavior of the operations.

For this purpose, we follow the BASIS (Behavioral Approach to the Specification of Information System) method [30], [15], which is an abstract model approach to specification, based on the ideas of Hoare, as refined for use in the Alphard programming language [31], [32]. BASIS has five major steps: information analysis, semantic specification, verification of the design specification, implementation, and verification of the implementation. The first step, information analysis, includes the specification of the objects and transactions involved in the specification to be built. This information is derived from the requirements analysis phase (and can be done at that time).

The second step (semantic specification) includes the specification of the logical rules or properties (constraints) of the real world system. This information includes not only the operations of the system, but also the legal states of the data. If the data start out in a legal or accurate state and only legal operations are applied, then the data will be guaranteed to have semantic integrity. (This specification can be verified as the next step.)

There are three main parts of a BASIS specification of semantic integrity: the image of the object, the invariant, and input and output constraints for each operation defined on each object. The image is a list of the attributes associated with the object along with constraints on the values of these attributes for instances of the object. The invariant is composed of the interattribute constraints, if any. This invariant can be replaced by placing such constraints in the input and output constraints for the operations. The operations are defined by the input and output constraints which characterize the effects of the operations, using Hoare's notations for preconditions and postconditions. The specification of the pre and post conditions is important for three reasons: 1) the checking of particular constraints is tied to particular operations, 2) the pre and post constraints for the operations act as a guide for the implementor, and 3) they are used to prove that the specification and implementation are correct.

Formal specifications are a valuable discipline and help to eliminate the ambiguity that is often present with informal specifications. Formal specifications are rarely requested by users, though, who normally prefer that the equivalent effort be given to development of the prototype or final system. Formal specifications may be difficult to write and are not easily understood. Furthermore, most users do not yet understand that they aid in the identification and removal of errors. Thus, they have little interest in the formal specifications of the operations.

The ability to formalize one's concept of a system is an important process (even if the process is not done on every system). Thus, the formal specification step is an important part of the USE methodology. In practice, the complete formalization is rarely used, but the USE methodology is guided by the ideas inherent in the BASIS approach. Furthermore, the methods and tools used in the USE methodology are all based on formalisms, such as state transition networks and the theory of relations.

VIII. Experience

The User Software Engineering methodology has evolved since the late 1970's and has been shown to be a practical method for the creation of interactive information systems. At first, the methodology relied upon manual creation and modification of the USE transition diagrams. At that time, it was useful primarily as a specification method, rather than as a system building tool. The transition diagram specification method was used successfully on several interactive medical applications.

The envisioned implementation language was PLAIN [33], designed to support the creation of interactive information systems. PLAIN is a Pascal-based language with features for string-handling, pattern-matching, exception-handling, and relational database management, in addition to a data abstraction mechanism. While PLAIN is valuable as an implementation language, our attention was increasingly drawn to the earlier stages of the development process and to the notions of external design and rapid implementation described in this paper.

Implementation of tools to support the USE methodology directly was undertaken in 1978. The Troll/USE relational database system was designed so that it could serve both as the backend to PLAIN and as a stand-alone relational system. Design and implementation of the Transition Diagram Interpreter and RAPID/USE was begun in 1980. In both cases, an important project goal was to produce software tools that could be distributed to others. As a result, the User Software Engineering distribution was begun jointly by the University of California, San Francisco, and the Vrije Universiteit, Amsterdam, in 1981. Initially, the distribution included only the Troll/USE relational DBMS. Now, in the fourth release, the distribution includes a vastly improved version of Troll/USE, along with the third version of RAPID/USE, the Troll/USE library, the TBE browser for Troll/USE relations, and some experimental software. Approximately 100 sites are using one of the two latest versions of the distribution, divided half and half between academic and industrial users.

Commercial interest in the User Software Engineering methodology and its supporting tools led to the creation of a commercial venture, Interactive Development Environments, Inc., which markets commercial versions of this software, plus the Transition Diagram Editor and other graphical editors described in this paper.

Until 1984, experience with the methodology and tools was fragmentary, and mostly confined to the original developers of the methodology. Availability of tools and tutorial materials were necessary to transfer the technology out of the research setting. RAPID/USE has now been used for some significant applications, including the system administrator's interface for an engineering workstation, a patient record-keeping system for a health maintenance organization, a general ledger accounting system, and a customer/order management system, in addition to applications developed within our own organization and the library system described in this paper. All but the first of these applications use Troll/USE as the database support for their application.

Now that there is a substantial user community, we are forming a USE Users' Group to serve as a forum for discussing the methodology and the tools. The first meeting of this Group is scheduled for mid-1986.

IX. EVALUATION

At this stage, evaluation of the methodology and tools is largely anecdotal. However, it is possible to give a subjective evaluation of the User Software Engineering methodology against the goals presented in Section II. Each of the goals is taken up in turn.

A. Functionality

Since User Software Engineering results in the creation of running systems, one could say that it covers the entire development process. In fact, though, the USE approach makes specific contributions only in the specification, design, and implementation phases, and relies heavily on integration with other approaches for analysis and testing. The identification of abstract data and abstract operations during the analysis phase supports the use of those abstract operations when one defines the external interface to the system.

B. Reliability

User Software Engineering makes a significant contribution to assuring the reliability of the interactive interface. First, the interface is formally specified and executable, making it possible to create a set of test cases to validate the interface. One can make certain that the IIS provides an error path from each node where erroneous user input may be received. The presence of these paths may be verified through inspection of the diagrams.

Second, RAPID/USE produces two logs: a *raw log* containing all of the user input from the execution of the program and a *transition log*, as described in Section V-C. The raw log may be saved and subsequently used as input to a later version of the IIS. A set of such logs can be added to a test suite for the system. The transition log can be used to obtain measures of node coverage and arc coverage for a given execution of the IIS, as well as information on user error frequency and task completion times.

A set of transition logs can assure that test coverage of the user interface was sufficient. The use of these logs, plus animation of the executing transition diagrams, is discussed at greater length in a related paper [34].

Third, the IIS is largely built upon two components: RAPID/USE and Troll/USE. These application development tools have been thoroughly tested and widely used. The amount of code to be written by the developer is relatively small, making it easier to test the program than if the equivalent system had been created *de novo* in a procedural programming language.

C. Usability

Usability of the resulting system is a key goal of User Software Engineering and the use of prototypes of the user interface may be regarded as an important contribution of the USE methodology. This notion of interface prototyping is rapidly gaining favor, and there is some preliminary evidence of this concept being introduced into other methodologies. We remain convinced by our experience that user involvement in the interface design process is a major factor in eventual user satisfaction with the system.

As noted in Section V-A, early attempts at user involvement were hindered by the lack of an executable prototype of the interface. Our own efforts to build a system for a glaucoma clinic (circa 1980) showed that transition diagrams and screen layout forms were inadequate for user understanding in the absence of the Transition Diagram Interpreter.

When end users (or surrogate end users) work with the prototype of the interface, it is possible to evaluate their experience, both objectively and subjectively. The objective information can be taken from the transition logs, while the subjective information comes from observation of the user, followed by an informal interview. Further refinement of this evaluation procedure is needed, since there is a wide variation in user skills and in motivation to use the system, especially in its early nonfunctional stages.

D. Evolvability

The separation of system specification into user interface, operations, and database is valuable for creating evolvable systems. For example, changes in the database schema typically do not affect the user interface; similarly, changes to the user interface rarely affect the database or the system operations. Thus, modifications can be isolated within the system. For example, a minor change in the user interface to a medium-sized system can often be found and corrected in a matter of seconds, with a new version of the executable user interface running within a minute.

At the same time, though, there are some difficulties with evolvability, particularly in maintaining consistent dialog styles through a set of subsystems or transaction types. Also, some changes to the specification may have far-reaching effects, requiring changes to the database, the operations, and the user interface. It is easy to make errors in the use of names for nodes, RAPID/USE variables, Troll/USE attributes, and program variables in the application code. We believe that introduction of a data dictionary can reduce the frequency of this type of problem; we have also found that multiple windows as found in many workstation environments make it easy to check for consistent use of names in different parts of the IIS.

E. Automated Support

User Software Engineering takes the position that software tools can be *integrated* into a structured software development methodology, rather than just placed into an available toolkit. While the infrastructure of the methodology is essential, it is the tools that make the methodology work. User involvement and interface prototyping are sound ideas, but they would be of little utility without the tools. The Transition Diagram Editor is an especially valuable addition to the USE toolset, reducing the need to learn the RAPID/USE syntax and eliminating some of the typing required to input the RAPID/USE language.

The USE tools are created as a set of components, many of which communicate via message passing. They are implemented on the Unix™ operating system.[6] This tool architecture supports two important aspects of tool development and use, namely

1) the ability for tools to communicate with and via a database (Troll/USE); and

2) the ability to extend tool capabilities without modifying existing tools; such extensions may be made either by the methodology's developers or by the methodology's users, since the tool interfaces are well-defined.

As with many other toolsmiths, we are continually seeking ways to provide additional automated support and to improve the existing tools. This objective continually provides many research and development projects. We are currently making modifications to Troll/USE to support long tuples ($> = 4$ kbytes); since Troll/USE already supports variable length strings, such a change will increase the usability of Troll/USE for developers and for end users.

We are also developing a "what-you-see-is-what-you-get" forms-based program for database entry, update, and retrieval. Such a tool will make it much easier to specify and to implement this important class of programs. This tool, RAPID/FORM, will generate a RAPID/USE script or executable program from a description of the form-based user interface and the associate database relations and attributes.

In summary, automated support for the USE methodology is very important, and we are pleased with the strategy that has been used for tool development and integration. Further development is aimed at simplifying the development process, and at extending the tool coverage to other aspects of that process.

™Unix is a trademark of AT&T Bell Laboratories.

[6]The USE tools are distributed by the University of California, San Francisco, by the Vrije Universiteit, Amsterdam, and by Interactive Development Environments, Inc., of San Francisco, which also provides support for the methodology and tools.

F. Improved Developer Productivity

Productivity is difficult to measure and has traditionally been measured in delivered source lines of code per unit of time. It is generally accepted that developers can deliver the same number of lines of code per day independent of the programming language.

By that measure, User Software Engineering can lead to a significant jump in developer productivity, since most of an interactive information system can be described either by the RAPID/USE dialog description language or by the Troll/USE data manipulation language. For a very small RAPID/USE example, we discovered that 35 lines of dialog description and data manipulation text required nearly 300 lines when reprogrammed in the C language. Furthermore, virtually none of the C language code was reusable, and it was necessary to eliminate one of the features available in the RAPID/USE version. It is apparent that creation and maintenance of 35 lines of RAPID/USE text, similar to that found in Fig. 10, is much simpler than creating and maintaining 300 lines of code in the C language.

The library example developed in this paper consists of approximately 1200 lines of RAPID/USE text, fewer than 100 lines of Troll/USE data manipulation scripts, and 30 lines of relational database definition.

It should also be noted that the RAPID/USE compiler is very fast, capable of processing more than 2000 lines of RAPID/USE input per minute on a Sun-2 Workstation or a VAX-11/750. Compilation of the library example takes approximately 30 seconds, while compilation and linking of the equivalent program in C or Pascal would take several minutes.

While we would not claim an order of magnitude improvement in productivity from User Software Engineering and its tools, such an improvement can be found for a portion of the development process, namely the design and implementation of the user interface. For the interactive systems that we have built, use of the methodology and tools has yielded an apparent factor of 3 to 4 gain in overall productivity, sharply reducing the time needed to produce a working system.

These results may be biased by our own expertise with the methodology and tools. The reported experience of others will be required before accurate estimates of productivity gains can be made. Nonetheless, initial anecdotal reports are extremely promising, and we hope that users of the USE methodology and tools will soon report on their experiences.

G. Reusability

As we continue to develop interactive information systems, consistent program schemas appear repeatedly. In the library system, we see the presence of a menu, followed by a multiway branch based on the user response. Similarly, a request for a yes-or-no response typically results in a three-way branch, corresponding to the yes case, the no case, and the error case. These "dialog schemas"

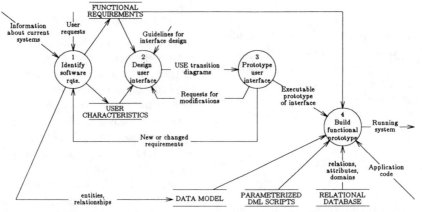

Fig. 16. Overview of the User Software Engineering methodology.

may be saved and reused in a variety of user interface designs. Similarly, entire diagrams may be reused.

We have observed that individuals and organizations develop personal styles of user interface design. These styles are captured in USE transition diagrams, which may then be repeatedly used. Further work is needed to support management of a library of reusable diagrams and dialog skeletons, but preliminary observations indicate that one can reuse part or all of a user interface design in the same way that one can reuse a piece of code.

X. CONCLUSION

The User Software Engineering methodology and its supporting toolset have been developed over the last ten years as an effective approach to the design and development of interactive information systems. The USE methodology has effectively integrated the design of user interfaces into a systematic development process and has created tools to support the rapid development and modification of prototypes of that interface.

The prototype variant of the USE methodology, as shown in Fig. 16, has proved to be especially valuable in improving the design of user interfaces, in constructing systems quickly, in improving the reliability of interactive information systems, and in providing users with a good framework to assist developers during the early stages of the development process.

The USE methodology supports the goals of functionality, reliability, usability, evolvability, reusability, automated support, and improved developer productivity by combining formal and informal methods for specification with extensive use of prototypes and a systematic software development process.

Current research and development on the User Software Engineering methodology is focused on extending the types of interactive media that can be supported by the specification method, on providing greater automated support for program generation, and on making the Unified Support Environment available on a large number of machines. All of these activities are intended to preserve the structure of the methodology while simplifying its use and reducing the effort needed to produce high quality interactive information systems.

REFERENCES

[1] A. I. Wasserman, "Information system development methodology," *J. Amer. Soc. Inform. Sci.*, vol. 31, no. 1, pp. 5–24, 1980.
[2] ——, "Software engineering environments," in *Advances in Computers*, vol. 22, M. Yovits, Ed. New York: Academic, 1983.
[3] M. Porcella, P. Freeman, and A. I. Wasserman, "Ada methodology questionnaire summary," *ACM Software Eng. Notes*, vol. 8, no. 1, Jan. 1983.
[4] B. Shneiderman, *Software Psychology*. Cambridge, MA: Winthrop, 1980.
[5] D. J. Streveler and A. I. Wasserman, "Quantitative measures of the spatial properties of screen designs," in *Proc. Interact '84 Conf.* Amsterdam, The Netherlands: North-Holland, 1984.
[6] T. W. Olle, H. G. Sol, and A. A. Verrijn-Stuart, Eds., *Information System Design Methodologies: A Comparative Review.* Amsterdam, The Netherlands: North-Holland, 1982.
[7] T. W. Olle, H. G. Sol, and C. J. Tully, Eds., *Information System Design Methodologies: A Feature Analysis.* Amsterdam, The Netherlands: North-Holland, 1983.
[8] J. M. Smith and D. C. P. Smith, "Conceptual database design," in *Tutorial: Software Design Techniques*, 4th ed., P. Freeman and A. I. Wasserman, Eds. Los Alamitos, CA: IEEE Comput. Soc., 1983.
[9] P. P.-S. Chen, "The entity-relationship model—Toward a unified view of data," *Trans. Database Syst.*, vol. 1, no. 1, pp. 9–36, Mar. 1976.
[10] M. Jackson, *System Development*. London: Prentice-Hall, 1983.
[11] M. Lundeberg, G. Goldkuhl, and A. Nilsson, *Information Systems Development—A Systematic Approach.* Englewood Cliffs, NJ: Prentice-Hall International, 1981.
[12] C. Gane and T. Sarson, *Structured Systems Analysis.* Englewood Cliffs, NJ: Prentice-Hall, 1979.
[13] D. L. Parnas, "A technique for software module specification with examples," *Commun. ACM*, vol. 15, no. 5, pp. 330–336, May 1972.
[14] O. Roubine and L. Robinson, "SPECIAL reference manual," SRI Int., Menlo Park, CA, Tech. Rep. CSG-45, 1978.
[15] N. G. Leveson, A. I. Wasserman, and D. M. Berry, "BASIS: A behaviorial approach to the specification of information systems," *Inform. Syst.*, vol. 8, no. 1, pp. 15–23, 1983.
[16] J. Roach, H. R. Hartson, R. W. Ehrich, T. Yunten, and D. H. Johnson, "DMS: A comprehensive system for managing human–computer dialogue," in *Proc. Human Factors in Comput. Syst.*, Mar. 1982, pp. 102–105.
[17] A. I. Wasserman, "User software engineering and the design of interactive systems," in *Proc. 5th Int. Conf. Software Eng.*, 1981, pp. 387–393.
[18] A. I. Wasserman and S. K. Stinson, "A specification method for interactive information systems," in *Proc. IEEE Comput. Soc. Conf. Specification of Reliable Software*, 1979, pp. 68–79.
[19] D. L. Parnas, "On the use of transition diagrams in the design of a user interface for an interactive computer system," in *Proc. 24th Nat. ACM Conf.*, 1969, pp. 379–385.
[20] R. J. K. Jacob, "Using formal specifications in the design of a human–computer interface," *Commun. ACM*, vol. 26, no. 3, pp. 259–264, Mar. 1983.
[21] D. Kieras and P. Polson, "A generalized transition network representation for interactive systems," in *Proc. CHI '83 Human Factors in Comput. Syst.*, 1983, pp. 103–106.

[22] A. I. Wasserman, "Extending state transition diagrams for the specification of human–computer interaction," *IEEE Trans. Software Eng.*, vol. SE-11, Aug. 1985.

[23] A. I. Wasserman and D. T. Shewmake, "Rapid prototyping of interactive information systems," *ACM Software Eng. Notes*, vol. 7, no. 5, pp. 171–180, Dec. 1982.

[24] A. I. Wasserman, D. T. Shewmake, and P. A. Pircher, "A RAPID/USE tutorial," Lab. Med. Inform. Sci., Univ. California, San Francisco, 1985.

[25] C. Mills and A. I. Wasserman, "A transition diagram editor," in *Proc. 1984 Summer Usenix Meeting*, June, 1984, pp. 287–296.

[26] C. J. Date, *An Introduction to Database Systems*, 3rd ed. Reading, MA: Addison-Wesley, 1982.

[27] M. R. Stonebraker and E. Wong, "The design and implementation of INGRES," *Trans. Database Syst.*, vol. 1, no. 3, Sept. 1976.

[28] D. D. Chamberlin *et al.*, "SEQUEL 2: A unified approach to data definition, manipulation, and control," *IBM J. Res. Develop.*, vol. 20, no. 6, pp. 560–575, Nov. 1976.

[29] M. L. Kersten and A. I. Wasserman, "The architecture of the PLAIN data base handler," *Software—Practice and Experience*, vol. 11, no. 2, pp. 175–186, Feb. 1981.

[30] N. G. Leveson, "Applying behaviorial abstraction to information system design and integrity," Ph.D. dissertation, Univ. California, Los Angeles, 1980. (Available as Tech. Rep. 47, Lab. Med. Inform. Sci., Univ. California, San Francisco.)

[31] C. A. R. Hoare, "Proof of correctness of data representations," *Acta Inform.*, vol. 1, no. 3, pp. 271–281, 1972.

[32] M. Shaw, Ed., *ALPHARD: Form and Content*. New York: Springer-Verlag, 1981.

[33] A. I. Wasserman, D. D. Sherertz, M. L. Kersten, R. P. van de Riet, and M. D. Dippe, "Revised report on the programming language PLAIN," *ACM SIGPLAN Notices*, vol. 16, no. 5, pp. 59–80, May 1981.

[34] A. I. Wasserman, P. A. Pircher, and D. T. Shewmake, "Building reliable interactive information systems," *IEEE Trans. Software Eng.*, vol. SE-12, pp. 147–156, Jan. 1986.

Software Design Techniques (IEEE Computer Society), with P. Freeman, and *Automated Tools for Information Systems Design* (North-Holland), with H.-J. Schneider.

Dr. Wasserman is the Editor-in-Chief of ACM's *Computing Surveys*, and a member of the Editorial Board of several other journals, including the *International Journal of Man-Machine Studies, Information Systems*, and the *Journal of Systems and Software*. He is a member of the Programme Committee for the IFIP Congress '86, Vice-Chairman of IFIP WG 8.1 (Design and Evaluation of Information Systems), and a former chairman of ACM's SIGSOFT. He is a member of the Association for Computing Machinery and the IEEE Computer Society.

Peter A. Pircher was born in Lucerne, Switzerland, in 1953. He received the M.S. degree in mathematics and computer science and the Ph.D. degree in computer science from the University of Zurich, Zurich, Switzerland.

From 1980 to 1983 he was a Research Assistant and Lecturer at the University of Zurich. His research included the design of a runtime environment for an interactive Pascal programming system. In 1983, after receiving a two-year grant from the Swiss National Science Foundation, he moved to San Francisco to continue his research on programming environments. He currently works as a Research Associate in the Department of Medical Information Science at the University of California, San Francisco.

David T. Shewmake (S'85) received the B.S. degree in physics from the University of Michigan, Ann Arbor, in 1974.

He is currently completing the Ph.D. degree in medical information science at the University of California, San Francisco. His research interests are in software engineering, human factors, and medical informatics.

Mr. Shewmake is a member of the IEEE Computer Society and the Association for Computing Machinery.

Martin L. Kersten received the Ph.D. degree in mathematics and computer science from the Vrije Universiteit, Amsterdam, The Netherlands, in 1985. His dissertation was on the subject of secure programming environments.

He is currently leading a database systems project at the Centrum for Wiskunde en Informatica, Amsterdam, and holds a faculty position at the Vrije Universiteit, Amsterdam. His research interests are in database management.

Dr. Kersten is a member of the Association for Computing Machinery and the Dutch society for informatics (NGI).

Anthony I. Wasserman (M'71) received the A.B. degree in mathematics and physics from the University of California, Berkeley, and the M.S. and Ph.D. degrees in Computer Sciences from the University of Wisconsin—Madison.

After three years in industry, he joined the University of California, San Francisco, where he is now Professor of Medical Information Science. Since 1970, he has also been Lecturer in the Computer Science Division at the University of California, Berkeley. He is also the founder and President of Interactive Development Environments, Inc. He is the architect of the User Software Engineering methodology and supporting toolset for the specification and design of interactive information systems. His research interests include software development methods, tools, and environments, human interaction with computers, and data management. He is the author of more than 60 papers and an editor of seven books, including *Tutorial:*

PERFORMANCE ENGINEERING: DOING IT "LATER" ON LARGE PROJECTS

Dr. Thomas E. Bell
Rivendel Consultants Inc.

ABSTRACT

The manager of a large system development project is responsible for ensuring that performance engineering is not deferred until "later." However, he may submit to the temptation for delay because performance engineering is difficult, because the technological skills needed for performance engineering are urgently needed elsewhere, because of a desire to avoid impacting other efforts, because of inappropriate analyses by performance people, or because of a curious fatalism about performance. A project manager should be particularly concerned about performance if interactive or real-time response is required, if throughput levels are required, if hardware resources are limited or not free, or if performance is truly important to users and their managers. Indicators of impending problems are presented for managers and project reviewers. They are organized by project phase to facilitate identification of trouble early rather than "later." Readers are invited to suggest revisions to the indicators.

Waiting until "later" to address computer performance problems is an expensive way to manage a large project. Near the end of a project (when "later" occurs), design decisions have been made in all major areas, implementation has been largely completed, and documentation efforts are almost through. A few minor changes can still be made, but any major changes result in major breakage (costly repair of "broken" design). Unfortunately, tardy performance engineering on a large project usually identifies shortcomings that require such changes, and can result in substantial schedule slips and large cost over-runs or (in some cases) project cancellation.

A large project, in the context of this paper, refers to a system development effort (perhaps involving hardware development but certainly software development) that includes from 20 to 300 people. This number of people always exceeds the span of control of a single manager (even at the bottom end) and forces a structured development process in order to control effort. In this environment a large number of problems may induce a Project Manager to delay performance engineering.

"Performance Engineering" involves at least four types of technical activities:

o   Evaluating requirements -- particularly those addressing performance,

o   Projecting performance and resource impacts of a proposed design -- whether software, or hardware and software,

o   Measuring the prototyped or implemented system to determine its performance and/or resource consumption, and

o   Suggesting alternatives that will improve performance and/or reduce resource requirements.

Performance engineering on a large project requires concentration of resources, and is frequently delayed either consciously or unconsciously. We need to understand the reasons that this may happen in order to cope with the situation.

REASONS TO DELAY

Because meeting performance requirements is one of a project manager's responsibilities, the temptation is to criticize him unmercifully for his folly in ignoring the issue. However, the manager of a large project is confronted with such an enormous set of problems that he will almost certainly fail to solve some of them; we need to understand why performance requirements are an area in which failure occurs so often.

DIFFICULTY

Performance engineering is a complex discipline where practitioners must understand the bulk of the technologies used in the project, must have used a variety of performance analysis techniques, and must have the insight to use the correct approaches along with the judgment to know when to demand design changes. Finding qualified people to do the job is hard, and culling out the ones that falsely claim expertise is even more difficult. In the crush of starting a project, it's easy to defer finding these people or assigning someone with inadequate skills.

TECHNOLOGICAL SKILL DIVERSION

Good performance engineers are well-qualified technologists who can solve a variety of difficult problems. When a difficult problem on the critical path requires increased skills, the natural response is temporarily to divert the performance engineers onto the critical problem. When the problem seems to be under control, the analysts can be returned to their main task -- or onto the next critical problem and then the next one and so on.

ZERO-IMPACT APPROACH

A challenging schedule is the rule rather than the exception for system development projects. Given a difficult schedule, disruptions can hardly be tolerated -- particularly if incentive fees or bonuses are expected this year. A performance engineer may be ignored or chastised if he recommends a disruptive design change that will result in failure to meet near-term schedule objectives. When a performance problem is identified, the development staff may protest that its current design is adequate, and that changes will have unacceptable schedule and cost impact. It is disruptive and unpleasant to challenge developers who believe they understand the performance implications of their design as well as an experienced performance engineer. It is painful to accept the certainty of a schedule slip now rather than the possibility of a schedule slip later. It's easier to defer the change until "later" and collect this year's fee or bonus. After all, who knows what might turn up before final delivery?

INAPPROPRIATE ANALYSIS

Unfortunately, some performance engineers are more interested in applying their favorite technique than in solving project performance problems. Some of them insist on measuring a system even if it is hardly designed yet. Others are so dedicated to continued simulation or analytical modeling that they demand to continue their work without revision even when initial operational results have already proven predictions wrong. When the analysis approach is inappropriate for the project's current phase, it is easier and less stressful for the project manager to ignore the entire issue than to devote the time needed to really resolve the issues of personnel competency and direction. It's easier to defer the problem until "later" while addressing issues that might result in immediate criticism from an outside management review.

FATALISM

Severe criticism can legitimately be directed toward the project manager who takes the attitude that "The performance will be what the performance will be." That is, he asserts that the job is to build functionality; the resulting performance is out of his control. Of course, it really is out of his control if he chooses to take no actions to control it. In such cases, unfortunate results (for both the project and its manager) are almost certain.

Failure to perceive performance engineering as one of the essential technical disciplines to be employed in a system development project is relatively consistent with the failure of many development policies and standards to require its use.

WHEN PERFORMANCE SHOULD BE A CONCERN

Performance engineering probably should not be a concern in some small software projects when code doesn't need to run operationally, but it should be a concern in large projects and any in which code will run in production. In particular, project managers should be especially concerned if one or more of the following is true:

1. Interactive or real-time response times are required.

2. Non-trivial throughput levels are required for a given amount of machine resources.

3. The project's software must run on its own hardware resource that is either specified or must be purchased out of the same budget as other development resources.

4. Incentive fees or bonuses are based on response time or throughput.

5. Senior customer/user personnel will observe the responsiveness of the system while it is performing tasks that, to them, are intuitively easy for a computer. Under these conditions, ignoring performance issues until "later" will very likely result in embarrassment to the project manager, his successor, and/or his superior before the project is completed.

SIGNS OF TROUBLE

Industry experience with large projects' performance has been adequate for us to identify some early indicators of performance problems that will be apparent "later." Reviewers can use them as a check-list, and project managers can use them for evaluating their performance engineering organizations. Special conditions exist in any large development project, so some indicators may be true even when performance engineering is being successfully performed. However, finding more than 25% true at any phase should be cause for concern, and finding more than 50% true should trigger corrective actions.

The indicators below are organized by phases of a project and are summarized in Appendix A. In general, the indicators for earlier phases also apply to all later phases. Therefore, for example, indicators 5 - 8 in addition to indicators 1 - 4 apply to a project nearing detailed design. Comments, explanations, and examples from industrial experiences are presented with the indicators.

PROPOSAL THROUGH SYSTEM DESIGN REVIEW

1. Performance commitments are made, but no gross-level resource budgets exist.

2. No Performance Engineering organization or plan exists (even within a System Engineering organization).

3. No personnel on the system design team have experience in solving performance problems in the anticipated hardware/software environment.

4. Consideration has not yet been given to the nature of performance data collection approaches/mechanisms for the system.

Comments, Explanations, and Cases

During the proposal and system design phases, optimism is great, and DP personnel typically over-promise in all areas. Frequently, the approach is to make any promise that can't be proven infeasible. Of course, it's extremely difficult to prove that a performance requirement can't be met, particularly if the necessary analysis has not yet been performed.

One of the most dangerous approaches is to select unfamiliar hardware, operating system, application system, or development environment and assume that its vendor is totally accurate in his claims that it will solve the historical problems of the old environment. Almost as dangerous, however, is entrusting design to people with no experience on the target system and/or experience in performance engineering.

For example, a very large military project selected a combination of hardware, operating system, and DBMS with which none of its people had any familiarity. (But it was really cheap!) The development personnel responded to the situation by building a layer of software over parts of the system unfamiliar to them (nearly all parts). Guess what: the performance impact was overwhelming. Eventually the project was cancelled because adequate performance was unattainable.

In another case, the project manager for an accounting system selected a fourth-generation language. Everything sounded wonderful for development, but even superficial performance analysis showed that the largest available machine could not process 24 hours of input in 24 hours. Another alternative was selected.

The System Engineer for another large project found his way to fame. He promised outstanding performance when describing the system to users during the proposal phase. After the "go-ahead" decision, his performance people examined the situation. In this case, "later" came early. The promises were proved to be infeasible. The System Engineer changed jobs and the users (who were astute enough to be skeptical anyhow) learned the truth early. Although exposure to the truth was unfortunately delayed a few months, it came early enough that users still had sympathy with the project personnel.

A sophisticated DBMS, offering nearly-relational access (whatever that means), was selected for an order entry system. The vendor had assured the users that adequate performance data were generated by the system. After installation, the data center (with the responsibility for making the product work) found that the data consisted of job accounting -- for the DBMS and all users as a single entity. The system works, but very slowly; the cause is not known.

Do any of the examples sound like the author has revealed your private secret? The chances are he hasn't, but maybe he has exposed some of the industry's dirty little secrets. We really don't know about the performance of lots of systems; we tend to fake it when we can; and some vendors aren't completely candid with us.

If you're a project reviewer, ask about specifics and don't accept bland assurances.

SYSTEM DESIGN REVIEW THROUGH PRELIMINARY DESIGN REVIEW

5. No simulation or analytical model has been developed to ensure the consistency of budgets, assumptions, and requirements.

6. Plans have not been made to ensure that resource consumption and elapsed time can be measured during implementation and integration.

7. None of the performance requirements has been questioned.

8. Adjustment of planned hardware and system software has not been proposed.

9. Examination of requirements has not included analysis of transaction frequencies, patterns of interaction, and projected loading derived from a detailed concept of operations.

Comments, Explanations, and Cases

During preliminary design (also called "high level design" and "general design") project personnel should be working almost frantically to understand the nature of their problems. If the person in charge of performance says "I can tell you for a fact that our performance is just fine, so we'd be wasting our time to do further analysis," give him high marks for faith and/or deception. Also, hold onto your wallet and prepare for the worst.

Without detailed, documented analysis, the necessary revisions to hardware/software architecture can't be identified. Changes will be lots and lots more expensive later, and they're almost certain to be needed.

Examining requirements for performance issues may be extremely difficult if the requirements have been specified in the classical hierarchial format. When, for example, a man-machine interactive system has been specified using the hierarchial format, the layout of each screen may be specified. For each screen, a comment may be given that response time shall be "adequate" or even that it shall not exceed two seconds. However, a variety of different paths through the ultimate system will typically present each screen of data, and many inputs (some with critical timing needs) will result in no output screens. In many cases, performance requirements need to be placed on paths through the system; hierarchial ordering is not a natural way to state these requirements. A performance engineer many need to examine the requirements carefully to discern the paths and to ensure that implicit and unstated performance needs are known before designers get too far in the design process.

For systems with particularly challenging or critical performance requirements, prototyping and performance evaluation of selected paths or subsystems may be highly desirable at this stage. Good performance engineers can usually identify some of parts of the system that are likely to be the sources of performance problems even at this early stage. Investigating these areas may provide early warnings so that requirements can be re-examined, and/or preliminary design effort can be concentrated on the most critical parts of the system. Certainly, though, this activity should not be delayed beyond the next phase of the project.

Now is the time to plan for later measurement. Quite likely, a few important changes can be made in the design or the project plan to provide data for giving early indications of problems later in the project life. Usually, the biggest payoff for consideration of data collection at this phase, however, is forcing design personnel to consider which performance problems will be most important (and therefore worthy of monitoring).

A critical on-line, financial reporting system for a major US manufacturing firm was being redeveloped and reimplemented (as a change from a stand-alone system) for integration into the firm's mainline systems. The objective of integration was so important that even simple models of total resource consumption were not used to check memory demands and paging requirements. The system encountered so many performance problems that its implementation was never completed. Involved corporate officers and their direct subordinates were severely embarrassed, and several left the firm.

In another case, a simple analytical model indicated that the design of an input module would lead to overload in a variety of conditions. The designer was very motivated toward project success, examined the model implications, and changed the design to one that was far more robust. On the same project, an outsider developed a simulation model indicating that the design would consume excessive CPU resources. Although initially skeptical, project personnel eventually accepted the implications and made a major revision in overall design.

PRELIMINARY DESIGN REVIEW THROUGH BEGINNING OF IMPLEMENTATION

10. Detailed (module-by-module) resource budgets do not exist.

11. End-to-end sequences with elapsed time budgets for individual modules have not been identified and documented for all response time requirements.

12. Initial benchmarking (with synthetic tasks or prototype code) has been deferred until "real code" exists; assumptions have been adopted as reality without empirical evidence.

13. Performance tools have not yet been identified for use in the system during and after implementation.

Comments, Explanations, and Cases

By this phase in a project's life, the pressure is great to proceed with implementation. Performance engineers on large projects are typically caught up in making snap decisions about implementation alternatives and trying to keep track of all the design decisions that developers are making. Too often, they withdraw into continuing the approaches that were appropriate in earlier phases.

This is the time to get specific about demands on the system, empirical verification of critical assumptions, and tools to use through acceptance testing. Demanding that operational concepts be detailed, however, can be interpreted as simply pursuing niceties that will delay implementation. The performance engineer must be both demanding and diplomatic. If the game is lost at this phase, the next real performance examination may well occur when performance disaster is looming.

The performance engineer should ensure that budgets are defined and that critical benchmarking has been performed to ensure that earlier models are realistic. He may find that the only effective means to bring reality to the paper design is a prototype. Unfortunately, some organizations have incorrectly defined the term "rapid prototyping" to mean only mocking up a series of displays. Such exercises are frequently useful for initial examination of user interfaces, but they are not useful for other purposes during design.

Goldberg[1] provides the following: "RAPID PROTOTYPING is the creation of an executable, but perhaps very inefficient, implementation (the implementation may be the specification itself) from a formal specification. Rapid prototyping allows the functionality of the system to be observed before development has occurred, significantly reducing maintenance performed to modify functionality after coding has occurred. Rapid prototyping helps identify code bottlenecks -- the critical regions of code that must be carefully optimized."

In one large project, performance personnel continued their earlier efforts into the detailed design phase. They continued detailing a simulation model down to the point that vendor personnel could not describe the remaining details. However, they did not readily undertake benchmarking studies, and pressed people to make estimates when empirical studies would have been both quicker and more useful. Eventually, they checked their model and were surprised by the great discrepancy between assumptions and reality.

In another case, performance engineering for a major subsystem had been deferred until "later" and implementation had proceeded. A couple of engineers happened to inquire about the situation and discovered that both revised loading projections and prototype software testing indicated that the design could never meet requirements. After a series of changes, a new design emerged. The subsystem will probably meet its required primary function, but performance remains questionable and is being monitored continually.

BEGINNING OF IMPLEMENTATION THROUGH BEGINNING OF INTEGRATION

14. Measurement tools are not in place and in use by both performance and development personnel.

15. Predicted performance has not been compared with initial measured performance; management reviews do not require that performance data be presented.

16. Corrective plans are not in place to respond to performance short-falls.

17. Initial workstation software has not been operated (even with extensive stubs) by human operators while measuring resource consumption and response time.

18. Hardware alternatives, system software alternatives, and application alternatives are not being considered to improve performance.

19. A complete set of hardware and system software has not yet been assembled and tested with benchmarks to ensure correct functionality and performance.

Comments, Explanations, and Cases

During implementation, opportunities abound for performance engineering to identify problems and correct them before they become critical. If tools are in place for general use, development personnel can probably be persuaded to use them or ask performance engineers to assist in their use. Unexpected issues will arise, and immediate solutions can be developed and applied so that further development is build on a foundation of software that performs well.

As parts of the system are brought up, unexpected performance effects will become apparent. Adjustments of hardware and software architectures will probably be desirable. The earlier the effects can be identified, the greater will be the options and, therefore, the less costly will be the fix. Identifying these effects can be hastened by running initial software (particularly workstation software) as early as possible. All the pieces of hardware and software should be assembled so that unexpected problems can be identified.

In one case, assembling the hardware during implementation showed that both tape and disk drives had design errors that became apparent with the software being implemented. The time before required deployment was long enough that design revisions to the hardware could be made by the vendors. Had identification of the effects been delayed, the project would have had a major crisis.

A project with heavy dependency on workstations did not begin examining performance until quite late. The design called for multiple windows to be active continually. Unfortunately, the hardware and software did not adequately support the number of windows, and the operational concept had to be changed after much of the interfacing software had been written. Significant breakage resulted.

BEGINNING OF INTEGRATION THROUGH END OF ACCEPTANCE TESTING

20. Lists have not been documented to record opportunities for performance improvement during this phase and after acceptance testing.

21. Intensive performance measurement efforts are not underway to understand the causes of anomalous results.

22. Everyone is certain that performance problems are all under control.

Comments, Explanations, and Cases

During Integration, further performance problems will be uncovered. Typically, the extent of overhead in the system will become apparent at this stage, and the implications of earlier compromises and design decisions will begin to be fully understood. Flows through application modules will take far longer than expected, and project personnel will have a variety of ideas for improving performance.

Given tight schedules, most of the improvement ideas can't be implemented immediately. Instead, they need to be recorded for future examination while the real causes of anomalies are examined. Then selection of the most appropriate changes can be selected.

Quite often, resources preclude implementing good ideas immediately, but the improvement ideas should be pursued as soon as possible. Unless the ideas are recorded, they will be lost in the course of normal personnel turn-over and new ideas crowding out the old ones.

Programmers may be among the most prideful people around. When the performance (both timing and reliability) of a major subsystem began creating severe problems during integration, a proud programmer fought vigorously to keep the performance people out of "his domain." He was successful in his battle. The issue is now reopened as people consider how the entire subsystem will be replaced; an easier solution would have been to fix the problems after determining the underlying causes but before completion of integration.

ACCEPTANCE INTO OPERATIONAL USE

23. Performance results (from built-in collection mechanisms) are not being reviewed by performance engineers and project management.

24. Lessons learned from the implementation are not being documented or otherwise passed to personnel who will do sustaining software engineering.

25. No sustaining performance management activity has been defined or established by operational management; routine performance reports are not yet in use by operational management.

26. The most critical performance short-falls have not yet been subjected to intensive analysis with the objective of developing both "quick-fix" and long-term solutions.

Comments, Explanations, and Case

After acceptance testing is successfully completed, the system goes into operational use. Often, many of the same people (sometime including the project manager) remain with the system as sustaining engineers. They must shift their orientation away from the internally-driven development priorities and toward externally-driven support priorities. This new operational orientation requires continually monitoring system status, keeping track of problems (and working them off), and ensuring that sustaining engineering is institutionalized.

If the temptation for delay has previously overcome project management, acceptance tests may have been only conditionally passed. A long list of performance exceptions will have been documented, and project personnel will need to work off these residual problems as soon as possible.

In a project with geographically-dispersed operational sites, upgrading performance became so expensive that upgrades were collected into a new release. This same approach is regularly used by many vendors; they release a product near its advertised availability date, and then make a future delivery with the performance fixes. In such cases, "later" solutions to performance problems may cause the firm extreme embarrassment and considerable lost sales.

CONCLUSION

The problem with waiting until "later" is that "later" has a distinct tendency to arrive at the time when functional and budgetary problems also arrive. At this time, both higher management and customers/users are strikingly unsympathetic to having performance short-falls announced. Corrective actions and possible revisions in requirements can frequently be accommodated if they are addressed in a timely fashion during the development.

The danger is that all functional requirements will be considered as implicitly critical; inability to satisfy even a few may be considered a major problem. On the other hand, all performance requirements may be considered as "nice but not necessary." In fact, however, it is usually more important that a system perform its primary task **with acceptable performance** than that it perform all its functional tasks -- with questionable performance. Not all functionality is on par with meeting performance requirements for the primary task/mission/function. Although functional problems are usually easier to prove early in the project life-cycle, performance problems frequently extend from early development through system replacement; developers tend to concentrate on the immediate, provable problems rather than the more important ones that they can leave until "later."

The indicators suggested above arise from a number of projects where adequate performance was required. The experiences of other practitioners may indicate that additional indicators are important, or that some of the suggested indicators are specific to certain types of projects. The author anticipates revising this paper and would appreciate suggestions that would assist in identifying performance issues early rather than later.

Project managers must maintain cognizance of the state of performance throughout development. They need to ensure that necessary actions are taken to avoid performance surprises "later."

ACKNOWLEDGEMENT

The author is indebted to Fred C. Manthey for his extensive suggestions to this paper. His comments led to a variety of explanations and additional indicators that were not originally identified. He used his extensive experience in managing large projects (and their performance) to improve the content and presentation of this paper.

REFERENCE

1. Goldberg, A. T., "Knowledge-Based Programming: A Survey of Program Design and Construction Techniques," IEEE Transactions on Software Engineering, SE-12:7 (July 1986), pp 752-753.

APPENDIX A

The indicators have been extracted from the paper into this appendix to aid managers and reviewers who may find a summary desirable. As in the body of the paper, these are ordered by phase of the project.

PROPOSAL THROUGH SYSTEM DESIGN REVIEW

1. Performance commitments are made, but no gross-level resource budgets exist.

2. No Performance Engineering organization or plan exists (even within a System Engineering organization).

3. No personnel on the system design team have experience in solving performance problems in the anticipated hardware/software environment.

4. Consideration has not yet been given to the nature of performance data collection approaches/mechanisms for the system.

SYSTEM DESIGN REVIEW THROUGH PRELIMINARY DESIGN REVIEW

5. No simulation or analytical model has been developed to ensure the consistency of budgets, assumptions, and requirements.

6. Plans have not been made to ensure that resource consumption and elapsed time can be measured during implementation and integration.

7. None of the performance requirements has been questioned.

8. Adjustment of planned hardware and system software has not been proposed.

9. Examination of requirements has not included analysis of transaction frequencies, patterns of interaction, and projected loading derived from a detailed concept of operations.

PRELIMINARY DESIGN REVIEW THROUGH BEGINNING OF IMPLEMENTATION

10. Detailed (module-by-module) resource budgets do not exist.

11. End-to-end sequences with elapsed time budgets for individual modules have not been identified and documented for all response time requirements.

12. Initial benchmarking (with synthetic tasks or prototype code) has been deferred until "real code" exists; assumptions have been adopted as reality without empirical evidence.

13. Performance tools have not yet been identified for use in the system during and after implementation.

BEGINNING OF IMPLEMENTATION THROUGH BEGINNING OF INTEGRATION

14. Measurement tools are not in place and in use by both performance and development personnel.

15. Predicted performance has not been compared with initial measured performance; management reviews do not require that performance data be presented.

16. Corrective plans are not in place to respond to performance short-falls.

17. Initial workstation software has not been operated (even with extensive stubs) by human operators while measuring resource consumption and response time.

18. Hardware alternatives, system software alternatives, and application alternatives are not being considered to improve performance.

19. A complete suite of hardware and system software has not yet been assembled and tested with benchmarks to ensure correct functionality and performance.

BEGINNING OF INTEGRATION THROUGH END OF ACCEPTANCE TESTING

20. Lists have not been documented to record opportunities for performance improvement during this phase and after acceptance testing.

21. Intensive performance measurement efforts are not underway to understand the causes of anomalous results.

22. Everyone is certain that performance problems are all under control.

ACCEPTANCE INTO OPERATIONAL USE

23. Performance results (from built-in collection mechanisms) are not being reviewed by performance engineers and project management.

24. Lessons learned from the implementation are not being documented or otherwise passed to personnel who will do sustaining software engineering.

25. No sustaining performance management activity has been defined or established by operational management; routine performance reports are not yet in use by operational management.

26. The most critical performance short-falls have not yet been subjected to intensive analysis with the objective of developing both "quick-fix" and long-term solutions.

WORKSTATION-BASED RAPID SIMULATION AIDS FOR DISTRIBUTED PROCESSING NETWORKS

Gary E. Swinson

TRW Defense Systems Group
1 Space Park, 02/1396
Redondo Beach, CA. 90278

ABSTRACT

Rapid simulation aids at TRW provide systems engineers with CAD/CAM type engineering workstation-based capabilities to quickly define and modify network architectures. In addition, they permit the systems engineer to analyze the performance of such networks using general purpose simulation tools hosted on backend processors. Application of rapid simulation aids assists in early conceptual understanding of newly conceived systems, speeds decisions concerning implementation, and helps reduce system development risk and cost. This paper describes a methodological framework for applying rapid simulation aids to the engineering of distributed processing networks, and illustrates the application of specific tools within this framework.

INTRODUCTION

The May 1981 Department of Defense report "Candidate R&D Thrusts for the Software Technology Initiative" states "Capabilities are needed for the rapid simulation of newly defined systems to judge their probable throughput, error rate, costs, etc. Rapid simulation will assist in early conceptual understanding, and speed decisions concerning implementation". The report further states that rapid simulation aids will reduce risk, generate cost savings, and potentially benefit users by fielding systems earlier.

The need for rapid simulation aids is particularly acute for the design of sophisticated distributed processing networks which are often large, complex, and difficult to evaluate before construction. The system engineering of these systems requires numerous tradeoffs involving architecture, functional allocation, performance, reliability, costs, etc.

Historical approaches to providing project specific simulation support typically involve the establishment of a separate simulation group to complement the system engineering organization. The function of this group is to extract from the systems engineering organization the description of a system under development, and to develop an automated model of the system. However, while the model is being built, the system engineering organization continues to evolve the system design so that the initial simulation model is out of date by the time it is completed. Thus, a second iteration is required to modify the simulation model to better represent the "latest" characteristics of the system design. As this catch-up process is repeated, possibly several times, the success of the simulation activities counts on the anticipated slow-down in the rate of design changes as the design matures. Thus, it is hoped that by the time the design activities are completed, simulation activities will have caught up sufficiently to provide useful analysis results.

The above scenario for performing project specific simulation activities fails to produce simulations which have an early influence on system designs. This results because simulation tools are designed for use by programmers and not by engineers. These tools typically employ abstract building elements such as "nodes" and "channels"; the resulting simulation products often require considerable translation to be converted into usable engineering products. In addition, although many of these programmer oriented tools represent significant modeling capabilities, their internal models are not easily transported to other projects or even to other development phases for the same project.

What is needed is a capability to rapidly respond to initial designs and design changes in order to make earlier and more effective use of simulation results within the design process. In short, rapid simulation aids are needed which:

- Provide rapid capabilities to define and modify descriptions of networks to be simulated

- Use intuitive engineering specifications to describe network architectures

- Generate simulation products which are directly usable within the engineering process

- Reduce distributed processing network simulation development costs by emphasizing the portability of simulation tools and network models

- Build on extensive simulation capabilities which are already available.

Within the TRW Defense Systems Group, we have responded to the recognized need for rapid simulation

EH0291-5/89/0000/0387$01.00 ©1984 IEEE

aids by investing in applicable research and development projects. In particular:

- Network characterization tools have been developed as part of our Network Engineering IR&D project

- Scenario representation and rapid simulation interface tools have been developed as part of our Rapid Simulation Aids IR&D project

- The Automatic Data Processing Equipment (ADPE) System Sizing and Simulation Tool (ASSIST) was developed as part of our Real-Time Battle Management IR&D project.

The network characterization and rapid simulation tools use interactive features of Sun engineering workstations to provide CAD/CAM type capabilities for describing network architectures. The ASSIST general purpose simulation tool is hosted on a backend processor which is networked with Sun workstations. Collectively, these tools permit systems engineers to quickly define and modify network architectures, and to analyze the performance of such networks using general purpose simulation tools.

This paper describes a methodological framework for applying rapid simulation aids to the engineering of distributed processing networks, and illustrates the application of specific tools within this framework. With the exception of the Display Processor tool, which is under development, all of the tools described herein are currently operational.

OVERVIEW

Figure 1 provides an overview of the rapid simulation aids tool set. The tools are hosted on Unix-based Sun processors and a VMS-based VAX processor. The principal development language for the workstation-based tools is Pascal. Unix and Pascal were selected to facilitate the development of portable tools, allow applicable software products from other TRW IR&D projects to be used by the rapid simulation aids, and permit use of available sophisticated engineering terminals such as the Sun workstations. The Suns are Motorola 68010-based processors that provide comprehensive high resolution graphics display functions, including user interaction via a "mouse" (Figure 2). The VMS-based VAX is included to permit rapid simulation aids access to the ASSIST simulation tool, which is hosted in the VMS environment.

The first three tool components -- Types and Network Characterization, and Scenario Generation -- build and maintain files which comprise the rapid simulation aids data base. This relational data base forms the core of the rapid simulation aids tool set; it serves the dual purpose of describing a network design and providing the system description needed to drive a network simulation. A set of generalized utility routines, programmed in C and Pascal, access the data base structure. The principle user of the rapid simulation aids data base is the Simulation Interface component.

TYPES CHARACTERIZATION

The Types Characterization component provides the tools to define and maintain static performance characterization data for the following types of hardware and operating system elements:

- Central Processing Units (CPUs)

- Disk controllers

- Disks

- Input/Output processors (IOPs) used to access communications buses

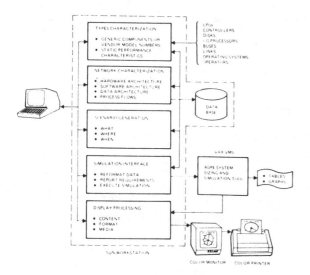

Figure 1. Rapid Simulation Aids
Functional Components

Figure 2. Sun Workstation

- Communications buses

- Communications links

- Arbitrary devices such as printers, modems, etc.

- Operating systems

- Operator stations.

Type characterization entries are typically referenced by manufacturer's name and model nomenclature (e.g., DEC VAX 11/780); these entries are maintained as a separate set of files within the rapid simulation aids data base. Figure 3 illustrates a typical template used to capture type characterization data.

An extensive library of type characteristics data has evolved from the repeated application of the rapid simulation tools. A composite library of type information is maintained by IR&D project personnel and passed on to each new project which uses the tools. Accordingly, it is now possible for many projects to satisfy most modeling parameter requirements from data readily available within the types characterization library.

NETWORK CHARACTERIZATION

The Network Characterization component provides the tools to define and maintain user conceptualizations of distributed processing network architectures. The process of describing a network architecture has been decomposed into four separate but related definition activities:

- Hardware architecture -- Propagates instances of hardware type entries to describe the hardware structure of the network architecture

- Software architecture -- Describes the static characteristics (e.g., load module size, priority) of

separately modeled software components and maps these components onto the hardware architecture

- Data architecture -- Identifies data files and messages and maps files onto the hardware architecture

- Process Flows -- Describes the dynamic flow of processes through the hardware and software components of the network architecture and identifies associated accesses to data architecture components.

Interactive graphic capabilities of Sun workstations are employed to define hardware, software, and data components of network architectures. Figure 4 illustrates a Sun graphic representation of a typical network hardware architecture. Auxiliary capabilities provided as part of the Sun graphics interface include specification entry, zoom features, stylized annotations, move element processing, etc. Figure 5 displays a typical template used to capture hardware element characteristics; note the use of the "type" entry to reference related library model parameters. Figures 6 and 7 illustrate Sun graphic representations associated with software architecture characterizations. Similar templates are used to capture data message and file characteristics. Interactive capabilities are also provided for mapping software and data components onto related hardware components (i.e., software modules onto processors/CPUs and data files onto disks).

A processing flow language, closely linked to the ASSIST simulation tool, facilitates the modeling of architecture process flows. The process flow language permits the engineer to control flow, describe resource utilization, and specify the collection of port-to-port timing statistics. The basic unit of the language is a thread which represents a flow of information through the system. Threads invoke network components which consume resources such as CPU cycles, disk

HWTYPE

Database: hwtyp   Mode: Modify

DISK TYPE	
Name	Fujitsu M2312K
Description	8 inch disk, 84.4 Mbytes
Time Between Failures (sec)	3.6e+7
Time To Repair (sec)	3.6e+2
Transfer Rate (bytes/sec)	1.229e+6
Rotational Latency (sec)	8.3e-3
Minimum Seek Time (sec)	5.0e-3
Average Seek Time (sec)	2.0e-2
Maximum Seek Time (sec)	4.0e-2
Exit	

Enter name for hardware type: Fujitsu M2312K

Figure 3. Type Characteristics Data Template

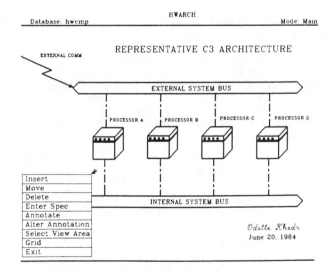

Figure 4. Hardware Architecture Display

REPRESENTATIVE C3 ARCHITECTURE

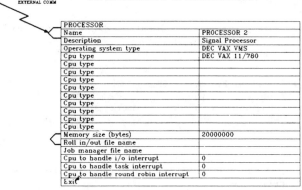

PROCESSOR	
Name	PROCESSOR 2
Description	Signal Processor
Operating system type	DEC VAX VMS
Cpu type	DEC VAX 11/780
Cpu type	
Cpu type	
Cpu type	
Cpu type	
Cpu type	
Cpu type	
Cpu type	
Cpu type	
Cpu type	
Memory size (bytes)	20000000
Roll in/out file name	
Job manager file name	
Cpu to handle i/o interrupt	0
Cpu to handle task interrupt	0
Cpu to handle round robin interrupt	0
Exit	

Use the mouse button to display the template.

Figure 5. Hardware Component Data Template

REPRESENTATIVE SOFTWARE ARCHITECTURE

PROCESSOR A

TASK A.1 TASK A.2 TASK A.3 TASK A.4

PROCESSOR B

TASK B.1 TASK B.2

PROCESSOR C

TASK C.1 TASK C.2 TASK C.3

PROCESSOR D

TASK D.1 TASK D.2 TASK D.3 TASK D.4

Gary S. Swinson
June 22, 1984

Figure 6. Software Architecture Display

accesses, communications bandwidth, and operator time. Threads can be modeled with a number of control structures which permit them to simulate control/data flows in real systems. These control structures include looping, concurrent processing, unconditional and probabilistic branching. Figure 8 illustrates a segment of a typical process flow.

SCENARIO GENERATION

The Scenario Generation component provides tools to define, review, and maintain descriptions of scenarios used to stimulate network process flows. This component uses a flexible, interactive "menu processing" front end to interface with the user. Extensive error checking and on-line help functions are included. Figure 9 illustrates a typical entry type menu used by the Scenario Generation module.

REPRESENTATIVE SOFTWARE ARCHITECTURE

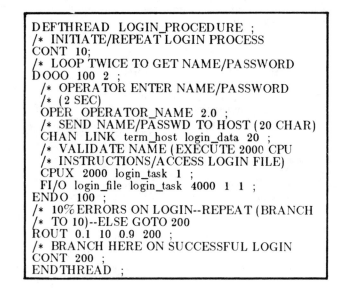

SOFTWARE TASK	
Name	Task A.2
Task Type (os/apps)	apps
Queue Type (fifo/lifo/lowpri/highpri)	fifo
Priority	10
Code Mix	7.00
Memory Required	1000000
Memory Status (fixed/rollout/norollout)	rollout
Spawning Allowed?	no
Exit	

Gary S. Swinson
June 22, 1984

Make any desired changes to this record; Choose "Exit" when done

Figure 7. Software Component Data Template

```
DEFTHREAD  LOGIN_PROCEDURE  ;
/*  INITIATE/REPEAT LOGIN PROCESS
CONT  10;
/*  LOOP TWICE TO GET NAME/PASSWORD
DOOO  100  2  ;
  /*  OPERATOR ENTER NAME/PASSWORD
  /*  (2 SEC)
  OPER  OPERATOR_NAME  2.0  ;
  /*  SEND NAME/PASSWD TO HOST (20 CHAR)
  CHAN  LINK  term_host login_data  20  ;
  /*  VALIDATE NAME (EXECUTE 2000 CPU
  /*  INSTRUCTIONS/ACCESS LOGIN FILE)
  CPUX  2000  login_task  1  ;
  FI/O  login_file  login_task  4000  1  1  ;
ENDO  100  ;
/*  10% ERRORS ON LOGIN--REPEAT (BRANCH
/*  TO 10)--ELSE GOTO 200
ROUT  0.1  10  0.9  200  ;
/*  BRANCH HERE ON SUCCESSFUL LOGIN
CONT  200  ;
ENDTHREAD  ;
```

Figure 8. Process Flow Segment

SIMULATION INTERFACE

Interactive portions of the Simulation Interface component use a menu processing front end to capture simulation run parameters (e.g., run duration) and reporting requirements. Figures 10 and 11 illustrate the menus used to perform these functions. The remaining portions of the simulation interface component translate designated portions of the user's rapid simulation aids data base into a format compatible with the ASSIST simulation tool input requirements.

The product of the Simulation Interface translation activities is an ASSIST-formatted input data stream

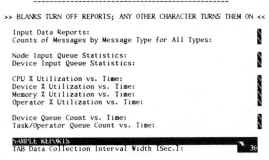

```
          SCENARIO TYPE CHARACTERIZATION
          ------------------------------

Scenario Name:                        ANALYST
Scenario Description:
Analyst Output Stimulus

Identify Where Scenario Occurs
        Component Type:               Processor
        Component Name:               Graphics

Thread Name:                          Analyst_Output

Message Name:                 Msg
Message Priority:        8    Message Size [Bytes]:        2

Start Time [Sec.]:              0   End Time [Sec.]:         3600


  >> SELECT <NEXT> TO DESIGNATE OCCURRENCE DISTRIBUTION PARAMETERS <<
```

A>bort, E>dit, or N>ext--

Figure 9. Scenario Characterization Menu

```
          DEFINE SIMULATION PARAMETERS
          ----------------------------

ASSIST File Name:        K021.inp
ASSIST User Path Name:
sptsun2\!/usr/demo/uucp

Desired Debug Level:                    0
Average Bytes per Rollin/Out:           0
Average Bytes per Job Manager I/O:      0

Simulation Start Time [Sec.]:           0
Simulation End Time [Sec.]:          3600


  >> SELECT NEXT TO SPECIFY SIMULATION REPORTING REQUIREMENTS <<
```

A>bort, E>dit, or N>ext--

Figure 10. Simulation Run Parameters Menu

resident on a Unix-based Sun workstation. A set of automated interface procedures has been developed which:

• Transfer ASSIST input data streams from their Unix-based Sun host to the VMS-based VAX hosting ASSIST

• Periodically execute an ASSIST handler on the VMS-based VAX to determine whether ASSIST data sets have been received; if such data sets are present, then the handler initiates the ASSIST execution

• Optionally notify the user when the ASSIST execution has been completed; subsequently, the user can retrieve the stored products of the ASSIST run by exercising inter-computer com-

```
      SPECIFY ASSIST SIMULATION REPORTING REQUIREMENTS
      ------------------------------------------------

>> BLANKS TURN OFF REPORTS; ANY OTHER CHARACTER TURNS THEM ON <<

  Input Data Reports:
  Counts of Messages by Message Type for All Types:        X

  Node Input Queue Statistics:                             X
  Device Input Queue Statistics:                           X

  CPU % Utilization vs. Time:                              X
  Device % Utilization vs. Time:                           X
  Memory % Utilization vs. Time:                           X
  Operator % Utilization vs. Time:                         X

  Device Queue Count vs. Time:                             X
  Task/Operator Queue Count vs. Time:                      X

SAMPLE REPORTS
  TAB Data Collection Interval Width [Sec.]:             36
```

A>bort, R>especify Reports, or S>ave--

Figure 11. Simulation Reporting Requirements Menu

munications utilities, or cause the simulation products to be printed on equipment tied to the VMS-based VAX system.

ASSIST SIMULATION

The ASSIST simulation is a TRW developed general purpose network simulation tool that contains a large library of built-in simulation models (Table 1). ASSIST also provides comprehensive reporting capabilities covering a large range of network analysis performance measures (Table 2). What ASSIST lacks is an effective user interface to permit direct interaction by engineers; the rapid simulation aids are intended to overcome this shortcoming of the simulation tool.

DISPLAY PROCESSOR

The Display Processor component of the rapid simulation aids tool set is still in development; it is the principle task associated with the 1984 Rapid Simulation Aids IR&D project. The display processor will permit the user to generate simulation products that can be incorporated directly into the engineering process. This requires that the user be able to control the content, format, and media associated with the simulation products. For example, it is desirable that the user be able to:

1. Designate one or more simulation-related output files to be displayed (i.e., content specification)

2. Indicate the format of the display outputs such as time lines, bar charts, pie charts, or probability distributions

3. Cause results to be displayed on a Sun color display monitor, color printer, or laser printer (i.e., media specification).

Table 1. Summary of ASSIST ADPE Modeling Capabilities

ADPE Hardware Models

- Any number of computers (arbitrary networks of processors)
- Any number of CPUs per computer
- Associated disk systems
- Operator stations
- Arbitrary devices
- Communications components

Operating System Models

- Multiprogramming
- Multiple CPU scheduling
- Priority and round robin task scheduling
- Multi-level interrupt processing
- Interprocessor communications
- Memory management including roll-in/roll-out

Software Tasks

- Task resource utilization (CPU, disk I/Os)
- Priority control
- Any assignment of tasks to processors
- Intertask communications
- Arbitrary level of user-supplied detail

The Display Processor is expected to be operational by the end of the third quarter of 1984.

EMPLOYMENT SCENARIO

Figure 12 depicts a typical scenario for employing rapid simulation aids. A set of system requirements and candidate architectures have been defined. The systems engineer utilizes the Sun workstation-based rapid simulation aids to input the hardware, software, data, and process flow components of the candidate architectures. System requirements yield loads and load mixes used to stimulate the simulated systems. When all inputs have been defined and saved in the project data base, the VAX-based ASSIST simulation tool is accessed, via the Sun workstation, to simulate and assess the performance of each candidate architecture.

The products of the ASSIST simulation runs will be tables and graphs which depict system performance responses to defined workloads. Typically, comparisons of simulated system performance with system requirements will yield one or more areas where a candidate architecture fails to perform adequately. This normally leads to proposed revisions in candidates architectures and a repetition of the simulation/analysis cycle.

Table 2. ASSIST Performance Measures

System Loads

- Number of messages versus time for any message type
- Message load on each model component

Operating System Data

- CPU overhead
- Number of service calls processed
- Number of interrupts
- Number of task swap roll-ins/outs

Software Statistics

- Task execution frequency
- Average task service time
- Resources consumed (CPU, I/O)

Resource Utilization

- Percent utilization versus time for any component in the model
- Number of transactions processed by any model component

Detailed Model Activities

- Printout of any simulator event by type by time
- Trace message flows

Response Time

- Minimum, maximum, average response time between any specified points in the model
- Plots of probability of achieving any required response time

Throughput

- Total number of jobs processed per time unit by any processor or model component

Queue Statistics

- Queue size (minimum, maximum, average) versus time for any queue
- Wait time in any queue

The ultimate goal of the rapid simulation process is to identify one or more preferred architectures (i.e, those which satisfy system performance requirements). These architectures can then be assessed for non-performance evaluation factors such as risk and cost to make a final architecture selection.

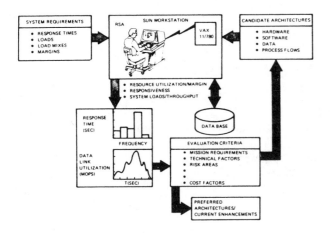

Figure 12. Use of Rapid Simulation Aids

CONCLUSIONS

Initial versions of the Rapid Simulation Aids became operational in December of 1983. To date, they have been or are being applied to half a dozen proposal and project simulation activities. Another dozen proposed uses of the tools are currently being evaluated.

The responsiveness of the tools has been outstanding. In a recent case, two architectural analyses associated with the same system were conducted. The first analysis involved an architecture with 35 hardware components, 24 software tasks, and 20 process threads; a single workload snapshot was examined. This analysis required one and one-half days to complete with an associated expenditure of two and one-half person days. The second architecture was an expansion on the first. It involved an architecture with 74 hardware components, 91 software tasks, and 32 process flows; five workload snapshots were examined. This analysis required three and one-half days to complete with an associated expenditure of eight person days. Based on the volume of inputs generated for the ASSIST simulation tool, it has been conservatively estimated that it would have taken at least four to six person weeks to have accomplished the same modeling activities without the rapid simulation aids. Furthermore, engineers were able to perform the modeling activities using rapid simulation aids without the need for programmer support.

In summary, our continuing involvement with rapid simulation aids has further substantiated the earlier assertion that application of these tools to distributed processing systems will:

● Assist in early conceptual understanding of system complexities

● Speed decisions concerning implementation

● Reduce development risk and cost.

ACKNOWLEDGMENTS

This overall research has benefited from associated and prior IR&D work within TRW's Defense Systems Group. In particular, the efforts of the Network Engineering project (D. Herzo, M. Sherbring, D. Sterba, R. Vossler, and S. Yamanaka) within the Software & Information Systems Division and the ASSIST-based, Real-Time Battle Management project (M. Kaur, J. Melde, and W. Priore) within the Systems Engineering & Development Division are acknowledged. The contributions of personnel supporting the Rapid Simulation Aids project (O. Khedr, P. Knutson, and S. Young) within the Software & Information Systems Division are likewise acknowledged.

SAFETY VERIFICATION IN MURPHY
USING FAULT TREE ANALYSIS*

Stephen S. Cha   Nancy G. Leveson   Timothy J. Shimeall

Department of Information and Computer Science
University of California, Irvine
Irvine, CA 92717

Abstract

MURPHY is a language-independent, experimental methodology for building safety-critical, real time software, which will include an integrated tool set. Using Ada as an example, this paper presents a technique for verifying the safety of complex, real-time software using Software Fault Tree Analysis. The templates for Ada are presented along with an example of applying the technique to an Ada program. The tools in the MURPHY tool set to aid in this type of analysis are described.

Introduction

A system or subsystem may be described as *safety-critical* if there are potential consequences of using the system that are so serious that it cannot be used at all unless the probability of a high-cost event (an accident) occurring is very low. For example, a system is usually considered safety-critical if some behavior of the system can result in death, injury, loss of equipment or property, or environmental harm. When computers are used to control safety-critical processes, there is a need to verify that the software will not cause or contribute to an accident. Until relatively recently, although computers were used in such potentially unsafe systems as aircraft, air traffic control, nuclear power, defense, and aerospace systems, a natural reluctance to add unknown and complex factors to these systems kept computers out of most safety-critical loops. However, the potential advantages of using computers are now outweighing apprehension (some might say good sense), and both computer scientists and system engineers are finding themselves faced with potential liability and with new government standards and requirements (e.g., MIL-STD-882B Notice 1 in the U.S.) that require certification of software safety to a degree not yet possible with current software engineering methods.

In safety-critical systems, it is not unusual to have reliability requirements of 10^{-5} to 10^{-9} probability of failure over a given period of time. This translates into requirements such as one failure per hundred years. Unfortunately, current software engineering technology cannot guarantee that such reliability is achieved for software (or, for that matter, even measured). Available evidence indicates that current software reliability figures are, at best, orders of magnitude less than required[2].

What can be done? One option is not to build these systems or not to use computers to control them. This option should be seriously considered by those making such decisions. The current rush to use computers to control nearly every type of device may involve a seriously unrealistic discounting of the potential risk. In some cases, reliability models based on totally unrealistic and unproven assumptions (e.g., Yount[14] which is based on an assumption that has been experimentally shown to be false[5]) are used to justify the use of computers. In others, the evaluation of risk appears to be based solely on optimism. One reasonable conclusion is that in safety-critical systems where the potential risk must be very low, computers should not be used as the sole source of control without highly reliable back-up systems and independent (non-software) protection against software control errors.

There are, however, systems where a realistic risk/benefit tradeoff might conclude that computer control is justified. For example, it is easier to justify the use of fly-by-wire systems in a military fighter aircraft than in a commercial aircraft. In these cases, a non-absolute approach to reliability may be possible. It is often not necessary for software to be completely correct in order for it to be safe; there are many types of failures possible in any complex system, with consequences varying from minor annoyance up to injury and death. For example, if the spacecraft software temporarily fails to archive some data for later analysis, the consequences are undesirable but not as serious as a failure involving the destruction of the spacecraft itself or non-fulfillment of the primary mission.

It seems reasonable to devise techniques that focus on those failures with the most serious consequences. Even if all failures cannot be prevented, it may be possible to ensure that the failures that do occur are of minor consequence or that even if a potentially serious failure does occur, the system will "fail safe" (i.e., fail in a manner that does not have unacceptable results).

This approach is useful under the following circumstances: (1) not all failures are of equal consequences and (2) there are a relatively small number of failures that are potentially serious. Under these circumstances, it is possible to augment traditional software engineering techniques that attempt to eliminate all errors with techniques that concentrate on potentially high-cost errors. These new techniques often involve a "backward" approach that starts with determining what are the unacceptable or high-cost failures of the software and then ensures that these particular failures do not occur or that their probability of occurrence is minimized. Another way of looking

---

*this work was partially supported by a MICRO grant co-funded by the State of California and Hughes Aircraft Company

Recommended by: O. Lecarme and W. Riddle

at this is that a "forward" analysis attempts to ensure that all possible reachable states of the system are correct whereas the goal of backward analysis is to ensure that particular incorrect states are not reachable. The latter is practical only under the above assumptions that there are a relatively small number of failures that are unacceptable and that these can be stated. In practice, this is usually the case even in complex systems. For example, this type of approach has been applied to nuclear power plants, commercial aircraft, and missile defense systems. For a description of some of the research on software safety, see Leveson[6].

The UCI Safety Project is developing an experimental methodology called MURPHY that will include an integrated tool set for building safety-critical, real-time software. There are currently three main areas of research: (1) software hazard analysis and requirements specification techniques; (2) verification, validation, and assessment of safety; and (3) software design and run-time environments. This paper describes a technique for safety verification of software. Previously, Leveson and Harvey[7] developed a technique called Software Fault Tree Analysis and applied it to Pascal, and Leveson and Stolzy[8] demonstrated its use on the Ada[†] rendezvous. This paper extends the technique to full Ada, provides an example of its use, and describes the tools currently completed and under development. Ada is used in this paper because many safety-critical software projects are currently planning to use Ada and also because it contains complex, real-time programming facilities that provide a good example of the technique. The approach, however, can be applied to any language.

Fault Tree Analysis

A hazard is a set of conditions (state) that has an unacceptable risk of leading to an accident, given certain environmental conditions. System safety analysis involves determining the hazards of a system and then either verifying that the hazardous state cannot be reached or that the risk is acceptable. There have been several system safety engineering techniques developed to accomplish this. One of these, Fault Tree Analysis (FTA), was developed in the early 1960's to analyze the safety of electro-mechanical systems[13]. Software Fault Tree Analysis[7] was derived from and extends FTA to systems containing computers as subcomponents. In FTA, a hazard is specified, and the system is then analyzed in the context of its environment and operation to find credible sequences of events that can lead to this hazard. The fault tree itself is a graphic model of various parallel and sequential combinations of faults (or system states) that will result in the occurrence of the predefined undesired event. The faults can be events that are associated with component hardware failures, human errors, or any other pertinent events that can lead to the undesired state. A fault tree thus depicts the logical interrelationships of basic events that lead to the hazard.

The basic procedure in FTA is to assume that the hazard has occurred and then to work backward to determine its set of possible causes. The root of the fault tree is the hazard and the necessary preconditions are described at the next level of the tree with either an AND or an OR relationship. Each subnode is expanded in a similar fashion until all leaves describe events

of calculable probability or are unable to be analyzed for some reason.

Once the fault tree has been built down to the software interface, the high level requirements for software safety have been delineated in terms of software behavior (usually involving outputs or lack of outputs) that could adversely affect the safety of the system. Unsafe software behavior may result from:

- failing to perform a required function, i.e., never executing the function or not producing an answer,

- performing a function not required, i.e., getting the wrong answer, issuing the wrong control instruction, or doing the right thing but under inappropriate conditions (for example, activating an actuator inadvertently, too early, too late, or failing to cease an operation at a prescribed time),

- failing to enforce required sequencing, e.g., failing to ensure that two things happen at the same time, at different times, or in a particular order,

- failing to recognize a hazardous condition requiring corrective action

- producing the wrong response to a hazardous condition.

After the hazardous software behavior has been identified in the system fault tree, Software Fault Tree Analysis (SFTA) can be applied at the design or code level to identify safety-critical items and components, to detect software logic errors, to determine the conditions under which fault-tolerance and fail-safe procedures should be initiated and to guide in the placement and content of run-time checks to detect hazardous software states, and to facilitate effective safety testing by pinpointing critical functions and test cases. If used in conjunction with a system simulator, the interfaces of the software fault tree can be examined to determine appropriate simulation states and events.

Software Fault Tree Analysis

SFTA works backward from the critical control faults determined by the system fault tree through the program code or the design to the software inputs. The approach is similar to the backward reasoning used in formal axiomatic verification, but with a much more limited goal. That is, SFTA attempts to verify that the program will never allow a particular unsafe state to be reached, although it proves nothing about incorrect but safe states. Most real-time embedded systems have two goals: (1) accomplishing a mission or function, while (2) not causing harm in the process. SFTA is aimed at only the second goal.

There are several reasons to separate the verification of these two goals. First, different approaches may apply. Furthermore, partial verification may be less costly and therefore more practical. Finally, government licensing agencies are often concerned only with safety with respect to granting a license to use the system. For example, government nuclear regulatory agencies are usually concerned with the safety of nuclear power plants but not with whether they put out a certain amount of power or earn money for the utilities running them. Most safety-critical systems now have government

†Ada is a registered trademark of the U.S. Department of Defense (Ada Joint Program Office).

licensing or certification requirements. Potential liability concerns also provide incentive to perform safety verification.

Because the goal is to prove that the software will not do something, it is convenient to use proof by contradiction. In SFTA, it is hypothesized that the software has produced an unsafe control action, and it is shown that this could not happen since the hypothesis leads to a contradiction. If a path is found through the software and out into the controlled system or its environment that does not contain a logical contradiction, then the hazard is reachable and this needs to be considered in the design of the system. For example in a SFTA of a scientific satellite control program[7], it was found that the satellite could be destroyed if the input sensors detected two sun pulses within 64 ms of each other. The appropriate action in this case is to use run-time assertions to detect such conditions and simply to reject incorrect or unsafe input. In other cases it might be most appropriate to redesign the program, to initiate software recovery routines, or to redesign non-computer parts of the system.

SFTA has been successfully applied in several real software projects. Its success appears to be related to the fact that it forces the analyst to look at the software in a slightly different way. That is, usually the programmer is concerned with what the software is required to do. SFTA forces the programmer or analyst to consider what the software is *not* supposed to do. It also starts from a separate specification (the system fault tree) and therefore can possibly find errors in the software requirements specification. The process of working backward through the software and out into the environment allows identification of the most critical assumptions about the environment. In the satellite example cited above, the designers and programmers had been entirely unaware that the software was based on an assumption about the minimum timing interval of the incoming sun pulses.

SFTA Applied to Ada Programs

SFTA starts with the hazardous output and works backward through the code. The analysis proceeds based on statement-specific templates for generating the tree. Because the technique makes use of the semantics of the language in which the algorithm is specified, the templates may be different for each language. The basic templates for Ada statements are shown in figures 1 through 16. The templates were designed by examining the statement semantics as defined in the Ada Language Reference Manual[1] and by analyzing the causes of frequently-made programming errors. In each template, it is assumed that the statement caused the critical event, and the tree is constructed by considering how this might have occurred.

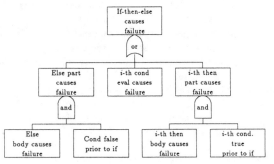

Figure 2: If-then-else Template

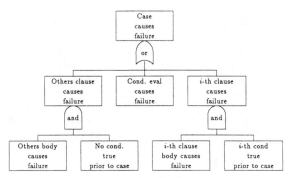

Figure 3: Case Template

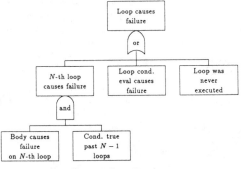

Figure 4: Loop Template

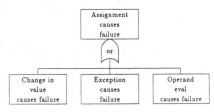

Figure 1: Assignment Template

Figure 5: Procedure Call Template

396

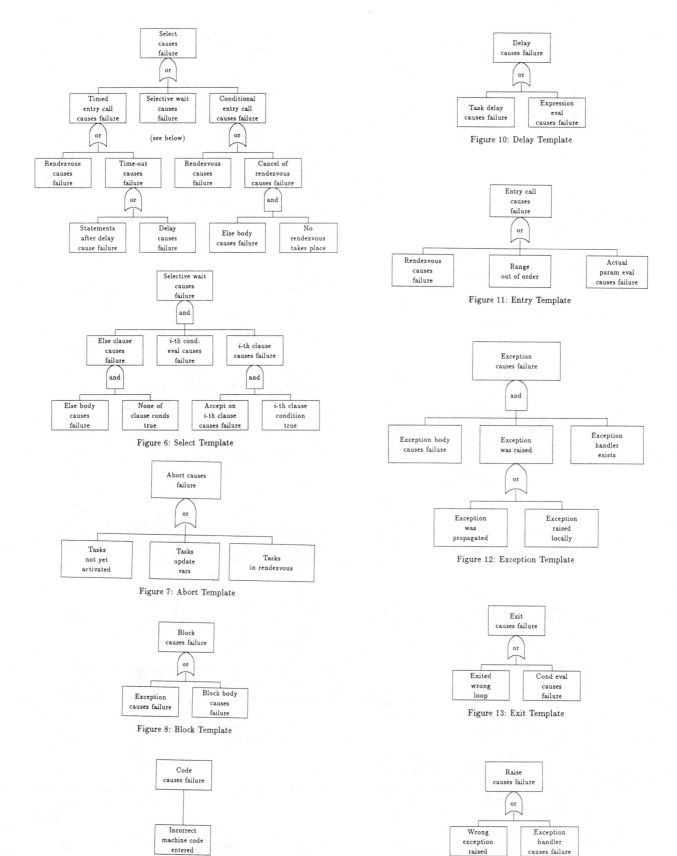

Figure 6: Select Template

Figure 7: Abort Template

Figure 8: Block Template

Figure 9: Code Template

Figure 10: Delay Template

Figure 11: Entry Template

Figure 12: Exception Template

Figure 13: Exit Template

Figure 14: Raise Template

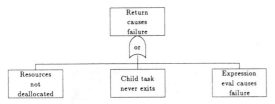

Figure 15: Return Template

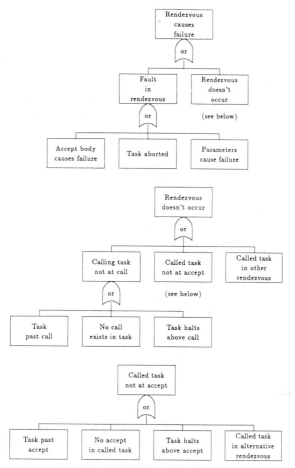

Figure 16: Rendezvous Template

As an example of how the templates are defined, consider the template for a rendezvous (figure 16). The event being analyzed (or 'failure') is caused by the rendezvous if either (1) the rendezvous not occurring could cause the failure or (2) the rendezvous does occur and a fault during the rendezvous could cause the failure. (If neither case holds, then the failure must have been caused by some prior statement, and the analyst must consider each prior statement in turn.) There are three ways a rendezvous could not occur: (1) the calling task may not be able to execute the entry call, (2) the called task may not be able to execute the accept, and (3) the called task may be able to execute the accept, but some task other than the calling task may have made an entry call on that accept and the called task proceeds with a rendezvous with this third

task. If none of these conditions hold, then the rendezvous will occur, and the analyst must consider whether a fault in the rendezvous could cause the failure. To aid in this process, three cases are present in the template for the analyst to consider. In the first case, the values passed as parameters to the rendezvous are inappropriate and thus cause the failure. In the second case, the body of the accept statement contains a fault, which causes the failure. In the last case, the Ada Language Reference Manual notes that if a called task is aborted while it is in a rendezvous, then an exception will be raised in the calling task. The analyst needs to consider whether this exception could lead to the event being analyzed. If help is desired in that case, the analyst could consult the exception template (figure 12).

The templates are based on the following assumptions:

- The Ada program being analyzed is free from any syntax errors.

- The implementation of the underlying virtual machines (e.g., compiler) are perfect. Although this may not be true, it simplifies the templates. If desired, fault tree analysis can be applied to the underlying virtual machines (software or hardware) to verify that they do not contribute to a hazard.

- The templates currently refer to faults made in the program body. The analysis of faulty declarations using fault trees is not included in this paper.

- Some statements, particularly **goto**, are difficult to analyze by a backward trace and are not included in this paper.

Perhaps the simplest way to explain the use of the templates is to illustrate it by analyzing an example problem:

A traffic light control system at an intersection consists of four (identical) sensors and a central controller. The sensors in each direction detect cars approaching the intersection. If the traffic light currently is not green, the sensor notifies the controller so that the light will be changed. A car is expected to stop and wait for a green light. If the light is green already, the car may pass the intersection without stopping. The controller accepts change requests from the four sensors and arbitrates the traffic light changes. Once the controller changes the light in one direction (east-west or south-north) to green, it maintains the green signal for five seconds so that other cars in the same direction may pass the intersection without stopping. Before the green light in any direction becomes red, it should remain in yellow for one second so that any car present in the intersection may clear. The light then turns to red while the light in the opposite direction turns green.

A sample Ada implementation of the problem is shown in figure 17. Due to the asymmetric nature of the Ada rendezvous (e.g., the called task does not know the identity of the calling task), an initialization (lines 17 through 19 and 45 through 47) is needed to assign a direction to each sensor. This direction is passed to the controller when each sensor requests the controller to change the lights. When a car approaching the

```
1   procedure traffic is
2     type direction is (east, west, south, north);
3     type color is (red, yellow, green);
4     type light_type is array (direction) of color;
5     lights : light_type := (green, green, red, red);
6     task type sensor_task is
7       entry initialize (mydir : in direction);
8       entry car_comes;
9     end sensor_task;
10    sensor : array (direction) of sensor_task;
11    task controller is
12      entry notify (dir : in direction);
13    end controller;
14    task body sensor_task is
15      dir : direction;
16    begin
17      accept initialize (mydir : in direction) do
18        dir := mydir;
19      end initialize;
20      loop
21        accept car_comes;
22        if (lights(dir) /= green) then
23          controller.notify (dir);
24        end if;
25      end loop;
26    end sensor_task;
27    task body controller is
28    begin
29      loop
30        accept notify (dir : in direction) do
31          case dir is
32            when east | west =>
33              lights := (green, green, red, red);    delay 5.0;
34              lights := (yellow, yellow, red, red);  delay 1.0;
35              lights := (red, red, green, green);
36            when south | north =>
37              lights := (red, red, green, green);    delay 5.0;
38              lights := (red, red, yellow, yellow);  delay 1.0;
39              lights := (green, green, red, red);
40          end case;
41        end notify;
42      end loop;
43    end controller;
44  begin
45    for dir in east..north loop
46      sensor(dir).initialize (dir);
47    end loop;
48  end traffic;
```

Figure 17: Ada Implementation of Traffic Light

intersection is detected, the sensor for the corresponding direction executes line 21. The actual passing of the car through the intersection is assumed to begin when the program execution passes line 24 of the sensor task.

The trees in this paper make use of three of the standard fault tree symbols. A rectangle indicates an event that needs to be analyzed further. A diamond indicates an event that is not further analyzed, either because it is inapplicable to the statement being analyzed or because a contradiction is found. Finally, an oval indicates a condition normal to the operation of the system that contributes to the failure.

The application of SFTA to this program is illustrated by analyzing the event where two cars travelling from the north and east of the intersection are present in the intersection simultaneously. The analysis proceeds by finding the causes of the event and their relationships.

There could be many ways two cars travelling north and east could be in the intersection simultaneously (figure 18). The authors have chosen to examine the case where the north car enters the intersection as the east car enters[‡]. After selecting the event to be analyzed, the next step in the analysis is to find recursively the possible subevents leading to the failure event. In this example, the authors have decided to

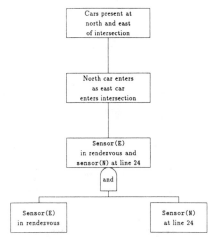

Figure 18: Top Level Fault Tree

explore (again, among several possibilities) the case where the sensor(east) task is in rendezvous with the controller task and the sensor(north) task bypassed the rendezvous point (null else). This implies that the signal was green when the car from the north approached the intersection, and it therefore entered the intersection without stopping. The tree indicates that the top event could happen if and only if both subevents occur.

In order to determine how the sensor(north) task bypasses the rendezvous point, it is necessary to trace the program backward from line 24 (figure 19). Since the immediately preceding statement is the **if** statement (lines 22 through 24), the **if** template is attached to the fault tree. A statement template is used here to offer the analyst suggestions as to how the specific statement might cause the fault. Since it is known that the sensor(north) task bypasses the rendezvous with the controller (then-part) and that the else-part does not have any statements, it is possible to immediately terminate the analysis along those two branches. The diamond symbol ("undeveloped event") is used to indicate this. The refinement of the leftmost branch is quite straightforward. For the task to bypass the rendezvous, lights(north) must be green. If the north sensor task checks this as the controller task changes lights at the request of the east sensor task, then a race condition will occur. To determine if this race condition is possible, it is necessary to examine the behavior of the east sensor task in the rendezvous with the controller.

The subevent "sensor(east) task in rendezvous" is analyzed in a similar way (figure 20). The template for the rendezvous is used here. Among the three possible causes, two are discarded immediately since the examination of the code indicates that there is no task abortion and that parameter evaluation (line 23) was not a direct cause of the event. While the former decision is obvious, the latter one represents a decision made by the analyst. The only branch left to explore further is the branch where the rendezvous body (line 33 through 35) causes the top event. The specification allows one second[§],

_____

[‡]In fact, the authors are aware of several other failure modes for this program. Only one possible case is explored as an example. Interested readers are encouraged to try to find the other failure modes.

[§]Another possible failure mode is where this time is insufficient. However, this is a specification error, not a programming error.

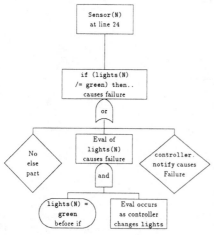

Figure 19: Sensor(North) at Line 24

33 is excluded. This leaves the statement

```
lights := (green, green, red, red);
```

on line 33 to be analyzed. The assignment template (figure 1) is used to analyze the statement. Two of the branches in the template are determined not to be applicable here. The third branch, "change in value causes failure", is chosen for further expansion. According to the specification, no light change is allowed from green to red without yellow occurring in between. However, if the preceding rendezvous was with the east or west sensor tasks, then line 35 would have set the state of the lights to (red, red, green, green). In this case, the assignment on line 33 would cause a change from green to red with no intervening yellow light.

In summary, the above fault tree analysis demonstrates that the above Ada code could contribute to the hazard (i.e., two cars, travelling at right angles to one another, are present in the intersection at the same time) if two successive rendezvous occur with the east or west sensor tasks and the north sensor task checks the state of the lights immediately prior to the second rendezvous. The complete fault tree is shown in figure 21.

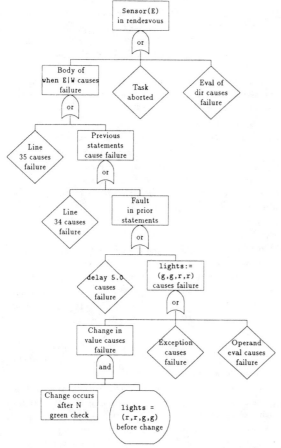

Figure 20: Sensor(East) in Rendezvous

during which the lights are yellow, for any car remaining in the intersection to clear. Therefore line 34 is excluded as a cause of the top event. By similar logic the delay statement on line

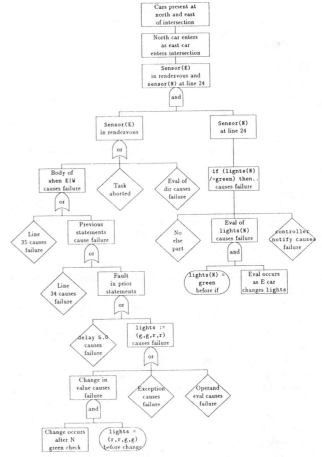

Figure 21: Final Fault Tree

In general, a software fault tree has one or both of the following patterns:

1. A contradiction is found. The construction of the fault tree (at least for this path) can stop at this point since the logic of the software cannot cause the event. The example given above does not deal with the problem of failures in the underlying implementation of the software, but this is possible. There is, of course, a practical limit as to how much analysis can and need be done depending on individual factors associated with each project. It is possible to include assertions or exception conditions in the code to catch critical implementation errors at run-time if run-time software-initiated or software-controlled fault-tolerance and fail-safe procedures are feasible. Note that the software fault tree provides the information necessary to determine which assertions and run-time checks are the most critical and where they should be placed. Since checks at run-time are expensive in terms of time and other resources, this information is extremely useful.

2. The fault tree runs through the code and out to the controlled systems or its environment. The example fault tree above shows one possible path to the hazard, and changes are necessary to eliminate it.

The technique illustrated above can be used to analyze any Ada program subunit. Analysis of tasks and the rendezvous are performed as demonstrated in the example, assuming that all communication is through a rendezvous. Although communication using shared global variables is not prohibited in the language definition, its use in tasks is unsafe since simultaneous reading and writing could result in an undefined and most likely undesirable state. Similarly, use of the goto statement is discouraged since it changes the control flow arbitrarily.

Analysis of procedures and function bodies is straightforward (see Leveson and Harvey[7] for a thorough explanation). Calls to procedures are analyzed using the procedure call template (figure 5). Since a procedure body is a sequence of simple or compound statements, it can be analyzed using the existing templates. Analysis of function calls is similar, and is part of the analysis of failures caused by expression evaluation. Packages and generics in Ada consist of subunit specifications and corresponding bodies. The bodies can be analyzed by examining the statements in each of the constituent packages, procedures and functions, as appropriate. It is necessary to include the initialization body of a package, and the effect of instantiation on a generic in the analysis.

The discussion above focuses on the application of the analysis procedure to Ada code. It is also possible to apply the same type of analysis to a design language. At the highest level of design, the analysis pinpoints the safety-critical components of the design. These can then be isolated for protection and further analysis, and fault-tolerance or other design features can be used. Careful design analysis has the potential for minimizing expensive verification procedures later in the development process.

Software Fault Tree Analysis also has important implications in the reuse of components and packages. Accidents often arise from problems in the interfaces between components of a system. A recent software problem causing the death of three people[3] involved the reuse of software components. The interface between components of a system is composed of the assumptions the components make about each other. In terms of one component, its interface is the set of assumptions it makes about its environment. A path through the component in a software fault tree can show the conditions in the environment under which that component will exhibit a certain behavior. If there is no such path through the software, then that behavior cannot occur. Even though reusable packages can themselves be highly reliable, this alone does not preclude the possibility of problems arising when those components are used within a particular system context.

Fault Tree Tools

Fault Tree Editor

The first tool in the MURPHY fault tree analysis tool set is an interactive screen-oriented fault tree editor[11,12]. This tool provides the analyst with the capability of creating or modifying fault trees in a structured manner. The editor performs no checking of the semantics of the fault tree generated. A version of the editor now in development will incorporate insertion of statement templates into the tree.

In figure 22 a screen image from a session with the editor is shown. The analyst has just changed the connector (or 'gate') between the node labelled 'E in rendez., N at null' and its children by selecting the 'and' item from a pull-down menu. Other options available to the analyst allow modification of node shape, changes in its screen position or relationship to other nodes in the tree, adding or deleting nodes in the tree, and saving the tree for future reference or modification. The editor also provides graphic output of the fault tree by invoking the fault tree artist.

Fault Tree Artist

The fault tree artist takes the output format used by the fault tree editor and the fault tree generator and produces a graph of the tree in a standard format. Using a set of layout algorithms[10], the artist handles the positioning of the tree on paper, dealing with off-page connections if the tree is too wide or too tall to fit on a single sheet. Three types of output are provided: WID, for wide line-printer forms (14 by 8.5 inches), LPT for narrow line-printer forms (8.5 by 11 inches) and PIC for output in the Pic[4] graphics language, which is translatable into either troff or TeX commands for final output. All fault tree illustrations appearing in this paper are produced by the fault tree artist.

Prototype Fault Tree Generator

A Fault Tree Generator is currently in development; it is the only tool that currently is not language-independent. This tool takes an Ada program as input and, based on that program and interaction with the analyst, produces a fault tree or group of fault trees as output. The initial prototype of this tool when completed will have two parts, a translator from Ada into an intermediate form and a tree generator to turn the intermediate form into a fault tree. Once the tree is generated, it could be displayed using the fault tree artist or edited using the fault tree editor.

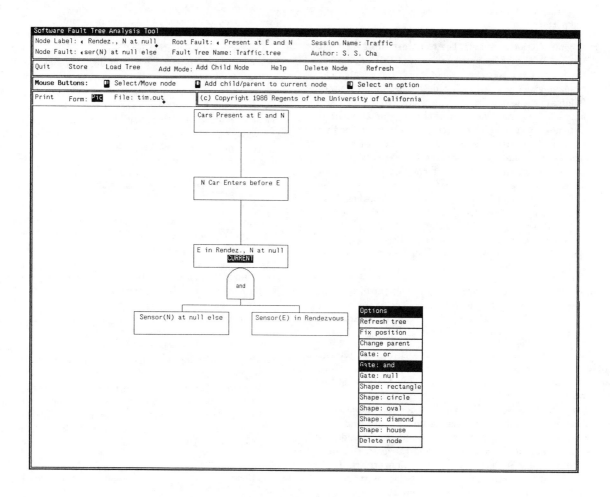

Figure 22: Sample Editor Session

Translator The first part of the fault tree generator is a translator that reads in an Ada program and translates it into a control-flow graph, annotated with the fault tree templates appropriate to each of the input statements. The translator is being built using the Lex/Yacc tools. As the graph is constructed, all of the statement-specific terms in the associated templates are replaced by the appropriate source fragment. For example, an Ada assignment statement would be translated into a control-flow graph node annotated with a copy of the template for assignment statements (see figure 1). In that copy of the template the words "left side" and "right side" would be replaced by the source text for the left and right hand sides of that assignment statement, respectively. This part of the translation task is being designed so that revisions of the templates can be easily incorporated (i.e., the templates are independent of the tool itself).

Prototype Tree Generation Once the translator has produced the annotated flow graph, the tree generator traverses the flow graph and generates a fault tree. The initial version of this part of the fault tree generator is highly interactive. The analyst supplies the initial (root) fault and a program location, specifies which statements are to be expanded as branches of the fault tree, and enters additional information (such as loop invariants) as necessary. At any point in this process, the existing tree can be saved for modification, display, printing or later development. Future versions of this tool are planned that will incorporate what has been learned from initial use of the tool and will increase the automation available to the analyst (such as including weakest-precondition predicate transformation).

Conclusion

A procedure for safety verification has been presented along with an example and a description of some prototype tools to aid the analyst. Since fault tree analysis was originally used to analyze safety in electromechanical systems, the technique being developed has the advantage of being able to link together the software system and the controlled system at the interfaces of the two, allowing the system to be analyzed as a whole. It can be used at various levels and stages of software development and, although not shown in this paper, can include failures in the underlying computer hardware. The basic technique of software fault tree analysis has been applied successfully in real projects on assembly language programs[9] and other simple sequential programs. This paper extends the analysis technique to include more complex, real-time language constructs.

The reader is cautioned, however, in expecting too much from the technique. The analysis is very human-oriented, and therefore its success will depend on the ability of the analyst. The tools can aid the analyst, but do not guarantee success. SFTA, as defined here, is basically a form of structured walk-through. Its success in previous usage appears to be related to the fact that the analyst is forced to view the program in a different fashion than is common during development, and this increases the chance for finding errors. An analogy might be that when one vacuums a rug in one direction only, one is likely to pick up less dirt than if the vacuuming occurs in two opposite directions. That is, the more different ways a program is examined, the more likely that errors will be found. Programmers during development tend to concentrate on what they want the program to do; SFTA requires consideration of what the program should *not* do. However, the technique itself requires knowledge and experience on the part of the analyst and is not a substitute for any other type of verification and validation procedures. SFTA is just one part of the MURPHY methodology. In order to build software systems with acceptable risk, it will be necessary to make changes to and apply special procedures throughout the entire software development process.

Acknowledgements

The authors would like to acknowledge the help of Dr. John Goodenough of the Software Engineering Institute who provided information from a survey of errors found in Ada programs.

References

[1] ANSI/MIL-STD-1815A-1983. *The Programming Language Ada Reference Manual.* American National Standards Institute, February 1983.

[2] Janet R. Dunham and John C. Knight. *Production of Reliable Flight-Crucial Software.* Technical Report 2222, NASA, November 1981.

[3] Ed Joyce. Software bugs: a matter of life and liability. *Datamation,* 88-92, 15 May 1987.

[4] B. W. Kernighan. Pic – a language for typesetting graphics. *Software – Practice and Experience,* 12(1):1–21, 1982.

[5] John C. Knight, Nancy G. Leveson, and Lois D. St.Jean. A large scale experiment in n-version programming. In *International Symposium on Fault Tolerant Computing Systems,* pages 135–139, June 1985.

[6] Nancy G. Leveson. Software safety: why, what, and how. *ACM Computing Surveys,* 18(2):121–163, June 1986.

[7] Nancy G. Leveson and Peter R. Harvey. Analyzing software safety. *IEEE Transaction on Software Engineering,* SE-9(5):569–579, September 1983.

[8] Nancy G. Leveson and Janice L. Stolzy. Safety analysis of ada programs using fault trees. *IEEE Transactions on Reliability,* R-32(5):479–484, December 1983.

[9] James W. McIntee Jr. *Fault Tree Techniques As Applied to Software (Soft Tree).* Technical Report, USAF, March 1983.

[10] E. M. Reingold and J. S. Tilford. Tidier drawing of trees. *IEEE Transaction on Software Engineering,* SE-7(2):223–228, March 1981.

[11] C. Rolandelli, T. J. Shimeall, C. Genung, and N. Leveson. *Software Fault Tree Analysis Tool User's Manual.* Technical Report 86-06, University of California, Irvine, February 1986.

[12] J. L. Stolzy. Software fault tree analysis tool. University of California, Irvine, December 1984.

[13] W.E. Vesely, F.F. Goldberg, N.H. Roberts, and D.F. Haasl. *Fault Tree Handbook.* U.S. Nuclear Regulatory Commission, nureg–0492 edition, January 1981.

[14] L. J. Yount, K. A. Lievel, and B. H. Hill. Fault effect protection and partitioning for fly-by-wire/fly-by-light avionics systems. In *AIAA Computers in Aerospace V Conference,* pages 275–284, AIAA, Long Beach, CA, October 1985.

Reprinted from *IEEE Transactions on Software Engineering*, Volume SE-12, Number 9, September 1986, pages 905–920. Copyright ©1986 by The Institute of Electrical and Electronics Engineers, Inc. All rights reserved.

On Hierarchical Design of Computer Systems for Critical Applications

PETER GABRIEL NEUMANN, SENIOR MEMBER, IEEE

Abstract—We consider here the design of computer systems that must be trusted to satisfy simultaneously a variety of critical requirements such as human safety, fault tolerance, high availability, security, privacy, integrity, and timely responsiveness—and to continue to do so throughout maintenance and long-term evolution. Hierarchical abstraction provides the basis for successive layers of trust with respect to the full set of critical requirements, explicitly reflecting differing degrees of criticality.

Index Terms—Abstraction, critical requirements, hierarchical design, kernels, reliability, safety, security, trusted subsystems.

I. INTRODUCTION

COMPUTERS are increasingly being used in life-critical environments (e.g., air-traffic control, space and missile systems, medical care) and other critical applications (e.g., involving valuable resources). However, the frequency of serious and even catastrophic disasters is also increasing—with various cases of loss of life.[1] Many more such problems can be expected. Because successful operation is dependent not only on the computer systems, but also on the overall operating environments, communications, *and* people in the loop, any weak link may potentially be destructive. However, in times of crisis, when both the systems and the people are stressed most, various combinations of problems may tend to interact and escalate the crisis (as in the case of Three Mile Island, which involved the confluence of at least *four* different equipment failures, one operator error, and some questionable judgment—see [23]).

In this paper the term *system* refers primarily to computer systems, while the term *environment* refers to the overall application—which in control contexts might otherwise be referred to as "the system." The term *critical requirements* is used generically here to represent any or all of a wide range of characteristics whose absence or diminished presence can result in serious consequences.

Critical computer-system requirements exist in different abstractions—from the end-user environment interface down, through various computer subsystems and operating systems, to the computer hardware. At the highest layer of abstraction, general requirements such as human safety or financial stability may be paramount. At lower layers of abstraction, the general requirements may translate into a variety of specific requirements such as guaranteed timely performance of the underlying computer operating system, freedom from deadlock and unacceptable degradation, automatic fault recovery or fault masking in the software and hardware, and adequate security (such as user privacy, system integrity, data integrity, and protection against intentional denials of services).[2] There are also external attributes on which critical behavior may depend, such as rapid mean time to repair of the system, either manually or automatically—particularly in response to unforeseen emergencies.

The satisfaction of highly critical requirements necessitates the use of extraordinary measures in system development. One design approach of particular interest here involves the structuring of a critical system into design layers such that flaws in, or misuse of, the higher-level layers cannot contaminate the lower layers (e.g., cannot undermine system reliability, security, and safety properties), and such that faults in the lower layers can be contained or recovered from without compromising operation of the higher layers. Such designs have been explored, but only for specific requirements—notably in the security community (e.g., security kernels and trusted computing bases) and to some extent in the fault-tolerance community.

Unfortunately, a sound design can be seriously compromised by a slightly defective implementation. For example, timing dependencies may become critical—particularly in distributed systems. Synchronization problems are especially difficult to anticipate, to prevent, and to recover from automatically in real time. Two valuable illustrations of unanticipated global failures are provided by the synchronization problem that delayed the launch of the first Space Shuttle [18] and by an accidentally propagated status-word virus that caused the complete collapse of the ARPANET [43].

Security, privacy, and integrity issues are closely interrelated with reliability and fault tolerance,[3] and both may

Manuscript received August 30, 1985; revised February 28, 1986.
The author is with SRI International, Menlo Park, CA 94025.
IEEE Log Number 8609733.

[1]See the quarterly issues of the ACM *Software Engineering Notes* for an ongoing catalog and documentation on many such problems, particularly the sections on Risks to the Public in Computer Systems.

[2]It is not the intent of this paper to elaborate upon and compare different requirements for safety, reliability, security, etc. For this reason, some imprecise terminology is used, with the understanding that any particular system should have precise definitions of the desired requirements. References are given to some such definitions.

[3]See Lampson [26] for a discussion of some of the interactions between security and reliability and the importance of dealing with both. Recent papers by Randell and Dobson [42], [13] also conclude that the mechanisms for achieving fault tolerance and security need to be interrelated.

EH0291-5/89/0000/0404$01.00 ©1986 IEEE

be compromised by seemingly unrelated or trivial system changes. In addition, although issues of safety overlap somewhat with security and fault tolerance in hardware and software, they require more than just the combination of those other requirements. A few examples follow of how critical system requirements are closely interrelated:

• A system that is not secure may have its fault tolerance undermined: an intruder may be able to crash it, or the system may run amok due to its lack of self-protection. Security must imply protection not only against intruders and authorized users, but against other parts of the system itself.

• A system that is not fault tolerant may have its security undermined: its behavior under uncovered fault modes is generally unknown.

• A system that lacks either fault tolerance or security may not be able to fulfill requirements for critical safety or guaranteed services.

• A system that is not safe to use (e.g., in a life-critical environment) could still satisfy the security and fault-tolerance requirements—although those attributes might then be somewhat irrelevant.

Safety requirements imply weak links above and beyond those that arise as security or fault-tolerance vulnerabilities. Some measure of security and fault tolerance seems necessary but not sufficient for safety. There are enormous problems in recognizing and adequately defining all of those requirements and in designing and implementing a system that can satisfy all of them with some meaningful measure of trustworthiness.

We seek here an integrated hierarchical framework for research into and development of critical systems. The design approach follows earlier work by Dijkstra, Parnas, and Hoare, among others, and seeks to align the layers of a hierarchical design constructively with critical requirements at each layer. The basic hypothesis is that appropriate use of hierarchical abstraction and encapsulation can lead to systems intrinsically better at satisfying critical requirements than conventionally designed systems, while also helping to reduce undesired side-effects and to isolate propagation of failures.

We first examine some different requirements and consider how they interact. We then consider the question of whether, for the computer systems and their operating environment along with their associated models, a single hierarchical framework could exist that simultaneously addresses all of the relevant requirements. Much has been learned by the security and fault-tolerance communities, but that knowledge by itself is not enough. New problems result from combining requirements—especially requirements that seem mutually antagonistic when approached separately.

Not only is a running system of concern, but also its use, administration, and maintenance. The entire physical environment in which the computer systems operate may also be critical, particularly in computer-controlled environments. The interactions between the environment and the computer systems are often a source of serious prob-

lems, as are the people involved. Furthermore, each change made to a system may potentially alter its behavior adversely, often in unexpected ways.

No system can ever be guaranteed to operate successfully in its environment all of the time, *under all possible circumstances*, especially when the underlying design assumptions fail to be satisfied. Thus, the social problems must also be kept in mind, as well as both the consequences of *doing it wrong* and the cost of *doing it right*. It is important to note that the local costs of doing it right may seem high in the short run, but may present great savings in the long run—especially if disasters that might otherwise occur can be avoided or reduced in scope.

II. HIERARCHIES

Some of the research on abstraction and encapsulation has been directed at hierarchical decompositions of a system design into *layers of abstraction* that enforce some form of *downward-only functional dependence*. (For example, see [12], [38], [41], [39], [35].)

In [39], Parnas considered various relations with which it is meaningful to talk about hierarchies, e.g., layer *A depends for its correctness on* layer *B*, or layer *A calls* layer *B*, or a combination of both that Parnas refers to as layer *A uses* layer *B* (first form).[4]

A hierarchy of properly encapsulated abstractions serves several purposes. It aids in the separation of policy (*what is to be done*) from mechanism (*how it is to be done*), e.g., it helps separate logical operations from physical resource management. Each successively higher layer can provide functionality that is more abstract, and more readily useful to the still-higher layers (and eventually to the ultimate user). It also can hide much of the seemingly irrelevant (but otherwise exposed) detail of the lower layers whose exposure can result in compromise, or whose inconsistent use can result in failures. Perhaps most importantly, it can provide a basis for an implementation that limits the extent of deleterious effects noted above.

In [40], Parnas reassessed the desired meaning of *A uses B*, recognizing that an interrupt handler (say) is not explicitly used, but is nevertheless depended upon. (Runtime support libraries provide a somewhat less implicit, but not always obvious, dependence.) In order to address implicit dependence, Parnas redefined the first form above to a second form of *uses*: *A requires the presence of a correct version of B*.

Recognition of implicit invocation is indeed important. However, the requirement for *correctness* in the definition the second form of *uses* is awkward, making it semantic in nature and difficult to interpret precisely. Several questions immediately come to mind. With respect to what set of requirements is correctness to be defined? A failure (i.e., apparently *noncorrect* behavior, in the sense of [33]) at a particular layer could be tolerated if it can be overridden by actions at a higher layer—as in the case of

---

[4]Models of hierarchies are considered by Berry *et al.* in [6] with *interpretation, enmasterization, virtualization, compilation,* and *software extension* as representative approaches to support abstraction.

dynamic (forward) fault recovery. (We could attempt a definition in which correctness was implied only with respect to the critical requirements for the particular model, but that introduces the additional problems of completeness of those requirements and the consistency of the different requirements from layer to layer.) What if the correctness requirements are incomplete at a particular layer, omitting something crucial? Then A could be said *not* to use B, even though B could compromise A. For example, a Trojan horse in B could cause side-effects not covered by the incomplete requirements.

A more mechanistic definition follows that avoids correctness, but that is still semantic in nature:

depends-upon: A is said to depend upon B whenever an action of B, or change to B, or total unavailability of B, can have an effect upon A.

Note that the effect upon A here need not imply any lack of consistency with A's requirements. However, this definition is still difficult to interpret precisely, in that the effect need not be explicit or directly visible to A—as in the case of a hidden side-effect.[5]

Consequently, as basically syntactic notion of *uses* is sought:

uses (third form!): *A uses B whenever it is syntactically possible that A depends upon B.*

This definition is intentionally intuitive, and admittedly dependent on one's algorithm for interpreting "syntactically possible." The reader should include both explicit and implicit invocations such as procedure calls, remote procedure calls, and asynchronous demon processes. (In the case of coroutines, A uses B, and B uses A.)

If there are no cyclic dependencies among the layers with respect to *uses*, the layers form a total ordering. (Note that any design is totally ordered if all layers with cyclic dependencies are collapsed into a single layer.) In the definitions of *uses* and *depends-upon*, we can also consider modules within each layer, and relations among modules rather than just among the layers themselves. In this case these relations provide a partial ordering among the modules rather than a total ordering among the layers.

For present purposes it is desirable that the design form a nontrivial hierarchy in which there is some sensible correspondence between the design layers (or modules) and the critical requirements. If, at each layer, either all modules are equally trustworthy (or untrustworthy), or there is only one module at that layer, then a linear ordering on

this relation is adequate. Throughout this paper, the term *hierarchy* can for simplicity be thought of as a linear layering, but could be a partial ordering—if that generality is meaningful.

The third form of *uses* is implied (for simplicity) throughout the rest of this paper, although its semantic variant *depends-upon* is alternatively useful (no pun intended). However, we make a distinction here between layer B having to be trusted (because, in the sense of A *depends-upon* B, if B does not do the right thing or does nothing at all, A may be unable to meet its requirements) and layer B actually being *trustworthy*. Trustworthiness is a measure of how much trust might justifiably be placed in a particular layer. Interesting cases where assumptions of trustworthiness are weak arise in Byzantine agreement, interactive consistency, and interactive convergence (e.g., [25], [24]). In such cases, a particular layer (e.g., implementing a Byzantine-agreement algorithm) would *use* certain lower-layer modules even if they were not trustworthy. However, depending on the algorithm, it would not *depend upon* all of them—it might, for example, tolerate k out of n that were faulty or malicious. Such a design is made unusually defensive to compensate for the possibility of locally noncompliant behavior, in order to achieve compliance at a higher layer. The distinction is significant in that, while analysis based on (the third form of) *uses* is syntactic in nature, that of trustworthiness is semantic.[6]

Experience to date with security and fault tolerance indicates that such a hierarchical structuring of a critical system is both possible and valuable in newly designed systems (but generally difficult to retrofit into a nonhierarchically designed system). Cyclic dependencies across different abstractions are in general potentially dangerous, and well as complicating analysis. However, they are easily avoided by careful design—e.g., by creating a virtual layer and a physical layer for the same abstraction (as in [35]).

An important set of design decisions involves what functionality must exist at each layer. What safety, fault-tolerance, and security mechanisms must be trustworthy at each layer, and with respect to what requirements? Are there meaningful generalizations of the security community's notion of a trusted computing base (TCB), which enforces a particular security policy? These questions are addressed below.

Somewhat related to layers of functional abstraction are various *degrees of criticality*. For example, Multics has a most critical innermost layer, a malfunction in which can cripple the entire system; then, layers whose malfunction can cripple only the executing user process; then, layers whose malfunction merely results in the user process being returned to command level, with some suitable error message. (In Multics, these layers are implemented using

---

[5]It is interesting to contrast *depends-upon* with the Goguen-Meseguer notion of *noninterference* [19]: B is *noninterfering* with A if and only if no operation of B can influence the future behavior of A—i.e., operations of B cannot be detected by A. This relation is used to model effects that must remain invisible in order to prevent security violations (e.g., the existence of an event at Top-Secret that must not be detectable by a Secret user). "B is noninterfering with A" seems close in meaning to "A does **not** depend upon B." However, A may depend upon B without A being able to detect such a dependence if B operates correctly. Also, noninterference does not address the case in which B stops functioning altogether. Furthermore, noninterference is generally not used hierarchically.

[6]See also [27], which defines a broad notion of *dependability* that encompasses various forms of reliability—including availability, maintainability, and safety.

TABLE I
RISKS: CONVENTIONALLY DESIGNED SYSTEM

Hierarchy of criticality; effects of HW/SW problems
2. Noncritical functions; disaster possible
1. Less-critical functions; disaster possible
0. Most-critical functions; disaster possible

TABLE II
RISKS: HIERARCHICALLY DESIGNED SYSTEM

Hierarchy of criticality *and* functionality; effects of problems
2. Noncritical functions; many disasters unlikely to be caused by noncritical (*e.g.*, untrusted) software due to sharply defined design isolation. Correctness of certain functions still an issue.
1. Somewhat-critical functions; sharply limited disaster, because of isolation and limited power
0. Most-critical functions; disaster possible but unlikely if system partitioned internally, critical hardware and software fault tolerant, simple enough to be extensively analyzed

concentric rings of protection in the hardware, so that there is a relationship—albeit *a posteriori*—between internal security and system availability. In addition, the segmented virtual memory permits compartmentation within each ring.) However, in most computer systems, relatively little attention seems to have been paid either to relative criticality or to abstraction, the consequences of which can be system malfunctions, deadlocks, fault recovery that is costly (in personnel, time, and/or unrecoverable data), occasional far-reaching outages or losses, security vulnerabilities, and general doubts as to what might happen in an unanticipated emergency. We consider here ways in which varying degrees of criticalities can be explicitly related to the layers of a design hierarchy.

Tables I and II suggest a comparison of ordinary practice with respect to criticalities. Table I represents a (grossly oversimplified) conventionally designed system. Here the criticalities are not necessarily related to the system design. In this case, any hardware burp or program flaw anywhere—even in supposedly system-independent application code—could cause a disaster such as loss of life, crash of the system, total deadlock among parts of the system, or collapse of system security. Weaknesses in the protection mechanisms or in fault-tolerance algorithms increase the likelihood of unanticipated problems. More generally, it is dangerous to try to build a sound application on top of an unsound operating system and flaky hardware. The von Neumann concept of building reliable systems out of unreliable components does not generalize to reliable, secure, and safe systems in which

the depended-upon systems can have their underlying assumptions violated, either accidentally or intentionally.[7]

Table II represents a generic system design in which the relative criticalities and the design hierarchy (e.g., for fault-tolerance, security, life-criticality, and evolution) are conceptually unified—that is, the most critical functions are those that are accorded much greater care, through defensive design. (Only three layers are shown, for simplicity.) Presuming that some sensible ordering of criticalities can be found (see below), this table is based on the existence of a generalized trusted computing base (GTCB) that attempts to enforce certain most-critical properties. That GTCB must be designed and implemented so that it is protected from higher-layer functions. The properties that the GTCB enforces must not be compromisable from outside the GTCB, and those properties should have been covered defensively by good design (including fault-tolerant hardware and software), careful implementation, thorough verification, audit facilities, and adequate recovery strategies in case all else fails. There are obviously problems in achieving such a GTCB, and one of the main purposes here is to see whether this concept is realistic. The success of such a design depends critically on the ability to decouple the requirements hierarchically, and to define a meaningful design layering.

Each layer of abstraction in a design structure may have a corresponding model defining the desired properties to be attained by that layer (e.g., human safety of the entire environment, immediate availability of most file-system files with sharply bounded delay otherwise, multilevel security of a trusted computing base, or single-error correction and double-error detection within a memory). In that the design layers must accommodate exceptions or failures unresolvable at that layer (e.g., detection of an apparent double error), the responses to exceptional conditions must also be modeled. Throughout, it must be explicitly recognized that the assumptions made at a particular layer may in fact not be satisfied, and some higher-layer check may be necessary. (A simple example involves the case of a triple error that is *mis*corrected as if it were a single error in the error-correction case noted above.) In addition, each layer of design abstraction may also have further internal layers of specifications, defining in detail the expected behavior of that design layer.

The precise distinction between model properties (e.g., assertions about properties of the interface to a layer) and specifications (e.g., functional relations on the state variables or algebraic relations among the inputs and outputs) is not always clear—but is not important to the discussion here. However, the examples may help to illustrate the differences.

---

[7]As an example, consider MVS, whose security weaknesses led to the development of SKK's ACF-2 and IBM's RACF. Although IBM systems running either ACF-2 or RACF on top of MVS appear superficially to be secure against penetration, they in fact do not stand up against attack once a user has logged in; they cannot prevent penetrations of the underlying operating system, which, in turn, can be used to circumvent either of these two superficial layers. For example, see [37].

The next three sections address, in order, relative degrees of criticality (Section III), layers of design abstraction (Section IV), and corresponding layers of models (Section V). Numerous examples are given. This leads to consideration of how relative criticalities can be accommodated within a hierarchical design, so that the critical requirements at each design layer can be satisfied simultaneously (in Section VI).

The conclusions (Section VII) suggest that this approach can provide greater assurance of satisfying the critical requirements, better manageability of the implementation, easier maintenance, and lesser likelihood of deleterious changes compromising the critical requirements.

III. DEGREES OF CRITICALITY

In this section, various examples are considered that illustrate differing degrees of criticality. The reader will note an intended relationship between the degrees of criticality and the layers of design abstraction, a relationship that is explored subsequently. However, it must be emphasized here that, unless we can do something dramatic in designing systems, the desired hierarchicalization of the degrees of criticality must be considered only as a conceptual ideal; most conventionally designed systems do not readily permit such an identification of criticalities that can be related to a design hierarchy (except in the degenerate sense of a flat hierarchy).

• Consider first Asimov's Three Laws of Robotics [1]. These laws have been dramatically employed by Asimov in writing science fiction, but are also of interest as an illustrative (albeit superficial) model of a set of safety requirements, stated as follows:

1) A robot may not injure a human being, or through inaction, allow a human being to come to harm.
2) A robot must obey the orders given it by human beings except where such orders would conflict with the First Law.
3) A robot must protect its own existence as long as such protection does not conflict with the First or Second Laws.

Table III is derived from these three laws. The three laws leave many conditions uncovered, e.g., conflicting orders from competing humans, or situations in which only some of the humans can be saved. Four illustrative degrees of safety are indicated in the table. The most critical (from a human point of view, at least) is the violation of the First Law, the next most critical being the violation of the Second or Third Law. Note that behavior satisfying all three laws is not necessarily correct behavior, as illustrated by the distinction between degrees 2 and 3 in Table III.[8]

• Table IV shows six illustrative degrees of behavior under faults, for some particular definition of *safe*. For the example, we assume that *safe* behavior does not in-

[8]An analogy with mandatory security policies—see below—is evident, where a set of properties must be globally enforced.

TABLE III
CRITICALITIES: HUMAN AND ROBOT SAFETY

Effects of Robot Action (after Asimov)

3. Compliant *and* correct behavior
2. Satisfaction of all three laws, but not necessarily correct operation
1. Injury or death of robot (violates Law 2 or 3), but never of humans (satisfies Law 1)
0. Injury or death of humans (violates Law 1)

TABLE IV
CRITICALITIES: PERFORMANCE UNDER FAULTS

Effects of Faults

5. System and application code not only safe but also correct
4. Fail-operational (safe with no degradation)
3. Fail-soft (safe with graceful degradation)
2. Fail-safe (anything goes if it is safe)
1. Fail-stop-safe (suspend operation before any unsafe behavior)
0. Fail-unsafe (unpredictable)

clude performance characteristics unless explicitly stated otherwise. In the table, degrees 2, 3, and 4 are fairly standard (e.g., see Leveson [30]). The other degrees are suggestive of additional degrees of criticality. *Note that safety is best defined in terms of the overall environment, although it is also meaningful to identify safety-related properties in terms of the computer system. Fail-unsafe* implies that system behavior is unpredictable. (In practice, there may be varying degrees of unsafe behavior, e.g., with partially confined damage.) *Fail-stop-safe* implies the system will stop before it can exhibit any unsafe behavior. *Fail-safe* behavior implies that the system may degrade in performance and may abandon noncritical functionality altogether; it may also defer or cease to perform certain critical functions, but its behavior will remain safe. (Fail-stop-safe is a limiting case of fail-safe, except when safety requires assured performance.) *Fail-soft* behavior implies that the system may degrade performance for functions that can wait. but will otherwise fulfill all of its critical requirements—and will remain safe. *Fail-operational* behavior suggests that the system continues to satisfy all of its safety requirements—including performance—despite faults to which the system is fault tolerant. If none of the critical requirements involves performance, fail-operational and fail-soft are equivalent. In each of the cases, there may be further degrees of criticality related to the layering of the critical requirements themselves, and dependence upon which faults are actually covered. (If safety requirements include performance requirements, or if we attempt to model several safety properties with varying priorities, then a partially ordered representation of criticalities seems more appro-

TABLE V
CRITICALITIES: COMPUTATIONAL SURVIVABILITY

Effects of HW/SW Problem

5. Actually adequate behavior
4. Apparently adequate behavior
3. May abort command, leave user intact
2. May crash one user job
1. May crash local system
0. May crash entire distributed system

TABLE VI
CRITICALITIES: NETWORK SURVIVABILITY

Effects of HW/SW Problem in Distributed Net

6. Actually flawless communication
5. Apparently flawless communication (with miscorrections)
4. Loss of one packet; if retry successful, no visible effect
3. Loss of one link between two nodes, reroute
2. Loss of a noncritical node and comm to attached hosts; reroute for hosts attached to multiple nodes
1. Loss of node/comm isolating attached hosts; impossible to reroute; delayed reception
0. Disruption of entire network (*e.g.*, ARPANET collapse)

TABLE VII
CRITICALITIES: IMPENETRABILITY

Effects of HW/SW Vulnerability

4. No possible adverse effects (hypothetical)
3. Penetration of one user login only; one user compromised, but others may be also, due to sharable resources or OS flaws
2. Penetration of one resource (file, server); can compromise all users who share it, *e.g.*, via a Trojan horse
1. Penetration of every user (*e.g.*, by virus or by unencrypted password file)
0. Penetration of system databases; forced crashes; coverup through altered audit trail

TABLE VIII
CRITICALITIES: EXPERT SYSTEM SOUNDNESS

Effects of HW/SW Problems in a Hypothetical Structured Expert System

3. Expert system completely sound for the given application
2. Rule base seems complete for critical use, but may give wrong or incomplete results, or be compromised by nonprimitive rules
1. Expert system kernel itself is sound with respect to rule interpretation (including its nonsubvertibility), irrespective of expert knowledge given to the system. Rule base may not be sound.
0. Underlying operating system is unsound, and can be used to compromise the expert system.

priate than the linear hierarchy shown in the table—but that complexity is beyond what is useful for the present illustration.)

• Table V gives six illustrative degrees of *computational survivability*, with successively less serious effects resulting from hardware or software problems (hardware faults, design errors, etc.) associated with the execution of code in the particular layer of the system. For example, a segmented virtual-memory, ring-structured hardware (e.g., Multics, SCOMP, and iAPX 286/386) can support this kind of a multilayer decomposition based on survivability. Note that designs of many conventional systems are not generally strict enough to guarantee that most faults can be sufficiently isolated, and indeed faults that logically appear to be high-layer (e.g., application-dependent rather than system-dependent) may have catastrophic consequences such as crashing the system or blocking network communications.

• Table VI shows seven illustrative degrees of *network survivability*. One might suspect that in a well-designed network, no malfunction of a single node of the network would be able to render the entire network useless. Note that such a case actually occurred in the ARPANET collapse of October 27, 1980, in which two slightly corrupted versions of a single status message acted as accidentally propagated viruses, infecting all nodes and causing the entire network to become flooded by highest-priority status messages that rapidly dominated all network traffic [43]. This event effectively brought the entire

net to a halt, as well as rendering it unmaintainable through the normal maintenance interface (from BBN in Cambridge using the net itself). A challenge in network design is to minimize or eliminate the chance of such a disaster; fault tolerance in the lower layers can help, but cannot provide complete guarantees.

• Table VII shows five illustrative degrees of *impenetrability* (and penetrability) in an operating system. At each higher degree, the idealized notion is that less damage can be done. As discussed below, many systems designs do not respect that.

• Table VIII shows four illustrative degrees of *soundness* in a knowledge-based system or *expert system*. This table suggests the difficult problem of designing and implementing an expert system so that its behavior remains controllable despite a variety of potential problems, such as 1) subversion by exploitation of underlying operating system problems to change the expert system itself, 2) incompleteness of the rule base, 3) failure resulting from addition of a contradictory rule or a rule of higher priority. (The use of heuristics of course adds a further measure of uncertainty.) An interesting research question is whether a layered structure such as that suggested in the table for the design can contribute to intrinsically safe expert systems, possibly along with corresponding design verification, e.g., demonstrating sufficient completeness of the system and of its rule base.

Implicit in each of these tables are certain assumptions about the isolation enforced by the underlying structure of the system and its applications. It is of course natural to begin this discussion with requirements and then talk about design. However, we see that we need a notion of the design before we can talk about the *effects* of the system. Thus, the above discussion considers conceptual degrees of criticality. In an actual system, the perceived hierarchy of critical effects may be grouped differently. The actual effects with respect to the critical requirements are reconsidered after the following examination of the role of the design.

IV. LAYERS OF DESIGN ABSTRACTION

The premise of this section is that hierarchies of abstract data types, with careful encapsulation and information hiding, can be valuable in organizing the design of a critical system. In this section, several illustrative design hierarchies are considered, and examples of existing systems cited.

For most current systems, the notion of degrees of criticality seems to be derived from the resulting system, i.e., observed *a posteriori*. Indeed this appears true for the examples in the preceding section—except for the last example, in which an attempt has been made to anticipate a hierarchical design of a critical expert system. It is expected that explicit *a priori* recognition of differing degrees of criticality in life-critical systems could have a significant impact on the design. In general, we desire that this recognition might go hand in hand with the development of the design.

Before attempting to consider whether various criticalities might be respected by a common design that accommodates all of the requirements at once, we first consider several examples of design hierarchies. Not surprisingly, security is a concern of many of these systems; extensive use of hierarchical decompositions to date has come from the security community—but then only from the viewpoint of security. However, that work has some significant impact on the other critical requirements considered here. In particular, the work to date on security provides some significant insights on how to design critical systems generally. People who have sought to achieve security beyond what was generally available in widely used operating systems a few years ago have been challenged to solve some nasty problems. Some of these solutions may actually lead to systems that provide a basis for some of the other critical applications, although the efforts to retrofit security into a nonsecure system are generally less productive.

An important concept here is that of *multilevel security* (MLS) [2], reflecting the notion of security clearances and classifications in which (say) Top-Secret, Secret, Confidential, and Unclassified labels (classifications) are affixed to every potentially visible piece of data, and similar labels (clearances) are associated with each individual. (Compartment labels may also be associated with each level.) A portion of the MLS policy involves the *no-adverse-flow policy*, that no information is permitted to flow to a lower level of security or laterally to another compartment at the same security level.[9] (See [16], [45].) An MLS policy is called a *mandatory security policy* because users cannot arbitrarily compromise that policy—e.g., they cannot give away or make copies in violation of no-adverse-flow. For any set of security labels, the system can enforce the security policy without knowing anything other than the labels representing classifications and clearances.

In multilevel secure systems, the lowest layers of the computer system typically provide a *security kernel* (implemented in hardware *and* software) that enforces the no-adverse-flow property except for certain privileged functions. On top of the kernel is implemented a set of trusted processes, so-called because they are privileged to violate no-adverse-flow selectively, but which enforce the desired MLS properties overall. (An example of such a trusted function is a downgrader or security-label changer, which creates an authorized adverse flow.) The kernel and all trusted software together from the Trusted Computing Base. (See [14].) In principle, if the TCB is properly designed and implemented, no program outside of the TCB should be able to compromise the TCB-enforced properties. On top of the TCB might be found non-security-related operating system functions, then programming languages, then system-provided application subsystems, then customer-provided environments, and then user software. Each successively higher layer of abstraction refines the facilities of the lower layers, and may provide finer-grained protection mechanisms more closely suited to the specific application.

Systems that do not support a mandatory security policy have several intrinsic problems, notably regarding propagation and revocation. For example, a user who is granted read access to something sensitive could copy it or simply make it accessible to others against the wishes of the originator. If granted write access, the user can write on request from other unauthorized users. Similarly, revocation of propagated rights can be difficult. In non-MLS systems, a user can often undermine the intended security without the system being able to counter it or indeed to be aware of it. This makes the burden of the operating system significantly greater—including the control of Trojan horses and viruses.

The hardware ring-structured protection mechanisms noted above in Multics, SCOMP, and iAPX 286/386 are particularly interesting.[10] The segmented-memory ring

[9]Mathematically speaking, the security levels (including compartments) are lattice-ordered.
[10]Multics has enforced MLS for many years (although not originally). On the other hand, the SCOMP was originally designed for MLS. Protection rings and security levels are essentially orthogonal issues, although MLS is typically implemented in the innermost rings. The Data General 10 000 series also has a ring-based architecture, although memory is not segmented within a ring—and there is no MLS.

structures—and more general domain protection mechanisms—can be used not only to provide isolation of users from the system, but also to protect the system from itself—increasing its fault tolerance. The Plessey System 250 used a capability-based generalization of rings to provide isolated domains for reliability purposes; each succeeding layer upwards requires longer to recover from faults, but needs to be invoked more rarely.

In fault-tolerant systems, similar layerings of functionality are found. Basic hardware may be configured into a fault-tolerant system kernel upon which successive layers of system and application code are built—relying on the fault tolerance of the kernel. Each successive layer again refines the facilities of the lower layers, and provides fault tolerance more closely suited to each application. Fault tolerance can be associated with each layer, appropriate to the particular level of abstraction.

For example, the Tandem fault-tolerant (''NonStop'') transaction-based operating system has a layering for synchronization purposes of communications, requester, server, disk processes, and a database (in descending order). This is a particularly interesting example, in that while the hierarchy results in a small loss of performance in a local system, it permits a 64-processor transaction system to operate at essentially 64 times the throughput of a single-processor system—despite a shared database [21]. A hierarchy combining synchronization and fault tolerance is also found in the transaction system described in [15].

An early example (1967) of a hierarchically designed system is the *THE* system. *THE* was based on a linearly ordered *uses* hierarchy for its process structure (also a *gives-work-to* hierarchy, in Parnas' terminology) enforcing a hierarchically prioritized synchronization strategy that guarantees the avoidance of deadlocks *between layers*; it is described by Dijkstra [12]. (It did not guarantee absence of deadlocks *within a layer*, and indeed such deadlocks did occasionally occur.)

Fault-tolerance techniques used at each layer in a hierarchical design can be largely invisible to the users of that layer. Bernstein [5] provides one example of a system (Sequoia) that attempts to do that.

The Paradox system (Ansa Software) is a query-by-example database manager that runs on IBM PCs and their equivalents. It is powerful, easy to use, and yet remarkably efficient. The system is quite large by PC standards, but highly structured into layers of virtual machines (primarily for purposes of managing complexity rather than security or fault tolerance). Self-optimization features in the database software permit high efficiency.

The use of hierarchical design structure to aid in system development and experimentation with alternative designs and in system evolution is considered by Goldstein and Bobrow [20].

In both security and fault-tolerance hierarchies, violations of the hierarchical encapsulation can occur as a result of unforeseen events such as uncovered hardware faults, synchronization dependencies, or distributed-sys-

TABLE IX
DESIGN LAYERS: MULTILEVEL SECURITY

Hierarchy of MLS Functionality and Effects of Compromise
3. End-user interface (restricted set of user functions); breaking restricted shell must not compromise MLS.
2. Subsystem interface; untrusted with respect to MLS, trusted with respect to applications; application security subvertible, but no MLS compromise; nonmandatory (discretionary) security may be subvertible.
1. MLS trusted subsystem interface (privileges masked); MLS subvertible through privileged trusted code.
0. MLS kernel interface -- Privileged functions for trusted subsystems, unprivileged otherwise; MLS compromise can result from kernel attack.

tem time-outs. If one mistakenly assumes perfect designs and implementations and sufficiently malfunction-free hardware, then any deviation from those assumptions can undermine the application. The big difference between allegedly secure systems and allegedly fault-tolerant systems today is that the former generally assume perfect hardware and try to demonstrate correctness of the software; the latter try to adapt to the hardware and the software not being perfect. Sensible design assumes the existence of real hardware faults and probably flawed software, and then anticipates what might happen if the assumptions are violated.

• Table IX shows a typical architectural decomposition of a multilevel secure (MLS) system, based on a no-adverse-flow kernel and some trusted subsystems that together are responsible for the maintenance of multilevel security. Layers 0 and 1—including the underlying hardware—constitute the trusted computing base. The table indicates some of the potential vulnerabilities at each layer.

Although the levels of multilevel security are not mandated in conventional computing systems (e.g., in unclassified or dedicated single-level systems), multilevel security is still a valuable concept. First, Lipner has shown that an MLS system can be useful even in unclassified environments [31], by taking advantage of the multilevel separation. Furthermore, the kinds of compartmentation available in MLS systems may be of great value in providing isolation in unclassified systems. Second, the MLS property illustrates the importance of having a mandatory policy that must not be compromised—whether it is a notion of security, fault tolerance, safety, or timely life-critical performance. The importance of the policy enforced by a secure trusted computing base is that higher layers cannot compromise the underlying policy—even accidentally. Thirdly, the notion of multilevel integrity (noted below) is of significant relevance in its own right, and can be better understood in the light of multilevel security.

TABLE X
DESIGN LAYERS: MULTILEVEL INTEGRITY

Hierarchy of Multilevel Integrity and Effects of Compromise
3. End-user interface; application integrity enforced
2. Subsystem interface; application integrity violated, but no MLI compromise
1. MLI trusted subsystem interface; Trojan horses installable that violate MLI
0. Integrity kernel interface; MLI compromisable

TABLE XI
DESIGN LAYERS: DISTRIBUTED SECURE SYSTEM

3. Users and user programs
2. UNIX operating system, with a distributed MLS file store
1. Newcastle Connection plus trusted network interface units for comm among UNIX systems, each with its own level of trust. (Each system assumes all users may be equally trusted.)
0. UNIX kernel for each UNIX system

Penetration and malfunction associated with each layer can have similar effects. However, note that, if the design and implementation are not sufficiently sound (e.g., they do not address security and fault tolerance of both software and hardware), a user or a malfunction could compromise the entire system from an outer layer. In other words, a single weak link—e.g., a flaw in the design, or a hardware malfunction—could compromise critical functionality, irrespective of the layer in which the running program was executing. Thus, strict isolation of most-critical functionality within the hierarchical design is a hope, but by no means a certainty—even with extensive analysis and formal verification. SCOMP [17] and KSOS [32] are two examples of systems supporting multilevel security. There are other kinds of trusted computing bases than MLS-kernel-based systems and separation kernels [46] for security applications, e.g., database systems and guards that guarantee job-stream separation.

• Table X shows a similar decomposition, based on a TCB that enforces a mandatory multilevel integrity (MLI). One such MLI policy is that due to Biba [7]—which is a formal dual of the MLS policy (although the names of the *integrity levels* are different from the names of the security levels). Integrity levels might be called Low-Trust, Medium-Trust, and High-Trust, implying a measure of *trustworthiness* associated with (say) a program or piece of data.) The corresponding no-adverse-flow integrity policy states (in essence) that a user at a particular level of integrity must never be permitted to depend upon a program or data whose integrity level is lower (less trustworthy), or—if at the same integrity level—whose integrity compartment is incompatible. That dual policy is fairly restrictive. A different mandatory integrity policy is used by the Secure Ada Target system (SAT), noted below. Implementation of integrity-level separation can be used to limit tampering with the system by less trustworthy individuals—and in combination with multilevel security can ensure that no Trojan horses, viruses, etc., can violate the MLS/MLI requirements (although other problems such as massive deletions could still occur).[11] An example of a problem that the MLI property solves is

protecting against the use of an untrustworthy program (e.g., a compiler or editor that contains a Trojan horse) by a more critical program. Considering the criticality of the applications, some form of system and data integrity is recommended. Lipner's argument also applies to MLI being suitable for commercial systems. Integrity is of particular interest in critical systems. This table also indicates some of the potential vulnerabilities at each layer.

• Table XI shows the hierarchy of the Distributed Secure System (DSS) [44], which is based on the UNIX™ United system and its network, the Newcastle Connection—which interposes a remote-procedure-call protocol between UNIX software and the UNIX kernel. In UNIX United, a collection of UNIX systems is organized into a network in which all communications among the different UNIX systems are provided by the Newcastle connection. DSS then puts a trusted network interface unit between each UNIX system and its network connection. The appearance of one MLS file system is provided, although it is implemented across all of the constituent UNIX file systems. The individual UNIX systems need not be trusted, in that each lives within a single MLS partition. In DSS, the Newcastle Connection does not have to be trusted for privacy (data are encrypted), but does have to be trusted for integrity and prevention of denial of service. (Configuration control and key management are of course also critical.)

• Table XII shows the abstract-machine hierarchy of the hardware/software design for a Provably Secure Operating System (PSOS) [35] that is based on a hierarchy of type managers. Each type manager is *solely* responsible for the management of its particular class of objects or resources (including whatever protection, fault tolerance, and distributed implementations are required). (That is the notion of *type safety*, not to be confused with *human* or *process safety*.) The internal details relevant to the implementation of each type are generally hidden. Protection is based on the use of nonforgeable objects called *tagged capabilities* that are used to control access to *all* objects (not just memory). In the PSOS design, a different policy can be enforced by each type manager, relevant to the objects that it manages. Honeywell's Secure Ada Target system (SAT) implements a suggestion of the PSOS

---

[11]Note that MLS by itself does not prevent Trojan horses that cause unauthorized altering of critical information, and that MLI by itself does not prevent unauthorized reading of information (in violation of MLS).

™UNIX is a trademark of AT&T Bell Laboratories.

TABLE XII
DESIGN LAYERS: PSOS

Layer	PSOS Abstraction or Function
16.	user request interpreter *
15.	user environments and name spaces *
14.	user input-output *
13.	procedure records *
12.	user processes*, visible input-output*
11.	creation and deletion of user objects*
10.	directories (*){c11}
9.	extended types (*){c11}
8.	segmentation (*){c11}
7.	paging {8}
6.	system processes and input-output {12}
5.	primitive input/output {6}
4.	arithmetic, other basic operations *
3.	clocks {6}
2.	interrupts {6}
1.	registers (*), addressable memory {7}
0.	capabilities *

```
   *    = functions visible at user interface.
  (*)   = partially visible at user interface.
  {i}   = module hidden by layer i.
  {c11} = creation/deletion hidden by layer 11.
```

TABLE XIII
DESIGN LAYERS: ISO OSI REFERENCE MONITOR HIERARCHY

Level	Typical protocols	Potential problems
7. Application	Electronic mail, EFTS	User behavior, application flaws, vulnerabilities visible from below
6. Presentation	FTP, Telnet, Virtual terminal, name servers, password management	Operating system, comm flaws, mail spoofs, viruses, remote maintenance spoofs, malevolent users, hardware failure, unencrypted headers, mailer ports with superuser status
5. Session	Ports, sockets, SNA, Courier (Xerox)	User synchronization, naming, viruses, spoofing, OS/comm bugs, hardware failure
4. Transport	TCP (DARPA), ISO/NBS/ECMA, NSP (DEC)	End-to-end protocol bugs, lack of transport encryption, flow control, os/comm bugs, hardware failure
3. Network, Internet	X75/X.25(Lev 3), IP (DARPA), RP (DEC)	Unprotected links and nodes, comm system bugs, untrusted gateways/nets spoofed connectivity, hardware failure
2. Link	HDLC(ISO), Ethernet, CMSA/CD contention, X.75/X.25(Lev 2), Cambridge ring, ADCCP (ANSI) BISYNC, SDLC (IBM) Token-ring, -bus,	Contention, saturation, ring breaks, denial of service, excessive traffic or retransmission, viruses, OS bugs, synchronization problems
1. Physical	V.35 (CCITT) RS 232, 449 (EIA) Mil-Std-188	Piggybacking, emanations, jamming, denial of service, traffic analysis, hardware failure

erable controversy over this particular hierarchy, which includes some standards for reliability. However, the hierarchy was established largely oblivious to security problems, and there are indeed serious potential problems with respect to security. The table suggests a few potential problems at each layer (i.e., ''level'' in OSI parlance).

Of these hierarchical designs, all bear some resemblance to the notion of hierarchical criticalities. In addition, a recent example of a design hierarchy for a multi-level-secure database management system satisfying an MLS/MLI policy is given in [11].

The hierarchical decompositions presented thus far illustrate some different design approaches for specific requirements. However, a system design should consider *all* of the relevant critical requirements simultaneously, in advance, including its application requirements—or else it must be shown that the application requirements can be decoupled without compromising performance (which is often not the case). Furthermore, the design and implementation for any critical requirement (e.g., fault tolerance or security) can generally be partitioned among different layers in the design and among different components in the distributed or centralized implementation of each layer, according to where the various mechanisms are most needed and can be most effective. However, where different requirements may interact or compete, commonality is required.

It is useful to note that there are two basically different ways of accommodating distributed implementations (whether for throughput, or reliability, or any other reason): *explicit* distribution, in which the user of an interface must know something about what is distributed and how, and *implicit* distribution, in which such knowledge is hidden by the interface. Note that the latter approach fits elegantly within the notion of encapsulated abstract data types (although the former approach is often favored for efficiency reasons). Implicit distribution minimizes various covert leakage channels whereby knowledge of the distribution permits inferences to be made. It also contributes significantly to long-term evolvability of a system and networks of systems. Therefore, that approach is favored here. In a hierarchy of type managers such as PSOS, one could provide implicitly distributed implementations of whichever type managers are appropriate.

Various design principles can be usefully invoked, a few of which are suggested as follows.

• Principle of least privilege. Each program module or user should be given only the privileges required for the purpose at hand. Superuser privileges are intrinsically dangerous, first because they are all powerful, and second because they usually bypass many of the controls and auditing mechanisms. Such mechanisms undermine the notion of associating diminishing criticalities with successive design layers. Privileges should be compartmentalized, rather than conferred globally. Domain-oriented designs implemented on a MLS domain architecture such as the SAT may be attractive for particularly critical systems.

reports, embedding the MLS property into the capability mechanism (see Boebert *et al.* [8]), thus gaining the benefits of enforcing a mandatory security policy. It also takes a different approach to mandatory integrity than the dual MLI policy noted above (see Boebert and Kain [9]), implementing it via hardware-enforced type safety. (Proofs of this enforcement of integrity are given in [22].)

• Table XIII summarizes the ISO Open Systems Interconnection (OSI) network hierarchy. There is still consid-

• Principle of information hiding. Unneeded implementation detail should be invisible from above each layer or constituent module. This encourages clean encapsulation, and actually helps implement the principle of least privilege if the encapsulation mechanism is sound. It also applies to communications to and from other components in a distributed system.

• Principle of preserving hierarchical orderings, including in distributed systems and networks. Dependence on less trustworthy components for implementing more critical functionality is to be avoided. No circuitous routes (e.g., to another site and back) should exist that would violate a local hierarchical ordering. Note that such an adverse dependence can arise if two hierarchies in a distributed system are incompatible (in which case a flaw in the hierarchy in one component can be used to compromise another), or if the communications are not hierarchy preserving. In distributed systems and networks, upper-layer protocols must not be able to violate lower-layer abstractions; furthermore, lower-layer protocols must not undermine the integrity of upper-layer protocols. This problem is exacerbated still further by the presence of untrustworthy distributed components and untrustworthy communications.

All three principles contribute to the notion of defensive design for critical systems, which tries to make the results at each layer resilient to undetected or unanticipated failures (and flaws) of lower layers, and which tries not to propagate its own errors upward.

V. LAYERS OF MODEL ABSTRACTION

As noted in Section II, there are two model types of particular interest in critical systems, models of properties (sometimes called requirements) and models of behavior (sometimes called specifications). Models of both types can be associated with each layer in a hierarchical design (or more generally, with each encapsulated unit in a structured design).

Although model hierarchies could be exhibited here for each of the above hierarchical designs, just three illustrations are given.

• Table XIV gives examples of properties appropriate at each layer in the design hierarchy achieved by combining Tables IX and X, where MLS and MLI properties are both enforced by a TCB. Note that the SCOMP system has undergone formal design proofs that its kernel specification (layer 0) satisfies the formal no-adverse-flow (except for the trusted processes and some storage channels) [47] and further proofs that its trusted process specifications (layer 1) satisfy another model relevant at that layer [3], which together imply the MLS property.

• Table XV gives examples of properties appropriate at various layers of the PSOS design. If each layer is looked upon as the type manager for a particular type of objects, then that layer must satisfy properties appropriate for objects of that type and for the type manager itself. The properties could relate to security, integrity, reliability, safety, timely responsiveness, etc. Thus in some

TABLE XIV
MODEL HIERARCHY: MLS/MLI

3. End-user interface: application-specific discretionary security and functional correctness
2. Subsystem interface: correctness properties
1. Trusted subsystem interface: e.g., privilege policy satisfied; no higher-layer Trojan horses can violate MLS/MLI; noncircumventable system auditing
0. Kernel interface: MLS/MLI with privilege mechanisms -- no violations for unprivileged use

TABLE XV
MODEL HIERARCHY: PSOS

Layer PSOS Abstraction and Model Property

n. User-created type manager: soundness
15. User spaces: search-path flaw avoidance
12. User processes isolated, I-O sound
11. User objects: no "lost objects" without capabilities
10. Directories: type safety, correct directory
9. Extended types: generic type safety
8. Segmentation: virtual memory gives proper segment, no residues after deletion, paging (layer 7) hidden
6. System processes: interrupts, I-O masked
4. Basic operations: correctly implemented
0. Capabilities nonforgeable, nonbypassable, nonalterable

sense, each type manager is a TCB for its objects, ensuring *type safety* of its objects as well.

• Table XVI gives examples of various layers of proof properties associated with the design of a Software-Implemented Fault-Tolerant system (SIFT). Some proofs have been carried out for a paper version of the SIFT system [34] (a simplified version of the system running at NASA Langley). The SIFT design uses allocation (in software) of each critical task to three different computers, with voting (in software) among the three. Transient errors are thus masked by the voting. Degraded performance is permitted. A typical flight might begin with 8 CPU's; any that fail permanently are deconfigured out of the system (again by the software). Fortunately, the portion of the code that must be trusted to maintain a failure probability less than 10^{-10} per hour is relatively small (less than 1000 lines of Pascal).[12]

Various safety properties can be considered in a similar vein. Those considered by Asimov and by Leveson (e.g.,

[12]If one of the algorithms is wrong, clearly triple-modular redundancy is of no help. For that reason, some efforts involve *n*-version programming—e.g., the space-shuttle backup computer system, which uses (more-or-less) independent algorithms on a separate computer. However, common faults may be found even in *n*-version programming. Furthermore, implicit assumptions are usually made that lower-layer abstractions are working correctly—e.g., that the hardware really works as supposed.

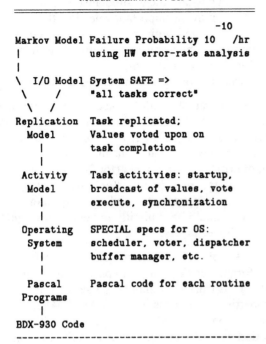

TABLE XVI
MODEL HIERARCHY: SIFT

```
                                            -10
Markov Model  Failure Probability 10   /hr
    |              using HW error-rate analysis
    |
  \ I/O Model  System SAFE =>
   \    /      "all tasks correct"
    \  /
Replication   Task replicated;
    Model     Values voted upon on
      |       task completion
      |
  Activity    Task actitvies: startup,
    Model     broadcast of values, vote
      |       execute, synchronization
      |
  Operating   SPECIAL specs for OS:
   System     scheduler, voter, dispatcher
      |       buffer manager, etc.
      |
   Pascal     Pascal code for each routine
  Programs
      |
 BDX-930 Code
--------------------------------------------
```

[28] and [29]) were not conceived within a hierarchical framework, rather being properties just of the application interface. Nevertheless, it is useful to consider them in attempting to hierarchicalize requirements for human safety. Table III suggests that a hierarchicalization of the degrees of criticality might make some sense for safety issues—although, as noted, the Asimov Laws are a gross oversimplification of the complexity of the safety problem.

VI. TOWARD A UNIFIED DESIGN APPROACH

In systems that are not hierarchically structured with realistic assumptions at each layer, flaws anywhere may potentially have side-effects that can compromise requirements globally—as suggested by Table I. Some fundamental questions remain to be answered regarding what must be trusted at each layer. For example, is safety intrinsically a user-interface issue, or does it manifest itself hierarchically at different layers? Is there a useful notion of a *safety-trusted computing base* responsible for enforcing a primitive safety policy that cannot be compromised from above? In many cases, safety could be compromised by faulty application code, even if the underlying system were completely sound. However, trustworthy lower layers of a system that provide security, fault tolerance, and some primitive forms of safety would be valuable.

As an example, consider traffic signals. A primitive safety policy might be that green lights shall never be indicated simultaneously in conflicting directions. A higher-layer safety policy might relate to mechanisms for sound handling of red, yellow, and green switching and priority interrupts, and a still higher layer might involve setting of parameters for light cycles and delays in light changes. The hierarchical decomposition, the design of the primi-

tive layer, and the implementation should attempt to guarantee that nothing at a higher layer can compromise the lower-layer policies.

Thus, it appears useful to seek a hierarchical layering under an extended notion of trust encompassing a variety of critical requirements, with correspondingly layered models that accurately reflect the desired safety properties of a system and its applications.[13] As with security and fault-tolerance, there are aspects of safety requirements at various layers in the hierarchy.

Mandatory security properties such as MLS/MLI can indeed be enforced by a TCB such that untrusted application subsystems cannot compromise MLS/MLI—subject to the satisfaction of the underlying assumptions. Unfortunately, the amount of hardware and software that must be trusted is not small; however, it is smaller than it would be without a TCB-conscious design. In the absence of such a mandatory policy, it is often difficult for a lower layer to enforce anything rigorous upon a higher layer, e.g., if the higher layer can compromise the integrity of the lower layers, or if the lower layer can itself be compromised directly. (The example of brokered indirect reading and writing is given above. An extreme example is provided by systems providing superuser privileges that bypass all protection; their use by ordinary users from unprotected domains, either accidentally or intentionally, represents a serious threat.) MLS/MLI policies are not the only solution, but conventional approaches permit potential compromises from a much larger body of code. They do not necessarily provide a simple solution, in that in many applications the size of the TCB is considerable.

Mandatory TCB properties similar to those for MLS/MLI are not as clearly evident for other requirements such as fault tolerance, safety and high availability—although there are certainly low-layer functionalities that could be conveniently overlaid onto an MLS/MLI hierarchy. Because safety cannot generally be formulated *solely* as a lower-layer system concept, significant portions of the application code may have to be correct or partially correct in order to provide appropriate safety.

We consider here an MLS/MLI TCB as the basis for a hierarchical critical system—although the MLS property may be used "commercially" as suggested by Lipner ([31]) rather than "militarily." The design of such a system is characterized by a coalescing of Tables IX and X, with corresponding properties at each layer such as are represented in Table XIV. Techniques are added at each layer for availability, fault-tolerance, correctness, safety, or other critical requirements. An illustrative set of techniques and properties at each layer is suggested by Table XVII. (For simplicity, only four layers are shown.) It must be noted that the GTCB indicated is not *totally* responsible for enforcing the critical system requirements (e.g., for security, safety and fault tolerance), but rather pro-

---

[13]Distributed-system research has defined still another notion of *safety* (used in the sense of *doing the right thing*), along with the notion of *liveness* (*doing it eventually, within a finite time bound*). The former notion appears here as correctness, i.e., consistency with requirements.

Layers of MLS/MLI, fault tolerance, availability,
correctness, safety, etc. See also Tables 9, 10, 14.

----

4. *User programs* (cannot compromise lower-level functionality)

3. *End-user interface*: application programs with varying
criticalities; application correctness (*e.g.*, for safety),
consistency checks on application; checkpoints and rollback;
noncritical administrative programs.

2. *Computer subsystem interface*: sound, secure, reliable, safe
subsystems consistent with requirements (subject to satisfaction
of underlying assumptions); administrative and operational
procedures within acceptable risks; nondenial of service for
time-critical and resource-critical safety; proper restoration
of subsystems after crashes; fair accounting procedures.

1. *GTCB*: Enforces MLS/MLI, primitive fault-tolerance,
additional safety properties; privilege mechanisms sealed off;
trusted servers; device recoverability; sound primitive atomic
actions for database transactions -- especially in distributed
implementations; fair scheduling; noncircumventable auditing
and reporting of system operations.
Integrity locks to detect undesirable system modifications.
System configuration -- restoration of sound system states
following malfunction, penetration, etc.

0. *MLS/MLI/FT/... kernel*: nonflow ensures nontrusted programs
cannot compromise security/integrity of the kernel objects;
security and fault-tolerance of the kernel enhance trusted
subsystems' ability to support primitive safety properties.
Software reliability -- sound synchronization and interrupt
handling, consistency checks, integrity checks on security
labels, rapid reboot for high availability, reliable and
fail-safe low-level communications.
Hardware reliability -- error-correcting codes, instruction
retry, reliable address calculation, bounds checks, security
label integrity, to guarantee no accidental alteration of
critical and/or sensitive data.

----

vides appropriate primitives. This reflects the problem
with secure systems in which, although only the TCB has
to be trusted to enforce MLS, some trust must be generally placed at each higher layer (if only for correctness of
functionality!)—although the design should be such that
the properties of the lower layers cannot be compromised
from above.

The use of MLS/MLI TCB as the basis for the GTCB
is not the only possible design strategy, but is a convenient one for present descriptive purposes. In addition to
providing support for the mandatory properties, it also has
the future potential that economical commercial systems
are expected to emerge for MLS/MLI.

There are clearly many design alternatives and corresponding tradeoffs in attaining a hierarchy (possibly a partial ordering rather than a linear ordering) that encompasses a diverse set of requirements. The design principles
noted above impose a few constraints on what is reasonable. Conferring least privilege, hiding unneeded information, and preserving hierarchical orderings help to
minimize (accidental or intentional) undesirable side-effects, and help allocate specific functionality to an appro-

priate layer—which should be low enough to be efficient
and high enough to suit the desired abstraction. Efficiency
considerations play an important role. But the concept of
what must be trusted with respect to each requirement,
with a corresponding layering of trust, is ultimately the
forcing function on the design.

The desired approach is summarized as follows:

A design hierarchy, ordered according to the *uses*
relation, should be established with both a model
hierarchy and associated relative criticalities in
mind. Each layer should contribute to the enforcement of critical requirements (for fault tolerance, security, safety, real-time performance characteristics, etc.) as appropriate, and the requirements at
each layer should be explicitly related to the requirements at lower layers.

Given a set of critical requirements, it is natural to ask
whether formal verification could play a role. If there were
a small GTCB trusted to maintain a set of primitive critical properties (as is possible with MLS/MLI), then design verification could indeed be attractive—although code
verification is still too agonizing except for small programs. In any event, design decompositions should be
sought that require only a small portion of the system to
be trusted (in the broader sense of the critical requirements). On the other hand, if the system design is such
that human safety (for example) could depend upon much
of the code, then there is very little hope for verification—
or for safety. Such a design would intrinsically be a disaster; the risks would be so great that such a computer
system should never be used to control a life-critical environment. Verification thus makes sense only when the
system design is structured so that only a few small components are really critical. Some recent background on
formal verification is found in [10].

In order to minimize the effect of uncovered hardware
faults, and to provide some of the (*vertical*) isolation of
critical functionality from less critical functions, a distributed architecture has some advantages if it is organized according to a criticality hierarchy—but with the
distributed components enforcing some *horizontal* isolation. In this case, it might appear that the hierarchical
unity could be relaxed among different components, e.g.,
if one component is security-critical and another is life-
critical. But the principle of preservation of local ordering
must be maintained. The interactions noted above among
different requirements must also be considered, as well as
the increased complexity of synchronization problems.

Misuse of modularity can be harmful, e.g., resulting in
inefficient implementations with many nested layers of
interpretation. A general-purpose GTCB may be inappropriate if a general-purpose system is to be implemented
on top of it. However, with appropriate software design
and suitable hardware, hierarchical designs can be implemented efficiently. Examples of Paradox and Tandem are
noted above. The PSOS design of Table XII provides another example, in which a single hardware instruction can

be used to implement a nonremote procedure call at layer 12—even though procedures at certain lower layers may be implemented in software!

Another important consideration is that any GTCB needed for real-time critical requirements (safety, for example) must be sufficiently rich to provide the necessary facilities (including any needed asynchronous and synchronous input–output options and other low-level control features—especially if transactions are to be supported). In order for this to be sufficiently efficient, suitable hardware support is likely to be necessary. Neumann *et al.* [35] and Bernstein and Siegel [4] address the attainment of efficiency despite hierarchical design.

VII. CONCLUSIONS

We have attempted a step toward the design, development, and modeling of systems that must simultaneously satisfy a variety of critical requirements. This is just a beginning. Unfortunately, readers not familiar with all of the areas of security, fault tolerance, and safety may find too much left unspecified to make the examples meaningful. But this simply reinforces the fact that design of critical systems must clearly reflect deep awareness of a wide range of concerns.

Hierarchical design can be of significant value in achieving isolation of critical parts of a computer system from less critical parts, with respect to such varied requirements as security, reliability, and safety—to mention a few. By accommodating all of the critical requirements within a unified hierarchy, a sensible ordering of degrees of criticality can be achieved that is directly and naturally related to the design structure. Distributed implementations of functionality and fault tolerance at any desired layer can be effectively masked. The resulting criticalities can then manifest themselves as explicit properties in the corresponding layers of models that must be satisfied at each design layer. The hierarchical approach also provides significant benefits in manual recovery from nontolerated faults when human intervention is unavoidable, in software maintenance, and in long-term evolution.

The generalized trusted computing base must not be looked upon as a panacea. It cannot provide the basis for fool-proof software written above it—although it can enforce MLS/MLI isolation and provide some useful primitives for fault tolerance, safety, and other critical requirements. Making all of the underlying assumptions explicit helps in identifying flaws that would otherwise result from incomplete, unsatisfied, or false assumptions at any layer in the system.

Satisfying a set of critical requirements is a problem not only of the computer system(s) but also of the operating environment. It requires a thorough design approach with considerable foresight. Problems otherwise left unsolved (e.g., hardware malfunctions, software bugs, and faulty assumptions) could ultimately have catastrophic effects such as resulting in unsafe behavior, security flaws, and system collapses. Unless significant structure and defensive design are present, such problems may propagate wildly. However, even in a highly structured system or a system whose distributed implementation provides strong isolation to reduce propagation, unforeseen failures can cause disaster. The examples of the ARPANET collapse and the first shuttle launch should be kept in mind as illustrative of the subtle nature of distributed-system problems. Besides, even the best design can be compromised by a poor implementation or by a poor choice of programming language (e.g., one that cannot intrinsically enforce abstraction, encapsulation, type safety, and safe synchronization). On the other hand, a bad design has consequences that permeate the lifetime of the system; it is often insurmountable.

A few other summary conclusions are in order.

• No system is ever going to be guaranteed to work properly all of the time, especially if it runs stand-alone.

• Humans in the loop may add to the problem rather than improve it—especially if they must operate under tight real-time constraints. Complex human interfaces undoubtably make matters worse.

• In a complex system, it is essentially impossible to predict all the sources of catastrophic failure. This is true even in well-engineered systems, where the sources of failure may be even more subtle. Risks may come from unexpected directions. A system that has run without serious failure for years may suddenly fail. Hardware may fail. Lurking flaws may surface. Software may fail because of changes elsewhere. False assumptions at any layer in the hierarchy—but particularly at the lowest layers—can be devastating.

• The notion that all critical concerns—security, reliability, etc.—can be confined to a small portion of a computer system or distributed system (e.g., a kernel) is a fantasy, particularly with conventionally designed computer systems. A realistic generalized trusted computing base—upon which the adequacy of system operation can depend—tends to be much larger, especially if a variety of requirements is encompassed. When human safety is a critical requirement, significant amounts of application code may have to be trusted. However, hierarchical design and careful distributed implementation—including the substructuring of the GTCB—can help considerably to confine bad effects.

• The notion that distributed control solves problems not easily solved with central control is also largely a myth—problems of updating, synchronization, concurrency, backup, verifiability, etc., may simply appear in different guises, and some may be much harder to analyze.

• The operating environment may contain risks that can defeat sound design and implementation—irrespective of how well engineered the computer systems are.

• Sound software engineering practice provides no easy answers. But even riskier are the archaic techniques often found in lowest-bidder efforts.

This paper suggests one further step toward developing computer systems that can better accommodate a range of critical requirements. But it is only one step. More work is needed to make these concepts precise, to address the many lurking problems, to model the desired critical requirements, and to show whether the concepts are indeed realistic.

Above all, it is vital to recognize that completely guaranteed behavior is impossible and that there are inherent risks in relying on computer systems in critical environments. The unforeseen circumstances are often the most disastrous.

Historical Note: In addition to deriving its inspiration from Parnas, Dijkstra, Hoare, and others, this article has been stimulated by the author's involvement in efforts somewhat dispersed in time: the hierarchical directory structure and process structures of Multics (1965–1969), an early effort to organize fault tolerance hierarchically (1972–1973, for an ARPA project, Contract N00014-72-C-0254), the hierarchical design of PSOS, with its domain-based hardware and software (1973–1980), and the writing of [36]. Most recently, a NASA effort to study the computing requirements for the Space Station (Contract NAS2-11864) provided a chance to look at the problem of designing critical systems from the broader perspective taken here.

REFERENCES

[1] I. Asimov, "Runaround," *Astounding Science Fiction*, Apr. 1941; also in *I, Robot* and *The Complete Robot*.

[2] D. E. Bell and L. J. La Padula, "Secure computer system: Unified exposition and multics interpretation," Mitre Corp., Bedford, MA, Rep. ESD-TR-75-306, Mar. 1976.

[3] T. C. V. Benzel and D. A. Tavilla, "Trusted software verification: A case study," in *Proc. 1985 Symp. Security and Privacy*, IEEE Comput. Soc., Oakland, CA, Apr. 1985, pp. 14–31.

[4] A. J. Bernstein and P. Siegel, "A computer architecture for level structured systems," *IEEE Trans. Comput.*, vol. C-24, pp. 785–793, Aug. 1975.

[5] P. A. Bernstein, "Sequoia: A fault-tolerant tightly-coupled computer for transaction processing," Wang Inst., Rep. TR-85-03, 1985.

[6] D. M. Berry, M. Erlinger, J. B. Johnston, and A. von Staa, "Models of hierarchical machine support," in *Formal Descriptions of Programming Concepts*, E. J. Neuhold, Ed. Amsterdam, The Netherlands: North-Holland, 1978, pp. 557–588.

[7] K. J. Biba, "Integrity considerations for secure computer systems," MTR 3153, Mitre Corp., Bedford, MA, Rep. MTR 3153, June 1975.

[8] W. E. Boebert, S. A. Hansohn, and W. D. Young, "Secure Ada target: Issues, system design, and verification, in *Proc. 1985 Symp. Security and Privacy*, IEEE Comput. Soc., Oakland, CA, Apr. 1985, pp. 176–183.

[9] W. E. Boebert and R. Y. Kain, "A practical alternative to hierarchical integrity policies," presented at the 8th Nat. Comput. Security Conf., NBS, Gaithersburg, MD, Oct. 1-3, 1985.

[10] S. Crocker and K. N. Levitt, Eds. "VERkshop III: Verification workshop," *ACM SIGSOFT Software Eng. Notes*, vol. 10, no. 4, pp. 1–136, Aug. 1985.

[11] D. E. Denning, S. G. Akl, M. Morgenstern, P. G. Neumann, and R. R. Schell, "Views for multilevel database security," in *Proc. 1986 Symp. Security and Privacy*, IEEE Comput. Soc., Oakland, CA, Apr. 1986, pp. 156–172.

[12] E. W. Dijkstra, "The structure of the THE multiprogramming system," *Commun. ACM*, vol. 11, no. 5, May 1968.

[13] J. E. Dobson and B. Randell, "Building reliable secure computing systems out of unreliable insecure components," in *Proc. 1986 Symp. Security and Privacy*, IEEE Comput. Sci., Oakland, CA, Apr. 1986, pp. 187–193.

[14] *Department of Defense Trusted Computer System Evaluation Criteria*, Comput. Security Center, Dep. Defense, Rep. CSC-STD-001-83, 1983.

[15] A. El Abbadi, D. Skeen, and F. Cristian, "An efficient fault-tolerant protocol for replicated data management," in *Proc. 4th SIGACT-SIGMOD Symp. Principles of Data Base Syst.*, ACM, 1985.

[16] R. J. Feiertag, "A technique for proving specifications are multilevel secure," Comput. Sci. Lab., SRI Int., Menlo Park, CA, Rep. CSL109, Jan. 1980.

[17] L. J. Fraim, "SCOMP: A solution to the multilevel security problem," *Computer*, vol. 16, no. 7, pp. 26–34, July 1983; reprinted in *Advances in Computer Security*, vol. 2, R. Turn, Ed. Dedham, MA: Artech House, 1984.

[18] J. Garman, "The bug heard 'round the world," *ACM SIGSOFT Software Eng. Notes*, vol. 6, no. 5, pp. 3–10, Oct. 1981.

[19] J. A. Goguen and J. Meseguer, "Security policies and security models," in *Proc. 1982 Symp. Security and Privacy*, Oakland, CA, Apr. 26–28, 1982, pp. 11–20.

[20] I. P. Goldstein and D. Bobrow, *A Layered Approach to Software Design*, D. R. Barstow, H. E. Shrobe, and E. Sandewall, Eds. New York: McGraw-Hill, 1984.

[21] J. Gray, "Why do computers stop, and what can be done about it?" Tandem Comput., Inc., Cupertino, CA, Tech. Rep. TR85.7, 1985.

[22] J. Haigh and W. Young, "Extending the non-interference version of MLS for SAT," in *Proc. 1986 Symp. Security and Privacy*, IEEE Comput. Soc., Oakland, CA, Apr. 1986, pp. 231–239.

[23] J. Kemeny et al., "Report of the President's commission on the accident at Three Mile Island," U.S. Government Printing Office, 1979.

[24] L. Lamport and P. M. Melliar-Smith, "Synchronizing clocks the presence of faults," *J. ACM*, vol. 32, no. 1, pp. 52–78, Jan. 1985.

[25] L. Lamport, R. Shostak, and M. Pease, "The Byzantine generals problem," *ACM Trans. Program. Lang. Syst.*, vol. 4, no. 3, pp. 382–401, July 1982.

[26] B. W. Lampson, "Redundancy and robustness in memory protection," in *Inform. Processing 74 (Proc. IFIP Congress 1974)*, 1974, pp. 128–132.

[27] J.-C. Laprie, "Dependable computing and fault tolerance," in *Dig. Papers, FTCS-15*, IEEE Comput. Soc., June 1985, pp. 2–11.

[28] N. G. Leveson et al., "Design for safe software," in *Proc. AIAA 21st Aerospace Sci. Meeting*, Amer. Inst. Aeronautics and Astronautics, Reno, NV, Jan. 1983.

[29] N. G. Leveson, "Software safety in computer controlled systems," *Computer*, vol. 17, no. 2, pp. 48–55, Feb. 1984.

[30] N. Leveson, "Software safety: Why, what, and how," Univ. California, Irvine, ICSD Tech. Rep. 86-04, 1986.

[31] S. B. Lipner, "Non-discretionary controls of commercial applications," in *Proc. 1982 Symp. Security and Privacy*, Oakland, CA, Apr. 26–28, 1982, pp. 2–10.

[32] E. J. McCauley and P. Drongowski, "KSOS: Design of a secure operating system," in *Proc. NCC*, June 1979; reprinted in *Advances in Computer Security*, R. Turn, Ed. Dedham, MA: Artech House, 1981.

[33] P. M. Melliar-Smith and B. Randell, "Software reliability: The role of programmed exception handling," *ACM SIGPLAN Notices*, vol. 12, no. 3, pp. 95–100, Mar. 1977; also in *Proc. Conf. Language Design for Reliable Software*, Raleigh, NC.

[34] P. M. Melliar-Smith and R. L. Schwartz, "Formal specification and mechanical verification of SIFT: A fault-tolerant flight control system," *IEEE Trans. Comput.*, vol. C-31, pp. 616–630, July 1982.

[35] P. G. Neumann, R. S. Boyer, R. J. Feiertag, K. N. Levitt, and L. Robinson, "A provably secure operating system: The system, its applications, and proofs," SRI Int., 2nd ed., Rep. CSL-116, May 1980.

[36] P. G. Neumann, "Experiences with *formality in software development*," in *Theory and Practice of Software Technology*, D. Ferrari, M. Bolognani, and J. Goguen, Eds. Amsterdam, The Netherlands: North-Holland, 1983, pp. 203–219.

[37] R. Paans and G. Bonnes, "Surreptitious security violation in the MVS operating system," Dep. Elec. Eng., Delft Univ. Technol., Delft, The Netherlands, 1984.

[38] D. L. Parnas, "On the criteria to be used in decomposing systems into modules," *Commun. ACM*, vol. 15, no. 12, Dec. 1972.

[29] ——, "On a 'buzzword': Hierarchical structure," in *Inform. Processing 74 (Proc. IFIP Congress 1974)*, 1974, pp. 336–339.

[40] ——, "Some hypotheses about the 'Uses' hierarchy for operating systems," Technische Hochschule Darmstadt, Mar. 1976.

[41] ——, "A technique for software module specification with examples," *Commun. ACM*, vol. 15, no. 5, May 1972.

[42] B. Randell and J. E. Dobson, "Reliability and security issues in distributed computing systems," in *Proc. Fifth Symposium Reliability in Distributed Software and Database Systems*, Los Angeles, CA, Jan. 1986.

[43] E. Rosen, "Vulnerabilities of network control protocols," *ACM SIG-SOFT Software Eng. Notes*, vol. 6, no. 1, pp. 6–8, Jan. 1981.

[44] J. M. Rushby and B. Randell, "A distributed secure system," *Computer*, vol. 16, no. 7, pp. 55–67, July 1983.

[45] J. M. Rushby, "The security model of enhanced HDM," presented at the 7th DoD/NBS Comput. *Security Initiative Conf.*, NBS, Gaithersburg, MD, Sept. 24–26, 1984.

[46] ——, "A trusted computing base for embedded systems," in *Proc. 7th DoD/NBS Comput. Security Initiative Conf.*, NBS, Gaithersburg, MD, Sept. 24–26, 1984, pp. 294–311.

[47] J. M. Silverman, "Reflections on the verification of the security of an operating system," in *Proc. 9th ACM Symp. Operat. Syst. Principles*, Oct. 1983, pp. 143–154; reprinted in *Advances in Computer Security*, vol. 2, R. Turn, Ed. Dedham, MA: Artech House, 1984.

Peter Gabriel Neumann (S'56–M'61–SM'85) received the A.B., S.M., and Ph.D. degrees from Harvard University, Cambridge, MA, in 1954, 1955, and 1961, respectively, and the Dr. rerum naturarum from the Technische Hochschule, Darmstadt, West Germany, in 1960.

He is Staff Scientist in the Computer Science Laboratory at SRI International, Menlo Park, CA, where he has been since 1971. He has been active in the computer field since 1953. His current research interests include computer systems, security, system vulnerabilities, and software engineering.

Dr. Neumann is Editor of the ACM SIGSOFT *Software Engineering Notes*, Chairman of the ACM Committee on Computers and Public Policy, and Coordinator of the on-line Forum on Risks to the Public in the Use of Computers.

*Management of
Computing*

*E. Burton Swanson
Editor*

Computer Backup Pools, Disaster Recovery, and Default Risk

YEHUDA KAHANE, SEEV NEUMANN, and CHARLES S. TAPIERO

*ABSTRACT: There is a growing popularity of computer
backup pools, where a few members share the ownership, or
right for service, of a computer center. Such a center stands
by to provide for the lost computing capacity of a member
suffering a computer breakdown and disaster recovery. The
efficiency of such a solution may be examined from various
points of view, such as costs, response time, reliability etc.
We focus on the reliability of such an arrangement. Two
types of default risks are discussed: the probability that the
center itself will break down when needed, so that it would
be unable to provide service (this is similar to the traditional
measure of a "probability of ruin") and a "perceived
probability of ruin" (the probability that a member will be
affected by the failure of the center). We borrow the concepts
of probability of ruin from the risk management and
insurance literature, in order to reach explicit relationships
between these probabilities and the pricing of a mutual
computer pool. It is shown that the membership fee for each
participant must be a function of both the payments of all
members and their loss (call for service) distributions,
reflecting thereby the simultaneity of and mutual
interdependence of members.*

1. INTRODUCTION

The growing dependence of large organizations on their
computers emphasizes the high loss potential in case of
interruption in the normal operation of their computers. Interruption of the computer center's services
may drastically affect the ability of the organization to
function, and to serve its customers. The loss may often
be higher than the direct loss of hardware and/or software (see for example Krauss [1980], Datapro [1983])
and in extreme cases may cause a long-term conse-
quential loss, perhaps even bankruptcy. The problems
arising from the shutdown of a large computer center
are especially complicated, due to the need for a special
environment (large area, power, wiring, cooling, communications etc.), and due to the long lead and installa-

tion times of computer hardware. It is not surprising,
therefore, that much attention is given to the protection
of computer centers. The means of protection include
physical means and financial instruments, such as insurance. Being indemnified for a financial loss through
insurance is not always sufficient to compensate for
other losses which are often more important, especially
when the survival of the firm is at stake due to a breakdown of its computer center.[1] Therefore, control of risk
is often preferred over insurance arrangements.

There are numerous technical and administrative
means to control the risk of physical damage to hardware and software. Data and software can be protected
easily by appropriate storage of backup tapes and disks
in another, separate, location. Other technological solutions (for example, dual processors)—usually based on
some sort of physical backup and requiring a substantial investment—are being employed to protect hardware systems.

There is a variety of solutions for large computer
backup centers (see, for example Reed (1980),
McDonald (1966), Datapro (1983)). They differ by
their response time, cost and reliability. Among the
most common solutions are:

(1) *"Hot Backup"* Maintaining an additional site,
which operates in parallel to the main installation,
and immediately takes over in case of a failure of
the main center.
(2) *"Warm Backup"* Maintaining another inactive
site ready to become operational within a matter of
hours.
(3) *" Split Site"* Two installations (each somewhat
smaller than a hot backup) are used. In case of
emergency one center can keep the organization
running by performing only jobs with high priority
(Dentay [1980], Datapro [1983]).

---

[1] Risk management literature often emphasizes the need for a simultaneous
optimization of risk financing (insurance) and risk control (such as pooling).
Under certain circumstances, a firm would prefer one method over the other,
whereas under other conditions a combination may be desirable. In this paper
no attempt has been made to address these issues.

(4) *"Cold Backup"* Maintaining empty computer premises ("empty shell") with the relevant support ready to accept the immediate installation of appropriate hardware. "Cold backup" is used when the recovery time is mainly affected by the need to install the infrastructure and support systems (electricity, communications, air conditioning, etc.), whereas the cost is mainly affected by the cost of the hardware (Reed [1980], Dentay [1980], Sullivan [1980]).

(5) *"Mutual Backup"* This is a mutual agreement between two computer centers, operated by different firms, which decide to assist each other in case of emergency on the basis of "best efforts." This appears to be the least expensive, but also the least effective arrangement, especially when both firms operate with similar peak loads, and where each has only a limited excess capacity.

(6) *"Pooling"* A solution which is gaining popularity is a pooling arrangement where a few members join into a mutual agreement concerning a computer center, which is standing-by idle to offer a service to any member suffering from interruption in its computer center. The idle computer center may be employed in the form of "cold" or "warm" backup. The center serves a pool of users, who share the ownership (or pay a certain membership fee to the owner of the facility). Such pooling is the focus of this paper.

In practice, such pools tend to serve members (users) similar in size and having similar needs, i.e., they all use computers of the same family. The differences in configuration of various members using the same basic family are typically insignificant as the equipment is standard, and can be purchased off-the-shelf in case of need. Otherwise, configuration differences can be handled by having some slack capacity in the backup center, in terms of peripheral equipment (disk drives, terminals, etc.).

Such pools are based on the ability to simultaneously serve more than one member in need. The capacity of the center is then shared among the users. The ability to share is facilitated by appropriate system software, by security arrangements, and by relevant contingency planning. The sharing arrangement has to be agreed upon in advance, and established on the basis of membership fees. The fees are a function of the service required and the quality of protection offered. The *quality of protection* is a parameter often overlooked in the analysis of this solution, and thus will be the focal point of our analysis in this paper.

2. RISK CONCEPTS

The membership fee that each member is willing to pay depends on several parameters, such as the expected capacity loss, and the significance of the computing power loss to the member organization. The membership fee depends, of course, also on the reliability of the system in providing a true backup service to the member. It is surprising that these relationships have, to the best of our knowledge, neither been recognized in theory or practice. The purposes of this paper are therefore: (a) to analyze these relationships; (b) to formulate an explicit pricing formula relating these parameters and the appropriate membership fee; and, (c) to enhance the understanding of certain tradeoffs which may affect the operation and functioning of computer backup pools, and may determine the size of the population they serve.

The analysis in this paper borrows the concept of probability of ruin and mutual insurance, from the risk management literature, in order to reach an explicit pricing formula. (See a recent paper on the failure of a mutual insurer by Tapiero, Kahane & Jacque [1986]).

The focus of our analysis is on the parameters affecting the willingness of organizations to join such a pool; we attempt to obtain an explicit relationship between the price the participating members are willing to pay for a given assumed probability of loss (due to the disruption of a computer center's operations), and the reliability of this backup center.

Loss-sharing arrangement contracts are often defined as transactions where members exchange uncertain "prospects" with certain ones at the cost of a "premium" (see Beard, Pentikainen and Pesonen [1972], Buhlmann [1970], Borch [1974]). In this context, the member faces no risk, once he has paid for the loss-sharing arrangement contract. Practically, however, there is always a tradeoff between the cost and the reliability of a backup service, which has to be considered by the potential participants and in the rate making process (Kahane [1979]).

The actual or perceived reliability of the backup arrangement may affect the participants' response to a particular membership fee policy. The optimal membership fee depends on the reliability (risk of failure) of the pool, which depends on the number of members participating in the pool (itself a function of the membership fee). The major contribution of this paper is the presentation and solution of this complex relationship.

In particular, we shall emphasize the similarity to the case of a mutual insurer, and introduce two notions of risk of failure, namely, the objective probability of the pool's being unable to provide service (due to breakdown, or its inability to serve the simultaneous calls for service from a number of members), and the perceived probability of the pool's default from the member's point of view (see also Tapiero, Kahane and Jacque [1986]). Thus, a member's decision may be guided by both the perceived, and the actual, probability of the pool's inability to serve the member. The paper assesses the effect of these two probabilities on the optimal membership fee.

The relationship between the membership fee and the risk of failure is analyzed in the following section, in which a model is presented and the risk of failure is defined and calculated. Particularly, we analyze a backup pool with N members (each being risk averter or risk neutral, and each facing a known risk, with at most one call for backup service per member during the period).

3. THE POOL MEMBER AND THE RISK OF FAILURE

3.1 *The Model.* Consider a pool which backs up N computer centers, each with initial computing capacity W_i (this capacity, like other variables of the model, could be expressed either in terms of real capacity, or be translated into equivalent monetary values). Each member is exposed to two risks: the risk of complete or partial business interruption to its own facility, and the risk that the backup center defaults when its services are needed. Each participant has a "utility" function $u_i(\cdot)$ which describes its benefit from the available computing capacity. The utility from computing capacity is increasing, but at a declining rate $[u' = \partial u_i(Z)/\partial Z \geq 0,$ $u_i'' = \partial^2 u_i(Z)/\partial Z^2 \leq 0]$ implying an increasing absolute risk aversion, $\Pi_i = -u_i''/u_i' > 0, i = 1, 2, \ldots, N$.

Each member $i(i = 1, 2, \ldots, N)$ is exposed to the risk $(p_i, \tilde{x}_i)$, where p_i is the probability of its computer center failure ("call for service") occurring within the period (at most one call for service is allowed per contracted backup period), and $\tilde{x}_i$ is the random variable describing the magnitude of the loss of computing power with known distribution functions $F(\cdot)$. Each member pays a periodical membership fee M_i[2] and these payments are used to purchase capacity in the backup center.

In practice, firms can often sustain a certain loss of computing capacity by simply deleting jobs with lower priority. Therefore, the model allows for the purchase of a "partial" protection. It is assumed that the backup center provides coverage on a proportional basis; for example, in case of a breakdown the member is entitled to be serviced for a loss of computing power of $(1 - \theta_i)x_i$ and retains $\theta_i x_i$, where θ_i is a "loss-sharing arrangement" ("coinsurance") factor.[3]

Calls for service occurring within the period are answered on a first–come, first–served basis. The pool arrangement may, however, default when the available backup computing capacity is insufficient to cover all calls, or when a technical problem interrupts the backup center's activities. The probability of this happening (the "probability of ruin") is denoted by B.[4]

It is possible that the backup pool will be unable to serve, and yet the individual member remains unaffected (since it has submitted no call for services, or

since it received service prior to the depletion of the computer pool's capacity). The "perceived probability of ruin" measures the probability of the members being affected by the pool's inability to serve. This probability is a function of the number of calls for service, their sizes, and the order in which the calls for services have occurred.

For convenience, we summarize the model's notations in Table I.

TABLE I. Notation

i = a subscript denoting computer center (member) $(i = 1, 2, \ldots N)$
u = utility
W = Initial computing capacity
p = probability of computer center failure
x = the magnitude of capacity loss (stochastic variable)
θ = proportion of the capacity loss being uninsured
M = membership fee (= "premium") measured in terms of capacity which could have been acquired for that price
B = The probability of backup center failure due to breakdown or due to excessive demand (call for service)
A = probability that a member will be affected by the backup center inability to serve
q = a "loading factor" (pool's costs)

Let A be the (conditional) probability that a member is affected by the pool's inability to serve. If θ_i is the coverage ratio of the ith member, and $E_{\tilde{X}_i, p_i}(\cdot)$ is the expectation operator over $\tilde{X}_i$ and p_i, then its expected utility with the backup arrangement is given by:

$$Eu_i = (1 - B) \underset{\tilde{X}_i, p_i}{E} U_i(W_i - M_i - \theta_i \tilde{X}_i)$$

$$+ B \left\{ (1 - A) \underset{\tilde{X}_i, p_i}{E} U_i(W_i - M_i - \theta_i \tilde{X}_i) \right.$$

$$\left. + A \underset{\tilde{X}_i, p_i}{E} U_i(W_i - M_i - \tilde{X}_i) \right\} \quad (1)$$

$$i = 1, 2, \ldots, N$$

Since p_i is the probability of a call for service occurring, (and $1 - p_i$ the probability of no call, i.e., $X_i = 0$), equation (1) yields the simpler expected utility (with $E_{\tilde{X}_i}(\cdot)$ the expectation operator over $\tilde{X}_i$, the ith member service).

$$Eu_i = (1 - p_i)U_i(W_i - M_i)$$

$$+ p_i(1 - B) \underset{\tilde{X}_i}{E} U_i(W_i - M_i - \theta_i \tilde{X}_i)$$

$$+ p_i B \left\{ (1 - A) \underset{\tilde{X}_i}{E} U(W_i - M_i - \theta_i \tilde{X}_i) \right.$$

$$\left. + A \underset{\tilde{X}_i}{E} U_i(W_i - M_i - \tilde{X}_i) \right\} \quad (2)$$

For a member to participate in pooling it is necessary that the expected utility (2) be greater than the expected utility of a "self-backup" arrangement, or

$$Eu_i \geq p_i \underset{\tilde{X}_i}{E} U_i(W_i - X_i) + (1 - p_i)U_i(W_i) \quad (3)$$

---

[2] The membership fee, M_i, is usually a monetary payment. However, it is more useful to measure it in units of capacity (i.e. the capacity which could be purchased for such a monetary payment).

[3] In practice, most centers will be fully covered for the loss of computing capacity, thus, $\theta = 0$ in most cases. The model in this paper allows, however, for the more general case of $\theta \neq 0$. This enables handling cases where the member is protecting only a certain percentage of its capacity, knowing that in case of emergency certain low priority uses could be eliminated.

[4] In practice, in such a case all users will be requested to cut their non-critical, and low priority jobs. Therefore, assuming an inflexible case of "ruin" makes the model somewhat unrealistic. An interesting issue which is deferred to another study is appropriate pricing formula. This will enable users to more effectively compete for the backup center services by offering higher marginal payments for their more valuable applications.

From equation (2), we note that Eu_i is expressed in terms of the default probability B of the computer backup pool and by the perceived (conditional) probability of default, both a function of the membership fees M_i, $i = 1, 2, \ldots, N$ paid by members, their coverage ratio ("coinsurance rates") θ_i, as well as other parameters, such as the pool's initial capacity (W_0), the loss severity distribution, the statistical dependence among risks etc. The level of the membership fee will be determined as the result of the simultaneous decisions made by all members taking into consideration all these parameters—thus, its computation can be quite complex.

Assume that A_i is the ith member's conditional probability of being affected by the backup center's default (if it occurs). In this case, equation (3) (together with (2)) can be solved for the fee and the probability of default. Straightforward computation yields:

$$A_i B \le \frac{\begin{aligned}&(1 - p_i)[U_i(W_i - M_i) - U_i(W_i)] \\ &+ p_i[EU_i(W_i - M_i - \theta_i \tilde{X}_i) - EU_i(W_i - \tilde{X}_i)]\end{aligned}}{\{EU_i(W_i - M_i - \theta_i X_i) - EU_i(W_i - M_i - X_i)\}}$$

$$i = 1, 2, \ldots, N \quad (4)$$

which expresses the relationships between the default risk actually faced by the ith member, and the member's fee M_i and coverage ratio θ_i, $i = 1, \ldots, N$; the product "$A_i B$" is the unconditional probability of default as assessed by the ith member. This default probability is, of course, the one relevant for computing the appropriate level of backup service and the membership fee. It can also be expressed as a function of the information available to the member regarding the reliability of the mutual backup arrangements, other members' risk, the statistical dependence of these risks etc. Thus, $A_i B$ is a function which would generally be written as:

$$A_i B = g_i(M_1, \ldots, M_N, \theta_1, \cdots \theta_N; \text{other parameters}) \quad (5)$$

$$i = 1, 2, \ldots, N$$

expressing the complexity of the decisions concerning the appropriate membership fee. Simple cases can, however, be used to obtain some initial insights regarding the relationship between the probability of the pool's failure faced by the member and the membership fee. Several cases are examined below.

CASE A. *Homogeneous Risk Neutral Members*   Let all pool members be homogeneous and with linear (risk neutral) utility function $U_i(z) = z$, $\forall i \in [1, N]$. Then, equation (4) is reduced to

$$AB \le [pX(1 - \theta) - M]/[X(1 - \theta)], \quad \text{or}$$
$$0 \le M \le (1 - \theta)X(p - AB) \quad (6)$$

where $X = E(\tilde{X}_i)$, $\forall i \in [1, N]$. When the inequality sign is replaced by equality, we obtain an expression for a "fair" membership fee ("actuarially fair premium"). Since AB is necessarily a function of both N, M, θ, and the distribution of the severity of the interruption, a

fair fee M is more complex than might be expected by just looking at equation (6). It is only in the special case of a "risk free" pool ($B = 0$), that $M \le p(1 - \theta)X$, which is analogous to the well-known condition for actuarially fair insurance premiums. In the more general case, when $AB > 0$, it is evident that the membership fee is smaller than in the (hypothetical) case of a pool which is guaranteed to be risk free.

In this special case $(1 - \theta)X \, AB$ can be interpreted as the fee the member is willing to pay to be insured against the default risk.

CASE B. *Homogeneous Members with a Quadratic Utility*   When all the members are homogeneous and have a quadratic (risk averse) utility function, such that: $EU(Z) = E(Z) - \Pi \, \text{var}(Z)$, where Π is a parameter of risk aversion then:

$$M \le [X(1 - \theta) + \Pi \sigma_x^2(1 - \theta^2)](p - AB) \quad (7)$$

where (X, σ_x^2) are the mean and variance, respectively, of a call for service if it occurs.

If $AB = 0$, we again obtain a standard and well known result for a fair fee, which increases due to the member's aversion to risk and its severity variance. This fee will decrease as a function of the coverage ratio θ; however, when $AB = 0$, then $[X(1 - \theta) + \Pi \sigma_x^2(1 - \theta^2)]AB$ is again the fee the member might be willing to pay to be insured against the default risk.

CASE C. *Exponential Utility (Constant Risk Aversion)*   Now assume that the members' utility is of the constant risk aversion type (for example, exponential), with risk parameter Π. The fair fee is found by

$$e^{\Pi M} \le \frac{(1 - p) - pG(\Pi)}{(1 - p) + pG(\Pi \theta) + AB[G(\Pi) - G(\Pi \theta)]} \quad (8)$$

where $G(\cdot)$ is the moment generating function $(E \exp(\Pi \tilde{X}))$ of the loss severity distribution. The fair fee M can be computed again (with difficulty) since AB is a function of M, N and the various parameters which affect the financial wealth of the pool.

In order to characterize such a distribution we shall assume that the backup pool has an initial capacity W_0 and that it collects a total fee of NM at the beginning of the period. The fee paid by each member is determined by

$$M = (1 + q)pE(X) \quad (9)$$

where q is the charge to cover the pool's costs ("loading factor") used by the pool (Tapiero [1984], Tapiero, Zuckerman and Kahane [1983]). Further, we shall assume that all members are homogeneous and all have complete information regarding one another. These restrictive assumptions will considerably simplify the computation of the default risk below.

3.2 The Perceived Default Risk and the Probability of Ruin.   Pooling is viewed as a collective process where N members, each paying a fee M_i, and selecting a coverage rate ("coinsurance") θ_i, are mutually "insured" against any losses covered by the contract, contingent on the pool's ability to meet the calls for service. At the beginning of the period, the pool's capacity is

$$W_0 + \sum_{i=1}^{N} M_i \qquad (10)$$

where

$$M_i = (1 + q)p_i \mathrm{E}(\tilde{X}_i)[1 - \theta_i].$$

Here, $\mathrm{E}(\tilde{X}_i)$ is the ith member expected call for service, p_i is the probability of a call, θ_i is the coinsurance rate, and q is the loading factor applied uniformly to all members. For homogeneous members, $M_i = M$, $p_i = p$, $\theta_i = \theta$ and $\mathrm{E}(\tilde{X}_i) = X$, $\forall i \in [1, N]$ and the pool's initial capacity is

$$W_0 + N[(1 + q)pX(1 - \theta)].$$

Now let j, a random variable, be the number of calls for service which occur during the period, each call giving rise to a loss of $\tilde{X}_k$, $k = 1, 2, \ldots j$ with identically and independently distributed severity with density function $dF(\cdot)$. Denote by $h(j)$ the probability distribution of j, and by S_n, the probability of the backup center being down (or exhausting its capacity), after the nth call. It follows that:

$$S_1 = 1 - F_1(\delta); \qquad \delta = (W_0 + NM)/(1 - \theta)$$

After the second and the nth call we obtain, respectively:

$$S_2 = F_1(\delta)[1 - F_2(\delta)]$$

$$\vdots \qquad (11)$$

$$S_n = \prod_{k=1}^{n-1} F_k(\delta)[1 - F_n(\delta)]$$

where $F_k(\cdot)$ is the cumulative distribution of the sum of k calls, each identically and independently distributed with distribution function $F(\cdot)$. Thus, the probability of default B is simply given by:

$$B = \sum_{j=1}^{N} \sum_{n=1}^{j} h(j)S_n \qquad (12)$$

which is the expectation that j calls occur and the probability event that default occurs after the nth call, $m \le j$. The expected number of calls which are not serviced due to default, is also given by

$$\sum_{j=1}^{N} \sum_{n=1}^{j} (j - n)h(j)S_n. \qquad (13)$$

This is the expected sum of the number of calls j, less the event that default occurs at the nth call. If all members have equiprobability of a call occurring, and j calls occur (while default occurs after the nth call), then $1 - n/j$ ($j > n$) is the probability that the member will not be covered when default occurs. In other words, the unconditional default risk is

$$AB = \sum_{j=1}^{N} \sum_{n=1}^{j} (1 - n/j)h(j)S_n. \qquad (14)$$

This latter expression is an estimate of a member's perceived probability of default in this mutual backup agreement. Combining this equation with (4), (11) and an appropriate (say binomial) distribution for $h(j)$, we obtain explicitly:

$$AB = \sum_{j=1}^{N} \sum_{n=1}^{j} \left(1 - \frac{n}{j}\right)\binom{N}{p}p^j$$

$$\cdot (1 - p)^{N-j} \prod_{k=1}^{n-1} F_k(\delta)[1 - F_n(\delta)^W] \qquad (15)$$

where

$$\delta = \{W_0 + N[(1 + q)pX(1 - \theta)]\}/(1 - \theta)$$

and for a "fair" loading factor q when the utility is of the mean-variance type (equation (7) for example):

$$(1 + q) \le \left[1 + \Pi(1 + \theta)\left(\frac{\sigma_x^2}{X}\right)\right]\left[1 - \frac{AB}{p}\right] \qquad (16)$$

which is solved for q by inserting (AB) from (15) into (16) and replacing the inequality sign in (16) by an equality sign to obtain the actuarial loading factor q.

Define the implicit function

$$Q = (1 + q) - \left[1 + \Pi(1 + \theta)\left(\frac{\sigma_x^2}{X}\right)\right]\left[1 - \frac{AB}{p}\right] = 0. \qquad (17)$$

Then by implicit differentiation we can assess the sensitivity of the required fair fee with respect to each of the parameters in (17). For example, $dq/d\theta = -[\partial Q/\partial \theta]/[\partial Q/\partial q]$ and

$$\frac{dq}{d\theta} = \frac{\Pi(\sigma_x^2/X)[1 - AB/p]}{-[\partial A/\partial \theta]/p][1 + \Pi(1 + \theta)(\sigma_x^2/X)]}{1 + (\partial AB/\partial q)/p} \qquad (18)$$

If $dq/d\theta < 0$, we can infer the relative effects of q and θ on the default probability. Due to the complicated functional form of AB (equation 15) this is a difficult task which can be accomplished by numerical analysis.

For a risk neutral member, it can be shown that $q \le -(AB/p)$, or the loading factor is slightly negative, expressing a default risk which is assumed by the member when joining into this mutual arrangement. In other words, the default risk will tend to reduce the fee the member might be willing to pay to enter into this mutual pooling arrangement. This relationship will be increased further when risk aversion is taken into account, implying that $q(\Pi) < q(0)$, or the loading calculated by (17) will be bounded by $q(0) = -AB/p$. It follows that the smaller the default risk, the larger the fee each member is willing to pay.

In case of a mean variance utility function (equation 17), a simple linear relationship is obtained:

$$\frac{dq}{dAB} = -\left[1 + \Pi(1 + \theta)\left(\frac{\sigma_x^2}{X}\right)\right]\frac{1}{p} < 0$$

This simple equation provides the net effect the default risk has on the member's willingness to pay or on the loading factor. For example, if we reduce the probability of the member's perceived default by (say) 20 percent, then $\Delta AB = -(.2)$ and the incremental change in the loading factor is

$$\Delta q = .2[1 + \Pi(1 + \theta)(\sigma_x^2/X)](1/p)$$

This increment is an increasing function of σ_x^2, Π and θ, and a decreasing function of p and X, respectively.

4. CONCLUSIONS

This study was intended to add insights and enhance the understanding of some interesting tradeoffs which exist in the choice of the optimal size (number of members served) of a computer backup pool, and the appropriate membership fees (= insurance "premiums"). Our results point out explicit tradeoffs and relationships between the default risk and fees required of members of a mutual computer backup pool.

Such relationships have not been investigated previously in the computer literature. When the number of members is large, risks tend to be very large (and possibly correlated), and the default risk might become considerable.

Under such circumstances, our analysis points out formulas which can be used to compute optimal membership fees. Due to the complexity of the model, explicit relationships may be obtained under certain restrictive assumptions. More realistic cases have to be analyzed with the aid of numerical analysis.

Other properties of the analysis point out the effects of parameters which tend to justify higher membership fees (for example, the variability of a computer center suffering a loss, the members' aversion to risk, and their willingness to "self insure" parts of the risk). On the other hand, the probability of loss, and the size of such a potential loss tend to reduce the loading factor, and hence the fees.

There are several problems of interest related to this paper which were not discussed, such as: the use of pooling arrangements among the pools themselves (similar to reinsurance arrangement in commercial insurance) in reducing (or perhaps eliminating) the default risk for members, the use of different types of computers, the use of insurance, the effects of information asymmetry and members' heterogeneity on fees and default risk, and so on. These are problems which we hope to pursue in future research.

Acknowledgments. We would like to thank the editor and anonymous referees for their helpful comments and suggestions. All the usual caveats apply.

REFERENCES
1. Beard, R.E., Pentikainen, T., and Pesonen, E. *Risk Theory*, Chapman & Hall, London, 1972.
2. Borch, K. *The Mathematical Theory of Insurance*, Lexington Books, Lexington, Mass., 1974.
3. Buhlmann, H. *Mathematical Methods in Risk Theory*. Grundlehren der Mathematischen Wissenschaften in Einzeldarstell, Bard 172, 1. 1970.
4. Cramer, H. Model building with the aid of stochastic processes. *Technometrics*, 6, 133–159. 1964.
5. Datapro Research Corp. *All About Disaster Recovery* 10. 83. 1983.
6. Dentay. Developing a contingency plan. *Data Management 18*, 1 (January 1980), 10–47.
7. Kahane, Y. The theory of insurance risk premiums—A re-examination in light of recent developments in capital market theory. *ASTIN Bulletin 10*, 2 (March 1979), 223–239.
8. Krauss, L.I. EDP contingency planning—how to survive a disaster. *Management Review 69*, 6 (June 1980), 19–26.
9. McDonald, D.L. *Corporate Risk Control*, Ronald Press Co., New York, 1966.
10. Reed, S. Disaster recovery operation research. *Data Management 18*, 1 (January 1980), 9–18.
11. Sullivan. A first recovery site corporation evolves. *Data Management 18*, 1 (January 1980), 15–16.
12. Tapiero, C.S., Kahane, Y., and L. Jacque, 1986, Insurance premiums and default risk in mutual insurance. *Scandinavian Actuarial Journal* (April 1986), 82–97.
13. Tapiero, C.S., Zuckerman, D., and Kahane, Y. Optimal investment-dividend policy of an insurance firm under regulation. *Scandinavian Actuarial Journal* (January 1983), 65–78.
14. Tapiero, C.S. Mutual insurance: A diffusion stochastic control problem. *Journal of Economic Dynamics and Control 7*, (1984) 241–260.

CR Categories and Subject Descriptors: K.6.0., K.6.2., K.6.4.
Additional Key Words and Phrases: Backup, claims process, compound Poisson, computer failure, computer risk management, membership fee, pooling, portfolios, probability of ruin, utility

Received 8/86; revised 6/87; accepted 9/87

Authors' Present Addresses: Yehuda Kahane and Seev Neumann, Faculty of Management, Tel Aviv University, Ramat Aviv, Tel Aviv, Israel 69978; Charles S. Tapiero, Graduate School of Business, Hebrew University, Jerusalem, Israel.

DEADLINE PRESSURE: HOW TO COPE WITH SHORT DEADLINES, LOW BUDGETS AND INSUFFICIENT STAFFING LEVELS

Tom GILB
Independent Consultant
Iver Holtersvei 2, N-1410 Kolbotn, Norway

Reprinted with permission from *Information Processing*. Edited by H.J. Kugler, 1986, pages 293–299. Copyright ©1986 by Elsevier Science Publishers B.V. All rights reserved.

All industrial software engineering environments are usually under very tight pressure to meet calender deadlines. The pressure is so intense as to tempt software professionals to follow primitive software practices, resulting in poor product quality, and even more real delays in getting satisfactory products to the market. This paper reviews a number of realistic strategies, with reference to practical experience, in dealing with this problem. The solutions are both common sense, political and technical in nature. They involve software metrics to define the real problem, evolutionary delivery and Fagan's Inspection method to correct process failures using early feedback. Ten guiding principles summarize the paper.

1. THE PROBLEM

1.1 The problem as viewed by the project manager's manager.

The big boss wants it.
A deadline has been established.
The pressure to deliver something, on time, is on.

There may well be some clear reason for the particular date chosen. It may be specified in a contract. It may be synchronized with other product developments. But, it could just be an arbitrary guesstimate. It could have simply been a rash promise by the project manager, made to impress his boss.

It is probable that the big boss really:

- would like to get even earlier delivery - of something, - has no clear unambiguous definition of what is to be delivered, - might accept later delivery of parts of the package, - has been misunderstood, as to what and when, - hasn't told the project manager what he really wants, yet, - is in the process of deciding differently about what and when.

All of these represent potential opportunities for relief of deadline pressure.

1.2 The problem as viewed by the project manager.

The project manager is caught between the pressures from above, and the finite productive capacity below him. You might wonder how intelligent people can voluntarily accept such lack of control over both their destiny and reputation.

The project manager feels that the demands from above are unreasonable. Further, that the resources, in terms of people, talent, budget, machinery and time for getting the job done, are inadequate.

But, the project manager is there to do as well as can be expected under the circumstances. And he will try to do so with the least pain to himself.

The project manager, either through ineptitude, or experience and cunning, has made sure that the exact nature of the project deliveries are perfectly unclear. This has the effect of allowing him to deliver something, really anything that is ready by the "deadline", and claim on-time delivery. Who can prove otherwise?

1.3 The problem as viewed by the project professional.

The people working for the project manager - the ones that have to do the real work - are perfectly prepared to let their boss worry about deadlines, as long as they can do whatever they most enjoy doing, the way they enjoy doing it. They realize that the project manager doesn't dare fire them or take similar drastic action (like training them) because that would destroy the project schedule.

Of course, as individuals each one of them would very much like to make a brilliant recognized contribution to the project. The problem is they are not sure what the project is all about, and they are pretty sure that somebody else will snatch the glory from them anyway. Better to save those brilliant efforts for when one starts ones own company.

If the project fails, they might get promoted to project manager. But the important thing is to not be <u>seen</u> to threaten the project.

1.4 The problem as viewed by the customer/user.

The recipient of the project output probably needs the results "yesterday". Your deadline, as project manager, is probably viewed as the longest acceptable wait time until the product is ready.

The "customer" might very well be willing to wait longer for 90% of the project results, if only 10% were delivered on time. They might even be willing to let some of that 10% be delivered later if 1% were delivered <u>much</u> earlier. It is perfectly possible that <u>they</u> really don't need 99% of what has been asked for. There are a lot of people out there who have a vested interest in building new systems, rather than improving old ones.

2. THE SOLUTIONS

2.1 Redefine the problem.

I have never yet walked into a project of any kind, anywhere in the world where I felt that the project deliveries were fully and completely defined.

I'm not saying that all projects should be <u>perfectly</u> defined in advance. There are both good and bad reasons for incomplete requirements specification. However, this lack-of-specification situation gives us a powerful tool for relieving deadline pressure, because it can put us in a position to "clarify" or "detail" the specifications in such a way as to make the delivery task easier.

Gerald M. Weinberg, in our book "Humanized Input"[1] made use of this principle when he formulated his "Zeroth Law of Unreliability"

" If a system doesn't have to be reliable, it can meet any other objective"

If a quality, like reliability, is not clearly specified - you can deliver the project earlier - if you "interpret" the quality requirement as "whatever it happens to be when the deadline arrives". This, coupled with an innocent "Ohhh ! You wanted <u>more</u> than two minutes between failures!", after the first complaints arrive, will solve the deadline problem initially. You are of course prepared to discuss a new schedule and project for enhancing

quality to the required levels - now clarified for the first time.

Whether or not "reliability" is defined is irrelevant. There are a large number of quality attributes [2]which probably have a dramatic influence on cost and schedule. You only need <u>one</u> of them to be unclearly specified to give you the opening you need.

The more quality requirement specifications that are added, the more uncertainty is introduced into the schedule estimation problem. In fact with ten or more demanding state-of-the-art quality requirements - you can be certain that the project can <u>never</u> be delivered.

The trick is to get the client to specify what they "dream of", rather than what they will want to pay for or wait for. They will always be tempted into this trap, and you will always have an excuse for non-delivery.

2.2 Don't work harder, work smarter.

It is natural, when faced with deadline pressure, to consider various ways of working harder. More overtime, reducing employee vacations, working weekends. Such a response designed to give the

impression of trying to meet the deadlines. But, lets face it, working harder defeats the <u>real</u> purpose of life, whatever it is.

There is no certainty that hard work will help the deadline at all. The real <u>problem</u> is the individual who made a promise for a deadline, without considering whether it was realistic at all. Unfortunately, this person is often the Chief Executive of the company.

So, you have to work smarter. This involves doing things mentioned elsewhere in this paper, such as,
  - redesigning for evolutionary delivery,
  - using Inspection of requirements and high-level design to find problems while they are small ones,
  - formally identifying the real goals, measurably,
  - sub-contracting the work to someone else.

2.3 Refuse! Make Counter-threats

Have you ever considered refusing to accept the deadline which someone is trying to impose upon you ? You can do so under the guise of loyalty to your boss. But do it in writing. An oral refusal can too easily be misunderstood or misused. Here is an example of a diplomatic formulation:

" I must unfortunately decline, at the present moment, to accept full responsibility for meeting the suggested deadline. I sincerely believe that this would result in you (your boss!) getting blamed for non-delivery at a later date. The project is as yet not clearly defined (it never is) and it is by no means clear that we have the resources (you never will) to complete it on the suggested schedule to the quality expected by the customer. We must not be caught making promises we cannot keep, no matter how great the pressure. What we will promise is to do the very best we can to deliver as early as possible, with the resources we have or are later granted."

If this diplomatic attempt to avoid responsibility doesn't work. Don't worry. The project is sure to be late, or some kind of a disaster. You can then prove that you were wise enough to disclaim responsibility in advance. If, by some miracle everything succeeds, you can safely assume that your disclaimer will be forgotten in the euphoria of success. And if it is remembered, you can safely say that it was luck or that certain factors became clearer after it was written.

2.4 If necessary, use the Counter-Threat.

A diplomatic disclaimer might not be enough to fool your boss. The "counter-threat" ploy may be necessary. The objective is to scare people into not imposing a really serious deadline. It might be along the following lines. (do not copy this text exactly each time - someone might get suspicious).

"I cannot but note the deadline that you have felt it necessary to impose. We will naturally do our very best to meet it. However, in your own interest please note the following problems which may occur as a result.

1. There is very little real chance of meeting this deadline. Can we afford the damage to our reputation?

2. If we do try to deliver something by this date it will most certainly have a quality level below what people will expect. Can we afford this damage to our reputation?

3. The attempt to meet an impossible deadline, upon which we have not been consulted or agreed to, will result in severe stress to our staff. We risk that our best people (who do all the real work) leaving us in frustration.

We do of course want to co-operate in any way we can to make a realistic plan, and to help estimate realistic resources for doing a job which will not threaten our standing as responsible professionals in the eyes of customers or the public."

2.5 Redefine the Solution.

If these tactics fail, don't despair! There are many avenues of rescue open to you. One is to redefine the solution so that it is easier to achieve than the one you were landed with.

This can be a dangerous path because solutions are often "Holy Cows" for somebody. However - just as often - the solutions are accidental and nobody really cares about the detailed solution type - as long as they achieve their real objectives. Somebody (you of course,) has to take the initiative to change the solution so that the deadline can be met.

The steps are as follows:

1. Trap your boss or customer into declaring that the proposed deadline is extremely critical (if it is not, your problem dissolves anyway).

2. Entice them into agreeing that the results of the project are more critical than the means by which it is accomplished. Few managers will admit to anything else. Establish in formal measurable terms the results to be accomplished (savings of time and money, improved service or sales etc.).

3. Show them that the presently suggested solution does not guarantee the achievement of these results. (No solution is ever guaranteed anyway).

4. Then, find an alternative solution which at least looks far more safe in terms of getting the results. For example such a solution is likely to be based on existing and known products or technologies, modified for your purposes. Possibly you can get some outside instance to guarantee the deadline for the modifications - in which case the monkey is off your back.

Naturally, you offer to manage the new effort. This gets you a reputation for sheer heroism in the face of impossible odds. When its all over, you can take the credit for the successful solution.

2.6 Define the solution yourself

Of course "redefining" the solution might seem a bit too much for the cases where no clear

428

solution has yet been defined. In this case you should make use of such an opportunity to get control over the solution definition before others do. They might suggest something which cannot be achieved within the deadline.

There is one cardinal rule when defining solutions. Make sure you have a clear idea of the objectives which top management has. This is likely to be different from what you boss told you the goals were.

Next, you want to do what engineers call "design to cost". This simply means that you must find a solution architecture which ensures that you deliver the results as expected. It is vital that you are prepared to go outside your normal specialty discipline to achieve this.

For example you may be a software engineer. The requirement may be for "zero defects" software. You may not feel capable of producing that within the deadline. So, you must be prepared to swallow your pride - but deliver a solution.

You must for example find a ready-made solution with "zero defect" (or near to it, because perfection is mighty hard to find in practice). Or, you need to find some reputable sub-supplier who will guarantee the result on time.

They will not of course be able to do it - but you can blame them afterwards. Your job amounts to writing a clear specification of what they will be attempting to deliver by the deadline. You should get them to guarantee this in a contract, or at least a letter or in writing.

You might feel more like a legal person than a technical person at this point, but remember - legal people cannot write technical specifications - and they don't care about your deadline pressure.

2.7 Get somebody else to do it.

There is an important strategy of making sure it is someone else who is under the deadline pressure. Remember, management doesn't really care who does things, as long as they get done. If you can, make a strong case for letting somebody else do the job - then pressure is off your back.

It is important that you consider taking main contractor responsibility. That is, you find, then you control, the sub-contractor. This gives you something to do and to look busy with - but of course the sub-contractor does all the real work. You just sit there with a whip.

3. THE TECHNOLOGIES OF THE SOLUTIONS

3.1 Evolutionary Delivery

The most powerful practical technique I have experienced for getting control over deadline pressure is evolutionary delivery[3]. The evolutionary delivery method is based on the simple observation that not everything is needed all at one initial delivery or deadline.

An example: The New Taxation System.

In one concrete case, a national taxation on-line system - we had a deadline six months hence. The initial project plan was to use a staff of one hundred technical people (programmers) for probably (nobody knew) three years to complete delivery of a totally new design. I worked out an alternative design based on making use of all the old data and programs, with a few politically interesting frills thrown in.
This idea alone, guarantees you will meet any deadline - but it is not nearly as much fun for the technologists who want to play with new toys. In this case there were ninety-eight programmers who wanted to learn a totally new programming language.
I made sure that I kept my eye on the essential deadline idea - that the Finance Minister was to see the new system in action personally in exactly six months. The new system was the old system, on a new computer mainly. Secondarily a "while-you-wait" access to their base of taxation data was desired. We provided a way using a copy of their current data. The Finance Minister had to wait one full second to get the data, using binary search on disks, with my modified solution, as opposed to 1/10th of a second with the previously committed 300 work-year solution.

They argued for a full three months about whether my simplistic solution could possibly work in such a large and complex environment. Then, using a handful of people they actually delivered successfully in three months.

3.2 USING FAGAN'S INSPECTION METHOD

"A stitch in time saves nine" says the old folk wisdom. Many of the problems in meeting deadlines for large projects are caused by the tail end backlash. This is the penalty you pay for poor quality control in the early stages of design and planning. The small details that were overlooked come back to haunt you - as you desperately try to fix the problems that pop up when you try to meet required quality levels or performance levels for delivery.

Conventional quality control [4] methods insist that "inspection" of product and process quality is a vital pre-requisite for being able to maintain the required cost and quality attributes of almost any development. Around 1972 Michael E. Fagan, of IBM in Kingston New York, began to transfer these methods to quality control of IBM software products. Nobody had tried to do this until then. In fact it was his training as a quality control hardware engineer which gave him the basic idea of applying "inspection" to software. It was an uphill battle at IBM, but very successful [5]. Although the method is widely recognized internationally, it will still take many more years before it is widely used.

The aspect of Inspection which is interesting in connection with deadline pressure is that it seems to have these repeatable general characteristics:

1. Delivery of major software projects is achieved in about 15% to 35% [6] less calender time than otherwise. This saving can also be translated into cost or work-power savings if desired[7].

2. The quality (in terms of defects removed) is measurably improved (by as much as one or two orders of magnitude) while this saving is made.

3. Improvements are cumulative, for several years. This is due to a process of management analysis of the time and defect statistics generated by inspection - combined with management taking change action to improve productivity [8].

Why does inspection save time and cost ?

It would be too much to explain all the details of inspection here. But, the basic reason why inspection saves resources is simple.

1. It can be used at early stages of design and planning - before conventional product testing can be used. Sixty percent of software bugs exist already at this stage, according to a TRW Study [9]. It identifies and cleans up defects which would cause much larger later repair costs. IBM data indicates as much as eighty-two times[10] more to correct software errors found late at the customer site, as opposed to early at design stages, if they were not found until much later.

2. The statistical data collected during the inspection process is carefully analyzed. This is much like Financial Directors analyze accounting data to get insights into a companies operational weaknesses. It is then used to suggest, and confirm the results of, major changes to the entire development or production process.

If the changes are implemented early enough in a project, they can impact the deadline of that project. If the changes are implemented late, or even after the project is completed - they can at least improve your ability to perform better on the following projects.[11].

3.3 Attribute Specification

Another technology for getting some control over deadlines and other resource constraints is, as indicated above, setting formal objectives for quality and resources in a formal measurable way.

The major reason why this impacts resources is that at the high levels of qualities desired by any user, even small improvements in a quality level, can cost disproportional resources.

So for example it took Bell Labs several years to move the best levels of availability they could report [12] from 99.9% to 99.98% for computerized telephone switching systems. The difference "0.08%" does not seem like a significant number in considering a project deadline. Both the above measures of system availability are "extremely high state of the art levels" if described in mere words. But that"little difference" cost Bell Labs (or AT&T) about eight years of research and development.

It is obviously vital for management to know exactly what levels their projects are aiming for in relation to the state of the art limits. If they don't have full control over those factors, then they do not have control over meeting deadlines.

Here are some principles of attribute specification:

1. All critical attributes of quality and resources should be established as measurable and testable requirements.
2. Any single critical attribute which management fails to control, is likely to be the Achilles Heel of the project - threatening cost and time resources.
3. All attributes should be specified at at least two parameters. The worst acceptable case for any system delivery - and the "planned level" - the one you hope to get to together with the others.

4. It is also quite useful to document, for all critical attributes, the "present system levels" and the known engineering limits or "state of the art limits". It is particularly these which give management a warning of unreasonable planned levels - and thus of impending schedule or cost problems.

5. Even with a first attempt at specification, be prepared to iterate towards a balanced specification of all the demands throughout the design and development process.

AN EXAMPLE OF ACTUAL APPLICATION OF THE PRINCIPLES OF THIS PAPER ON A LARGE PROJECT

One large (multi-thousand work-years, years of effort, $100 million dollars cost) software project in Europe asked me what they could do to avoid overrunning their deadline, a year from then, by more than two years.

Part of my advice was to break the project down, even at this late stage, into evolutionary deliveries. In this case the software critical to the initial and high-volume products to go before the very low volume product software which had been coupled to the same deadline.

Another part of my advice was to use Fagan's Inspection method on their work.

A third component of my advice was to define the worst case quality levels and performance levels more precisely. They had to differentiate between those software components which needed high quality levels, and those that were not as critical. Most of the volume of the software was not as critical as the central "real-time" components - and they had failed to make that distinction in their planning! They were quite simply committed to far too high a quality level, too early, for too much of their project product.

THE RESULTS

After eleven months, in November 1985, one month before the "impossible deadline", this group reported to me that their first useful delivery had been operating for two continuous weeks without any problems. There were certainly many reasons for this , not all of which I have depth knowledge. But evolutionary extraction was certainly a key element.

4.0 SUMMARY

Let me sum up what I have tried to say, as guiding principles of resisting deadline pressure.

1. The Deadline Mirage.
Rethink the deadline given to you - it may not be real.

2. The Solution Mirage.
Rethink the solution handed to you - it may be in the way of on-time delivery.

3. The Other Viewpoint.
Rethink the problem from other peoples point of view -it will help you simplify your problem and convince them to agree with you.

4. The Expert Trap.
Don't trust the experts blindly - they will cheerfully lead you to disaster.
Be sceptical and insist on proof and guarantees.

5. The All-at-once Trap.
Remember, nobody needs all of what they asked for by the deadline - they would simply like you to provide the miracle if possible.

6. The Real-Needs Principle.
Don't damage your credibility by bowing to pressure to make impossible promises. Increase your credibility by fighting for solutions which solve the real needs of your bosses and clients.

7. The Ends Dictate The Means.
If the deadline is critical and seems impossible otherwise - don't be afraid to change the solution.

8. The Principle of Conservation of Energy.
If deadlines are critical, make maximum use of existing systems and "known technology" - avoid research-into-unknowns during your project.

9. The Evolutionary Delivery Principle.
Any large project can be broken down into a series of earlier and smaller deliverables - don't give up - even if you have to change the technical solution to make it happen.
Keep your eye on results - not technologies.

10. The "don't blame me" Principle.
If you succeed using these principles, take the credit - give your boss and these ideas some credit in a footnote. If you fail - you obviously didn't apply these principles correctly (don't mention my name, mention your boss's, if you must blame somebody. Management is always at fault.)

REFERENCES

[1] T. Gilb & G. M. Weinberg, Humanized Input: Techniques for Reliable Keyed Input, QED Information Sciences, Inc., 170 Linden St., Wellesley Mass USA 02181. ISBN 0-89435-073-0, 1984

[2] Gilb, T., Principles Of Software Engineering Management, Addison-Wesley, ca. 1987. This contains chapters on quantitative definitions of software qualities, as well as chapters on Inspection and Evolutionary Delivery discussed in this paper.

[3] Tom Gilb, Evolutionary Delivery versus the Waterfall Model, ACM Software Engineering Notes, July 1985, p. 49-61

[4] See for example J M Juran (Editor), Quality Control Handbook, Third Edition, McGraw Hill, ISBN 0-07-033175-8, 1974.

[5] In 1979 Fagan was awarded a $50 thousand personal "Outstanding Contribution Award" by IBM in recognition of the success of his variant of the method in improving IBM software quality and cost.

[6] See for example the 35% difference measured on about 30 of 60 projects at IBM Federal Systems Division, as reported in IBM Systems Journal Number One 1977 (Felix and Walston article).

[7] Other examples of savings are reported in M E Fagan, "Design and code inspections to reduce errors in program development", IBM Systems Journal Number Three 1976, page 182-211.

[8] These points are supported by various IBM Technical publications authored by Horst Remus of IBM San Jose from 1978 to 1983.

[9] T. A. Thayer et al, Software Reliability, North-Holland, TRWSeries 2. 1978, ISBN 0-444-85217-4. Page 80.

[10] According to data collected by the author at IBM Santa Teresa Labs from Ken Christiansen in 1979. Another factor observed by IBM earlier was 62 x. Same principle as "An ounce of prevention is worth a pound of cure".

[11] R. A. Radice et al, A Programming Process Architecture, IBM SJ Vol. 24, No. 2, p.79-90. also, C. L. Jones, A process-integrated approach to defect prevention, p.151-167.

[12] Communications of ACM about mid 1984, as I recall.

Section 4: Implementing Risk Management

4.1: Risk Management in the Software Life Cycle

4.1.1: Life-Cycle Roles of the Customer and the Developer

The primary responsibility for software-risk management is shared by the customer for a software product and by the developer or contractor. Figure 4.1 shows the primary–risk-management functions each participant performs throughout the software life cycle, by using the competitive-contract mode of software acquisition (internal software developments follow the same basic principles, but differ in implementation detail).

The most important initial risk-management product is the life-cycle risk-management plan. It is primarily the responsibility of the customer, but it is very useful to involve the developer community in its preparation as well.

It addresses not only the development risks that have been the primary topic of this tutorial, but also operations and maintenance risks. These include such items as staffing and training of maintenance personnel; discontinuities in the cutover from the old to the new system; undefined responsibilities for operations and maintenance facilities and functions; and insufficient budget for planned life-cycle improvements or for corrective, adaptive, and perfective software maintenance. The magnitude and distribution of these costs are covered in Chapter 30 of [Boehm, 1987].

The other highlight in Figure 4.1 is the importance of proposed developer risk-management plans in competitive source evaluation and selection. Emphasizing the realism and effectiveness of a bidder's risk management plan increases the probability that the customer will select a bidder who clearly understands the project's critical success fac-

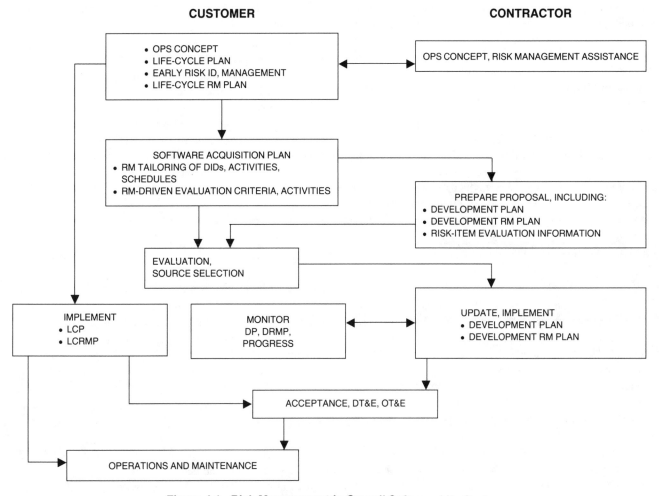

Figure 4.1: Risk Management in Overall Software Life Cycle

tors, and who has established a development approach that satisfactorily addresses them. (If the developer is a noncompetitive internal organization, it is equally important for the customer to require and review a developer risk-management plan.)

Two of the three articles in this section of the tutorial provide examples of this customer-developer approach to software-risk management. The FAA example [Basili et al., 1987] primarily addresses the establishment of the life-cycle risk-management plan and the risk-management aspects of source selection procedures. The small ICBM example [Peschel, 1987] also addresses some of the resulting risk assessments jointly addressed by the customer and the contractors. The third article [Wolff, 1989] describes the application of a risk management approach to an internal non-contract software development.

4.1.2: Risk-Oriented Software–Process Models

The main function of a software process model is to establish the order in which a project performs its major tasks (prototypes, specifications, increments, reviews, etc.), and to establish the transition criteria for proceeding from one task to the next.

A software project that uses a process model that operates independently of risk considerations will run into serious difficulties when it encounters high-risk elements. The most frequent recent example has been the attempt to use a pure document-driven "waterfall" model on user-intensive systems. The waterfall model relies on a series of written specifications as the transition criteria between phases to define the requirements and design of the product to be developed.

For user-intensive systems, however, there are major risks that users will not understand the implications of the written specifications, or that they will use the specifications to insert a lot of unnecessary gold-plate into the system's requirements. Thus, a process model that uses risk considerations to determine the ordering of project tasks can incorporate such tasks as rapid prototyping, in order to resolve user-interface risks before they become embedded in system and contract specifications.

4.1.2.1: The Spiral Model

The initial definition of a risk-driven software process model has been the spiral model presented in the [Boehm, 1988] and [Boehm-Belz, 1988] articles in Section 1 of this tutorial. Figure 4.2 shows the version of the spiral model discussed in the latter article. A project that uses the spiral model will elaborate its definition of both the software product and the software process in a series of cycles.

Each cycle of the spiral elaborates the product and process objectives and constraints; elaborates the alternative product and process solutions; evaluates and prioritizes the alternatives with respect to the objectives and constraints; and identifies and resolves the major risks that a potentially attractive alternative solution will satisfy the product and process objectives and constraints. Based on the risk-resolution results, the project can then eliminate unpromising product and process alternatives, and can refine the most attractive one(s). The process refinement constitutes a set of plans for future cycles. These are then reviewed and, given a commitment to proceed, further elaborated in the next cycle.

More detailed descriptions of the spiral model cycles and steps are given in the articles in Section 1, along with a summary of the most extensive experiences in using the model.

4.1.2.2: Experience with the Spiral Model

An overall summary of the experience with the spiral model is that it has been excellent for complex, dynamic internal projects requiring a good deal of flexibility, but that it provides more flexibility than is convenient for many situations.

Thus, for example, in the straightforward contract procurement of a low-risk inventory-control system, the spiral model provides more degrees of freedom than most managers wish to deal with. In such cases, either a straightforward waterfall model for a unique custom product, or a straightforward evolutionary-development model for a system that can be based on a commercial-inventory-control software product, are easier for people to understand and work with.

In either case, the simpler process model can establish more specific up-front definitions than the spiral model uses for such items as contract provisions, product acceptance criteria, internal milestones, and cost-schedule control limits. The spiral model approach keeps these options open for as long as possible. By analogy to software compilation and execution models, the spiral model is gaining the sort of flexibility one typically obtains from late-binding strategies, at the corresponding cost in simplicity and efficiency achievable via more early-binding approaches.

4.1.2.3: Using the Spiral Model as a Process Model Generator

In the previously described inventory-control example, however, something like the spiral model is needed to achieve the right early finding: i.e., to analyze the process objectives, constraints, and alternatives to determine whether to use a waterfall or an evolutionary-development-process model for the project. This consideration leads to the conclusion that the spiral model can be used as a *process model generator* for simpler and more efficient specialized process models.

By applying the spiral model process-determination steps to various combinations of key project characteristics, or *critical process drivers*, one can use the spiral model to derive a process-model decision table, as shown in Figure 4.3. This decision table determines the best process model to use on a project as a function of the project's critical process drivers. It thus allows risk considerations to deter-

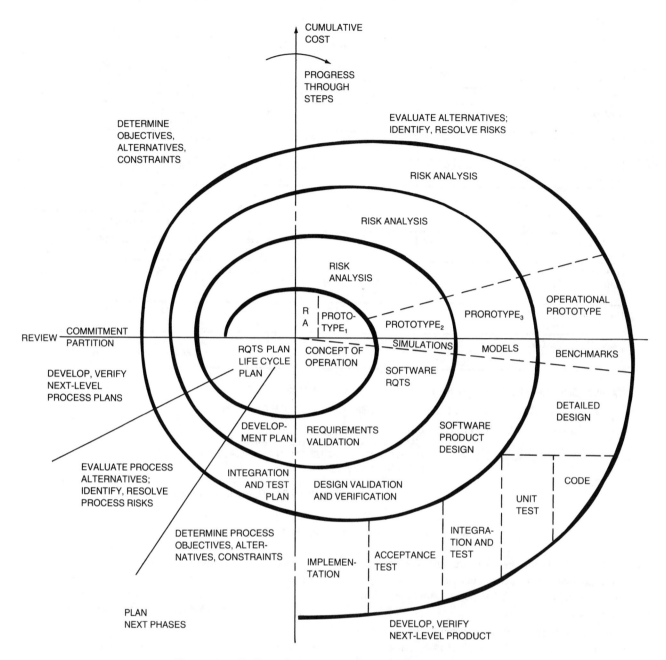

Figure 4.2: Refined Spiral Model of the Software Process

mine the most appropriate process model for a project, but it does this determination in advance, thus also securing the efficiency and simplicity advantages of early process-model binding to the project.

The following steps show how the spiral model process-determination steps in the lower left part of Figure 4.2 are applied to determine the most appropriate process model for each combination of project critical process drivers:

- *Determine process objectives and constraints:* These constitute the project's process drivers. Some examples are to develop a product-engineered version of the software in 18 months; ensure that the product will satisfy a given class of users; and use commercial off-the-shelf (COTS) software wherever possible

- *Identify process model alternatives:* These would include the currently familiar process models such as the waterfall model, incremental development, and proto-typing/evolutionary development; plus mixes of process models that might better fit COTS-dominated software systems

- *Evaluate process model alternatives with respect to objectives and constraints; identify risks:* In many cases, this evaluation will produce a clear, low-risk choice of a particular process model that fits the process drivers. In other cases, potentially attractive alternatives may have risks of a mismatch to the process drivers: e.g., an attractive COTS-oriented solution may have major uncertainities about the COTS product's maturity, performance, or scalability to large systems

OBJECTIVES, CONSTRAINTS			ALTERNATIVES		MODEL	EXAMPLE
GROWTH ENVELOPE	UNDERSTANDING OF RQTS.	ROBUSTNESS	AVALAIBLE TECHNOLOGY	ARCHITECTURE UNDERSTANDING		
LIMITED			COTS		BUY COTS	SIMPLE INVENTORY CONTROL
LIMITED			YGL, TRANSFORM		TRANSFORM OR EVOL. DEVEL.	SMALL BUSINESS — DP APPLICATION
LIMITED	LOW	LOW		LOW	EVOL. PROTOTYPE	ADVANCED PATTERN RECOGNITION
LIMITED TO LARGE	HIGH	HIGH		HIGH	WATERFALL	REBUILD OF OLD SYSTEM
	LOW	HIGH			RISK REDUCTION FOLLOWED BY	COMPLEX SITUATION ASSESSMENT
		HIGH		LOW	WATERFALL	HIGH-PERFORMANCE AVIONICS
LIMITED TO MEDIUM	LOW	LOW- MEDIUM		HIGH	EVOLUTIONARY DEVELOPMENT	NEW DECISION SUPPORT SYSTEM
LIMITED TO LARGE			LARGE REUSABLE COMPONENTS	MEDIUM TO HIGH	CAPABILITIES-TO-REQUIREMENTS	ELECTRONIC PUBLISHING
VERY LARGE					RISK REDUCTION & WATERFALL	AIR TRAFFIC CONTROL
MEDIUM TO LARGE	LOW	MEDIUM	PARTIAL COTS	LOW TO MEDIUM	SPIRAL	SOFTWARE SUPPORT ENVIRONMENT

CONDITIONS FOR ADDITIONAL COMPLEMENTARY PROCESS MODEL OPTIONS

— *DESIGN-TO-COST OR SCHEDULE:* FIXED BUDGET OR SCHEDULE AVAILABLE

— *INCREMENTAL DEVELOPMENT:* EARLY CAPABILITY NEEDED

(ONLY ONE CONDITION IS SUFFICIENT)

LIMITED STAFF OR BUDGET AVAILABLE
DOWNSTREAM REQUIREMENTS POORLY UNDERSTOOD
HIGH-RISK SYSTEM NUCLEUS
LARGE TO VERY LARGE APPLICATION
REQUIRED PHASING WITH SYSTEM INCREMENTS

Figure 4.3: A Software Process Model Decision Table

- *Analyze risks:* In the previous example, the risk analysis could involve reference-checking the COTS product, or benchmarking it for performance, scalability, and/or ease of adaptation

- *Use risk analysis results to determine the project-tailored process model:* This involves integrating the best mix of process model alternatives to satisfy the project's process drivers. This step may produce a process model for the entire life cycle, or it may produce a process plan for the next phase, deferring portions of subsequent process decisions until the next round of the spiral

A process model decision table; critical process drivers: Figure 4.3, a process model decision table, is a summary of experiences to date in using the spiral model as a process model generator. It shows how certain key characteristics of the system's objectives, constraints, and alternatives determined during the early spiral model cycles can be used to establish the most effective process model for the project. These key characteristics, or critical process drivers, are:

- *Growth envelope:* This refers to the likely limits of a system's size and diversity over the course of its life cycle. A limited growth envelope implies a low risk of using limited-domain solution approaches such as COTS products, transform capabilities or fourth-generation languages (4GL's). A large growth envelope makes these limited-domain solution approaches very risky

- *Understanding of requirements:* The lower (weaker) the level of system requirements understanding, the more essential are process models emphasizing prototyping and evolutionary development, as opposed to a requirements specification-driven process model such as the waterfall, which has a high risk of developing correct software to the wrong requirements

- *Robustness:* Systems that need to be highly robust and error-free encounter high risks from informal process models such as evolutionary prototyping. More rigorous process models such as the waterfall reduce these risks, although they may need to be preceded by less formal phases addressing requirements-understanding or architecture-understanding risks

- *Available technology:* If technology such as COTS, transform, or 4GL capabilities cover a system's growth envelope, it determines the most attractive process model for a system. A related process model is the "capabilities-to-requirements" model, in which the availability of powerful, easy-to-adapt capabilities strongly influences the system requirements

- *Architecture understanding:* The lower the level of system architecture understanding, the higher the risk of a pure top-down waterfall approach. On the other hand, a high level of architecture understanding lowers a risk of evolutionary development: That the system evolves in directions that the architecture cannot support

There are additional critical process drivers such as budget and schedule limitations and the existence of a high-risk system nucleus, which lead to other process model alternatives such as incremental development and design-to-cost. These critical process drivers and process model alternatives are treated differently than the others in Figure 4.3, since incremental development and design-to-cost can be used in concert with, rather than in place of, any of the other process model alternatives.

Process model decision table contents: The process model decision table shown as Table 4.3 shows the results of applying the spiral model paradigm to the critical-process drivers to determine the most appropriate process model for various combinations of critical-process drivers. The process models generated in Figure 4.3 are:

- *Buy COTS:* This is a simple process model often overlooked in the enthusiasm to design and build something new, or because of the inertia involved in applying administrative procedures designed for custom-developed software

- *Transform:* This model uses the specification rather than the design or code as the basis for evolution, and relies on the availability of a capability to automatically transform the specifications into design and code [Balzer-Cheatham-Green, 1983]. If such a capability spans the system's growth envelope, the transform model is most appropriate

- *Evolutionary development:* This involves developing an initial approximation to a desired software product, and evolving it into the desired product based on usage feedback [McCracken-Jackson, 1982]. This is a highly effective, low-risk approach if the system's growth envelope is covered by a 4GL, or if the system requirements are poorly understood in a situation where the architecture is well-understood (a low risk that the system will evolve into a configuration poorly supported by the architecture)

- *Evolutionary prototyping:* This model is similar to evolutionary development, except that a prototype-quality system (low robustness) is acceptable, and the system architecture is generally poorly understood

- *Waterfall:* The sequential requirements-design-code-test-maintain model [Royce, 1970]

- *Risk reduction/waterfall:* The waterfall model, preceded by one or more phases or spiral model cycles focused on reducing the risks of poorly understood requirements or architecture, technology uncertainties, potential performance or robustness shortfalls, etc.

- *Capabilities-to-requirements:* This model reverses the usual requirements-to-capabilities sequence inherent in the waterfall and related models. It begins with an assessment of the envelope of capabilities available from COTS or other reusable components, and then involves adjusting the requirements wherever possible to capitalize on the existing capabilities

- *Spiral:* This involves continuing to use the spiral model through the entire development cycle

- *Incremental development:* This involves organizing the development into a series of increments of functional capability rather than a single-shot development. This is the preferred approach under various conditions shown in Figure 4.3, such as the existence of a high-risk system nucleus, which should be developed and proven in an initial increment before investing in applications software dependent on the nucleus

- *Design to cost or design to schedule:* This approach involves prioritizing the desired system capabilities and organizing the architecture to facilitate dropping lower-priority capabilities as one finds that their development does not fit within one's available budget or schedule. As mentioned earlier, this approach and incremental development can be used in concert with the other process models in Figure 4.3

As an example of the use of Figure 4.3, consider a typical high-performance avionics system, in which the performance objectives are well-understood but sufficiently ambitious that there is only a low level of understanding with respect to the best architectural alternative for achieving the objectives. This means that there is a high risk of proceeding with a waterfall-type model without some previous risk-reduction activities to ensure an appropriate architecture and an achievable level of performance. However, the high robustness objective means that there is a high risk of applying a less rigorous approach such as evolutionary prototyping or evolutionary development. Also, there are currently no available COTS products, transform capabilities, or 4GL's which cover the application.

Given these risk patterns in the system objectives and alternatives (row 6 in Figure 4.3), the best process model involves a two-phase approach: a risk reduction phase to analyze, simulate, and/or prototype alternative architectures, followed by a rigorous waterfall-model phase once the preferred architecture is determined. Further, if there were additional process drivers such as a limited budget or a series of pre-planned product improvements, an incremental development and/or a design-to-cost approach would also be appropriate.

4.1.2.4: Mapping Early Risk Resolution Steps to Contract Milestones

The second phase of the two-phase approach for complex systems such as advanced avionics software is a straightfor-

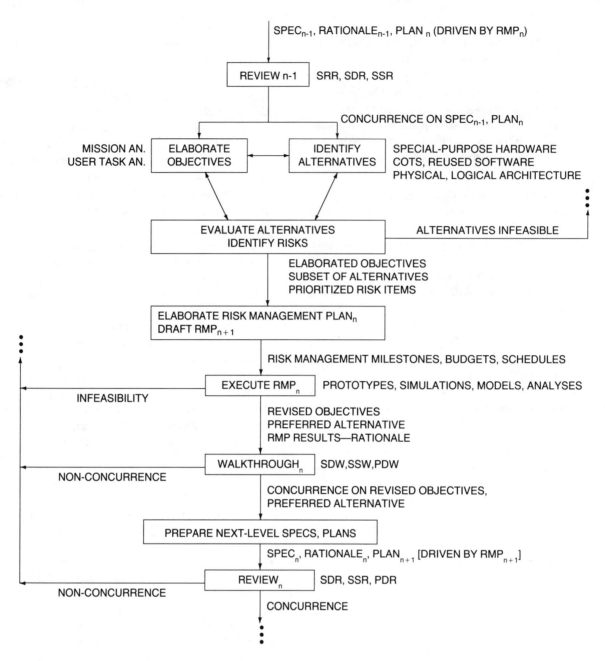

SPEC$_{n-1}$, RATIONALE$_{n-1}$, PLAN$_n$ (DRIVEN BY RMP$_n$)

| REVIEW n-1 | SRR, SDR, SSR |

CONCURRENCE ON SPEC$_{n-1}$, PLAN$_n$

MISSION AN. | ELABORATE | IDENTIFY | SPECIAL-PURPOSE HARDWARE
USER TASK AN. | OBJECTIVES | ALTERNATIVES | COTS, REUSED SOFTWARE
PHYSICAL, LOGICAL ARCHITECTURE

EVALUATE ALTERNATIVES
IDENTIFY RISKS   ALTERNATIVES INFEASIBLE

ELABORATED OBJECTIVES
SUBSET OF ALTERNATIVES
PRIORITIZED RISK ITEMS

ELABORATE RISK MANAGEMENT PLAN$_n$
DRAFT RMP$_{n+1}$

RISK MANAGEMENT MILESTONES, BUDGETS, SCHEDULES

INFEASIBILITY   EXECUTE RMP$_n$ PROTOTYPES, SIMULATIONS, MODELS, ANALYSES

REVISED OBJECTIVES
PREFERRED ALTERNATIVE
RMP RESULTS—RATIONALE

WALKTHROUGH$_n$ | SDW,SSW,PDW

NON-CONCURRENCE

CONCURRENCE ON REVISED OBJECTIVES,
PREFERRED ALTERNATIVE

PREPARE NEXT-LEVEL SPECS, PLANS

SPEC$_n$, RATIONALE$_n$, PLAN$_{n+1}$ [DRIVEN BY RMP$_{n+1}$]

REVIEW$_n$ | SDR, SSR, PDR

NON-CONCURRENCE

CONCURRENCE

Figure 4.4: Mapping of Risk Management Steps to Contact Milestones

ward waterfall approach. The first phase will most often consist of several spiral-type cycles of early product definition.

A more specific elaboration of the steps in these early phases is provided in Figure 4.4, which translates the more flexible spiral model steps into milestones compatible with such standard acquisition milestones as the system requirements review (SRR), system design review (SDR), software specification review (SSR), and software preliminary design review (PDR).

Figure 4.4 shows the process of going from the review of one level of definition of a software product (either a specification, an executing portion of the product, or a mix of both) to the review of the next level of definition of the product. The review covers the current definition of the product and the plan for the next phase or cycle, which is strongly driven by the risk-management plan for the phase (to begin the process, an initial version of these is generated). If the successive products are primarily system and software requirements and design specifications, then the reviews will follow the SSR-SDR-SRR-PDR sequence identified in Figure 4.4.

If the review process produces a concurrence on and a commitment to the plan for the next cycle, then the next steps involve an elaboration of the objectives and constraints for the software product and process, an identification of alternative approaches for satisfying the objectives within the constraints, an evaluation of the alternatives, and a risk assessment activity. This risk assessment activity includes

438

the risk identification, risk analysis, and risk prioritization steps discussed in Section 2 of this tutorial. The following step involves the elaboration and refinement of the risk-management plan for the current cycle, plus a draft of a risk-management plan to cover the primary risk-management functions to be performed during the following cycle (including the necessary budget and schedule for performing them).

Once the risk-management plan is executed (along with risk monitoring and any necessary corrective actions), the resulting revised objectives, preferred alternatives, and their rationale are covered in a technical walkthrough involving the key developer, customer, user, and maintainer participants. A non-concurrence on the results of the walkthrough will cause an iteration of the appropriate previous steps. Given a concurrence, the project will proceed to develop the next level of definition of the product (specification, executing portion, or mix) and the plan for the next cycle, which is driven by the draft risk management for the next cycle.

Thus, Figure 4.4 provides a roadmap for using risk management techniques to navigate through the first phase of the two-phase "risk reduction followed by the waterfall" process model. The project's relative risk exposure factors provide guidance on when and what to prototype, simulate, benchmark, or V&V; and on how much of these activities will be enough.

4.1.2.5: Summary

The previous discussion of risk-oriented process models can be summarized as follows:

- A software project using a process model that operates independently of risk considerations will run into serious difficulties when it encounters high-risk elements

- For very complex, dynamic in-house projects, the spiral model provides the flexibility and risk-orientation necessary to apply the right process options at the right time

- For less complex, less dynamic, or contract specification-driven projects, the spiral model often has more flexibility than is convenient to use. However, something like the spiral model is needed to choose a specialized process model that is sensitive to the project's high-risk elements

- The use of the spiral model as a process model generator has produced a process model decision table (Figure 4.3), which enables a project to use its high-risk elements or critical-process drivers to determine an appropriate and efficient pre-defined process model for its needs

- The most complex of these pre-defined process models is a "risk resolution followed by waterfall" model. An elaboration of this model has been developed (Figure 4.4) to provide a specific mapping of its front-end risk-reduction steps to familiar contract milestones and reviews

4.2: Overview of Tutorial Articles

Section 4 contains three articles that deal with the implementation of risk management. The first article, "Implementing Risk Management: A Program Office Perspective" [Peschel, 1987], summarizes a software risk-management approach taken by a very large, complex, reliability-critical program, the U.S. Small ICBM Program. The number of large, interacting systems and contractors, the use of advanced technology, and the national criticality of the system's performance have required the program office to be both highly innovative and very careful in program management. This led the program to be one of the pioneers in the use of risk management, for both software and the other computer components included under the term mission critical computer resources (MCCR).

The article provides a summary of the use of risk management during the various phases of MCCR definition and development. It shows a list of the top-eight risk items identified during the risk assessment activities. These were expanded into a larger set of 19 potential problems that were summarized and addressed as follows:

- Cause of problem
- Impact if not addressed
- Mitigation actions under consideration
- Actions taken

These potential problems then entered a thorough risk monitoring and corrective action process.

The article also identifies a number of the advanced techniques used for risk management on the program. Pages 10 and 11 describe the use of nuclear safety cross check analysis (NSCCA) and performance analysis and technical evaluation (PATE) to resolve operational reliability, survivability, safety, and performance risks. Page 13 summarizes the primary risk reduction options used to resolve the major sources of software risk, by using categories similar to those in Air Force Pamphlet 800-45 [AFSC, 1988] (included in Section 2 of this tutorial) and the ones used in the tutorial text: cost, schedule, operational, technical, and support. It concludes with a useful set of lessons learned in applying this risk-management approach over several years.

The second article, "Use of Ada for FAA's Advanced Automation System (AAS)" [Basili et al., 1987], is an excerpt of the risk management portions from the larger report of that name. The study was commissioned by the U.S. Federal Aviation Administration (FAA), which wanted an assessment of the use of the Ada programming language on its next-generation air-traffic control system, the advanced automation system.

The excerpt begins with the executive summary, which describes the study's context and identifies the main conclusions and recommendations. The primary recommendation was that the FAA use Ada on the AAS, subject to several conditions including the use of an Ada risk-management plan.

The remainder of the excerpt is the risk management portion: The Ada risk areas identified, and the recommended actions the FAA should establish to resolve the risks. The Ada risk areas identified included the impact of tasking, run-time support system, and other Ada features on real-time performance; the impact of exceptions, elaboration, and other Ada features on reliability and availability requirements; software size concerns; Ada support environment concerns; and staffing, management, and cost-schedule concerns. The primary risk management actions recommended were the use of risk management plans; employing an Ada exercise as part of source selection; establishing a development process focused on designs expressed in compilable Ada; and extensive benchmarking of Ada compilers and support capabilities.

Overall, the report provides a good example of the results of a risk identification activity focused on a particular project issue: the use of Ada. It is important to note that the existence of Ada risks was compatible with a recommendation to use Ada. The risks were felt to be manageable, and Ada's other advantages more than compensated for the risks.

The third article, "The Management of Risk in System Development: 'Project SP' and the 'New Spiral Model'" [Wolff, 1989], summarizes an application of the risk-driven spiral model to an internally-developed commercial information system: the Praxis Company Information System (PCIS).

The first spiral cycle of the PCIS development involved a fairly high-level determination of system requirements and alternative implementation approaches. Several data management alternatives were evaluated. The plan for cycle 2 was to use a commercial database management system (DBMS) to develop an operational prototype PCIS, with an option to migrate to a database machine in later cycles.

The second cycle was implemented; it provided good feedback on the PCIS requirements, but was too slow for full operational use. Thus, the plan for the third spiral cycle was to migrate a refined PCIS onto the database machine, given a satisfactory outcome of a further short database machine risk analysis.

The basic conclusion from the experience was that the spiral model provided a reasonably good framework for the PCIS project. However, some needed improvements were identified: a need to carry forward objectives, plans, etc. from cycle to cycle; a need for hierarchical relationships and for spawning "spirals within spirals;" and a need for more specific guidance in the planning process.

The PCIS experience led to the formulation of a variant of the spiral model called the new spiral model. It envisions the software process as an accumulation of a knowledge base of project-related objectives, alternatives, specifications, plans, executing components, and related objects. This knowledge base is refined and elaborated into the desired operational product via a collection of spiral-type cycles.

The steps in this "new spiral model" are:

1. Gather new knowledge and add it to the knowledge base.
2. Review, analyze, and rationalize the knowledge base.
3. Execute any plans that are ready to go.

Step 1 corresponds to the upper left quadrant in the original spiral model. Step 2 collects the remaining three quadrants into a single step. Step 3 involves the triggering of spiral sub-cycles when their triggering conditions are met.

Similar concepts of expressing the spiral model artifacts as an expanding object base, and treating portions of risk management plans as executing process programs [Osterweil, 1987] are expressed in the [Boehm-Belz, 1988] paper in Section 2 of this tutorial. The Wolff paper [Wolff, 1989] carries these concepts to a greater level of detail, and presents an attractive candidate scheme for software project knowledge representation with its "Project SP" notation. The scheme still needs further development to serve as a base for production software projects, but it holds promise for such usage in the future.

4.3: Summary

The most important thing for a software project to do is to get focused on its critical success factors.

For various reasons, including the influence of previous software management guidelines, projects get focused on activities that are not critical for their success. These frequently include writing boilerplate documents, exploring intriguing but peripheral technical issues, playing politics, or trying to sell "the ultimate system."

In the process, critical success factors get neglected, the project fails, and nobody wins.

The key contribution of software risk management, and the Theory-W context in which it is applied, is to create this focus on critical success factors—and to provide the techniques that enable the project to deal with them.

The spiral model and its derivatives presented in this section establish a risk-oriented approach that embeds the project's critical success factors into its life-cycle activities. The risk assessment and risk-control techniques presented in Sections 2 and 3 provide the specific capabilities needed to implement the risk-oriented approach.

Risk management is not a cookbook approach. To handle all of the complex people-oriented and technology-driven success factors involved in software projects, a great measure of human judgment is required.

Good people, with good skills and good judgment, are what make software projects work. Risk management can provide you with some of the skills, and a good conceptual framework for sharpening your judgment. I hope you find these useful on your next software project.

IMPLEMENTING RISK MANAGEMENT A PROGRAM OFFICE PERSPECTIVE

A. Peschel
System Development Division

September 1987

SMALL ICBM OPERATIONAL SOFTWARE

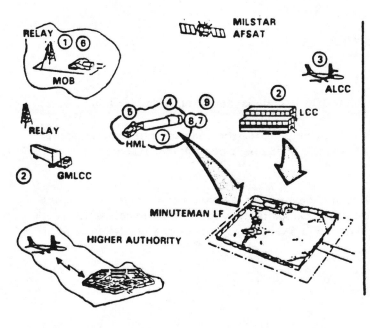

1. CODE PROCESSING SOFTWARE

2. LAUNCH CONTROL CENTER SOFTWARE

3. AIRBORNE LAUNCH CONTROL SOFTWARE

4. LAUNCHER CONTROL SOFTWARE

5. VEHICLE CONTROL SYSTEM SOFTWARE

6. WEAPON SECURITY SOFTWARE

7. MISSILE FLIGHT SOFTWARE

8. MISSILE GROUND SOFTWARE

9. OPERATIONAL TARGETING SOFTWARE

441

PROGRAM MANAGER: AIR FORCE BALLISTIC MISSILE OFFICE

The Small ICBM Weapon System is a land-mobile force of strategic nuclear missiles positioned topside on MINUTEMAN bases. To achieve survivability against nuclear attack, each mobile launcher may be dispersed upon warning. Additionally, critical functions of the computer electronics are hardened.

Small ICBM software supports code processing at a Main Operating Base; launch operations control at fixed and mobile launch control centers; launch operations control at Airborne Launch Control centers; launcher control at the mobile launcher; vehicle control for the tractor-launcher; weapon system security at the Main Operating Base; missile flight control at the missile; missile ground mobility operations at the launcher; and missile targeting at the launcher.

As Program Manager, Air Force Ballistic Missile Office must acquire software that is reliable, secure and nuclear safe within tight constraints on computer memory/throughput and on program schedule to IOC.

MCCR* RISK MANAGEMENT OBJECTIVES

IDENTIFY AREAS THAT INTRODUCE SUBSTANTIAL RISK TO PROGRAM OBJECTIVES

DETERMINE SPECIFIC CAUSES OF HIGH-LEVEL RISKS

IDENTIFY ACTIONS TO ELIMINATE OR MITIGATE RISKS

SELECT PREFERRED FALL-BACK ACTIONS

MONITOR HIGH-RISK AREAS AND CONTROL TIMELY CORRECTIVE ACTION PROCESS

*MISSION CRITICAL COMPUTER RESOURCES.

Like other Program Offices, BMO has performed MCCR risk management activities for a long time.

The recently issued Air Force Regulation AFR 800-14 emphasizes the need for greater formality in risk management activities in the context of life cycle management of computer resources in systems.

In conducting the Small ICBM Program, BMO has anticipated this emphasis and has implemented a risk management program which identifies risk areas, pinpoints their cause, determines risk mitigation actions, selects preferred courses of action, and monitors risk areas to control a timely corrective action process.

PRE-FSD CONSIDERATION OF SMALL ICBM MCCR RISK (1984 – 86)

1985		1986			
3Q	4Q	1Q	2Q	3Q	4Q

```
WEAPON SYSTEM
STUDIES

        ASSOCIATE CONTRACTOR
        STUDIES

            INDEPENDENT MCCR
            ARCHITECTURE STUDIES

                TAILORED STANDARDS AND
                APPLICATION OF REGULATIONS

                SYSTEM MCCR INTEGRATION

                    MCCR RISK ANALYSIS
```

FSD DECISION △

MCCR Risk Management activities started early in the Small ICBM Concept Exploration/ Demonstration and Validation Phase. Early Weapon System Studies provided insight into required system functions and MCCR implementation in similar systems such as PEACEKEEPER.

Associate Contractor C/DV Studies included parallel, competitive studies of system/subsystem requirements, architectures and development plans. An assessment study for the use of Ada was also performed.

Two parallel, independent MCCR architecture studies were performed to focus exclusively on MCCR issues — particularly issues concerning standardization and software development. BMO provided assumptions concerning requirements allocation and programmatic constraints to permit this very early focus.

Based on all these independent study inputs, BMO selectively tailored standards, synthesized integrated MCCR concepts, baselined top-level MCCR requirements, developed Prime Item Development specifications, and prepared all FSD procurement documents.

MCCR Risk analyses played a continuing role in RFP development and Source-Selection to remove FSD contracting risk.

INDEPENDENT MCCR ARCHITECTURE STUDIES

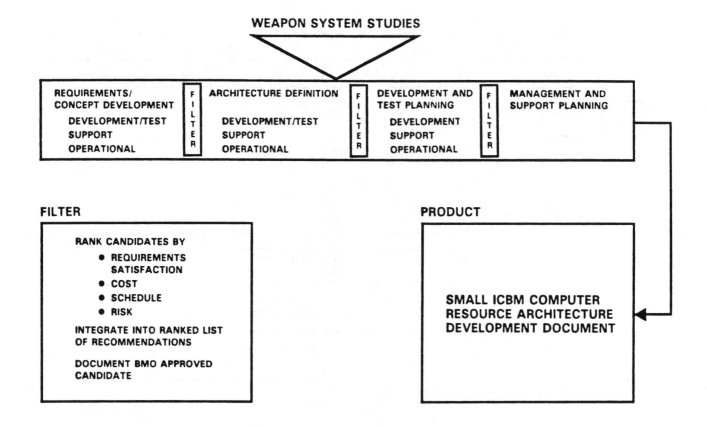

Two independent MCCR architecture studies addressed risk formally. The Statement of Work explicitly required three MCCR concept-architecture-implementation recommendations to be developed — each with a greater level of study detail.

BMO approval of a list of assumptions assured adequate control of study scope, depth, and direction. A BMO approval filter was applied to ranked list recommendations for concepts, architectures, and implementation, each in turn.

Candidate rankings for risk were required separately and integrated with criteria for cost, schedule, and requirements satisfaction.

A Data Item Description was specially created for the MCCR Architecture Development Document to discipline the documentation of incremental study findings. This facilitated document review and integration of MCCR study findings by three Weapon Control System and two Hard Mobile Launcher competitor studies.

The MCCR study results were performed first independently for BMO and then provided to all competitors.

MCCR RESULTS (APR 86)

RISK
ASSESSMENT

- Ada LANGUAGE

- LAUNCH CONTROL OFFICER MAN-MACHINE INTERFACE

- ALLOCATION OF PROCESSOR MEMORY/THROUGHPUT MARGINS

- AINS ACCOMMODATION STRATEGY AT HARD MOBILE LAUNCHER (HML)

- SECURITY/SAFETY CERTIFICATION

- NEW TECHNOLOGY DEVELOPMENT

- MCCR INTEGRATION MANAGEMENT

- SOFTWARE QUALITY DEFINITION

EARLY RISK ASSESSMENT RESULTS SUPPORTED SYSTEM/SUBSYSTEM SPECIFICATION AND RFP DEVELOPMENT

RESULTS PROVIDED TO COMPETITORS

Early MCCR risk assessments were formulated by members of the Program Office as part of the System Requirements Review activities.

Risk areas considered were

- Ada Language because of compiler maturity concerns

- Launch Control Officer Man Machine Interface because workload projections exceeded those for PEACEKEEPER

- Allocation of processor memory/throughput margins because of severe constraints

- Alternate Inertial Navigation System computer processing strategy because BMO needed to protect selection of this new technology option

- Security/Safety Certification because failure to adequately address these during requirements and design could lead to delays in IOC

- New Technology Development for Processors because of a tradeoff in hardened MIL-STD-1750A processors versus shielded "proven family" processors

- MCCR Integration Management because failure to structure an adequate Interface Control Program could lead to serious integration and IOC schedule problems

- Software Quality Definition because the new software development standard MIL-STD-SDS requires consideration of software quality factors in addition to functionality and performance

These risk assessments supported subsystem specification and RFP development. Results were provided to competitors.

DOCUMENTATION OF POTENTIAL PROBLEMS

LIST OF 19 POTENTIAL PROBLEMS

CAUSE OF PROBLEM

IMPACT IF NOT ADDRESSED

MITIGATION ACTIONS CONSIDERED

ACTIONS TAKEN

INITIAL ASSESSMENT OF RISK: LOW, MEDIUM, HIGH

The early risk assessments were expanded into a larger set of potential problems.

Each potential problem was documented on a single page addressing:

- Cause of problem
- Impact if not addressed
- Mitigation actions under consideration
- Actions taken

Each potential problem was assessed as having high, medium or low risk potential.

Low risk implies low expectation of negative program impact requiring normal management control.

Medium risk implies medium expectation of negative program impact requiring medium priority planned or formal corrective action.

High risk implies high expectation of negative program impact requiring high priority planned or formal corrective action.

CRLCMP* DRAFT

NO SPECIFIC RISKS IDENTIFIED THAT WOULD JEOPARDIZE FSD START

SEVERAL RISK AREAS REQUIRING MANAGEMENT ATTENTION

- DECISIONS IMPACTING REQUIREMENTS STABILITY
- GFE AVAILABILITY
- PROGRAMMATIC DEFINITIONS IMPACTING SOFTWARE AND TESTING
- AVAILABILITY OF FACILITIES FOR TESTING
- Ada AND DEVELOPMENT TOOLS

DURING FSD, START RISK MONITORING IN HIGH POTENTIAL PROBLEM AREAS

*COMPUTER RESOURCE LIFE CYCLE MANAGEMENT PLAN.

MCCR risk assessment results were formally documented in a draft of the Computer Resource Lifecycle Management Plan and per AFR 800-14.

The FSD decision itself is partially based on formal assessment that risk areas have been sufficiently minimized and are low enough to proceed with the program.

Usually there will be other risk areas which are not under full control of the Program Office. Risk areas which were identified as requiring continuing management attention included:

- Decisions that impact requirements stability

- Arrangements for the availability of GFE

- Programmatic definitions impacting software and testing, particularly those related to interoperability

- Arrangements for the availability of test facilities

- Use of Ada and development tools

Finally, there will be high potential risk areas that will be singled out for careful monitoring based on lessons learned experience.

PROBLEM AREAS

HIGH POTENTIAL

REQUIREMENT DEFINITION AND STABILITY

SCHEDULE/COST

PROOF-OF-CONCEPT AND PROOF-OF-DESIGN

PRODUCT SUPPORTABILITY

CONTRACTOR CAPABILITY AND PROGRAM CONTROLS

PROGRAM OFFICE VISIBILITY

HIGHER ORDER PROGRAMMING LANGUAGE

POTENTIAL SHORTFALLS IN TECHNICAL OBJECTIVES

STANDARDS FOR PROCESSES AND PRODUCTS

AVAILABILITY OF FACILITIES, GFE ITEMS, AND INTER-AGENCY SUPPORT

Risk analysts supporting BMO have developed a checklist of high potential problems areas to better focus MCCR risk monitoring activities during FSD.

A template was created which named each potentially high risk problem area, identified possible causes and defined options for avoiding or mitigating them. The checklist presented here and the templates used AFR 800-14 risk appendix and other source material as a point of departure.

Incorporated into these templates are the insights gained from previous lessons learned. The checklist factors are shown in the slide.

There is no priority assignment implied in this listing.

It is recommended that each Program Office develop such a risk monitoring template for its own use.

ANALYSIS AND TEST OBJECTIVES OVERVIEW

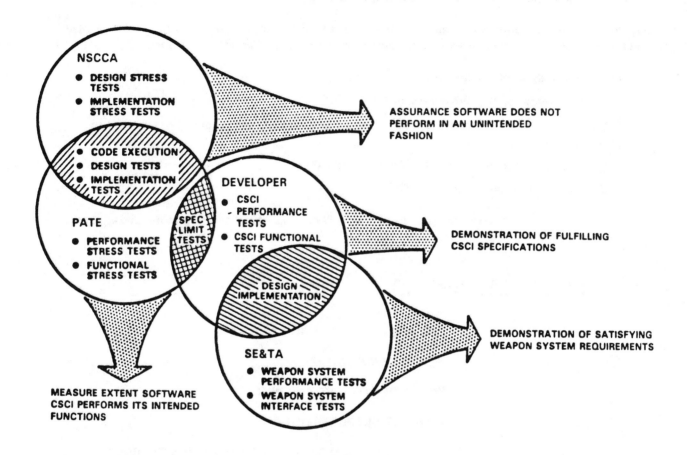

It is important that software technical analysis and test activities be designed so as to surface and resolve risks in a timely manner. Of particular concern is software nuclear safety.

BMO has been innovative in creating structured Associate Contractor relationships which include:

- NSCCA (Nuclear Safety Cross Check Analysis) to assure that software does not perform in an unintended fashion which could jeopardize nuclear safety

- PATE (Performance Analysis and Technical Evaluation) to measure the extent that software performs its intended function

- DEVELOPER to demonstrate fulfillment of CSCI (Computer Software Configuration Item) specification

- SE&TA (Systems Engineering and Technical Assistance) to demonstrate satisfaction of weapon system requirements

NUCLEAR SAFETY CROSS-CHECK ANALYSIS/ PERFORMANCE ANALYSIS AND TECHNICAL EVALUATION

NSCCA/PATE TASKS	MINIMUM ESSENTIAL TOOLS	LEVEL OF ANALYSIS CRITERIA (NSCCA)	LEVEL OF ANALYSIS CRITERIA (PATE)
SOFTWARE TOOL DEVELOPMENT SOFTWARE REQUIREMENTS ANALYSIS SOFTWARE DESIGN ANALYSIS CODE ANALYSIS TEST PLANNING TEST CONDUCT SOFTWARE/SYSTEM EVALUATION NSCCA DEMONSTRATION TWO-MAN CONTROL NSCCA ONLY	REQUIREMENTS/DESIGN ANALYSIS SUPPORT SOURCE CODE ANALYZERS OBJECT CODE ANALYZERS TEST EXECUTION AND ANALYSIS SUPPORT SUPPORT TEST TOOLS PERFORMANCE SIMULATION AND ANALYSIS	SOFTWARE CRITICAL AREA IDENTIFICATION REQUIREMENTS ADEQUACY/ ROBUSTNESS DOCUMENT ANALYSIS SIMULATION/TEST FOR CRITICAL VULNERABILITIES DISCREPANCY REPORT CLOSEOUT --------------1--- INDEPENDENT "CRITICAL" ALGORITHM DEVELOPMENT "CRITICAL" SYSTEM/ THREAD TESTING --------------2--- INDEPENDENT DEVELOPMENT RESOLUTION OF DIFFERENCES ADDED SYSTEM/THREAD TESTING --------------3---	SOFTWARE PRODUCIBILITY RISK RISK-PRIORITIZED REQUIREMENTS ADEQUACY/ ROBUSTNESS CODE/DESIGN VERIFICATION TEST ADEQUACY/RISK CSCI-LEVEL SIMULATION/ TEST FOR KNOWN RISKS DISCREPANCY REPORT CLOSEOUT ------------------1--- ANALYSIS/TEST FOR HIGH RISK AREAS SUPPLEMENTAL TEST FOR CRITICAL AREAS INDEPENDENT SOFTWARE RMA ANALYSIS/PREDICTION ------------------2--- SELECTIVE TESTING ON REAL HARDWARE SOFTWARE RMA VERIFICATION TESTING ------------------3--- INDEPENDENT DEVELOPMENT; RESOLUTION OF DIFFERENCES SUPPLEMENTAL TEST FOR ADEQUACY/ROBUSTNESS SELECTIVE, FULL THREAD SYSTEM/SOFTWARE TESTING ------------------4---

NOTE: LEVEL OF ANALYSIS CRITERIA ARE ADDITIVE.

BMO's approach to analysis and test using an independent NSCCA/PATE Program has contributed to defining the current DoD policies for Independent Verification and Validation contracting.

For the Small ICBM Program, BMO has further formalized NSCCA/PATE Program definition by creating explicit standards for:

- NSCCA/PATE analysis and test tasks to be performed upon Development Contractor deliverables

- Minimum essential tools to be used to perform the analysis and test tasks

- The criteria level to be applied for nuclear safety analysis/test

- The criteria level to be applied for performance analysis and technical evaluation

NSCCA/PATE analysis and test is strongly driven by risk considerations.

PATE activities include independent relability analysis, prediction, and test.

There is considerable use of simulators to drive CSCI testing to minimize reliance on ASCON and integrated test facilities.

COMPUTER RESOURCE MANAGEMENT

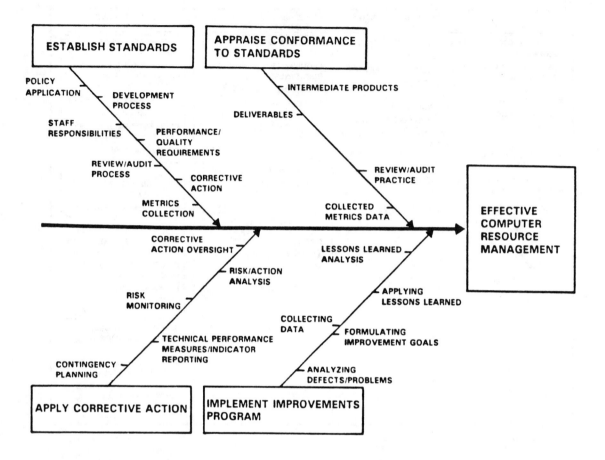

Risk management is but one aspect of effective computer resource management which consists of:

- Establishing standards for listed items

- Appraising conformance to standards of listed items

- Applying corrective action by performing the actions listed

- Implementing an Improvement Program by performing the listed items

Risk management plays a dominant role in development process planning and in driving a timely corrective action process.

RISK MITIGATION PLANNING OPTIONS*

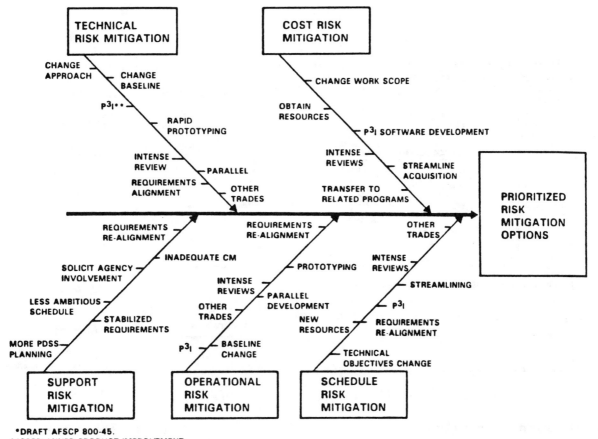

*DRAFT AFSCP 800-45.
**PREPLANNED PRODUCT IMPROVEMENT.

Software risk management included risk identification, cause-effect analysis, impact assessment and mitigation course of action planning.

This template has been created using AFSCP Draft Pamphlet 800-45 as source material. It will be refined according to BMO Lessons Learned to help identify criteria for future contingency planning.

Software risk has been divided into technical, cost, support, operational, and schedule areas. The template is presented in the form of a cause-effect diagram.

For example, to mitigate technical risk one could change one's approach; change baseline; perform rapid prototyping; adopt Pre-planned Product Improvement; activate an intensive review process; initiate parallel developments; re-align requirements; or initiate other trade study actions.

At any point in the program one can use this template to identify possible courses of action to mitigate risk in a particular area.

Then one can assess whether a possible course of action is actually still available to one.

And finally, program impact analysis can be performed to help prioritize courses of mitigation action.

RISK-DRIVEN CORRECTIVE ACTION PROCESS

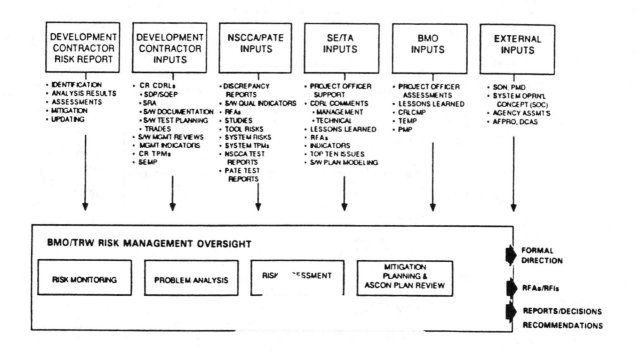

BMO is beginning to implement .... process shown here.

FSD Development Contract' ....
management indicators, con... ..... data packages.

NSCCA/PATE contractor inputs include discrepancy reports, quality indicator reports, tool risk and system MCCR risk assessments.

SE&TA contractor inputs include direct support to Project Officers, comments against contract deliverables, RFAs/RFIs, and indicator analysis reports.

Program Office inputs include project officer assessments, lessons learned, and system level management plans.

External agency inputs include directives, requirements, assessments, comments, and support.

Risk management oversight activities are directed towards providing needed formal direction, issuing appropriate RFAs/RFIs, and producing necessary reports, decisions, and recommendations.

RISK MANAGEMENT INTEGRATION

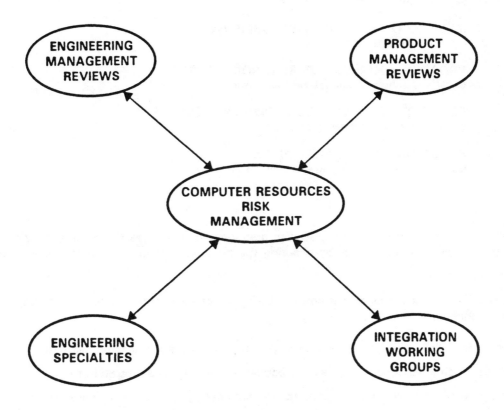

Directives, regulations, and guidebooks to implement risk management are only guides to action. To be effective, risk management must be integrated into the total Program Office management process.

This means participation in — and contributions to — engineering management reviews, product management reviews, engineering specialty activities and integration working groups such as the CRWG (Computer Resource Working Group), TPWG (Test Planning Working Group), ICWG (Interface Control Working Group), and others.

It is important to assure that risk management discipline contributes to overall management effectiveness without creating unproductive, adversarial relationships.

INGREDIENTS FOR SUCCESS

START EARLY IN PROGRAM AND FOLLOW THROUGH
CAPTURE/APPLY LESSONS LEARNED

SEEK INDEPENDENT ADVICE
ADAPT AND INTEGRATE

USE CHECKLIST/TEMPLATE STANDARDS
DEPEND ON LESSONS LEARNED

REQUIRE INDICATOR AND RISK REPORTING
PERIODIC, MEANINGFUL; RECOGNIZE RESPONSIBILITY AND AUTHORITY RELATIONSHIPS

INSIST ON CONSTRUCTIVE MANAGEMENT PROCESS
PREVENT ADVERSARIAL RELATIONSHIPS

IMPROVE QUALITATIVE ASSESSMENTS
QUANTIFY WHERE POSSIBLE

BROADEN SOURCES FOR RISK NOMINATION
CAREFULLY SCREEN, PRIORITIZE AND DISPOSITION

FORMALIZE CORRECTIVE ACTION PROCESS
USE RISK LIST MANAGEMENT TECHNIQUE

FOCUS ON FAILURE PREVENTION
USE HIGHLY EXPERIENCED STAFF; EMPHASIZE TEAMWORK

A fundamental concern is to prudently apply risk management principles to improve BMO's overall acquisition management process, thereby assuring the greatest likelihood of Small ICBM program success.

In applying the MCCR risk management process BMO has already learned a number of important lessons. These include:

- Start early, follow through — make sure you capture and apply lessons learned

- Seek as much independent advice as practical — but plan to adapt and integrate

- Use checklists and templates. This helps to formalize application of lessons learned

- Require formal indicator and risk reporting — make it periodic, meaningful and sensitive to disclosure criteria

- Ensure constructive — not adversarial — contractor relationships

- Improve qualitative assessments through documentation, review, and quantification

- Broaden sources for nominating risks — but carefully screen, prioritize and disposition

- Formalize corrective action using risk list management techniques

- Focus on failure prevention by using highly experienced personnel with teamwork as principal emphasis

Use of Ada®
for
FAA's Advanced Automation System (AAS)

Dr. Victor R. Basili
Dr. Barry W. Boehm
Judith A. Clapp
Dale Gaumer
Dr. Maretta Holden
Arthur E. Salwen
John K. Summers

April 1987

MTR-87W77

SPONSOR:
Federal Aviation Administration
CONTRACT NO.:
DTFA01-84-C-00001
PROJECT:
1763C

Approved for public release; distribution unlimited.

The MITRE Corporation
Civil Systems Division
7525 Colshire Drive
McLean, Virginia 22102-3481

INTRODUCTION

In 1981, the Federal Aviation Administration (FAA) embarked on a comprehensive plan for modernizing and improving the United States Air Traffic Control (ATC) system. The Advanced Automation System (AAS) is the largest of over ninety projects in this National Airspace System (NAS) Plan; it is also the most software-intensive, with over a million lines of code expected to be developed. The Acquisition Phase contractor for AAS will be asked to select a single high order computer language for use on the project. Anticipating that the contractor might select Ada, and citing lack of FAA experience with Ada, the FAA's Deputy Associate Administrator for NAS Programs, ADL-2, asked The MITRE Corporation to organize and participate in a study. He asked that leading MITRE and non-MITRE software experts be assembled to address the use of Ada for AAS.

This report documents the findings and recommendations of the study participants.

CHARACTERIZING A SOFTWARE DEVELOPMENT

The use of the very best in software engineering is imperative for large, critical, and complex systems such as AAS. Therefore, the study participants' consensus view of how a software development might proceed on such large procurements is outlined. Next, the benefits of the described approach are discussed, along with the advantages offered by Ada in achieving them. Based on this framework, qualified recommendations on the use of Ada for AAS are provided.

Elements of an Ada Software Development

While there is more than one way to use Ada in support of good software engineering, one reasonable way to proceed is to use Ada in a software development process characterized by a composite of the following elements:

- Compilable designs

- Small, expert design team up front

- Benchmarks, prototyping, and incremental development

- Appropriate milestones and deliverables

- Early access to mature development environments
- Training in Ada and software engineering

- Ada-oriented Software Development Plan

The above approach also provides a framework for discussing risk and risk reduction activities (as summarized below).

Advantages of an Ada Software Development

Use of Ada does not inevitably lead to good software engineering; a sound development approach must be followed. However, if properly used, Ada provides a natural vehicle for employing sound software engineering practices.

Ada use stimulates a more effective development approach. The richness of the language, which also contributes to the rigor of Ada as a design notation, is a major reason for this. In addition, the multiple individual walk-throughs provide shorter, more focused reviews than a monolithic Critical Design Review (CDR) would provide. Ada also offers greater continuity of activities across phases of a project. Furthermore, the thoroughness of automated compiler checking permits many flaws to be uncovered early in the development process, which in turn permits high-risk elements to be addressed early in the framework of the total design.

Lower life-cycle costs, enhanced software readability and traceability, improved maintenance productivity and system evolution, and software with higher quality and increased reliability are expected benefits of such an Ada development approach. Actual project experience shows that expectations of a shorter, smoother integration phase can be realized. Unfortunately, because Ada technology is new, no large Ada systems are available for verifying the expected life-cycle advantages.

Compilable designs written in Ada Program Design Language (PDL) provide all the advantages of other-language PDLs, and much more. For example, other high order languages do not require compiler checking of module interfaces. In addition, the use of Ada syntax provides increased rigor for interface definitions; compiler checking ensures that these interfaces will be used consistently.

The machine-readable deliverables resulting from compilable designs can be generated with minimal extra effort, since they are produced as a natural outgrowth of the development process. They result in a single representation of the design; manual translations of the products of one phase into the notation of the next (with the inevitable mistranslation errors) are no longer needed. Thus there is better traceability between the products of a given phase and those of the succeeding ones throughout the development process. There is also better traceability between documentation delivered to the customer, and the system that the documentation purports to describe. Finally, the machine-readable deliverables can be more easily reviewed; in fact, automation can be used to assist in the review process.

Using Ada on AAS: Recommendations

The study participants concluded that the size and complexity of AAS make software engineering, and not the programming language, the key issue. Moreover, if properly used, Ada best facilitates good software engineering practices and a sound software development process. Therefore, the study participants unanimously recommended that the FAA commit to Ada as the appropriate choice for AAS, given four strong qualifications to ensure that Ada's potential is realized:

- The software development process must be modified; the FAA and contractors must use an approach tailored to take advantage of modern software engineering practices and the support that Ada provides for them.

- It should be expected that appropriate selective use of non-Ada code within the framework of an Ada design may be necessary when Ada is found to be inadequate.

- Contractor readiness for an Ada software development must be evaluated.

- Positive risk reduction activities must be undertaken addressing the risk areas associated with Ada.

The large system nature of AAS makes it well suited for the advantages offered by Ada; no other language offers more advantages. If one of the likely alternative languages were chosen, the large system problems posed by AAS would remain, but many of Ada's advantages would not be available for addressing them.

At the same time, it should be noted that the advantages offered by Ada will not accrue by default; positive steps must be taken to realize them. It is of particular importance that both contractor and customer be well-trained in Ada technology. If positive steps are not taken, or if risk reduction activities indicate significant problems (e.g., compilers are inadequate), then the advantages of Ada usage will be outweighed by the associated risks. In such a case, the recommendation to use Ada would not stand. If the FAA commits early to Ada, risks can be assessed early in the development process. Problem areas thereby uncovered can be addressed in a timely fashion, or if need be, a fallback position can be pursued without wasted cost and effort having accrued.

IDENTIFIED RISK AREAS

Although Ada offers the potential of significant advantages on AAS, its proper use can only diminish the risks, not eliminate them. Some of the risks arise from the newness of the Ada technology; others, however, are not peculiar to Ada. The identified risk areas include the following:

- Ability to meet real-time and availability requirements--The hardware architecture, run-time systems, and the need for proper use of Ada's features and non-Ada code pose risks to meeting the demanding AAS performance requirements.

- The inherent large size of the AAS software--The inability of compilers to handle large quantities of code has been a key problem area on other Ada projects.

- Adequacy of computing resources--Ada projects are typically heavy users of development resources.

- Customer readiness--The newness of Ada technology and its many differences pose risks of whether a customer is prepared to award and monitor an Ada contract.

- Software support systems on development and target machines-- Their lack of maturity provides increased risk on an Ada procurement.

- Personnel and management--Risk areas on any software procurement include staffing profiles and experience, and management commitment and flexibility.

- Schedule and cost--There is virtually no historical database of Ada projects to provide guidance.

Early risk reduction activities are needed to address the above risks; appropriate risk reduction activities were recommended by the study participants where possible. However, it is realized that, even given very good early risk reduction awareness and associated activities, there will be inevitable modifications to the software environments for the system being developed. Thus the contractors should document in their plans an approach for addressing problems when they arise, and should allocate sufficient time and money resources for proceeding with the documented approach.

To summarize, the proper use of Ada can reduce some of the risks inherent in a large software development. However, the residual risks that remain must be addressed.

ADDRESSING THE RISKS

In addition to specific risk reduction activities designed to address individual risk areas, the following general risk reduction activities are recommended:

- Each contractor's proposal should be required to include a <u>Risk Management Plan</u>.

- Each contractor's proposal should be required to include an Ada-oriented <u>Software Development Plan</u>.

- A <u>software engineering exercise</u> should be conducted. First, the FAA would define a software problem. Then the contractors would be asked to solve it using their AAS personnel, software methodologies, and toolsets. This would test the contractors' planned methodologies and their ability to design and implement software using them. The results could be used by the contractors to improve their methodologies, and by the FAA as technical criteria for assessment in making the Acquisition Phase contract award, as an adjunct to the technical evaluation of the proposals.

- The AAS contractors should be required to develop <u>compilable Ada designs</u> for their proposed systems and deliver them to the FAA in machine-readable format. A corollary to this recommendation is that the FAA should thoroughly review the Ada designs.

- <u>Benchmarks</u> should be required on development and target machines to address many of the identified risks.

NEAR-TERM FAA ACTIVITIES

Multiple near-term FAA activities must be undertaken to realize the benefits of an Ada development and to address the inherent risks:

- The FAA must develop in-house expertise and access outside expertise in Ada and in software engineering.

- The FAA should prepare and dry run a software engineering exercise.

- The FAA should revise the AAS milestones to reflect an Ada development process (e.g., replace a monolithic CDR with incremental reviews).

- The FAA must develop a strategy for implementing the recommendations that it chooses to undertake. For example, benchmarks must be selected, and criteria for evaluating the results must be established.

- The FAA must assess the feasibility of a fixed price contract, if one is being considered for AAS. In doing so, the FAA should consider whether the estimated costs are realistic and known with a high degree of certainty, and whether design and requirements are thorough and stable. Where these conditions are not met, a cost plus contract--or a contract with a mix of fixed price and cost plus components--should be used to provide the needed flexibility.

- Schedule revision may be necessary for the FAA and contractors to carry out activities needed to ensure a successful software development effort on AAS.

- The FAA should bring the software maintenance organization on board now. The long-term success of the AAS program depends upon the early, active involvement of this organization. Recommended near-term activities for it include the following: writing of a Software Maintenance Plan, involvement in training and preparation of a software engineering exercise, and support in preparing the Request for Proposals (RFP) and Statement of Work (SOW).

- The FAA must prepare for awarding an Acquisition Phase contract and monitoring the post-award development activities. Training, development of contract award criteria, and establishment of FAA computing facilities are needed. Criteria need to be set for each intermediate product at each milestone so that project tracking can occur.

3.0 IDENTIFIED RISK AREAS

Although Ada offers the potential of significant advantages on AAS, its proper use can only diminish the risks, not eliminate them. Many of the risks arise from the newness of the Ada technology: staff must be trained in Ada, tools must be developed and mature, and there are no historical data for estimating cost and schedule. However, it will be noted that many of the risk items are not peculiar to Ada; they would apply even if another language were chosen as the implementation vehicle.

This section of the report addresses the risk areas identified by the study participants. Details are provided on the risk items within these areas, and appropriate risk reduction activities are recommended where possible. Both Ada-specific and general software engineering recommendations are provided, though the latter are couched in the context of using Ada. These recommendations can be used by both the FAA and the contractors: by the FAA as guidance in writing the Request for Proposal (RFP) and Statement of Work (SOW), evaluating proposals, and monitoring contracts; by the contractors as input to consider in establishing their development process.

It should also be noted that only the AAS procurement was considered in formulating these recommendations, and their applicability should thus be considered appropriate only in that context. Nonetheless, the general nature of the identified risks implies that the recommendations may have applicability in a larger context, and could serve as the starting point for formulating risk reduction activities on other large procurements.

3.1 Ada Performance Risks

Ada was designed to be used for meeting the performance req of real-time systems. However, risks remain in this area to be addressed if Ada is to be employed effectively. performance risks are considered--real-time and should be noted that these risks are likely to as compilers mature.

3.1.1 Meeting Real-T

AAS demanding real-time performance requirements. Ind study participant noted, a timely but imprecise indication pending midair collision would be far superior to a precise cation given after the fact.

Four real-time performance risk items were identified and are discussed below.

3.1.1.1 Impact of Tasking. The foremost real-time performance risk item identified was the use of the Ada tasking feature. Even though object code generated by Ada compilers is generally as efficient as that generated from other high order languages, industry experience leads to two concerns about tasking: its object code often has poor run-time performance, and there is a tendency to over-rely on it.

To address tasking risks, execution speeds of various tasking features should be measured on the target machines. Based on these measurements, contractor Risk Management Plans should provide a methodology for the use of tasking; should indicate how performance bottlenecks resulting from tasking will be avoided, and how they will be detected and attributed to tasking when they do occur; and should provide alternative paradigms that may have to be substituted for tasking.

Even ignoring its performance implications, Ada tasking has the same risks that apply to any other concurrency facility. The problems addressed by tasking are generally complex, and it is difficult to design solutions such that there is no possibility of deadlock, starvation, etc. among competing and cooperating tasks. Furthermore, tasking is one of the most difficult Ada features to learn. Therefore, there should be a methodology for its controlled use. Using tasking only where it is specifically needed can reduce the associated risks. When this is done, tasking expertise can be limited to a few senior designers for higher-level use, and need not be of concern to most of the coders as they implement lower levels of the code. Controlled use can also simplify debugging since tasking errors can be difficult to find and repair.

3.1.1.2 <u>Impact of Storage Management</u>. Industry experience indicates risks involved in meeting Ada's implicit need for the availability of a large contiguous memory. The use of overlay techniques on a 16-bit architecture may in all likelihood prove too restrictive. Therefore, hardware maturity would be evidenced by the availability of large contiguous memory. Moreover, the allocation and deallocation of storage for tasks and other dynamic entities is of concern.

To address these risks, run-time storage management (i.e., the allocation and deallocation of storage) and the amount of space required by the run-time support system should be checked. If this is not done, the amount of working storage for application software may be considerably less than was planned when the hardware memory was sized. It is further recommended that the Risk Management Plans use the results of such checks to show that the memory subsystems of the chosen hardware families are appropriate for Ada, or to indicate what work-arounds will be employed for overcoming the problems.

3.1.1.3 <u>Impact of Run-Time Support System</u>. Even if Ada's features, such as tasking, are used in an optimal fashion, and the compiler generates efficient code for them, the run-time support system on the target machines poses a run-time performance risk. System services, and the methods for invoking them, must be able to meet real-time requirements. This is, of course, true for any real-time system; it is of particular concern on an Ada development because of the newness of, and lack of experience with, the Ada run-time support systems.

3.1.1.4 <u>Impact of Under-Use or Over-Use of Non-Ada Code</u>. As noted earlier, there was unanimous agreement that in spite of all of Ada's advantages, there may still be areas of AAS that will require the use of non-Ada code. Low-level display software (but not the graphics applications built on top of it), device drivers, and in-line expansion of assembly language bit manipulation routines were cited as possible areas where non-Ada code may be needed for meeting real-time requirements. Anticipating such needs in a Risk Management Plan should be considered a positive sign of contractor awareness. Furthermore, the proposed use of commercially available tools should be considered positively, whether or not such tools happen to be written in Ada.

On the other hand, there is also the risk that performance will be used as a convenient excuse for justifying an over-reliance on non-Ada code. Since experience indicates that it is very difficult to anticipate where performance bottlenecks will develop, benchmarks should be used to help make this determination. Another possible approach is to design the entire system in Ada, providing Ada code for all package specifications. Then in those areas where performance becomes a problem, the package bodies can be recoded in another language, with the result that the non-Ada code will be developed in the context of an Ada design.

To address the above risks, the contractors' plans should include methodologies for using non-Ada code if required. These methodologies should also document which other languages will be used for the non-Ada code, and should reflect performance issues, as well as the difficulty of interfacing non-Ada code to Ada. For example, in some instances there are indications that interfacing to high order languages may be more difficult than interfacing to assembly language. This leads to three recommendations on non-Ada language selection:

- The FAA waiver process for using non-Ada code should be flexible enough to allow its use when appropriate.

- If a contractor has already identified where non-Ada code will be needed, through the use of benchmarks or other activities, or has at least developed the benchmarks for doing so, this should be considered positively.

- The methodologies should provide for tool sets that can be used in determining where performance bottlenecks arise.

  Demonstrations of the early availability of such tools and their level of sophistication should be part of the FAA's evaluation process.

3.1.1.5 <u>Summary of Real-Time Performance Risks</u>. As the discussion in the preceding subsections indicates, early risk reduction activities are needed to ensure that AAS real-time performance requirements can be met. These activities are needed to identify which risks are of serious concern in the hardware/software environment chosen by the contractor, whether or not Ada is used. If these concerns are not addressed by prior satisfactory experience with the same systems on similar projects, then benchmarks are needed. They should be used to determine how tasking and other paradigms are best employed, to identify memory constraints and work-arounds for them, to indicate where non-Ada code should be provided, and to determine whether the run-time support system can support large systems development.

3.1.2 <u>Meeting System Availability Requirements</u>

AAS has very stringent availability requirements, with only three seconds of down-time allowed per year. This is an area where Ada is seen as a strength. However, two aspects of the language--exceptions and elaboration--should be considered in designing the system, for they offer the potential to improve reliability. In addition, the run-time support subsystem, previously cited as a real-time performance risk, poses availability risks as well.

3.1.2.1 <u>Impact of Exceptions</u>. The first aspect of Ada to be considered with respect to reliability is the Ada exception feature, which is used to trap error conditions. In designing reliability into AAS, careful attention must be paid to such conditions, regardless of the chosen language. If Ada is used, the role for exceptions in handling these conditions must be considered. If all of the conditions are not considered, then Ada will perform default handling of the error, which may cause the error to propagate upward. This will result in loss of the local information needed for handling the error and could even stop the system. Note that such error effects are typical of other languages, which generally do not provide any exception-handling capability to the application programmer. Therefore, Ada provides the capability to eliminate system stoppage when an exception occurs, but there is considerable risk because it is very difficult to ensure that all possible exceptions have been properly anticipated.

Another concern regarding exceptions arises from compiler optimization, which can re-order, or even eliminate, statements in the object code. Thus the order in which exceptions are invoked, and the information that is available to the exception handlers, can be implementation-dependent. The result is a danger of unpredictable behavior. Furthermore, if some of the testing takes place on the development machines, there is a risk that development and target machines will optimize differently, resulting in different execution time behavior for the same code. (See also Section 3.4.5 for other risks involving differences between development and target machines.)

The contractors should show evidence of fully understanding how exception handling works on their machines. Their methodology should address mechanisms for dealing with the cited concerns and for using exceptions. Exceptions should be used for true error conditions, and not as a convenient way to implement normal occurrences, such as end-of-file or loop termination.

3.1.2.2 Impact of Elaboration. The second aspect of Ada that should be considered with respect to reliability is elaboration, a run-time process that takes place when a program unit is invoked. Depending upon the error-recovery techniques employed in AAS, the elaboration time during restarts of the system could be too time-consuming. Unless the compiler provides pre-elaboration (i.e., the results of the elaboration execution are mostly attained before the software is loaded into the target), stringent availability requirements may not be met.

3.1.2.3 Impact of Run-Time Support System. The run-time support system on target machines poses availability risks since it is the foundation upon which application code is executed. If bugs contained within such systems cause the software to abort, then meeting AAS availability requirements may be at risk, regardless of how bug-free the application code may be. The newness of the Ada run-time systems, coupled with their required high level of sophistication (Ada real-time support systems, unlike those associated with other high order languages, are effectively mini operating systems), makes this a particular concern. Even the compilers pose risks because their relative newness increases the likelihood that object code will be incorrectly generated from correct source code. Thus it is important that contractors demonstrate the reliability of their support systems and be sufficiently familiar with them to find work-arounds when troubles arise. Demonstrated previous use of the same hardware/software environments on large projects should be considered a plus.

However, regardless of what precautions are taken, the newness of the Ada environments increases the likelihood of bugs. Therefore, it is important that the contractors have a viable, documented plan for working with vendors and having problems fixed in a timely manner, as they arise (see also Section 3.4.6).

3.2 Risks Arising from AAS Software Size

The largeness of the AAS software—hundreds of thousands of lines of code—results in its own risks. These often arise because the experiences gained on small systems simply do not scale up to larger amounts of software in a practical amount of time. Although such risks would also arise in non-Ada developments, the use of Ada makes them potentially more troublesome because of the newness of the Ada compilers, environments, and tools.

3.2.1 Compiler Limits—a Key Problem Area

The first software size risk, which has caused significant problems on other procurements, is the ability of the compiler to handle large amounts of code in the context of the chosen hardware/software environment. For example, a compiler may work quite well on a small- to medium-sized application, but run out of internal heap space without warning when a very large compilation is attempted. It is therefore essential that benchmarks be applied early for stressing the large system aspects of the chosen compiler, on exactly the same hardware/software environment that will be used for application code development.

Several options must be considered in choosing such benchmarks. First, it must be determined which ones will be chosen by the contractor and which by the FAA. For those chosen by the FAA, a previous large Ada project could be supplied. The contractors would make minimal modifications and then compile the benchmark to demonstrate that the compiler correctly handles large quantities of code. Another possibility for an FAA-supplied benchmark is a synthetic one whose overall characteristics (e.g., number of packages, number of procedures per package, nesting depth, interdependencies arising from "with" statements) are similar to those anticipated for AAS. Since such a benchmark is intended as a compilation test and not as a run-time test, stubs could be provided for the package bodies. In some cases, these stubs could be constructed in such a way that they would stress the compiler for memory space or for time.

Even if the compiler has no internal size limitations, its speed may result in de facto limits as to how much code can be handled. The same is true for the linker, library manager, and other tools: they may be too slow to handle large volumes of code. Thus benchmarks are needed on all these development tools to ascertain how quickly they can handle large volumes of code.

Other types of compiler limits manifest themselves at run time. For example, a compiler implementation may support a limited amount of dynamically spawned tasks. These limits should be known early in the procurement, so that designs can be constrained to remain within these limits, or steps taken to increase them.

3.2.2 Resource Adequacy of Development and Target Machines

The adequacy of computing resources is another risk because Ada developments typically require more development resources than do non-Ada ones, partly because of the large amounts of checking that must be performed by the compiler. (This should not be confused with the efficiency of the generated code; in fact, the more efficient the generated code is on the target machines, the more computing resources are required to produce it on the development machines.) In effect, one is trading off large personnel costs and time at integration for more complete computer checking throughout the software development. Machine time is traded for human labor, and reliability is gained in the process.

An important aspect of resource adequacy is how the contractors intend to proceed with their designs. Because of the interdependencies among modules arising from the use of "with" statements, a small system change can result in large recompilation ripple effects; total recompilations of a week's duration or longer have been observed for very large systems with slow compilers. Early benchmarks should be carried out indicating the time required for such recompilations. Furthermore, the development methodology should address this issue and display an awareness of the need for stable top-level designs before larger staffs are brought on board for parallel development activities: a week of idle time forced by total recompilation is more costly the larger the team size. Other issues to be addressed by the methodology include the necessity for deferring some design changes until the next major recompilation, the use of incremental compilers, and the availability of tools that indicate what the effects of a particular change will be. This information, combined with compilation speed benchmark results, enables management to make informed decisions about proceeding with design changes or deferring them.

There is also a need to address the adequacy of computing resources on host and target machines. One concern, for example, is that sufficient disk space must be provided to hold the anticipated number of system releases (including source code, object code, and on-line documentation) that will be required at any given time. By comparing the planned resource usage with that actually encountered, controlled resource growth over the project life cycle can be achieved. The adequacy of the computing resources for the number of development personnel and the anticipated number of recompilations must be considered as well. This includes central processing unit (CPU) speeds, the amount of memory, and the number of workstations to be made available. Again, tracking of projections with actual experience provides the mechanism for informed growth planning.

3.3 FAA Readiness for Contract Monitoring

Considering the newness of Ada technology and the many differences inherent in an Ada development process, there is a risk on any Ada procurement that the customer will not be ready to award the contract or to monitor and manage the project. An understanding of Ada and software engineering is needed so that contractor and customer can communicate, with the result that the activities, the design notation, and the items being tracked (e.g., number of package specifications) have meaning for the customer. Furthermore, there is a risk that lack of readiness could jeopardize the development process. For example, unnecessary deliverables could be called for, or a contractor could be unfairly penalized for identifying and proposing positive risk reduction activities.

Contractor readiness is also needed to make informed decisions about waivers for the use of non-Ada code (see Section 3.1.1.4), and to tailor DOD-STD-2167. In the latter case, there is a risk of not allowing the contractor to tailor this standard towards an Ada development process.

3.4 Software Support System Risks

Software support systems are the foundation upon which code is developed and executed. Thus they are a key concern—on both the development and target machines. Always a risk item, they are especially so on an Ada development because of their newness. This is particularly true on the target machines, since vendors often put most of their emphasis on the development environment; support for the target machine may be limited to a cross-compiler back-end for their product line. The result can be a "bare-bones" target environment not suitable for testing and running a large system.

Indeed, the history of Ada indicates that a likely problem area is the unavailability of environments with adequate maturity; this has been the cause of failures on past projects. Therefore, an early assessment, such as through the use of benchmarking, is made of the environments. If they prove to be unacceptable, there is still time to find alternatives; if their inadequacies are manageable, steps can be taken to find work-arounds or to have the environments mature on the job through corrective measures.

Guidance in addressing environment risks is available. For example, the Software Engineering Institute is working on criteria for evaluating environments, and the National Aeronautics and Space Administration (NASA) Space Shuttle program has undertaken development of its own Software Support Environment.

3.4.1 Functionality

There is a risk that insufficient functionality will be available in the support environment. This risk pertains whether or not Ada is used. In fact, incomplete toolsets are a common problem in the software industry. On an Ada development, this may be especially true since the newness of the technology means inadequate time may have been available for developing the toolsets. (See also Section 2.1.6.3 for a characterization of an Ada toolset.)

3.4.2 Performance

As discussed in Sections 3.1.1.3 and 3.1.2.3, the support systems present risks for meeting real-time and availability requirements.

3.4.3 Maturity

Ada technology has clearly advanced to the point where production quality compilers are available for use on a wide range of computer architectures. Nonetheless, the maturity of a compiler and its associated tools and environment remains a concern for any particular hardware suite; overall maturity of the technology is of little solace if the technology is unavailable, or is not of production quality, on the hardware chosen for the application. "Maturity" is hard to define, but implies, at a minimum, being bug-free, having the ability to work with large amounts of code, and offering a comprehensive set of tools. Validation of a compiler is necessary, but validation alone is insufficient to ensure production quality.

A mechanism for handling exponential compile time growth would be considered evidence of maturity. Elaboration should be optimized for real-time systems. A demonstrated mechanism or technique for interfacing with other languages should be available.

Since maturity cannot be achieved rapidly (e.g., several years are needed for compilers to attain maturity), prior successful use of the exact hardware/software environment on other large projects is advan-

tageous. If this experience is not available, then other techniques
(e.g., benchmarks) will be needed. Early availability (see
Section 3.4.4) and contractor preparedness for modifications (see
Section 3.4.6) will also allow maturity to be achieved.

3.4.4 Early Availability on Development and Target Machines

The early availability of a run-time support system, on both target
and host machines, is essential. Although such availability is strongly
recommended regardless of what language is used, it is especially
important for Ada: because of the difficulty in producing Ada compilers,
there is a history of projects never achieving access to satisfactory
compilers and support systems for the chosen hardware/software environments. Therefore, an early demonstration of such availability should be
required of the contractors. Such demonstration should include
satisfactory results from the compiler sizing benchmarks discussed in
Section 3.2.1.

3.4.5 Portability

Although it is not anticipated that AAS code will be reused on other
projects, two types of portability within AAS are of concern. The first
of these--the ability to transfer code from development to target
machines--is essential if some of the testing takes place on development
machines. The second type--the ability to transfer code from one major
subsystem (e.g., the Initial Sector Suite System [ISSS]) and reuse it on
another (e.g., the Tower Control Computer Complex [TCCC])--is desirable.

Many Ada features were designed to enhance portability, and the use
of a validation suite was intended to enforce it. Indeed, Ada is more
portable than other high order languages. Nonetheless, operating system
dependencies remain, and Chapter 13 of the Ada language reference manual
(U.S. Department of Defense, 1983), allows for machine dependencies. For
example, code optimization schemes used by the compiler may result in
different run-time behavior for exceptions on development and target
machines. The contractors should demonstrate an awareness of these
differences, perhaps through the use of benchmarks.

In order to ensure that the developed code will run on the target
machines, the contractors should provide an early assessment of the
commonality of Ada's implementation-specific aspects on target and
development machines. The results of such an assessment should be
incorporated in their methodology guidelines on minimizing the use of
implementation-specific features. Where such features are necessary,
their use should be limited to the common intersection only.

In some cases, such an assessment may indicate that an essential
feature is lacking. If this is so, then early access to such information
allows the contractor to have this feature developed in a timely fashion,
or to find alternative compilers. The commonality assessment can also
address the impact of optimization on such items as exception handling
(see Section 3.1.2.1), testing, and program correctness.

3.4.6 Contractor Preparedness for Inevitable Modifications

Early demonstrations of tool capabilities, such as through the use
of benchmarks, are considered important since surprise limitations late

in the life cycle can have disastrous consequences. However, it is realized that, even given very good early risk reduction awareness and associated activities, some tailoring of the environments to the system being developed is inevitable on systems as large as AAS. (This is true whether or not Ada is employed.) Thus the contractors should document in their plans an approach for addressing problems when they arise, and should allocate sufficient time and money resources for proceeding with the documented approach. One attractive solution, which has been used previously, is to have all tool and environment vendors under subcontract on the procurement, in order to ensure responsiveness. It may even be desirable to provide them with work areas on the contractor's development system so they can verify and fix bugs quickly. This is preferable to a cumbersome Problem Trouble Reporting procedure in which difficulties must be overcome in reproducing bugs on a different system before the bugs can be fixed.

To summarize, an indication that troubles are anticipated in the support environments should not be considered a weakness in the proposals, but rather realistic addressing of a risk. This is not a contradiction to the early availability recommendation in Section 3.4.4: enabling existing environments/compilers to mature is acceptable; developing new ones from scratch is not.

3.5 Personnel Risks

Several risks regarding contractor personnel have been identified, as discussed below.

3.5.1 Ada, Software Engineering, and Large System Experience

For the contractors to proceed successfully with AAS, it is necessary that staff have sufficient experience and training. Software engineering training is needed--not just Ada training. The Ada experts repeatedly stressed to the study participants that such training is needed for management personnel as well as for development personnel. (See also Section 3.3 on the importance of a prepared customer.)

Sufficient lead time must be allowed for the requisite expertise to be acquired. For example, estimates range from six months to several years for the time needed to get programmers up to speed on Ada and the associated methodologies. Thus a one-week training course after contract award, while better than nothing, does not suffice.

3.5.2 Staffing Profile with a Small Experienced Front End

In order to achieve the full benefits of a sound software engineering approach, including a stable top-level design with well-defined inter-faces, a small team of experienced designers is needed up front. Again, sufficient lead-time is needed for bringing this team on board, and more than Ada experience is required. Judicious use of such people up front allows successful deployment of a much larger team of less experienced personnel later in the life cycle.

3.5.3 Commitment to AAS and Retaining the Team

The contractors should indicate a commitment to retaining key personnel needed to exercise control over the design and implementation throughout the project (see Section 2.1.2). For example, it is important

that the participants in a software engineering exercise (see
Section 4.3) continue to play key roles throughout the development
process. Because of the relative scarcity of Ada personnel, attrition
issues, always a problem on software development, are particularly acute.
The contractor needs to indicate what incentives will be used to retain
key personnel and how personnel will be replaced if lost.

3.5.4 Subcontracting Approach

The relationship of the contractor to its subcontractor personnel is
important. All training and experience requirements that apply to the
contractor apply equally to the subcontractors. The latter should,
moreover, be as proficient as the contractor in the chosen software
development methodology, and their use of it should be enforced. Software development methodologies should show how the subcontractors are
truly part of the development team (e.g., indicate their participation in
the design and review process).

The contractor/subcontractor relationship is of concern on any
procurement. The newness of Ada methodologies that allow full realization
of the Ada potential makes this relationship of particular concern on an
Ada development effort.

3.5.5 Commitment to Tool Usage, Including Management Tools

A sophisticated toolset is no advantage if it goes unused. For
example, simply dropping a six-inch user manual on a manager's desk will
not be sufficient to guarantee use of a project tracking tool. Training
can be considered evidence of a commitment to using the provided tools.
Another indicator is a track record of prior usage, which also helps
ensure tool maturity.

3.6 Management Risks

Strong, disciplined management is essential for success in any large
software development process. For example, all personnel must be familiar
with, and use, the chosen methodology. The managers must understand the
methodology well enough to enforce it, and to permit refinements when,
but only when, they are necessary. As new personnel are brought into the
project, they, too, must become part of the project culture.

One of the advantages of an Ada development process is that prototyping and the rigorous design notation will make design flaws more
readily apparent earlier in the development process. However, realizing
the benefit of this potential advantage requires that the contractor have
flexible management to act upon this information. As work at lower
levels of the project reveals top-level design flaws, management must be
willing to back up and correct the higher-level problems. Flexible
management is also needed to forgo the use of the design methodology in
the limited number of cases where it is not applicable; for example,
object-oriented design may not be appropriate in implementing well-defined
communications protocols. Furthermore, nice-to-have, but inessential,
design changes may have to be deferred to reduce the number of major
recompilations. Management flexibility is also needed in approaching the
use of non-Ada code. For example, even though guidelines may suggest the
use of C over assembly language for implementing a certain function, the
use of assembly language may be necessary if productivity will suffer
because of difficulties in interfacing the C code to Ada.

Implicit in the preceding discussion on the need for flexible contractor management is that FAA procedures allow for this flexibility to occur without the contractors' expending undue effort in gaining permission. Even if the contractors have properly approached the use of non-Ada code, they may perceive an implied stigma in asking the FAA for waivers from using a single language. Also, as noted in Section 3.1.1.4, the FAA waiver process for using non-Ada code should be flexible enough to allow it to be invoked when appropriate. Moreover, timely FAA responses to requests for waivers should be given. Thus the FAA may want to consider the use of general guidelines rather than case-by-case waivers.

3.7 Schedule and Cost Risks

3.7.1 No Historical Data Available

Schedule and cost risks, always high on a software procurement, are increased for an Ada development. The newness of Ada means that no major procurements have gone through an entire Ada development process, including the maintenance phase. Thus there is no familiar application or environment that can be used for guidance in generating AAS cost and schedule estimates. This is the foremost cost and schedule risk resulting from the use of Ada.

3.7.2 Lines of Code a Poor Estimation Technique

Software estimation techniques have traditionally centered around lines of code estimates. There has always been controversy as to what constitutes a "line of code": Should comments be included? blank lines? data statements or only executable lines of code? Unfortunately, the situation is worse in Ada. The most apparent, but probably least important, complication is that there is not a one-to-one mapping between Ada statements and source lines. For example, an if-then-else statement can span multiple lines; conversely, multiple statements can appear on the same line, although this practice is generally frowned upon. An easy solution to this problem is simply to count semicolons. However, this solution ignores more significant issues. The extreme strong typing in Ada requires that all data structures be clearly laid out in "type" statements and that all variables be declared. This is not done in some of the older languages such as FORTRAN and JOVIAL. The cost and schedule effects of producing such statements, relative to the effects of producing a line of executable code, have yet to be determined. Fortunately, past experiences in Pascal may provide guidance in this area. Conventions, such as those provided in Boehm, 1981 (p. 59), should be established for counting lines of code. Whatever convention is chosen, its consistent use throughout the project life cycle is essential.

A more significant issue is how to count package specifications, since there are no corresponding constructs in other languages. At first glance, specifications may seem somewhat insignificant since, in size, they may be only one-quarter to one-third as large as the corresponding package bodies. However, this perception is deceptive, because they are more difficult to write. This, in turn, is because they embody important design aspects such as encapsulation, information hiding, and data abstraction, and even form the structure of the overall software architecture. In fact, they may often be written by the design team early in the project, and are thus not produced during the formal coding process. Furthermore, some of the information in package specifications is repeated if there is a corresponding body. Should such code be counted doubly? Again, there is no right answer here, but at a minimum the contractors should show awareness of the problems and provide an intelligent means for addressing them. Counting the semicolons may be a naive approach.

By far the most serious impact on estimation techniques is the use of Ada generics. When properly used, generics are a boon to productivity, since a single line of code can be used to tailor and reuse ("instantiate") a code template generated elsewhere on the project. How such instantiated code should be counted is an open question--as a single line of code, or as the perhaps thousands of lines that it generates? Even writing the generic template poses estimation problems, since writing such a template takes somewhat more effort than writing the equivalent nongeneric version; the payoff comes in its reuse. Because of these difficulties, on some previous Ada procurements, contractors used other estimates (e.g., staff months), and then "backed out" an equivalent line of code measure corresponding to the the measure being used. Such "lines of code" might correspond to the number that would have been produced on, say, a FORTRAN project; however, they do not necessarily correspond to those actually produced on an Ada procurement. Unfortunately, we have no experience to serve as a basis for mapping FORTRAN lines of code into those for Ada, or for determining the relative amounts of effort needed to produce them.

In summary, the limited past history with Ada means that there is no prior project experience to draw on; such historical data are the cornerstone of popularly used commercial models. In lieu of this experience database, one is forced to resort to analogous experience with other languages. However, the more significant the estimation problem becomes, the less guidance is available in relating this problem to experiences gained with other software development languages. Nonetheless, if Ada is to be used on AAS, the FAA may want to consider alternative measurement techniques. Ada-oriented measures, such as number of completed package specifications or bodies, may be more appropriate. The advantage of using such Ada-tailored techniques is that the same ones can be employed throughout the life cycle, including the design phase, to derive early quantitative measures of progress.

3.7.3 Impact of Ada Methodology and Milestones

The revised milestones resulting from incremental development provide a natural development progression, reflecting the fact that different parts of the system achieve maturity and completion at different times. However, this approach tends to blur the distinction between various phases. Again, there are no historical data available to indicate the resultant cost and schedule impact.

3.7.4 Tracking

The ability to track a project is essential since such feedback can be used to provide early warning of needed changes. Past experience indicates that far too often, both contractor and customer fail to track progress and update costs based upon that tracking. Failure to track could be especially troublesome on an Ada development, because the lack of prior experience makes initial estimates less reliable.

Thus it is strongly recommended that both contractor and customer commit to a tracking process that will enable them to learn from the experience database being generated throughout the procurement. At all times, indicators of planned vs. actual progress should be available. Machine-readable deliverables provide the opportunity for doing this with the assistance of automation; for example, the number of package specifications (planned and actual) could be tracked vs. time.

In summary, to realize the tracking potential offered by an Ada-oriented development requires the following:

- That the proper measures be defined

- That the proper tools for providing these measures be developed

- That both contractor and customer commit to using these tools in a tracking process

3.8 Other Risk Areas

Several other risk areas have been identified, as discussed below.

3.8.1 User Interface and Graphics

Acceptance of the finished AAS product by air traffic control personnel is essential for its success. Achieving such acceptance, and meeting the goal of increased controller productivity, requires an outstanding user interface to the system, regardless of the language used to implement it. Such interface development requires multiple iterations with the controllers in the loop. Thus the use of prototyping is strongly encouraged in this area. As is noted earlier in Section 3.6, management flexibility is the key; the ability to back up and address mistakes is particularly crucial. One possible impediment to such flexibility would be the use of a fixed-cost contract (see Sections 5.5 and 5.6). Since a requirement such as "be user friendly" is difficult to define precisely, the use of a fixed-cost approach in this area can easily lead to a "design to cost" solution.

Another risk in this area is the question of whether Ada is the most appropriate language for implementing graphics; as assessment may be needed to determine whether another high order language or assembly language would be more appropriate, at least for the low-level routines such as device drivers.

3.8.2 Ada Orientation of Design Specifications

One risk is that the design specifications will not be suited to an Ada procurement. The RFP should allow for, and the contractors should propose, machine-readable deliverables that are a natural consequence of a compilable design process. Other types of deliverables could be worse than useless; not only are they costly, but their production detracts from the more meaningful work that is needed.

3.8.3 Ada Orientation of Software Development Plans

The methodologies proposed in the Software Development Plans should show cognizance of, and exploit, the many differences that will result with an Ada procurement. A "business as usual" proposal will mean that

473

all of Ada's risks will be inherent in the procurement without the offsetting advantages.

3.9 Risk Summary

The proper use of Ada can reduce some of the risks on a large software development described in this section. However, the residual risks that remain must be addressed. This section of the report has focused on specific risk items organized into eight general areas. Wherever possible, solutions addressing the specific risk items have been proposed. In Section 4, some general risk reduction activities are recommended for addressing risks in a broader context.

4.0 ADDRESSING THE RISKS

This section of the report recommends five general risk reduction activities: Risk Management Plans, Software Development Plans, a software engineering exercise, compilable designs, and benchmarks. If properly carried out, they can minimize the effects of the risks identified in Section 3.

4.1 Require Contractors to Develop Risk Management Plans

Recommendation: The contractors should be required to submit Risk Management Plans as part of their proposals.

The Risk Management Plans should address each of the risk items identified in Section 3 of this report; in addition, they should identify and address other risks. For each item, the following material should be included in the plans:

- Documentation of the item, including an indication of its significance

- A risk resolution approach, including milestones and schedules

- Assignment of responsibility to individuals or organizations

- Identification of the resources (personnel, computing, and other) required for addressing the risk item

The plans for the individual items should be coordinated with each other and with the overall Software Development Plan.

4.2 Require Contractors to Develop Software Development Plans

Recommendation: The contractors should be required to submit Ada-oriented Software Development Plans as part of their proposals.

Any program as large and complex as AAS should require a Software Development Plan, encompassing material beyond the scope of this study. Nonetheless, the plan should indicate how Ada will affect the software development process and should include the following Ada-oriented material:

- A methodology showing how Ada is used, including the following:

  - Use of the the language's tasking, exception, and generic features

  - An approach for handling the ripple effects arising from redesign

  - An approach towards total recompilations

- A substantial tailoring of DOD-STD-2167, if that standard is used on AAS

- An emphasis on the use of benchmarks, prototyping, and incremental development, with a clear indication of the relationship between the results of these activities and the overall methodology

- An approach for using non-Ada code (see Section 3.1.1.4 for specific recommendations)

- A discussion on the use of Ada-oriented tools

- A method for transferring the Ada technology and methodologies to all the subcontractors involved in the software development effort

- An approach for reusable software that includes the following:

  - Development of reusable software

  - Identification and incorporation of available reusable software

To summarize, the Software Development Plan should contain material that characterizes a sound development approach, such as the one described in Section 2 of this report. Its contents should be familiar to all development personnel, and its use should be enforced throughout the software development.

4.3 Conduct a Software Engineering Exercise

Recommendation: A software engineering exercise should be conducted.

A software engineering exercise (sometimes informally termed a "contractor take-home exam") is a novel approach to risk reduction. The recommendation for its use is based on initial indications of its viability and success.

Briefly, in conducting a software engineering exercise, the FAA would define a software problem that the contractors would then be asked to solve. In carrying out the exercise, the contractors would be required to use their AAS personnel, their software methodologies, and their toolsets. More details follow.

The study participants recognize that they are not familiar with the detailed software progress to date by the design competition contractors, the software related deliverables provided during the course of the competition, or the detailed plans for expected deliverables to the time of contract award. As a result, the actual performance of the software exercise by the contractors may vary from the description below, but the intent of the exercise is very significant, and its conduct should be required by the FAA.

4.3.1 Description of the Exercise

A software engineering exercise would be carried out as described below.

4.3.1.1 <u>Preparing the Exercise</u>. First, the FAA would prepare a short problem statement, perhaps four pages, defining the requirements for a relatively small-scale software development effort. It is important that such a problem statement be tailored towards the AAS application, addressing some of the perceived risks of AAS. In fact, if properly constructed, the exercise could have spin-offs, perhaps a prototype, that would have been developed anyway, somewhere else on the AAS procurement. Thus, problem statements written for exercises on other procurements are probably not appropriate for AAS.

It should be noted that preparing the problem statement would not be an easy undertaking. If the problem were too simple, the results could be misleading: the contractor could use a few expert software engineers for the exercise, whose performance would not be indicative of what could be expected from the entire contracting team on the AAS procurement. Conversely, if the exercise were too complex, then little progress would be made on it during the limited time allowed. (Even worse, so much time and effort could be devoted to the exercise that it would detract from the overall AAS development effort.)

To best ensure that the problem statement is of proper scope, it is strongly recommended that an FAA team dry run the exercise before presenting it to the contractors. Doing so could uncover defects in the problem statement, so it could be revised before presentation to the contractors. A dry run could also provide the FAA with insight into the problem, allowing for better evaluation of the contractors' results.

4.3.1.2 <u>Conducting the Exercise</u>. The contractors would be given the problem statement and asked to carry it out. Only a limited amount of time, perhaps three weeks, would be allotted for this purpose. To obtain meaningful results, it is essential that the exercise employ key AAS personnel who will be involved on the actual procurement, as well as the software development methodologies and toolsets defined in the Software Development Plan. Typically, ten contractor staff members, including subcontractor representation, would be involved.

During the exercise, the contractors' activities would be in the form of an inverted triangle. That is, compilable Ada would be used to develop the following: a top-level design and software architecture for the entire problem, a partial detailed design, and code for perhaps one key thread. The entire effort would be documented in accordance with AAS documentation standards.

4.3.1.3 <u>Timing of the Exercise</u>. The exercise would be carried out after proposal submission, but before contract award. Thus, the contractors would not have to split their team between two activities-- responding to the RFP and carrying out the exercise. Furthermore, the software engineering exercise activities would then dovetail nicely with other procurement activities: while the contractors are preparing their responses to the RFP, the FAA can be preparing the exercise. Then while the FAA is performing technical evaluation of the proposals, the contractors can be carrying out the exercise.

It is suggested that the exercise be required as an adjunct to the RFP response; however, it could be FAA-funded as part of the DCP risk reduction activities taking place between April 1987 and the Acquisition Phase contract award.

4.3.1.4 <u>Evaluating the Exercise</u>. The final step of the exercise would be an FAA evaluation of the exercise results, in accordance with AAS contract monitoring procedures.

4.3.2 <u>Results of the Exercise</u>

A software engineering exercise would have several results. First, it would provide a test of the contractors' planned methodologies; this is because the contractors would be required to adhere to those methodologies in carrying out the exercise. Second, it would provide a test of the contractors' ability to design and implement software using their methodologies. Third, the results could be used by the FAA as technical criteria for assessment in making the Acquisition Phase contract award, as an adjunct to the technical evaluation of the proposals. Finally, the exercise could result in an improved Software Development Plan; any contractor activities deviating from those laid out in the plan during this, its initial use, would have to be documented.

4.3.3 <u>Benefits of the Exercise</u>

There are many benefits to be realized from conducting a software engineering exercise.

First, by requiring that the contractors adhere to their Software Development Plans, the FAA would, in effect, be requiring them to turn "dead" paper plans into living methodologies. In so doing, the contractors would undoubtedly find flaws in those plans. Thus, necessary revisions to the plans should be allowed, provided that such revisions are well documented and become part of the final Software Development Plans used on AAS. This would result in better, partially tested, methodologies for use on the actual procurement. Similarly, problems with the various toolsets could be identified early, thereby removing them from the critical path of the AAS development effort.

Another benefit resulting from the exercise is that contractor and subcontractor personnel would be forced to become familiar with the methodologies and tools they had proposed for use on AAS. Thus the exercise team members would become experts who would serve as an important nucleus of expertise for the larger procurement effort. The exercise would also serve as a partial mechanism for keeping the integrated software team together and current on AAS during the time between proposal submission and contract award.

A corresponding benefit would result for FAA personnel: based on their experiences in evaluating the exercise results, the FAA would gain familiarity with its own contract monitoring procedures, and could modify them if necessary. As part of this evaluation, the FAA could assess the adequacy of the deliverable requirements, and determine whether they should be altered. A spin-off benefit of the exercise is that an FAA dry-run of it would provide valuable training in software engineering and in Ada.

Another benefit is that the exercise results would provide the FAA with an opportunity to observe how the two contractors perform on a real-world problem. Proposing compilable PDL designs is desirable, but actually producing them on such a problem would provide greater assurances.

Finally, FAA review of the exercise would indicate whether the Software Development Plans were followed and how many revisions were needed to carry out the exercise. This could, in turn, indicate the viability of the plans and of the contractors' commitment to using them.

4.4 Require Compilable Designs

Recommendation: The AAS contractors should be required to develop compilable Ada designs for their proposed systems and deliver them to the FAA in machine-readable format.

As discussed in Section 2, compilable designs are an essential part of an Ada software development. They may also be considered part of the risk reduction activities. Therefore, this recommendation on compilable designs stands even if it means that some or all of the existing designs must be redone.

A corollary to this recommendation is that the FAA should thoroughly review the Ada designs. This review should include verification of compilability, and a check of how much of the design appears in comments as opposed to how much is expressed in Ada. In effect, an Ada-oriented PDR is called for. The size of this activity is not necessarily as large as it may at first appear. Because of the compactness and rigor of Ada notation, it is anticipated that a redesign in Ada would be considerably more compact than any corresponding English-oriented designs that may previously have been produced. Furthermore, if a moderately sophisticated toolset were employed, much of the deliverable documentation could be generated automatically from the Ada designs, and would not have to be regenerated.

As noted earlier, compilable top-level designs are considered a big plus. Their advantages include providing evidence of the contractors' ability to perform, providing early consistency checking of the design, and providing the opportunity for the use of tools as part of the FAA reviews. For more details on these and other advantages, see Section 2.2.3.

4.5 Benchmarks Should be Used

Recommendation: Benchmarks should be required for use in addressing many of the identified risks.

Benchmarks were previously suggested as a means of achieving risk reduction for many of the items discussed in Section 3. For the contractors, they identify problem areas, which can then be remedied; for the FAA, they provide an indication of contractor readiness. Because of their importance, benchmarks are discussed in some detail in the following three subsections.

4.5.1 Use of Benchmarks on Development Machines

On the development machines, early application of benchmarks is needed to address the large system size aspects of the AAS procurement. For example, the compilers should be stressed to their limits to find out how large a system they can successfully compile.

Similarly, the library and configuration management tools should be stressed to determine their adequacy for a large system procurement. Since there will be a large team of developers, the tool assessment should include tests of simultaneous access by multiple users.

Early benchmarks demonstrating the functionality of the support environment should be carried out as well. These can be used to generate changes to the system in time for development activities.

Benchmarks measuring performance are needed for ascertaining how much code can be compiled within a given amount of time. Measurements on disk space, and on memory and CPU utilization, are needed. A determination can thereby be made as to the adequacy of the hardware resources assigned to development personnel.

4.5.2 Use of Benchmarks on Target Machines

The large system aspect of AAS should also be addressed by target machine benchmarks. For example, if spawned tasks are to be used, then the run-time limit of the number of such tasks that can be run on the target machine must be ascertained, and the system design constrained to be within those limits. Similarly, memory limitations should be ascertained.

Target machines frequently have only "bare-bones" environments, as contrasted with the often much richer environments on the development machines. Thus benchmarks addressing the adequacy of the development machine toolset are needed.

AAS must run under the framework of the target machine run-time support system. Thus this system poses risks with regard to both performance and reliability, and benchmarks are needed to address these two areas. Performance measures on the target machine can be used in determining how best to employ tasking; the results from similar benchmarks on the development machine would be largely meaningless. These performance measures can also ascertain memory constraints imposed by the hardware, and determine whether enough memory has been provided. In addition, performance measures can give an indication of where non-Ada code should be used. Benchmarks illustrating the best mechanisms for interfacing to non-Ada code are needed as well.

Fairly elaborate benchmarks may be needed to test graphics and the user interface. For example, as part of the efforts involved in prototyping various user interfaces, measurements of the graphics hardware performance (e.g., time needed to refresh a screen or to zoom) should be obtained.

4.5.3 Use of Benchmarks That Run on Both Machines

Benchmarks that run on both development and target machines are needed to identify which Ada features are supported differently on the two machines. Results from early application of such benchmarks can be be fed back into the Software Development Plans and methodologies. In some cases, this information would take the form of prohibitions (e.g., "Don't use feature X because it is not supported on all the machines."). In other cases, some restrictions might have to be invoked (e.g., "The largest-sized array that will fit on all machines is <n> words; thus no array should be larger than that, even though there is no practical limit to the size of arrays on the development machines."). Assuming the availability of adequate documentation, these benchmarks might be simple verifications of documented limits.

4.6 Summary

The use of Ada, or any other language, on a large systems development has many inherent risks. However, recent experience indicates that these risks are manageable if properly addressed. To this end, the above recommendations for risk reduction activities have been provided.

REFERENCES

Boehm, Barry W (1981), Software Engineering Economics, Englewood Cliffs, NJ: Prentice-Hall.

Booch, Grady (1987), Software Engineering with Ada, Menlo Park, CA: The Benjamin/Cummings Publishing Company.

Bryan, Doug (January, February 1987), "Dear Ada", Ada Letters, VII:1, pp. 25-28.

Buhr, R.J. (1984), System Design with Ada, Englewood Cliffs, NJ: Prentice-Hall, Inc.

Castor, Virginia L. (1985), Issues To Be Considered in The Evaluation of Technical Proposals from The Ada Language Perspective, AFWAL-TR-85-1100, Wright-Patterson Air Force Base, OH.

Humphrey, W.S. et al. (1987), Assessing the Software Engineering Capability of Contractors, Pittsburgh, PA: Software Engineering Institute.

The Institute of Electrical and Electronics Engineers, Inc, IEEE Recommended Practice for Ada As a Program Design Language, IEEE Std 990-1987, New York, NY.

U.S. Air Force (1984), Software Development Capability/Capacity Review, Wright-Patterson Air Force Base, OH.

U.S. Army (1984), Ada Training Curriculum, Fort Monmouth, NJ: Center For Tactical Computer Systems.

Weiderman, Nelson et al. (1987), Evaluation of Ada Environments, Pittsburgh, PA: Software Engineering Institute.

U.S. Department of Defense (17 February 1983), Reference Manual for the Ada Programming Language, ANSI/MIL-STD-1815A-1983.

The Management of Risk in System Development: 'Project SP' and the 'New Spiral Model'

J. Gerard Wolff

School of Electronic Engineering Science, University of Wales, Dean Street,
Bangor, Gwynedd, LL57 1UT, UK. Telephone: +44 248 351151 ext 2691.

1: Abstract

The article discusses the development of complex products, with a particular emphasis on software, and focuses on the problem of how to manage the risks in the development process.

A number of models of the development process are described including Boehm's Spiral Model, which has risk management as a central theme.

An example is described where Boehm's Spiral Model has been tried. The strengths and weaknesses of the model are discussed in the light of this experience.

In the last part of the article, a notation called 'Project SP' is presented as a means of recording the progressively growing knowledge base of a project and the areas of uncertainty and associated risk.

Also described is the New Spiral Model, derived from Boehm's model and designed to be used in conjunction with Project SP. The New Spiral Model appears to preserve the advantages of the previous model and appears to remedy its weaknesses.

Associated issues are described and discussed.

2: Introduction

Many products of modern technology — cars, aeroplanes, computing systems — have proved to be very useful. But the development of products like these is complicated — and there are risks [11]. There are many examples — from Concord to Nimrod — to illustrate the hazards in the development of new complex systems. In the software industry — which is what I know best — cost overruns and the wasted effort represented by projects which are abandoned at a late stage, or whose deliverables are never used, are notorious.

This article considers the process of designing and developing complicated systems, especially software, and discusses how the risks in development and the overall cost of development can be minimised.

In many ways, software provides a paradigm for all kinds of design and development. Software is pure information and, as such, it captures the essence of all kinds of design. Software systems are often very complicated (although the same is increasingly true of integrated circuits). The main difference between software and hardware systems is that, with software, there is no significant process of 'production'. Once the design is complete, multiple copies may be made very easily. This difference has some bearing on the design process — and this will be briefly discussed. But the model of design and development proposed in this article is general enough to cover all kinds of system.

In the next section I briefly examine a small range of models of design and development giving special attention to Boehm's 'Spiral Model' and its approach to the management of risk. Then I describe and discuss a project at Praxis (where I was employed until recently) where the Spiral Model has been tried. In the following section, the New Spiral Model is presented. It is derived from the Spiral Model and includes a notation, called 'Project SP', for tracking the status of a project from start to finish. The article concludes with a discussion of some related issues.

3: Models of System Development

In order to manage any kind of system development, including small projects, it is necessary to have some kind of model of the development process, preferably one which is explicit and precise. In this section, I will first briefly review some of the more popular models and then I will describe and discuss Boehm's Spiral Model at more length.

- **The Waterfall Model:** This model of system development (see, for example, [4]) is one of the oldest and is still popular. In this model, a project proceeds in an essentially fixed sequence of 'stages'. A typical sequence is:

1. Project inception: defining objectives and constraints on the project.
2. Planning.
3. Specification of requirements for the system.
4. Design meaning definition of the software at some high level of abstraction.
5. Coding, meaning the production of an executable program.
6. Testing and integration.
7. Release of the system to the client.

At any stage (except the first) it is possible to return to the previous stage and rework it. More radical backtracking is discouraged because of the management problems which that entails.

The Waterfall Model marries naturally with the principle of *top-down design*. In top-down design, there is a more or less fixed progression in the design process from the definition of the largest abstract components of the design to the progressively more detailed elaboration of each part and its component parts. As with the Waterfall Model, some backtracking is accommodated, provided it is not too radical.

- **The Two-Legged Model:** In this model (see, for example, [7]) the process of design and development is divided into two 'legs': 'abstraction' and 'reification'. Abstraction leads from users' requirements to a formal specification of a system while reification is a process of progressively translating a specification into some kind of runnable 'implementation'. This translation process is sometimes called 'refinement'.

  Associated with the concepts of abstraction and reification are the concepts of 'validation' and 'verification'. The former means establishing that the specification conforms to the users' requirements while the latter means proving that the implementation conforms to the specification. There has been a marked tendency in discussions of this model and in its applications for abstraction and validation to receive much less attention than refinement and verification.

- **The Prototyping Model:** This model and variants of it are described in [6]. One of the main motivations for this model is the recognition that prospective users of a system are rarely able to define their requirements fully in one operation. Users also often find it difficult to define what they want in abstract or verbal terms independent of some working system: "I'll know it when I see it" (IKIWISI). A prototype provides a means for users to say more precisely what they do or do not want. The general idea, then, is to construct a series of prototypes, to allow prospective users to examine each one, and say what changes they want in the next one.

  Prototyping can also provide a means for system designers to clarify other aspects of a system: how it should be structured for easy modification or maintenance; how best to optimize the performance of the system; and so on.

  In the Throw-it-away variant, all prototypes are discarded; the delivered system is the last system in the sequence. In the Evolutionary and Incremental variants, software is carried forward from stage to stage and the functionality of the system is progressively refined and increased. The Evolutionary Model allows deletion and changes from stage to stage while the Incremental Model allows only additions.

  There is a natural affinity between the Evolutionary and Incremental Models and object oriented design (see, for example, [1], [5]). The mechanism of *inheritance* in such languages as Simula, Smalltalk and LOOPS provides a streamlined way of integrating new software with old. Because it supports the creation of 'well structured' designs, object orientation facilitates the process of changing designs.

3.1: Boehm's Spiral Model

Boehm [2] claims, with some justice, that the Spiral Model embraces most other models as special cases. It is a more general view of the process of design and development than other models and can apparently be applied to a wide range of types of project. But it is not so general as to be vacuous: it provides useful disciplines and constraints on the way development is done.

According to the model, a project should comprise a series of **cycles** or **rounds**. The steps in each cycle are broadly these:

1. Define **objectives** for the cycle.
2. Identify **constraints**, eg budgetary constraints and timescales.
3. Identify **alternative** means of meeting objectives (eg design A, design B, reuse, buy etc).
4. Evaluate alternatives with respect to objectives and constraints and, for each alternative, identify areas of uncertainty and the corresponding **risks**.
5. Decide how to **resolve** risks (eg construct a prototype, consult an expert, do a simulation, administer a user questionnaire, build system) and then do the chosen task.
6. Gather and review the **results** of the risk resolution exercise.
7. **Plan** the next cycle.
8. Review the plan and make a **commitment** to it.

The main differences between this model and the more traditional approaches are these:

- There is explicit recognition for alternative means of meeting the objectives of a project.

- The identification of risks associated with each alternative, and the ways in which those risks may be resolved, are brought centre stage. With traditional approaches, the easy bits of a project may be done early and the areas of uncertainty left till later — and this can give a spurious impression of progress. A risk driven approach to development more readily avoids this pitfall.

- The division of a project into cycles with a 'commit' step at the end of each cycle, means that there is explicit provision for changes in the direction of a project or the termination of a project, at any stage, in the light of what has been learned since the start of the project. By contrast with 'big bang' approaches to system development, the cyclic approach enables a limit to be placed on the risks which have to be accepted at any time.

- The model accommodates types of activity (eg consulting an expert or library research) which are often valuable in reaching the objectives of a project but which have no place in other models.

4: The PCIS Project

In Praxis we have tried using the Spiral Model in an internal project to develop the "Praxis Company Information System" (PCIS). The experience that we gained with the Spiral Model seems to be useful and worth reporting.

The development of business information systems is, of course, fairly well understood and the project is not intrinsically risky. Nevertheless we found that the framework provided by the Spiral Model has been valuable and has enabled us to retreat from potential pitfalls before any strong commitment was made.

What has been done maps fairly well to the model although there have been some areas of uncertainty as we learned to interpret and apply the model. As we used the model, some weaknesses became apparent and these are discussed below.

Our application of the Spiral Model included the Evolutionary Model as a subset. We felt that it would be rash to try to gather all requirements before producing any working system because of the IKIWISI phenomenon and because the needs of a company like Praxis, which is growing fast, do change as time goes by. We envisaged that several of the cycles of the Spiral Model would each be largely concerned with the development of a 'prototype' or 'version', to be evaluated by prospective users and, in most cases, carried forward into the next cycle for refinement and enhancement.

4.1: The First Cycle

The objective defined for the project at the outset, which applied throughout the project, was to "develop an information system to meet the needs of Praxis management".

It seemed necessary to start the project off with a fairly conventional gathering of requirements from prospective users of the system but, because we envisaged evolutionary development, this first gathering of requirements was not done in exhaustive detail. An outline data model was constructed together with an outline description and analysis of the functions to be performed and a description of the 'non-functional' attributes required in the system.

This first gathering of requirements was regarded as part of the process of defining the objectives and constraints on the project.

The next four steps in the model were covered by a study called "Analysis of Options and Risks." In this study, we identified a set of alternative means of meeting the objectives:

- Sub-contract the work to another systems house. Since we are, ourselves, a systems house, this option did not look very plausible. But we felt it would be useful, nevertheless, to weigh the pros and cons.

- Do the work ourselves. On this basis, we identified four alternative means of developing the system:
  - Use software DBMS "A" and its 4GL tools.
  - Use software DBMS "B" and its 4GL tools.
  - Use database machine "C" and its 4GL tools.

- Assemble a collection of packages to serve the various functions of the company.

Criteria for evaluation were derived from the initial study of requirements and the options were investigated and evaluated against them. Examples of criteria for evaluating the proposed vehicles for the system include: cost of the vehicle, ease of use of the development tools (and corresponding cost of development effort), the quality of the user interface, the existence or otherwise of mechanisms to preserve the integrity of data in the face of hardware failures, and so on. The criteria may be seen as 'risks': if an option does not meet one or more of the criteria then the final system is likely to be unsatisfactory.

The best option appeared to be to do the work ourselves using the database machine "C", perhaps after some further investigation of the machine.

However, there were constraints which dictated a slightly different course. We already had a licence for software DBMS "A" and, for budgetary reasons, there was little prospect of getting the database machine soon. There was also a need to gain experience with DBMS "A."

Consequently, we planned to do the first one or two versions of the PCIS with software DBMS "A", and also do some further investigation of "C." If, after further investigation, "C" was still looking good, we would re-write the system on it and continue with it in subsequent cycles.

This longer-term plan was the basis of the shorter term plan prepared for the next cycle: to develop a first version of the PCIS to serve the needs of the company in the areas of marketing and sales.

The plan was reviewed and a commitment made to it.

4.2: The Second Cycle

The objective of the second cycle was the development of the first version of the PCIS under the constraint that it should use DBMS "A."

No significant alternatives presented themselves in this cycle and, with a qualification described below, we did not see significant areas of risk requiring investigation. The cycle constituted a fairly straightforward development of the first version of the PCIS. Detailed requirements were gathered from relevant staff, a running system was developed using the 4GL tools, and the system was carefully evaluated by the prospective users of the system. This evaluation led to the definition of changes required in future versions and new features needed.

The evaluation of the first version of the PCIS and the definition of changes required in future versions may be regarded as the first part of the Third Cycle: these activities are part of the process of defining the next set of objectives in the project.

The idea that there was no apparent risk in this cycle should perhaps be qualified by the thought that the development of the first version of the PCIS may, itself, be seen as an exercise in the reduction of uncertainty and the resolution of risk. Before the development is undertaken, there is a degree of uncertainty about what form the system will take and about how well it will work; this uncertainty is reduced or removed by constructing and evaluating the system. In this spirit, the cycle - and the project - were reviewed.

The main conclusion of the review of 'results' was that DBMS "A" is much less satisfactory than we had anticipated. Its main defect is unacceptably slow response times on our equipment even with very little data in it and few users. A new and bigger machine could, of course, be bought for it but this option needs to be set against the apparently preferable option of buying dedicated hardware - the database machine.

The slow response times with DBMS "A" could, of course, have been discovered without actually developing a version of the PCIS. In retrospect, it might have been wiser to conduct some tests on the DBMS as a risk resolution exercise prior to building the first version of the system. However, the development of the first version of the PCIS was not wasted effort because it sharpened our understanding of users' requirements in several other areas, especially the user interface.

On the strength of the review, the Third Cycle was planned to take in a further short investigation of the database machine and its tools, and a decision on its purchase. In this Third Cycle, a new version of the PCIS is to be developed using the new system, drawing on the knowledge gained in developing and evaluating the first version. The definition of these objectives, like the definition of changes required in future versions of the PCIS, may be regarded as the first stage in the Third Cycle.

4.3: Discussion

To date, the Spiral Model seems to have been a reasonably good framework for the PCIS project. But there is a need for more clarity in some areas, or changes in the model. These will now be described.

1. There is a need to define more clearly how longer term objectives and plans may be carried forwarded from cycle to cycle and integrated with the shorter term objectives and plans. An example of a long term intention which needed to be carried forward into later cycles is our early decision in the PCIS project to migrate to database machine "C" after one or two versions of the PCIS produced using software DBMS "A," provided that further evaluation of the database machine was satisfactory.

2. There seems to be a need to provide for hierarchical relationships and for 'spirals within spirals':

   - Within a cycle, the process of resolving risks may be regarded as a spiral in its own right: there should be objectives and there is likely to be alternative means of meeting the objectives, each with risks which may need to be resolved. The model needs to be applied recursively.

   - Similar remarks apply to the planning activity within each cyle. That planning may itself be modelled on a spiral model has been noted and discussed by Boehm and Belz [3]. Other points about how planning relates to the Spiral Model are made below.

   - Alternatives may easily demand a hierarchical structure. The alternatives shown in section 4.1 are one example. As another example, one of the alternative means of resolving risks - "consult an expert" - may itself be broken down into a set of alternatives: "consult Susan," "consult Joe" etc.

3. As we saw in section 4.2, there may not be obvious major alternatives in a cycle. And it is not very obvious that developing a version of a system is 'risk resolution' in quite the same sense as investigating alternative vehicles for the system.

4. Not only may the planning activity within each cycle of the Spiral Model be modelled on a spiral model but several of the other activities in each cycle — defining objectives, identifying constraints, identifying alternative ways of meeting objectives, identifying risks and deciding how to resolve risks - may themselves be regarded as planning activities. Moreover, the Spiral Model may itself be regarded as a skeleton plan for a project. There is, in general, a need to define more clearly how any planning done within the model relates to the model itself.

5: 'Project SP' and the 'New Spiral Model'

In this section a notation and a new version of the Spiral Model are described. They seem to meet most of the problems with the Spiral Model which were noted above.

5.1: 'Project SP': A Notation for Project Management

This section introduces a simple notation called 'Project SP' which is an informal variant of the SP computer language, described elsewhere [10].

Project SP, which is similar to BNF, may be used for recording the progressively growing **knowledge base** for a project. This includes the objectives of the project, constraints on the project, alternative means of meeting objectives, the areas of risk and uncertainty, planned activities on the project and the information gathered to reduce uncertainty and resolve risks. The last-mentioned category includes information about the design of the system being developed. Boehm and Belz [3] have also proposed using a data store in conjunction with the Spiral Model.

Here is the notation:

- (...) - A sequence of items or 'ordered AND object' (OAO). This includes the normal sequencing of words in English sentences.

- [...] - An 'unordered AND object' (UAO): a group of items where order is not defined.

- {...} - An 'OR object' (ORO): the items between the curly brackets represent alternatives.

  Each option may be marked with a 'per cent' ('%') or 'weight' showing the apparent strength of the case for choosing that option: 0% means that the option should never be chosen while 100% means that it should always be chosen.

If the weights in an ORO total to 100% then it represents an **exclusive** OR relation. If weights within an ORO total more than 100% then it represents an **inclusive** OR relation. If all the weights within an ORO are, individually, 100% then the structure is equivalent to a UAO.

- * - A star placed after an item shows that the item may be repeated.

- ? - Question marks show where more informtion appears to be needed, the strength of the need being shown by the number of question marks.

- Indendation may be used to improve readability.

5.2: An Example

As an example to introduce the uses of Project SP, Figure 1 shows how the notation may be used to describe the knowledge base for the PCIS project at the time of writing. This and other examples are discussed in the following sections. In the Figure, sets of three dots ("...") are used to show where information has been left out to save space.

5.3: The Uses of Project SP

The ways in which Project SP may be used are described here with illustrations from Figure 1 and other examples.

5.3.1: Groupings of Objects

OAOs and UAOs both serve to group their constituent objects. UAOs are used where there is no spacial or temporal ordering of the constituents. One example in Figure 1 is the evaluation criteria for the vehicle for the PCIS. Another is the grouping of any object with its label or identifier (see below).

OAOs are used where there is some kind of spacial or temporal ordering of constituents. Examples in Figure 1 are the ordering of activities in a project plan and the order of words in English text. The relevance of Project SP to planning is discussed more fully below.

5.3.2: Identifiers and References

The notion of 'identifier' has no formal significance in Project SP. Indeed, any object may be identified by any of its constituents which is sufficiently distinctive. However, as a matter of psychology, it is often convenient to regard one of the constituents of an object as being primarily an identifier or lable for that object.

The relationship between an identifier or label and what it identifies seems to be best represented as an unordered AND relationship. In Project SP, any object may be labelled by bracketing it with its label within a UAO, eg [Fred (...)]. If the object being labelled is itself a UAO then the inner brackets may be dropped.

Since the identifier and what it identifies are constituents of a UAO, they may be written in any order. However, for the sake of readability and easy comprehension, it is convenient to put the identifier first. Examples in Figure 1 of the labelling of objects in this way include [DBMS-A...] and [objectives-1...].

A reference to any object may be created by using its identifier as a constituent by itself within a UAO. Examples in Figure 1 include [objectives-1] and [UI]. The latter example is a reference to the user interface, one of the criteria for evaluation listed elsewhere in the structure.

References may be used to avoid recording a structure more than once when it appears in more than one context. The examples in the last paragraph illustrate this use in Figure 1.

References may also be used when incorporation of a large data object at a given point would be cumbersome and would make the organization of the whole structure less easy to see. Examples of this second use of references are the numbers in square brackets, eg [42.1-1.0], which are reference numbers for Praxis documents. The text of any such document is not incorporated directly in the main structure.

5.3.3: Uncertainty in the Knowledge Base

OROs in Project SP provide a means of representing uncertainty in a project. As described earlier, the weights on items within a ORO (figures with '%') show the apparent strength of the case for choosing that option. Whenever weights are less than 100% and more than 0% there is a corresponding uncertainty in choosing.

An example in Figure 1 of the use of the ORO in this way is the choice between the development work in-house and contracting it out to another systems house. In this example, the in-house option is itself broken down into a number of subsidiary options.

Question marks in Project SP provide a second means of representing uncertainty or ignorance within a knowledge base. Of course, we can never be sure that our knowledge of any one thing is complete: there is a metaphorical question mark attaching to every object in every knowledge base. The use of question marks in Project SP is intended to show the perceived strength of the need to find out more in this or that part of the knowledge base. Exactly how one makes such judgements is itself a significant question mark in our understanding of systems development.

5.3.4: 'Deletion' or 'Replacement' of Objects

The intention with Project SP is that information should never be destroyed within the structure — unless it is a simple error in editing the structure or if it is redundant. In the latter case, where an object has been replicated in more than one context, all instances except one 'master' copy may be replaced by references to that master copy.

If one object supercedes another in the knowledge base then the two objects should be formed into an ORO, with the later item marked as 100% and the superceded item marked as 0%. If, at some later stage in the project, the old item seems useful again, then the weights may be adjusted to show this.

```
[(The PCIS Project)
    [(project management)
        [(The Spiral Model)
            [cycle ((step-1 ...)(step-2 ...) ...)]* ]
        [(project plan)
            (
                [(the first cycle)
                    [define [objectives-1]]
                    [identify [constraints-1]]
                    [2.1-1.0]
                    ...]
                [(the second cycle)
                    [define [objectives-2]]
                    [identify [constraints-2]]
                    [2.2-1.0]
                    ...]
                [(the third cycle)
                    [define [objectives-3]]
                    [identify [constraints-3]]
                    ???]
            )]]
    [(requirements for the PCIS)
        [objectives-1
            [(overall objective for the project) ...]
            [("Preliminary Specification of Requirements for the PCIS")
                [41.1-1.0]]]
        [objectives-2
            [("Requirements Statement for the PCIS, Version 1")
                [42.2-1.0]]]
        [objectives-3
            [("Requirements Statement for the PCIS, Version 2")
                [42.3-1.0]]]]
    [(constraints on the development of the PCIS)
        [constraints-1 [time ...][cost ...]
        [constraints-2 [time ...][cost ...](use DBMS "A")]
        [constraints-3 [time ...][cost ...](use database machine "C")]]
    [(mode of development)
        (
        [(sub-contract the work) 20% [90.1-1.0]]
        [(do the work in house) 80%
            [(vehicle for the PCIS)
                [(evaluation criteria) [90.1-1.0]
                    [(available from any one terminal) ...]
                    [(high level of integration) ...]
                    [(access control) ...]
                    [(preservation of integrity) ...]
                    [(accessability of information) ...]
                    [(user interface) UI [42.3-1.0]
                        [(bandwidth of visual display)
                            (size of screen)
                            (windowing)
                            (efficient scrolling)]
                        [(flexibility in production of hard copy)
                    (landscape printing)
                    (printing of screens and reports
                     'on the fly')]]
                    [(capital and recurrent costs) ...]
                    [(development facilities) DF ... ]
                    [(performance, response times) PF ... ]
                    [(distributed working) ...]
                    [(adaptability to changing needs) ...]
                    [(documentation and training) ...]
                    [(maturity of system) ...]
                    [(other considerations) ...]]
                (
```

Figure 1:   A representation in Project SP of the knowledge base of the PCIS project at the time of writing.

```
            [DBMS-A 15%
                [90.1-1.0]
                [(experience of second cycle)
                    [[PF] poor]
                    [[UI] (poor; there are limitations on
                        the production of hardcopy and in
                        the formatting of forms and reports)]
                    [[DF] (not easy to learn but tolerably
                        easy to use once learned; X's
                        help-line is poor)]
                    (other aspects of DBMS-A appear
                        to be acceptable)]]
            [DBMS-B 25%
                [90.1-1.0]
                (experience on project xxxx)]
            [(a collection of packages)[90.1-1.0] 10%]
            [(database machine) 50%
                {
                [(database-machine-C) ??? 80%
                    [90.1-1.0]
                    [(XX's experience) ...]
                    [(meeting at Praxis, 22/2/88)[24.6]]
                    [[UI] ???]
                    [[PF] ??]
                    [[DF] ???]]
                [other ?? 20%]}]
            }]]}]
    [PCIS
        {
        [PCIS-1
            (for marketing and sales)
            [DBMS-A]
            (executable specification)
            [("High level design for the PCIS, version 1")
                [42.1-1.0]]
            [("User guide for the PCIS, version 1")
                [42.2-1.0]]]
        [PCIS-2 ???]
        }]
]
```

Figure 1 (continued)

If an object is to be 'deleted' and nothing put in its place then it should be formed into a selection where its alternative is a UAO which is empty except for its 100% weight, eg [...{[0% Fred (...)],[100%]}...]. An acceptable shorthand is simply adding a 0% weight to the object which is to be demoted — without incorporating it in an ORO.

To preserve all information in the knowledge base even when it is out of date may seem cumbersome but it is no different from what has been normal practice for many years with conventional, paper-based filing systems. Of course, many computerised databases are designed for the deletion and over-writing of information but this is likely to change as storage technology improves and the advantages of non-overwriting systems like ADAM [10] are seen.

A main reason for never destroying information in the knowledge base is that one can always backtrack if necessary. Another important reason is that one can always construct an 'audit trail' for a project. This can be useful in project debriefing and in case of dispute if that unfortunate contingency arises.

5.3.5: Representing the Structure of Software Systems

Project SP is an informal version of the SP computer language, described in [12]. The SP language is intended as a 'broad spectrum' language with a wide range of uses including data storage and retrieval, software specification and design, representation of rules for expert systems, logic programming and others. If the potential of SP is realised — and a research programme is needed to establish how and how far one simple language can serve such a wide range of applications — it may be possible to represent the whole structure of a developing software system with one notation which is the same as is used for other parts of a project knowledge base.

Figure 1 shows information about the PCIS in only the barest outline, with references out to Praxis documents where the real meat of the information about the structure of the system is stored. It would take us too far afield to discuss fully how SP or Project SP could be used more directly to represent the structure of the PCIS (there is relevant discussion in [12]) but some brief indication of the possibilities is warrented here:

- Project SP embraces the concepts of 'sequence' (OAO), 'selection' (ORO) and 'iteration' ('*') which are widely recognised as basic organizing principles in software (see, for example, [7]). Iteration does not feature in SP but an equivalent effect may be achieved by using recursion. The UAO construct may provide a means of representing 'concurrency' in software systems.

- SP and Project SP apparently lend themselves to the efficient representation of versions or variants of software systems. In other words, they have potential to facilitate configuration management. The mechanisms which will serve the 'object oriented' concepts of classes, sub-classes and inheritance of attributes (see [12]) will also serve to keep track of the several versions of a software system which usually arise in system development. A simple example appears in Figure 1 where the versions of the PCIS are represented as constituents of an ORO — alternative realisations of the PCIS.

5.3.6: Representation of Plans

In keeping with the 'wide spectrum' remarks in the last section, there is potential in Project SP to represent plans directly in the knowledge base. The main constructs recognised in project planning also appear in the notation:

- A sequence of activities in a plan may be represented using an OAO.

- A UAO may be used to represent activities which are independent of each other in much the same way that it may be used to represent concurrency in software. Independence of activities corresponds to the slightly innaccurate use of the term *parallel* in project planning. 'Parallel' activities may be performed in parallel or they may be performed in some arbitrary sequence, depending on the resources available and the required timescales.

- An ORO may be used to represent activities which are **alternatives** in a plan. This is not very common in ordinary projects but the concept is recognised in the term 'contingency planning'. Where there are alternatives in a plan there is a need to know how to choose between the options. This can be achieved by associating each option with a condition which must be satisfied before that option can be chosen. In Project SP, each alternative course of action should be enclosed within an OAO together with its corresponding condition or conditions:

```
{
    (condition-1 action-1)
    (condition-2 action-2)
    (condition-3 action-3)
    ...
}
```

The similarity between the organizing principles recognised in project planning and those recognized in software design is interesting in its own right. It also reinforces Osterweil's argument [9] that "Software processes are software too". If project planning is to be seen as "process programming" then it will be convenient and elegant if the notation used to describe a software product can also be used to describe the process by which that product is created. Whether or not that can be achieved with SP or Project SP remains to be seen.

5.4: The New Spiral Model

Given the use of Project SP to record the growing knowledge base of a project, Boehm's model may be recast in a modified form.

In the New Spiral Model (NSM), there are two fundamental operations or activities: (1) gathering new knowledge and adding it to the knowledge base; (2) reviewing, analysing and rationalising what is in the knowledge base. There will usually also be the **execution** of plans described within the knowledge base. Here is a fuller description.

1. Gather new knowledge and add it to the knowledge base. "New knowledge" in this context can mean any or all of the following kinds of knowledge:

   - Knowledge about the **objectives** of a project or activity.

   - Knowledge about **ignorance** and corresponding **risks.** This is not as paradoxical as it sounds. For example, anyone with experience with computers and similar technology knows that, for any proposed new piece of equipment, one ought to find out how reliable it is, the callout time for maintenance, the cost of maintenance, the availability of spares, and so on. Knowing what one needs to find out is part of the skill of system development.

     Defining gaps in one's knowledge is closely related to the definition of **objectives** for an activity or project. A requirement to "support the production and maintenance of company accounts" is a gap waiting to be filled by a suitable system. The gaps in one's knowledge about any proposed new piece of equipment are objectives for corresponding activities to plug those gaps: "find out about reliability", "find out about callout times", etc.

   - Knowledge gleaned from various sources about **constraints** on a project or subsidiary activity, eg budgets and timescales.

   - Knowledge about **methods** of meeting objectives within the given constraints; where there is more than one method for an objective these represent the kind of **alternatives** which feature in Boehm's Spiral Model.

     A method, together with such information as start and end dates and staff assignments, is the kind of information which is normally represented in some kind of network of **activities** or PERT chart. As indicated above, SP or Project SP may also provide a means of representing this kind of knowledge, including sequences of activities (OAOs), independent or 'parallel' activities (UAOs) and alternatives or contingencies (OROs).

Gathering information about methods and corresponding activities, incorporating it in the knowledge base, reviewing, analysing and rationalising it (see below) is what is normally meant by **planning.**

Knowledge about methods includes such hum-drum things as how to make a journey to visit a client, how to obtain information from libraries, and so on. Knowledge about methods also includes knowledge about the several models of system development - including the NSM itself!

If knowledge about methods is supplied from the experience of members of the project team, as it often will be, it is not, in that sense, 'new'. However, in terms of the project's knowledge base it is new knowledge. Unless it is trivial, everyday knowledge, it needs to be recorded explicitly regardless of whether it comes from some external 'expert' or from within the team.

- Knowledge about the developing system. For most projects this is the main 'deliverable' of the project. It includes such things as high level design, low level design, source code, maintenance documentation, user guides and so on.

- Records of any commitments made to project plans.

2. Review, analyse and rationalise the knowledge base. This activity includes any or all of the following kinds of activity:

- Look for redundancy in the knowledge base and reduce it where possible. Where objects are replicated, references may be used to reduce redundancy, as described earlier. Examples of searching for redundancy in a knowledge base and reducing it include the process of 'normalising' data models and the processes needed to achieve 'good structure' in the design of software (see [12]).

- Review objectives against the results of system development to see whether the objectives have been met.

- In the light of any new knowledge gained since the previous cycle, review the weights attaching to the constituents of OROs.

- Identify areas of uncertainty, ignorance and risk and decide where further investigation is needed.

3. **Execute** any plans which are ready to go. A plan is ready to go if it has been created and reviewed, if a commitment has been made to it and if all pre-conditions attaching to it are satisfied. Pre-conditions include such things as the completion of previous activities on which the plan depends (eg the delivery of equipment), the availability of relevant staff, reaching the start date, and so on. 'Execute' in this context is analogous to 'eval' in Lisp.

Figure 2 represents the main points in foregoing description of the NSM using the Project SP notation.

The 'activities' object in Figure 2 describes the two basic operations in each cyle of gathering new knowledge and then reviewing, analysing and rationalising it. Under each heading there is an ORO describing the options. One or more of these options may be chosen on each cycle.

The [define [activities]] object is the 'planning' or 'process programming' operation. It means fleshing out the bare bones of the basic [activities ...] object in the NSM with the more detailed descriptions of activities needed to make a project go, using any available knowledge about methods.

As already noted, knowledge about methods can include the NSM itself. Thus the NSM may reappear within itself as, for example, when a major project has been planned to contain one or more sub-projects. The model can be applied at any level.

Notice that the application of the NSM within itself means that it can be used in the creation of project plans. In other words, it can be included within the [define[activities]] object. Boehm and Belz [3] have, in a similar way, proposed using the Spiral Model in the development of project plans.

With or without this kind of recursive application of the model, Project SP accommodates an hierarchical structuring of activities within activities, with sequence, selection, concurrency and iteration at any level.

5.5: Discussion

To quote a well-known phrase, "forewarned is forearmed": the reduction of risk is closely related to the reduction of ignorance or the building of knowledge.

The idea behind the use of Project SP and the NSM is to treat a development project as a progression from relative ignorance to relative knowledge. The design of a computing system (or anything else) is a form of knowledge and the process of creating a design may be seen as a process of knowledge accretion. Likewise, all the other aspects of a development project - the model of development, objectives, constraints, user's requirements, project plans, and knowledge about equipment and facilities - are forms of knowledge which typically grow as the project proceeds.

Areas of uncertainty in a development project take two forms in Project SP: alternatives in a selection or straightforward gaps in knowledge (represented by question marks). Uncertainty is reduced when an alternative is chosen or when a gap in the structure is plugged.

Project SP and the NSM together meet the points made in section 4.3:

1. Short and long term objectives and plans may be recorded in the knowledge base and carried forward from cycle to cycle.

2. Hierarchical relationships are naturally accommodated in the notation. Selections within selections are shown

```
[NSM
     [activities
          (
          [((gather new knowledge)
               {
               [define [objectives]]
               [identify [constraints]]
               [define [activities]]
               [record [commitments]]
               [create [deliverables]]
               }]
          [(review, analyse and rationalise the knowledge base)
               {
               (look for redundancy and remove where possible)
               (review objectives against deliverables)
               (review and adjust weights on the constituents of OROs)
               (identify areas of uncertainty and risk)
               }]
          (execute planned activities which are ready to go)
          )*
          [constraints ?]
          [commitments ?]
          ]
     [deliverables
          [objectives ?]
          {
          [report ?]
          [(high level design) ?]
          [(low level design) ?]
          [(source code) ?]
          ...
          }]
     ]
```

Figure 2:   The New Spiral Model represented using Project SP

in Figure 1. The NSM is itself one of the candidate 'methods' which may be used in any part of a structure of planned activities and at any level. In other words, the NSM can be applied recursively to create 'spirals within spirals.'

3. Risk reduction may be achieved by any kind of gain in relevant knowledge. Sometimes this relates to alternatives but it may equally well be the plugging of gaps in knowledge - and that includes gaining knowledge by building a system.

4. The relationship between 'planning' and the NSM is this:

   • The NSM is itself a skeleton plan.

   • The NSM replaces three activities in Boehm's model with a single 'process programming' activity for fleshing out the skeleton with the more detailed descriptions of activities needed to make the plan practical. The three activities which are replaced are: the identification of alternative means of meeting objectives, deciding how to resolve risks, and 'planning'.

6:   Related Issues

In this section, I pick up some loose ends from what I have said and discuss them briefly.

6.1:   The Spiral Models and Iteration in Design

As we have seen, the idea of **iteration** features not only in the spiral models but in the prototyping model as well. In the spiral models iteration serves a management need to limit the risk to which a project is exposed at any time. In the prototyping model, iteration is probably serving the rather different needs of the design process:

   • Iteration seems to suit end users best. A major reason is IKIWISI but there is the related reason that potential users of a system naturally examine and re-examine their requirements in the process of thinking them out.

   • In a similar way, it is psychologically natural for designers to iterate in the process of thinking out the best organization for a design. Drafting and re-drafting has always been required in all kinds of design - from graphic art to the writing of articles and books.

Whatever the reasons for iteration, it is accommodated very well within the spiral models.

6.2:   Should One Always Concentrate on High Risk Areas First?

As we have seen, there are good reasons why a project should focus on areas of ignorance and risk. However, in the design process, it sometimes seems better to design the best understood parts first. For example, in object oriented design it is recognised (see [1]) that one should first identify and define the most salient classes in the system and should later add the less salient classes, whether they be at higher or lower levels of abstraction.

I believe this contradiction is more apparent than real. There is a difference between recording things which you already know and working out something new. As a result of discussions with users, a designer will know things about the form which the system must take and these things need to be recorded. Recording them explicitly in a partial design is quite consistent with the principle of seeking out areas of uncertainty. One cannot see the areas of uncertainty clearly unless one has recorded what one already knows.

6.3: The Design of Other Kinds of System

The ideas which have been presented seem to have a fairly wide scope and should prove useful in the development of systems where there are significant components which are not software.

The main difference between hardware and software is that hardware systems are usually less 'malleable' than software systems. A significant commitment of resources is often required in the construction of hardware systems.

This feature has been a reason for the traditional notion that 'design' always precedes 'construction'. When the software industry first developed, it was natural to borrow this idea. And it flourished because, until recently, significant resources were required in the creation of software systems and there was a consequent need to get the 'design' right before embarking on 'implementation'.

Modern tools and the increasing performance of computers for a given price is progressively reducing the resources required in the creation of a working software system. There is, consequently, more scope to adopt new methods of working which take advantage of this new flexibility.

Of course, it was never entirely true in the hardware world that design necessarily preceded construction. The creation of prototypes has been a part of engineering methodology from the earliest days. Brunel built prototypes where there was uncertainty about design. And the construction of any one bridge, for example, may be regarded as a trial run for the design and construction of bridges which come later. The eighteenth century bridge at Pontypridd, which at the time was the longest single span in the world, fell down three times during construction before a successful design was found.

These observations confirm the validity of the iterative principle in the world of hardware development and suggest that the spiral models can indeed apply to the development of systems other than software.

7: Conclusion

In this article, I have tried to identify key concepts in the management of system development which will reduce risks, reduce the cost of failure and thus reduce the overall cost of developing complex systems.

I hope that other people will try out the ideas which I have described and report their experiences and new thinking in the future.

8: Acknowledgements

I am grateful to all those involved in the PCIS project, in development work, reviewing, or as prospective users of the system - Dave Allen, David Bean, Tim Huckvale, George May, Jane Northcote, Martyn Ould, Stephen Robertson, Tony Voss - for cooperation in the application of a new management model and for constructive comments on the model and earlier drafts of this article. I am also grateful for very useful comments and suggestions from an anonymous referee.

9: References

[1] Birtwistle, G.M., Dahl, O-J., Myhrhaug, B., and Nygaard, K.: *Simula Begin*, Van Nostrand Reinhold, New York, 1979.

[2] Boehm, B.W.: "A Spiral Model of Software Development and Enhancement," *ACM Sigsoft Software Engineering Notes*, 1986, **11**, (4) pp. 14–24.

[3] Boehm, B.W. and Belz, F.: "Applying Process Programming to the Spiral Model," *Proceedings of the Fourth Software Process Workshop*, Devon, England, May 1988.

[4] Buckle, J.K.: "Software Configuration Management," MacMillan, New York, 1982.

[5] Cook, S.: "Languages and Object-Oriented Programming" *Software Engineering Journal*, 1986, **1**, (2), pp. 73–80.

[6] Hekmatpour, S. and Ince, D.: "Rapid Software Prototyping," *Open University Technical Report 86/4*, The Open University, 1986.

[7] Jackson, M.A.: *Principles of Program Design*, Academic Press, Calif., 1975.

[8] Lehman, M.M.: "A Further Model of Coherent Programming Processes," *Proceedings of the IEEE Software Process Workshop*, Feb. 1984, pp. 27–33.

[9] Osterweil, L.: "Software Processes Are Software Too," *Proceedings of the Ninth International Conference on Software Engineering*, Monterey, Calif., 1987.

[10] Peeling, N.E., Morison, J.D., and Whiting, E.V.: "ADAM: An Abstract Database Machine," *RSRE Report No. 84007*, Royal Signals and Radar Establishment, 1984.

[11] Wingrove, A.: "The Problems of Managing Software Projects," *Software Engineering Journal*, 1986, **1**, (1), pp. 3–6

[12] Wolff, J.G.: "Simplicity and Power: Some Unifying Ideas in Computing," to appear in *The Computer Journal*.

Chapter 5: Annotated Bibliography and References

[AFSAB, 1983]. U.S. Air Force Scientific Advisory Board, *Report on the High Cost and Risk of Mission Critical Software*, December 1983.

A set of recommendations for improvements in U.S. Air Force software technology and acquisition strategy, including specific emphasis on software risk management.

[AFSC, 1988]. U.S. Air Force Systems Command, "Software Risk Abatement," *AFSC/AFLC Pamphlet 800–45*, 1988.

Contained in Section 2 of this tutorial. Provides comprehensive guidelines for applying software-risk-abatement techniques, including top-level risk assessment techniques and a good set of risk-identification checklists.

[AFSC, 1988a]. U.S. Air Force Systems Command, "Software Independent Verification and Validation," *AFSC/AFLC Pamphlet 800–5*, May 20, 1988.

Contains techniques for determining an appropriate level of software independent verification and validation (IV&V) as a function of software error criticality and risk. Also contains guidelines for applying IV&V across the software life cycle.

[Arrow, 1971]. K.J. Arrow, *Essays in the Theory of Risk Bearing*, North Holland, New York, 1971.

A classic economic treatment of the fundamentals of risk analysis.

[Babel, 1985]. P.S. Babel, *Software Development Capability/Capacity Reviews*, U.S. Air Force, Aeronautical Systems Division, 1985.

A good checklist of questions and techniques for evaluating an organization's software development capability.

[Balzer-Cheatham-Green, 1983]. R. Balzer, T.E. Cheatham, and C. Green, "Software Technology in the 1990's: Using a New Paradigm," *Computer*, November 1983, pp. 39–45.

Presents an alternative software life-cycle process model based on updating specifications rather than on design or code, assuming the existence of capabilities for transforming the specifications into design and code.

[Basili et al., 1987]. V.R. Basili, B.W. Boehm, J.A. Clapp, D. Gaumer, M. Holden, and J.K. Summers, "Use of Ada for FAA's Advanced Automation System (AAS)," *MITRE Corp., MTR-87W77*, MITRE Corp., Bedford, Mass., April 1987.

Portions of this report are contained in Section 4 of this tutorial. Provides an example of the application of software risk management techniques to a large project management issue: the use of Ada on the FAA-AAS.

[Bell-Raiffa-Tversky, 1988] D.E. Bell, H. Raiffa, and A. Tversky, *Decision Making*, Cambridge University Press, Cambridge, Mass., 1988.

A collection of current survey papers and research papers on decision-making principles, including several papers on decision-making under risk and uncertainty.

[Bell, 1987]. T.E. Bell, "Performance Engineering: Doing It 'Later' on Large Projects," *CMG Transactions*, Winter 1987, pp. 75–82.

Contained in Section 3 of this tutorial. Provides a valuable set of checklists, with examples, of the most frequent performance risk items; and identifies performance engineering techniques for dealing with them.

[Boehm, 1974]. B.W. Boehm, "Software System Design and Development; Top-Down, Bottom-Up, or Prototype?" *Proceedings, TRW Symposium on Reliable, Cost-Effective, Secure Software*, TRW, Redondo Beach, Calif., March 1974, pp. 4–79 — 4–81.

Contained in Section 2 of this tutorial. An initial approach to applying risk and decision-theory techniques to resolve software process model issues.

[Boehm, 1976]. B.W. Boehm, "Software Engineering," *IEEE Transactions on Computers*, December 1976, pp. 1226–1241.

An overview of software engineering, organized around an extended version of the waterfall model with embedded verification and validation steps to address risk items.

[Boehm, 1981]. B.W. Boehm, *Software Engineering Economics*, Prentice Hall, Englewood Cliffs, N.J., 1981.

Chapters 19 and 20 on risk analysis are contained in Section 2 of this tutorial. Also presents the constructive cost model (COCOMO) for software cost estimation, a useful tool for software-risk identification, analysis, and prioritization.

[Boehm, 1984]. B.W. Boehm, "Verifying and Validating Software Requirements and Design Specifications," *Software*, January 1984, pp. 75–88.

An approach to performing risk management as a verification and validation (V&V) function. Assesses the relative efficacy of candidate risk resolution techniques in addressing various classes of risk items.

[Boehm, 1987]. B.W. Boehm, "Improving Software Productivity," *Computer*, September 1987, pp. 43–57.

Summarizes techniques and leverage factors in improving software productivity, including reduction of current high software-rework costs via risk-management techniques.

[Boehm, 1988a]. B.W. Boehm, "A Spiral Model of Software Development and Enhancement," *Computer*, May 1988, pp. 61–72.

Contained in Section 1 of this tutorial volume. Describes a risk-driven software process model. Experience with the spiral model is discussed in Subsection 4.4.1.

EH0291-5/89/0000/0493$01.00 ©1989 IEEE

[Boehm, 1988b]. B.W. Boehm, "Rapid Prototyping, Risk Management, 2167, and the Ada Process Model," *Proceedings, U.S. Army-AWIS Ada Symposium,* TRW, Inc., Fairfax, Va., September 1988.

Contained in Section 1 of this tutorial. Outlines how spiral model and risk-management techniques can be tailored to government acquisition standards and Ada.

[Boehm et al., 1978]. B.W. Boehm, J.R. Brown, H. Kaspar, M. Lipow, G.J. MacLeod, and M.J. Merritt, *Characteristics of Software Quality,* North Holland, New York, 1978.

An early study providing techniques for characterizing desired software properties, with checklists and techniques for addressing software quality risks.

[Boehm-Gray-Seewaldt, 1984]. B.W. Boehm, T.E. Gray, and T. Seewaldt, "Prototyping vs. Specifying: A Multi-Project Experiment," *IEEE Transactions on Software Engineering,* May 1984, pp. 133–145.

Results of an experiment comparing the use of a waterfall and a prototyping-oriented software process model. The waterfall approach better addressed product and process control risks; the prototyping approach better addressed user-interface and gold-plating risks.

[Boehm-Belz, 1988]. B.W. Boehm and F.C. Belz, "Applying Process Programming to the Spiral Model: Lessons Learned," *Proceedings, 4th International Software Process Workshop,* ACM, Inc., New York, 1989.

Contained in Section 1 of this tutorial. Discusses experiences with and extensions to the spiral model.

[Boehm-Ross, 1989]. B.W. Boehm and R. Ross, "Theory W Software Project Management: Principles and Examples," *IEEE Transactions on Software Engineering,* July 1989 (to be published).

Contained in Section 1 of this tutorial. Presents a theory of software project management focused on creating and sustaining win-win conditions for all of the software project participants, including a focus on identifying and managing risks of creating win-lose or lose-lose situations.

[Bowen-Wigle-Tsai, 1985]. T.P. Bowen, G.B. Wigle, and J.T. Tsai, "Specification of Software Quality Attributes," *RADC TR-85–37* (3 vol), RADC, Griffiss AFB, New York, February 1985.

A thorough set of assessment criteria for software quality factors. A bit cumbersome to apply, but very good for quality checklists.

[Brown, 1986]. R.V. Brown, "Managing Diffuse Risks from Adversarial Sources with Special Reference to Computer Security," *Proceedings, 9th National Computer Security Conference,* NBS, Gaithersburg, Md., 1986.

Characterizes computer security assets and vulnerabilities, and techniques for computer-security risk assessment and control.

[Carey-Mason, 1983]. T.T. Carey and R.E.A Mason, "Information System Prototyping: Techniques, Tools, and Methodologies," *INFOR—The Canadian Journal of Operational Research and Information Processing,* August 1983, pp. 177–191.

Contained in Section 3 of this tutorial. Categorizes, surveys, and analyzes prototyping approaches and techniques. A good early-1980s state-of-the-art review.

[Cha et al., 1988] S.S. Cha, N.G. Leveson, and T.J. Shimeall, "Safety Verification in MURPHY Using Fault Tree Analysis," *Proceedings, 10th International Conference on Software Engineering,* IEEE Computer Society Press, Washington, D.C., April 1988, pp. 377–386.

Contained in Section 3 of this tutorial. Describes a methodology and set of tools for identifying and analyzing risks of software faults in safety critical systems.

[Covello-Mumpower, 1985]. V.T. Covello and J. Mumpower, "Risk Analysis and Risk Management: An Historical Perspective," *Risk Analysis,* June 1985, pp. 103–120.

A nice short history of risk analysis and risk management since the Babylonians in 3200 B.C.

[DSMC, 1983]. Defense Systems Management College, "Risk Assessment Techniques," *DSMC Handbook,* July 1983.

The portion of this handbook covering risk analysis techniques is contained in Section 2 of this tutorial. Provides a good introduction to risk assessment, covering technique selection, implementation, presentation of results, and related policy directives.

[Dyer, 1987]. W.G. Dyer, *Team Building: Issues and Alternatives* (2nd ed), Addison-Wesley, Reading, Mass., 1987.

Presents checklists and techniques for team building activities, with examples of their use and discussion of frequent issues and problem areas.

[Edgar, 1982]. J.D. Edgar, "Controlling Murphy: How to Budget for Program Risk," *Concepts,* Summer 1982, pp. 60–73.

Contained in Section 2 of this tutorial. A good summary of the practical use of cost risk management techniques in government system acquisitions.

[Garvey-Powell, 1988]. P.R. Garvey and F.D. Powell, "Three Methods for Quantifying Software Development Effort Uncertainty," *Journal of Parametrics,* March 1988, pp. 76–92.

Contained in Section 2 of this tutorial. Provides some techniques for software-cost risk analysis. Some are still somewhat theoretical, but the RISCOMO tool provides a very practical approach.

[Gilb, 1986]. T. Gilb, "Deadline Pressure: How to Cope with Short Deadlines, Low Budgets, and Insufficient Staffing Levels," *Proceedings, 1986 IFIP Congress,*

North-Holland, New York, September 1986, pp. 293–299.

Contained in Section 3 of this tutorial. Identifies a number of practical techniques for avoiding or resolving software project schedule or budget risks.

[Gilb, 1988]. T. Gilb, "Estimating the Risk," Chapter 6, *Principles of Software Engineering Management*, Addison-Wesley, Reading, Mass., 1988, pp. 71–82.

Contained in Section 1 of this tutorial. Provides some useful risk management principles and examples. Other parts of the book provide some good approaches for establishing software quality objectives, and managing the risks of not achieving desired quality objectives.

[Heckel, 1984]. P. Heckel, *The Elements of Friendly Software Design*, Anderson, Ind., Warner Books, 1984.

A practical book, with many good examples and counter-examples, on how to avoid unfriendly user-interface risks.

[Hertz-Thomas, 1983]. D.B. Hertz and H. Thomas, *Risk Analysis and Its Applications*, Wiley, New York, 1983.

A comprehensive general textbook on risk-analysis principles and techniques.

[Hertz-Thomas, 1984]. D.B. Hertz and H. Thomas, *Practical Risk Analysis*, Wiley, New York, 1984.

Extensive case studies illustrating the risk analysis principles and techniques in [Hertz-Thomas, 1983].

[Hoffman, 1986]. L.J. Hoffman, "Risk Analysis and Computer Security," *Proceedings, 9th National Computer Security Conference*, NBS, Gaithersburg, Md., 1986.

Discusses computer security risk analysis options and needs.

[Humphrey et al., 1987]. W.S. Humphrey et al., "A Method for Assessing the Software Engineering Capability of Contractors," *CMU Software Engineering Institute Report CMU/SEI-87-TR-23*, Carnegie Mellon Univ. Press, Pittsburgh, Penn., 1987.

Contained in Section 2 of this tutorial. Presents an effective instrument for assessing the relative maturity level of a software development organization, and discusses techniques for applying it.

[Jones, 1986]. T.C. Jones, *Programming Productivity*, McGraw-Hill, New York, 1986.

Contains much valuable quantitative information on improving software productivity, including reduction of software rework costs.

[Kahane et al, 1988]. Y. Kahane et al., "Computer Backup Pools, Disaster Recovery, and Default Risk," *ACM Communications*, January 1988, pp. 78–83.

Contained in Section 3 of this tutorial. Presents an economic analysis of alternative approaches to providing computer backup pools to insure against the risk of computer center failure.

[Leveson, 1986]. N.G. Leveson, "Software Safety: What, Why, and How," *ACM Computing Surveys*, June 1986, pp. 121–163.

A very thorough survey article on techniques for assessing and resolving software safety risk items.

[McCracken-Jackson, 1982]. D.D. McCracken and M.A. Jackson, "Life Cycle Concept Considered Harmful," *ACM Software Engineering Notes*, April 1982, pp. 29–32.

Describes the evolutionary development process model, and how it addresses some of the risks frequently not addressed by the waterfall model.

[McCrimmon-Wehrung, 1986]. K.R. McCrimmon and D.A. Wehrung, *Taking Risks*, The Free Press, New York, 1986.

Contains an excellent introduction and literature survey on risk and risk analysis, followed by a summary of extensive research in risk quantification.

[McFarlan, 1981]. F.W. McFarlan, "Portfolio Approach to Information Systems," Harvard Business Review, September-October 1981, pp. 142–150.

Contained in Section 1 of this tutorial. Discusses the importance of risk management in managing one's portfolio of information system applications. Identifies risk dimensions and techniques for dealing with them.

[Mantei-Teorey, 1988]. M.M. Mantei and T.J. Teorey, "Cost-Benefit Analysis for Incorporating Human Factors in the Software Lifecycle," *ACM Communications*, April 1988, pp. 428–439.

Contained in Section 2 of this tutorial. A good example of cost-benefit analysis of a particular set of software human-factors risk resolution activities.

[NBS, 1979]. U.S. National Bureau of Standards, "Guidelines for Automatic Data Processing Risk Analysis," *FIPS Pub 65*, NBS, Gaithersburg, Md., August 1979.

Focuses on operational risk analysis, particularly on reliability and security. Provides procedures and forms for risk analysis and cost-benefit analysis of risk-resolution techniques.

[Neumann, 1986]. P.G. Neumann, "On Hierarchical Design of Computer Systems for Critical Applications," *IEEE Transactions on Software Engineering*, September 1986, pp. 905–920.

Contained in Section 3 of this tutorial. Presents a set of system and software-design principles and techniques for avoiding the occurrence of software reliability and safety risks.

[Neumann, 1988]. P.G. Neumann (ed), "Risks to the Public in Computers and Related Systems," *ACM Software Engineering Notes*, April 1988, pp. 5–18.

Contained in Section 1 of this tutorial. Provides examples of software-oriented risk items.

[NSAM, 1987]. National Security Agency, "NSA/CSS Software Product Standards Manual," *NSAM 81–3*, April 1, 1987.

A recently updated version of this manual with greater emphasis on prototyping and incremental development.

[NSIA, 1987]. National Security Industry Association, *Pro-*

ceedings, NSIA Conference on Software Risk Management, Los Angeles, Calif., September-October 1987.

Contains presentations on overall software-risk management and on a wide range of specialty risk-management topics; cost, performance, reliability, Ada, contractor selection, supportability.

[Osterweil, 1987]. L. Osterweil, "Software Processes Are Software Too," *Proceedings, Ninth International Conference on Software Engineering,* Association for Computing Machinery, Inc., New York, March 1987, pp. 2–13.

Presents the significant concept that software processes may advantageously be expressed as programs, and that software environments can become more powerful and pro-active by incorporating the capability of executing process programs.

[Parnas, 1979]. D.L. Parnas, "Designing Software for Ease of Extension and Contraction," *IEEE Transactions on Software Engineering.,* March 1979, pp. 128–137.

Discusses the very effective information-hiding approach to minimizing the risks of building hard-to-modify software.

[Peschel, 1987]. A. Peschel, "Implementing Risk Management: A Program Office Perspective," *Proceedings, NSIA Conference on Software Risk Management,* September-October 1987.

Contained in Section 4 of this tutorial. An example of the application of software risk management techniques to the acquisition of extensive software for the U.S. Air Force Small ICBM Program.

[Putnam-Fitzsimmons, 1979]. L.H. Putnam and A. Fitzsimmons, "Estimating Software Costs," *Datamation,* September 1979, pp. 189–198. Continued in *Datamation,* October 1979, pp. 171–178, and November 1979, pp. 137–140.

Contains an application of the PERT statistical range-estimation technique to software product sizing.

[Raiffa, 1968]. H. Raiffa, *Decision Analysis: Introductory Lectures on Choices under Uncertainty,* Addison-Wesley, Reading, Mass., 1968.

A classic textbook on decision analysis, including its associated risk-analysis techniques.

[Rothfeder, 1988]. J. Rothfeder, "It's Late, Costly, and Incompetent—But Try Firing a Computer System," *Business Week,* November 7, 1988, pp. 164–165.

Contained in Section 1 of this tutorial. Provides examples and information on the frequency of high-risk "runaway" software projects.

[Royce, 1970]. W.W. Royce, "Managing the Development of Large Software Systems: Concepts and Techniques," *Proceedings, Wescon,* August 1970. Also in *Proceedings, ICSE 9,* IEEE Computer Society Press, Washington, D.C., 1987.

The initial presentation of the waterfall model. Includes a "build it twice" step as an early risk management approach.

[Ruthberg-Fischer, 1986]. Z.G. Ruthberg and B. Fischer, "Work Priority Scheme for EDP Audit and Computer Security Review," *NBS Report NBSIR 86–3386,* July 1986.

Part of this report is contained in Section 2 of this tutorial. Provides an elaboration of the McFarlan portfolio approach to risk management. Particularly good on checklists and guidelines for identification and assessment of software reliability and security risks.

[Smith-Mosier, 1986]. S.L.Smith and J.W. Mosier, "Guidelines for Designing User-Interface Software," *MITRE Corp., MTR 10090,* MITRE Corp., Bedford, Mass., August 1986.

An extensive and very good set of principles and checklists for user interface design.

[Swinson, 1984]. G.E. Swinson, "Workstation-Based Rapid Simulation Aids for Distributed Processing Networks," *Proceedings, IEEE COMPCON F'84,* 1984.

Contained in Section 3 of this tutorial. Describes a rapid simulation tool for analyzing performance risks in complex, distributed systems.

[Tate, 1988]. P. Tate, "Risk! The Third Factor," *Datamation,* April 1, 1988, pp. 58–64.

Contained in Section 1 of this tutorial. Provides examples of corporate software risk factors, particularly in the computer security and reliability areas.

[Wasserman et al., 1986]. A.I. Wasserman et al., "Developing Interactive Information Systems with the User Software Engineering Methodology," *IEEE Transactions on Software Engineering,* February 1986, pp. 326–345.

Contained in Section 3 of this tutorial. Describes a representative example of the use of a prototyping support system and methodology focused on interactive information systems.

[Willett, 1951]. A.H. Willett, *The Economic Theory of Risk and Insurance,* University of Pennsylvania Press, Pittsburgh, Penn., 1951.

A classic book on the insurance-oriented approach to risk management. First published in 1901.

[Williams-Heins, 1976]. C.A.Williams and R.M. Heins, *Risk Management and Insurance,* McGraw-Hill, New York, 1976.

A more recent textbook on the insurance-oriented approach to risk management. Covers general techniques for risk measurement, risk control, risk financing, types of insurance, insurance contracts, and insurer selection.

[Wolff, 1989]. J.G. Wolff, "The Management of Risk in System Development: 'Project SP' and the 'New Spiral Model,'" *Software Engineering Journal,* May 1989.

Contained in Section 4 of this tutorial. Summarizes the experience of applying the spiral model to an internally-developed commercial information system, and provides some good candidate approaches for improving the spiral model.

NOTES

NOTES

NOTES

NOTES

NOTES

IEEE Computer Society Press Titles

MONOGRAPHS

Analyzing Computer Architectures
Written by Jerome C. Huck and Michael J. Flynn
(ISBN 0-8186-8857-2); 206 pages

Branch Strategy Taxonomy and Performance Models
Written by Harvey G. Cragon
(ISBN 0-8186-9111-5); 150 pages

Digital Image Warping
Written by George Wolberg
(ISBN 0-8186-8944-7); 340 pages

Implementing Configuration Management:
Hardware, Software, and Firmware
Written by Fletcher J. Buckley
(ISBN 0-7803-0435-7); 256 pages

Information Systems and Decision Processes
Written by Edward A. Stohr and Benn R. Konsynski
(ISBN 0-8186-2802-2); 368 pages

Integrating Design and Test —
CAE Tools for ATE Programming
Written by Kenneth P. Parker
(ISBN 0-8186-8788-6); 160 pages

Optic Flow Computation:
A Unified Perspective
Written by Ajit Singh
(ISBN 0-8186-2602-X); 256 pages

Physical Level Interfaces and Protocols
Written by Uyless Black
(ISBN 0-8186-8824-2); 240 pages

Real-Time Systems Design and Analysis
Written by Phillip A. Laplante
(ISBN 0-7803-0402-0); 360 pages

Software Metrics:
A Practitioner's Guide to
Improved Product Development
Written by Daniel J. Paulish and Karl-Heinrich Möller
(ISBN 0-7803-0444-6); 272 pages

X.25 and Related Protocols
Written by Uyless Black
(ISBN 0-8186-8976-5); 304 pages

TUTORIALS

Advances in ISDN and Broadband ISDN
Edited by William Stallings
(ISBN 0-8186-2797-2); 272 pages

Architectural Alternatives for Exploiting Parallelism
Edited by David J. Lilja
(ISBN 0-8186-2642-9); 464 pages

Artificial Neural Networks —
Concepts and Control Applications
Edited by V. Rao Vemuri
(ISBN 0-8186-9069-0); 520 pages

Artificial Neural Networks —
Concepts and Theory
Edited by Pankaj Mehra and Banjamin Wah
(ISBN 0-8186-8997-8); 680 pages

Autonomous Mobile Robots:
Perception, Mapping and Navigation — Volume 1
Edited by S. S. Iyengar and A. Elfes
(ISBN 0-8186-9018-6); 425 pages

Autonomous Mobile Robots:
Control, Planning, and Architecture — Volume 2
Edited by S. S. Iyengar and A. Elfes
(ISBN 0-8186-9116-6); 425 pages

Broadband Switching:
Architectures, Protocols, Design, and Analysis
Edited by C. Dhas, V. K. Konangi, and M. Sreetharan
(ISBN 0-8186-8926-9); 528 pages

Readings in
Computer-Generated Music
Edited by Denis Baggi
(ISBN 0-8186-2747-6); 232 pages

Computer Arithmetic I
Edited by Earl E. Swartzlander, Jr.
(ISBN 0-8186-8931-5); 398 pages

Computer Arithmetic II
Edited by Earl E. Swartzlander, Jr.
(ISBN 0-8186-8945-5); 412 pages

Computer Communications:
Architectures, Protocols, and Standards
(Third Edition)
Edited by William Stallings
(ISBN 0-8186-2712-3); 360 pages

Computer Graphics Hardware:
Image Generation and Display
Edited by H. K. Reghbati and A. Y. C. Lee
(ISBN 0-8186-0753-X); 384 pages

Computer Graphics: Image Synthesis
Edited by Kenneth Joy, Nelson Max, Charles Grant,
and Lansing Hatfield
(ISBN 0-8186-8854-8); 380 pages

Computer Vision: Principles
Edited by Rangachar Kasturi and Ramesh Jain
(ISBN 0-8186-9102-6); 700 pages

Computer Vision: Advances and Applications
Edited by Rangachar Kasturi and Ramesh Jain
(ISBN 0-8186-9103-4); 720 pages

Current Research in Decision Support Technology
Edited by Robert W. Blanning and David R. King
(ISBN 0-8186-2807-3); 256 pages

Digital Image Processing (Second Edition)
Edited by Rama Chellappa
(ISBN 0-8186-2362-4); 816 pages

Digital Private Branch Exchanges (PBXs)
Edited by Edwin Coover
(ISBN 0-8186-0829-3); 394 pages

Domain Analysis and Software Systems Modeling
Edited by Ruben-Prieto Diaz and Guillermo Arango
(ISBN 0-8186-8996-X); 312 pages

Formal Verification of Hardware Design
Edited by Michael Yoeli
(ISBN 0-8186-9017-8); 340 pages

Groupware: Software for Computer-Supported
Cooperative Work
Edited by David Marca and Geoffrey Bock
(ISBN 0-8186-2637-2); 600 pages

Hard Real-Time Systems
Edited by John A. Stankovic and Krithi Ramamritham
(ISBN 0-8186-0819-6); 624 pages

For further information call toll-free 1-800-CS-BOOKS or write:

IEEE Computer Society Press, 10662 Los Vaqueros Circle, PO Box 3014,
Los Alamitos, California 90720-1264, USA

IEEE Computer Society, 13, avenue de l'Aquilon,
B-1200 Brussels, BELGIUM

IEEE Computer Society, Ooshima Building, 2-19-1 Minami-Aoyama,
Minato-ku, Tokyo 107, JAPAN

Knowledge-Based Systems:
Fundamentals and Tools
Edited by Oscar N. Garcia and Yi-Tzuu Chien
(ISBN 0-8186-1924-4); 512 pages

Local Network Technology (Third Edition)
Edited by William Stallings
(ISBN 0-8186-0825-0); 512 pages

Nearest Neighbor Pattern Classification Techniques
Edited by Belur V. Dasarathy
(ISBN 0-8186-8930-7); 464 pages

Object-Oriented Computing,
Volume 1: Concepts
Edited by Gerald E. Petersen
(ISBN 0-8186-0821-8); 214 pages

Object-Oriented Computing,
Volume 2: Implementations
Edited by Gerald E. Petersen
(ISBN 0-8186-0822-6); 324 pages

Real-Time Systems
Abstractions, Languages, and Design Methodologies
Edited by Krishna M. Kavi
(ISBN 0-8186-3152-X); 550 pages

Reduced Instruction Set Computers (RISC)
(Second Edition)
Edited by William Stallings
(ISBN 0-8186-8943-9); 448 pages

Software Design Techniques (Fourth Edition)
Edited by Peter Freeman and Anthony I. Wasserman
(ISBN 0-8186-0514-6); 730 pages

Software Engineering Project Management
Edited by Richard H. Thayer
(ISBN 0-8186-0751-3); 512 pages

Software Maintenance and Computers
Edited by David H. Longstreet
(ISBN 0-8186-8898-X); 304 pages

Software Management
(Fourth Edition)
Edited by Donald J. Reifer
(ISBN 0-8186-3342-5); 656 pages

Software Reengineering
Edited by Robert S. Arnold
(ISBN 0-8186-3272-0); 688 pages

Software Reuse — Emerging Technology
Edited by Will Tracz
(ISBN 0-8186-0846-3); 400 pages

Software Risk Management
Edited by Barry W. Boehm
(ISBN 0-8186-8906-4); 508 pages

Standards, Guidelines and Examples on System
and Software Requirements Engineering
Edited by Merlin Dorfman and Richard H. Thayer
(ISBN 0-8186-8922-6); 626 pages

System and Software Requirements Engineering
Edited by Richard H. Thayer and Merlin Dorfman
(ISBN 0-8186-8921-8); 740 pages

Systems Network Architecture
Edited by Edwin R. Coover
(ISBN 0-8186-9131-X); 464 pages

Test Access Port and Boundary-Scan Architecture
Edited by Colin M. Maunder and Rodham E. Tulloss
(ISBN 0-8186-9070-4); 400 pages

Visual Programming Environments: Paradigms and Systems
Edited by Ephraim Glinert
(ISBN 0-8186-8973-0); 680 pages

Visual Programming Environments: Applications and Issues
Edited by Ephraim Glinert
(ISBN 0-8186-8974-9); 704 pages

Visualization in Scientific Computing
Edited by G. M. Nielson, B. Shriver, and L. Rosenblum
(ISBN 0-8186-8979-X); 304 pages

Volume Visualization
Edited by Arie Kaufman
(ISBN 0-8186-9020-8); 494 pages

REPRINT COLLECTIONS

Distributed Computing Systems:
Concepts and Structures
Edited by A. L. Ananda and B. Srinivasan
(ISBN 0-8186-8975-0); 416 pages

Expert Systems:
A Software Methodology for Modern Applications
Edited by Peter G. Raeth
(ISBN 0-8186-8904-8); 476 pages

Milestones in Software Evolution
Edited by Paul W. Oman and Ted G. Lewis
(ISBN 0-8186-9033-X); 332 pages

Object-Oriented Databases
Edited by Ez Nahouraii and Fred Petry
(ISBN 0-8186-8929-3); 256 pages

Validating and Verifying Knowledge-Based Systems
Edited by Uma G. Gupta
(ISBN 0-8186-8995-1); 400 pages

ARTIFICIAL NEURAL NETWORKS TECHNOLOGY SERIES

Artificial Neural Networks —
Concept Learning
Edited by Joachim Diederich
(ISBN 0-8186-2015-3); 160 pages

Artificial Neural Networks —
Electronic Implementation
Edited by Nelson Morgan
(ISBN 0-8186-2029-3); 144 pages

Artificial Neural Networks —
Theoretical Concepts
Edited by V. Rao Vemuri
(ISBN 0-8186-0855-2); 160 pages

SOFTWARE TECHNOLOGY SERIES

Bridging Faults and IDDQ Testing
Edited by Yashwant K. Malaiya and Rochit Rajsuman
(ISBN 0-8186-3215-1); 128 pages

Computer-Aided Software Engineering (CASE)
(2nd Edition)
Edited by Elliot Chikofsky
(ISBN 0-8186-3590-8); 184 pages

Fault-Tolerant Software Systems:
Techniques and Applications
Edited by Hoang Pham
(ISBN 0-8186-3210-0); 128 pages

Software Reliability Models:
Theoretical Development, Evaluation, and Applications
Edited by Yashwant K. Malaiya and Pradip K. Srimani
(ISBN 0-8186-2110-9); 136 pages

MATHEMATICS TECHNOLOGY SERIES

Computer Algorithms
Edited by Jun-ichi Aoe
(ISBN 0-8186-2123-0); 154 pages

Distributed Mutual Exclusion Algorithms
Edited by Pradip K. Srimani and Sunil R. Das
(ISBN 0-8186-3380-8); 168 pages

Genetic Algorithms
Edited by Bill P. Buckles and Frederick E. Petry
(ISBN 0-81862935-5); 120 pages

Multiple-Valued Logic in VLSI Design
Edited by Jon T. Butler
(ISBN 0-8186-2127-3); 128 pages

IEEE Computer Society

IEEE Computer Society Press Publications

Monographs: A monograph is an authored book consisting of 100-percent original material.

Tutorials: A tutorial is a collection of original materials prepared by the editors, and reprints of the best articles published in a subject area. Tutorials must contain at least five percent of original material (although we recommend 15 to 20 percent of original material).

Reprint collections: A reprint collection contains reprints (divided into sections) with a preface, table of contents, and section introductions discussing the reprints and why they were selected. Collections contain less than five percent of original material.

Technology series: Each technology series is a brief reprint collection — approximately 126-136 pages and containing 12 to 13 papers, each paper focusing on a subset of a specific discipline, such as networks, architecture, software, or robotics.

Submission of proposals: For guidelines on preparing CS Press books, write the Editorial Director, IEEE Computer Society Press, PO Box 3014, 10662 Los Vaqueros Circle, Los Alamitos, CA 90720-1264, or telephone (714) 821-8380.

Purpose

The IEEE Computer Society advances the theory and practice of computer science and engineering, promotes the exchange of technical information among 100,000 members worldwide, and provides a wide range of services to members and nonmembers.

Membership

All members receive the acclaimed monthly magazine *Computer*, discounts, and opportunities to serve (all activities are led by volunteer members). Membership is open to all IEEE members, affiliate society members, and others seriously interested in the computer field.

Publications and Activities

Computer **magazine:** An authoritative, easy-to-read magazine containing tutorials and in-depth articles on topics across the computer field, plus news, conference reports, book reviews, calendars, calls for papers, interviews, and new products.

Periodicals: The society publishes six magazines and five research transactions. For more details, refer to our membership application or request information as noted above.

Conference proceedings, tutorial texts, and standards documents: The IEEE Computer Society Press publishes more than 100 titles every year.

Standards working groups: Over 100 of these groups produce IEEE standards used throughout the industrial world.

Technical committees: Over 30 TCs publish newsletters, provide interaction with peers in specialty areas, and directly influence standards, conferences, and education.

Conferences/Education: The society holds about 100 conferences each year and sponsors many educational activities, including computing science accreditation.

Chapters: Regular and student chapters worldwide provide the opportunity to interact with colleagues, hear technical experts, and serve the local professional community.